Handbook
of
Workplace Spirituality
and
Organizational
Performance

Handbook
of
Workplace Spirituality
and
Organizational
Performance

edited by

Robert A. Giacalone and
Carole L. Jurkiewicz

M.E. Sharpe
Armonk, New York
London, England

Library of Congress Cataloging-in-Publication Data

Handbook of workplace spirituality and organizational performance / edited by Robert A.
Giacalone and Carole L. Jurkiewicz.
    p. cm.
   Includes bibliographical references and index.
   ISBN 0-7656-0844-8 (alk. paper) ISBN 0-7656-1743-9 (pbk. : alk. paper)
    1. Work—Religious aspects. 2. Employees—Religious life. 3. Management—
Religious aspects. I. Giacalone, Robert A. II. Jurkiewicz, Carole. L., 1958–

   BL65.W67 H36 2002
   291.1'785—dc21

2002030889

Printed in the United States of America

CONTENTS

CONTENTS vii

LIST OF TABLES AND FIGURES

TABLES

FIGURES

FOREWORD

Albert Einstein was supposedly once asked: "If you could ask God one question, what would that question be?" Einstein quickly responded that he would ask God *how* the universe began, because after that, the rest would all be math. However, after further reflection, Einstein said he would ask God *why* the universe began, because then he would know the meaning of his own life.

Today's interests in spirituality begin with this same reflective engagement that Einstein proposed: the exploration of the inner territory and the search to know more about the meaning of life and our purpose in some grander scheme. This volume on workplace spirituality and organizational performance, in bringing together and focusing multiple perspectives, takes a much needed first step toward building a foundation for exploring the age-old tensions between individual freedom and organizational constraints: Can I be who I am regardless of whether I am at home, or at the workplace, or in a place of worship? Can I be who I am regardless of whether I am with family and friends, or with my managers, direct reports, coworkers, suppliers, vendors, customers, and competitors, or with my spiritual neighbors and fellow congregants?

Throughout our studies and seminars (Kouzes and Posner 2002) we've asked thousands of people to list the historical leaders they most admired—leaders they could imagine themselves following willingly. While no single leader receives a majority of the nominations, the two most frequently mentioned are Abraham Lincoln and Martin Luther King, Jr. While these two leaders lived a century apart from one another, they both faced times of national struggle. Mahatma Gandhi, Jesus, Mohammed, Moses, Golda Meir, Eleanor Roosevelt, Franklin D. Roosevelt, and Mother Teresa are other historical leaders who've made the list.

What do these admired leaders have in common? In reviewing the list of individuals nominated for most admired leader, we found that the entire list was populated by people with strong beliefs about matters of principle. They all had spent long periods of time confronting their inner selves, wrestling with and resolving inner doubts, encountering their spiritual and transcendent beliefs so that they could emerge with the necessary courage and conviction to handle the conflicts and complexities of external hardships and challenges. They all had an unwavering commitment to principles. They all were passionate about their causes. The message is clear. We admire those who speak out. We admire, and are willing to follow, those who stand up for their beliefs. People expect their leaders to speak out on matters of value and conscience. But how can you speak out if you don't know what to speak about? How can you stand up for your beliefs, if you don't know what you stand for?

Recently when Jim Kouzes and I were discussing the list of historical leaders, we pondered where the calling for leadership began. Jim said: "I think leadership begins with discontent." I replied that this "was too dark a view for me. I think leadership begins with caring." Jim: "Why don't we look up the word *caring* in the dictionary." We grabbed the volume off the shelf, and opened it to "care." The first meaning was: "suffering of mind: GRIEF." There it was: Suffering and caring, discontent and concern, all come from one source. Deep within ourselves there is something we hold dear, and if it's ever violated, we'll weep and wail. We'll fight to the death to secure it, grieve if we lose it, and shriek with joy when we achieve it. In time, we came to realize that though our words were different, what Jim and I were saying was the same—that leadership begins with something that grabs hold of you and won't let go.

Where leaders must go to find their voice is within. You have to explore your inner territory. You have to take a journey into those places in your heart and soul where you hide your treasures, and then let them out to play. You have to examine them on your own and then bring them out to the forefront. We take a few steps in this direction when we ask and answer for ourselves such questions as: What do I *stand* for? What do I *believe* in? What am I *discontent* about? What makes me *weep* and *wail*? What makes me *jump for joy*? What *keeps me awake* at night? What's *grabbed hold* and won't let go? Just what is it that I really *care about*? It's important to reflect upon questions such as these.

Why's this so critical? In one study we asked people to consider the clarity with which they understood their own values, the clarity with which they understood the values of their organization, as well as their levels of organizational commitment, satisfaction, motivation, esprit de corps, and the like. While the data affirmed that clarity about organizational values was important, what we found was that its significance paled in comparison to clarity of personal values. Take the dimension of commitment: People who knew what they believed in, but had never heard the corporate credo, were *more likely* to stick around than those people who'd heard the organizational litany but had never listened to their own inner voice.

How can this be? How can people who are very clear about their own values be committed to a place that has never posted its organizational values? Think about it. Have you ever had the feeling that "This place is not for me"? Have you ever walked into a place, immediately gotten the sense that "I don't belong here," and just walked right out? On the other hand, have you ever just known that you belong, can be yourself, and that "This is the right place for me." It's the same way with our workplace. There comes a point when we just know whether it is or isn't a good fit with our values and beliefs, even if there was no lecture on the organization's credo. It all boils down to this: We won't stick around a place for very long when we feel in our heart and in our soul that we don't belong.

Clarity about personal values is more important in our attitudes about work than is clarity about organizational values alone. Ultimately it's people who decide if the organization is a great place to work. Those individuals with the clearest personal values are better prepared to make choices based on principle—including deciding whether the principles of the organization fit with their own personal principles! The data also tell us that sending the executive team off on a retreat to chisel out the organization's values, making corporate videotapes about those principles, conducting seminars on them, or handing out laminated wallet cards imprinted with the values all matter very little *unless* we also make sure that we ask individuals what they value and believe.

The answer to the question of "What do I care about?" comes only when we're willing to take a journey through our inner territory—a journey that'll require opening doors that are shut, walking in dark spaces that are frightening, and touching the flame that burns. But at the end is a truth. Discovering what we care about is like finding one's voice, and this is something that every artist understands. Every artist knows that finding a voice is most definitely not a matter of technique. It's a matter of time and a matter of searching—soul searching.

Several years back we attended a retrospective of Richard Diebenkorn's work with an artist friend, Jim LaSalandra. Toward the end of the gallery walk, LaSalandra made this observation: "There are really three periods in an artist's life. In the first we paint exterior landscapes. In the second, we paint interior landscapes. In the third, we paint our selves. That's when you begin to have your own unique style." This made for an important art appreciation lesson—it applies equally to the appreciation of the art of leadership—and this perspective might similarly be applied to this volume of readings.

As scholars we are primarily focused on what we see outside of ourselves—on painting exterior landscapes—and so exploring and documenting systematically and scientifically the connections between workplace spirituality and organizational performance is extremely valuable. We are indebted to the editors and authors within who have taken this absolutely essential first step, and they've done so in a first-rate fashion. My hope is that after building this foundation, framing the side walls, and putting on the roof, we'll turn our attention to what's going to go inside.

Barry Z. Posner
Dean and Professor of Leadership
Leavey School of Business
Santa Clara University
Santa Clara, CA

REFERENCE

Kouzes, J.M., and B.Z. Posner. (2002). *The Leadership Challenge,* 3d ed. San Francisco: Jossey-Bass.

PREFACE

The majority of our waking hours, and certainly our hours of greatest effort, are spent at work. The work we do, and the environment in which we do it, is integral to our self-concept, and this affects the quality of our lives outside of work as well. We seek satisfaction through our work both in terms of the contributions we make and the manner in which we make them. To facilitate this satisfaction is to stimulate individual effort and, in doing so, to maximize organizational performance.

The intrinsic drive to grow in skill and self-actualization has been long established in a variety of disciplines in the social and hard sciences. Individuals, for the most part, desire opportunities to learn and advance themselves, to feel valued about the contribution they are making to a group, and to experience in so doing a growth in spirit, a sense of connection to the enigma of what our purpose on earth may be. We know this ineffable feeling of joy when through work we attain personal strivings for meaning. Perhaps it has come in bits and spurts throughout our careers, or perhaps for long periods in certain organizations and working with particular people. The experience seems to transcend both our task at hand and the commonalities of the workplace, and it aligns us with something meaningful that we know but cannot articulate. We work longer and harder during these periods yet seem to come away refreshed and energized rather than depleted and drained. The experience of meaningfulness carries over to our personal lives, and we feel better about ourselves and about our interactions with others. These are the memories or experiences we cling to, what we want to recreate and sustain in our work environments. Described by some as "flow," "in the zone," "a peak experience," or "when things just clicked," it is the time when we are driven to our best efforts, overlook insignificant distractions, and seek to find symbiotic methods of problem solving.

We also know when that sense of connection between spirit and work is absent. We are too familiar with the consequent disassociation and disconnect between that toward which we naturally strive and that which is our day-to-day lot. It is the experience of doing what needs to be done for the sake of our careers, because of a needed paycheck, or because we have come to believe that this is the "natural order" of things. Many have come to accept as normal a lack of fulfillment at work beyond the necessary monetary reward and occasional step up the ladder, which itself seems often disconnected from effort and unpredictably whimsical. While we might long for the spirit–work connection, the time we feel most alive, we may come to believe that it is magical in nature and that the confluence of the two appears out of nowhere and disconnects without reason.

The purpose of this book is to explore the possibility that the spirit–work connection is not based on happenstance but on definable, measurable aspects of the work environment. These aspects can then be extrapolated as a separate area of study, as has been done with such other areas of study as motivation, leadership, and human resource management. Just as organizations can learn to more effectively motivate, lead, and manage people, so too can they excel at creating and sustaining the spirit–work connection toward the common end of maximizing organizational performance. It is not magic. It is not religion. It is not an idiosyncratic belief system. It requires objective investigation that is no less problematic or essential than the scientific pursuits of other areas of organizational study.

This book is the beginning of a scientific investigation into the role "spirituality" plays in workplace performance. Each chapter approaches workplace spirituality from the authors' individual areas of expertise, connecting it to the greater body of literature in a particular field. Collectively, these chapters provide a framework for inquiry and, we hope, an impetus for further study on the role of spirit in organizational outcomes. We anticipate that it also will spur scientific work to determine whether the spirit–work connection extends beyond the workplace to affect families, groups, and society as a whole. The answers to these issues can only be found if scholars choose to advance this new frontier of organizational science.

We would like first to thank the authors of these chapters and their extraordinary efforts toward developing a new science of workplace spirituality. We would also like to recognize Harry Briggs, our editor at M.E. Sharpe, who epitomizes in his work that which spirituality embodies: integrity, responsibility, autonomy, and sincerity. Finally and most importantly, we wish to express our gratitude and love for our families and friends, who inspire us always and from whom we get the courage to reach beyond our grasp.

Robert A. Giacalone
Carole L. Jurkiewicz

THEORETICAL DEVELOPMENT
OF WORKPLACE SPIRITUALITY

CHAPTER 1

TOWARD A SCIENCE
OF WORKPLACE SPIRITUALITY

ROBERT A. GIACALONE AND CAROLE L. JURKIEWICZ

INTEREST IN WORKPLACE SPIRITUALITY

Interest in workplace spirituality is growing at an accelerated rate. Academicians (Cavanaugh 1999; Sass 2000), practitioners (Laabs 1996), and the public in general (Zukav 1989) have evidenced this through popular, scholarly, artistic, and journalistic endeavors. A variety of reasons have been proffered for this heightened attention. Though little substantive data exists to support any of the contentions, attempts to explain the phenomenon can be clustered into three thematic areas.

One theme focuses on social and business changes as sources of turmoil, which in turn spur individuals to seek spiritual solutions to the consequent tension (e.g., Mitroff and Denton 2000). Cash, Gray, and Rood (2000) assert that the catalyst is an unstable work environment, one characterized by downsizing, reengineering, and new technologies, that has increased employee distrust in organizations (Murray 1995). This distrust, as reflected through their employers' policies, has made employees see themselves as expendable resources (Cohen 1996). This diminished view of self and work exacerbates feelings of social alienation and fear, compelling the employee to search for deeper meaning in life (Ali and Falcone 1995) and thus integrating a spiritual–work identity. A related theme focuses on the need for employees to seek satisfaction beyond measures of production (Izzo and Klein 1998), a function of a cultural shift driven by the "baby boomers" as their careers matured in an environment of growing commercial instability (Flynn 1996; Russell 1996). Some scholars have argued that workplace spirituality increases employee opportunities to experience a higher sense of service and personal growth (Hawley 1993), to maximize conceptions of self-worth and inherent uniqueness (e.g., DiPadova 1998), and thus is a motivator unto itself.

A second theme suggests a profound change in values globally. Neal (1998) argues that evidence of a growing social consciousness as reflected in business culture indicates a spiritual renaissance in the United States, exemplified best by a developing sense of corporate social responsibility. Inglehart (1997) argues that diminishing economic gains characteristic of the latter part of the twentieth century cannot create many additional, materialistic satisfactions. The search for something more has resulted in a quest for postmaterialist assets, of which spirituality may be one manifestation. This is supported by research suggesting that increasing numbers of individuals in developed Western nations are seeking self-actualization as opposed to material security (Abramson and Inglehart 1995; Inglehart 1997; Jurkiewicz and Massey 1997; Plummer 1989).

A final theme focuses on the broader spiritual changes taking place in connection with growing interest among Americans in Eastern philosophies (Brandt 1996), though what may have precipitated the trend specifically is unclear. Many (e.g., Eck 2001; Van Biema 1997; Zinsmeister 1997) attribute this interest to societal shifts toward diversity and increasing interest in other cultures. Others (e.g., Koehn 1999; Fox-Genovese 1999; Yuet-Ha 1996) view the impetus as corporate multinationalism and the consequent effort to integrate Eastern and Western managerial practices. Some (Billington 1997; Barnhart 1997; Callicott 1989; Rolston 1975) view it as a natural evolutionary step toward higher levels of karmic understanding that naturally spill over into the workplace. Certainly evidence that Eastern influences have permeated popular culture in the United States is evident in such lifestyle choices as cuisine (Surak 2001), fashion, and architecture (Yang, Gan, and Hong 1997).

The surging interest in spirituality likely culminates from a combination of these and other factors. Regardless of the cause, workplace spirituality has spurred curiosity beyond the capacity of scholars to keep pace either theoretically or methodologically. Elementary attempts at a noetic understanding of workplace spirituality began in the early 1990s as evidenced in books, articles, and special journal issues or sections. Organizational consultants have also embraced the value of workplace spirituality for their clients, with some consultants (Barrett 1998) taking a more pragmatic, data-based approach, and others providing training seminars and coaching on the topic.

As is common in new endeavors, "the emerging body of academic literature on spirituality in organizations exhibits more breadth than depth" (Sass 2000, 195). This proliferation of ideas with no discernible set of rules constitutes a normal research tradition while simultaneously presenting a frustrating circumstance for objectivists. As Kuhn (1970) explains,

> Recognizing that frustration, however, makes it possible to diagnose its source. Scientists . . . can . . . agree in their *identification* of a paradigm without agreeing on, or even attempting to produce, a full *interpretation* of *rationalization* of it. Lack of a standard interpretation or of an agreed reduction to rules will not prevent a paradigm from guiding research. Normal science can be determined in part by the direct inspection of paradigms, a process that is often aided by but does not depend upon the formulation of rules and assumptions. Indeed, the existence of a paradigm need not even imply that any full set of rules exists. [Italics in the original.]

Development of a paradigm involves an extensive process of conceptual assimilation and, as has been repeatedly demonstrated, more than one theoretical construction can always be imposed upon a given collection of data (Kuhn 1970). This drive toward nomotheism and the attendant frustration represents "the essential tension" implicit in all scientific research (Kuhn 1959, 162). Intellectual foraging for confirmation or falsification thus ensues to build consensus for a predominant way of viewing the data and offering a framework into which elements of the data can be placed toward a normative understanding of the phenomenon. Some first steps in this process toward an ontology of workplace spirituality are offered here.

A Scientific Inquiry into Workplace Spirituality

It is essential first that workplace spirituality be separated from "soaring rhetoric" (Sass 2000, 198), denominational polemics, and the faith blanket in which it is frequently cloaked. The goal is neither to confirm nor disconfirm particular belief systems but, rather, to separate scientific inquiry from such suppositions entirely. This effort explores methods by which workplace spirituality might be objectively studied in ascertaining its utility to work organizations and their stakeholders.

Claims that such scientific investigation is impossible and "prevents spirituality, religion, and work researchers from accurately detailing both theoretical and behavioral understanding" (Fornaciari and Dean 2001, 338) are undermined by decades of research in psychology and spirituality that have systematically and effectively employed the scientific method (e.g., Paloutzian 1996). Substantive efforts to develop empirical assessments and measurement tools for workplace spirituality (e.g., Ashmos and Duchon 2000) provide further evidence to reject this impediment. Yet even with this empirical base, workplace spirituality is still equated by some scholars with particular religious or faith-based doctrines. While for many scholars the two are arguably separate constructs (Cavanaugh 1999), populist notions tend to meld them into a generalized conception of workplace spirituality as faith-based business. It is essential that this distinction between populist beliefs and epistemological inquiry be clarified before engaging in a more explicative dialogue.

Separating Religion from Workplace Spirituality

To many people the process of separating religion from spirituality is effortless; to others it is equivalent to surgically dividing conjoined twins. Yet, spiritual concerns are not synonymous with religious ones; spiritual concerns are separate from participation in and the sharing of beliefs with any particular religious groups (Veach and Chappell 1991). Additionally, viewing workplace spirituality through the lens of religious tradition is divisive: it excludes those who do not share in the denominational tradition (Cavanaugh 1999) and conflicts with the social, legal, and ethical foundations of business and public administration (Nadesan 1999). Adherence to a religious workplace orientation can lead to arrogance that a particular company, faith, or even nation is somehow "better" or worthier than another. Such insolence is given voice by Nash (1994, 61) quoting a Christian evangelical businessman: "When you look at the success of the American economic system in relation to the poorer countries of the world, you have to believe it's more than good luck. You feel there is some connection with God's will." Such a view implicitly disparages those who do not subscribe to similar beliefs and presumes poorer nations are disassociated from God(s).

But the term spirituality has developed a negative religious connotation (see Mitroff and Denton 2000) as a function of the way it has been used and experienced by the general public. Individuals have extrapolated from such corrupt television evangelists as Jimmy Swaggart and Jim Bakker and such religion-invoking politicians as Jesse Jackson and Al Sharpton to the entire domain of spiritual pursuits. The spirituality attached to such devotional-based endeavors is more a religiosity driven by *fear* (of eternal damnation, divine retribution, loss of a reference group) rather than *trust* (as workplace spirituality is configured) (Corrington 1989; Pargament 1999). The spirituality associated with such dogmatic, profit-centered prosletyzing can diminish a person's capacity for a good life (from a resulting obsessiveness), takes on the form of self-righteousness, and is frequently used as a political tool against others (Nadesan 1999). Translating religion of this nature into workplace spirituality can foster zealotry at the expense of organizational goals, offend constituents and customers, and decrease morale and job satisfaction for employees.

Fundamentally, because religious doctrine is based on faith, the rigors of proof necessary for scientific study do not apply. One can espouse any belief as divine providence without need for substantiation. For example, under the rubric of papal infallibility, the Pope can make a decree on matters of faith without having the legitimacy of his decree questioned, at least among devout Catholics. Organizational principles are not so readily embraced. The disciplines of management and administration are premised on a positivist scientific model and admonish against embracing nonverifiable approaches to understanding workplace behavior. Workplace spirituality based on religion is ill-defined and untestable and therefore cannot contribute to a scientific body of knowledge. Application of religious principles to the workplace is tantamount to physicians practicing medicine based upon idiosyncratic religious beliefs rather than scientifically proven protocols. While one can certainly take a religious approach, the absurdity of doing so is no less apparent for organizational science than it is for medical practice.

In moving toward a scientific understanding of workplace spirituality, this chapter is divided into two parts. The first addresses the weaknesses to date in the development of spirituality generally and workplace spirituality particularly as areas of study. The second suggests methods for strengthening these areas and establishing a common language, a theoretical map of the new paradigm.

WEAKNESSES IN THE DEVELOPMENT OF WORKPLACE SPIRITUALITY AS A DISTINCT AREA OF STUDY

From our vantage, the key weaknesses hampering the emergence of a scientific study of workplace spirituality are fourfold: (1) the lack of an accepted, conceptual definition; (2) inadequate measurement tools; (3) limited theoretical development; and (4) legal concerns.

Defining Workplace Spirituality

The roots of workplace spirituality lie in spirituality as an isolate, an amorphous megatrend identified by Naisbitt (1982) nearly two decades ago (Hoge 1996). Spohn (1997) notes that there are a great variety of spiritualities, ranging from New Age practices to Twelve-Step programs. In fact, spirituality can have many meanings, ranging from religion to "anything intangible" to the occult (DiPadova 1998) and, as a dimension of human experience, can include a variety of values, attitudes, perspectives, beliefs, and emotions (Elkins, Hedstrom, Hughes, Leaf, and Saunders 1988).

The absence of a clear definition of spirituality is not for lack of effort. Table 1.1 provides a representative listing of some of the many definitional attempts to date. While most include a descriptor of transcendence, ultimacy, or divinity, other components of the definitions vary greatly. Some treat spirituality as a behavior (the personal expression), others as an objective reality (that which involves ultimate and personal truths), others specifically describe it as a "subjective experience." In some definitions it is described as a search (emerging from moments in which the individual questions the meaning of personal existence), while in others it is "an animating force" or a "capacity." The lack of a consensus in defining spirituality poses a significant conceptual impediment to achieving an understanding of workplace spirituality.

Identifying the scope of dimensionality is essential in moving toward a consensus definition. Table 1.2 develops a typology of the definitional components found in the literature. Ten discrete dimensions of spirituality are outlined, and brief explanations are given, along with the citations. A meta-analysis of this data would be most helpful in advancing the study of workplace spirituality but is beyond the scope of this endeavor. Still, we hope this typology may encourage further investigation and assessment.

Just as spirituality is ambiguous in scope, more so is a definition of what constitutes workplace spirituality (see Kahnweiler and Otte 1997; McGee 1998). The lack of clarity in defining spirituality in isolate is only compounded by extrapolating it to the workplace (Sass 2000). One approach is to define workplace spirituality in terms of its component parts, as Ashmos and Duchon

Table 1.1

A Representative Sampling of Definitions of Spirituality in the Literature

Definition of spirituality	Source
The personal expression of ultimate concern	Emmons (2000)
That which involves ultimate and personal truths	Wong (1998), p. 364
How the individual lives meaningfully with ultimacy in his or her response to the deepest truths of the universe	Bregman and Thierman (1995), p. 149
The presence of a relationship with a higher power that affects the way in which one operates in the world	Armstrong (1995), p. 3
Our response to a deep and mysterious human yearning for self-transcendence and surrender, a yearning to find our place	Benner (1989), p. 20
A way of being and experiencing that comes about through awareness of a transcendent dimension and that is characterized by certain identifiable values in regard to self, life, and whatever one considers to be the ultimate	Elkins et al. (1988), p. 10
A transcendent dimension within human experience . . . discovered in moments in which the individual questions the meaning of personal existence and attempts to place the self within a broader ontological context	Shafranske and Gorsuch (1984), p. 231
A subjective experience of the sacred	Vaughn (1991), p. 105
A personal life principle which animates a transcendent quality of relationship with God	Emblen (1992), p. 45
The human dimension that transcends the biological, psychological, and social aspects of living	Mauritzen (1988), p. 118
That vast realm of human potential dealing with ultimate purposes, with higher entities, with God, with life, with compassion, with purpose	Tart (1975), p. 4
That human striving for the transforming power present in life; it is that attraction and movement of the human person toward the divine	Dale (1991), p. 5
Pertaining to the innate capacity to, and tendency to seek to, transcend one's current locus of centricity, which with transcendence involves increased knowledge and love	Chandler and Holden (1992)
The animating force that inspires one toward purposes that are beyond one's self and that give one's life meaning and direction	McKnight (1984), p. 142

Table 1.2

The Dimensionality of Spirituality

Spiritual dimension	Description	Source
Spiritual well-being	The affirmation of life in a relationship with God, self, community and environment that nurtures and celebrates wholeness.	Ellison (1983); Moberg, (1984)
Spiritual transcendence	Capacity of individuals to stand outside of their immediate sense of time and place to view life from a larger, more objective perspective.	Piedmont (1999)
Spiritual development	The process of incorporating spiritual experiences that result ultimately in spiritual transformation.	Chandler and Holder (1992)
Spiritual wellness	Spiritual wellness represents the openness to the spiritual dimension that permits the integration of one's spirituality with the other dimensions of life, thus maximizing the potential for growth and self-actualization.	Westgate (1996), p. 27
Spiritual needs	Any factors necessary to establish and or maintain a person's dynamic personality relationship with God (as defined by that individual) and out of that relationship to experience the forgiveness, love, hope, trust, and meaning and purpose in life.	Stallwood and Stoll (1975), p. 1088
Spiritual distress	A disruption of the life principle that pervades a person's entire being and that integrates and transcends one's biological and psychosocial nature.	Kim et al. (1987), p. 314
Spiritual intelligence	Abilities and competencies that may be part of an individual's expert knowledge. These include the capacity to transcend the physical and material, the capacity to be virtuous, and the ability to experience heightened states of consciousness, sanctify everyday experience, and utilize spiritual resources to solve problems.	Emmons (2000)
Spiritual (religious) self-consciousness	The extent to which individuals reflect on their faith and beliefs.	Leak and Fish (1999)
Spiritual growth	Reflective of the gratification of individual needs, especially "belonging," and those of a higher order such as a sense of achievement.	Burack (1999)
Spiritual health	Optimal function is the enhancement of spiritual oneness with whatever a person considers to be more than oneself as an individual with reason, experience, and intuition; the ongoing development of an adherence to a responsible ethical system.	Stroudenmire, Batman, Pavlov, and Temple (1986)

(2000) have done: (1) a recognition that employees have an inner life; (2) an assumption that employees desire to find work meaningful; and (3) a commitment by the company to serve as a context or community for spiritual growth. Yet even if one were to accept these components, they do not entail a method for operationalization. Are we to presume that an employee's inner life at work is qualitatively different from their inner life at home or elsewhere? Or is workplace spirituality rather an aggregate cluster of personal components and, if so, which components should be included? Essentially, does workplace spirituality constitute either distinctly individual or organizational components, or is it an amalgamation of both? Such distinctions are important if the study of workplace spirituality is to be distinguished from studying spirituality in other contexts.

Measuring the Value of Workplace Spirituality

Culture is a causal variable in the growth and development of an organization and, more specifically, is a determinant of labor productivity essential to the predictive and explanatory power of economic theory in competitive markets (Altman 2001). It is viewed as an additional variable in the production function on par with capital stock, technological change, and human capital (Altman 2001), an extension of Weber's (1958) notions as articulated in *The Protestant Ethic and the Spirit of Capitalism*. Becker (1998) introduced the notion of culture as an explicit component of social capital that affects utility, building upon Buchanan's (1994) work that establishes culture as a facilitator or impediment to the quantity and quality of the work effort. Data unequivocally suggests that spirituality-based organizational cultures are the most productive, and that by maximizing productivity they confer organizational dominance in the marketplace (Reder 1982). Cultural factors related to workplace spirituality have been shown to override the economic-political environment as an influence on worker productivity, ethics, values, exercise of authority, innovation, etc. (Altman 2001; Becker 1998). Individual effort is discretionary and is positively correlated with policies that entail consequences, support the individual, challenge them to grow, reward progress and innovation, and restrain inefficiencies—largely policies embodied in a spirituality-based workplace (Buchanan 1994). "Culture can affect the level of per capita real output produced in an economy and therefore the level of per capita material wealth as well as differences in per capita wealth advanced by different economies at any given time" (Altman 2001, 267). While the spirituality of the individual, the organization, or both can be measured tangentially through cultural assessments and policy analysis, a discrete measure is needed to directly correlate variable levels of spirituality with organizational performance.

To facilitate this measurement, precise measures and valid instruments are needed (see Paloutzian 1996). Instead, justification for studying the topic has heretofore been premised on observations such as "we need to integrate spirituality into management . . . no organization can survive for long without spirituality and soul" (Mitroff and Denton 1999, 1991), and Goodpaster's (1994) "call for the reintegration of work and spirituality . . . it is not more or less than the human face of capitalism that is at stake" (61). Such observations, however well-intentioned, contribute more to the lack of precision in measurability rather than knowledge. Although other researchers have called for a greater focus on spirituality (e.g., Biberman and Whitty 1997; Bolman and Deal 1995; Russell 1989; Scherer and Shook 1993), effort is needed to increase precision and integration in delineating concepts, rather than adding to rhetoric that simply enlarges the volume of discussion.

Precise measurement, *using validated instruments*, can help organizations understand the utility of workplace spirituality. The scientific study of workplace spirituality must be founded on sound theoretical justification of its utility. Researchers must effectively demonstrate the utility of spirituality in the workplace by framing it as a question of value-added: How does spirituality help us to undertake work processes more effectively? Such utility can be shown on two bases: practical and ethical.

Practical Utility

Identifying the practical implications of workplace spirituality is perhaps the most fundamental method of demonstrating utility. Researchers must show how spiritual variables impact work-related processes. Similar questions have been addressed in spirituality research, but clear empirical substantiation has been lacking. Some authors (e.g., Neck and Milliman 1994) believe that spirituality can enhance intuitive abilities, increase innovation, enhance teamwork and employee commitment, and facilitate a more powerful vision. Trott's (1996) correlation of affective commitment, perceived personal competence, affiliation, autonomy, and higher order need strength (Meyer and Allen 1991) with properties of spiritual well-being (connectedness in relationships, value placed on self-determination, the desire to live up to one's potential) (Hungelmann, Kenkel-Rossi, Klassen, and Stollenwerk 1985) provides a promising start. Additionally, Chandler and Holden's (1992) conclusion that spirituality in the workplace can impact long-term behavioral change is a strong contribution, though the issue of whether spirituality alone accounts for this variance remains unaddressed. While a relationship between spirituality and overall quality of life has been argued (see Campbell 1976; Diener 1984; Fox 1994; Paloutzian and Kirkpatrick 1995), strong empirical support of this connection has yet to be reported in mainstream research (see Trott 1996).

Demonstrating practical implications would provide organizations with a tangible understanding of how spiritual variables are connected to a host of organizational variables. Research has suggested a link between organizational concerns with spirituality (manifested in such issues as optimism, orientation toward giving, acceptance of diversity) with an increase in employee enthusiasm, effort, collaboration, creativity, performance, etc. (e.g., McKnight 1984; Bracey, Rosenblum, Sanford and Trueblood 1990). A causal relationship has yet to be clarified, however, as does an evaluation of the magnitude of spirituality's impact. From a human resources perspective, relating tangible outcomes such as a more symbiotic person–job fit, increased productivity, reduced turnover, and enhanced recruiting-and-retention success with a spiritually centered organizational culture would provide a strong testament to its value (Braus 1992; Izzo and Klein 1998).

There is evidence that workplace spirituality may help to explain both overt (resources) and subjective (increased ethicality) economic gains (Zinnbauer, Pargament, and Scott 1999); employees who view their work as a means to advance spiritually are likely to exert greater effort than those who see it merely as a means to a paycheck. Research suggests employees empowered through policies associated with workplace spirituality are more productive (Reich 1981), with the greatest productivity gains seen at the level of unskilled labor (Freeman 1994). At the other end of the hierarchy, Himmelfarb (1994) suggests that leaders who view their work as a means to advance spiritually, at the individual or group level, lead the organization to higher levels of performance. This is a key area for exploration in understanding the impact of workplace spirituality across the hierarchical spectrum.

Although spirituality-related work practices such as gainsharing, job security in encouraging calculated risks, narrower wage and status differentials, processes for effective worker input into the organization's decision-making processes, and guarantees on individual workers' rights have been widely correlated with higher rates of growth in labor productivity (e.g., Ichniowski et al. 1996; Gordon 1996; Buchele and Christiansen 1995; 1999; Reich 1981), it is the organizational environment that determines the extent to which these and other similar practices are likely to be adopted (Levine 1995). Most organizational environments resist such changes even when confronted by empirical data supporting their efficacy (Altman 2001). Usually attributed to mistrust between managers and subordinates and a fear of power sharing and loss of personal influence on the part of decision-makers, there are considerable short-run costs in adopting a new set of long-term policies and procedures, particularly when managers are measured on the basis of short-term results (Kochan, Katz, and McKersie 1986; Gordon 1996). However, a large and growing body of data suggests that costs associated with shifting to a spirituality-based work culture are more than offset by measurable productivity gains (e.g., Marshall 1994; Campbell and Sengenberger 1994; Feis 1994; Wilkinson 1994; OECD 1996; Gordon 1996). Cultural change of this type is effected primarily through education (Weber 1958), though the economic environment plays a role (Altman 2001), and an influential individual changing him/herself can serve as a catalyst in spurring broader change (Himmelfarb 1994). Personal power bases are threatened with a change in culture that empowers others, notwithstanding the evidence supporting the financial advantages of making the shift. Therefore, it is not surprising that the move to a spirituality-based workplace is usually made in periods of crisis or reorganization when power hierarchies are normally disrupted, and such proven innovations as a spirituality-based culture are more readily adopted as conferring strategic advantage (Altman 2001).

Ethical Utility

The utility of spirituality could also be demonstrated in terms of positive ethical impact along with measurable benefits to the organization's effectiveness and efficiency. At the individual level, research has suggested a positive causal relationship between spirituality-based value orientations, ethics, and work performance (e.g., Fox 1994; Forsyth 1992; Kohlberg 1981; Rest 1980; Ramos 1972). At the organizational level are such issues as that posed by Kanter (1977), who speaks of the "the myth of separate worlds," a management philosophy that elevates goal achievement at work to a spot of preeminence and devalues an employee's home life. The extent to which management policies that epitomize spiritual values increase organizational performance without damaging an employee's home life could provide an excellent justification of utility.

Limited Theoretical Development

An elemental weakness in the development of a workplace spirituality paradigm is the lack of a sound theoretical base. Pargament (1999), working within the comparatively more rigorous area of psychology, has described much of the spirituality literature as ungrounded; Sass (2000) has echoed this criticism for workplace spirituality. Much of the literature on workplace spirituality has indeed taken a "soft" approach to the topic. Benevolently motivated writers speak from a personal perspective about love, compassion, mutual support, and caring without grounding their beliefs in a strong foundation of theoretical and empirical work. This rightfully leads many readers to view them as promoting a cause rather than advancing scientific knowledge. Other writers appear to disregard the existing empirical foundations of workplace spirituality entirely and instead try to "reinvent the wheel," overlooking the essentiality of rooting their work within or in relation to existing concepts. As a result of both of these predominant approaches, workplace spirituality is largely disassociated from the more mainstream topics in the scholarly literature and (as discussed above) in organizational life more generally. If it is to emerge as a mainstream topic of study, future studies on workplace spirituality must be integrated into more traditional areas of investigation.

Legal

Potential legal repercussions of workplace spirituality represent critical concerns for researchers and practitioners, leading organizations and scholars to dismiss considerations of the construct based upon the word "spirituality" itself. The word has many connotations, some of which no serious scholar or professional wants to invite into their work. Yet the word also encompasses a body of interdisciplinary research of potential importance to organizations of all types and sizes. The idiom, "throwing the baby out with the bathwater" seems appropriate here in cautioning those who equate all spirituality work with the dogmatic, proselytizing, ethereal machinations most of us abhor, rather than the serious study of a set of policies and practices that can advance both organizations and individuals. The former viewpoint has had deleterious consequences.

As Moberg and Brusek (1978) have noted, the constitutional separation of church and state in the United States (abetted by a lack of government funding for research), has shied many researchers away from this area of inquiry. Putting the scarcity of government funding aside, legal concerns appear to be at the crux of these fears and fall into two categories: separation and accommodation. Both are based upon faulty assumptions.

First is the impression that spirituality and religion are synonymous, no doubt emanating from populist notions equating the two concepts. If religion and spirituality are viewed as separate constructs, research and practice becomes far less intimidating to those uncomfortable mixing faith-based beliefs and objectivist truths. Second is the assumption that what we know about spirituality is purely philosophical rather than scientifically based, and making practical decisions on the basis of animistic notions is unsupportable in our society (Guba's [1990] notions notwithstanding). Reviewing the state of published research on workplace spirituality to date, one would be hard pressed to mount a plausible argument to counter such a stance. Certainly, as is advocated here, a scientific approach to future research would render this assumption feckless. Lastly is the supposition that implementing spirituality-based principles at work will adversely impact or otherwise disadvantage employees and, hence, be illegal. Here one needs to refer to other organizational domains. Employment tests, a staple of human resource management, are also potentially illegal when used in a way that adversely impacts particular groups. Yet just as employment tests are carefully scrutinized for fairness and studiously implemented, similar care can and should be exercised with applications of spirituality-based principles, and all policies or programs that affect employees.

Concern for separation of work and spiritual domains is further compounded by a parallel concern for the accommodation of employee's spiritual needs at work. While the potential for abuse is clear, particularly in the form of religious harassment (e.g., Hitchens 2000), the need to accommodate spiritual issues is nonetheless important in maximizing both productivity and satisfaction. Cash, Gray, and Rood (2000), who provide a framework for dealing with spiritually-related work accommodations, cite studies demonstrating that organizations are actively making reasonable accommodations for employee spirituality (recognizing social and personal growth needs, and acceptance of diverse beliefs and self-expression). Certainly, accommodations of any sort should reinforce the organizational mission of an innovative, progressive, productive culture. Giving preferential treatment to one group over another, or accommodating one while imposing upon another is not aligned with either the study or application of workplace spirituality. The need to balance separation and accommodation is fungible for organizations with and without a spirituality-based culture and entails an inherent bias that limits investigation, as discussed in the following section.

TOWARD A SCIENCE OF WORKPLACE SPIRITUALITY

The preceding section delineated four issues that stood as impediments to the development of a science of workplace spirituality. In this section, we will discuss how these weaknesses might be overcome by (1) approaching the definition of workplace spirituality with an intent to clarify; (2) examining the question of utility by immersing workplace spirituality into larger global changes; (3) demonstrating how workplace spirituality might be grounded within a number of interdisciplinary literatures; and (4) working with the biases against spirituality, heretofore labeled as legalistic concerns.

Clarification of Meaning

If, before researchers used the term "workplace spirituality," there was a general consensus as to its meaning, many of the problems of this new field of study would not exist. But, as Spohn (1997) has noted, the discipline of spirituality is still seeking a definitive character (Kahnweiler and Otte 1997; Konz and Ryan 1999; McGee 1998), making a scientific assessment difficult.

The dimensions of spirituality can be conceived in two opposing ways (Emmons 2000), each contraindicating the other. One approach is the study of spirituality's passive, static, and traitlike qualities, similar to possessions (like beliefs) or actions (as in rituals) that remain relatively constant over time. Conversely, spirituality can be conceived of as dynamic—a set of skills, resources, capacities, or abilities that are evolving and developing and interact with the external environment. In a static conceptualization, one expects greater longitudinal consistency in the data, making it a dependent variable; in a dynamic conceptualization, greater divergence is anticipated, and, thus, it would be treated as an independent variable. In this dual conceptualization the ontology of workplace spirituality closely resembles the literature on power, or more accurately *pouvoir*, meaning it can be rightfully approached as either a noun (something one has), or a verb (a force one exerts), embodying both contradictory elements at once. Studies in workplace spirituality have tended toward one approach or the other, as summarized in Table 1.3, with examples from the literature clearly oriented toward either attribution or action.

Although research must necessarily focus on either attribute or action, a working definition of workplace spirituality must represent a consensus of these perspectives if it is to have utility. The substantive aspect must evoke manifestations of beliefs, emotions, practices, and relationships while the functional aspect focuses on the practical purpose spirituality serves for an individual or within an organizational context. The functional aspect would address, for example, the connection between spirituality and absenteeism, productivity, turnover, ethicality, health, stress, and leadership, while the substantive aspect would focus on the diversity of spiritual beliefs and practices and their impact on the functional variables. With this understanding, we offer the following working definition of workplace spirituality: *Workplace spirituality is a framework of organizational values evidenced in the culture that promotes employees' experience of transcendence through the work process, facilitating their sense of being connected to others in a way that provides feelings of completeness and joy.*

Table 1.3

Manifestations of Spirituality: Attributes Versus Activities

Spiritual attributes	Spiritual activities
Broader worldview	Acting on positive attitudes and relationships with the world
Intention to live with integrity	Acting virtuously
Intention to develop sacred relationships	Living out one's deep personal values
A belief that there are multiple levels of reality that are not readily apparent	Acting with altruistic love and action
Confidence that life is deeply meaningful	Affirming what is essential through service
Confidence that one's own existence has purpose	Acting with authenticity
A sense of responsibility to life itself	Ability to live with inconsistencies and contradictions in one's life
A sense of inner truth	Accepting life and others on their own terms
Greater capacity to love	Transcending physical and material aspects of existence
A recognition of divine presence in ordinary activities	Experiencing a heightened state of awareness
A deep awareness of human suffering, pain, and death	Utilizing spiritual resources to solve difficulties
An integrating factor within personality	Embracing the experiences that life provides as opportunities for growth
Desiring meaning and purpose	Seeking personal integration
Having a source of yearning	Self-actualization
Desiring to make a difference	Living in the moment
Desiring to create a meaningful world	Going beyond one's self-interests
Desiring inner peace	Needing to contribute to the betterment of others
Desiring truth	
Having a strong sense of community	
Having a strong sense of social justice	

Positioning Workplace Spirituality Within a System Context

The first part of this chapter delineated the need to demonstrate utility by linking workplace spirituality to tangible aspects of the work environment. The impact of spirituality, from this standpoint, can be evidenced most easily through acropetal changes in performance measurement, turnover, and productivity.

There is yet another way to demonstrate this utility, however, that focuses on environmental dynamism. From this vantage, workplace spirituality is more easily understood within a holistic context: a system of interwoven cultural and personal values and changes that impact all aspects of life, including organizational life. Zinnbauer, Pargament, and Scott (1999) argue for this broader view, admonishing that seeing spirituality solely as an individual phenomenon is to treat it as occurring in a social vacuum. Sass's (2000) view purports that spirituality can be understood at a variety of levels, ranging from the individual to the organization.[1] The interconnectedness of these levels provides us with a true systemic understanding of how spirituality can differentially impact the workplace at both the micro and macro levels. Thus, to comprehend the full utility of workplace spirituality, one must examine the interplay between individual and organizational spiritual values. We posit that the greater the congruity across these levels, the increased likelihood that an individual will experience transcendence through their work and, thus, demonstrate the presence of workplace spirituality. Conversely, considerable value incongruity between the levels suggests an absence of spirituality in the workplace resulting from a poor job–person fit, with attendant expression through decreased performance and increased conflict. Evidence of increasing divergence between individual and organizational values, both in the United States and abroad as detailed below, is likely a key catalyst for the growing interest in workplace spirituality.

Changing Values: Postmaterialism, Integral Culture, and New Paradigm Thought

Evidence points to pervasive value changes emerging both nationally and internationally, reflecting a comprehensive shift in worldview (see Ray and Rinzler 1993). Three converging areas of literature describe the nature of these changes: political science values research on postmaterialism (e.g., Inglehart 1977, 1997); the demographic work of Ray (1996, among others) on the emergence of integral culture; and the interdisciplinary work on changing social and business paradigms (Ray and Rinzler 1993; Lichtenstein 2000; Giacalone and Eylon 2000). This growing interest in workplace spirituality appears to mirror changes in values across the globe.

Inglehart's (1977, 1990) work provides evidence of a significantly greater propensity to favor postmaterialist societal values over more materialist ones. Postmaterialist values are epitomized by concerns for social equality; increased participation in important decisions impacting one's life; increased desire for freedom, increased concern for quality-of-life, self-expression, sense of community, and environmentalism. On the other hand, materialist values express concern for prosperity, security, and control (Inglehart 1977).

Postmaterialists are gradually becoming the dominant population segment in the workplaces of postindustrial societies (Abramson and Inglehart 1992, 1995; Inglehart and Abramson 1994). This widespread trend toward postmaterialism in developed democracies (Inglehart [1977] 1990) has been growing steadily over the past three decades (Abramson and Inglehart 1995; Inglehart 1997). According to Inglehart (1997), in 1970–1971, materialists outnumbered postmaterialists by a ratio of 4 to 1; by 1990 that ratio had shifted to 4 to 3.

The increase in postmaterialist values parallels the increase in material security in developed nations, reflecting on a larger scale Maslow's (1998) notion that upon attainment of material comfort and safety, individuals seek out higher-order fulfillment. Unlike Maslow, however, Inglehart (1977, 1990) believes that the importance of postmaterialist values remain with an individual even if their degree of comfort and safety decline. Older employees who tend to hold materialist values (raised under conditions of greater scarcity and insecurity) are being replaced by younger employees (raised under conditions of greater economic security) who demonstrate postmaterialist values (Inglehart 1977, 1990; Thau and Heflin 1997; Tulgan 1995; Jurkiewicz and Fogel 1999).

The implications of this shift are enormous. DeGraaf and Evans (1996, 608) note that postmaterialism "is important and its implications are far reaching . . . it (is) nothing less than a culture shift . . ." in which quality of life rather than material possessions are a fundamental driving force. This postmaterialist culture shift is one of the most highly fixed of social science generalizations (e.g., Warwick 1998), and one that is arguably inherently more spiritual (Inglehart 1997).

A second area of literature approaches these changing values from a demographic stance. Ray (1996, 1997) found an emerging value structure in the United States that he labels "cultural creatives." These cultural creatives, who had not been identified in prior studies, tend to be more idealistic and spiritual, concerned with relationships and psychological development, altruistic, environmentally concerned, and socially conscious in their desire to create a positive future for all. They tend to be less concerned with making a lot of money, express disenchantment with the idea of accumulating excess possessions, are middle- to upper-middle class, and are likely to be college graduates. Cultural creatives place strong emphasis on having new and unique experiences. This group comprises about 24 percent of the U.S. adult population, or about 44 million people.

Cultural creatives fall into two subgroups. "Core cultural creatives" (about 20 million people) are concerned with their inner lives and have a strong penchant for social activism. Their values are systems-oriented, ecological, and spiritual in focus. They are characterized by globalism and xenophilism, self-actualization, social conscientiousness, and social optimism. "Green cultural creatives" (about 24 million people) are more intensely eco-focused and socially concerned from a more secular view, generally viewing nature itself as sacred, with only an average interest in abstract spirituality. In general, both subgroups evidence postmaterialist values in their beliefs and activities.

New paradigm thought provides a third body of literature that deals with changing values. Unlike the trendy, futuristic discussions that turned the phrase "new paradigm" into a mantra for self-aggrandizement, new paradigm thought is an interdisciplinary, critical approach to accepted methodological and philosophical assumptions. New paradigm thought rejects materialistic values; focuses on such postmaterialist and cultural creative concerns as ecology and quality of life; and uses an integrative, collaborative, systems view that focuses on interconnectedness, interdependence, and qualitative aspects of phenomena. In particular, a theme throughout virtually all of new paradigm thought is spirituality: its existence, manifestation, and importance (see Ray and Rinzler 1993). New paradigm thought is constituted on the synergy of such diverse disciplinary perspectives as biology (Sheldrake 1981, 1988; Maturana and Varela 1987), psychology (Frankl 1962; Vaughn 1979), ecological studies (Hawken 1994), futurism (Henderson 1991; Maynard and Mehrtens 1993), physics (Bohm 1980; Prigogine and Stengers 1984; Wheatley 1992), religion (Fox 1994; Hawley 1993; Macy 1991), and systems theory (Capra 1993; Jaworksi 1996; von Bertlanffy 1973). These perspectives, increasingly accepted among scholars in a variety of interdisciplinary settings, provide evidence of a significant change in mindset across the globe. Giacalone and Eylon (2000), who summarized the premises of new paradigm thought, identified what they call the analytic transformation as particularly relevant to workplace spirituality. Inherent to this transformation of values is an epistemological acceptance and incorporation of qualitative data (augmenting quantitative data [e.g., Autry 1991; Fox 1994]), spiritual/intuitive data (amplifying rational data [Bellah et al. 1985; Briskin 1998; Conger 1994; DeFoore and Renesch 1995; McCormick 1994; McKnight 1984; Mirvis 1997; Orsborn 1992]), and holistic approaches (as separate from symptomatic ones [Capra 1982, 1993; Capra, Steindl-Rast, and Matus 1991]). As applied to the workplace, this transformation is seen in the balancing of economic, quality of work life, and social responsibility concerns (DeFoore and Renesch 1995), along with a shift in leadership style moving from autocratic to inspirational and servant-centered (Block 1993; Greenleaf 1977; Jaworski 1996).

Overall, broad value changes, characterized by spirituality and spiritually-oriented ideals, are becoming embedded in societies around the world. Although these changes are not equally distributed across the globe (Inglehart 1990, 1997; Ray 1996, 1997), their numbers represent a population segment that organizations cannot afford to disregard. As values transform, the foundations of materialism and other conventional modernist values (Ray 1996, 1997) decrease in importance. In fact, if one accepts the trajectory of change identified by Inglehart (1997), postmaterialists will outnumber materialists in the coming decade. Organizations will thus need to reconsider everything, from products to services, and rewards to punishments if they are to remain viable (Reder 1982; Becker 1998).

Research Immersion: The Interdisciplinary Context of Workplace Spirituality

As noted in the first part of this chapter, spirituality research is tethered by its lack of grounding in theoretical and empirical literature. This has not only hampered development of the field, but in a profound way has artificially reduced its importance. But framed within existing research, a scientific assessment of spirituality becomes more plausible. Much as Emmons (2000) argues that the concept of spiritual intelligence enhances spirituality research by grounding it in the literature of psychological intelligence, we argue that the study of workplace spirituality can be advanced by placing it within the context of multidisciplinary research. Table 1.4 identifies some of the key research areas and their connection to specific aspects of spirituality.

The convergence between areas such as forgiveness, hope, and spirituality is self-evident; even from a nonscientific stance, these topics have been associated with spiritual concerns. Alternatively, concepts such as generativity, agency, and communion are almost exclusively entrenched in the scientific literature and appear to be excellent proxies for spiritually-oriented ideas such as transcendence, nonspirituality, and the desire for connection, respectively. Building upon the research findings of these (and similarly related) areas can help to immerse spirituality research, theory, and practice in developed fields of inquiry. Immersion in such work bolsters the development of the workplace spirituality paradigm and helps to distinguish workplace spirituality from (and integrate it with) related concepts.

Legal Concerns in Moving Toward a Scientific Approach to Workplace Spirituality

The concern over legal repercussions, as previously discussed, appear omnipresent whenever the terms "spirituality" and "workplace" coexist. But what is asserted as a legal issue may not be the reason for ignoring workplace spirituality. Teasing apart the nuanced arguments in this area, a variety of distinct countenances can be identified, some legal, some philosophical, and some simply undiscerning. Although legal issues are asserted, we believe that these mask underlying stances that individuals, both academic and practitioner, hold regarding spirituality.

At present, we see three potential stances that could be taken regarding the role of spirituality in the workplace: *the parallel relationship*, *the adversarial relationship*, and *the integrative relationship*. These convictions posit clear, definable positions on what the role of spirituality is, could be, or should be in organizations.

In a *parallel stance*, spirituality and the workplace are seen as pertaining to different domains,

Table 1.4

Interdisciplinary Links to Workplace Spirituality

Research area	Description	Representative literature	Relevance for workplace spirituality
Generativity	An adult's interest in and commitment to making a positive and creative contribution to future generations (Erikson 1950).	Mansfield and McAdams (1996)	Interest in and commitment to future generations demonstrates transcendence and a desire to create a more meaningful world.
Agency and communion	Agency reflects individual existence (includes self-assertion, self-expansion, self-control, and self-direction), and communion reflects the participation of the individual in the larger whole (includes group participation, cooperation, attachment, and connections and emphasizes the creation of unions).	Bakan (1966); Helgeson (1994)	Communion demonstrates a desire to go beyond one's self-interests, a need to contribute to the betterment of others.
Ethics and social responsibility	Moral behavior in work-related settings.	Frederick (1994); Kennedy and Lawton (1998)	Commitment to ethics and social responsibility demonstrates a capacity to be virtuous, a sense of responsibility to life itself.
Materialism	A value that represents the importance that possessions play in an individual's life.	Belk (1985); Richins and Dawson (1992)	Lower levels of materialism should be associated with transcendence.
Work values	Work values reflect the importance that people give to particular outcomes at work.	Roe and Ester (1997); Sagie, Elizur, and Koslowsky (1996)	May correlate with such values as the need to contribute to the betterment of others, community orientation, sense of social justice.
Workaholism	Workaholism is a behavior pattern in which individuals spend a great deal of time in work activities that often result in detrimental impacts on social and family life.	Scott, Moore, and Miceli (1997); Robinson (2000)	High levels of workaholism may be inversely related to spiritual concerns if the workaholism is directed toward self-interest, and positively related to a broader worldview, desire to find meaning and purpose, and attain social justice if the workaholism is directed toward helping others.

Social movements	The study of social movements focuses on how particular social factions develop and evolve.	Benford and Snow (2000)	Understanding of social movements have helped scholars to understand the workplace spirituality movement and its direction.
Morphic fields	Morphic fields are nonvisible fields that guide systems under their influence toward specific goals or end points.	Sheldrake (1981); (1988)	Such intangible aspects of spirituality as love and the sense of inner truth may be related to morphic fields.
Servant leadership	Servant leadership is a model of leadership in which serving others is the primary priority.	Greenleaf (1977)	Servant leadership should be positively related to positive attitudes and relationships with the world, and affirmation of the essential through service, desire to make a difference, and the desire to go beyond one's own self-interest.
Work–life balance	Work–life balance is a desire to establish greater equality in the time and energy spent on work and life activities.	Berry and Rao (1997); Caproni (1997); Hall and Richter (1988); Vincola (1998)	Work–life balance may be associated with the desire for meaning and purpose, the intention to develop sacred relationships, and the need to contribute to the betterment of others.
Downshifting	Downshifting is a trend among workers that seeks to slow down their work lives and/or break out of jobs that are in a corporate setting.	Laabs (1996)	May be associated with the desire for meaning and purpose, the intention to develop sacred relationships, and the need to contribute to the betterment of others.
Voluntary simplicity	Voluntary simplicity refers to a choice to limit expenditures on consumer goods and cultivate postmaterialist values.	Etzioni (1998)	May be associated with a heightened state of awareness, transcendence, a belief in multiple levels of reality, and a desire to create a meaningful world.
Family responsive workplaces	Initiatives undertaken by organizations that are designed to be supportive toward families.	Glass and Estes (1997)	May be related to a strong sense of social justice, a commitment to altruistic love and action, and a capacity to transcend physical and material aspects of existence.

and it is assumed that no relationship exists between spirituality and the workplace. This does not prescriptively assert that there *should be* no relationship, but rather that workplace issues and spirituality issues reside in different worlds, using different languages. The contention is that no substantive connection between the two exists: a change in one has no impact on the other. The argument is similar to the one made against the study of business ethics (Shaw and Barry 2000). This assumption precludes scientific assessments of workplace spirituality.

In an *adversarial stance*, spirituality and the workplace are perceived as belonging apart. Here, the argument is prescriptive: there should be no relationship between spirituality and the workplace. Proponents of this stance may point to the potential antagonism and hostility resulting from the intersection of work and spiritual domains. For some, the position emanates from the view that there is a conflict between a rationalist, positivist world and one based in transcendent intangibles that obviates study. In other cases, the stance may be a function of seeking to control a particular version of a sacred worldview, such that allowing nonreligious notions of spirituality into the workplace might help to validate alternative spiritual views that threaten deeply held personal beliefs. Still others may take this stance in order to prevent legal problems they see arising from the entry of spiritual concerns into the workplace. But the conclusion for those who hold an antagonistic stance is the same: workplace spirituality should not be a valid area for inquiry.

Finally, in the *integrative stance*, the concepts of workplace and spirituality are seen as *potentially* connected. This capacity is based on scientific work demonstrating a relationship among spirituality and other facets of life (e.g., Paloutzian 1996). In this stance, the hypothesis is that there is a causal relationship between spiritual variables and workplace outcomes that should be investigated and understood. Those holding an integrative stance admit that the proponents of a parallel stance may be correct: unlike the connections between spirituality and such variables as physical and mental health (e.g., Anandarajah 2001; Koenig 1998), there may be no relationship between spirituality and the workplace. Similarly, proponents of the integrative stance concede that the introduction of spiritual variables into the workplace may result in either ameliorative or deleterious results. The approach here is that the relationship is worthy of empirical investigation to determine if a connection exists, and if so, what the nature of that interaction entails.

What separates those holding an integrative stance from others is twofold. First, they assert that spirituality can and must be subjected to the same scrutiny as other variables in the organizational sciences. Because spirituality is pivotal to the lives of so many people and has been shown to impact many facets of life (see Paloutzian 1996), it is myopic to dismiss its impact on the workplace without justification. Given the long history of organizational research on such intangibles as leadership, power, and affect, repudiating spirituality because it is similarly intangible, is ungrounded. Second, the integrative stance does not assume that faith is an adequate substitute for science within the domain of organizational life. If the administration and management of organizations have been predicated to date on scientific principles, one cannot use a different yardstick for spiritual variables. The discoveries may coalesce with or may counter issues of faith, or they may be consistent with or contradictory to personally held beliefs; the issues of faith and personal beliefs are irrelevant. Much as there may be those who adhere to authoritarian versus participatory leadership, we would not expect to expunge discoveries about either form of leadership simply because one group or the other "likes" some results and "dislikes" others.

Thus, the integrative stance asserts that the value of studying workplace spirituality is not to invoke a particular faith (or an atheistic/agnostic counterpart), but to scientifically assess whether

Table 1.5

Hypothetical Connections Between Workplace Spirituality and Areas of Organizational Interest

Potential criteria of interest	Representative connections
Recruitment	Do organizations need to recruit spiritual employees in different ways?
Self-presentation	Does spirituality impact how individuals present themselves to colleagues and managers both in terms of self-presentational style and quantity of self-presentation?
Ethics	What is the relationship between spirituality and ethical decision making?
Health insurance claims	Does the relationship between spirituality and health similarly relate to health insurance claims?
Creativity/innovation	Are spiritual individuals more creative, as some (e.g., Ray 1996) have suggested?
Antisocial/Prosocial behaviors	Given their value structure, do spiritual employees demonstrate more prosocial behaviors and/or fewer antisocial behaviors?
Public relations	What are the public relations repercussions to those organizations embracing or rejecting spirituality?
Leadership	Do spiritual employees possess a different leadership style (e.g., servant leadership)?
Job satisfaction	To what extent is a person's job satisfaction impacted by spirituality?
Work group cohesion/group dynamics	Given the role that concern for others can play in spirituality, how do spiritual employees impact work group cohesion?
Work-family issues	What is the relationship between spirituality and concern with work-family balance?
Motivation/reward systems	Are spiritual employees motivated by different factors than nonspiritual employees?

it affects the functioning of organizations. The outcome of these assessments cannot be decided a priori, be premised on personal predilections, or avoided out of fear of legal repercussions or discomfort with potential findings. As with all scientific studies that have generalizability and validity, they must be rooted in the facts we have at hand, building upon those toward a body of knowledge. If concepts related to spirituality are to play a role in organizational science, it must be on their own merit and separate from any bias of their proponents or detractors.

Therefore, we see the scientific study of workplace spirituality focused on a pivotal question: Is spirituality significantly related to various aspects of organizational behavior and performance, and if so, how? As a point of departure in answering this question, Table 1.4 introduces potential areas for research, their relevance, and representative literatures. Carefully designed research focusing on these and other variables can move us toward a new paradigm of study that is based on the same scientific principles (and fraught with the same controversies) that have historically characterized the organizational sciences.

CONCLUSION

In developing the discipline of workplace spirituality, Kuhn's (1970, 111–112) words capture the point in time at which we find ourselves:

> Led by a new paradigm, scientists adopt new instruments and look in new places. Even more important[ly], during revolutions, scientists see new and different things when looking with familiar instruments in places they have looked before . . . when the normal-scientific tradition changes, the scientist's perception of his environment must be re-educated—in some familiar situations he must learn to see a new gestalt. After he has done so, the world of his research will seem, here and there, incommensurable with the one he had inhabited before.

The scientific study of workplace spirituality may bring forth a new development in the organizational sciences, one hopefully unfettered by legal and religious phobias. The potentially groundbreaking nature of this research leaves no doubt that if significant relationships are discovered, a new understanding of the workplace will emerge that could redefine our ontological stance. The challenge of investigating these relationships is great, but more daunting is the leap over *vox populi* notions of workplace spirituality to that of a science in its own right.

It is important to note that organizational scientists are not charting the spiritual waters alone. A concomitant literature on spirituality in the natural sciences is moving toward paradigmatic definition (e.g., the journal *Science and Spirit*). Just as the organizational sciences emerged from the methods and approaches of the natural and social sciences, investigations into workplace spirituality will no doubt mirror theirs, allowing both disciplines to symbiotically bolster each others' findings. We therefore ought to proceed with confidence, recognizing that those who have paved this path for us before are paving it for us again, but knowing that our own direction can transform individual and organizational life in ways unrestricted by natural laws. Our intention in this effort is to remove some of the obstacles on the path.

NOTE

1. The reader is directed to Sass (2000) for a full discussion of spirituality at these levels.

BIBLIOGRAPHY

Abramson, P.R., and R. Inglehart. (1992). "Generational Replacement and Value Change in Eight Western European Societies." *British Journal of Political Science* 22: 183–228.
———. (1994). "Generational Change: Cohort Effects and Period Effects." In *Solidarity of Generations: Demographics, Economic and Social Change and Its Consequences*, ed. H. Becker and Piet Hermkens. Amsterdam: Thesis, 71–109.
———. (1995). *Value Change in Global Perspective*. Ann Arbor: University of Michigan Press.
———. (1996). "Formative Security, Education, and Postmaterialism: A Response to Davis." *Public Opinion Quarterly* 60: 450–455.
Ali, A.J., and T. Falcone. (1995). "Work Ethic in the USA and Canada." *Journal of Management Development* 14: 26–33.
Altman, M. (2001). *Worker Satisfaction and Economic Performance*. Armonk, NY: M.E. Sharpe.
Anandarajah, G. (2001). "Spirituality and Medical Practice: Using the HOPE Questions as a Practical Tool for Spiritual Assessment." *American Family Physician* 63: 81–89.
Armstrong, T.D. (1995). "Exploring Spirituality: The Development of the Armstrong Measure of Spiritu-

ality." Paper presented at the annual convention of the American Psychological Association, New York, August.

Ashmos, D.P., and D. Duchon. (2000). "Spirituality at Work: A Conceptualization and Measure." *Journal of Management Inquiry* 9: 134–145.

Autry, J.A. (1991). *Love and Profit.* New York: Morrow.

Bakan, D. (1996). *The Duality of Human Existence: An Essay on Psychology and Religion.* Chicago: McNally.

Barnhart, M.G. (1997). "Ideas of Nature in an Asian Context." *Philosophy East and West* 47, no. 3: 417–433.

Barrett, R. (1998). *Liberating the Corporate Soul.* Boston: Butterworth-Heinemann.

Becker, G.S. (1998). *Accounting for Tastes.* Cambridge, MA: Harvard University Press.

Belk, R.W. (1985). "Materialism: Trait Aspects of Living in the Material World." *Journal of Consumer Research* 12: 265–280.

Bellah, R.N.; R. Madsen; W.M. Sullivan; A. Swidler; and S.M. Tipton. (1985). *Habits of the Heart.* Berkeley: University of California Press.

Benford, R.D., and D.A. Snow. (2000). "Framing Processes and Social Movements: An Overview and Assessment." *Annual Review of Sociology* 26: 611–639.

Benner, D.G. (1989). "Toward a Psychology of Spirituality: Implications for Personality and Psychotherapy." *Journal of Psychology and Christianity* 5: 19–30.

Berry, T.O., and J.M. Rao. (1997). "Balancing Employment and Fatherhood: A Systems Perspective." *Journal of Family Issues* 18: 386–402.

Biberman, J., and M. Whitty. (1997). "A Postmodern Spiritual Future for Work." *Journal of Organizational Change Management* 10: 130–138.

Billington, R. (1997). *Understanding Eastern Philosophy.* New York: Routledge.

Block, P. (1993). *Stewardship: Choosing Service over Self-Interest.* San Francisco: Berrett-Koehler.

Bohm, D. (1980). *Wholeness and the Implicate Order.* London: Routledge and Kegan Paul.

Bolman, L.G., and T.E. Deal. (1995). *Leading with Soul: An Uncommon Journey of Spirit.* San Francisco: Jossey-Bass.

Bracey, H.; J. Rosenblum; A. Sanford; and R. Trueblood. (1990). *Managing from the Heart.* New York: Dell.

Brandt, E. (1996). "Corporate Pioneers Explore Spirituality." *HR Magazine* (April): 82–87.

Braus, P. (1992). "What Workers Want." *American Demographics* (August): 30–37.

Bregman, L., and S. Thierman. (1995). *First Person Mortal: Personal Narratives of Illness, Dying, and Grief.* New York: Paragon.

Briskin, A. (1998). *The Stirring of Soul in the Workplace.* San Francisco: Berrett-Koehler.

Buchanan, J.M. (1994). *Ethics and Economic Progress.* Norman: University of Oklahoma Press.

Buchele, R., and J. Christiansen. (1995). "Worker Rights Promote Productivity Growth." *Challenge: The Magazine of Economic Affairs* 38: 32–37.

———. (1999). "Labor Relations and Productivity Growth in Advanced Capitalist Economies." *Review of Radical Political Economies* 31: 87–110.

Burack, Elmer H. (1999). "Spirituality in the Workplace." *Journal of Organizational Change Management* 12: 280–291.

Callicott, J.B. (1989). "The Metaphysical Implication of Ecology." In *Nature in Asian Traditions of Thought,* ed. J.B. Callicott and R.T. Ames. Albany: State University of New York Press.

Campbell, A. (1976). "Subjective Measures of Well-being." *American Psychologist* 31: 117–124.

Campbell, D., and W. Sengenberger. (1994). "Labour Standards, Economic Efficiency and Development: Lessons from Experience with Industrial Restructuring." In *International Labour Standards and Economic Interdependence,* ed. W. Sengenberger and D. Campbell. Geneva: International Labour Organization, 421–439.

Capra, F. (1982). *The Turning Point.* Toronto: Bantam.

———. (1993). "A Systems Approach to the Emerging Paradigm." In *The New Paradigm in Business,* ed. M. Ray and A. Rinzler. New York: Tarcher Books, 230–237.

Capra, F.; D. Steindl-Rast; and T. Matus. (1991). *Belonging to the Universe.* San Francisco: HarperSanFrancisco.

Caproni, P.J. (1997). "Work/Life Balance: You Can't Get There from Here." *Journal of Applied Behavioral Science* 33: 46–56.

Cash, K.C.; G.R. Gray; and S.A. Rood. (2000). "A Framework for Accommodating Religion and Spirituality in the Workplace." *Academy of Management Executive* 14: 124–134.

Cavanaugh, G.F. (1999). "Spirituality for Managers: Context and Critique." *Journal of Organizational Change Management* 12: 186–199.

Chandler, C.K., and J.M. Holden. (1992). "Counseling for Spiritual Wellness: Theory and Practice." *Journal of Counseling and Development* 71: 168–176.

Cohen, G. (1996). "Toward a Spirituality Based on Justice and Ecology." *Social Policy* (Spring): 6–18.

Conger, J., ed. (1994). *Spirit at Work: Discovering the Spirituality in Leadership.* San Francisco: Jossey-Bass.

Corrington, J.E. (1989). "Spirituality and Recovery: Relationships Between Levels of Spirituality, Contentment, and Stress During Recovery from Alcoholism in AA." *Alcoholism Treatment Quarterly* 6: 151–165.

Dale, E. S. (1991). *Bringing Heaven Down to Earth.* A Practical Spirituality of Work (American University Studies, Series 7, Theology and Religion, vol. 83). New York: Peter Lang.

DeFoore, B., and J. Renesch, eds. (1995). *Rediscovering the Soul of Business.* San Francisco: New Leaders Press.

DeGraaf, N.D., and G. Evans. (1996). "Why Are the Young More Postmaterialist?" *Comparative Political Studies* 28: 608–635.

Diener, E. (1984). "Subjective Well-being." *Psychological Bulletin* 95: 542–575.

DiPadova, L.N. (1998). "The Paradox of Spiritual Management: Cultivating Individual and Community Leadership in the Dilbert Age." *Journal of Management Systems* 10: 31–46.

Eck, D.L. (2001). *America: How a "Christian Country" Has Become the World's Most Religiously Diverse Nation.* San Francisco: HarperCollins.

Elkins, D.N.; L.J. Hedstrom; L.L. Huhges; J.A. Leaf; and C. Saunders. (1988). "Toward a Humanistic-Phenomenological Spirituality: Definition, Description, and Measurement." *Journal of Humanistic Psychology* 28: 5–18.

Ellison, C. (1983). "Spiritual Well-being: Conceptualization and Measurement." *Journal of Psychology and Theology* 11, no. 4: 330–340.

Emblen, J.D. (1992). "Religion and Spirituality Defined According to Current Use in Nursing Literature." *Journal of Professional Nursing* 8: 41–47.

Emmons, R.A. (2000). "Is Spirituality an Intelligence? Motivation, Cognition, and the Psychology of Ultimate Concern." *International Journal for the Psychology of Religion* 10: 3–26.

Erikson, E. (1950). *Childhood and Society.* New York: Norton.

Etzioni, A. (1998). "Voluntary Simplicity: Characterization, Select Psychological Implications, and Societal Consequences." *Journal of Economic Psychology* 19: 619–643.

Feis, H. (1994). "International Labour Legislation in the Light of Economic Theory." In *International Labour Standards and Economic Interdependence*, ed. W. Sengenberger and D. Campbell. Geneva: International Labour Organization, 29–55.

Flynn, G. (1996). "Xers vs. Boomers: Teamwork or Trouble?" *Personnel Journal* 75: 86–90.

Fornaciari, C.J., and K.L. Dean. (2001). "Making the Quantum Leap: Lessons from Physics on Studying Spirituality and Religion in Organizations." *Journal of Organizational Change Management* 14: 335–351.

Forsyth, D.R. (1992). "Judging the Morality of Business Practices: The Influences of Personal Moral Philosophies." *Journal of Business Ethics* 11: 461–470.

Fox, M. (1994). *The Reinvention of Work: A New Vision of Livelihood for Our Time.* San Francisco: HarperCollins.

Fox-Genovese, E. (1999). "Multiculturalism in History: Ideologies and Realities." *ORBIS* 43, no. 4: 531–543.

Frankl, V. (1962). *Man's Search for Meaning: An Introduction to Logotherapy.* New York: Washington Square Press.

Frederick, W.C. (1994). "From CSR$_1$ to CSR$_2$: The Maturing of Business and Society Thought." *Business and Society* 33: 150–164.

Freeman, R.B. (1994). "A Hard-Headed Look at Labour Standards." In *International Labour Standards and Economic Interdependence*, ed. W. Sengenberger and D. Campbell. Geneva: International Labour Organization, 79–92.

Giacalone, R.A., and D. Eylon. (2000). "The Development of New Paradigm Values, Thinkers, and Business: Initial Frameworks for a Changing Business Worldview." *American Behavioral Scientist* 43: 1217–1230.

Glass, J.L., and S.B. Estes. (1997). "The Family Responsive Workplace." *Annual Review of Sociology* 23: 289–313.

Goodpaster, K.E. (1994). "Work, Spirituality, and the Moral Point of View." *International Journal of Value-based Management* 7: 49–62.

Gordon, D.M. (1996). *Fat and Mean: The Corporate Squeeze of Working Americans and the Myth of Managerial Downsizing.* New York: Free Press.

Greenleaf, R.K. (1977). *Servant Leadership: A Journey in the Nature of Legitimate Power and Greatness.* New York: Paulist Press.

Guba, E.G. (1990). *The Paradigm Dialog.* Newbury Park, CA: Sage.

Hall, D.T., and J. Richter. (1998). "Balancing Work Life and Home Life: What Can Organizations Do to Help?" *Academy of Management Executive* 11: 213–233.

Hawken, P. (1994). *The Ecology of Commerce.* New York: HarperCollins.

Hawley, J. (1993). *Reawakening the Spirit at Work: The Power of Dharmic Management.* San Francisco: Berrett-Koehler.

Helgeson, V.S. (1994). "Relation of Agency and Communion to Well-being: Evidence and Potential Explanations." *Psychological Bulletin* 116: 412–428.

Henderson, H. (1991). *Paradigms in Progress.* Indianapolis, IN: Knowledge Systems.

Himmelfarb, G. (1994). *On Looking in the Abyss: Untimely Thoughts on Culture and Society.* New York: Knopf.

Hitchens, C. (2000). "God at Work." *Free Inquiry* 20: 5–6.

Hoge, D.R. (1996). "Religion in America: The Demographics of Belief and Affiliation." In *Religion and the Clinical Practice of Psychology,* ed. E.P. Shafranske. Washington, DC: American Psychological Association, 21–41.

Hungelmann, J.; E. Kenkel-Rossi; L. Klassen; and R. Stollenwerk. (1985). "Spiritual Well-being in Older Adults: Harmonious Interconnectedness." *Journal of Religion and Health* 24: 147–153.

———. (1996). "Focus on Spiritual Well-being: Harmonious Interconnectedness of Mind-Body-Spirit-Use of the JAREL Spiritual Well-Being Scale." *Geriatric Nursing* 17: 262–266.

Ingersoll, R.E. (1994). "Spirituality, Religion, and Counseling: Dimensions and Relationships." *Counseling and Values* 38: 98–112.

Ichniowski, C.; D. L. Kochan; C. Olson; and G. Strauss. (1996). "What Works at Work: Overview and Assessment." *Industrial Relations* 35: 299–333.

Inglehart, R. (1977). *The Silent Revolution: Changing Values and Political Styles Among Western Publics.* Princeton, NJ: Princeton University Press.

———. (1990). *Culture Shift in Advanced Industrial Society.* Princeton, NJ: Princeton University Press.

———. (1997). *Modernization and Postmodernization: Cultural, Economic and Political Change in 43 Societies.* Princeton, NJ: Princeton University Press.

Inglehart, R., and P.R. Abramson. (1994) "Economic Security and Value Change, 1970–1993." *American Political Science Review* 78: 336–354.

Izzo, J., and E. Klein. (1998). "The Changing Values of Workers: Organizations Must Respond with Soul." *Helathcare Forum Journal* (May/June): 62–65.

Jaworksi, J. (1996). *Synchronicity: The Inner Path of Leadership.* San Francisco: Berrett-Koehler.

Jurkiewicz, C.L., and S.A. Fogel. (1999). "Are GenXers All That Different? Generational Comparisons of Preferred Job Characteristics." *Journal of Public Affairs and Issues* 3: 5–32.

Jurkiewicz, C.L., and Tom K. Massey, Jr. (1997). "What Motivates Municipal Employees: A Comparison Study of Supervisory vs. Non-supervisory Personnel." *Public Personnel Management* 26: 367–377.

Kahle, L.R.; B. Poulos; and A. Sukhdial, A. (1988). "Changes in Social Values in the United States During the Past Decade." *Journal of Advertising Research* 35–41.

Kahnweiler, W., and F.L. Otte. (1997). "In Search of the Soul of HRD." *Human Resource Development Quarterly* 8: 171–181.

Kanter, R.M. (1977). *Work and Family in the United States: A Critical Review and Agenda for Research and Policy.* New York: Sage.

Kennedy, E.J., and L. Lawton. (1998). "Religiousness and Business Ethics." *Journal of Business Ethics* 17: 163–175.

Kim, M.J.; G.K. McFarland; and A.M. McLane. (1987). *Pocket Guide to Nursing Diagnoses.* St. Louis, MO: Mosby.

Kochan, T.A., H.C. Katz, and R.B. McKersie. (1986). *The Transformation of American Industrial Relations.* New York: Basic Books.

Koehn, D. (1999). "What Can Eastern Philosophy Teach Us About Business Ethics?" *Journal of Business Ethics* 19, no. 1: 71–80.

Koenig, H. (1998). *The Handbook of Religion and Mental Health.* San Diego: Academic Press.

Kohlberg, L. (1981). *The Philosophy of Moral Development.* Cambridge, MA: Harper and Row.

Konz, G.N.P., and F.X. Ryan. (1999). "Maintaining an Organizational Spirituality: No Easy Task." *Journal of Organizational Change Management* 12: 200–210.

Kuhn, T.S. (1959). *The Essential Tension: Selected Studies in Scientific Tradition and Change.* Chicago: University of Chicago Press.

———. (1970). *The Structure of Scientific Revolutions.* Chicago: University of Chicago Press.

Laabs, J. (1996). "Downshifters." *Personnel Journal* (March): 62–76.

Leak, G.K., and S.B. Fish. (1999). "Development and Initial Validation of a Measure of Religious Maturity." *International Journal for the Psychology of Religion* 9: 83–103.

Levine, D.I. (1995). *Reinventing the Workplace: How Business and Employees Can Both Win.* Washington, DC: The Brookings Institution.

Lichtenstein, B.M.B. (2000). "Valid or Vacuous? A Definition and Assessment of New Paradigm Research in Management." *American Behavioral Scientist* 43: 1334–1366.

Macy, J. (1991). *World As Lover, World As Self.* Berkeley, CA: Parallax Press.

Mansfield, E.D., and D.P. McAdams. (1996). "Generativity and Themes of Agency and Communion in Adult Autobiography." *Personality and Social Psychology Bulletin* 22: 721–731.

Marshall, R. 1994. "The Importance of International Labour Standards in a More Competitive Global Economy." In *International Labour Standards and Economic Interdependence*, ed. W. Sengenberger and D. Campbell. Geneva: International Labour Organization, 65–78.

Maslow, A.H. 1998. *Toward a Psychology of Being.* New York: Wiley.

Maturana, H.A., and F.J. Varela. (1987). *The Tree of Knowledge: The Biological Roots of Understanding.* Boston: Shambhala.

Mauritzen, J. (1988). "Pastoral Care for the Dying and Bereaved." *Death Studies* 12: 111–122.

Maynard, H.B., and S.E. Mehrtens. (1993). *The Fourth Wave: Business in the Twenty-First Century.* San Francisco: Berret-Koehler.

McCormick, D. (1994). "Spirituality and Management." *Journal of Managerial Psychology* 9: 5–8.

McGee, J.J. (1998). "The Emergence of Secular Corporate Spirituality." Paper presented at the Academy of Management, San Diego, August.

McKnight, R. (1984). "Spirituality in the Workplace." In *Transforming Work: A Collection of Organizational Transformation Readings*, ed. J.D. Adams. Alexandria, VA: Miles River, 138–153.

Meyer, J.P., and N.J. Allen. (1991). "A Three-Component Conceptualization of Organizational Commitment." *Human Resource Management Review* 1: 61–98.

Mirvis, P. (1997). "'Soul Work'" in Organizations." *Organization Science* 8: 193–206.

Mitroff, I.I., and E.A. Denton. (2000). *A Spiritual Audit of Corporate America.* San Francisco: Jossey-Bass.

Moberg, D.O., and P.M. Brusek. (1978). "Spiritual Well-being: A Neglected Subject in Quality of Life Research." *Social Indicators Research* 5: 303–323.

Murray, M. (1995). "Tackling Workplace Problems with Prayer." *Wall Street Journal* (Eastern Edition), October 19, B-l, B-12.

Nadesan, M.H. (1999). "The Discourses of Corporate Spiritualism an Evangelical Capitalism." *Management Communication Quarterly* 13: 3–42.

Naisbitt, J. (1982). *Megatrends.* New York: Macmillan/Merrill.

Nash, L. (1994). *Believers in Business.* Nashville, TN: Nelson.

Neal, C. (1998). "The Conscious Business Culture." *Creative Nursing* 4: 5–7.

Neck, C.P., and J.F. Milliman. (1994). "Thought Self-Leadership: Finding Spiritual Fulfillment in Organizational Life." *Journal of Managerial Psychology* 9: 9–16.

OECD. (1996). "Trade, Employment and Labour Standards: A Study of Core Worker' Rights and International Trade." Paris: OECD.

Orsborn, C. (1992). *Inner Excellence: Spiritual Principles of Life-Driven Business.* New York: New World Library.

Paloutzian, R.F. (1996). *Invitation to the Psychology of Religion*, 2d ed. Boston: Allyn and Bacon.

Paloutzian, R.F., and L.A. Kirkpatrick. (1995). "Introduction: The Scope of Religious Influences on Personal and Societal Well-being." *Journal of Social Issues* 51: 1–11.

Pargament, K.I. (1999). "The Psychology of Religion and Spirituality? Yes and No." *International Journal for the Psychology of Religion* 9: 3–16.

Piedmont, R.L. (1999). "Does Spirituality Represent the Sixth Factor of Personality? Spiritual Transcendence and the Five-Factor Model." *Journal of Personality* 67: 985–1013.

Plummer, J.T. (1989). "Changing Values." *Futurist* 7–13.

Prigogine, I., and I. Stengers. (1984). *Order Out of Chaos: Man's New Dialogue with Nature*. New York: Bantam.

Ramos, A.G. (1972). "Models of Man and Administrative Theory." *Public Administration Review* 32: 241–246.

Ray, P.H. (1996). *The Integral Culture Survey: A Study of Transformational Values in America*. Sausalito, CA: Institute of Noetic Sciences.

———. (1997). "The Emerging Culture." *American Demographics* (February): 28–32.

Ray, M., and A. Rinzler, eds. (1993). *The New Paradigm in Business*. New York: Tarcher.

Reder, M.W. (1982). "Chicago Economics: Permanence and Change." *Journal of Economic Literature* 20: 1–38.

Reich, M. (1981). *Racial Inequality: A Political-Economic Analysis*. Princeton, NJ: Princeton University Press.

Rest, J.R. (1980). "Basic Issues in Evaluating Moral Education Programs." In *Evaluating Moral Development*, ed. L. Kuhmerker, M. Mentknoski, and V.L. Erickson. Schenectady, NY: Character Research Press, 113–120.

Richins, M.L., and S. Dawson. (1992). "A Consumer Values Orientation for Materialism and Its Measurement: Scale Development and Validation." *Journal of Consumer Research* 19: 303–316.

Robinson, B.E. (2000). "Workaholism: Bridging the Gap Between Workplace, Sociocultural, and Family Research." *Journal of Employment Counseling* 37: 31–47.

Roe, R.A., and P. Ester. (1999). "Values and Work: Empirical Findings and Theoretical Perspective." *Applied Psychology: An International Review* 48: 1–21.

Rolston, H., III. (1975). "Can the East Help the West to Value Nature?" *Philosophy East and West* 37: 172–190.

Roof, W.C. (1993). *A Generation of Seekers: The Spiritual Journeys of the Baby Boom Generation*. San Francisco: HarperSanFrancisco.

Russell, P. (1989). "The Redemption of the Executive." *Leadership and Organization Development Journal* 10: 1–4.

Russell, C. (1996). "War Between Generations?" *American Demographics* 18: 4–5.

Sagie, A.; D. Elizur; and M. Koslowsky. (1996). "Work Values: A Theoretical Overview and a Model of Their Effects." *Journal of Organizational Behavior* 17: 503–514.

Sass, J.S. (2000). "Characterizing Organizational Spirituality: An Organizational Communication Culture Approach." *Communication Studies* 51: 195–207.

Scherer, J., and L. Shook. (1993). *Work and the Human Spirit*. Spokane: Scherer.

Scott, K.S.; K.S. Moore; and M.P. Miceli. (1997). "An Exploration of the Meaning and Consequences of Workaholism." *Human Relations* 50: 287–314.

Shafranske, E.P., and R.L. Gorsuch. (1984). "Factors Associated with the Perception of Spirituality in Psychotherapy." *Journal of Transpersonal Psychology* 16: 231–241.

Shaw, W.H., and B. Barry. (2000). *Moral Issues in Business*, 8th ed. Belmont, CA: Wadsworth.

Sheldrake, R. (1981). *A New Science of Life: The Hypothesis of Formative Causation*. London: Blond and Briggs.

———. (1988). *The Presence of the Past: Morphic Resonance and the Habits of Nature*. New York: Vintage Books.

Spohn, W.C. (1997). "Spirituality and Ethics: Exploring the Connections." *Theological Studies* 58: 109–124.

Stallwood, J., and R. Stoll. (1975). "Spiritual Dimensions of Nursing Practice." In *Clinical Nursing*, ed. I.L. Geland and J.Y. Passos. New York: Macmillan.

Stroudenmire, J.; D. Batman; M. Pavlov; and A. Temple. (1986). "Validation of a Holistic Living Inventory." *Psychological Reports* 57: 577–578.

Surak, J.G. (2001). "Eastern Influence." *Food Technology* 55: 19.

Tart, C. (1975). "Introduction." In *Transpersonal Psychologies*, ed. C.T. Tart. New York: Harper and Row, 3–7.

Thau R.D., and J.S. Heflin. (1997). *Generations Apart*. New York: Prometheus Books.

Tischler, L. (1999). "The Growing Interest in Spirituality in Business." *Journal of Organizational Change Management* 12: 273–279.

Trott, D.C. (1996). "Spiritual Well-being of Workers: An Exploratory Study of Spirituality in the Workplace." Dissertation, Graduate School of the University of Texas at Austin.

Tulgan B. (1995). *Managing Generation X: How to Bring Out the Best in Young Talent*. New York: Nolo Press.

Van Biema, D. (1997). "Buddhism in America: An Ancient Religion Grows Ever Stronger Roots in a New World, with the Help of the Movies, Pop Culture, and the Politics of Repressed Tibet." *Time*, October 13, 72–80.

Vaughn, F. (1979). "Spiritual Issues in Psychotherapy." *Journal of Transpersonal Psychology* 23: 105–119.

Veach, T.L., and J.N. Chappell. (1991). "Measuring Spiritual Health: A Preliminary Study." *Substance Abuse* 13: 139–149.

Vincola, A. (1998) "Work and Life: In Search of the Missing Links." *HR Focus* (August): S3–S4.

von Bertlanffy, L. (1973). *General System Theory*, rev. ed. New York: George Braziller.

Warwick, P.V. (1998). "Disputed Cause, Disputed Effect: The Postmaterialist Thesis Re-Examined." *Public Opinion Quarterly* 62: 583–609.

Way, N. (1999). "Juggling and Struggling." *BRW*, October 22, 68–75.

———. (2000). "Father of All Quality Control." *BRW*, January 28, 70–72.

Weber, M. (1958). *The Protestant Ethic and the Spirit of Capitalism: The Relationship Between Religion and the Economic and Social Life of Modern Culture*. New York: Scribner's.

Westgate, C.E. (1996). "Spiritual Wellness and Depression." *Journal of Counseling and Development* 75 (September/October): 26–35.

Wheatley, M. (1992). *Leadership and the New Science: Learning About Organization from an Orderly Universe*. San Francisco: Berrett-Koehler.

Wilkinson, F. (1994). "Equality, Efficiency and Economic Progress: The Case for Universally Applied Equitable Standards for Wages and Conditions of Work." In *International Labour Standards and Economic Interdependence*, ed. W. Sengenberger and D. Campbell. Geneva: International Labour Organization, 61–86.

Wolcott, I. (1996). *A Nice Place to Work: Small Business and Workers with Family Responsibilities*. Melbourne, Australia: Australian Institute of Family Studies.

Wong, P. T. P. (1998). "Implicit Theories of Meaningful Life and the Development of the Personal Meaning Profile (PMP)." In *Handbook of Personal Meaning: Theory, Research, and Practice*, ed. P. T. P. Wong and P. Fry. Mahwah, NJ: Lawrence Erlbaum, 5.

Yang, J.; D. Gan; and T. Hong, eds. (1997). *Eastern Standard Time: A Guide to Asian Influence on American Culture from Astro Boy to Zen Buddhism*. Boston: Houghton Mifflin.

Yuet-Ha, M. (1996). "Orientating Values with Eastern Ways." *People Management* 2: 28–31.

Zinnbauer B.J.; K.I. Pargament; and A.B. Scott. (1999). "The Emerging Meanings of Religiousness and Spirituality: Problems and Prospects." *Journal of Personality* 67: 889–919.

Zinsmeister, K. (1997). "Days of Confusion." *American Enterprise* 8: 4–8.

Zukav, Gary. (1989). *The Seat of the Soul*. New York: Simon and Schuster.

CHAPTER 2

BUSINESS AND THE SPIRIT

Management Practices That Sustain Values

JEFFREY PFEFFER

One would think that managing people in ways consistent with building and maintaining their spirit would be an uncontroversial idea. After all, there has been increasing interest in workplace spirituality and management practices that help develop people (e.g., Ashmos and Duchon 2000; Mitroff and Denton 1999; Mirvis 1997). This interest derives in part from the importance of work organizations in people's lives today—"people are spending more of their time working and number among closest friends their coworkers" (Mirvis 1997, 198). At the same time, waves of downsizing (Cappelli 1999), increased turnover, more people working as temporaries and contractors (Pfeffer and Baron 1988), and more frequent changes in ownership have created employees who are less loyal and committed and are angrier and more disaffected, working in places characterized by "fear, pressure, and impermanence" (Mirvis 1997, 198). Even as these changes in the workplace are occurring, writers have argued that organizations that are values-based and values-driven are "built to last" (Collins and Porras 1994) and are better able to engage the hearts and the minds of their people (O'Reilly and Pfeffer 2000).

Because people spend a lot of their life at work and partly derive their social identity from their workplace, what happens to them on the job is important for their mental and physical health and well-being (e.g., Cartwright and Cooper 1997). Aside from any social welfare benefits from managing people better, there is a substantial and growing body of evidence suggesting that an organization's management practices have important effects (both statistically and substantively) on such economic outcomes as quality, productivity, and profitability (e.g., Pfeffer 1998; Becker and Huselid 1998). Although the specific dimensions identified by various researchers vary somewhat, most of those writing about high-commitment or high-performance management practices identify at least the following as constituting the foundations of such a model: (1) employment security and mutual commitment, (2) selective recruiting for cultural fit as well as skill, (3) an investment in training and developing the skills and capabilities of employees, (4) decentralization of decision-making and the delegation of substantial responsibility, often to self-managed teams, (5) pay and other rewards that are contingent on group and organizational, as well as individual, performance, and (6) sharing information broadly with people inside the company (e.g., Pfeffer 1998). The argument is that these management practices elicit discretionary effort from people as well as making it possible for people to both learn and develop and use their skill and knowledge to benefit their organizations.

The positive effects of using high-performance or high-commitment work practices have been observed in numerous industries including: automobile assembly (MacDuffie 1995), apparel manufacturing (Dunlop and Weil 1996; Bailey 1993; Appelbaum et al. 2000; Abernathy et al. 1999), oil refineries (Ricketts 1994), integrated steel manufacturing (Ichniowski, Shaw, and Prennushi 1997), steel minimills (Arthur 1994), semiconductor fabrication (Brown 1996; Sattler and Sohoni 1999), telephone call centers (Batt 1999), medical electronic instruments and imaging (Appelbaum et al. 2000), banking (Delery and Doty 1996), as well as in multicompany studies that span industries (e.g., Huselid 1995; Welbourne and Andrews 1996; Burton and O'Reilly 2000; Hannan et al. 2000; Youndt et al. 1996).

Nor are the positive effects of employing high-performance work practices limited to companies operating in the United States. The positive economic benefits of using high-commitment or high-performance work arrangements have been observed for organizations operating in such countries as Germany (Bilmes, Wetzker, and Xhonneux 1997), Korea (Lee and Miller 1999), Japan (Ichniowski and Shaw 1999), and the United Kingdom (Wood and de Menezes 1998). Moreover, the importance of how firms manage the employment relationship has been found not only for large, established companies, but also for small, entrepreneurial firms. For instance, a longitudinal study of entrepreneurial companies in the Silicon Valley found that those companies founded under a "commitment" model were twelve times more likely to advance to a successful initial public offering during the study period compared to firms not founded under a commitment model (Burton and O'Reilly 2000), and not one of the firms with a commitment approach to managing people failed during a five-year period (Hannan et al. 2000).

The study of high-technology companies by Burton and O'Reilly (2000) speaks to the importance of values as well as management practices in affecting organizational outcomes. Their research found that there was an effect not just of specific management practices, but also of the founder's values on success, measured as time to the initial public offering. Companies with people-centered values, operationalized by the founder's espousing a commitment model of attachment between the company and its people, performed better. There was also an effect of high-commitment organizational practices on performance, as well as an interaction such that companies with both people-centered values and high-commitment practices enjoyed even greater performance.

These results help to account for some recent findings (e.g., Cappelli and Neumark 2001) that did *not* uncover a positive relationship between management practices and company financial performance. The work by O'Reilly and his colleagues (Burton and O'Reilly 2000; O'Reilly and Pfeffer 2000) suggests that management practices, by themselves, may not be enough to ensure improved performance. Employees look not only at *what* is done, but also at the motivations and beliefs that underlie management approaches. If managers are trying to do the right thing, people will give them some room for mistakes; conversely, good management practices implemented with malevolent intent may not produce such positive results. As George Gallup noted long ago, people are judged by their intentions, not just by their results: "People tend to judge a man by his goals, by what he's trying to do, and not necessarily by what he accomplishes or how well he succeeds" (quoted in Edelman 1964, 78). If management approaches are premised on nonemployee-centered beliefs, people will see through that, and the company may not benefit from implementing the management techniques.

Although the *idea, concept,* or *theory* of managing people in ways that build and sustain values and their spirit may not seem controversial, when this idea or intention is confronted with the realities of what is actually going on in many workplaces, as well as much conventional wisdom about management practices, there are enormous discontinuities. Terkel's (1985) interviews with working people showed that many people work in places that wound their spirits. For example, the CEO of a health care software development company sent an e-mail to his employees complaining that because the parking lot was too empty early in the morning, in the evening, and on weekends, they weren't working hard enough, and he threatened them with layoffs, cuts in benefits, and other potential punishments if they didn't shape up (Wong 2001). He also gave them a deadline: "You have two weeks . . . Tick, tock" (Wong 2001). This incident is just one example of the many companies that manage through fear and stress (e.g., Pfeffer and Sutton 2000).

Many widespread and widely advocated management practices are destructive to the employees' spirits. In this chapter, I first review what the research literature suggests *are* important characteristics that people seek in their work. I then propose some management practices that are consistent with building values and enriching people's spirit, and contrast them with what is currently occurring in organizations and often advocated by management consultants and writers. Finally, I make the argument that because people spend so much of their time in formal organizations, and organizations are so important to their social identities, there is an imperative to make organizations more consistent with human values and psychology, and as a byproduct, more effective as well.

WHAT PEOPLE VALUE AT WORK: DIMENSIONS OF THE SPIRIT

We should probably begin with a definition of "spirit": "spirit comes from the Latin word *spiritus* meaning 'breath.' It is defined as 'the vital principle or animating force traditionally believed to be within living beings' " (Anderson 2000, 16). What elements define this vital force, at least as it is manifest in organizational workplaces? According to an interview and questionnaire study of human resource and line executives, the most important thing that gives people meaning and purpose in their jobs is "the ability to realize my full potential as a person" (Mitroff and Denton 1999, 85). Abraham Maslow (1954) described this as self-actualization. Most people love to learn and develop competence and mastery. That's what impels little children to learn to walk and to explore the world in which they live. One of the reasons developing skill is so important is that it provides a way of enhancing one's self-concept, and the self-enhancement motive is quite strong (Steele 1988; Tesser 1988). So, people often seek in their work the ability to develop and master new skills and competencies and to learn new things, thereby becoming more competent and knowledgeable and realizing their full potential.

Many people seek not only competence and mastery in their work, but also to do work that has some social meaning or social value. A study of 696 people in four midwestern hospitals, undertaken to develop a measure of workplace spirituality, concluded that having work that was meaningful and purposeful was one of the most important dimensions of this construct (Ashmos and Duchon 2000). Two items in the meaning at work scale were: "I see a connection between my work and the larger social good of my community" and "The work I do is connected to what I think is important in life" (Ashmos and Duchon 2000, 143). This workplace dimension is clearly consistent with building organizations that stand for something and that have an overarching purpose or mission, a theme prominent in contemporary writing about building great companies (e.g., Collins and Porras 1994).

A third important dimension that people value at work is being able to feel part of a larger community or being interconnected. "Part of being alive is living in connection to other human beings" (Ashmos and Duchon 2000, 136). People value their affiliations at work. Having good colleagues and being associated with a good organization were both highly rated dimensions in

Mitroff and Denton's (1999) study of what provided people with meaning in their work. Both case and survey evidence are consistent with the view that one's colleagues are an important source of job satisfaction (Locke 1976; Smith, 1992). Particularly as people spend more time at work (Schor 1991) and as work becomes an ever more important source of social identity, who one works with and, more importantly, the nature of those social relations in the workplace, loom ever more important. As Mirvis (1997, 198) has noted, "lacking continuity and connection in so many other settings, many naturally look to their organization as a communal center."

The fourth important dimension of what people value at work that is quite consistent with building the spirit is being able to live and work in an integrated fashion. The advent of bureaucracy and scientific management were designed to separate ascriptive, personalistic dimensions from the workplace. People were to be judged on what they did and how they performed, not who they were. Although bureaucratic control (Edwards 1979) embraced the laudable goal of ending the evaluation of people based on such irrelevant characteristics as race, gender, social background, and social ties to higher-level managers, as it was implemented, the result came increasingly to be the requirement for people to leave part of themselves at the door and to become someone else at work. People are not only rational, sentient beings; they also have emotions and feelings that obviously affect their attitudes and behavior. To deny this aspect of people on the job meant that "managers and other employees were expected to complete their allotted tasks without involving their essential self" (Ackers and Preston 1997, 678).

But leaving part of oneself at the doorway to work every day is quite difficult, effortful, and at, times, stressful. Kahn et al.'s (1964) classic study of role conflict described one form of conflict as inter-role—the contradictory demands made for behavior by the different roles a single individual occupies, such as the conflict between being a good parent and being a good employee. Kahn and his colleagues also described person-role conflict, which occurred when people's work roles required them to do and be things that were inconsistent with their basic beliefs and self-concept. The Kahn et al. study documented the stress that occurred when individuals faced conflicting demands and had to somehow resolve them. Trying to compel people to be "different" than who they are on the job is not only stressful and uses energy, it essentially sends a message that who people really are is not what the organization wants or desires on the job. Such a message obviously contradicts people's desire for self-enhancement and their drive to maintain self-esteem. And, the message is quite destructive of the human spirit in that it denies the value of people as they are, sending a signal that they need to be someone different, and compelling them to behave in ways different from their essential nature.

MANAGEMENT PRACTICES THAT BUILD AND DESTROY
VALUES AND THE SPIRIT

We can examine and evaluate management practices on the basis of how each is logically (and empirically) consistent or inconsistent with the four fundamental dimensions of what people seek in the workplace: (1) interesting work that permits them to learn, develop, and have a sense of competence and mastery, (2) meaningful work that provides some feeling of purpose, (3) a sense of connection and positive social relations with their coworkers, and (4) the ability to live an integrated life, so that one's work role and other roles are not inherently in conflict and so that a person's work role does not conflict with his or her essential nature and who the person is as a human being. Using this perspective provides a somewhat different, but nonetheless complementary lens on a number of management practices. These ideas about what people want at work also help us understand why some management practices work, and why others do not.

Mission, Values, and the Dictum to Maximize Shareholder Value or Profit

It has come to be taken as accepted wisdom and good management practice to run companies solely for the benefit of shareholders, with the concomitant emphasis on maximizing shareholder value and profits. Although many companies have adopted statements of mission or values, for too many these are simply platitudes to be hung on walls or put on small cards to be carried in wallets, but not something to be actually implemented and lived. Commenting on how few companies took their mission statements seriously, author Eileen Shapiro described a mission statement as "a talisman, hung in public places, to ward off evil spirits" (Shapiro 1995, 15). There are, however, several problems with managing just for the interests of shareholders and ignoring the importance of mission and values.

First, maximizing profit or shareholder value is not an objective that very often stirs people's imaginations or emotions, even if the employees are also shareholders. People want to make a difference in the world and to engage in meaningful activities, and the mere accumulation of value or assets—which will invariably and inevitably be left behind at death anyway—does not provide a compelling rationale or motivation to inspire people. Second, it is not clear why, in the contemporary world, maximizing shareholder value makes strategic business sense. Most observers of the contemporary scene maintain that what is really scarce is not capital, but talent and knowledge. If we are indeed in a "war for talent," to use the McKinsey phrase (Chambers et al. 1998), then it would seem that focusing solely on returns to capital makes little or no economic sense. If the winners will be those companies that are best able to attract, retain, and motivate their people, then management practices or philosophy that ignore or downplay people compared to capital cannot be a recipe for success.

Third, as Aoki (1988) has demonstrated using a game-theoretic approach, operating companies for the benefit of both shareholders and employees can lead to better decisions than simply trying to maximize share price. That is because "in order to generate the organizational quasi rent [exceptional profits], both bodies [shareholders and employees] need each other's commitment to the accumulation of financial and human assets" (Aoki 1988, 155).

Fourth, it is not at all clear, from either a legal or a logical standpoint, why capital should receive a higher priority than other stakeholders in the company, such as labor. As Dennis Bakke, the CEO of AES (the largest independent power producer in the world and a company that does live its values) asks, "Where does capital come from?" If you earn income, some you spend and some you save. Those savings can be used to purchase stocks, bonds, or other financial instruments. In other words, capital, for an individual or a country, comes from the residual of income earned but not spent. But seen in that way, capital is simply the result of past labor. Why should *past* labor receive a higher priority than *current* labor?

Nor is there some legal obligation to maximize stock price without regard to other constituencies (Bagley and Page 1999). "Thirty states have enacted statutes intended to permit (and, in the case of Connecticut, to require) consideration of other constituencies" in corporate decision-making by boards of directors (Bagley and Page 1999, 921). These laws have been passed in part in recognition of the fact that share prices do *not* always reflect a company's real value or profitability, so that making decisions only on the basis of capital market considerations is unwise. "Delaware courts, among others, have continually expressed skepticism over the accuracy of viewing the trading prices of shares as a reflection of the corporation's 'intrinsic value,' and consequently, the degree to which directors can use those trading prices as a guide to action" (Bagley and Page 1999, 920).

Finally, stock price and profits are *outcomes*. Not focusing on the processes—including managing by using values that engage the hearts and minds of people—that produce those outcomes causes problems. Reichheld (1996) has shown that superior profit performance comes from having loyal customers, and loyal customers come from having loyal, long-term employees. By focusing on building employee and customer retention, companies outperform their peers, and this is a result of how they manage the value proposition they create. Southwest Airlines did not begin with an objective to build a company that is worth more than the rest of the U.S. airline industry combined—although it currently is. It began with an objective of taking care of its people and its customers, and the rest followed as a consequence. Not focusing on the processes that produce results, but instead obsessively focusing on the goal, is a prescription for frustration and management problems.

Companies that excel at engaging the hearts and minds of their people not only *have* values, they *live* them, thereby providing an element of the sacred in the everyday working environment. AES, for instance, has four core values of fun, fairness, integrity, and social responsibility. The company evaluates itself partly on how well it is succeeding in living its values, something it discusses in its annual report. And the company will adhere to its values even at the cost of profit, a fact that has caused the Securities and Exchange Commission to ask the company to list "adherence to AES values" as a risk factor in its offering prospectus. AES also has a general objective to carefully steward resources, a more specific mission to help provide electricity to the world, and a goal to be the leading global power company. The company operates all over the world including in places, such as Brazil and Argentina, that experience periodic currency crises and economic problems that adversely affect the price of AES's stock. When the company is questioned about why it operates in such economically risky places, it answers in terms of its mission to provide electricity to the world, something that can fundamentally change people's lives and their economic well-being. "The essence of AES's mission to the world makes it inevitable that we will endeavor to serve in areas that some consider unstable" (AES 1998, 15).

How does living by its mission square with a company's achieving profits? Profits are obviously necessary for a company to survive, but to Bakke and the people of AES, profits are not the "be all, end all" of a company:

> Profits are to a corporation much like breathing is to life. Breathing is not the goal of life, but without breath life ends. Similarly, without turning a profit, a corporation, too, will cease to exist. (Bakke 1996, 5)

The rationale for AES's existence as a company is "to help individuals make a difference in the world that they could not otherwise make" (AES 1997, 6). This way of operating infuses work at AES with meaning. As one AES person stated, "I am comfortable in the knowledge that we are making a difference and that what I do matters. I am proud to be a part of the team" (AES 2000, 5). The result is a company where people stay even when they can afford to leave and a competitive advantage in attracting and retaining talent.

Autonomy and Decision-Making Responsibility

If you think carefully about it, most management practices such as setting budgets, annual performance reviews, meetings and reports charting progress toward some goal, and measurements and incentive compensation schemes are about controlling and directing behavior. These management practices are not simply for providing feedback so that people can guide their own actions more effectively. Indeed, the very definition of management includes: "to control and direct" and "to make and keep (one) submissive" (Merriam-Webster 1981, 1372). But such an approach is inconsistent with individuals realizing their full potential and achieving a feeling of mastery and competence. In a world in which some are told what to do by others, the self-esteem of those doing the telling may be enhanced, but those being told are not likely to develop much belief in their worth, competence, or value.

That is why studies of job design have typically found that autonomy is the most important factor influencing motivation and job satisfaction (e.g., Hackman and Oldham 1980). And that is why one of the more important management practices to build people's spirits involves letting them actually make decisions—important decisions—about organizational direction and resource allocations. Most companies are run under the principle of hierarchy: those higher up must know more and be more competent and therefore, most important decisions should be left to them to minimize the risks of mistakes. But operating in this way, although consistent with Taylorism and the idea of separating planning from doing, leaves the majority of people as passive recipients of direction rather than as active decision-making agents.

This is not how AES operates. In that company, the maintenance group in the Thames, Connecticut, plant volunteered to be responsible for investing about $12 million in debt reserves; Paul Burdick, a mechanical engineer without an MBA, led the financing for the $404 million Warrior Run project in Maryland; a financing of about $350 million in Northern Ireland was managed by a team led by two control room operators; and Oscar Prieto, a chemical engineer who had worked for AES for just two years in his first job in the electric power industry, was given the task of leading AES's involvement in Brazil, and after eighteen months was in charge of about one-quarter of the company's total assets (O'Reilly and Pfeffer 2000, 163). At AES, supervisors are taught to give away their power and to become servant leaders. This is because AES believes that if someone's supervisor makes a decision for that person, the person doesn't have a job. Part of being human entails making decisions and exercising responsibility, and if someone can't do that, the person cannot really experience full humanness.

·At New United Motors (NUMMI), the Toyota-General Motors joint venture that took over a closed GM manufacturing plant in Fremont, California, and improved productivity by about 50 percent while dramatically improving quality, absenteeism, and turnover, the key to success was simple: engage the minds, as well as the hands, of people who had worked in the plant for decades and consequently possessed vast stores of tacit knowledge. Not only did unleashing the knowledge of front-line people enhance business results, it improved the spirit in the plant and turned a workforce plagued by alcoholism and drug abuse into a model for the industry.

There is little doubt that management practices that take responsibility and decision-making away from people harm their spirit. Conversely, delegating real autonomy to people permits them to flourish and grow, thereby realizing more of their untapped potential.

Self-Managed Teams

Implementing self-managed teams has several desirable effects. First of all, the research evidence strongly suggests that teams are an effective way to organize work. "Two decades of research in organizational behavior provides considerable evidence that workers in self-managed teams enjoy greater autonomy and discretion, and this effect translates into intrinsic rewards and job satisfaction; teams also outperform traditionally supervised groups in the majority of . . . empirical studies" (Batt 1996, 340). A longitudinal field study of the implementation of self-managed teams in a manufacturing plant observed a 38 percent reduction in the defect rate and a 20 percent increase in productivity (Banker et al. 1996).

Second, teams provide peer-based monitoring and control, which is both more acceptable and less costly, as well as being less threatening to self-esteem than hierarchical control. "Instead of management devoting time and energy to controlling the workforce directly, workers control themselves" (Graham 1995, 97). At NUMMI, front-line people appreciated the fact that they were able to organize and direct themselves and that the front-line supervisors were seldom visible on the factory floor.

Teams also provide social support and advice to people exercising responsibility and making decisions. Being able to access others for their expertise and advice helps to assure better quality decisions, as the research literature suggests that collective judgments are often of higher quality (Davis 1969). And, teams take some of the burden and loneliness off of people who need to exercise judgment in uncertain situations. In fact, Festinger (1954) noted that people seek social support under conditions of uncertainty. A team-based structure automatically puts such social support close at hand.

With respect to what people seek in their work environment, a team-based structure provides several things. Most obviously, it helps people achieve a sense of connection to others, because they work with others to achieve joint objectives. The literature has shown that working together toward a common objective helps build interpersonal liking and stronger interpersonal ties (Leavitt 1978, ch. 20). Second, by substituting peer support for hierarchical control, self-managing teams help to maintain positive self-images and feelings of worth. Although team-based control is still control, being guided by one's peers in a joint decision-making exercise maintains more autonomy and sense of control over one's work environment than being told what to do by the boss. In these ways, a team-based structure helps to build people's spirit at work.

Collective Forms of Reward and Recognition

Although individual pay or recognition for individual performance is a popular prescription for the design of compensation and reward systems (e.g., Lazear 1995), more collective forms of reward are at once frequently more effective and more consistent with people's desires to achieve connection with others in the workplace.

One of the most frequently heard complaints from human resource managers and compensation and other consultants is how hard it is to get supervisors to differentiate in their raises between the best and worst performers. Instead of seeing this behavior as some sort of "problem," one might ask: "What does this tendency to pay people more equally (than the experts suggest you should) imply about people in organizations?" One thing that it certainly suggests is that, left to their own preferences, people prefer a more equal distribution of rewards, which is precisely what various studies have found (Leventhal 1976; Leventhal, Michaels, and Sanford 1972). Given a choice, for instance in an experimental setting, subjects will invariably allocate rewards more equally than would be warranted if they based reward allocations strictly on performance differences (Leventhal et al. 1972). The literature suggests that these more egalitarian reward allocations are undertaken in an effort to enhance social solidarity and the maintenance of positive social relations. In other words, people, when given a choice, make decisions about reward allocations that help maintain closer interpersonal ties, and these allocations are frequently more equal than implied on the basis of differences in performance.

And, there is evidence that more egalitarian reward allocations may not be completely misguided decisions on the part of people who obstinately refuse to reward differential individual performance differentially. In a study of the consequences of reward distributions in academic departments, Pfeffer and Langton (1993) found that the larger the amount of pay dispersion (more inequality in pay), the lower the job satisfaction. They also found that paying for performance and greater pay inequality were associated with *lower* research productivity and a smaller likelihood of working collaboratively. This latter result means that pay inequality diminishes the social ties in the workplace, something that most people, seeking connection with others on the job, do not prefer. Other studies of the effects of reward distributions have found that more inequality promotes more turnover, particularly for those farther down in the salary distribution (Pfeffer and Davis-Blake 1992). Bloom (1999) found that inequality in the salaries paid to baseball players on a team negatively affected a number of different outcomes ranging from won-loss percentage to attendance as well as measures of individual player performance.

One need not pay people without regard to performance, however. The important distinction is to pay people more collectively rather than individualistically on the basis of how well the whole organization or their subunit performs. This fundamental idea underlies such pay systems as profit sharing, gain sharing, employee stock ownership, and bonuses based on plant or company-wide performance. In each of these instances, pay is very much at risk. But pay is not determined by how well one person does in competition with another, but instead by how well the total system performs. A more collective reward structure diminishes the internal competition that retards knowledge sharing and helping others (e.g., Pfeffer and Sutton 2000; Lazear 1989), a big problem in interdependent systems. It also helps to develop a greater sense of community and common fate, thereby increasing the strength of social bonds of people to the organization and to each other.

Let People Be Who They Are and Use and Develop Their Gifts and Skills

Consider the following paradox. Many companies hire experienced executives and experienced technical people for their knowledge and skill, acquired through years of practice. But once hired, these people are frequently subjected to rules, procedures, controls, and told "that's the way we do things here," as a consequence denying them the ability to fully use the very experience and knowledge that caused them to be hired in the first place. The implicit assumption behind much of what organizations do seems to be that people cannot be trusted to use their talents in the interests of the organizations, that instead they need to be told what to do and monitored to be sure that they do it. Moreover, the presumption is that people ought to be molded into some predetermined view of what a good employee is.

But such an effort to control and tell people what to do as they are being molded confronts the reality of psychological reactance (Brehm 1966). Reactance theory holds that people rebel against constraints, in part to assert their freedom. It is the psychological equivalent of the law of physics that states that every action causes an opposite and equal reaction: attempts to mold, shape, and control provoke resistance. In turn, this resistance then justifies even more elaborate efforts to control and mold, and so the cycle continues. Moreover, attempts to control and monitor also unleash the self-fulfilling prophecy (Archibald 1974) and a mutually reinforcing cycle of behavior. As Strickland (1958) nicely described the process, the only way to know if you can trust some one is to trust them. In his study, subjects who randomly monitored one subordinate (actually a confederate of the experimenter) more closely came to believe that this person needed more close oversight and could not be trusted as much. And someone who is monitored may come to believe he or she cannot be trusted and, as a result, act in an untrustworthy way. Consequently, "views about human nature have important practical consequences. . . . [O]ur beliefs about human nature help shape human nature itself" (Frank 1988, 237).

Organizations that seek to nurture people's spirit in the workplace don't just let them do anything they want or act without direction. Instead, they help people understand what is expected and what they need to do to contribute to the organization, but they let the individuals decide how to accomplish the tasks and how to contribute in their own way to the collective effort. Three examples illustrate the point.

1. At The Men's Wearhouse, the highly successful retailer of off-price, tailored men's clothing (such as suits and sport coats) as well as casual wear, the company believes it is in the people business, not the suit business. This means "the company's job is to help people understand others, listen better, and develop excitement about helping themselves and their teammates reach their potential as persons" (O'Reilly and Pfeffer 2000, 85). Much of the training at Suits University is not just about how to sell or the specifics of men's clothing, but about how to be a better person and more available and accessible for one's friends, family, and colleagues. The company's mission statement includes "having fun and maintaining our values. These values include nurturing creativity, growing together, admitting to our mistakes, promoting a happy, healthy lifestyle, enhancing our sense of community and striving to become self-actualized people" (O'Reilly and Pfeffer 2000, 86). The company believes its success lies in unlocking the untapped human potential present in all people. At one time, Charlie Bresler, in charge of human resources, had the title of Executive Vice President of Human Development. Unlocking individuals' potential involves letting people be creative and become self-actualized. The company's success comes from its outstanding levels of customer service and its relatively low losses due to theft. These results, in turn, come from having people who are not only proud to be at the company, but feel that they are becoming better people for their experience of working at The Men's Wearhouse.

2. SAS Institute, the largest privately owned software company in the world, believes that its employees will have three or four careers over their working lives. The company wants them to have all of their careers at SAS. The company encourages people to learn and develop—there is a lot of training—and it also encourages people to move laterally as their skills and interests dictate. As David Russo, formerly the head of human resources, explained:

> There are no silos. . . . Everything is based on a tool kit. If your tool kit fits this division's model for business and you want to do that, chances are pretty good you'll get to do that. And if two years later you see something else you want to do and it's across three organizational boundaries, you get to do that. (O'Reilly and Pfeffer 2000, 115)

Note that the company's idea of career planning relies heavily on people finding their own interests and expressing them as they move across activities at SAS where (a) they can contribute to the company and (b) they can fulfill their own desires for what kind of work they want to do.

3. As a third example, consider the Wild Hare restaurant, run by executive chef Joey Altman and recognized as one of the premier restaurants on the San Francisco peninsula. When someone is hired into the Wild Hare, Joey explains his vision for the restaurant, the kind of dining experience he is hoping to create, not just with the food but also with the ambience, the service, the entire experience. Then he lets people figure out how to use their particular talents and interests to make that vision come alive. As he explains his management philosophy about service:

> As far as service goes, I realize that I have ten waiters and ten different people. I don't want Darrell to be like Joanie, and Joanie, I don't want you to be like Susie, and Susie, I don't want you to be like Paul. Paul, I want you to be the best Paul you can be. Susie, I want you to be the best Susie you can be. I just want you all to be knowledgeable and use your strengths of your personality to be the best.

None of these organizations is inefficient or out of control. Each operates on the premise that people will do a good job if they know what they need to do and are given the tools and training to succeed. Each provides direction and information about what the business objectives are and then helps people find a way—their own way—to contribute to the organization's success. In this way, each of these companies let people be themselves even as they connect with their teammates and contribute to the success of the whole.

Providing a Way for People to Fulfill Their Family and Other Social Obligations

Particularly in the Silicon Valley, high-technology culture of the late 1990s, working long, almost endless hours was a sign of one's importance—if you had to be on site all the time, it must mean the company could not survive without you. Working long hours was also presumably a signal of commitment to one's employer, indicating that work came first, before other interests and obligations. It got to the point where people would come to work after hours or on the weekend, for instance, at Apple Computer, just to sign in and then leave to do other things. Note, for instance, the Cerner CEO's comments equating hours with the quality of work and commitment to the company:

> We are getting less than 40 hours of work from a large number of our . . . EMPLOYEES . . . The parking lot is sparsely used at 8 a.m.; likewise at 5 p.m. . . . NEVER in my career have I allowed a team which worked for me to think they had a 40-hour job" (Wong 2001, 1). Neal Patterson's recommendation: "I STRONGLY suggest that you call some 7 AM, 6 PM and Saturday AM team meetings. . . . My measurement will be the parking lot. . . . The pizza man should show up at 7:30 PM to feed the starving teams working late." (F . . . Company.com, 2001)

Although one's job is important, we have important social ties with others not in the workplace—people such as spouses, friends, children, parents, and so forth. Organizations that compel people to choose between having a successful career and a life, between loyalty to the company and the commitments to one's friends and family, not only create role conflict, but potentially impoverish people's lives and their spirit. I recall seeing a former Stanford MBA student about nine years after she had graduated. "How's your social life?" I inquired. "I don't have one," was the response, "I'm married to Apple Computer."

The relentless time demands of work, particularly by many so-called "new economy" companies, has had the unintended and undesirable effect of essentially foreclosing those companies to women. Relatively few female Stanford MBA graduates are still employed full time ten to fifteen years after their graduation, and this is a population of immensely talented, highly educated, and motivated people who nonetheless cannot resolve the conflicts between being an employee and having a life and commitments outside of work. Many of the accommodations made to enhance work–life balance, things such as health clubs and concierge services at the job site, merely make it easier to never leave work. Cell phones, computers at home, and other technologies that enhance access have increasingly blurred the boundaries between work and nonwork. It is hard to know how studies that demonstrate the increasing time devoted to work can actually be reliably completed, given that for many people, particularly in managerial and professional occupations, being on-call or involved with the company are activities that easily interpenetrate presumably nonwork and even vacation time.

But none of this—the excessive time demands, the forced choice between the company and one's life, and the role conflicts thereby created—are inevitable or even useful. SAS Institute, located in Cary, North Carolina, is the largest privately owned software company in the world, with sales in excess of $1.1 billion. The company's software provides statistical analysis and data mining and data warehousing that is used by more than 80 percent of the *Fortune* 500 and more than 90 percent of the 100 largest companies in the United States. Although part of a highly dynamic and competitive market, SAS is famous for its 35-hour workweek; its generous, family-oriented benefits; and its onsite day care facility. People are encouraged to visit their children during the day, to eat lunch with them in one of the company cafeterias, to coach their sports, to be involved in their education. More than a few SAS employees are married to other people who work for the company. The spacious grounds are used for picnics on the weekends, and the company's facilities, including its swimming pool and athletic facilities, are open to families as well as the employees. The philosophy is simple:

> The best way to produce the best and get the best results is to behave as if the people who are creating those things for you are important to you. . . . It just means you take care of the folks who are taking care of you. (O'Reilly and Pfeffer 2000, 107–108)

SAS realizes that the people who are important to its employees are their family members, domestic partners, and those for whom they have responsibility. Recognizing this fact, SAS Institute removes much of the workday stress and strain from employees, in part by providing benefits and services that help them effectively meet their family commitments, but more importantly, by recognizing that people have lives and interests outside of work and honoring those obligations also.

SAS Institute has enjoyed more than twenty-four consecutive years of double-digit growth, a license renewal rate of more than 95 percent, and many product awards. The company has won numerous awards for its workplace practices. The two things are connected—its employee loyalty has enabled it to achieve outstanding customer satisfaction and customer retention. SAS's management style has produced a turnover rate consistently below 5 percent and a workplace that attracts more than thirty, and frequently more than fifty, applicants for each vacant position—all of this in the software industry that is not known for its low turnover, surfeit of talent, or being family-friendly. By building a company where people can have both a job and a life, SAS Institute nurtures the spirit of its people and creates a more benign world for them even as it produces better results for its customers.

Driving Fear and Abuse Out of the Workplace

W. Edwards Deming's (1986) prescription to drive out fear seems to be honored in the breach in many contemporary workplaces. And no wonder. Some of the meanest, most abusive bosses have been lauded in the business press and on Wall Street. When Al Dunlap, nicknamed "Chainsaw" for his massive layoffs at Scott Paper and Sunbeam, was hired by Sunbeam, the stock price soared by 60 percent, "the largest jump in the exchange's history" (Byrne 1999, 11). Frank Lorenzo, who took Continental Airlines into bankruptcy twice and destroyed Eastern Airlines as he fought implacably with the unions and the employees, was hailed by the press as a business genius; and he was even sought out as a source of advice on labor relations by the head of Air France—even after his horrible track record. *Fortune* used to run a list of the toughest bosses. Somehow it must seem macho, tough, or hard headed to inspire fear in the workforce. I have had more than one manager state that without a certain amount of fear, people get soft or lazy. An occasional layoff or firing, an occasional tirade, keeps people on their toes, so the theory goes.

But a management style based on fear ultimately doesn't work. First, it discourages people from telling the truth and bringing news, including bad news, to the boss. This means that companies operate without knowing what is actually going on. Second, fear encourages people to look out only for themselves and their immediate self-interest. They will not worry too much about the company, or their colleagues, in their drive for self-preservation. Third, fear drives good people out of the organization, thereby depriving the company of the talent required to prevail under competitive conditions. Fourth, fear demoralizes people, causing them to withdraw and give up even if they stay in the company, thereby reducing efforts and knowledge applied for the organization's benefit.

All of this can be seen in the case of Linda Wachner, the now-deposed CEO of Warnaco, an apparel maker that wound up in bankruptcy. Her management style made liberal use of fear, intimidation, and abuse:

> Mrs. Wachner also developed a reputation for demoralizing employees by publicly dressing them down for missing sales and profit goals or for simply displeasing her. Often . . . the attacks were personal rather than professional. (Kaufman 2001, 1)

The consequence: poor performance that many observers directly attributed to her approach to managing people:

> . . . Mrs. Wachner's style has hurt and perhaps even killed the company . . . her personal criticism of employees . . . has led to excessive staff turnover and robbed the company of talent it needed to maintain quality operations. Warnaco has, for example, employed three chief financial officers at the Authentic Fitness division in five years, five presidents of Calvin Klein Kids in three years and three heads of Warnaco Intimate Apparel in four years. (Kaufman 2001, 1)

Nor are these results an unusual consequence of fear. Dunlap was fired from Sunbeam when a massive accounting fraud was uncovered, a fraud encouraged by his drive for "numbers" at any price. Frank Lorenzo lost his job at Continental and has been precluded from holding an executive position in the airline industry because of a management approach that sought victory over the company's employees at any price, a scorched earth policy that ruined customer service as well as financial results.

Fear and intimidation are anathema to building spirit in the workplace. Fear makes people feel bad about themselves, each other, and the company. It breaks them down, not as part of some socialization process, but simply for the joy it gives those doing the intimidating in seeing others squirm and suffer.

Companies that build spirit treat people with dignity and respect, as people, not simply as economic agents or as factors of production. Southwest Airlines will fire employees who are rude to customers or cruel to each other. AES has built a culture of forgiveness, and The Men's Wearhouse has made "admitting mistakes" one of its core values. At SAS Institute, almost no mistake is punished, because the company wants to encourage creativity and innovation. Companies would be well served to model themselves after these examples and rid themselves of managers who succeed at the expense of the dignity and happiness of others.

AN AGENDA FOR WORKPLACE CHANGE

We spend a lot of time at work. We have and make friends at work. We are identified, in part, by where we work and what we do. The vast majority of people earn their livelihoods at work, in a job where they work for others. Although this was not always so (Boulding 1968), it is now taken for granted. The economic well-being of ourselves and our communities depend on the decisions organizations make, about how to organize, where to locate, and how to compete with other organizations both nearby and in other countries. It is obvious but true—organizations are important.

But there is an implication of these truisms that people sometimes don't want to face: If organizations are ubiquitous and important, then we cannot be neutral as to what goes on in them and their effects on those who work in them. Roy Adams (1999, 1) has stated this position most elegantly:

> In the 1930s and 40s a lot of bad things happened in the world. The holocaust is probably the most well remembered . . . at the end of the war the nations of the world agreed to establish an international moral code of right and wrong behavior. . . . The code said that racism and sexism were wrong. . . . It said that no one should be victimized for practicing a religion or for expressing their political convictions. . . . It said that it was wrong to exploit children for monetary gain, and it was wrong to use force or threats to compel people to work without their willing consent. The code said that "human rights and fundamental freedom are the birthright of all human beings."

These fundamental human rights and moral precepts do not disappear when one becomes an employee. We have, therefore, a moral obligation to work to ensure that our places of employment build rather than break down the human spirit. Max De Pree (1989, 9), the former chief executive of furniture manufacturer Herman Miller, commented on the role of leadership in organizations: "Leaders don't inflict pain; they bear pain." These are words to keep in mind as we observe contemporary workplaces.

We have come to somehow, almost unconsciously, accept the idea that the ends justify the means. If organizations need to be centralized, lean and mean, impermanent, and control-oriented in order to succeed in the marketplace, this is the way it is, and we need to accept these facts. What this chapter has suggested is that the premise is wrong and so is the conclusion. As to the premise, the evidence continues to grow that organizations that have and live by their values, that put people first, and that manage using high-commitment work practices outperform those that don't. Levering and Moskowitz (2000, 83), who compiled the *Fortune* list of the 100 best companies to work for in America, reported that "public companies on the list rose 37% annualized over the past three years, compared with 25% for the S&P 500." In 1998, Grant (1998, 81) reported that "of the 61 companies in the group [on *Fortune*'s best places to work list] that have been publicly traded for the past five years, 45 yielded higher returns to shareholders than the Russell 3000." How much evidence do we need before we begin to act on the basis of these data?

And the conclusion is also wrong. An individual's desire and right to be treated with dignity at work, to be able to grow and learn, to be connected to others, and to be a whole, integrated person cannot simply be sacrificed for economic expediency. For once we start down that path, where do we stop in justifying the treatment of people for economic results?

We have an obligation, a duty, to build organizations that help build people's spirits, not destroy them. An example of such an organization is ServiceMaster, the enormously successful provider for such home and industrial services as termite control, home warranties, lawn care, and cleaning. The company's former CEO and chairman, William Pollard, wrote a book entitled *The Soul of the Firm*. Excerpts from that book, printed in the company's 1995 annual report, speak to how we should and must think about companies and their relationships with their people:

> If we focused exclusively on profit, we would be a firm that had failed to nurture its soul. Eventually . . . firms that do this experience a loss in direction and purpose of their people, a loss in customers, and then a loss in profits. Both people and profit are part of our mission. . . . Business is not just a game of manipulation that accomplishes a series of tasks for a profit with the gain going to a few and with the atrophy of the soul of the person producing the results. . . . The soul-less, adversarial . . . environment should not be the model of the future. (ServiceMaster 1995, 18)

REFERENCES

Abernathy, F.H.; J.T. Dunlop; J.H. Hammond; and D. Weil. (1999). *A Stitch in Time*. New York: Oxford University Press.

Ackers, P., and D. Preston. (1997). "Born Again? The Ethics and Efficacy of the Conversion Experience in Contemporary Management Development." *Journal of Management Studies* 5: 677–697.

Adams, R. (1999). "Labor Rights As Human Rights: Implications of the International Consensus." Paper presented at the Annual Meeting of the Industrial Relations Research Association, New York City, January.

AES Corporation. (1997). *Annual Report*. Arlington, VA: AES.

———. (1998). *Annual Report*. Arlington, VA: AES.

———. (2000). *Annual Report*. Arlington, VA: AES.

Anderson, P. (2000). "This Place Hurts My Spirit!" *Journal for Quality and Participation* 16–17.

Aoki, M. (1988). *Information, Incentives, and Bargaining in the Japanese Economy*. Cambridge, UK: Cambridge University Press.

Appelbaum, E.; T. Bailey; P. Berg; and A.L. Kalleberg. (2000). *Manufacturing Advantage: Why High-Performance Work Systems Pay Off*. Ithaca, NY: ILR Press.

Archibald, W.P. (1974). "Alternative Explanations for Self-fulfilling Prophecy." *Psychological Bulletin* 81: 74–84.

Arthur, J.B. (1994). "Effects of Human Resource Systems on Manufacturing Performance and Turnover." *Academy of Management Journal* 37: 670–687.

Ashmos, D.P., and D. Duchon. (2000). "Spirituality at Work: A Conceptualization and Measure." *Journal of Management Inquiry* 9: 134–145.

Bagley, C.E., and K.L. Page. (1999). "The Devil Made Me Do It: Replacing Corporate Directors' Veil of Secrecy with the Mantle of Stewardship." *San Diego Law Review* 36: 897–945.

Bailey, T. (1993). "Organizational Innovation in the Apparel Industry." *Industrial Relations* 32: 30–48.

Bakke, D.W. (1996). "Erecting a Grid for Ethical Power." *Marketplace* (May–June).

Banker, R.D.; J.M. Field; R.G. Schroeder; and K.K. Sinha (1996). "The Impact of Work Teams on Manufacturing Performance: A Longitudinal Field Study." *Academy of Management Journal* 39: 867–890.

Batt, R. (1996). "Outcomes of Self-directed Work Groups in Telecommunications Services." In *Proceedings of the Forty-Eighth Annual Meeting of the Industrial Relations Research Association*, ed. P.B. Voos. Madison, WI: Industrial Relations Research Association, 340–347.

Batt, R. (1999). "Work Organization, Technology, and Performance in Customer Service and Sales." *Industrial and Labor Relations Review* 52: 539–564.

Becker, B., and M. Huselid. (1998). "High Performance Work Systems and Firm Performance: A Synthesis of Research and Managerial Implications." *Research in Personnel and Human Resources Management*, vol. 16. Greenwich, CT: JAI Press, 53–101.

Bilmes, L.; K. Wetzker; and P. Xhonneux. (1997). "Value in Human Resources." *Financial Times*, February 10, 12.

Bloom, M. (1999). "The Performance Effects of Pay Dispersion on Individuals and Organizations." *Academy of Management Journal* 42: 25–40.

Boulding, K. (1968). *The Organizational Revolution: A Study of the Ethics of Economic Organization.* Chicago: Quadrangle Books.

Brehm, J.W. (1966). *A Theory of Psychological Reactance.* New York: Academic Press.

Brown, C. (1994). *The Competitive Semiconductor Manufacturing Human Resources Project: First Interim Report.* Berkeley, CA: Institute of Industrial Relations, University of California, Berkeley.

Burton, M.D., and C. O'Reilly. (2000). "The Impact of High Commitment Values and Practices on Technology Start-ups." Unpublished paper, Sloan School of Management, Massachusetts Institute of Technology, Cambridge.

Byrne, J.A. (1999). *Chainsaw: The Notorious Career of Al Dunlap in the Era of Profit-At-Any-Price.* New York: HarperCollins.

Cappelli, P. (1999). *The New Deal at Work.* Boston: Harvard Business School Press.

Cappelli, P., and D. Neumark. (2001). "Do 'High Performance' Work Practices Improve Establishment-Level Outcomes?" *Industrial and Labor Relations Review* 54: 737–775.

Cartwright, S., and C.L. Cooper. (1997). *Managing Workplace Stress.* Thousand Oaks, CA: Sage.

Chambers, E.G.; M. Foulon; H. Handfield-Jones; S.M. Hankin; and E.G. Michaels III. (1998). "The War for Talent." *McKinsey Quarterly* 3: 44–57.

Collins, J.C., and J.I. Porras. (1994). *Built to Last: Successful Habits of Visionary Companies.* New York: Harper Business.

Davis, J.H. (1969). *Group Performance.* Reading, MA: Addison-Wesley.

Delery, J.E., and D.H. Doty. (1996). "Modes of Theorizing in Strategic Human Resource Management: Tests of Universalistic, Contingency, and Configurational Performance Predictions." *Academy of Management Journal* 39: 802–835.

Deming, W.E. (1986). *Out of the Crisis.* Cambridge: Massachusetts Institute of Technology, Center for Advanced Engineering Study.

De Pree, M. (1989). *Leadership Is an Art.* New York: Doubleday.

Dunlop, J.T., and D. Weil. (1996). "Diffusion and Performance of Modular Production in the U.S. Apparel Industry." *Industrial Relations* 35: 334–355.

Edelman, M. (1964). *The Symbolic Uses of Politics.* Urbana: University of Illinois Press.

Edwards, R.C. (1979). *Contested Terrain: The Transformation of the Workplace in the Twentieth Century.* New York: Basic Books.

Festinger, L. (1954). "A Theory of Social Comparison Processes." *Human Relations* 7: 117–140.

Frank, R.H. (1988). *Passions Within Reason: The Strategic Role of the Emotions.* New York: Norton.

Graham, L. (1995). *On the Line at Subaru-Isuzu.* Ithaca, NY: ILR Press.

Grant, Linda. (1998). "Happy Workers, High Returns." *Fortune,* January 12, 81.

Hackman, J.R., and G.R. Oldham. (1980). *Work Redesign.* Reading, MA: Addison-Wesley.

Hannan, M.T.; J.N. Baron; G. Hsu; and O. Kocak. (2000). "Staying the Course: Early Organization Building and the Success of High-Technology Firms." Unpublished paper, Graduate School of Business, Stanford University, Stanford, CA.

Huselid, M.A. (1995). "The Impact of Human Resource Management Practices on Turnover, Productivity, and Corporate Financial Performance." *Academy of Management Journal* 38: 635–670.

Ichniowski, C., and K. Shaw. (1999). "The Effects of Human Resource Management Systems on Economic Performance: An International Comparison of U.S. and Japanese Plants." *Management Science* 45: 704–721.

Ichniowski, C.; K. Shaw; and G. Prennushi. (1997). "The Effects of Human Resource Management Practices on Productivity: A Study of Steel Finishing Lines." *American Economic Review* 87: 291–313.

Kahn, R.L.; D.M. Wolfe; R.P. Quinn; and J.D. Snoek. (1964). *Organizational Stress: Studies in Role Conflict and Ambiguity.* New York: Wiley.

Kaufman, L. (2001). "Question of Style in Warnaco's Fall." *New York Times,* May 6, sec. 3, 1.

Lazear, E.P. (1989). "Pay Equality and Industrial Politics." *Journal of Political Economy* 97: 561–580.

———. (1995). *Personnel Economics.* Cambridge: Massachusetts Institute of Technology Press.

Leavitt, H.J. (1978). *Managerial Psychology,* 4th. ed. Chicago: University of Chicago Press.

Lee, J., and D. Miller. (1999). "People Matter: Commitment to Employees, Strategy and Performance in Korean Firms." *Strategic Management Journal* 20: 579–593.

Leventhal, G.S. (1976). "The Distribution of Rewards and Resources in Groups and Organizations." In *Advances in Experimental Social Psychology,* vol. 9, ed. L. Berkowitz. New York: Academic Press, 91–131.

Leventhal, G.S.; J.W. Michaels; and C. Sanford. (1972). "Inequity and Interpersonal Conflict: Reward Allocations and Secrecy About Reward as Methods of Preventing Conflict." *Journal of Personality and Social Psychology* 23: 88–102.

Levering, R., and M. Moskowitz. (2000). "The 100 Best Companies to Work for." *Fortune*, January 10, 82–110.

Locke, E.A. (1976). "The Nature and Causes of Job Satisfaction." In *Handbook of Industrial and Organizational Psychology*, ed. M.D. Dunnette. Chicago: Rand McNally, 1297–1349.

MacDuffie, J.P. (1995). "Human Resource Bundles and Manufacturing Performance: Organizational Logic and Flexible Production Systems in the World Auto Industry." *Industrial and Labor Relations Review* 48: 197–221.

Maslow, A.H. (1954). *Motivation and Personality*. New York: Harper.

Mirvis, P.H. (1997). "'Soul Work' in Organizations." *Organization Science* 8: 193–206.

Merriam-Webster. (1981). *Webster's Third New International Dictionary*. Springfield, MA: Merriam-Webster.

Mitroff, I.I., and E.A. Denton. (1999). "A Study of Spirituality in the Workplace." *Sloan Management Review* 83–92.

O'Reilly, C.A., and J. Pfeffer. (2000). *Hidden Value: How Great Companies Achieve Extraordinary Results with Ordinary People*. Boston: Harvard Business School Press.

Pfeffer, J. (1998). *The Human Equation: Building Profits by Putting People First*. Boston: Harvard Business School Press.

Pfeffer, J., and J.N. Baron. (1988). "Taking the Workers Back Out: Recent Trends in the Structuring of Employment." In *Research in Organizational Behavior*, vol. 10, ed. B.M. Staw and L.L. Cummings. Greenwich, CT: JAI Press, 257–303.

Pfeffer, J., and A. Davis-Blake (1992). "Salary Dispersion, Location in the Salary Distribution, and Turnover Among College Administrators." *Industrial and Labor Relations Review* 45: 753–763.

Pfeffer, J., and N. Langton. (1993). "The Effect of Wage Dispersion on Satisfaction, Productivity, and Working Collaboratively: Evidence from College and University Faculty." *Administrative Science Quarterly* 38: 382–407.

Pfeffer, J., and R.I. Sutton. (2000). *The Knowing-Doing Gap: How Smart Companies Turn Knowledge Into Action*. Boston: Harvard Business School Press.

Reichheld, F.F. (1996). *The Loyalty Effect*. Boston: Harvard Business School Press.

Ricketts, R. (1994). "Survey Points to Practices That Reduce Refinery Maintenance Spending." *Oil and Gas Journal* (July 4): 37–41.

Sattler, L., and V. Sohoni. (1999). "Participative Management: An Empirical Study of the Semiconductor Manufacturing Industry." *IEEE Transactions on Engineering Management* 46: 387–398.

Schor, J.B. (1991). *The Overworked American*. New York: Basic Books.

ServiceMaster. (1995). *Annual Report*. Downers Grove, IL: ServiceMaster.

Shapiro, Eileen. (1995). *Fad Surfing in the Boardroom*. Reading, MA: Addison-Wesley.

Smith, P.C. (1992). "In Pursuit of Happiness: Why Study Job Satisfaction?" In *Job Satisfaction*, ed. C.J. Cranny, P.C. Smith, and E.F. Stone. New York: Lexington Books, 5–19.

Steele, C.M. (1988). "The Psychology of Self-affirmation: Sustaining the Integrity of the Self." In *Advances in Experimental Social Psychology*, vol. 21, ed. L. Berkowitz. San Diego: Academic Press, 261–302.

Strickland, L.H. (1958). "Surveillance and Trust." *Journal of Personality* 26: 200–215.

Terkel, S. (1985). *Working*. New York: Ballantine.

Tesser, A. (1988). "Toward a Self-evaluation Maintenance Model of Social Behavior." In *Advances in Experimental Social Psychology*, vol. 21, ed. L. Berkowitz. San Diego: Academic Press, 181–227.

Welbourne, T., and A. Andrews. (1996). "Predicting Performance of Initial Public Offering Firms: Should HYM be in the Equation?" *Academy of Management Journal* 39: 891–919.

Wong, E. (2001). "A Stinging Office Memo Boomerangs: Chief Executive Is Criticized After Upbraiding Workers By E-Mail." *New York Times*, April 5, C-1.

Wood, S., and L. de Menezes. (1998). "High Commitment Management in the U.K.: Evidence from the Workplace Industrial Relations Survey, and Employers' Manpower and Skills Practices Survey." *Human Relations* 51: 485–515.

Youndt, M.A.; S.A. Snell; J.W. Dean, Jr.; and D.P. Lepak. (1996). "Human Resource Management, Manufacturing Strategy, and Firm Performance." *Academy of Management Journal* 39: 836–866.

CHAPTER 3

THE HUMAN SIDE OF SPIRITUALITY

RIANE EISLER AND ALFONSO MONTUORI

Many of us want to infuse our lives with deeper meaning. We want to be of service, to feel connected to one another and to our Mother Earth. We want deeper relationships and a sense of greater purpose. These are some of the motivations behind the talk today about imbuing our life, and our work, with spirituality.

But what does spirituality mean? Does it mean going to synagogue on Friday or church on Sunday, or alternately, going to "New Age" workshops to learn meditation, chanting, or other spiritual practices? Is the talk about spirituality in the workplace just anther fad? Or does it signal a potentially important development for business and, beyond this, for society?

The answers to these questions largely depend on how spirituality is defined and applied. In this chapter, we propose that spirituality is defined and applied very differently depending on its larger cultural and social context.

Specifically, we place spirituality in the larger context of what one of us (Eisler 1987, 1995, 2000) has identified as a partnership or dominator model of beliefs, structures, and relationships. We propose that—although most of us are still used to thinking of the choices for our future in terms of right versus left, capitalist versus communist, or secular versus religious—underneath the currents and countercurrents of human history lies the dynamic tension between these two basic possibilities for structuring relations. However, the distinction between the dominator and partnership models is not only a matter of politics and economics. It is a matter of how relations are structured in all spheres of life—from our intimate parent–child and gender relations to our workplace relations to our relations with our Mother Earth. And it is a distinction that plays out in two very different ways of conceptualizing and applying spirituality.

In the dominator view, spirituality is abstracted from daily life. It enables people to withdraw from what is happening around them. This kind of spirituality may help individuals cope with the chronic injustices and miseries that are inherent in a dominator model of relations—in the fear-and-force-backed ranking of man over woman, man over man, race over race, and nation over nation, which can only be maintained by inflicting or threatening pain. But it does not change much, if anything, in real life.

By contrast, the kind of spirituality that is appropriate for a partnership model of relations is not only transcendent, but also immanent. It is a spirituality that informs our day-to-day lives with caring and empathy. It does not place man and spirituality over woman and nature—or vice versa. And it provides basic teachings about empathy, respect, and nonviolence as alternatives to both a lack of standards and the use of spirituality to incite hate, scapegoating, and violence.

This is very important today. On the one side—as in earlier times when the dominator model, with its "holy wars," witch burnings, and other barbarities, was more firmly in place—we still have those who incite hate, scapegoating, and violence under the guise of spirituality. On the other, we have those who contend that there are no real standards of conduct, that we should not be "judgmental," and that all standards are merely cultural constructs that vary from time to time and place to place.

This second view is justified by some proponents of postmodernism, deconstructionism, or cultural relativism, as well as by some New Age teachings that we should not judge what is good or evil. It reflects a rebellion against "moral" rules that frequently have been unfair and all too often have been inhuman—rules developed in earlier times that were more oriented to the dominator model of society. It also reflects the fact that there are indeed cultural variations in what is considered moral and right, and that much blood has been shed in the name of moral righteousness.

But we humans need standards. Even arguing that all standards are relative is articulating a kind of standard, negative though it may be.

Distinguishing between the kind of standards appropriate for partnership or dominator relations can help us navigate through much of the moral confusion of our time. It can also help us integrate spirituality into our day-to-day lives—into the world where we relate and live—including our workplaces.

Indeed, to even talk about bringing spirituality into the workplace is an important part of the movement toward a partnership way of working and living.

But how can we prevent this talk about spirituality in the workplace from being diluted into no more than another diversion, an entertainment? How can we imbue the workplace and the way business is done with partnership spirituality? And if we do, will this really have positive effects not only on how we feel and how we relate to one another and to nature, but also on economic productivity and business effectiveness?

Montuori and Purser (2001) have reviewed the applications of humanistic psychology (HP) in the workplace. They found that despite the great importance placed on concepts originating in HP, and particularly the work of Abraham Maslow (in organizational development, for instance), the concepts have been used in such a way that their deeper underlying implications have been ignored. They argue that in some ways HP has been co-opted to fit into a larger corporate philosophical framework to which HP itself was quite opposed. Some aspects of HP have been applied very extensively, but very often almost as a feel-good smokescreen, given that the deeper implications of HP, such as the importance of a democratic workplace, have by and large been completely ignored. In other words, the surface elements of HP, and of human relations approaches in general, have been used, but the HP philosophy has not impacted the overarching level of strategic decision-making, where, as Montuori (2000) argues, the fundamental paradigm is still rational economic with strong-man implementation (cf. Pfeffer and Vega 1999). Furthermore, the excessive focus on the psychological aspects of HP, understood as a series of "tools" or "processes" for personal development, occurred at the expense of the structural changes required to make deeper changes. For instance, a technique such as active listening could be applied as a tool to give the impression that one was listening, rather than a profound attempt to democratize communication in the workplace (Montuori and Purser 2001).

Spirituality in the workplace runs the same risk as HP. While it is impossible to prevent ideas from being misused or trivialized, we propose that the dominator/partnership continuum represents a framework that can help us avoid this. We believe that unless there is more of a change from a dominator to a partnership model, there is a much greater likelihood that spirituality in the workplace will suffer the same fate HP—and all the other movements that addressed the so-called "soft" side of management and business operations.

THE PARTNERSHIP/DOMINATOR CONTINUUM

Let us begin by outlining what forms the core of our argument, namely the implications for the workplace and all other aspects of our lives of two modes of social relations—the partnership model and the dominator model.

An age-old distinction in thinking about organizations is between tasks and relationships. Every organization has certain tasks to perform and certain relationships to foster and maintain.

In recent years, increasing importance has been placed on the development and maintenance of relationships. One of the most important trends today—drawing from systems and complexity theories, creativity research, psychology, and organizational and management theories—is a shift from focusing on isolated objects to looking at their context, from examining separate parts to focusing on relationships. There is a growing recognition that life and culture exist in and as a web of inter-relationships. In business too there is a growing focus on relationships, both relationships inside organizations and relationships between businesses and their social and natural environment.

On the old assembly line, relationships between workers were considered irrelevant—in fact, in Frederick Taylor's mechanistic model, they were to be avoided. The assumption was that "gangs of men" could only cause trouble. Divide and rule was the order of the day. In today's economy, with the key economic role of service organizations where relationships are key, the role of relationships can no longer be overlooked.

The very differentiation between tasks and relationships is beginning to break down. With flatter, less hierarchical organizations, for instance, it is increasingly the case that task and relationship are one and the same. Tasks are networked, interrelated, and complex, rather than linear in an assembly-line model. There is almost no such thing as a task that does not involve relationship and communication, that does not involve motivating, influencing, listening, explaining, contextualizing, and so on.

The fundamental questions then become: What is the nature and experience of relationships? Are they essentially hostile, win–lose, domination–submission? Or are they geared toward mutual benefit, coevolution, and partnership? And which kinds of relationships are more appropriate and beneficial for business?

Eisler (1987, 1995, 2000; Eisler and Loye 1998) addresses these issues by identifying two contrasting models of social systems: the dominator model and the partnership model. Dominator systems are fear-based, characterized by rigid hierarchies of domination (where power is equated with giving orders that must be obeyed) an ethos of conquest (including the "conquest of nature"), a high degree of institutionalized or built-in violence and abuse, male domination, and contempt for "soft" or stereotypically feminine values such as empathy and caring. Partnership systems are trust-based, characterized by equalitarianism and "flatter," less top-down, more flexible hierarchies of actualization (where power is guided by "soft" values), a low degree of violence and abuse built into the system, and gender equality and equity.

No organization orients completely to the partnership or dominator model, hence, the term partnership/dominator continuum. But the degree to which it orients to either model profoundly affects everything—including how the workplace, management, and spirituality are constructed.

If we look at the modern workplace from this perspective, we see that it was in critical ways patterned to conform to the requirements of a dominator rather than a partnership type of social organization. The organizational model of the "well-oiled machine" represented the mechanical, clockwork universe that we associate with the Industrial Age. But this mechanical universe was about more than just machines. It was a universe patterned after the core elements of the dominator model: a top-down, authoritarian structure where rankings of "superiors" over "inferiors" are held together primarily by fear, with the men at the top of the organizational hierarchy dominating those below them, men dominating women, fear as the major motivator for workers, and industrial machines essentially war machines designed to do "battle" with the competition.

Like the slaves, serfs, and foot soldiers of the pre-Industrial Age, the rank and file of workers in these dominator structures were still expected to use their bodies to do whatever they were ordered to do. They were not supposed to think, much less change the orders they received in any way, and there was no place for such stereotypically feminine values as caring and nurturance.

That is not to say that there were no women in these dominator structures. In fact, in the early days of the Industrial Revolution, women and children were among the first to work in unbelievably unhealthy, unsanitary, and unsafe workplaces—as grimly illustrated by the infamous Triangle Shirt Waist Company fire, in which 146 women lost their lives because the doors were locked so that they could not take breaks. But while women and children were hired because they could be paid lower wages and were considered more docile and pliable than men, they had little if any voice in their workplace's design or décor—and neither did soft values.

The physical structures of this workplace were designed to conform to the dominator ideal of "real masculinity" in their inattention to matters stereotypically relegated to women, such as décor or comfort. From the dingy nineteenth-century mills and sweatshops to the angular twentieth-century office complexes, workplaces were properly devoid of bright colors, soft textures, green plants, flowers, and other "feminine frills." The organizational structure and management styles were likewise supposed to be masculine, that is, they too expressed what in dominator model thinking is considered appropriate for "real men"—control, detachment, aggression, "toughness" (Eisler 1991).

The human costs to both men and women of this imbalanced, fear-based, institutionally insensitive, and all too often abusive and dehumanizing way of organizing and managing business, and the social and economic structure that it reflected, were enormous. But it was said, and generally believed, to be necessary for economic productivity. In short, it was believed that top-down structures and a culture guided by "hard" rather than "soft" values were required if workers were to be productive.

Now a growing business, organization development, and management literature—as well as real life case histories—document that these once hallowed beliefs, and the structures that go along with them, are not spurs but rather impediments to productivity and creativity.

In the age of the so-called "knowledge-worker," but more importantly, in an age of democratic values, the old dominator "command-and-control" model is not only inappropriate; it is becoming increasingly dysfunctional. Bureaucratic rigidity is deadly for organizations that wish to navigate successfully in a rapidly changing environment where teamwork, innovation, and flexibility are key factors. Furthermore, workers in a democratic society should not be treated in ways that reduce them to being cogs in a machine.

The growing awareness that we urgently need new mindsets, structures, and behaviors has helped to move the workplace toward the partnership model as the template for a more humane and effective way of working and doing business. But, as we will see in the next sections, there is great resistance to this movement—resistance that also threatens to subvert the movement to imbue the workplace with spirituality into no more than just another temporary fad.

TOWARD A PARTNERSHIP WORKPLACE

We read a great deal today about teamwork, about leaders as facilitators rather than cops or controllers, about valuing diversity, about a more humane and socially and environmentally conscious way of doing business, about a move from rigid top-down structures to more flexible hierarchies—hierarchies of actualization rather than domination (Eisler 1987, 1995, 2000). In bits and pieces some of these ideas have gradually been put into practice.

For example, as early as the 1960s at a Volvo plant in Sweden, workers' teams were organized that met together and decided how they wanted to divide their jobs, when to stop and start the assembly lines, and even what hours to work. The result of leaving the traditional top-down structure behind was both far higher productivity and a much lower number of defects. Similarly, as Brian Dumaine (1990) reports in an article called "Creating a New Company Culture," in DuPont's plant in Towanda, Pennsylvania, where managers called themselves "facilitators, not bosses," productivity increased by a huge 35 percent. What made this plant so exceptionally productive was once again that it was organized in self-directed work teams where employees found their own solutions to problems, set their own schedules, and even had a say in hiring, and where managers were not cops or controllers but, rather, facilitators and nurturers of employees' capabilities—a partnership rather than dominator management style.

This movement toward a partnership style of management, emphasizing motivation and participation rather than coercion and rote obedience, is also beginning to bring about a redefinition of leadership. Max DePree, former CEO of Herman Miller and author of the book *Leadership Jazz*, argues that the signs of leadership are among the followers. "Are they reaching their potential?" he asks; "Are they learning?" "Are they achieving the desired results?" "Are they serving?" "Do they manage change gracefully?" "Do they manage conflict?"

These are very different kinds of questions from the ones leaders might have asked even twenty years ago. They reflect important changes in consciousness, focusing attention on human beings, human relations, and human development. And there is a growing literature showing that organizations that put these "soft" values into practice are extremely successful.

For example, Pfeffer and Vega (1999) write that organizations that put people first have a higher degree of financial success. They cite a 1996 study of 702 firms that found that a one standard deviation improvement in the human resources system was associated with an increase in shareholder wealth of $41,000 per employee.

Pfeffer and Vega (1999) identified some of the key human resource practices involved in making these companies successful. These included employment security, self-managed teams, and decentralization as basic elements of organizational design, comparatively high compensation contingent on organizational performance, extensive training, reduction of status differences, and sharing information—in other words, some of the key elements of a more partnership-oriented organizational structure and culture.

It all seems so simple, Pfeffer and Vega (1999) write. And in some ways it is.

But then why aren't more organizations doing this? What are the obstacles? According to Pfeffer and Vega, the primary obstacles are what they term "perverse norms," such as the idea that good managers are mean and tough and that management consists mainly of detached analysis (formulation) backed up by muscle (implementation/enforcement).

This mentality of fear and force is of course a heritage from earlier more dominator-oriented times. Indeed, it is inherent in organizations that still orient primarily to the dominator model.

Unless we address these "perverse norms," progress toward partnership organizations will be very slow. There will continue to be talk about a more humane workplace, about a shift from rigid hierarchies to more flexible heterarchies, and about social and environmental responsibility.

But management styles will continue to be dominating and disempowering rather than nurturing and empowering. Even flatter organizations will still be racked by dominator power games and nonempathic and insensitive relationships that sap people of vitality and creativity. And—as was starkly evident in recent tobacco, petrochemical, and gas and electricity industry exposés—business policies will often ignore environmental and social damage, and sometimes deliberately cause it.

THE SPIRITUAL AND EMOTIONAL CHALLENGE OF PARTNERSHIP

This is all very well, you may say, but what does it have to do with bringing spirituality into the workplace? Actually, it has a great deal to do with it. Think of the values and behaviors that the great spiritual leaders of world traditions have preached. Haven't they almost uniformly preached empathy, nurturance, and caring? And aren't these precisely the kinds of values that make it impossible to maintain rigid rankings of domination and submission ultimately backed up by fear or force? In short, aren't these spiritual values systematically impeded by the beliefs, rules, and structures characteristic of the dominator-oriented workplace that were the norm in earlier times?

So just as we were told that a top-down authoritarian workplace was required to get things done, we were told that such values as empathy, nurturance, and caring are not "practical," that getting things done requires that managers be "tough," emotionally detached, and "rational" rather than "soft" or emotionally engaged.

The talk today of a more spiritually enlightened workplace and way of doing business—one where respect for human dignity and human rights and more socially and environmentally responsible policies take central stage—is an important partnership trend. But, as Pfeffer's and Vega's observations about perverse norms highlight, shifting to the partnership rather than the dominator model as the norm is a huge emotional and spiritual challenge.

There is today a general, though at times grudging, recognition that "soft" values are vital for an organization to succeed. At the same time, the perverse norms regarding what constitutes good management are precisely the kind of norms that, by focusing on quantification and "strong man" tactics, block any dealings with this "soft" side. And these norms are embedded in deeply entrenched notions of what is appropriate not only in business but in life—unconscious mental and emotional maps that are extremely resistant to change. So it is much easier to focus on some of the more exotic phenomena associated with spirituality than getting to the core of the kinds of issues we need to address to create a more enlightened workplace and business culture.

An understanding of the underlying dynamics that keep dominator rather than partnership relations in place points to the need to address issues that usually are not considered in the business and organizational development literature. For example, consider that the so called "human element" of work has typically been referred to as the "soft" side of management—and that in the dominator model anything considered soft or stereotypically feminine is not deemed appropriate for "real men" and for the organizations they head. Consider also that a core component of the dominator model we have inherited from earlier, more authoritarian and rigidly male-dominated times is the ranking of the male half of humanity over the female half—and with this, the ranking of anything stereotypically associated with masculinity over anything stereotypically associated with femininity.

Before going further into the minefield of gender roles and relations that this association of "soft" with women and "tough" with men leads to, we want to emphasize that when we say stereotypically, we mean just that. Some men are more empathic and caring than some women, just as some women are more assertive and logical than some men. What we are dealing with is not anything inherent in women and men (Fausto-Sterling 1985). It is rather what is considered normal in a dominator mindset, which considers it normal for men to rule over women (and "inferior" men)—with the result that qualities such as empathy, caring, and nonviolence are only considered appropriate for "weak" men (sissies, wimps) and an occasional saintly or spiritual male such as Jesus or Buddha.

The point is that in a world where the vast majority of those who own and manage business and other organizations are male, the failure to address these kinds of issues in any serious discussion of a more humane and therefore more efficient workplace—much less a workplace imbued by spirituality—ignores some of the most resistant of the "perverse norms" that stand in the way of getting where we want to go.

The problem is that in the socialization we have inherited from more rigid dominator times, male identity is defined as not being like a woman. Indeed, men are defined in opposition to women, and women in opposition to men. The commonly used term "the opposite sex" reveals how pervasive this is.

Because of this oppositional identity, discussions of gender, and particularly ones that suggest a change from rigidly stereotyped male and female behaviors to the development of a broader range of behaviors on a continuum between stereotypically male and female ones can appear very threatening. It has been our experience that there is no subject more sensitive in the workplace, or elsewhere, than gender—that when this subject comes up, so do very deep-seated and strongly felt emotions because, particularly for men but for women too, issues of gender strike at the core of most people's identity or sense of self.

Whether we like it or not, the very values that we consider the highest spiritual goals of humanity—empathy, caring, nonviolence—are in dominator thinking inextricably intertwined with what those who still today hold most leadership and management positions—men—should avoid as being feminine, and hence "weak." They are precisely what men have been told *not* to be like through an extensive process of socialization, through gender-specific role models, toys, and—for those who deviate—ridicule, and even worse.

Moreover, the norm in dominator structures has been that leadership is the exclusive province of men. So even when an "exceptional" woman reaches the top, the model for her has been a "tough" leadership style. For example, Margaret Thatcher was sometimes called "the best man in England."

"SOFT" AND "HARD" BEHAVIORS AND POLICIES

Does this mean that partnership organizations are all soft and cuddly, with never any strife or conflict? Of course not. There is conflict in both partnership- and dominator-oriented organizations. But in the dominator-model conflict is both suppressed from the top and fomented among those on the bottom to maintain top-down hegemony. And because any questioning of orders, and hence conflicting views, needs, and aspirations, are suppressed in dominator structures, there is not only a choking of important information flow, but also the periodic eruption of conflict in extreme ways, such as coups to take over leadership positions. By contrast, in the partnership model conflicting views, needs, and aspirations can be more freely expressed. As a result, information flows far more easily and effectively, and conflict can lead to creative solutions to problems rather than to a clamping down of control from the top.

Similarly, competition exists in both the dominator and partnership models. But they too take different forms. In the dominator model, we find what is termed "dog-eat-dog" competition even though of course dogs don't eat dogs. The goal is to beat opponents, to put them out of business, to win at all costs. Why? Because in the dominator model there is no option other than being on top or bottom—there is no partnership alternative. By contrast, competition in the partnership model is more achievement or growth oriented—as is characteristic of what Maslow called the self-actualizing personality. But again the question is: "What kinds of behaviors are supported or inhibited by an organization's rules and policies—behaviors conducive to dominator or partnership relations?"

Does partnership suggest that there will be no differences between women and men? Of course not. But dominator gender stereotypes will no longer encase women and men in the straightjackets of rigid roles that force both genders to deny and distort part of their humanity. Extensive research shows that creative individuals are not locked into stereotypical gender roles and move far more flexibly along the spectrum of behaviors defined as stereotypically masculine or feminine (Barron 1990). And creative organizations need creative individuals, individuals who can express their "soft," empathic, human side whether they are male or female.

To pay attention to the human side does not mean not paying attention to such everyday organizational realities as production schedules and budgeting. It does, however, mean that in paying attention to these issues, human considerations are not ignored, and partnership ethical standards are not violated.

Bringing partnership spirituality into the workplace can help us move in this direction. Indeed, by bringing partnership spirituality into the world of business, we will be changing the "perverse norms" Pfeffer and Vega point to as obstacles to business success. We will be helping to change not only attitudes and behaviors, but also rules and structures. We will, to borrow Clement L. Russo's words (1984, 1985), help transform the "daily humiliations of work into an activity that gives meaning, direction, and self-fulfillment" and that provides "the opportunity to cooperate with others in a common enterprise that stimulates respect, creativity, and commitment that will ultimately benefit everyone."

But to bring spirituality into the workplace, we need to examine our deepest assumptions—including even our deeply held assumptions about gender and identity. If we do not address these kinds of issues, even though they may at first glance seem irrelevant, and even though they may stir up fierce emotional resistance, bringing spirituality into the workplace—or into other aspects of our day-to-day lives—will not be successful except in superficial ways.

KEYS TO PARTNERSHIP SPIRITUALITY

As we have briefly outlined, partnership spirituality suggests something that is quite different from the more traditional view of spirituality. It suggests that a privileged place to engage in a transformative practice is precisely the domain of everyday human relationships and everyday practices—that rather than becoming more detached, we become more involved in the workplace, with its stresses and strains, its creative challenges, its issues of authority, strategy, performance, and responsibility.

Spirituality does not have to be something that just provides an escape from life—including a dehumanizing workplace. Nor does it have to be a phenomenon that is confined to the individual.

Partnership spirituality is not just an "intrapsychic" phenomenon, where one has to "change oneself" before one can "change the world." Such a position is obviously problematic, particularly because a central point of many spiritual New Age philosophies is that everything is interconnected. Yet many of these teachings do not address our relationships with others.

Certainly there is a legitimate criticism to be made of those who would change the world without at the same time seeking to change and grow themselves. Many of the problems with charismatic leaders and social movements have involved a fervent desire to fight some injustice only to find that the methods involved in this fight have become almost or even as despicable as the injustice itself, or that organizations with lofty goals fall victim to the same kind of political infighting and power-grabbing that other organizations experience.

So we also have to ask ourselves: "What would it really mean to just change oneself, and not in any way change or affect the "outside" world?" Whether we meditate or engage in some transformative practice or not, we are always already in the world, and therefore we are always already acting in the world. For many meditators, the pleasant experiences during the meditative practice are quickly gone once they return to the world and to not always pleasant interactions with other people. That translates, all too often, into being spiritual while one is meditating or performing rituals, or whatever practice one engages in, and then being very different "in the real world"—meaning a dominator world.

There's no escaping the world, and to put action "on hold" while we await enlightenment is not possible even if we decide to become hermits. We affect the world, to some extent, with our every action. Of course, we even affect the world through nonaction.

Partnership spirituality is therefore not the kind of "spectator" spirituality that stands outside the world. It is both immanent and transcendent, informing our day-to-day relations with partnership values. In the language used by Charlene Spretnak (1999), it is "embodied and embedded."

Partnership spirituality does not, by any means, propose we forego such transformative practices as meditation or prayer. But rather than view the meditative space as the privileged one, and the world around us as that which pulls us out of the desired state, from a partnership perspective the world of human interactions is the very place where we learn and grow.

Nor is partnership devoid of standards, like some New Age teachings that define themselves in opposition to what was perceived to be the moralizing and moralistic aspects of organized religion, with all its "thou shalt nots." Quite the contrary, at the heart of partnership spirituality is the standard that empathy, caring, and responsibility are not only more humane, but in the long term, more effective.

Creating partnership organizations and developing partnership spirituality, be it in the workplace or in our lives outside of work, is a process that requires ongoing learning. It is a process that involves cognition (thinking), emotion (feeling), and conation (will). It is both inner and outer directed. And it requires action.

Drawing from Eisler's (2002) new book, *The Power of Partnership,* we outline four keys to partnership spiritual education that every one of us can use.

1. *Developing our human capacity to listen to our own inner wisdom is the first basic component of partnership spiritual education.*
   Meditation and prayer, which can combine intense concentration and "letting go," can take us past the noise of the old dominator tapes we all carry to connect with what is most evolved in us—our capacity for empathy and caring rather than indifference or hate. Many spiritual traditions and disciplines have practices that can help us overcome dominator programming. However, looking inward is not enough. Looking outward is equally important.
2. *Learning to become fully conscious of others and what is happening around us is the second basic component of partnership spiritual education.*
   Being sensitive to others enables us to live our spirituality outside of ourselves. Without this mindfulness, spirituality becomes little more than self-indulgence. Without active engagement with others, all our efforts at self-cultivation will come to naught. An emerging interest in emotional intelligence and other ways of defining intelligence in a more relational manner are but the tip of the iceberg here.
3. *Learning partnership moral standards of empathy, caring, and responsibility—both for ourselves and others—is the third basic component of partnership spiritual education.*

Using the analytical lenses of the partnership/domination continuum makes it possible to sort and evaluate the often contradictory rules and commands we have inherited from earlier, more domination-oriented times. This is an essential component of spiritual education, as it helps us successfully navigate through the moral "rudderlessness" of our time. It helps us see the difference between what social psychologist David Loye calls partnership moral sensitivity and dominator moral insensitivity (Loye 1999).

4. *Learning to put partnership moral standards into practice is the fourth basic component of partnership spiritual education.*

   Today's workplace provides us with an opportunity for spiritual growth—to see ourselves in action and address problems, both technical and psychological, organizational and social. We can all learn the skills and habits that make for relations based on empathy and respect rather than control and submission.

The spiritual teachings from many religious traditions focus on love. But in the dominator model, these teachings of love become abstract, detached from real life, distorted, fragmented, and all too often stunted to meet the requirements of a way of structuring relations into rankings of "superiors" over "inferiors" ultimately backed up by fear and force.

This does not mean that there are no differences in position in partnership structures. There are still parents and children, teachers and students, bosses and employees. But the relationships between them are mutually respectful, informed by empathy and caring. And these partnership standards—of respect, empathy, and caring—are also expressed in the rules and policies of organizations, in how business practices affect both our social and natural environment.

CONCLUSION

The workplace spirituality movement offers the opportunity for foundational change at a time when—be it economically, socially, or environmentally—the dominator model is increasingly dysfunctional. There is mounting evidence that a more humane workplace and organizational structure is more productive, flexible, and creative. There is also mounting evidence that "business as usual" is environmentally unsustainable. A way of doing business that ignores the harm it does to humans and to nature is increasingly being rejected by thinking people all over the world.

As business rules and workplace practices change, as the workplace shifts more toward the partnership model, we will see both more personal growth and the creation of a more humane workplace and society. Imbuing the world of business with partnership spirituality will not solve all our problems. But it will gradually change what is considered normal and right.

There are an almost overwhelming number of spiritual approaches, techniques, and practices in the world today. Partnership spirituality in the workplace provides us with a framework to orient ourselves. It points to the necessity for both inner and outer transformation and allows us to contextualize specific practices within a larger framework that provides us with touchstones about key aspects of human existence.

Many of the well-intentioned efforts to address the human elements in organizations have been coopted or used in a superficial, feel-good manner. Understanding the core differences between the partnership and dominator models can help us make the changes needed for a more humane and at the same time more productive and creative workplace. The challenge of transforming the workplace is in key respects a spiritual challenge. If we put partnership spirituality into action, business success and the highest human aspirations can meet.

REFERENCES

Barron, F. (1990). *No Rootless Flower*. Cresskill, NJ: Hampton Press.

DePree, M. (1993). *Leadership Jazz*. New York: Dell.

Dumaine, B. (1990). "Creating a New Company Culture." *Fortune* (January): 15.

Eisler, R. (1987). *The Chalice and the Blade*. San Francisco: Harper and Row.

———. (1991) . "Women, Men and Management." *Futures* 23, no. 1 (January/February): 3–18.

———. (1995). *Sacred Pleasure*. San Francisco: HarperCollins.

———. 2000). *Tomorrow's Children*. Boulder, CO: Westview Press.

———. (2002). *The Power of Partnership*. Novato, CA: New World Library.

Eisler, R., and D. Loye. (1998). *The Partnership Way*. Brandon, VT: Holistic Education Press.

Fausto-Sterling, A. (1985). *Myths of Gender*. New York: Basic Books.

Loye, D. (1999). "Can Science Help Construct a New Global Ethic? The Development and Implications of Moral Transformation Theory." *Zygon* 34, no. 3: 221–235.

Montuori A. (2000). "Strategy and/as Organizational Change: Reconceptualizing Evolution, Adaptation, and Environments." Academy of Management Conference, OD Track, Toronto, August.

Montuori A., and R. Purser. (2001). "Humanistic Psychology in the Workplace." In *Handbook of Humanistic Psychology*, ed. J.F.T. Bugental, K. Schneider, and J. Pierson. Thousand Oaks, CA: Sage, 635–644.

Pfeffer, J., and J.F. Vega. (1999). "Putting People First for Organizational Success." *Academy of Management Executive* 13, no. 2: 37–45.

Russo, C.L. (1984/1985). "Productivity Overview: Recognizing the Human Dimension." *ReVISION* 7, no. 2 (winter/spring): 68–73.

Spretnak, C. (1999). *The Resurgence of the Real*. New York: Routledge.

CHAPTER 4

SPIRITUALITY AND MARKETING

An Overview of the Literature

DARYL MCKEE

INTRODUCTION

There are markets for almost anything and everything imaginable. There are markets for goods, services, experiences, events, property, information, and ideas. People market themselves as brands (e.g., Martha Stewart). Organizations market their corporate identities. Places are marketed as business locations or tourist attractions. There are markets for products that some people consider good (like medical care and counseling), bad (like pornography and gambling), sacred (like religious relics), and mundane (like groceries and motor fuel).

What role then does spirituality have in marketing? Spirituality has been variously defined as a "search for meaning and values, which includes some sense of the transcendent" (Bruce and Novinson 1999, 163) and as "the basic feeling of being connected with one's complete self, others, and the entire universe" (Mitroff and Denton 1999, 83). Some would consider anything related to the process of buying or selling as the antithesis of spirituality, as inherently "profane" in a spiritual sense.

Yet it is argued by some that spirituality involves creating a more ethical and humane workplace (Gunther 2001); by extension, this would also seem to apply to a more ethical and humane marketplace. This orientation seems similar to the concept of "societal marketing," which involves conducting the marketing function in a way that "preserves or enhances the consumer's and society's well-being" (Kotler 2000, 25).

Most people spend a substantial amount of their time in market exchange: evaluating their needs, assessing product options, purchasing, "consuming" or using products and services, obtaining after-sale services or adjustments, and discussing consumption-related experiences with vendors or friends. Marketing encompasses much of many people's personal and professional lives. The extent to which the marketplace is humane and ethical should then have a substantial impact on people's life worlds.

The purpose of this chapter is to examine the role of spirituality in marketing. Marketing is a "societal process by which individuals and groups obtain what they need and want through creating, offering, and freely exchanging products and services of value with others" (Kotler 2000, 8). This process involves a seller and a buyer: supply and demand. It operates at the level of individual participants, groups of participants, and society. Thus, this chapter will examine the role of spirituality on both sides of the market equation and at each of these levels (Table 4.1).

Table 4.1

Spirituality Issues in Marketing

Level of analysis	Demand	Supply
Individual function	Expression of individual spiritual needs.	Meet individual spiritual needs through goods and services.
Spirituality issues	Asceticism vs. consumption. Fragmentation of spiritual needs.	Proliferation of spiritually related products. Sacralization process.
Market function	Aggregate demand into groups of consumers that can be be addressed efficiently and effectively.	Develop firms that can address consumer needs.
Spirituality issues	Spirituality-based market segmentation.	Development of organizations that care about employees.
		Developments of employees that care about customers.
		Spiritually based positioning of firms.
Society function	Support the spiritual needs of a trans-generational population within its evolving cultural framework.	Maintain a social and institutional fabric that supports exchange.
Spirituality issues	Deterioration of trust in the United States.	Globally expanding need for market-based trust.

INDIVIDUAL-LEVEL ISSUES

At the core of any market exchange system is a focal dyad: the individual buyer with a need coupled with the individual supplier of a product purported to meet that need. The "product" in a market exchange can be a good, service, idea, or set of beliefs. Thus, spiritual beliefs are marketed per se, in exchange for simple acceptance, allegiance, or altruistic feelings of having done something good. Spiritual ideas and services—including religious affiliations—are marketed in much the same way as everyday or "profane" products. In addition, profane products can be made sacred, or "sacralized."

The purpose of this section is to clarify the relationship between marketing and spirituality at the level of individual consumers, both in terms of their needs (demand) and the products intended to satisfy those needs (supply).

Demand

For the individual person, two issues relating to spirituality and marketing seem particularly important. One issue is the role of consumption in the everyday life of the consumers and the extent to which it inhibits, or enhances, their spiritual development. A second issue is the expansion and fragmentation of expressed spiritual needs among people, particularly in the United States.

Asceticism Versus Consumption

The tension between spirituality and consumption links back at least as far as Plato's distinction between soul and body, or spiritual versus material existence. Objects and services are provided in the material world, and spiritual existence is nonmaterial. Most religions associate spirituality with asceticism, that is, self-denial of material pleasures. Similarly, modern philosophers like Fromm (1976) attack social norms that encourage acquisitiveness, or "radical hedonism," on the grounds that it discourages community and individual social development. He argues that self-identity based on possessions exposes an individual to ultimate loss: "If I am what I have and if what I have is lost, who then am I?" (76). He suggests that developing an identity based on sharing, giving, and sacrificing should replace identity based on ownership. Similarly, Schor (1998) argues that hedonic consumption displaces attention to family, community, and religious affiliations.

Other philosophers argue that it is the disconnection between production and consumption that leads to spiritual damage. Kovel (1991) argues that the way production and consumption are bound together in primitive cultures builds the spiritual into everyday life; thus, "the universal exists in and cannot be split from the concrete particular" (23). Similarly, Borgmann (2000) suggests that self-production of goods and services, associated with technically primitive settings, encourages spiritual identity with objects. He argues that "sophisticated and impenetrable machinery" of production has "changed the nature of consumption fundamentally" (420). This separation between production and consumption is argued to diminish the spirituality inherent in preparing and using the objects that sustain and enhance life and living.

This argument becomes politicized in that producers (labor) are separated from consumers (owners), creating societal classes and corrupting individual motivation. Kovel (1991) notes with Marx that the separation of labor from capital displaces the focus of society from people to things. Marx argues that capitalist society encourages a propensity to acquire objects, which he terms a commodity fetish (Marx [1867] 1978). He argues that by separating work from ownership, capitalism alienates workers from the objects of their labor.

On the other hand, some scholars argue that the possession and consumption of products helps people define themselves. Wallendorf and Arnould (1988) distinguish "favorite object attachment" from ordinary material possessiveness. They suggest that these "favorite objects" give people a way to achieve individual expression through mass-produced objects. The meanings associated with these objects also link the owner to selected reference groups (McCracken 1986). Wallendorf and Arnould (1988) demonstrate that this process occurs across significantly different cultures. Sartre (1943) takes this a step further with his argument that possessions are all-important in understanding who we are. He suggests that people develop and express a sense of being through the things that they own. In the modern marketing literature, Belk (1988) similarly suggests that "we are what we have," and that this may be "the most basic and powerful fact of consumer behavior" (160). He suggests that the objects that we deliberately collect over time provide us with personal histories, inform us of who we are, give us a sense of personal direction.

In general, however, the tension along the asceticism–hedonic consumption spectrum requires individual people to find a balance consistent with their own developmental needs. As material beings, humans cannot survive on a purely spiritual basis. On the other hand, major elements of the marketplace and society encourage the maximization of consumption. Ultimately, the balance point is determined at the level of the individual.

It can be argued that the spirituality of consumers affect their consumption practices. Dwayne Ball and his colleagues (Ball et al. 2001) develop this argument in terms of Fowler's stages of faith development model (Fowler 1991). Fowler suggests that adults develop through up to four stages of faith. Briefly, the stages—and a brief characterization of each—are as follows:

1. Synthetic conventional—the individual shows a growing awareness of other religions and belief systems;

2. Individuating reflective—a core identity emerges that forms the foundation for subsequent connection to the eternal;
3. Conjunctive faith—a need develops for a stronger relationship with "direct" reality, unmediated by symbols; and
4. Universalizing faith—center of concern shifts from oneself to others.

Ball et al. (2001) suggest that, as an individual progresses through these stages of development, he will be less concerned in his purchasing behaviors about benefits to the self and more concerned about the well-being of others. They also suggest that the relationship between perceived benefits to self or others and consumption behaviors will be moderated by commitment to spiritual development.

In summary, it seems that a continuum between asceticism and hedonic consumption is accepted in the marketing literature, and that spirituality is seen as calling people toward asceticism while popular marketing appeals call them toward purchasing and consumption. Yet both extremes seem unrealistic in a world that is increasingly complex and environmentally challenged. Perhaps some middle ground, centered around "authentic consumption" reflecting personal history and idiosyncratic needs, may offer a realistic compromise for thoughtful consumers.

Fragmentation of Spiritual Needs

In addition to the tradeoff between asceticism and hedonic consumption, people also face the issue of increasingly fragmented spiritual needs. The openness of market economies fosters the expansion and diversity of consumer needs. Markets tend to encourage development of a cafeteria line of goods and services—product "breadth and depth"—that evokes the development of correspondingly diverse needs among consumers. Spiritual needs do not seem to be an exception to this tendency. As Roof notes:

> A global world offers an expanded religious menu: images, rituals, symbols, meditation techniques, healing practices, all of which may be borrowed eclectically, from a variety of sources such as Eastern spirituality, Theosophy and New Age, Witchcraft, Paganism, the ecology movement, nature religions, the occult traditions, psychotherapy, feminism, the human potential movement, science, and, of course, all the great world religious traditions. (Roof 1999, 73)

The compartmentalization of spirituality from other aspects of life, together with the open market for spiritual solutions, is seen by some as leading to a "shopping behavior approach" to spiritual development. Historically, spirituality was seen as woven throughout one's life-world, held in place by its centrality to the total personality and by its expression throughout the work, family, leisure, and other components of that world. Some contemporary critics argue that modern spirituality is not central to one's life-world, but is instead compartmentalized off from other aspects of one's life. This is seen as leading to low commitment to any particular spiritual system, with corresponding freedom to pick-and-choose among a variety of practices.

This freedom, combined with the plethora of spiritual "products" on the market, may lead to adoption of a wide range of spiritual beliefs. For example, Robert Wuthnow (1998) describes one twenty-six-year-old woman:

> She was raised Methodist, attended synagogue regularly with one of her friends, joined a Quaker meeting in college, was baptized in an Orthodox church during a trip to Russia,

practices Buddhist meditation, and participates about once a month in a Native American sweat lodge ceremony. (Wuthnow 1998, 41)

Wuthnow (1998) terms this eclectic approach to spiritual development "multiphrenic," which he defines as a type of religious orientation that is based on participation in multiple religious communities and built on a variety of moral foundations.

There appears to be little empirical research on the effects of this fragmented approach to spirituality on individuals or society. On the one hand, personalized spiritual pluralism would appear consistent with the openness of Western society. Certainly, selected traditions offer specific benefits. For example, people turn to such spiritual practices as meditation to reduce stress, increase health, and improve psychological well-being (Chandler et al. 1992; Elkins 1999; Idler 1987).

On the other hand, some scholars argue that conceptualizing spirituality from a consumer perspective is flawed, in that it shifts the relevant issues from moral striving to purchasing and consuming, from community salvation to individual transcendence, and from political change to individual mysticism (Cushman 1995). A deep-rooted focal tradition within which one has a historical base may provide the individual with a firmer basis for spiritual growth than a shopping cart full of off-the-shelf beliefs. Psychologist Kenneth Gergen (1991) refers to the latter, an individual who is torn in multiple directions of belief to the point where he loses his center, as a "saturated self."

Supply

An abundant and varied supply of goods and services are produced in response to the individual-level demand for the spiritual. In part, this demand relates to products *about* the spiritual, such as books on spirituality, religious music, and similar products. Beyond this, the search for things that are themselves spiritual is not met by simple production alone. Rather, spirituality—or sacredness—is conferred to certain objects and acts through a process of sacralization (Belk et al. 1989).

Proliferation of Spiritually Related Products

There has long been a market for relics, religious paraphernalia, and other sacred objects. Persons attending religious fairs and pilgrimages have sought to purchase sacred and spiritual objects for centuries (Turner and Turner 1978). In more modern times, spiritual needs have elicited production of a wide range of products. About 25 percent of the books listed on the New York Times best-seller list are said to be on spiritual topics (Taylor 1994). *The Road Less Traveled*, a book on spirituality by psychiatrist M. Scott Peck, has been on the best-seller list for 571 weeks. Other books on spirituality include *Embraced by the Light*, Betty J. Eadie's tale of a woman's near-death experience, and *The Celestine Prophecy*, James Redfield's story of a spiritual quest in Peru.

Spiritual information and entertainment is also packaged electronically. There are Nintendo Bible games, a CD-ROM entitled "Charlton Helston's Voyage Through the Bible," and a music CD titled "Chant," which was recorded by the reclusive Benedictine monks of Santo Domingo de Silos (Miller 1994). It is also possible to purchase a brown-hooded pullover, similar to the one the monks wear, but bearing a chant logo.

Spiritual services are offered by a variety of nonprofit and for-profit organizations. The fourth edition of *The Diagnostic and Statistical Manual of Mental Disorders,* the standard reference book used by mental health professionals and insurance companies for categorizing illnesses, includes "spiritual emergencies" as a new category. Previously, experiences beyond the normal were considered "abnormal" and treated with the corresponding pharmaceutical and therapy regimens. The new category indicates the potential existence of the need for spiritual rather than traditional medical assistance. As Graber and Johnson (2001) note, "spirituality is re-emerging as a relevant factor in serving the sick and disabled" (40).

In an apparent contradiction to the argument that asceticism and hedonic consumption constitute a continuum, O'Guinn and Belk (1989) suggest that in some instances society has reconciled materiality and spirituality by becoming more worldly and sacralizing consumption. Based on a review of Heritage Village, USA, home of the Praise the Lord (PTL) ministry, the authors identify this as "the first time that theology has incorporated luxurious consumption goals so directly and explicitly" in a setting associated with spirituality (237).

Products that address spiritual needs are not necessarily sacred, of course. The spiritual is defined primarily in terms of a relationship to "spirit" or "sacred matters," while the sacred is defined as "worthy of reverence and respect" (*Webster's New Collegiate Dictionary* 1997). Belk and his colleagues (Belk et al. 1989) suggest that the sacred can best be understood in contrast to the profane, or ordinary. They posit that sacred objects, places, or acts are distinguished by twelve properties: hierophany, kratophany, opposition to the profane, contamination, sacrifice, commitment, objectification, ritual, myth, mystery, communitas, and ecstasy and flow.

1. *Hierophany* is the idea that the sacred selectively shows itself to people, to some but not necessarily to everyone, as being of a "wholly different order" that does "not belong to our world" (Beane and Doty 1975, 141). As such, people do not create sacred things; sacred things reveal themselves.
2. *Kratophany* is the powerful ambivalence—combining strong approach and strong avoidance qualities—inherent in the sacred. The sacred combines good and desirable attributes with fear and dread (Durkheim [1896] 1975).
3. *Opposition to the profane*, or things of everyday life, is said to be inherent in the sacred. Contact with the profane destroys the essential attributes of the sacred (Durkheim 1953).
4. *Contamination* generally refers to the spread of positive sacredness rather than evil, or negative sacredness. "Objects blessed through sacred ritual are thus said to be contaminated with sacredness" (Belk et al. 1989).
5. *Sacrifice* is said "to prepare one to commune with the sacred, bring about a strong degree of commitment to sacred experience, and indicate appropriate deference" to the sacred (Belk et al. 1989).
6. *Commitment* is focused emotional attention to the sacred. Collective formation of shared commitment to the sacred is said to be the basis for societal integration (Durkheim 1915 [1902]; Weber [1920] 1962).
7. *Objectification* represents an object in a sacred or transcendent frame of reference (Mol 1976). Notes Belk and his colleagues (1989, 7), "A stone may continue to appear as a stone, but it is a sacred object when its origin is understood through a creation myth to be the tear of an animal."
8. *Ritual* consists of the rules of conduct about how one should approach sacred objects (Durkheim 1915). Ritual protects the individual from the negative powers of the sacred, and it protects the sacred from profane contact.
9. *Myths* are the stories about the sacred used to socialize participants to a collective understanding of the sacred (Kirk 1970).
10. *Mystery* is an essential element of the sacred and comes out of man's desire for extra-rational experiences and meaning.

11. *Communitas* is the temporary freedom from normal social hierarchies and roles that allows participants to share in a ritual experience with the camaraderie of status equality (Belk et al. 1989; Turner 1972).

12. *Ecstasy and flow* are states of being facilitated by the sacred. Ecstacy is a momentary transcendent experience separate and above the common pleasures of everyday life (Greeley 1985). Flow is a continuing sense of absolute involvement where individual experiences a loss of self-awareness and a total focus of attention on activity, such as a spiritual ceremony (Csikszentmihalyi 1975).

Sacralization Process

Mass-produced products are inherently devoid of spirituality. However, mundane objects can be "made sacred." For example, Moore notes that "when traditional cultures carve elaborate faces and bodies on their chairs and tools, they are acknowledging the soul in everyday things" (Moore 1993, 76). Belk et al. (1989) indicate that there are at least seven ways in which an object can be made sacred, that is, sacralized. These include: ritual, pilgrimage, quintessence, gift-giving, collecting, inheritance, and external sanction.

1. *Ritual* transforms an object symbolically from ordinary to sacred. One aspect of ritual transformation is singularization, the process by which a commodity is differentiated (or decommoditized) into one's own. As an example, Belk et al. (1989) describe the process of transforming a new house into a home by the placement of personal objects like family photographs and so on.

2. *Pilgrimage* is a journey to a site where one experiences sacredness. A family trip to a historical destination like Washington, DC, might qualify as a secular pilgrimage to the sacred.

3. *Quintessence* refers to an object's "rare and mysterious capacity to be just exactly what ought to be" (Cornfeld and Edwards 1983). Examples of such objects, according to Cornfeld and Edwards (1983), are Swiss Army knives, Ray ban sunglasses, and Coca-Cola. Popular outrage over the change in the formula of Coca-Cola in 1985 could be attributed to the drink's near-sacred status (Oliver 1986).

4. *Gift-giving* confers sacredness to an object by embedding it with relational properties.

5. *Collecting* instills a sacred or spiritual dimension to an object by including it in a collection, to which it adds completeness (Belk et al. 1988). The process of searching for, finding, arranging, and displaying objects added to a collection confers on them sacred status.

6. *Inheritance* of an object brings with it sacred status through sentimental associations with past family members.

7. *External sanction* refers to sacralization by an external authority. For example, "that tourists bowed to the external authority of museums was evident in their quiet, reverential tones and formal conversations concerning the importance of relics on display" (Belk et al. 1989, 21).

Overview

The relationship between spirituality and individual-level demand for goods and services is not simple. While spirituality is defined in terms of nonmaterial and eternal reality, individual people exist in a particular real world. In this world, even the communication of spiritual issues is facilitated through a variety of mundane physical technologies, including the printing of books and electronically disseminated messages. Beyond this, spiritual communities have developed and promulgated a variety of sacred objects. Even further, spiritual advisors suggest that self-production or adaptation of things can enhance their spiritual meaning. While this does not contradict the distinction between spiritual existence and hedonic consumption, it does suggest that these differences lie along a continuum rather than being split into a simple dichotomy.

Further, it seems reasonable to suggest that one's spirituality is likely to affect one's consumption behavior. Given that people express their deepest needs and desires in part through the purchase of certain goods and services—ranging from expensive cars to anonymous charitable donations—then it seems reasonable to argue that their pattern of consumption will change with their level of spiritual development.

From the supply side, the continued expansion of open market economies around the world—and the globalization of these markets—has led to a proliferation of spiritual goods and services. Further, objects from a variety of sources can be sacralized to meet the spiritual needs of individuals.

MARKET-LEVEL ISSUES

Examining spirituality from the standpoint of groups of people with similar needs and the organizations that supply those needs might again appear antithetical to the subject of spirituality itself. However, utilization of marketing research techniques to cluster the population based on spirituality provides a more detailed understanding of its heterogeneous nature on this issue. Further, if businesses are to follow ethical and humane practices, it may help to understand them from a spiritual perspective.

Demand

One of marketing's major disciplinary contributions is the concept of market segmentation (Biggadike 1981), and it appears that there are several different market segments to the religious/spiritual population. While research in this area is limited, Zinnbauer and his colleagues (1997) provided an interesting overview of this issue based on empirical research. Their findings suggest that religiousness and spirituality are two different orientations. This approach is consistent with the distinction between religious and spiritual identities proposed by Roof (1999, 178). Some of the characteristics associated with each orientation are illustrated in Figure 4.1 and described below.

Spiritual and Religious

The dominant segment was the "spiritual and religious" group, which comprised 79 percent of the Zinnbauer et al. (1997) study. This group shared characteristics with the remaining "spiritual but not religious" and "religious but not spiritual" groups. In addition, it appeared particularly strong on both intrinsic religiousness—referring to internally focused spirituality—and praying in places other than inside a church. Roof (1999, 178) considered this group to consist of both "mainstream believers" as well as "born-again Christians."

When compared to the smaller spiritual but not religious group, the spiritual and religious group reported a higher number attending church, as well as a higher number praying outside of church. In addition, the subject's parents had higher reported church attendance during their own

Figure 4.1 **Major Segments to the Religious/Spiritual Population**

		Low Religiousness	High Religiousness
Spirituality	High	Spiritual not religious Noncompetitive Mystic	Spiritual and religious Intrinsically religious Pray outside church New Ager Group experience of spirituality High income Well educated
	Low	Secularist Nonspiritual atheists and agnostics	Religious not spiritual Self-sacrificing Interdependent Self-righteous Authoritarian Religious family heritage

Low   High

Religiousness

childhoods. In terms of religious/spiritual variables, the spiritual and religious group had a substantially higher "self-rated religiousness" and religious orthodoxy. Finally, in terms of psychosocial variables, the spiritual and religious group was higher on "right-wing authoritarianism," interdependence with others, and self-sacrifice for others.

Spiritual but not Religious

The next largest segment, the "spiritual but not religious" group, consisted of individuals who considered themselves as spiritual, but who chose not to align themselves with organized religions. Multiple studies confirm the distinct identity of this group (Mitroff and Denton 1999; Roof 1999; Zinnbauer et al. 1997). In the Zinnbauer study this group comprised 21 percent of the study sample. Roof (1999) identified this group as "metaphysical believers" and "spiritual seekers."

Two sets of variables distinguished the spiritual but not religious group. They were significantly higher than other groups on "New Age beliefs and practices" and "mystical experiences." They were also significantly higher on "group experiences related to spiritual growth" and "independence from others." This spiritual but not religious segment identified by Zinnbauer et al. (1997) is similar to the "highly active seekers" segment of baby boomers identified by Roof (1999). This latter group consisted of individuals who had developed a highly individualized spirituality while explicitly rejecting organized religion. These individuals tended to be better educated and to be raised by parents who attended religious services less frequently, compared to the more traditionally religious population.

The correlational profile developed by Zinnbauer et al. (1997) found spirituality to be significantly and positively correlated to: education and income ($r = 0.15$ and 0.12, respectively; $p < 0.01$ and $p < 0.05$, respectively), group experience related to spiritual growth ($r = 0.27$; $p < 0.01$), "hurt by clergy" ($r = 0.12$; $p < 0.05$), New Age beliefs and practices ($r = 0.24$; $p < 0.01$), and mystical experiences ($r = 0.27$; $p < 0.01$). On the other hand, spirituality was found to be negatively related to religiousness ($r = -0.18$; $p < 0.01$) and individual competitiveness ($r = -0.18$; $p < 0.01$).

Religious not Spiritual

It would seem plausible to speculate the existence of a third segment: religious not spiritual. Indeed, Roof (1999) posits a category of "dogmatists" which have no spiritual identity but a religious identity and includes "fundamentalists, institutionalists, moralists, and neotraditionalists" (178).

While not specified in the Zinnbauer et al. (1997) study, one might expect that in a large sample one might identify individuals with a religious tradition who are strong on self-righteousness and authoritarianism, but low on spirituality. In such a group, one might find the spiritual basis of religion diminished or absent, leaving only the organizational and disciplinary aspects of traditional religion.

Based on their correlation analysis, Zinnbauer et al. (1997) found that religiousness was positively correlated with church attendance ($r = 0.45$; $p < 0.01$), mother's and father's church attendance during the subject's childhood ($r = 0.26$ and 0.23, respectively; $p < 0.01$), religious orthodoxy ($r = 0.40$; $p < 0.01$), right-wing authoritarianism ($r = 0.27$; $p < 0.01$), self-righteousness ($r = 0.16$; $p < 0.01$), interdependence with others ($r = 0.11$; $p < 0.05$), and self-sacrifice for others ($r = 0.15$; $p < 0.01$). On the other hand, religiousness was negatively related to independence from others ($r = -0.18$; $p < 0.01$).

Secularists

Roof (1999) termed those without a spiritual or religious identity as "secularists." While not specified in the Zinnbauer et al. (1997) study, individuals who are low on both religiousness and spirituality would presumably include nonspiritual atheists and agnostics. The proportion of the population in the atheist/agnostic group varies from culture to culture. In the United States about 95 percent of the population claims to believe in God, versus 50 percent of the population in Western Europe (Gunther 2001; Roof 1993). This seems to imply a relatively small (less than 5 percent) atheist/agnostic group in the United States, versus a larger group (50 percent) in Western Europe. However, one could be an atheist or agnostic and still have strong spiritual beliefs.

Large-sample studies might identify nuances within this framework, in terms of subsets of these four groups. However, the key point is that the felt need for spirituality and religiousness is unevenly distributed throughout the population, taking on different characteristics in different segments of the population. This diversity of needs creates diverse market and service opportunities.

SUPPLY (FIRM-LEVEL) SPIRITUALITY

From the perspective of market-level supply (i.e., the level of the firm), the concern of marketing as it relates to spirituality is the development of organizations that address the needs of both employees and customers for an ethical and humane workplace and marketplace. Among the issues that emerge in this domain are: (1) development of organizations that care about ethical and humane treatment of employees; (2) development of employees who genuinely care about ethical and humane treatment of customers; and (3) positioning of organizations in terms of value-based issues.

A conceptual framework that helps to integrate thinking about the role of spirituality in an organization's relationship with its employees, its customers, and other key groups that have a vested interest in its behavior is stakeholder theory. Stakeholder theory is based on the premise that organizations have relationships with multiple constituent groups that all have intrinsic value (Jones and Wicks 1999). The intrinsic value argument—that all legitimate stakeholders should be treated as "ends" in themselves rather than as a "means" for the firm to use to achieve its own ends (Evans and Freeman 1983)—is a key element of stakeholder theory.

While there is a presumption that a balanced approach to managing stakeholders' interests leads to long-term competitive advantage and profitability, there is little empirical support for this position (Griffin and Mahon 1997). Donaldson and Preston (1995) conclude that, ultimately, the defense of stakeholder theory is normative: "The plain truth is that the most prominent alternative to stakeholder theory (i.e., the 'management serving the shareholders' theory) is morally untenable" (88).

As such, a stakeholder perspective is a logical outcome of the marketing concept of the firm. The marketing concept, as a business philosophy and operating heuristic, holds that the firm should resolve trade-offs "in favor of the customer and the long run" (Biggadike 1981, 623). Webster (1992) argues that this concept must be expanded to include a wider range of internal and external stakeholders to the firm, such as employees, customers, and strategic partners. Indeed, Lusch and Laczniak (1987) demonstrate empirically that the marketing concept and stakeholder concept can be seen as denoting a single, underlying business orientation.

Development of Organizations That Care About Employees

Perhaps the central issue in the relationship between the organization and its employees is work per se. In that regard, spirituality at work may best be understood in contrast to the "scientific" management of labor associated with "taylorism"—breaking work down to the efficient performance of limited tasks. Arguably, this approach to labor management leads to employee isolation and alienation (Bolman and Deal 1995).

By contrast, spirituality at work is based on "recognition that employees have an inner life that nourishes and is nourished by meaningful work that takes place in the context of community" (Ashmos and Duchon 2000, 137). This is consistent with the finding that employees find meaning and purpose in their jobs when their work allows them to reach their full potential, when they are associated with a good or ethical organization, and when their work is interesting (Mitroff and Denton 1999).

An organizational mission centered on a socially acceptable goal, when properly aligned with individual career goals that provide employees with an on-the-job route to self-actualization, enacts a viable framework for organizational spirituality (Nadesan 1999). Such a framework implies employee empowerment. As Elmes and Smith (2001) note, "with concepts like attunement to self and others, synchronicity, and holographic design, empowerment discourse appeals to Americans' desires not only to have control over their lives, but also to identify themselves with something more perfect, prosperous, and good" (44).

Organizations that pursue morally based missions with which employees can identify, and which employees are empowered to pursue, are also likely to enjoy the benefits of employee self-selection, both inbound and outbound. According to "Image Theory," morally motivated individuals will tend to join firms that espouse and practice corresponding values because it is compatible with their value images (Lee and Mitchell 1994). On the other hand, "opportunists will tend to leave moral firms because they may become frustrated with 'irrational' (moral) decision making" (Jones 1995, 419).

Development of Employees That Care About Customers

An organization's caring for its employees is the foundation for employees caring for customers. Employees treat customers in the way that they feel management is treating them. The chain-of-service model developed by Heskett and his colleagues (Heskett et al. 1994) suggests that caring-level service to customers can only be fostered by caring treatment of employees.

Customer caring is a logical outgrowth of customer orientation. Customer orientation has been defined as " the sufficient understanding of one's target buyers to be able to create superior value for them continuously" (Narver and Slater 1990, 21). Customer orientation can assume a range of behaviors, from mundane to heroic. However, when deeply held employee values are aligned with a customer-focused organizational mission, the result can elevate work beyond the mundane to the status of a "calling." An extreme example of caring-based service may be seen in the following example:

> When riots swept through Jakarta in 1998, leaving more than 500 people dead, most air-
> lines and other businesses deserted the center of the Indonesian capital. Claire Hatton kept
> the office she managed for British Airways there open, telling the *London Times* "I will stay
> here as long as I am needed and there are people wanting to leave." ("BA Woman Rescues
> 2,000 in Jakarta," 1)

This incident illustrates a level of customer orientation that transcends a simple economic exchange. It raises the fundamental issue of when and how people care for others. Research suggests that individual caring is a result of both environmental and personality characteristics (Batson 1990). People care when they are in a communal relationship with others and when they have empathy for the plight of others (Hoffman 2000). Such caring is further supported by an altruistic personality (Oliner and Oliner 1988), internalized pro-social values (Batson 1989; Staub 1989), and a predisposition to care based on moral reasoning (Kitchener 1991; Kolhberg 1976).

Positioning of Organizations on Value-Based Issues

Organizations position themselves in the minds of customers and potential customers, employees and potential employees, and other existing and potential stakeholders through customer-oriented strategies, advertising (Hirschman 1990/1991), public relations, and acts of "moral imagination" (Jackson 1999, 68). Such positioning moves can align the firm and its products with deeply held stakeholder values. Such alignment can result in sales, self-selected employment applications, and other forms of organizational support.

For example, advertising is used to position Kellogg's Strawberry Squares, a breakfast cereal, as a natural product. In advertisements for the products, whole strawberries—stems and all—fall into a bowl of cereal, consumed by people in flannel shirts, eating on a wooden porch beside a garden. In this way "the ties of the product to sacred nature are expressed through rural iconography" (Hirschman 1990/1991). Similarly, the religious ties of HM Health Services, which include two hospitals in Ohio, is part of its advertising message. Founded by Catholic nuns, HM Health Services targets middle-income women aged twenty-five to fifty-four in a predominantly Catholic area. Consumers who evaluated the advertisements said they "felt reassured knowing the health-care provider is grounded in a spiritual mission" (Harrison 1997, 28).

Public acts can also confirm an organization's espoused values. In its statement of values, Merck states that its number one value is "preserving and improving human life. All of our actions must be measured by our success in achieving this goal. We value above all our ability to serve everyone who can benefit from the appropriate use of our products and services, thereby providing lasting consumer satisfaction" (http://www.merck.com/overview/philosophy.html). Merck determined that a drug could be developed to cure river blindness, which afflicts millions of people in less-developed countries, but that neither public nor private funding was available to purchase it. The company decided to develop and distribute the drug, although doing so surpassed any requirement of "minimal morality" (Jackson 1999, 68).

Overview

The clustering of people into groups based on their spirituality and/or religiosity—or lack thereof—establishes a minimal framework for understanding differences in spiritual wants of the population. From the supply side of the exchange equation, the concern of marketing as it relates to spirituality is to develop organizations that address the needs of both employees and customers for an ethical and humane workplace and marketplace. At some fundamental level, this may be accomplished by developing organizations that care about ethical and humane treatment of employees, and employees who share the same concerns about their customers. In addition, the positioning of organizations in terms of value-based issues may serve to efficiently align customers with supplying organizations that share the same general predispositions.

SOCIETAL-LEVEL ISSUES

Ultimately, the role of marketing—or any other social function—is to support the needs, both spiritual and mundane, of a trans-generational population within an evolving cultural framework (Table 4.1). If marketing fails to support the needs of current and future populations, within the value system accepted by the general culture, then it loses legitimacy as a social institution.

Just as marketing affects society, a variety of social forces and trends affect how marketing functions within a given social system. The purpose of this section is to describe two sets of societal trends—one at the level of demand and the other at the level of supply—that could have a substantial impact on the extent to which future marketing systems are humane and ethical.

Both sets of trends described in this section relate to the concept of social capital. Social capital involves social networks and their accompanying norms of reciprocity and trustworthiness. As Putnam notes, "where physical capital refers to physical objects and human capital refers to properties of individuals, social capital refers to connections among individuals" (Putnam 2000, 19).

Apparently, Lyda J. Hanifan, the state supervisor for rural schools in West Virginia, made the first published reference to social capital. Writing in 1916, she noted the economic value of trust-based cooperation among organizations and individuals, commenting that "the community as a whole will benefit by the cooperation of all its parts, while the individual will find in his associations the advantages of the help, the sympathy, and the fellowship of his neighbors" (Hanifan 1916).

Two major trends appear to be developing which affect social capital in the marketplace in profound ways. One of these trends, on the demand side, relates to the degeneration of trust at the level of individuals and institutions among citizens in the United States. The second trend, on the supply side, relates ironically to increasing requirements for trust in business-to-business relationships. Both sets of trends would seem to impact the ethical and humane functioning of markets in society.

Demand

Degeneration of Trust

The research of sociologist Robert Putnam (2000) suggests that trust of institutions and individuals in the United States appears to be declining. Civic disengagement, individual isolation, reduced commitment to religious and other organizations, and lack of knowledge about public affairs appear likely to accompany this growing distrust. This alteration of the social fabric appears to be unprecedented in U.S. society, and not part of some normal generational maturation process.

A central measure of this growing distrust is that only 40 percent of the post–baby boom generation (born in the 1970s) believe "most people are honest," compared to 60 percent of the baby boomers (born during 1946–60) and more than 70 percent of those born before 1945 (Putnam 2000). Repeated surveys over time demonstrate that these generational cohort beliefs are relatively stable. Each cohort group's level of trust remains at approximately the same level throughout their lives.

Despite the expansion of information technology, the post–baby boom generation is substantially less knowledgeable about public affairs. Putnam notes that this is a recent development: "From the earliest opinion polls in the 1940s to the mid-1970s, younger people were at least as well informed as their elders were, but that is no longer the case. . . . Today's under-thirties pay less attention to the news and know less about current events than their elders do today or than people their age did two or three decades ago" (Putnam 2000, 36).

Individual isolation is not just from information, but also from actual contact with others. It is a shift from communality to personal autonomy. Putnam notes that much of this isolation is due to declining participation in faith-based communities, which he terms "the single most important repository of social capital in America" (Putnam 2000, 96). He notes that about half of all association memberships, personal philanthropy, and volunteer work is religiously based. He terms churches incubators for social skills that are then generalized to other forms of social engagement.

This pattern of distrust and isolation portends problems for marketing, which requires a minimal level of trust and reciprocity to function well. Markets work best in situations where there is open and ongoing communications, as well as generally accepted and observed norms of behavior. Effective within-group and between-group communications provides participants in a market with an opportunity to develop and maintain a reputation. An inability to establish a reputation—due to a breakdown of interpersonal communications—leads to an inability to build value. Similarly, observation of norms allows market participants to develop expectations of consistent exchange behavior. Failure of a community to adhere to behavioral norms diminishes participants' ability to predict exchange outcomes, which also diminishes the expected value of exchange.

As Putnam notes: ". . . people who trust others are all-around good citizens, and those more engaged in community life are both more trusting and more trustworthy. Conversely, the civically disengaged believe themselves to be surrounded by miscreants and feel less constrained to be honest themselves" (Putnam 2000, 137). As a result, the entire marketing system becomes less ethical and humane.

Supply

Need for Market-Based Trust Expanding Globally

Even as trust deteriorates at a personal level in the United States, the need for trust—particularly in business-to-business exchange—grows worldwide. Belief in reciprocation of ethical and humane business practices is a precondition for establishment of effective market economies (Rossouw 1998). Thus, the success of the market economies proliferating in Eastern Europe, South Africa, and Asia requires the corresponding establishment of a network of trust. However, the emergence of democracies is often associated with an increase in unethical business practices and deterioration of trust (Rossouw 1998). This pattern suggests that the need for market-based trust will grow worldwide in the emerging market economies.

Transactions have costs (Williamson 1975). Lack of trust and trustworthiness among exchange partners increases the costs of exchange by increasing the need for more detailed contract development, policing of contract implementation, and dispute resolution.

Unfortunately, for newly emerging market economies, interfirm trust is particularly important in volatile and uncertain environments (Noordewier et al. 1990). In relatively stable environments, where the relevant social, economic, technical and other factors are reasonably simple and predictable, contracts and contractual enforcement mechanisms may be sufficient to ensure that agreements will be honored. However, when relevant environmental factors are unstable—as they are more likely to be in emerging market economies—it may be impossible to predict, specify, and contractually resolve all relevant contingencies in advance. At some basic level, trust may be a precondition for developing business-to-business exchange, particularly in volatile markets.

Development of trust and trustworthiness among exchange partners allows for the creation of an interdependent workflow and value creation (Holm et al. 1999). Parties to a trust-based system of exchange can develop idiosyncratic assets that expose them to risk, while increasing the value-creation capability of the entire system. Similarly, parties to a trust-based system of exchange can openly communicate information—about costs, market opportunities, relational problems, and the like—that allow for optimization of the combined partnership (Strutton et al. 1993).

Trust allows parties to an exchange to expand their relationship, in terms of the diversity and intensity of linkages between firms, and to depend on the terms of the relationship. Trust allows for improvements in quality (by reducing the variability associated with multiple partners), increased adaptability (by reducing the need for extended contracting), and decreased cost (by reducing the need for inspections and other policing of contractual terms). Customer relationships are also associated with customer satisfaction, loyalty, word-of-mouth behaviors, and increased purchasing (Reynolds and Beatty 1999). These factors in turn help to build the firm and its trade partners and the trust within the relevant trade system.

However, the failure to establish trust in a market system can have the reverse effects, inhibiting the formation of effective business systems, diminishing quality and market adaptability, and raising costs. Like individuals, businesses that fail to trust one another can develop preemptive opportunistic behaviors—and unethical practices—that reinforce a destructive cycle of change.

Overview

It is clear that societal trends can impact the marketing function. In this section I have attempted to develop an argument that trust will have an impact on U.S. and world markets. Within the United States, it seems plausible to argue that the deterioration of trust could have a detrimental impact on the level of ethical behavior within the system as well as consumers' ability to derive satisfaction from the system. Globally, I argue that the ability to build trust within emerging economies may relate to the effectiveness of emerging democratic market economies.

SUMMARY

The purpose of this chapter has been to examine the role of spirituality in marketing, interpreted as responding to consumers' spiritual and mundane needs within the context of an ethical and humane marketplace. Both sides of the supply-and-demand market equation were examined from the perspectives of individual participations, groups of participants, and society. The role of spirituality was specified at each level, together with an examination of selected related issues.

At the individual level, spirituality has a deep influence on both demand and supply. What we want (demand) is affected by a fundamental trade-off between asceticism and hedonic consumption, as well as a continuing fragmentation of spiritual needs among some. These needs are responded to by a proliferating supply of spiritually related products. In addition, people confer spiritual meaning to products through a process called sacralization.

At the market level, it is possible to cluster people into groups based on their spirituality and/or religiosity, or lack thereof. From the supply side, the concern of marketing as it relates to spirituality is to develop organizations that address the needs of both employees and customers, as well as other stakeholders for an ethical and humane workplace and marketplace. In addition, the positioning of organizations in terms of value-based issues may serve to efficiently align customers with supplying organizations that share the same general interests.

Finally, at the level of society, marketing can be seen to influence—and be influenced by—critical social trends. Markets require a "social matrix" that includes an effective means of communications, a system of order that precludes dishonesty, a currency, and a mechanism for the enforcement of promises (Macneil 1980). Beyond that, "humane and ethical" markets require at least a minimal level of trust in one's trade partner, as well as a foundation for trustworthiness on each side. In the United States, there is reason to believe that social trust—and social capital—may be eroding. At the global level, it seems more required than ever.

REFERENCES

Ashmos, Donde P., and Dennis Duchon. (2000). "Spirituality at Work: A Conceptualization and Measure." *Journal of Management Inquiry* 9, no. 2 (June): 134–145.

"BA Woman Rescues 2,000 in Jakarta." (1998). *London Times*, May 19, 1.

Ball, Dwayne; Ronald Hampton; Athinodoros Chronis; and Matt Bunker. (2001). "The Development of Spirituality and Its Effects on Consumer Behavior." In *2001 AMA Educators' Proceedings, Enhancing Knowledge Development in Marketing*, ed. Greg W. Marshall and Stephen J. Grove. Chicago: American Marketing Association, 3–6.

Batson, C.D. (1989). "Personal Values, Moral Principles, and a Three-Path Model of Prosocial Motivation." In *Social and Moral Values: Individual and Societal Perspectives*, ed. N. Eisenberg, J. Reykowski and E. Staub. Hillsdale, NJ: Erlbaum, 213–228.

———. (1990). "How Social an Animal?: The Human Capacity for Caring." *American Psychologist* 45, no. 3 (March): 336–346.

Beane, Wendell C., and William C. Doty, eds. (1975). *Myths, Rites, and Symbols: A Mircea Eliade Reader*, vol. 1. New York: HarperCollins.

Belk, Russell W. (1988). "Possessions and the Extended Self." *Journal of Consumer Research* 15, no. 2 (September): 139–168.

Belk, Russell W.; Melanie Wallendorf; and John F. Sherry, Jr. (1989). "The Sacred and the Profane in Consumer Behavior: Theodicy on the Odyssey." *Journal of Consumer Research* 16, no. 1 (June): 1–38.

Belk, Russell W.; Melanie Wallendorf; John Sherry; Morris Holbrook; and Scott Roberts. (1988). "Collectors and Collections." In *Advances in Consumer Research*, vol. 15, ed. Michael Houston. Provo. UT: Association for Consumer Research, 548–553.

Biggadike, E. Ralph. (1981). "The Contributions of Marketing to Strategic Management." *Academy of Management Review* 6, no. 4: 621–632.

Bolman, L., and T. Deal. (1995). *Leading with Soul.* San Francisco: Jossey-Bass.

Borgmann, Albert. (2000). "The Moral Complexion of Consumption." *Journal of Consumer Research* 26 (March): 418–422.

Bruce, Willa, and John Novinson. (1999). "Spirituality in Public Service: A Dialogue." *Public Administration Review* 59, no. 2 (March/April): 163–169.

Chandler, Cynthia K.; Janice Miner Holden; and Cheryl A. Kolander. (1992). "Counseling for Spiritual Wellness: Theory and Practice." *Journal of Counseling & Development* 71 (November/December): 168–175.

Cornfeld, Betty, and Owen Edwards. (1983). *Quintessence: The Quality of Having It.* New York: Crown.

Csikszentmihalyi, Mihaly. (1975). *Beyond Boredom and Anxiety.* San Francisco: Jossey-Bass.

Cushman, Philip. (1995). *Constructing the Self, Constructing America: A Cultural History of Psychotherapy.* Boston: Addison-Wesley.

Donaldson, Thomas, and Lee E. Preston. (1995). "The Stakeholder Theory of the Corporation: Concepts, Evidence, and Implications." *Academy of Management Review* 20, no. 1 (January): 65–91.

Durkheim, Emile. [1902] (1915). *The Elementary Forms of the Religious Life.* London: Allen and Unwin.

———. (1953). *Sociology and Philosophy,* trans. D.F. Pockock. London: Cohen and West.

———. [1896] (1975). *Durkheim on Religion: A Selection of Readings with Bibliographies and Introductory Remarks,* trans. J. Redding and W.S.F. Pickering. London: Routledge and Kegan Paul.

Eadie, Betty J. (1994). *Embraced by the Light.* New York: Bantam Books.

Elkins, David N. (1999). "Spirituality: It's What's Missing in Mental Health." *Psychology Today* (September/October): 45–48.

Elmes, Michael, and Charles Smith. (2001). "Moved by the Spirit: Contextualizing Workplace Empowerment in American Spiritual Ideals." *Journal of Applied Behavioral Science* 37, no. 1 (March): 33–50.

Evans, W., and R.E. Freeman. (1983). "A Stakeholder Theory of the Modern Corporation: Kantian Capitalism." In *Ethical Theory and Business,* ed. T. Beauchamp and N. Bowie. Englewood Cliffs, NJ: Prentice-Hall, 75–93.

Fowler, James W. III. (1991). "Stages in Faith Consciousness." In *New Directions for Child Development.* New York: Jossey-Bass, 27–45.

Fromm, Erich. (1976). *To Have or To Be.* New York: Harper and Row.

Gergen, Kenneth. (1991). *The Saturated Self: Dilemmas of Identity in Contemporary Life.* New York: Basic Books.

Graber, David R., and James A. Johnson (2001). "Spirituality and Healthcare Organizations." *Journal of Healthcare Management* 46, no. 1 (January/February): 39–50.

Greeley, Andrew M. (1985). "Unsecular Man: The Persistence of Religion." New York: Schocken.

Griffin, J.J., and J.F. Mahon. (1997). "The Corporate Social Performance and Corporate Financial Performance Debate: Twenty-five Years of Incomparable Research." *Business and Society* 36: 5–31.

Gunther, Marc. (2001). "God & Business." *Fortune* 144, no. 1 (July 9): 60–80.

Hanifan, Lyda Judson. (1916). "The Rural School Community Center." *Annals of the American Academy of Political and Social Science* 67: 130–138.

Harrison, Jennifer. (1997). "Advertising Joins the Journey of the Soul." *American Demographics* 19, no. 6 (June): 22–28.

Heskett, James L.; Thomas O. Jones; Gary W. Loveman; W. Earl Sasser, Jr.; and Leonard A. Schlesinger. (1994). "Putting the Service-Profit Chain to Work." *Harvard Business Review* (March–April): 165–174.

Hirschman, Elizabeth C. (1990/1991). "Point of View: Sacred, Secular, and Mediating Consumption Imagery in Television Commercials." *Journal of Advertising Research* (December/January): 38–43.

Hoffman, Martin L. (2000). *Empathy and Moral Development: Implications for Caring and Justice.* Cambridge: Cambridge University Press.

Holm, Desiree Blankenburg; Kent Eriksson; and Jan Johanson. (1999). "Creating Value Through Mutual Commitment to Business Network Relationships." *Strategic Management Journal* 20: 467–486.

Idler, Ellen L. (1987). "Religious Involvement and the Health of the Elderly: Some Hypotheses and an Initial Test." *Social Forces* 66, no. 1 (September): 226 238.

Jackson, Kevin T. (1999). "Spirituality as a Foundation for Freedom and Creative Imagination in International Business Ethics." *Journal of Business Ethics* 19: 61–67.

Jones, Thomas M. (1995). "Instrumental Stakeholder Theory: A Synthesis of Ethics and Economics." *Academy of Management Review* 20, no. 2: 404–437.

Jones, Thomas M., and Andrew C. Wicks. (1999). "Convergent Stakeholder Theory." *Academy of Management Review* 24, no. 2 (April): 206–221.

Kirk, G.S. (1970). *Myth.* Cambridge: Cambridge University Press.

Kitchener, Richard F. (1991). "Jean Piaget: The Unknown Sociologist?" *British Journal of Sociology* 42, no. 3 (September): 421–442.

Kolhberg, L. (1976). "Moral Stages and Moralization: The Cognitive-Development Approach." In *Moral Development and Behavior: Theory, Research, and Social Issues,* ed. T. Lickona. New York: Academic Press, 31–53.

Kotler, Philip. (2000). *Marketing Management.* Upper Saddle River, NJ: Prentice Hall.

Kovel, Joel. (1991). *History and Spirit: An Inquiry into the Philosophy of Liberation.* Boston: Beacon Press.

Lee, T.W., and T.R. Mitchell. (1994). "An Alternative Approach: The Unfolding Model of Voluntary Employee Turnover." *Academy of Management Review* 19: 51–89.

Lusch, Robert F., and Gene R. Laczniak. (1987). "The Evolving Marketing Concept, Competitive Intensity and Organizational Performance." *Journal of the Academy of Marketing Science* 15, no. 3 (fall): 1–11.

Macneil, Ian R. (1980). *The New Social Contract, An Inquiry into Modern Contractual Relations.* New Haven, CT: Yale University Press.

Marx, Karl. [1867] (1978). *Capital: A Critique of Political Economy*, vol. 1, trans. Ben Fawkes. Harmondsworth, UK: Penguin.

McCracken, Grant. (1986). "Culture and Consumption: A Theoretical Account of the Structure and Movement of the Cultural Meaning of Consumer Goods." *Journal of Consumer Research* 13 (June): 71–84.

Miller, Cyndee. (1994). "People Want to Believe in Something." *Marketing News* 28, no. 25 (December 5): 1–2, 19.

Mitroff, Ian I., and Elizabeth A. Denton. (1999). "A Study of Spirituality in the Workplace." *Sloan Management Review* (summer): 83–92.

Mol, Hans. (1976). *Identity and the Sacred: A Sketch for a New Socio-Scientific Study of Religion.* New York: Pilgram.

Moore, Thomas. (1993). "Care of the Soul." *Psychology Today* 28, no. 30 (May–June): 76–77.

Nadesan, Majia Holmer. (1999). "The Discourses of Corporate Spiritualism and Evangelical Capitalism." *Management Communications Quarterly* 13, no. 1 (August): 3–42.

Narver, John C., and Stanley F. Slater. (1990). "The Effect of a Market Orientation on Business Profitability." *Journal of Marketing* (October) 20–35.

Noordewier, Thomas G.; George John; and John R. Nevin. (1990). "Performance Outcomes of Purchasing Agreements in Industrial Buyer-Vendor Relationships." *Journal of Marketing* 4, no. 54 (October): 80–93.

O'Guinn, Thomas C., and Russell W. Belk. (1989). "Heaven on Earth: Consumption at Heritage Village, USA." *Journal of Consumer Research* 16, no. 2 (September): 227–238.

Oliner, S.P., and Oliner, P.M. (1988). *The Altruistic Personality: Rescuers of Jews in Nazi Europe.* New York: Free Press.

Oliver, Thomas. (1986). *The Real Coke, the Real Story.* New York: Viking Penguin.

Peck, M. Scott, M.D. (1978). *The Road Less Traveled: A New Psychology of Love, Traditional Values and Spiritual Growth.* New York: Simon and Schuster.

Putnam, Robert D. (2000). *Bowling Alone: The Collapse and Revival of American Community.* New York: Simon and Schuster.

Redfield, James (1993). *The Celestine Prochecy: An Adventure.* New York: Warner.

Reynolds, Kristy E., and Sharon E. Beatty. (1999). "Customer Benefits and Company Consequences of Customer-Salesperson Relationships in Retailing." *Journal of Retailing* 75, no. 1: 11–32.

Roof, Wade Clark. (1993). *A Generation of Seekers: The Spiritual Journeys of the Baby Boom Generation.* San Francisco: Harper.

———. (1999). "Spiritual Marketplace: Baby Boomers and the Remaking of American Religion." Princeton, NJ: Princeton University Press.

Rossouw, Gedeon J. (1998). "Establishing Moral Business Culture in Newly Formed Democracies." *Journal of Business Ethics* 17: 1563–1571.

Sartre, Jean-Paul. (1943). *Being and Nothingness: A Phenomenological Essay on Ontology.* New York: Philosophical Library.

Schor, Juliet B. (1998). *The Overspent American.* New York: Basic.

Staub, E. (1989). "Individual and Societal (Group) Values in a Motivational Perspective and their Role in Benevolence and Harmonizing." In *Social and Moral Values: Individual and Societal Perspectives*, ed. N. Eisenberg, J. Reykowski, and E. Staub. Hillsdale, NJ: Erlbaum, 45–61.

Strutton, David; Lou Pelton; and James R. Lumpkin. (1993). "The Influence of Psychological Climate on Conflict Resolution Strategies in Franchise Relationships." *Journal of the Academy of Marketing Science* 21, no. 3: 207–215.

Taylor, Eugene. (1994). "Desperately Seeking Spirituality." *Psychology Today* (November/December): 55–68.

Turner, Victor. (1972). "Passages, Margins, and Poverty: Religious Communitas." *Worship* 46, no. 7: 390–412.

Turner, Victor, and Edith Turner. (1978). *Image and Pilgramage in Christian Culture: Anthropological Perspectives.* Oxford, UK: Basil Blackwell.

Wallendorf, Melanie, and Eric J. Arnould. (1988). " 'My Favorite Things': A Cross-Cultural Inquiry into Object Attachment, Possessiveness, and Social Linkage." *Journal of Consumer Research* 14, no. 4 (March): 531–547.

Weber, Max. [1920] (1962). *The Sociology of Religion.* Boston: Beacon Press.

Webster, Frederick E. Jr. (1992). "The Changing Role of Marketing in the Corporation." *Journal of Marketing* 56 (October): 1–17.

Webster's New Collegiate Dictionary. (1997). Springfield, MA: Merriam-Webster.

Williamson, Oliver. (1975). *Markets and Hierarchies: Analysis and Antitrust Implications.* New York: Free Press.

Wuthnow, Robert. (1998). "Morality, Spirituality, and Democracy." *Society* 34 (March/April): 37–43.

Zinnbauer, Brian J.; Kenneth I. Pargament; Brenda Cole; Mark S. Rye; Eric M. Butter; Timothy G. Belavich; Kathleen M. Hipp; Allie B. Scott; and Jill L. Kadar. (1997). "Religion and Spirituality: Unfuzzying the Fuzzy." *Journal of the Scientific Study of Religion* 36, no. 4: 549–564.

CHAPTER 5

ORGANIZATIONAL INTERACTIONS

A Basic Skeleton with Spiritual Tissue

IRIS VILNAI-YAVETZ AND ANAT RAFAELI

Organizing is based on recurring interactions among multiple dyads and groups of people. Interactions may be purely functional, intended at accomplishing performance goals. They may also be purely social, intended at addressing the social needs of organizational members. And they may take the form of some hybrid of the two, likely the most frequent type of interactions in organizations: Interactions intended at accomplishing some formal task also include a social element. Organizations necessarily evolve as a result of the interactions they comprise. Interactions imposed by external, formal structures pave the way to the evolution of other forms of interactions. Both externally defined and emergent interactions ultimately define the quality of an organization (Feldman and Rafaeli 2001). All interactions may have spiritual qualities. In this chapter we advance an analytical framework that allows a separation between what we call the functional or basic skeleton of an interaction, and the social or spiritual tissue that can accompany this skeleton.

Our analysis as presented here is inductive and conceptual, providing an analytic framework. This analysis draws, however, from both our review of the literature and several sets of qualitative as well as quantitative data. These data focused, intentionally, on a rather mundane interaction between bus drivers and passengers, our assumption being that routine and mundane interactions can reveal very basic patterns that are likely to occur in more complicated forms in less mundane settings and interactions. We specifically draw on three sets of data: in-depth interviews with bus drivers, structured surveys of bus drivers and passengers, and extensive observations of interactions between bus drivers and passengers. We begin by briefly reviewing available conceptualizations of interactions in organizations. We then briefly discuss additional concepts that can facilitate analyses and the understanding of interactions, as well as the view of interactions as scripted patterns of behavior. These reviews provide the prelude to our introducing and illustrating our key thesis about the tissue that constructs the spiritual qualities of interactions.

CONCEPTUALIZATION OF INTERACTIONS IN ORGANIZATIONS

Conceptualizations of interactions have considered multiple groups of interactants—leaders and subordinates, employees and customers, employees and coworkers, customers and other customers, to mention but a few. Previous analyses have suggested different classifications for interactions (Bitner, Booms, and Stanfield Tetreault 1990; Dwyer, Schurr, and Oh 1987; Gremler and Gwinner 2000; Gutek, Bhappu, Liao-Troth, and Cherry 1999; Gutek 1995, 1997, 1999; Iacobucci

1998; Price, Arnould, and Tierney 1999; Solomon, Surprenent, Czepiel, and Gutman 1985). In this extant body of research, however, a common dichotomy can be observed between a basic, somewhat "narrow" type of interactions and a more extensive, elaborate, or "broad" type.

The dichotomy is best captured by Clark and Mills (1993) who speak about two basic modes of interaction—communal and exchange. The exchange mode is one where a transaction is governed by the quest to accomplish a task and a desire for and expectation of immediate and comparable repayment for benefits given previously. The communal mode, in contrast, is governed by the desire for social belonging and is accompanied by expectations for mutual responsiveness to one's needs. In Clark and Mill's (1993) analysis, an individual participating in a communal interaction demonstrates a general concern for the other person.

This dichotomy is echoed in the work of Gutek and her colleagues (Gutek 1995, 1997, 1999; Gutek et al. 1999) who suggest that interactions between employees and customers can be classified into two main groups: "encounters" between two strangers are sporadic service encounters between customers and random service providers. "Relationships," in contrast, are recurring interactions between customers and service providers who actually come to know each other on a deeper, more personal level. Parsons (1976)—who analyzed interactions among office workers—argued that most such interactions are work-oriented, although office work does embody informal social interactions. Price, Arnould, and Tierney (1999) similarly suggested a continuum between transactional relationships and interpersonal relationships, proposing a model of three dimensions of service interactions: duration of interaction, affective content, and the level of proxemics among participants. Connecting this model to Gutek's analysis, interactions that are short, unemotional, and occur in public (e.g., cinema tickets sales or bank transactions) can be defined as encounters; and interactions that have some continuity and involve emotion and intimacy (e.g., massage, river rafting) can be defined as relationships.

Lovelock and Wright (1999) further defined service delivery as ranging from "continuous relationships" to "sporadic transactions," while the type of contract with the organization is defined as "subscriber" or "no formal relationships." This conceptualization produces four possible combinations that, according to Lovelock and Wright (1999), involve a different structure of service interactions and fit different types of businesses. Liljander and Strandvik (1995) used the typology of "episodes" and "relationships," where the former (episodes) describes a one-time exchange of value between two parties with no prior or subsequent interaction, while the latter describes a relationship that is continuous in nature and is characterized by commitment, loyalty, and trust.

Thus, although diverse theory and research has examined interactions among individuals in organizational contexts, a common undertone of this work distinguishes between some basic mode of interaction that is brief, episodic, and devoid of deep emotion and an alternative mode that involves some recurrence and produces a sense of shared history, as well as an emotional connection among participants. A large part of previous work has focused on interactions between customers and service providers, where monetary exchange is often an integral part. Importantly, the exchange of money is typically assumed to be an element of exchange or a business interaction. But money may also facilitate "relationship" or "communal" interactions, as is the case, for example, with tipping behaviors. Tips are typically *not* an essential component of an interaction between customers and service providers but, rather, a form of expressing gratitude by the customer to the service provider (Garrity and Degelman 1990; Lynn and Latane 1984; Lynn, Zinkham, and Harris 1993; Starr 1988). Whyte (1948) and Spradley and Mann (1975) both documented the social-emotional role that tipping can play for service providers. Tipping behaviors are therefore a form of monetary activity included in communal relationships.

ADDITIONAL CONCEPTS FACILITATING ANALYSES OF INTERACTIONS

A seemingly unrelated body of work examined other organizational relations, such as those between leaders and followers or between employees and organizations. Yet this work also reveals a dichotomy between brief and purely businesslike interactions and more intimate, longer-term and interpersonally based interactions. In analyses of leadership, for example, Fiedler (1978) characterized managers as task versus people oriented, and Bass and Avolio (1993) and Yukl (1998) spoke of transactional versus transformational leadership. The "transactional leadership" concept represents leaders focused on short-term interactions with employees, based on rewards and productivity. The "transformational" leader concept, in contrast, represents leaders focused on deep, continuous relationships, characterized by consideration and a development of interpersonal relations.

Similarly, analyses of organizational contracts distinguish between "transactional" contracts, which are formal–legal contracts between employees and organizations, and relational or psychological contracts, which include the emotional and psychological commitment of employees (Rousseau and McLean-Parks 1993; Schein 1980). Hofstede's (1991) analysis of cultural values and differences focuses on relations between individuals and their communities. But this analysis also includes a distinction between "individualism" and "collectivism" that, again, focuses on the difference between brief and exchange interactions and deep and emotional relationships.

Thus, across diverse lines of organizational research discussions of interactions ensue, and a distinction is recognized between some brief, formal mode that is presumably devoid of a deep emotional experience and an alternative and more emotional and personally involving mode. We view this distinction as central to the understanding of interactions in organizations. We further suggest that this distinction can be viewed as separating elements of interactions that are spiritual from those that are not. To understand this separation, a view of interactions as scripted patterns of behavior is helpful. As elaborated next, a view into interactions as scripts suggests that rather than distinct forms of interactions, the case may be that analyses of interactions need to refer to two components of any interaction.

INTERACTIONS IN ORGANIZATIONS AS SCRIPTS

A second common thread in the diverse analyses of interactions is the implicit reference that interactions comprise predictable yet distinct sequences of behaviors. The "cognitive script" concept was suggested by Schank and Abelson (1977) to capture this predictability and has been recognized as central to research in and of organizations (Gioia and Poole 1984; Lord and Kerman 1987; Poole, Gray, and Gioia 1990; Wofford 1994), and especially the organization of service delivery (Humphrey and Ashforth 1994; Shoemaker 1996; Solomon et al. 1985). Within a body of work that considered service interactions as instantiation of cognitive and behavioral scripts (Dwyer et al. 1987; Halpern 1994; Liljander and Strandvik 1995; Solomon et al. 1985) the distinction between two modes of interactions is also recognized. Halpern (1994), for example, documented two types of scripts in the selling process—a "business" script and an "interpersonal relations" script. In a similar vein, Leigh and McGrew (1989) documented the existence of two parallel scripts—a "professional" script, comprising business actions, and a "personal" script, which includes, for example, greeting, smiling, shaking hands, or making small talk.

"SKELETON" VERSUS "TISSUE" SCRIPTS OF INTERACTIONS

We suggest that the distinction between the scripts of interaction actually implies that all interactions hold a common structure that includes two conceptually distinct parts. The first part, the foundation that we label *the skeleton of an interaction*, is some basic essential core that is similar to the "business" script in Halpern's (1994) conceptualization, or to the "exchange" idea in Clark and Mill's (1993) theory. The second, the added-on texture, which we call *the tissue of an interaction*, accompanies the core or the skeleton and, according to our research, is informal and introduces spiritual qualities to interactions. Both the skeleton and the tissue are scripts, and both involve both participants in any interaction. But, as will be elaborated next, there are fundamental and recognizable differences between the skeleton and the tissue script. These differences make the distinction between them conceptually, empirically, and managerially useful.

The "Skeleton" Script

The "skeleton" script is a basic script that includes some essential content of exchange relations among partners to interactions. This script comprises behaviors addressing the main business action of partners to an interaction without which the interaction would not be viewed as existing. For example, the behavior of ordering from a waiter is the fundamental element or the skeleton of restaurant interactions between waiters and customer. People can dine in a restaurant without performing this behavior, but they would not be viewed as interacting with a waiter. That in some restaurants payment is made to the waiter while in others payment is made to a cashier reflects the fact that the skeleton may vary between organizations that otherwise seem similar.

Our studies identify four statements that can be made about the skeleton: (1) The behaviors it comprises are recognized by participants as elements of routine interactions. (2) The behaviors it comprises are taken for granted and therefore frequently *not* mentioned in descriptions of extraordinary or extreme interactions. (3) There is agreement among all participants to an interaction about the behaviors comprising the skeleton (Vilnai-Yavetz and Rafaeli 2003). However (4) these behaviors are likely to be explicitly noted only if an interaction somehow goes astray. People thus seem to treat skeleton behaviors like the hygiene factors of work conceptualized by Herzberg (1966): They are not noticed until they are somehow jeopardized. Because of the topic of this volume, we focus in the remainder of the chapter on what we have learned about tissue behaviors.

The "Tissue" Script

The "tissue" script comprises overtly social behaviors that cannot substitute for the skeletal behaviors but, rather, follow or somehow accompany them. Behaviors comprising the tissue script can either improve or deter from the quality of the experience of partners to the interaction. Thus, patrons and waiters can be nice or nasty to each other while dealing with the ordering of the food. In both cases, their social (or antisocial) behaviors are tissue that accompanies the skeleton script of ordering from or paying the waiter.

Various bodies of literature have identified behaviors that fit our concept of tissue of interactions, though the focus has typically been on tissue that improves the experience of interaction participants. Organ (1990), for example, suggested a concept of "organizational citizenship" arguing that employees with deep psychological commitment exhibit behaviors that make a contribution both to the organization and to fellow workers and customers beyond the formal demands defined by their role. Included in this concept of "organizational citizenship" are, for example, behaviors of helping others or saving resources. In this theoretical framework, formal role demands can be viewed as the skeletal script, while the extra role behaviors represent the tissue of the relationship between employees and the organization. Indeed, additional analyses explicitly speak of "pro social" and "extra role behaviors" (George and Bettenhausen 1990; Manrai 1993).

A prototypical tissue behavior is cooperation. Building on Baron's (1994) analysis, interpersonal cooperation similarly can be viewed as behavior that is not essential to an interaction and therefore is not the skeleton but does determine the quality of interactions as "the tissue" typically does. Additional tissue elements can include expression of positive emotion, including eye contact and smiling (Rafaeli and Sutton 1987, 1989), creating social affiliation (Dube et al. 1995; Russell and Mehrabian 1978), and communicating willfully with others (Kuller 1991). In the study of consumer behavior, Manrai (1993) distinguishes between routine behaviors that are part of the formal role and additional behaviors, such as helping others, that are beyond job requirement. Here again, such nonroutine elements comprise the tissue of consumer interactions.

The tissue script may, however, hamper rather than enhance the experience of an interaction. In this case as well, behaviors manifested in the script are *not* central or essential to the execution of the interaction, but their display by participants in the interaction produce negative outcomes. Included here, for example, are behaviors of aggression, rudeness, and carelessness (Forgas 1999; Glomb 2001) or behaviors defined as employee withdrawal (Hanisch and Hulin 1990, 1991), including tardiness, unwillingness to help others, or deterring communication or coordination with others (Cote 1999).

TISSUE OF INTERACTION AS SPIRITUAL ELEMENTS

Why does the idea of tissue and skeleton of interactions belong in this volume on spirituality? We have come to learn that the tissue script is what introduces spirituality into routine organizational interactions. In spirituality we refer to individuals' concept of what is the best, of what it means to help others be their best, and what it means to feel a sense of connectedness with work and coworkers. Tissue behaviors are precisely the behaviors that either promote or hinder such spiritual desires. Tissue elements are the added-on elements that accompany the cores or skeletons of interpersonal interactions and that add a spiritual flavor to interactions. Such accompanying can facilitate the interaction, introducing a positive tone, which is what happens when one partner to an interaction is pleasant, polite, or empathetic. However, accompanying tissue can hamper the positive flow of the interaction, introducing a negative tone, which is what happens when one partner is aggressive, rude, or impatient.

In this way, the tissue of interaction comprises elements that move interpersonal relations from being formatted as an exchange to being formatted as communal in Clark and Mill's (1993) conceptualization. Similarly, tissue elements distinguish between encounters and relationships in Gutek's (1997) conceptualization. Indeed, communal relations in Clark and Mill's (1993) conceptualization and relationships in Gutek's conceptualization have a spiritual overtone.

THE RELATIONSHIP BETWEEN THE "SKELETON" AND THE "TISSUE" OF INTERACTIONS

Our choice of metaphors—skeleton and tissue—is not random. Rather, it represents our assumption that the skeleton is an essential and shared foundation of a distinct type of interaction so that any and all interactions of this type must have this skeleton. Skeletal behaviors are those without which a certain type of interaction does not exist. As noted above, ordering from a waiter is such a skeleton of interactions between waiters and restaurant patrons. Similarly, in our studies of public transportation bus drivers in Israel (where passengers pay the driver when they board the bus), we found that the one behavior that all drivers and all passengers viewed as essential in order for an interaction between driver and passenger to occur was payment.[1]

The idea of a skeleton is analytically useful because interactions can be defined as similar to the extent that they share this skeleton. Tissue or each of the tissue components, in contrast, may or may not be apparent in a specific episode of a prototypic interaction, and interactions may occur without an appearance of tissue behaviors. But the tissue is what generates the emotional tone of an interaction, much like the tissue of a human body establishes the nature of an individual's appearance. Thus, similar tissue may appear atop different skeletons, and similar skeletons can be accompanied by different tissue.

As in the human body, the skeleton is a foundation and operates as a dichotomy: It either does or does not exist. If it does not exist, conceptually the interaction does not exist. The tissue, in contrast, is a more complex notion in that each of its components may or may not appear. A large and varied set of behaviors can compose the tissue, including verbal, paraverbal, and nonverbal behaviors. To illustrate, performance evaluation discussions between a sales clerk and her manager (a specific type of work interaction) are premised on a manager appraising an employee's job performance. In these meetings, however, the manager may or may not smile, be courteous, be assertive, praise or thank the employee for her performance. These would all be "tissue" behaviors, and their appearance or lack thereof cannot negate the fact that an interaction occurs, although they are likely to influence the tone of the interaction.

Different interactions will likely compose different tissue behaviors, but also participants in an interaction may disagree about whether elements of a tissue should be manifest in a certain type of interaction. For example, a passenger may not thank a driver assuming that the driver was merely doing his job so should not be thanked. In this vein, Rafaeli (1989) reports that employees do not feel they should smile to customers because they (the employees) are paid to process merchandise, not to be nice to customers. Thus, a tissue script is not always fully activated in a specific manifestation of an interaction. The extent to which this script is activated depends on multiple factors, such as status relations among participants. Whether an interaction is between a manager and an employee, an employee and another employee, or an employee and a customer is likely to influence the nature of the activated tissue script (Leigh and McGrew 1989; Halpern 1994). Other factors may include cultural norms of behavior (Hall 1987; Hall and Hall 1990; Schwartz 1992, 1996) as well as professional standards (Abbott 1993; Bazerman and Paradis 1991) regarding what is and is not appropriate or even acceptable to an interaction. Becker, Geer, Hughes, and Strauss (1961), for example, describe how medical doctors learn professionally acceptable tissue behaviors to accompany medical diagnoses.

In short, the base of any interaction is "the skeleton," which exists in any occurrence of an interaction and therefore defines a specific type of interaction. The skeleton is similar to what Clark and Mills (1993) defined as an exchange mode of interpersonal interactions and what Rousseau and McLean-Parks (1993) called the transactional mode of a contract between individuals and organizations. It includes giving and receiving processes, which construct the foundation of a transaction. The "tissue" accompanies this "skeleton" in some cases but comprises behavior that can accompany different skeletons. Tissue behaviors include commitment, loyalty, and willingness to help and are thus similar to behaviors included in the communal mode of interaction identified by Clark and Mills (1993). However, contrary to prior conceptualizations, we suggest that the processes comprising skeletal and tissue behaviors are *not* mutually exclusive or extreme ends of one continuum. Rather, *skeleton and tissue behaviors are different elements of the very same interaction, similar to the skeleton and tissue of the body of any living organism.*

Initial empirical support for this idea of the "skeleton" and "tissue" scripts is evident in a study by Sutton and Rafaeli (1988). This study reported that in stressful conditions employees tend to primarily perform formal job requirements, or "the skeleton" of the job. In contrast, when stress is low, according to Sutton and Rafaeli (1988), employees tend to express positive emotion, smile, and thank customers, in addition to performing their formal duties. Thus, in the report by Sutton and Rafaeli (1988) the skeleton—of providing basic customer service such as accepting payment and bagging groceries—appeared in all manifestations of interactions between grocery store clerks and their customers. The tissue, in contrast, appeared only in some interactions, those occurring during what Sutton and Rafaeli (1988) identified as "slow times" in the store. Thus, the business script—the skeleton—is included in *every* business interaction while the friendship script is activated only when at least one side of the interaction views the situation as appropriate for social interactions (see also Leigh and McGrew 1989 and Halpern 1994).

CAN TISSUE BEHAVIORS BECOME A PART OF THE SKELETON?

There can be an appropriation of tissue behaviors into the skeleton. When organizations or clients expect certain behaviors as fundamental elements of employees' role, they are attempting to define the skeletal behaviors of a role. McDonald's, for example, trains employees to smile and greet customers, defining these smiles as an essential part of the job (Ritzer 2000). Disneyland similarly maintains formal rules regarding displayed emotion as part of employees' roles. Van Maanen (1995, 295) cites from the rules book of the University of Disneyland:

> First, we practice the friendly smile. Second, we use only friendly and courteous phrases. Third, we are not stuffy—the only Misters in Disneyland are Mr. Toad and Mr. Smee.

Similarly, retail outlets have been seen to post signs or make employees wear tags saying "$5.00 if I don't smile and ask you how you are doing today" (Rafaeli and Sutton 1987, 1989). Such requests essentially coopt tissue elements into the skeleton of the job required from employees. The integration of tissue into the skeleton may be motivated by customer expectations, wherein the smiles of employees have become fundamental (skeletal) elements of good customer service.

However, although it may look as if tissue behaviors become part of the skeleton, this is not necessarily true because these behaviors do not necessarily appear in all interactions. In social welfare occupations, tissue elements, such as smiling and helping, may be argued to be the skeleton of the interaction between employees and clients. When agents such as social workers or nurses perform only technical parts of their job (e.g., filling forms, distributing welfare checks, or taking blood tests), it is often argued that they are not performing their job. But employees can stop smiling or being empathetic while they cannot stop filling forms or taking blood tests. This has been argued to occur, for example, among burnt-out employees (Maslach and Leiter 1997) and among employees working under high pressure (Sutton and Rafaeli 1988; Rafaeli and Sutton 1990).

Thus, although there may be some overlap between skeletal and tissue behaviors, our definition of the qualities of the two sets of behaviors clarifies where a particular behavior belongs. If a behavior is mentioned by all participants and is taken for granted by participants as integral to an interaction, it is a skeletal behavior. Other behaviors are tissue behaviors. As we argued before and elaborate next, tissue behaviors are the behaviors that introduce spirituality into interactions in organizations.

Table 5.1

Spiritual Tissue Elements: Examples from a Critical Incidents Study

Type of communication	Influence on experience of interaction partners	
	Improving the experience	Damaging the experience
Verbal	Greeting Thanking Sending a letter of thanks to the driver or praising him Expressing concern about driver Talking to or joking with driver	Swearing Complaining Lack of or poor communication with driver (e.g., language problems)
Paraverbal	Laughing Talking politely and courteously Sitting in back reducing crowding	Being annoyed or irritated Yelling Smoking
Nonverbal	Smiling Acting in a friendly way Cooperating with driver Giving driver candy	Frowning Acting inconsiderately Ignoring others' requests

WHAT DO WE KNOW ABOUT THE SPIRITUAL TISSUE OF INTERACTIONS?

There is a multitude of behaviors that may dress up the skeleton, and individual and situational variations determine precisely which of these behaviors occur in a given interaction. Importantly, the tissue comprises behaviors, not thoughts or feelings that accompany interactions. Thus, we are not talking about how people feel during an interaction, a notion that has been explored by studies of "affective scripts" (Conway and Bekerian 1987; Demorest and Alexander 1992; Karniol and Ben Moshe 1991; Russell 1987) but, rather, about what people do during an interaction. However, tissue behaviors do tend to influence how people feel during interactions.

Tissue behaviors may be verbal (greeting, answering a question), nonverbal (eye contact, touching, helping to carry luggage) and paraverbal (talking politely, speaking loudly) (Oksenberg, Coleman, and Cannell 1986). They also may improve or enhance the quality of the experience of partners to an interaction, as well as hamper or damage this experience, as summarized in Table 5.1. Table 5.1 specifically includes examples of tissue behaviors extracted from our study of critical incidents of good and bad passengers as described by bus drivers, following the methods described by Bitner, Booms, and Mohr (1994). As evident in Table 5.1, tissue behaviors may either improve an experience or damage it. Spiritual tissue behaviors are not necessarily rare or unusual. They are simply not part of the formally prescribed routine interaction. Precisely this combination defines the spiritual tissue of interactions—behaviors that are (1) not essential for an interaction to ensue, but (2) recognizable, when they occur, to all interaction participants. Thus, although Table 5.1 cites quotes from specific informants, similar examples will be evident in reports from other informants.

There is a certain pattern to the emergence of the specific tone of spiritual tissue. The pattern involves some trigger, which leads to ensuing behaviors that, in turn, produce the emotional overtone of the interaction. Both the trigger and the ensuing behavior can be viewed as parts of the tissue of the interaction, the emotion being their respective spiritual outcome. Consider the following brief description by a driver of "the worst passenger" he ever met:

> The bus was delayed for almost an hour. A passenger boarded the bus and said to me that I was a moron, and I immediately answered that she should calm herself down and that in my bus there is no swearing. She got on and swore at every opportunity, and there was another passenger who got up and told her to shut up.

This report is from one driver, but its elements of the story, including the triggering event of the bus being late and the emergent behaviors of a passenger being annoyed and nasty at the driver was related in multiple reports. Similarly, a recurring narrative we encountered was of customers making special, personal, or illegal requests from a driver. The driver's reaction in all these stories produced a certain set of tissue behaviors—swearing, yelling, rudeness, and so forth—which established the emotional tone of the interaction. Consider another example of a narrative:

> A young passenger asked me to let him off at a point that is not a formal stop. When I refused to stop there, and told him that I was not allowed to do that, he got annoyed and angry, to the point of yelling, swearing, and being physically violent.

In this example as well, the triggering event is clear (the customer request for a special stop), as are the tissue elements of behavior of both driver and passenger and the emergent emotional tone of the interaction. As evident in these two examples, we found that tissue behaviors can be grouped according to the triggering events. A typical set of triggering events, evident in the above example, involved demands for special or unusual attention from the driver, frequently demands that call for some violation of formal organizational rules. Interestingly, however, such violations can produce both positive and negative emotional overtones. Positive overtones occur, for example, when a passenger asks to be let off outside a formal stop and the driver agrees, leading the passenger to report very positive tissue behaviors and a positive emotional tone of the interaction. Negative overtones occur when a passenger asks to be let off outside a formal stop, and the driver does not agree, leading the passenger to report very negative tissue behaviors producing a negative emotional tone of the interaction. In both cases, the driver was asked to violate formal rules, and the behaviors of both driver and passenger are tissue behaviors because they are not essential for the trip.

Tissues of interactions can also be categorized according to the behaviors they embody. Tissue behaviors can include verbal demands or paraverbal aspects such as yelling or swearing. In studying bus drivers and passengers, we also found tissue behaviors of accusations of incivility or even racial discrimination, which introduced a negative tone into the interaction. But tissue behaviors may also improve the interaction experience when they include, for example, complimenting, encouraging, or joking as part of an interaction.

As evident in our analysis so far, three issues should be highlighted with respect to tissue elements of interactions: First, tissue elements are recognized as *plausible* elements of an interaction by multiple participants. Second, these elements are *not deemed* essential to the fulfillment of the formal goals of the interaction and do not always appear when the interaction occurs. Third, tissue behaviors *influence the affective tone* of the interaction. It is this pattern of influence that leads us to view the tissue as introducing a spiritual element to interactions.

Most central is the fact that tissue behaviors can be conceptually divorced from the goals of the interaction. People can be nice, polite, helping, and say thank you to anyone, not only to a bus driver. People can also be nasty, impolite, or impatient with anyone. As shown, these elements may be positive or negative, meaning they may produce positive or negative emotion or pleasantness and unpleasantness (Russell and Mehrabian 1977). However, the spiritual tissue does influence the quality of an interaction.

Positive elements that bear a positive influence on the interaction have the potential to support the accomplishment of the formal task at hand, or the goal of the interaction, by aligning the interaction with the correct script. As with many other things, therefore, spirituality may not be a necessary part of formal organizational operation, but it can bear an influence on such operations. The following, again from our study of bus drivers, illustrates this point:

> During a very long trip I was tired because I had only a very short stop during the long ride. The passengers understood my situation and tried to help. They offered me food and drink, were really nice to me, and helped me find my way when I made a mistake and took a wrong turn.

As evident in this description, there is a spiritual quality to the tissue because of the emotional tone that it produces. Both the passengers and the driver in this example very likely felt a sense of uplifting from the common experience. Similarly, in the following report of a driver, the spiritual tissue of the interaction bears a positive influence on the interaction and supports the accomplishment of the formal task:

> During an ordinary trip warm relationships with a few passengers were formed. We were talking, passing information, and telling jokes. When another customer, at the back of the bus, lit a cigarette (which was forbidden), one of my "new friends" told him to put it out, and it allowed me to concentrate on driving instead of on fighting with passengers.

In this story the situation described combines a positive emotional tone of the interaction with an enhancement in the quality of task performance. Thus, the spiritual quality of the tissue does influence goal accomplishment. In a similar vein, Price, Arnould, and Tierney (1999) focused on an extreme case of service relationships and described interactions formed during a rafting trip. They documented empathy, communication, intimacy, friendship, and emotional reactions as integral to such interactions. Their study suggests that these spiritual elements bring both participants in the interaction to perform beyond the call of duty. The service provider gives something in addition to his or her formal role (smile, social invitation, good advice, etc.) and the customer does the same, by reacting with something that is more than payment. Thus, spiritual behaviors can turn any interaction into a successful one.

In sum, although not essential, tissue behaviors can help or facilitate the accomplishment of formal, skeletal organizational tasks by introducing a positive, emotional tone to role interactions. The spiritual tissue sets up the emotional qualities of the interaction, which is part and parcel of quality task accomplishment.

IMPLICATIONS FOR RESEARCH AND MANAGEMENT

We have suggested a conceptual framework for the analysis of interactions. The framework distinguishes between a skeleton, or the core behaviors essential to and addressing the goals of a specific interaction, and additional elements that we label tissue behaviors, which we suggest introduce spirituality into interactions. Both the skeleton and the tissue are scripts, and both involve multiple participants in any interaction. One builds on the other, the skeleton being the core upon which the tissue builds. Yet, we wish to suggest that, similar to the skeleton and tissue of a human body, both are somehow important to interactions.

Since the skeleton relates to the immediate task of the individuals involved, as well as the organization in which they operate, it may appear to be more important. The tissue, in this light may seem to be peripheral, or unimportant. Indeed, without the skeleton the mere existence of the interaction can be challenged. Organizational operations that depend on interactions are likely to be jeopardized when the skeleton of an interaction is compromised, positioning the skeleton as critical to organizational functioning. Yet the skeleton is where technology can often replace people. Banking interactions, for example, have been to a large extent substituted by interactions with technology in the form of automated teller machines (ATMs), deposit boxes, and electronic banking. The interaction we chose to study—between drivers and passengers—has also been stripped of its skeleton in those countries where passengers do not pay the driver.

But the tissue is what produces the texture and the emotion of an interaction, establishing the spiritual experience of an interaction. Tissue is what determines how people *feel* during and after an interaction. As with the human body, while the skeleton keeps the interaction together, the tissue keeps it alive. It is the tissue that gives an interaction its flavor, introducing spirit into an exchange. The tissue recognizes the partners to the interaction as human beings. The tissue may not be directly addressing organizational goals, but it does promote other important goals. Factors such as felt or displayed feelings of employees or customers, satisfaction or dissatisfaction, commitment or alienation, citizenship or lack thereof are all influenced by the tissue. It would therefore be inappropriate to say that the tissue is not important to organizations. We see multiple theoretical and applied implications to our analysis, as we discuss below.

Toward Future Research

Our analysis suggests an extensive research agenda regarding spirituality in interactions. One question that demands attention regards the precise mapping of skeletal versus tissue behaviors of multiple interactions, and the consequent identification of spiritual (tissue) elements of interactions. We can suggest that such mapping should separate between verbal (what is said), paraverbal (how it is said), and nonverbal issues (Oksenberg, Coleman, and Cannell 1986) and also between multiple aspects of nonverbal behaviors such as facial or postural issues (Bartel and Saavedra 2000). Such mapping will provide insights about what organizational goals are accomplished by various interactions and what spiritual contributions these interactions make. For example, Schwartzman (1989) and Feldman and Rafaeli (2001) suggest that interactions in various organizational meetings intended to promote decision-making goals actually promote more spiritual ends of connections among participants. Stripping meetings of their tissue elements, which may be performed in the interest of more effective decision-making, may strip them of their tissue, leading to a stripping of their spiritual contributions.

Once mapping of skeleton and tissue of interactions is accomplished, it can also pave the way to understanding which tissue behaviors improve upon interactions and which in turn are damaging to interactions. That some tissue elements are positive while others are negative is evident, for example, in the description of Gersick, Bartunek, and Dutton's (2000) analysis of positive and negative relationships among academic professionals. They illustrated that relationships are central to professional's performance, but that not all professional interactions necessarily improve role performance. Caution is required here, however, because the notion of improvement is problematic because not all behaviors that appear positive necessarily promote organizational goals. Sutton and Rafaeli (1988) and Rafaeli (1989), for example, argue that behaviors that appear to be positive (e.g., smiling) do not always promote organizational goals while behaviors that may appear neutral or even negative (e.g., nastiness) do not always hamper interactions. They report that mild rudeness by customer service employees was actually perceived by both employees and customers as facilitating the customer service interaction because they were speeding it up.

A second research direction regards the respective appearance of skeleton and tissue. Under what conditions does a skeleton appear without any tissue? Are there conditions in which the tissue overrides the skeleton? Are there conditions that inspire tissue behaviors that are damaging rather than enhancing interactions? Our analysis suggests that tissue behaviors are contextual, meaning that whether or not they appear depends on parameters of a particular situation. Whether skeleton behaviors appear is less negotiable because they seem to be essential foundations of an interaction. If a customer does not pay for merchandise, for example, some basic element of organizational performance is compromised. The definition of skeleton behavior was that they appear as a routine part of an interaction. Tissue behaviors, in contrast, may or may not appear in a given instance of an interaction depending on a host of factors such as who else is present, or where or when the interaction is taking place. Given such contextuality of tissue behaviors, research is needed to identify conditions that inspire spiritual tissue, and to separate them from conditions that bring about tissue that is damaging to individual and organizational goals.

The separation between skeleton and tissue of interactions also bears methodological implications for studies of interactions. It suggests that studies that somehow rely on data about routine interactions are likely to reveal skeletal properties, while studies that rely on data about interactions that are in some way special, atypical, or extreme are likely to unravel tissue behaviors. Spirituality in interactions will likely be lost if only routine transactions are examined. Yet, our examples from our study of bus drivers reveal that even a mundane interaction, such as between a bus driver and passenger, can be shown to include spiritual elements. Thus studies of interactions must complement techniques that focus on the routine (e.g., observations and surveys) with techniques that focus on the unusual (e.g., critical incidents).

Toward Spirituality in Management of Interactions

From a managerial perspective our analysis reflects dynamics of service delivery wherein there are certain behaviors that a service process cannot do without and other behaviors that somehow add flavor to the process. In the case of bus drivers the basis is payment by passengers, for example. But organizational reward systems do not always recognize the distinction between tissue and skeleton. Employees may, for example, be reprimanded for *not* exhibiting certain tissue behaviors, as is the case when passengers complain about a rude driver. Thus, the analysis suggests a potential inconsistency in the management of service providers: Interactions are frequently delineated by the skeletal behaviors, yet implicit expectations (of management and customers) exist for tissue behaviors (e.g., friendliness). Reward programs that focus on the skeleton rather than the tissue (Kerr 1975) can produce frustration for employees and maladaptive processes for organizations.

However, the definition and measurement of whether or not the skeleton is manifest in an interaction is far easier than a definition or measurement of whether or not the tissue is manifest. Customers may complain that a service provider is not polite, but the employee may argue that he or she is being polite. Disagreements about the quality of the tissue are therefore far more difficult to resolve than disagreements about the skeleton. Encouraging in this regard is Bartel and Saavedra's (2000) illustration that inter-judge reliability can be established regarding positive emotional displays.

Separating skeleton from tissue elements is also critical in order to identify what must go on even in stressful situations. When a bus is loaded with passengers and driving is difficult, a driver can stop joking with passengers but should not stop collecting payment. In general, recognition is necessary of behaviors that should not be compromised under any circumstances, that is, skeleton behaviors. In this vein, when employees burn out from customer service, the skeleton *is typically not* jeopardized, but tissue behaviors are compromised (Maslach and Leiter 1997).

Also important managerially is a distinction between employees' tasks and role responsibilities and their behavior vis-à-vis interactions that their job entails. In the case of bus drivers the separation is between driving the bus safely and interacting with customers. This may be viewed as a matter of level of analysis issue (Rousseau 1985). The former is at the individual (employee) level; the latter is at the interpersonal (dyadic) level. Management of the former, the employee, focuses on skills and abilities of the employees and includes selection and training in technical aspects of the job. Management of the latter must focus on two groups of people—employees and customers—because the behavior of one partner to an interaction is necessarily influenced by the behavior of the other partner. When a job entails interpersonal interactions, management must include analyses of these interactions in skills training programs. Thus, Bowen (1986) speaks of customer participation as a key foundation of service delivery. Mills and Morris (1986) and Bowen (2000) speak of customers as partial employees and Mills, Chase, and Margulis (1983) speak of employees as partial customers.

Our analysis brings forth the argument that a focus only on the individual level may be problematic in two ways. First, it might improve the employee's technical skills (better driving abilities), but this is not sufficient because it ignores the interpersonal elements of the job. Second, even if a dyadic view of the job is maintained, selection and training programs must recognize not only skeleton behaviors, but also tissue behaviors because they determine the spiritual tone of interaction.

Finally, managerial attention needs to focus on the implications of introducing technology as a substitute for human interaction for skeleton and tissue of interactions. Technology typically performs technical, skeletal rather than tissue properties of interactions. This does not mean that tissue behaviors are becoming unimportant but, rather, that more effort is required in order to keep tissue elements "alive" (Hallowell 1999). As Hallowell (1999) describes, such efforts are essential if the human nature of organizational participants is to be recognized.

Electronic and computer communication can replace some of the skeleton of organizational interactions. A customer can send an order through the Internet and receive the product home in a few days without any social contact. In such electronic commerce, people (employees and customers) may not see, talk, or smile to each other. The emergence of displayed emotions in electronic media [e.g., when :-) is inserted to represent a smile] illustrates that people need the tissue elements even in the electronic or cyber context. Emergent electronic communities in cyberspace seem to reinforce our notion that a skeleton divorced of tissue is likely to die. Seidel, Dukerich, and Bertolotti (2001), for example, talk about different types of relationships among organizational members and focus on communal relationships among individuals, contributing voluntarily to a wide network of independent computer programmers. The network they describe is knitted together only by a social contract. Seidel et al. (2001) illustrate how the skeletal behaviors (programming an additional patch for shared software) combine with tissue behaviors (forming a voluntarily social network that helps, encourages, and supports its members) to form a new type of organizational relationship. The relationship may be the relationship that will predominate the future, technological world that is primarily based on Web rather than face-to-face communication.

Adding our skeleton and tissue concepts to this description allows us to analyze and understand the uniqueness of cyberspace relationships. When interactions are computer-mediated, participants need to put in much more effort in order to maintain the impression that they are interacting in a "regular" way (Panteli 2001). The importance of the tissue is thus significantly elevated, perhaps to the point that it will become skeletal. As noted by Hallowell (1999), the need to keep the "human moment" in technology-based business is increasingly important to effective organizational operations.

In traditional managerial issues, and even more in the computer-mediated communication context, mentoring is a good example in which our concepts of skeleton and spiritual tissue can be helpful for analysis. Mentoring is a type of a relationship that builds on multiple formal and informal interactions. In mentoring and socialization interactions, there are spiritual needs (such as social support and friendliness) that the skeleton (skills training and learning of rules and norms) cannot meet. Ragins (1997) distinguished between two types of functions and behaviors employed by mentors—the "career development" behaviors (coaching, providing challenging assignments, etc.) that parallel to our concept of "skeleton," and the psychosocial functions (acceptance, opportunity to discuss personal problems, etc.), which form the base for the "spiritual tissue" behaviors. The boundary between tissue and skeleton is unclear in this case, as mentoring includes, in nature, both learning formal things about the job and organization and social-emotional support for the individual; but the importance of the terms "skeleton" and "tissue" increases. Ragins (1997) describes a mentoring process through e-mail and other electronic media, in which time and geographic constraints are avoided and the transfer of more information is enabled, thus facilitating the skeleton behaviors. The effectiveness of this process and the problems that it involved, we claim, can be understood if the notions of skeleton and tissue are applied.

In short, we suggest that separating skeleton from tissue elements of interactions is critical in order to maintain effective organizational interactions. Recognizing the spiritual tissue of interactions, and its influence on organizational operations can be a critical step toward understanding and enhancing organizational spirituality.

NOTE

We thank Techiya Ramati, Danit Kram, and Taly Schimmel for their help in data collection.

1. Included were all behaviors associated with payment such as giving or receiving change or a receipt.

REFERENCES

Abbott, A. (1993). "The Sociology of Work and Occupations." *Annual Review of Sociology* 9: 187–209.

Baron, R.A. (1994). "The Physical Environment of Work Setting: Effects on Task Performance, Interpersonal Relations, and Job Satisfaction." *Research in Organizational Behavior* 16: 1–46.

Bartel, C.A., and R. Saavedra. (2000). "The Collective Construction of Workgroup Moods." *Administrative Sciences Quarterly* 45: 197–231.

Bass, B.M., and B.J. Avolio. (1993). "Transformational Leadership: A Response to Critiques." In *Leadership Theory and Research: Perspectives and Directions*, ed. M.M. Chemers and R. Ayman. New York: Academic Press, 49–79.

Bazerman, C., and J. Paradis, eds. (1991). *Textual Dynamics of the Professions: Historical and Contemporary Studies of Writing in Professional Communities*. Madison: University of Wisconsin Press.

Becker, H.; B. Geer; E.C. Hughes; and A. Strauss. (1961). *Boys in White: Student Culture in Medical School*. Chicago: University of Chicago Press.

Bitner, M.J.; B.H. Booms; and L.A. Mohr. (1994). "Critical Service Encounters: The Employee's Viewpoint." *Journal of Marketing* 58: 95–106.

Bitner, M. J.; B.H. Booms; and Stanfield Tetreault, M. (1990). "The Service Encounter: Diagnosing Favorable and Unfavorable Incidents." *Journal of Marketing* 54: 71–84.

Bowen, D. (2000). "The 'Customer As Employee' Revisited." Paper presented at the Quality in Services (QUIS 7) Conference, Karlstad, Sweden, June.

Bowen, D.E. (1986). "Managing Customers As Human Resources in Service Organizations." *Human Resources Management* 25: 371–384.

Clark, M., and J. Mills. (1993). "The Difference Between Communal and Exchange Relationships: What It Is and Is Not." *Personality and Social Psychology Bulletin* 19: 684–691.

Conway, M.A., and D.A. Bekerian. (1987). "Situational Knowledge and Emotions." *Cognition and Emotion* 1, no. 2: 145–191.

Cote, S. (1999). "Affect and Performance in Organizational Settings." *Current Directions in Psychological Science* 8, no. 2: 65–68.

Demorest, A.P., and I.E. Alexander. (1992). "Affective Scripts As Organizers of Personal Experience." *Journal of Personality* 60, no. 3: 645–663.

Dube, L.; J.C. Chebat; and S. Morin. (1995). "The Effects of Background Music on Consumers' Desire to Affiliate in Buyer-Seller Interaction." *Psychology and Marketing* 12, no. 4: 305–319.

Dwyer, F.R.; P.H. Schurr; and S. Oh. (1987). "Developing Buyer-Seller Relationships." *Journal of Marketing* 51: 11–27.

Feldman, M.S., and A. Rafaeli. (2001). "Organizational Routines As Sources of Connections and Understandings." *Journal of Management Studies* 39, no. 3: 309–333.

Fiedler, F.E. (1978). "The Contingency Model and the Dynamic of the Leadership Process." In *Advances in Experimental Social Psychology*, vol. 11, ed. L. Berkowitz. San Diego, CA: Academic Press, 59–112.

Forgas, J.P. (1999). "On Feeling Good and Being Rude: Affective Influences on Language Use and Request Formulations." *Journal of Personality and Social Psychology* 76, no. 6: 928–939.

Garrity, K., and D. Degelman. (1990). "Effects of Server Introduction on Restaurant Tipping." *Journal of Applied Social Psychology* 20: 168–172.

George, J.M., and K. Bettenhausen. (1990). "Understanding Pro-social Behavior, Sales Performance and Turnover: A Group-Level Analysis in a Service Context." *Journal of Applied Psychology* 75: 698–709.

Gersick, C.J.G.; J.M. Bartunek; and J.E. Dutton. (2000). "Learning from Academia: The Importance of Relationships in Professional Life." *Academy of Management Journal* 43, no. 6: 1026–1044.

Gioia, D.A., and P.P. Poole. (1984). "Scripts in Organizational Behavior." *Academy of Management Review* 9, no. 3: 449–459.

Glomb, T.M. (2001). "Workplace Anger and Aggression: Informing Conceptual Models with Data from Specific Encounters." *Journal of Occupational Health Psychology* 7, no. 1: 20–36.

Gremler, D.D., and K.P. Gwinner, K. P. (2000). "Customer-Employee Rapport in Service Relationships." *Journal of Service Research* 3, no. 1: 82–104.

Gutek, B.A. (1995). *The Dynamics of Service—Reflections on the Changing Nature of Customer/Provider Interactions*, 1st ed. San Francisco: Jossey-Bass.

———. (1997). "Dyadic Interaction in Organizations." In *Creating Tomorrow's Organizations*, ed. C.L. Cooper and L.E. Jackson. New York: John Wiley, 139–155.

———. (1999). "The Social Psychology of Service Interactions." *Journal of Social Issues* 55, no. 3: 603–617.

Gutek, B.A.; A.D. Bhappu; M.A. Liao-Troth; and B. Cherry. (1999). "Distinguishing Between Service Relationships and Encounters." *Journal of Applied Psychology* 84, no. 2: 218–233.

Hall, E.T. (1987). *Hidden Differences: Doing Business with the Japanese*. Garden City, NJ: Anchor Press/Doubleday.

Hall, E.T., and M.R. Hall. (1990). *Understanding Cultural Differences: Germans, French, and Americans*. New York: Intercultural Press.

Hallowell, E.M. (1999). "The Human Moment at Work." *Harvard Business Review* 58, no. 1: 1–6.

Halpern, J.J. (1994). "The Effect of Friendship on Personal Business Transactions." *Journal of Conflict Resolution* 38, no. 4: 647–664.

Hanisch, K.A., and C.L. Hulin. (1990). "Job Attitudes and Organizational Withdrawal: An Examination of Retirement and Other Voluntary Withdrawal Behaviors." *Journal of Vocational Behavior* 37, no. 1: 60–78.

———. (1991). "General Attitudes and Organizational Withdrawal: An Evaluation of a Causal Model." *Journal of Vocational Behavior* 39, no. 1: 110–120.

Herzberg, E. (1966). *Work and the Nature of Man*. Cleveland, OH: World Publishing.

Hofstede, G. (1991). "I, We and They." *Cultures and Organizations: Software of the Mind*. London: McGraw-Hill, 49–78.

Humphrey, R.H., and B.E. Ashforth. (1994). "Cognitive Scripts and Prototypes in Service Encounters." *Advances in Services Marketing and Management* 3: 175–199.

Karniol, R., and R. Ben Moshe. (1991). "Drawing Inferences About Others' Cognitions and Affective Reactions: A Test of Two Models for Representing Affect." *Cognition and Emotion* 5, no. 4: 241–253.

Kerr, S. (1975). "On the Folly of Rewarding for A While Hoping for B." *Academy of Management Journal* 18, no. 4: 769–783.

Kuller, R. (1991). "Environmental Assessment from a Neuropsychological Perspective." In *Environment, Cognition, and Action: An Integrated Approach*, ed. T. Garling and G.W. Evans. New York/Oxford: Oxford University Press, 111–147.

Lacobucci, D. (1998). "Customer Service Interaction—Poor Customer Service and Prescriptions for Improvement." In *Servicescapes—The Concept of Place in Contemporary Markets*, ed. J.F. Sherry Jr. Chicago: NTC Business Books with the American Marketing Association, 515–538.

Leigh, T., and P.F. McGrew. (1989). "Mapping the Procedural Knowledge of Industrial Sales Personnel: A Script-Theoretic Investigation." *Journal of Marketing* 53: 16–34.

Liljander, V., and T. Strandvik. (1995). "The Nature of Customer Relationships in Services." In *Advances in Services Marketing and Management*, vol. 4, ed. T.A. Swartz, D.E. Bowen, and S.W. Brown. Greenwich, CT: JAI Press, 141–167.

Lord, R.G., and M.C. Kerman. (1987). "Scripts As Determinants of Purposeful Behavior in Organizations." *Academy of Management Review* 12, no. 2: 265–277.

Lovelock, C.H., and L.K. Wright. (1999). *Principles of Service Marketing and Management*, 1st ed. Englewood Cliffs, NJ: Prentice-Hall.

Lynn, M., and B. Latane. (1984). "The Psychology of Restaurant Tipping." *Journal of Applied Social Psychology* 14, no. 6: 549–561.

Lynn, M.; G.M. Zinkham; and J. Harris. (1993). "Consumer Tipping: A Cross-Country Study." *Journal of Consumer Research* 220: 478–488.

Manrai, L.A. (1993). "Mood Effects in Services: An Integrated Conceptual Model." In *Advances in Services Marketing and Management*, vol. 2, ed. T.A. Swartz, D.E. Bowen, and S.W. Brown. Greenwich, CT: JAI Press, 151–174.

Maslach, C., and M.P. Leiter. (1997). *The Truth About Burnout*. San Francisco: Jossey Bass.

Mills, P.K.; R.B. Chase; and N. Margulis. (1983). "Motivating the Client/Employee System As a Service Production Strategy." *Academy of Management Review* 8, no. 2: 301–310.

Mills, P.K., and J.H. Morris. (1986). "Clients As 'Partial' Employees of Service Organizations: Role Development in Client Participation." *Academy of Management Review* 11, no. 4: 726–735.

Oksenberg, L.; L. Coleman; and C.F. Cannell. (1986). "Interviewers' Voices and Refusal Rates in Telephone Surveys." *Public Opinion Quarterly* 50: 97–111.

Organ, D.W. (1990). "The Subtle Significance of Job Satisfaction." *Clinical Laboratory Management Review* 4, no. 1: 94–98.

Panteli, N. (2001). "Impressions and Boundaries Within Virtual Organizations." Paper presented at the annual meeting of the European Group of Organizational Studies (EGOS), 17th Colloquium, Subtheme: Managing Boundaries in Organizations, Lyon, France, July.

Parsons, H.M. (1976). "Work Environments." In *Human Behavior and Environment: Advances in Theory and Research*, vol. 1, ed. I. Altman and J.F. Wohlwill. New York: Plenum Press, 163–209.

Poole, P.P.; B. Gray; and D.A. Gioia. (1990). "Organizational Script Development Through Interactive Accommodation." *Group and Organization Studies* 15, no. 2: 212–232.

Price, L.L.; E.J. Arnould; and P. Tierney. (1999). "Going to Extremes: Managing Service Encounters and Assessing Provider Performance." In *Managing Services Marketing: Text and Reading*, ed. J.E.G. Bateson and K.D. Hoffman. London: Dryden Press, 249–266.

Rafaeli, A. (1989). "When Cashiers Meet Customers: An Analysis of the Role of Supermarket Cashiers." *Academy of Management Journal* 22, no. 2: 245–273.

Rafaeli, A., and R.I. Sutton. (1987). "The Expression of Emotion As Part of the Work Role." *Academy of Management Review* 12, no. 1: 23–37.

———. (1989). "The Expression of Emotion in Organizational Life." In *Research in Organizational Behavior*, vol. 11, ed. L.L. Cummings and B.M. Staw. Greenwich, CT: JAI Press, 1–42.

———. (1990). "Busy Stores and Demanding Customers: How Do They Affect the Display of Positive Emotion?" *Academy of Management Journal* 33, no. 3: 623–637.

Ragins, B. (1997). "Diversified Mentoring Relationships in Organizations: A Power Perspective." *Academy of Management Review* 22, no. 2: 482–521.

Ritzer, G. (2000). *The McDonaldization of Society*. Thousand Oaks, CA: Pine Forge Press.

Rousseau, D.M. (1985). "Issues of Level in Organizational Research: Multi-level and Cross-level Perspectives." In *Research in Organizational Behavior*, vol. 7, ed. L.L. Cummings and B.M. Staw. Greenwich, CT: JAI Press, 1–38.

Rousseau, D.M., and J. McLean-Parks. (1993). "The Contracts of Individuals and Organizations." In *Research in Organizational Behavior*, vol. 15, ed. L.L. Cummings and B.M. Staw. Greenwich, CT: JAI Press, 1–45.

Russell, J.A. (1987). "Comments on Articles by Frijda and by Conway and Bekerian." *Cognition and Emotions* 1, no. 2: 193–197.

Russell, J.A., and A. Mehrabian, A. (1977). "Evidence for a Three-Factor Theory of Emotions." *Journal of Research in Personality* 11: 273–294.

———. (1978). "Approach-Avoidance and Affiliation As Functions of the Emotion-Eliciting Quality of an Environment." *Environment and Behavior* 10, no. 3: 355–387.

Schank, R.C., and R.P. Abelson. (1977). *Scripts, Plans, Goals and Understanding*. Hillsdale, NJ: Erlbaum.

Schein, E.H. (1980). *Organizational Psychology*, 3d ed. Englewood Cliffs, NJ: Prentice-Hall.

Schwartz, S.H. (1992). "Universals in the Content and Structure of Calues: Theoretical Advances and Empirical Tests in 20 Countries." *Advances in Experimental Social Psychology* 25: 1–65.

———. (1996). "Value Priorities and Behavior: Applying of Theory of Integrated Value Systems." In *The Psychology of Values: The Ontario Symposium*, vol. 8, ed. C. Seligman, J.M. Olson, and M.P. Zanna. Hillsdale, NJ: Erlbaum, 1–24.

Schwartzman, H. (1989). *The Meeting: Gatherings in Organizations and Communities*. New York: Plenum Press.

Seidel, M.D.L.; J.M. Dukeritch; and F. Bertolotti. (2001). "Managing Boundaries in the E-Commerce Age." Paper presented at the annual meeting of the European Group of Organizational Studies (EGOS), 17th Colloquium, Subtheme: Managing Boundaries in Organizations, Lyon, France, July.

Shoemaker, S. (1996). "Scripts: Precursor of Consumer Expectations." *Cornell Hotel and Restaurant Administration Quarterly* 37, no. 1: 42–53.

Solomon, M.R.; C. Surprenent; J.A. Czepiel; and E.G. Gutman. (1985). "A Role Theory Perspective on Dyadic Interactions: The Service Encounter." *Journal of Marketing* 49: 99–111.

Spradley, J.P., and B.J. Mann. (1975). *The Cocktail Waitress: Woman's Work in Man's World*. New York: Knopf.

Starr, N. (1988). *The International Guide to Tipping*. New York: Berkeley.

Sutton, R.I., and A. Rafaeli. (1988). "Untangling the Relationship Between Displayed Emotions and Organizational Sales: The Case of Convenience Stores." *Academy of Management Journal* 31, no. 3: 461–487.

Van Maanen, J. (1995). "The Smile Factory: Work at Disneyland." In *Psychological Dimensions of Organizational Behavior*, ed. B.M. Staw. Englewood Cliffs: NJ: Prentice-Hall, 290–302.

Vilnai-Yavetz, I., and A. Rafaeli. (2003). "Analyzing Interactions: Separating the Skeleton from the Tissue." Paper in progress, Technion–Israel Institute of Technology, Haifa, Israel.

Whyte, W.F. (1948). "Human Relations in the Restaurant Industry." New York: Wiley.

Wofford, J.C. (1994). "An Examination of the Cognitive Processes Used to Handle Employee Job Problems." *Academy of Management Journal* 37, no. 1: 180–192.

Yukl, G.A. (1998). *Transformational and Cultural Leadership, Leadership in Organizations*. New York: Prentice-Hall, 324–350.

CHAPTER 6

INSTITUTIONALIZED SPIRITUALITY

An Oxymoron?

BLAKE E. ASHFORTH AND MICHAEL G. PRATT

Nearly fifty years ago, Ohmann (1955) pondered how individuals could worship a God(s) on weekends and then "worship . . . mammon [riches] Mondays through Fridays" (34). Indeed, if emerging contemporary evidence is to be believed, many individuals are defining themselves as "seekers" (Lofland and Stark 1965) who are less willing to consign their spirituality to nonwork hours and domains. As such, the search for spiritual fulfillment, or spiritual strivings (Emmons 1999), appears to be increasingly manifested in work settings (Cash and Gray 2000; Gunther 2001; Mirvis 1997; Mitroff and Denton 1999).

The individual employee, however, is hired into an existing work setting that comes with institutionalized ways of not only acting, but of valuing, thinking, and even feeling. By "institu- tionalized," we mean an enduring reality that is "out there," external to any one person (Zucker 1977). This notion of an institutionalized work setting raises an intriguing question: To what extent can an individual explore his or her particular spirituality within a prefabricated organiza- tional reality? In short, is institutionalized spirituality an oxymoron?

We broach this question as follows. First, we briefly explore the meaning of spirituality. Sec- ond, we discuss the tensions between spiritual strivings and institutionalized work settings. Third, we argue that despite these tensions, many workplaces approximate spirituality, whether through enabling individuals, partnering with them, or directing them. We examine the pros and cons of each approach and speculate on the future of spirituality in work organizations.

WHAT IS SPIRITUALITY?

Many scholars have struggled to define spirituality within the work context, without achieving consensus (Ashmos and Duchon 2000; McKnight 1984; Neal 2000; Neck and Milliman 1994). Based inductively on our reading of this literature, we suggest that spirituality at work has at least three major dimensions. The first is *transcendence* of self, a connection to something greater than oneself (Clark 1958, as cited in McCormick 1994). As such, spirituality represents an expansion of one's boundaries to encompass, for example, other people, causes, nature, or a belief in a higher power. The second dimension is *holism and harmony*. Holism is an integration of the various aspects of oneself (e.g., identities, beliefs, traits) into a roughly coherent and consistent self (see also "passionate reason," Vaill 1990, 338), whereas harmony is the sense that the inte- gration of the various aspects is synergistic and informs one's behavior. Holism and harmony presume a certain degree of self-insight and are associated with terms such as authenticity, balance, and perspective. The desire for holism and harmony is one reason why many people are unwilling to consign their spirituality to off-work domains. The third dimension of spirituality at work is *growth*, a sense of self-development or self-actualization, a realization of one's aspirations and potential. Evans (1990, as cited in Wong 1998, 365) argues that spirituality is "connected to what I *am* and what I must *become*." This dimension gives spirituality a dynamic flavor. If transcendence leads to connection, and holism and harmony to coherence, then growth leads to completeness.

Insofar as holism, harmony, and growth represent a transcendence of one's usual limits (Conger 1994), then the term transcendence can provide an overall shorthand for the various dimensions of spirituality. Indeed, transcendence addresses the four major motives of newcomers in organizational settings, as posited by Ashforth (2001): namely, identity (who am I?); meaning (why am I here?); belonging and control (via connection to a more powerful cause or collective). Thus, we will use the term transcendence throughout the chapter to refer to being part of something greater, synchronizing diverse facets of self and self-actualization.

Spirituality As State and Process

Spirituality is often conceptualized as a noun—a state of being—as implied by terms like connection, holism, and self-actualization. Spirituality, however, can also be thought of as a verb—a process—in the sense that the journey itself is part of the meaning. In particular, seeking transcendence may be viewed as an ongoing and open-ended process, a personal journey of exploration and discovery where the destination is unclear and the paths are emergent (e.g., Bolman and Deal 1995; Palmer 1994; Vaill 1990). Unlike religion, which "is about answers . . . spirituality is about questions" (Mirvis 1997, 197). Spirituality as a process, therefore, is highly subjective and fluid and often idiosyncratic. Whereas some enact spirituality in such religious practices as prayer, others enact it through helping others, exploring nature, or countless other ways.

This multiplicity of open-ended paths in turn underscores the importance of spiritual strivings, the ways in which individuals pursue transcendence. It is important to note that spiritual strivings are not dependent on grand actions and goals. Because spirituality is defined as a connection to something transcendent, seemingly small acts can have enormous personal meaning if they are indeed perceived to have such a connection (Emmons 1999).

ARE SPIRITUAL STRIVINGS CONSISTENT WITH INSTITUTIONALIZED SETTINGS?

We argue that spiritual strivings are basically *in*consistent with institutionalized settings in at least two ways: the locus of spirituality and the focus of spirituality.

Locus of Spirituality

Spirituality, as the state and process of transcendence, is necessarily about the individual: extending the boundaries of the self, striving for holism and harmony of the self, and developing the self. And, as noted, spirituality is often described as a personal and often idiosyncratic journey of the self. In short, the locus of spirituality resides in the individual.[1] An organization, of course, can prompt an individual's journey, channel his or her path, and suggest the "appropriate" lessons to be derived. Indeed, as we will argue, strong culture organizations—where values, beliefs, and norms are widely shared and deeply held—do just that. Nonetheless, it is the individual who must be ready, able, and willing to embark on the journey; who must take (if not choose) the actual steps; and who must internalize and somehow reconcile the lessons (if not recreate them) with his or her preexisting values and beliefs. Organizations can trigger and shape spiritual strivings, but the individual necessarily remains the locus.

Because its locus is the individual, spiritual seeking may be at odds with an organization's mandate. Organizations are collectives that require their members to mesh to some degree, to share a common culture and perspective: Unbridled individuality in the form of idiosyncratic spiritual journeys is thus a potential threat to the coherence of the organization.

Focus of Spirituality

Spirituality, as a process, is an end in itself (i.e., it does not require completion); and spirituality, as transcendence, pertains to intangibles. In contrast, organizations focus more on outcomes and on tangibles; processes and intangibles are regarded as means to ends, not as ends in themselves. Organizations are fueled by the "institutional logic of capitalism" (Friedland and Alford 1991, 248): They are enmeshed in a competitive struggle to commodify human activity for the marketplace. Spirituality alone cannot sustain an organization: Even avowedly spiritual organizations such as Tom's of Maine (Chappell 1993) and ServiceMaster (Pollard 1996) must turn a profit. As a result, an organization's vision of the individual tends to be strongly conditioned by the mission that enables its existence, the corporate culture that evolves to facilitate the mission, the necessarily localized perspective from which the organization operates, and the instrumental purposes for which the individual was hired. Despite frequent claims to the contrary, an individual is defined foremost as an organizational member and role occupant (e.g., accountant, pipe-fitter, salesperson), not as a unique, flesh-and-blood person. In short, organizations tend to offer a relatively atomistic rather than holistic vision of the individual. Thus, although organizations often help individuals address two aspects of transcendence—extending self-boundaries and developing the self—they are often ill-equipped to help individuals address the third: holism and harmony.

Further, organizations have unavoidable secular issues and are thus necessarily concerned with many tangibles. Whether an auto manufacturer, a hospital, or a police force, organizations have bricks and mortar (or clicks), equipment, supplies, and so on, and must churn out goods or services in an effective and efficient manner. In the workaday frenzy of organizations, spiritual matters tend to get squeezed out by the demands of the moment. Organizational priorities trump individual ones, and doing replaces choosing and reflecting. The abstract notion of spirituality is often less salient than the urgent press of concrete and pragmatic concerns.

The Dilemma

Because of the locus (individual) and focus (intangibles, process) of spirituality, work organizations are not readily compatible with spiritual strivings. That said, many studies indicate that a resonance between the individual and organization, or person–organization (P–O) "fit," facilitates work adjustment and positive outcomes for the individual and organization alike (Kristof 1996; Saks and Ashforth 2002).

P–O fit is often operationalized as the degree of congruence between the individual and organization in values, beliefs, and practices. Given the relatively high percentage of individuals who believe in God (up to 95 percent in the United States), and given resurging interest in workplace spirituality (Gunther 2001), it stands to reason that organizations may want to reflect spiritual values as a means of facilitating member fit. Indeed, the search for meaning and the need for being part of "something greater than oneself" have been posited to be major motivations for why individuals identify with organizations (Pratt 1998). As Mirvis (1997) put it, the drive to engage "the whole person at work . . . *must take account of people's spiritual life and its collective potential*" (203, his emphasis).

However, two barriers stand in the way of more fully integrating spirituality into work practices. First, as we have argued, work organizations are not readily compatible with spiritual strivings. Second, although appealing to some, there are undoubtedly employees who are disturbed by what they see as an inappropriate blurring of personal issues and the workplace (Mirvis 1994). The bulk of our paper addresses how organizations attempt to manage this dilemma by *approximating* spirituality. That is, we discuss how organizations facilitate spiritual strivings within the constraints imposed by the institutionalized setting.

APPROXIMATING SPIRITUALITY

Although spirituality is intensely personal, it need not be private (Palmer 1994; Scott 1994); and although spirituality tends to be idiosyncratic, it is often predicated on shared experiences, values, and beliefs. A typical organization embodies (or at least espouses) a certain identity and attendant goals, values, beliefs, and norms; in short, it stands for *something* (Albert and Whetten 1985; Ashforth and Mael 1996). That something provides potential spiritual hooks for the individual, particularly for connection and growth.

In this section, we argue that organizations can be arrayed on a continuum of approaches to spirituality, ranging from those that involve relatively high individual control to those that involve relatively high organizational control. In addition to the two extremes, which we label "enabling" and "directing," we discuss a middle position, "partnering." Our model is depicted in Figure 6.1.

It should be noted that we are focusing on organizations that have evidenced some receptiveness to spirituality, that is, that have gone beyond mere lip service or tolerance to actually displaying at least sympathy for—if not outright encouragement of—spiritual strivings and practices in the work context. Many organizations, of course, have not. An instructive analogy can be drawn from the receptiveness of work organizations to work–family issues. When concerns about work–family balance arose some years ago, organizations generally appeared uneasy and often resistant to what was seen as an unwarranted intrusion of the personal sphere into the proprietary. As pressure continued and work–family issues became mainstream concerns, many organizations relented and evinced greater tolerance; some even came to encourage work–family balance, and some effectively coopted individuals through work–family initiatives (e.g., Hochschild 1997). We see parallels with spirituality; namely, that many organizations are currently displaying the same halting receptiveness toward spirituality, and some—with or without good intentions—are using spiritual strivings to coopt the individual.

ENABLING

The left side of the continuum represents high individual control. Here, an organization can be said to be *enabling*: It acknowledges spiritual strivings and allows individuals to discover their own idiosyncratic transcendence, whether through prayer groups, meditation, yoga, journaling, spiritual retreats, or other means. The organization does not impose a particular worldview on the individual, at least with regard to spiritual matters. Instead, the organization may be merely a passive site for spiritual strivings or may be more active in providing resources for their realization. Work itself may be incidental to these strivings or directly implicated in them. Regardless,

Figure 6.1 **Approximating Spirituality: Organizational Types**

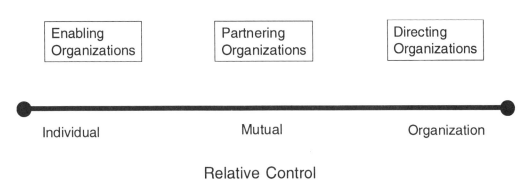

Relative Control

Note: This figure pertains only to organizations that are at least somewhat receptive to spirituality.

management tends to be indulgent, allowing individuals to find their own spiritual niche and depth according to their idiosyncratic needs and paths.

For example, employees at the World Bank sit in a semicircle for an hour each week and talk about such spiritual issues as attaining "soul consciousness" (Galen and West 1995); Tom's of Maine invites diverse spiritual leaders, from Native American tribal elders to divinity professors, to speak to employees (Brandt 1996); Taco Bell and Pizza Hut have hired chaplains to administer to employees' spiritual needs (Conlin 1999); Boeing had 500 top managers listen to a poet for three days a month as part of an executive training program (Galen and West 1995); and Monsanto has utilized experts to teach Buddhist meditation practices during their corporate retreats (Tworkov 2001). Similarly, World Vision has "weekly chapel meetings, morning devotions, group retreats and individual sessions with the spiritual-formation manager, if people feel they need personal direction" (Laabs 1995, 76).

Pros and Cons of Enabling

The primary benefit of enabling is *personalization*: It allows the individual to decide whether or not to undertake a spiritual journey at work, and if so, what paths to take. Personalization is likely to foster a sense of spiritual fulfillment along with commitment toward the workplace that enabled it. An indulgent environment is also likely to enhance diversity in spiritual practices and in the religious backgrounds that sometimes fuel them. This diversity can bring many benefits, such as creative thinking. Indeed, for better and for worse, spiritual inquiries may even lead some individuals to start questioning the identity and practices of the organization itself (e.g., Are they consistent with my beliefs? How might they be changed?) and to hold the organization to a higher standard.

Given that enabling allows for a wide variety of spiritual practices, the indirect benefits for the organization may be offset if enacting these practices makes members feel dissimilar to others in the organization, thus weakening the individual–organization bond (Ashforth and Mael 1989; Pratt 1998). The potential for interpersonal conflict and alienation is especially high when personal spiritual practices are made visible.

Further, in serving as a benign platform for spiritual strivings, the enabling organization may appear to implicitly sanction any and all spiritual practices. The 1996 (U.S.) Equal Employment

Opportunity Commission addressed employee requests for time off for religious observance, company space and time for religious activities, and permission to display religious materials, wear religious dress and symbols, and proselytize coworkers (Cash and Gray 2000). Although U.S. employers are legally required to accommodate "reasonable" spiritual requests, the receptive climate of the enabling organization may encourage many diverse requests, raising troubling questions about whether and where to draw a line. Finally, despite the permissive nature of the enabling organization, some individuals may feel implicit pressure to display their spirituality in the workplace or to conform to the spiritual practices of their superiors or peers. Permissiveness may be seen by some as a license to proselytize, and what was once an idiosyncratic, voluntary activity may gain normative momentum and seem mandatory.

DIRECTING

The right side of the continuum represents high organizational control, and we refer to the organization as *directing*. The organization effectively imposes its preferred cosmology on individuals, a cosmology that is intimately tied to the mission and practices of the organization itself. A cosmology is an overarching theoretical framework, perhaps tied to ultimate—and thus unverifiable—truths, "defining who one is (identity) and who belongs (membership), what matters (values) and what is to be done (purpose), how and why things hang together . . . to constitute 'reality' and 'truth' (ideology), [and] how one is embedded in that reality and connects to what matters and what is to be done (transcendence)" (Ashforth and Vaidyanath in press, 5). A cosmology is, in Ohmann's (1955) memorable words, a "skyhook . . . an abiding faith around which life's experiences can be integrated and given meanings" (34). As such, a cosmology grounds and justifies the selection of values, beliefs, strategies, ethics, decisions, spiritual practices, and so on (McGee 1998).

Typically, directing organizations have strong cultures that provide clear and often distinctive hooks for spiritual strivings. If enabling is about bottom-up exploration and heterogeneity, directing is about the top-down imposition of homogeneity. The idiosyncratic spirituality that is encouraged in the enabling organization veers into an institutionalized religion in the directing organization.

Given the religious pluralism of society, directing organizations are likely to appeal to a relatively narrow segment of job seekers and are unlikely to be publicly held firms (Cavanagh 1999). Organizations that tend toward the directing end of the spectrum may include ServiceMaster whose founder "dedicated his business to serving the Lord," and whose corporate office sports a statue of Jesus washing the feet of his disciples (Gunther 2001, 64). They may also include Domino's Pizza, whose philosophy under founder Thomas Monaghan was "God, family, and Domino's Pizza" (Rosenberg 2001, 1). More dramatic examples of organizations that take this approach are such network marketing organizations (NMOs) as Amway and Mary Kay, Inc.—many of whom espouse Christian principles (Biggart 1989). To illustrate, NMOs often require distributors to adhere to a set of ethical principles that include references to Christian tenets such as the "Golden Rule," and admonish distributors to put God before one's business concerns (Pratt and Rosa 2001). Moreover, many groups of Amway distributors use prayer during their business meetings, and some sponsor evangelical services at the end of long training seminars in order to provide members the opportunity to publicly declare that Jesus Christ is their savior (Pratt 2000a).

The Levers of Directing

A variety of levers may be used to encourage internalization of the cosmology. First, recruit selection emphasizes P–O fit more than technical skills or person–job fit (Schneider 1987; Wagner-

Marsh and Conley, 1999). Given the distinctiveness of the organization, P–O fit is enhanced by targeting individuals who are likely to be attracted to what the organization embodies. Thus, the organization selects individuals with commensurate values and beliefs or who have strong spiritual strivings (Pratt 2000b). For example, although NMOs such as Amway do not require their members to be Christian, the members should be willing to conduct their business using Christian principles (Pratt 2000a).

Second, directing organizations tend to socialize individuals using a cyclical process of sensebreaking and sensegiving (see "institutionalized socialization"—Ashforth 2001; Van Maanen and Schein 1979). In its fully articulated form, recruits' incoming identities, values, and beliefs are challenged via sensebreaking practices (thus fomenting a desire for change); managers and peers model the espoused culture, and recruits are encouraged to form personal attachments with these models (perhaps to the exclusion of former friends and families—i.e., encapsulation); recruits are exposed to particular situations and a strong ideological context that provides clear, organizationally endorsed interpretations (thus using sensemaking to normalize practices that may otherwise seem unorthodox); and recruits' adoption of the cosmology is shaped and reinforced through rewards, primarily social (see Pratt 2000b).

A third lever for encouraging internalization of the cosmology is ongoing normative control, which maintains the salience of the cosmology. Normative control is enacted through substantive management (i.e., material change in organizational practices, including strategies, structures, technologies, budgets, information systems, reward systems, physical settings, and so forth) and symbolic management (i.e., the ways in which the organization is portrayed, including vision and mission statements, historical narratives, metaphors, rituals, traditions, heroes, and so on) (Ashforth and Vaidyanath in press; Pfeffer 1981). These various levers signal what matters and what is to be done; provide self-aggrandizing interpretations of past, present, and future events; inspire devotion to the cause; and inoculate newcomers against the views and doubts of outsiders.

Finally, transformational leadership is often used to encourage internalization of the organization's cosmology, particularly where the cosmology is a function of the leader's vision, values, and beliefs (Bass 1985; Graham 1991). As Kanungo and Mendonça (1994) put it, "the leader is the soul of the organization" (192). According to Bass and Avolio (1990), transformational leaders galvanize intrinsic desires for change via idealized influence, inspirational motivation, intellectual stimulation, and individualized consideration. In particular, transformational leaders foster transcendence by harnessing spiritual strivings to the leader's vision, grounding those strivings in concrete goals and behaviors, and encouraging identification with the leader and his or her values and beliefs (Dehler and Welsh 1994; Kanungo and Mendonça 1994). Richard DeVos and Jay Van Andel of Amway, Mary Kay Ash of Mary Kay, Inc., and Thomas Monaghan of Domino's Pizza may all qualify as visionary leaders who have striven to infuse members with a particular cosmology. Together, selection, socialization, normative control, and transformational leadership create intense and relentless pressure to become an exemplar of the organization.

Pros and Cons of Directing

Given that most individuals are leery of corporate religions (Mitroff and Denton 1999), it may seem counterintuitive that individuals would subject themselves to the rigors of a directing organization. However, as Iannaccone (1994) argues regarding strict churches, strong cultures breed strong commitment by screening out those whose commitment is only half-hearted (Why subject myself to this?) and encouraging a sort of emotional contagion among those who remain. Such practices as inducing organizational members to display "strange" beliefs and behaviors, to socialize with one another rather than outsiders, to develop organization-specific identities and skills, and so forth—practices that entail, in short, a sacrifice—reinforce a distinction between "us" and "them," effectively raising the barriers to entry *and* exit. Ironically, it is the very strictness of the organization that persuades members to adopt its cosmology.[2]

There are several benefits of a directing approach. For one, modern life has been characterized as highly fragmented; as a result, members' efforts are often divided between different life domains. For those members whose values, beliefs, or spiritual strivings are consistent with the organization's cosmology, directing may facilitate a deep sense of spiritual fulfillment, spiritual community and belongingness, workplace identification, and a greater sense of wholeness, leading to enhanced motivation and organizational citizenship behaviors (Pratt 2000a). Directing organizations, therefore, may do more to approximate holism and harmony *for individuals with consonant beliefs* than do other organizational types. Further, the shared cosmology is likely to enhance unity and coordination and thereby achievement of the organization's goals (O'Reilly and Chatman 1996).

That said, we believe that wariness toward directing organizations is warranted. On the individual side, members who have not internalized the cosmology may feel highly pressured to do so—to become a convert (Mirvis 1997; Nadesan 1999; Young 1994). Also, insofar as the cosmology is founded on claims to ultimate truths that cannot be tested, members may be misplacing their faith and abnegating their critical thinking. Moreover, members may "overadapt" to the unique cosmology offered by the organization, making it difficult to work elsewhere or even to psychologically exit the organization in the event of, say, a layoff or retirement. A spirituality predicated on an organization that cannot always be there for the individual is a risky spirituality (Mael and Ashforth 2001).

On the organizational side, the unique cosmology, coupled with rigorous selection, socialization, normative control, and transformational leadership is likely to limit diversity and perhaps adaptability (Mitroff and Denton 1999). Consensus on the "right way"—particularly if that way is thought to be anchored in ultimate truths—may induce myopia, resistance to change, and even arrogance (Ashforth and Vaidyanath in press). Ashforth and Vaidyanath (in press) add that corporate religions are inclined to sacralize the means by which they pursue their sacred ends, thus further increasing the likelihood of resistance to change. Moreover, given our earlier discussion of the focus of spirituality, the cosmology may be corrupted by such unavoidable secular concerns as the need to raise capital and manufacture and market products, or it may be manipulated cynically by power holders for their own self-interests (e.g., Butterfield's [1986] critique of Amway). Finally, the unique cosmology of—and public wariness toward—corporate religions may undermine external legitimacy, although members' perception of being persecuted may increase *internal* legitimacy. Indeed, to gain external legitimacy and avoid legal challenges, a directing organization may rely on euphemisms like "mission," "values," "ethics," and "concerns" (Conlin 1999; Galen and West 1995).

We have sketched the two extremes of Figure 6.1—relatively high individual control and relatively high organizational control—and noted the pros and cons of each. But what about the middle ground between these two extremes? What might it entail and how might it compare to the extremes?

PARTNERING

The middle ground of Figure 6.1 represents a territory of shared control—indeed, because power is not zero-sum (Tannenbaum and Cooke 1979), the middle ground may represent high individual control *and* high organizational control. Here, we refer to the organization as *partnering*.

Spirituality is a meld of active bottom-up and top-down processes, although not in a mechanistic or legalistic manner. Spirituality is jointly authored or socially constructed as members explore their spirituality within a facilitative context. Thus, unlike in directing organizations, spiritual *strivings* are paramount, and the resulting spiritual practices and "outcomes" (e.g., beliefs) are likely to be emergent and open-ended. Further, in directing organizations, the system is stable, and it is the individual that must adapt; in enabling organizations, the individual finds his or her own path, and the system again remains stable or changes only indirectly; however, in partnering organizations, the opportunity is created for the individual and organization to coevolve. Also, given the top-down element of partnering, spirituality is likely to be more communal and less idiosyncratic and diverse than in enabling organizations, although it may remain pluralistic. And given the organizational involvement in partnering, spirituality is likely to implicate both the work of the individual and the collective context of the organization.

Because partnering occupies the broad middle ground of Figure 6.1, we believe that it can come in many shades—some partnering attempts may border on enabling, whereas others may border on directing. Moreover, we propose that partnering strategies are most likely to be used at an organization's founding, when the culture of the organization is beginning to form, or when an organization is attempting to forge new policies regarding spirituality.

Because of the unique challenges involved in partnering, a special type of leadership may be needed. Specifically, *servant leadership* and its variants, where leaders desire to humbly serve rather than lead their followers (Block 1993; DePree 1989; Greenleaf 1996a, b), are likely to bring partnering to fruition. Although the construct has not been rigorously researched, its proponents hold that servant leaders emphasize, among other things, a holistic approach to work, self-awareness and development, empowering and collaborating, true listening and constructive feedback, and—like transformational leaders—articulating a vision and inspiring trust. With the emphasis on holism, development, and vision, servant leadership has an avowedly spiritual flavor (Greenleaf 1996b; Lee and Zemke 1993; Wagner-Marsh and Conley 1999). Servant leadership is neither directing nor enabling because it encourages individuals—and leaders—to explore their spiritual strivings in concert with the organization's mission and workings (Nadesan 1999).

For example, Scott (1994) and Wisely and Lynn (1994) describe an intervention for trustees of not-for-profit institutions. The trustees are encouraged to reflect on the institution's history, mission, and place in the larger community, and on the meaning of trust. Trustees exchange personal and communal stories that explore the institution's identity, culture, and future and each trustee's deeper, idiosyncratic connections with the institution. In surfacing and strengthening personalized connections, the process presumably enables the trustees to extend personal boundaries and strive for holism and growth. The personal becomes the communal and vice versa. Similarly, Mirvis (1997) discusses a program that began with Shell Oil's top ten executives and cascaded down to 200 executives and then to middle management. The participants recorded their personal and career histories, and created a plaster cast of their face that they decorated with symbols of their journey and growth. The masks (and their associated stories) were shared with colleagues and are mounted in offices throughout Shell.

Pros and Cons of Partnering

As the middle ground between enabling and directing, partnering involves a meld of their advantages and disadvantages. The bottom-up involvement in the social construction of spirituality may be experienced as somewhat empowering (more so than under directing, though not necessarily less so than under enabling), leading to some personalization of spirituality and a resulting sense of spiritual fulfillment and personal development. And the top-down involvement, although potentially limiting empowerment and spiritual diversity, may foster a sense of spiritual community and belongingness (more so than under enabling, though not necessarily less so than under directing) and, thereby, unity and coordination. Because individuals and the organization coevolve, both are likely to remain more adaptable than under directing, and the organization is less likely to lose external legitimacy. Nonetheless, the potential for the individual to overadapt to the emergent cosmology and to be manipulated by cynical power holders remains very real.

Further, the pressure to display spiritual strivings and to conform to an emergent spirituality is likely to be stronger than under enabling. Partnering represents a problematic alchemy of the spirituality of many individuals and the organization itself. As a process, partnering is analogous to herding cats and may easily tip into directing. As Nash (1994) says of employee personal development programs, "As long as companies are initiating and bankrolling such programs, they will tend to structure them with a bias toward their own perceived interests" (189). This bias may be implicit, but nonetheless real. For example, Nash discusses a whitewater rafting trip where nonswimmers were pressured to participate for the sake of personal growth and teambuilding. Because spirituality is harnessed to organizational purposes, it is a *contingent* spirituality.

In sum, we posit a continuum of approaches that organizations can use to approximate spirituality (see Figure 6.1). We argue that these approaches differ in terms of whether they are primarily top-down, bottom-up, or some combination thereof; and suggest that each approach brings with it a unique set of pros and cons, as summarized in Table 6.1.

DISCUSSION

As interest grows in the intersection of spirituality and the workplace, so too do questions about their compatibility and the social desirability of such a marriage. Does it make sense to speak of an institutionalized spirituality—or is the very notion of spirituality antithetical to institutionalized settings? We argued that spiritual strivings are in fact basically inconsistent with such settings because the locus of spirituality is necessarily the individual, and the focus of spirituality is partly on process as an end in itself, whereas institutions are necessarily concerned with collectively constructed, tangible outcomes. Thus, just as spirituality cannot be completely institutionalized without compromising its locus and focus, so institutions cannot be completely "spiritualized" without sacrificing their collective and corporeal form. Spirituality and institutions are like Venn diagrams that cannot totally overlap without one eclipsing the other.

That said, we further argued that institutions may approximate spirituality through an array of approaches that differ in the degree of control arrogated by the organization. At one end, enabling organizations arrogate little control, allowing individuals, if they wish, to pursue their own spiritual journeys. At the other end, directing organizations arrogate great control, imposing a preferred cosmology on all. In between are partnering organizations that share control, where spirituality is mutually authored by individuals and the institution.

Which approach is best? Just as we cannot say that one major religion is better or more valid than another, we cannot pronounce on what approach or organizational cosmology is necessarily better or more valid in terms of its spiritual properties: One person's passion is another's poison. As summarized in Table 6.1, each approach has certain advantages and disadvantages, and each is capable of attracting individuals who resonate with that approach. And this is true not only of the *content* of the approach (what is believed), but of the *process* as well (how spirituality is sought or indulged). Whereas some are attracted by the diverse spiritualities that are possible in the enabling organization, others are attracted by the distinctive spirituality of the directing organization.

Table 6.1

Major Pros and Cons Associated with Organization Types

Enabling organizations	Partnering organizations	Directing organizations
Pros		
Personalization of spirituality—spiritual fulfillment	Some personalization of spirituality—spiritual fulfillment	For those whose spiritual strivings are consistent with the organization—spiritual fulfillment
Spiritual diversity	Spiritual community—unity and coordination	Spiritual community—unity and coordination
Questioning the organization itself		
Cons		
Perceived dissimilarities among members—potential conflict	Pressure to display spirituality and conform	Pressure to convert
Implicit sanctioning of any and all spiritual practices	Overadapt to emergent cosmology	Potentially misplaced faith
Potential pressure to display spirituality and conform	Susceptible to manipulation	Overadapt to cosmology
		Limited diversity and adaptability
		Susceptible to corruption and manipulation
		Potential loss of external legitimacy

What we *can* say is that directing organizations—and perhaps some forms of partnering organizations—that are predicated on a one-best-way cosmology seem to incur the most costs for individuals and organizations. Ironically, these organizations may also best approximate spirituality—for individuals with similar spiritual strivings—by approximating holism and harmony, as well as connectedness and growth. Given the inherent incompatibility between spiritual and organizational concerns, perhaps attempts to link them tightly—as in directing organizations—must always involve a trade-off. Success in approximating spirituality for some members may necessitate failure in achieving certain organizational interests (e.g., adaptability, job satisfaction for all members).

We also predict that most individuals—but clearly not all—will prefer enabling organizations and some forms of partnering organizations over directing organizations. There are three major reasons: First, self-determination remains a prized value for many; second, individuals tend to endorse spirituality more so than organized religion (Mitroff and Denton 1999); and third, there remains a contemporary echo from the twentieth-century compartmentalization of work and spirituality.

Regardless of whether an organization is enabling, partnering, or directing, it is imperative that individuals have reasonably full and accurate foreknowledge of the organization's spiritual orientation (e.g., through realistic job previews), that their informed consent be secured for any spiritual programs, and that they be allowed to opt out or withdraw without penalty (Mirvis 1997; Young 1994). Part of the reason that so-called "cults" invite suspicion is that many use highly deceptive recruitment and socialization practices, disguising their true nature and intent while the individual is indoctrinated (O'Reilly and Chatman 1996).

What might the future hold for spirituality in the workplace? Given the pace of change and the erosion of some traditional societal pillars (e.g., community participation, extended families), there is likely to be continuing turbulence in the "market economy" of religion (Stark and Finke 2000). Just as this turbulence has spawned a variety of New Age spiritual forms, it seems to also be spawning a variety of work-based spirituality initiatives. This ferment will likely continue, especially in light of the long work hours and psychological involvement often demanded of today's employees (Schor 1991). As noted, individuals are likely to be particularly receptive to enabling and some partnering organizations because of their emphasis on individualism. However, some individuals will continue to be attracted to directing organizations precisely because they offer a collective of like-minded seekers and a redeeming mission beyond the paycheck. And as change continues to undermine the utility of bureaucratic, technical, and hierarchical controls, the normative control afforded by corporate-sponsored spirituality will become more attractive to organizations. In short, there will likely be increases in all three forms of spiritual "approximation," particularly as the technology of spiritual socialization evolves.[3] Spiritual strivings, by their very nature, are conducive to a variety of spiritual forms, and thus the enabling, partnering, and directing organizations may all fare well in the years ahead.

NOTES

We thank Bob Giacalone, Carole Jurkiewicz, and Glen Kreiner for their very helpful comments on an earlier draft of the chapter.

1. This emphasis on individualism, of course, is consistent with a prized ethic in many Western societies. However, it should be noted that other societies prize collectivism (Triandis and Trafimow 2001) and thus may define spirituality in more collective terms.Accordingly, this argument about the locus of spirituality may be less central in some cultures. That said, many spiritual philosophies in "collective" cultures still maintain the centrality of the individual achieving salvation (e.g., exiting the "wheel of rebirth," achieving nirvana, becoming one with the universe) through their own efforts. Others may *help* a person achieve enlightenment, but they cannot achieve enlightenment *for* him or her.

2. Iannacone notes, however, that there are diminishing returns to strictness: At some point, the demands of a strong culture outweigh the perceived benefits to members.

3. We may also see a rise in new forms of work–faith linkages, such as organizations whose purpose is to better bridge the divide between the spiritual and the secular. For example, organizations such as the Business Leaders for Excellence, Ethics, and Justice, consisting of Chicago-area businesspeople, and the Avodah Institute (Avodah is Hebrew for both "work" and "worship"), headed by a former IBM executive, attempt to find "God in work" by gathering individuals across, rather than within, organizations (Gunther 2001). We may also expect a continuation of the trend toward creating investment funds that cater to investors of particular religious or moral backgrounds (Rosenberg 2001).

REFERENCES

Albert, S., and D.A. Whetten. (1985). "Organizational Identity." In *Research in Organizational Behavior*, vol. 7, ed. L.L. Cummings and B.M. Staw. Greenwich, CT: JAI Press, 263–295.

Ashforth, B.E. (2001). *Role Transitions in Organizational Life: An Identity-Based Perspective*. Mahwah, NJ: Erlbaum.

Ashforth, B.E., and F.A. Mael. (1989). "Social Identity Theory and the Organization." *Academy of Management Review* 14: 20–39.

———. (1996). "Organizational Identity and Strategy As a Context for the Individual." In *Advances in Strategic Management*, vol. 13, ed. J.A.C. Baum and J.E. Dutton. Greenwich, CT: JAI Press, 19–64.

Ashforth, B.E., and D. Vaidyanath. (in press). "Work Organizations As Secular Religions." *Journal of Management Inquiry*.

Ashmos, D.P., and D. Duchon. (2000). "Spirituality at Work: A Conceptualization and Measure." *Journal of Management Inquiry* 9: 134–145.

Bass, B.M. (1985). *Leadership and Performance Beyond Expectations*. New York: Free Press.

Bass, B.M., and B.J. Avolio. (1990). "The Implications of Transactional and Transformational Leadership for Individual, Team, and Organizational Development." In *Research in Organizational Change and Development*, vol. 4, ed. W.A. Pasmore and R.W. Woodman. Greenwich, CT: JAI Press, 231–272.

Biggart, N.W. (1989). *Charismatic Capitalism: Direct Selling Organizations in America*. Chicago: University of Chicago Press.

Block, P. (1993). *Stewardship: Choosing Service Over Self-Interest*. San Francisco: Berrett-Koehler.

Bolman, L.G., and T.E. Deal. (1995). *Leading with Soul: An Uncommon Journey of Spirit*. San Francisco: Jossey-Bass.

Brandt, E. (1996). "Corporate Pioneers Explore Spirituality." *HR Magazine* 41, no. 4: 82–87.

Butterfield, S. (1986). *Amway: The Cult of Free Enterprise*. Montreal: Black Rose Books.

Cash, K.C., and G.R. Gray. (2000). "A Framework for Accommodating Religion and Spirituality in the Workplace." *Academy of Management Executive* 14, no. 3: 124–133.

Cavanagh, G.F. (1999). "Spirituality for Managers: Context and Critique." *Journal of Organizational Change Management* 12: 186–199.

Chappell, T. (1993). *The Soul of a Business: Managing for Profit and the Common Good*. New York: Bantam Books.

Clark, W.H. (1958). *The Psychology of Religion*. New York: Macmillan.

Conger, J.A. (1994). "Introduction: Our Search for Spiritual Community." In *Spirit at Work: Discovering the Spirituality in Leadership*, J.A. Conger and Associates. San Francisco: Jossey-Bass, 1–18.

Conlin, M. (1999). "Religion in the Workplace: The Growing Presence of Spirituality in Corporate America." *Business Week*, November 1, 150–154, 156, 158.

Dehler, G.E., and M.A. Welsh. (1994). "Spirituality and Organizational Transformation: Implications for the New Management Paradigm." *Journal of Managerial Psychology* 9, no. 6: 17–26.

DePree, M. (1989). *Leadership Is an Art*. New York: Doubleday.

Emmons, R.A. (1999). *The Psychology of Ultimate Concerns: Motivation and Spirituality in Personality*. New York: Guilford Press.

Evans, C.S. (1990). *Soren Kierkegaard's Christian Psychology: Insights for Counseling and Pastoral Care*. Grand Rapids, MI: Zondervan.

Friedland, R., and R.R. Alford. (1991). "Bringing Society Back in: Symbols, Practices, and Institutional Contradictions." In *The New Institutionalism in Organizational Analysis*, ed. W.W. Powell and P.J. DiMaggio. Chicago: University of Chicago Press, 232–263.

Galen, M., and K. West. (1995). "Companies Hit the Road Less Traveled: Can Spirituality Enlighten the Bottom Line?" *Business Week* (June 5): 82, 84–85.

Graham, J.W. (1991). "Servant-Leadership in Organizations: Inspirational and Moral." *Leadership Quarterly* 2, no. 2: 105–119.

Greenleaf, R.K. (1996a). *On Becoming a Servant-Leader: The Private Writings of Robert K. Greenleaf*, ed. D.M. Frick and L.C. Spears. San Francisco: Jossey-Bass.

Greenleaf, R.K. (1996b). *Seeker and Servant: Reflections on Religious Leadership: The Private Writings of Robert K. Greenleaf*, ed. A.T. Fraker and L.C. Spears. San Francisco: Jossey-Bass.

Gunther, M. (2001). "God and Business." *Fortune* 144, no. 1 (July 9): 58–61, 64, 66, 68, 70, 72–73, 76, 78, 80.

Hochschild, A.R. (1997). *The Time Bind: When Work Becomes Home and Home Becomes Work*. New York: Metropolitan Books.

Iannaccone, L.R. (1994). "Why Strict Churches Are Strong." *American Journal of Sociology* 99: 1180–1211.

Kanungo, R.N., and M. Mendonça. (1994). "What Leaders Cannot Do Without: The Spiritual Dimensions of Leadership." In *Spirit at Work: Discovering the Spirituality in Leadership*, J.A. Conger and Associates. San Francisco: Jossey-Bass, 162–198.

Kristof, A.L. (1996). "Person-Organization Fit: An Integrative Review of its Conceptualizations, Measurement, and Implications." *Personnel Psychology* 49: 1–49.

Laabs, J.J. (1995). "Balancing Spirituality and Work." *Personnel Journal* 74, no. 9: 60–62, 64, 66–68, 70, 72, 74, 76.

Lee, C., and R. Zemke. (1993). "The Search for Spirit in the Workplace." *Training* 30, no. 6: 21–28.

Lofland, J., and R. Stark. (1965). "Becoming a World-Saver: A Theory of Conversion to a Deviant Perspective." *American Sociological Review* 30: 862–875.

Mael, F.A., and B.E. Ashforth. (2001). "Identification in Work, War, Sports, and Religion: Contrasting the Benefits and Risks." *Journal for the Theory of Social Behaviour* 31: 197–222.

McCormick, D.W. (1994). "Spirituality and Management." *Journal of Managerial Psychology* 9, no. 6: 5–8.

McGee, J.J. (1998). "Corporate Spirituality: An Interdisciplinary Conversation." Paper presented at the annual meeting of the Academy of Management, San Diego, August.

McKnight, R. (1984). "Spirituality in the Workplace." In *Transforming Work: A Collection of Organizational Transformation Readings*, ed. J.D. Adams. Alexandria, VA: Miles River Press, 138–153.

Mirvis, P.H. (1994). "Human Development or Depersonalization? The Company As Total Community." In *A Fatal Embrace? Assessing Holistic Trends in Human Resources Programs*, ed. F.W. Heuberger and L.L. Nash. New Brunswick, NJ: Transaction, 127–154.

———. (1997). "'Soul Work' in Organizations." *Organization Science* 8: 193–206.

Mitroff, I.I., and E.A. Denton. (1999). *A Spiritual Audit of Corporate America: A Hard Look at Spirituality, Religion, and Values in the Workplace.* San Francisco: Jossey-Bass.

Nadesan, M.H. (1999). "The Discourses of Corporate Spiritualism and Evangelical Capitalism." *Management Communication Quarterly* 13: 3–42.

Nash, L.L. (1994). "Reflections: Ethical Questions Every Company Should Ask About Personal Development Programs." In *A Fatal Embrace? Assessing Holistic Trends in Human Resources Programs*, ed. F.W. Heuberger and L.L. Nash. New Brunswick, NJ: Transaction, 181–196.

Neal, J. (2000). "Work As Service to the Divine: Giving Our Gifts Selflessly and with Joy." *American Behavioral Scientist* 43: 1316–1333.

Neck, C.P., and J.F. Milliman. (1994). "Thought Self-Leadership: Finding Spiritual Fulfillment in Organizational Life." *Journal of Managerial Psychology* 9, no. 6: 9–16.

Ohmann, O.A. (1955). "'Skyhooks': With Special Implications for Monday Through Friday." *Harvard Business Review* 33, no. 3: 33–41.

O'Reilly, C.A., and J.A. Chatman. (1996). "Culture As Social Control: Corporations, Cults, and Commitment." In *Research in Organizational Behavior*, vol. 18, ed. B.M. Staw and L.L. Cummings. Greenwich, CT: JAI Press, 157–200.

Palmer, P.J. (1994). "Leading from Within: Out of the Shadow, Into the Light." In *Spirit at Work: Discovering the Spirituality in Leadership*, J.A. Conger and Associates. San Francisco: Jossey-Bass, 19–40.

Pfeffer, J. (1981). "Management As Symbolic Action: The Creation and Maintenance of Organizational Paradigms." In *Research in Organizational Behavior*, vol. 3, ed. L.L. Cummings and B.M. Staw. Greenwich, CT: JAI Press, 1–52.

Pollard, C.W. (1996). *The Soul of the Firm.* New York: HarperBusiness.

Pratt, M.G. (1998). "To Be or Not to Be? Central Questions in Organizational Identification." In *Identity in Organizations: Building Theory Through Conversations*, ed. D.A. Whetten and P.C. Godfrey. Thousand Oaks, CA: Sage, 171–207.

———. (2000a). "Building an Ideological Fortress: The Role of Spirituality, Encapsulation and Sensemaking." *Studies in Cultures, Organizations and Societies* 6: 35–69.

———. (2000b). "The Good, the Bad, and the Ambivalent: Managing Identification Among Amway Distributors." *Administrative Science Quarterly* 45: 456–493.

Pratt, M.G., and J.A. Rosa. (2001). "Transforming Work-Nonwork Ambivalence Into Commitment in Network Marketing Organizations." Working paper, University of Illinois.

Rosenberg, Y. (2001). "Keeping the Faith: A Growing Number of Faith-Based Funds Are Catering to Religious Investors." *Fortune.com:* www.fortune.com (August 3).

Saks, A.M., and B.E. Ashforth. (2002). "Is Job Search Related to Employment Quality? It All Depends on the Fit." *Journal of Applied Psychology* 87: 646–654.

Schneider, B. (1987). "The People Make the Place." *Personnel Psychology* 40: 437–453.

Schor, J.B. (1991). *The Overworked American: The Unexpected Decline of Leisure.* New York: Basic Books.

Scott, K.T. (1994). "Leadership and Spirituality: A Quest for Reconciliation." In *Spirit at Work: Discovering the Spirituality in Leadership*, J.A. Conger and Associates. San Francisco: Jossey-Bass, 63–99.

Stark, R., and R. Finke. (2000). *Acts of Faith: Explaining the Human Side of Religion.* Berkeley, CA: University of California Press.

Tannenbaum, A.S., and R.A. Cooke. (1979). "Organizational Control: A Review of Studies Employing the Control Graph Method." In *Organizations Alike and Unlike: International and Interinstitutional Studies in the Sociology of Organizations*, ed. C.J. Lammers and D.J. Hickson. London: Routledge and Kegan Paul, 183–210.

Triandis, H.C., and D. Trafimow. (2001). "Cross-National Prevalence of Collectivism." In *Individual Self, Relational Self, Collective Self*, ed. C. Sedikides and M.B. Brewer. Philadelphia: Psychology Press, 259–276.

Tworkov, H. (2001). "Contemplating Corporate Culture." *Tricycle: Buddhist Review* (summer): 83–89.

Vaill, P.B. (1990). "Executive Development As Spiritual Development." In *Appreciative Management and Leadership: The Power of Positive Thought and Action in Organizations*, S. Srivastva, D.L. Cooperrider, and Associates. San Francisco: Jossey-Bass, 323–352.

Van Maanen, J., and E.H. Schein. (1979). "Toward a Theory of Organizational Socialization." In *Research in Organizational Behavior*, vol. 1, ed. B.M. Staw. Greenwich, CT: JAI Press, 209–264.

Wagner-Marsh, F., and J. Conley. (1999). "The Fourth Wave: The Spiritually-Based Firm." *Journal of Organizational Change Management* 12: 292–301.

Wisely, D.S., and E.M. Lynn. (1994). "Spirited Connections: Learning to Tap the Spiritual Resources in Our Lives and Work." In *Spirit at Work: Discovering the Spirituality in Leadership*, J.A. Conger and Associates. San Francisco: Jossey-Bass, 100–131.

Wong, P.T.P. (1998). "Spirituality, Meaning, and Successful Aging." In *The Human Quest for Meaning: A Handbook of Psychological Research and Clinical Applications*, ed. P.T.P. Wong and P.S. Fry. Mahwah, NJ: Erlbaum, 359–394.

Young, M.B. (1994). "Hard Bodies, Soft Issues, and the Whole Person: Personal Development Programs in the United States." In *A Fatal Embrace? Assessing Holistic Trends in Human Resources Programs*, ed. F.W. Heuberger and L.L. Nash. New Brunswick, NJ: Transaction, 17–48.

Zucker, L.G. (1977). "The Role of Institutionalization in Cultural Persistence." *American Sociological Review* 42: 726–743.

CHAPTER 7

THE EXPERIENCE OF WORK

Spirituality and the New Workplace

GORDON E. DEHLER AND M. ANN WELSH

> It seems that the day of openly discussing spirituality in
> the workplace is about to arrive.
> —*Cowan (1993, 59)*
>
> It may seem strange to you, as it does to me, to consider
> spirit as something connected to work.
> —*Moxley (2000, 8)*

INTRODUCTION

The evolution toward the "new economy" over the past decade has now turned the corner into the new millennium. The pace and scope of change has been dramatic, transforming Vaill's (1989) description of the business environment as "permanent whitewater" into a stark reality. Driven largely by technological advances, all levels of society have been impacted—from global communities to national economies, from industries to organizations, from work units to individual workers. Much of the attention has centered on the structural aspects of the new economy, particularly the integration of capital markets with technology breakthroughs that inspired dot-com ventures and nudged traditional organizations out of their status-quo orbits. The result, of course, is still in flux as the future unfolds. However, two key lessons are evident.

First, the turbulent environment is driving new ways of thinking and transforming work arrangements. Rather than adapting old solutions to new problems, surviving in the new economy requires a shift in thinking—in essence, adopting a new "paradigm" more amenable to the pace of discontinuous change occurring in a rapidly shrinking global milieu. Thus, the emergence of a "new business paradigm" (e.g., Ray and Rinzler 1993) has prompted a transformation from Newtonian to quantum thinking (Zohar 1997).

Organizationally, one central characteristic associated with this transformation of perspective is the movement toward flatter, more flexible structures. Thanks to dramatic breakthroughs in technology, information flows more freely throughout organizations and is now accessible to everyone rather than being hoarded within the hierarchy. This disrupts traditional power relationships and necessitates the redesign of work—essentially resulting in a movement toward democratizing organizations. The implication for workers in new paradigm organizations is a distinct move toward "knowledge work," which typically involves project-based tasks characterized by problem defining as well as problem solution, increased interdependence with coworkers

108

through collaborative interaction in teams and groups, and endeavors mediated by information technology.

Despite the recent demise of many dot-com firms (not all "new economy"), one irrefutable learning is this: The organizational landscape has been *permanently altered*—there is no turning back to the tried-and-true ways of the past (e.g., Lewis 2001). Thus, the first lesson indicates that the unprecedented rate of change is generating new organizational arrangements characterized by new perspectives on organizing.

The second lesson associated with this transformation concerns the person–work relationship—particularly the psychological, emotional, and spiritual responses that people experience in the conduct of their jobs. Although this topic has a long history in the organization and management theory literature, there has been a proliferation of attention and subsequent articles in the popular press as well as practitioner and academic journals in recent years. Richards (1995) describes this new take on work life in terms of four "energies": physical, mental, emotional, spiritual.

Physical aspects of the work setting have been addressed in the literature under the umbrella of organization and management theory, the Hawthorne studies being one well-known example. The mental, or cognitive, aspect has long been the focus of industrial-organizational psychologists, the precursor of the organizational behavior discipline. Fineman's (1993) view of organizations as "emotional arenas" opened the door to incorporating the emotional component of work in understanding organizational phenomena. Spiritual energies, however, have been less prevalent in the study of organizations. Referred to as the "last corporate taboo" (McDonald 1999, 46), numerous authors (e.g., Richards 1995; Vaill 1989) and journals (e.g., Ottaway 1994) ushered in a proliferation of literature on the topic.

The transformation of organizational arrangements, designed to put meaning into people's work—through mission statements and attention to vision and values—is going to have an emotional impact on people. Today's firm wants the employee to serve a purpose, not just to have a job (Mohrman et al. 1998). Thus, the second lesson is that people bring their *whole* selves to this new workplace—and as a result organizations *must* address the physical, mental, emotional, *and spiritual* needs of their workers (Dehler and Welsh 1994).

This chapter utilizes a framework grounded in the work of Pine and Gilmore (1998), who posit that economic progress has passed through three stages—agrarian, industrial, and service economies—into a fourth stage: the experience economy. Our intention is to extend their ideas into the *experience of work*. The following discussion elaborates historically the changing nature of work design in the industrial, service, and experience economies. These evolving work arrangements dramatically alter people's relationship with their work in each era—ultimately changing the way work is experienced. This can be seen most clearly in the arena of spirituality.

FROM YESTERDAY'S WORKPLACE TO THE NEW WORKPLACE: INDUSTRIAL-, SERVICE-, AND EXPERIENCE-BASED WORK LIVES

In the following sections, we recount the evolution of the work experience from the industrial era and the service economy into the current experience-based world. Our intent is not to attempt a new version of an often-told history, but to highlight relevant aspects of work life consistent with Pine and Gilmore's (1998) framework. There are many excellent sources for the twentieth century's evolution of organizational life, particularly the transformation from traditional forms of management to self-management, from the rule of hierarchy to participation in all facets of organizing. Purser and Cabana (1998) contend that the "knowledge revolution is making conventional management obsolete," leading to a new paradigm based largely on the emergence of knowledge work—"people who think for a living rather than simply following directions" (4–5).

Thus, our design for the following three subsections is to draw from Pine and Gilmore's schema to paint a picture of organizational and work life *as experienced* by workers. Our discussion addresses views on spirituality in the workplace within the broad and admittedly generalized historical context of each era, including general economic conditions, organizing principles, work design, the role of individuals in the work of the organization, and their relationship to their work. While the industrial and service economies are not insignificant, our emphasis will emerge on the present—the experience-based economy.

The Industrial Era: Weberian Bureaucracy, Taylorism, and Compliance

The Industrial Revolution could be characterized as the era of the producer. With the exodus from the farms of the agrarian society to the factories of the city, advances in transportation, communication, and machinery fostered mass production and urbanization. Industrialization for better or worse spawned a growing middle class and enhanced quality of life. The economy grew and expanded. "Professional management" emerged along with developments in work design and organizing that generated economies of scale, which created the possibility of mass markets and mass consumption.

Organizationally, Taylor's principles of scientific management found an audience in industrial society and, linked with Weber's elaboration of bureaucracy, generated the efficiencies consistent with views of the organization-as-machine. Not surprisingly, those best able to invent, develop, and fine-tune *machines*—engineers—were the first professional managers.

Thus, the major corporations of the day tended to be manufacturers who converted natural resources into tangible products using production methods designed to produce a high volume of standardized products, that is, commodities. Differentiating features were superficial, at best, and little attention was paid to market segmentation. Organizational structures were essentially governed by command-and-control hierarchies with clear distinctions between supervisory and line personnel. Managers were paid to think, make decisions, and give direction to subordinates.

Work design was deterministic, employing mass production technologies in order to produce an increasing number of products at lower cost per unit. Job fragmentation consistent with scientific management turned line workers into replaceable parts in a mechanistic process, quickly trained to do simplistic, boring, repetitive jobs. Supervisory responsibilities focused on surveillance to reduce any tendency for employees to slack off or to be creative in their highly regulated jobs. In essence, work tasks were designed to be simple; complex tasks were the purview of those in management.

Work as experienced by individual employees was tedious and revolved around a militaristic ethic of taking orders. The substance of "doing" work was compliance with supervisory directives, conformity to job descriptions, organizational rules, and imposed standards. In return for compliance, workers in the large industrial giants anticipated employment until retirement as long as they stayed in role.

Views on spirituality can only be speculation, of course. Of particular relevance, the emergence of the Human Relations School of management offers some insight. History has been quite critical of the Human Relations movement, not so much for its integration of social, psychological, and contextual influences on human behavior in the workplace, but of the underlying management philosophy. This was an era where workers' primary contribution was physical presence, for example, manual labor. Workers were expected to check their brain at the door—managers were responsible for any thinking required. Thus, historical sense making has criticized the Human Relations School for its manipulative intentions: Attend to workers' sociopsychological well-being, including job satisfaction, for its impact on the bottom line—not because it is the "correct" or humane thing to do. There was no real shift in thinking. Biberman and Whitty (2000) note "that the human relations movement, organization development, and its attendant concepts developed as a reaction to the prevailing modernist (traditional) paradigm, and existed within it, rather than trying to create a new paradigm" (356).

The conclusion, then, can be drawn that spirit and spirituality were not part of the explicit work experience for the majority of employees. The organization–worker relationship was essentially one of inducement–contribution exchange: money for physical labor. Assumptions underlying the motivation and expectations of both employer and employee were largely economically based. The worker's role was to put in time according to an externally imposed routine, earn a wage for family support and survival, and not be concerned with energy or meaning in connection to their job.

The Service Era: Mass Customization, the Organization Man, and Identification

If the industrial era belonged to the producer, the service era belonged to the customer. The ability for organizations to deliver intangible offerings to customers, on demand, characterized this period. Driven largely by new approaches to marketing, mass markets were disaggregated, so goods and especially services could be customized based on demographic and psychometric segmentation, that is, the domain of consumer behavior.

Dramatic improvements in information technology provided a catalyst for delivering services to clients. The emergence of financial services and a host of other personal service industries (e.g., day care, fast food, higher education) fed the increasing pace of busy, two-income lifestyles. In many respects, the principles of Taylorism and Weberian bureaucracy were merely adapted from manufacturing into this service-based economy. Efficiencies still guided "customized" products because categorization of clients allowed for the creation of a set of offerings from which clients could "choose" based on their needs and desires. For example, customers order their own "customized" pizza for delivery to their door but from a constrained choice set determined by Domino's. While differentiating features are the benefits perceived by clients, customization itself is built into organizational routines—mass customization (e.g., Gilmore and Pinc 1997; Schonfeld 1998) became possible through the integration of information technology and production processes. In essence, efficiencies are achieved because the most popular choices are derived from market research, then created "spontaneously" upon demand rather than inventoried or stockpiled as in the industrial era—the key factor being speed in terms of order turnaround time. Individual or small batch processes became possible in everything from restaurants to book publishing to online catalog shopping.

The major corporations of the day shifted from such manufacturers as GM and GE to providers that generated service-based products, such as Xerox, IBM, McDonalds, and TGI Fridays. Clients selected providers based on attributes related to convenience, speed, dependability, and benefits to themselves personally as opposed to features based in the products. Unfortunately, not much really changed organizationally. Governance continued in the command-and-control model, albeit under the umbrella of customer-first rhetoric, maintaining the hierarchy that constituted a traditional career promotional path.

As work itself became more complex, work design was also impacted by the emergence of the service-based economy. Work design was still driven by a Taylorist managerial philosophy, although work processes were less deterministic as standard offerings were configured into services "customized" for clients. Increased emphasis was placed on individual initiative and problem solving in selecting and accessing the most appropriate offering for customers.

The experience of work evolved for the employee as well. Rather than the "check your brain at the door" mentality, more workers were expected to "think"—to engage their cognitive abilities in support of and in relation to production of both manufactured and service-based products. Compliance evolved to identification (Kelman 1958) as workers' relationship to their organizations became mental in addition to physical—the evolution from body to mind, hands to heads.

The classic "Organization Man" (Whyte 1956) bridged the industrial and service eras. In the former, he (most explicitly *he*) was the staff soldier—a mental worker—perhaps an accountant or PR flak surrounded by workers engaged in the *real* work of organizations, that is, physical labor. In the service era, he (and increasingly "she") moved from roles in support of production toward doing the new work of the organization: providing service products directly to clients. The Organization Man became Tom Rath, "*the* man in *the* gray flannel suit" in the 1956 film (Pink 2001, 59) where the quintessential office worker adopted the identity of the organization. Now, who people "were" changed from assembly line worker or craftsman to IBM or Xerox employee. The psychological contract shifted from inducement–contribution exchange based mainly in wages and benefits to institutional values. Assimilation into the organizational value and belief system solidified one's place in the "family"—personal identity connected the individual to the organization. And the relationship endured from hiring to retirement in many large organizations.

Spirituality in the service era was still not an acknowledged concept. Essentially, emotional and spiritual life was partitioned out from organizational life. People adapted by having a work life and a personal life—*separately*. It was a big deal when the two lives collided, for example, when the boss visited for dinner or a backyard neighborhood cookout. Rationality was distinct from emotion, privileged as the mechanism by which "membership" in the company continued until retirement. Organizational values and beliefs were adopted by individuals as a condition of employment. Internal, personal values were subsumed by external, organizational values. "I work on the line" evolved to "I work for IBM."

Spirituality in terms of meaning and purpose was more likely to be provided by religion and faith outside of work life. This perspective was consistent with the Protestant work ethic, whose foundation continues to influence Western culture. The Puritan view "discouraged fun and frivolity and prized frugality and self-sacrifice" (Pink 2001, 65). Work, then, was an endeavor, often construed as unpleasant, to which people accommodated themselves—not a source of fulfillment. "Fun" or "play," as emotionally satisfying, happened only outside of work, not *within* it.

Thus, it is not surprising that current traditional business periodicals such as *Business Week* and *Fortune* confound religion with spirituality in their talk about importing religion into organizational life. Emotions, feelings, and spirituality are foreign to the traditional understandings of *work life* driven by rationality. In essence, from this view the only significant difference between the Organization Man of a half-century ago and today is that it includes the Organization Woman.

The Experience Era: Relationships, Free Agents, and Internalization

Moving forward from the eras of the producer and the customer, the experience economy is characterized by the *relationship* forged between the creator of services and the consumer. In particular, the provider's ability to integrate its services with the customer's needs generates an *experience* that itself becomes the differentiating variable in today's world. An organization's ability to customize a service or product is an imperative, yet not sufficient, condition to meet unique customer requirements. Instead, the challenge is to create an opportunity for consumers to *personalize their experience* in collaboration with the organization.

The classic example is Disney theme parks. The magic and enjoyment of the experience is unique to each visitor based on how they interact with the park. While products and services are in fact delivered, their success is based on the *experience* visitors derive from their interaction with the park. This trend is increasingly evident particularly in formerly "static" venues such as museums, aquariums, and galleries that are now designing "interactive" exhibits to engage visitors in experiences that are absorbing, imaginative, and emotional while expanding the mind (e.g., Dahle 2000). In many instances the intent is to create an educational experience by converting formerly passive viewing into a learning experience that the visitor takes away as "knowledge." For instance, the South Carolina Aquarium's explicit, stated mission is "education": the visitors' experience in interacting with the facility is grounded in "learning."

Other examples are numerous. In retail, at its Wolfsburg, Germany, headquarters, Volkswagen is creating Autostadt, an automotive theme park and new-car pickup center. Conceptualized by a theme-park design consultant to "create experiences that simply can't ever be replicated" elsewhere, the objective is to make an "emotional connection that can really affect purchase decisions and loyalty" (Kirsner 2000a, 138–142). Jungle Jim's in Cincinnati turns a mundane trip to the grocery store into an experience with a jungle pond outside—complete with elephant, giraffe, and flamingos with sound effects—and a mechanical wolf singing Elvis tunes inside. The Library of Congress invites people to visit its Web site and "play around." The ferry across the Irish Sea dramatically alters the traditional passive and monotonous journey by providing passengers with a variety of experiential options from eating at a full-service cafeteria, shopping in the ship's store, watching a movie, or enjoying a pint in the bar.

These examples demonstrate how it is possible for customers to create their own unique interaction that provides enjoyment *in the experience itself* beyond the basic utilitarian objective. The ultimate objective is to foster "experiences that are so distinctive, so compelling, that they stand out" and cannot be duplicated (Kirsner 2000b, 186).

EXPERIENCING THE NEW ECONOMY: LIVING AND WORKING IN THE NEW WORKPLACE

While there are many dimensions that could be offered to describe the New Economy, three are particularly relevant to our discussion of the experience economy: environmental turbulence, information technology, and the democratization of organizations. Without doubt, the pace of change in today's world is relentless. The half-life of products grows shorter, new product development cycle times are contracting, and advantages to first movers are fewer. Technology speeds the flow of information, both within and across organizations. Information available to everyone puts pressure on innovators and makes follower strategies based on economies of scale more viable. And finally, in order to take advantage of greater information access and distribution, organizations are becoming flatter so that they can respond more flexibly and with greater speed to rapidly changing environments. These aspects, as well as many others, provide a context whereby customers can create their own unique experience.

Organizations have responded by viewing their offerings, including tangible goods, as services; for example, General Motors is not an auto manufacturer but a provider of transportation.

But more importantly, the people who work for these new economy organizations become knowledge workers who not only apply their expertise to the tasks at hand, but also must employ emotional labor in the conduct of their jobs (e.g., Hochschild 1983). As organizations become flatter, not only do workers need to build communication skills to collaborate with coworkers, but with customers as well. That is, increasingly more workers come in contact with the actual users of their products and services. Visitors to the Waterford Crystal factory in Ireland view workers directly as they undertake their crafts of glassblowing and glass cutting. Master craftsmen are available to interact directly with visitors, answering questions and demonstrating their skills. This changes the traditional worker role from one of isolation from the consumer to being part of the consumer's experience.

The nature of work in the new economy also changes the relationship between workers and organizations. Traditional relationships based on mutual loyalty are being replaced by "free agents" (Pink 2001). Free agents essentially shift their loyalty to the work they do in connection with employers on a project basis. This does not preclude long-term relationships with employers, but the nature of the psychological contract shifts from long-term expectations to a series of short-term renewable relationships based on knowledge rather than employer identification or physical presence. In fact, if expertise and organization-specific knowledge is vital to organizations, it is in their interest to retain valued employees over the long term.

As workers forge new careers based on skill and expertise rather than organizational membership, work itself takes on a greater emotional component. Instead of being the means to the end, the work that people do becomes the end. That is, *doing the work* serves as a source of enjoyment, satisfaction, and fulfillment. Purpose and meaning are more closely linked to what we do—embedded in our endeavors more deeply and with greater emotional connection. This revolves around "*why* we do what we do" rather than "*how* we do what we do" (Richards 1995, 65, emphasis in original). The answer leads into the realm of spirituality.

SPIRITUALITY'S OWN SEARCH FOR MEANING

The notion of spirituality has been invoked in a variety of contexts, including work itself (Richards 1995), the workplace (Mitroff and Denton 1999a, 1999b), organizational transformation (Dehler and Welsh 1994), leadership (e.g., Moxley 2000; Vaill 1998), and management education (Dehler and Neal 2000; Delbecq 2000). If recent business press cover stories (Conlin 1999; Gunther 2001) and newspaper accounts (e.g., Broadway 2001) are an indicator, the topic is generating heightened interest beyond academics to the realm of practitioners.

While there are a variety of definitions of spirituality, the perspective on spirit and spirituality *in the context of work*, and the one employed in this chapter, remains grounded in our earlier work (Dehler and Welsh 1994). We do not claim that this is *the* (only) definition nor the "correct" one.[1] Our position is that when spirit is described as a search for meaning, aspirations beyond instrumentality, deeper self-knowledge, or transcendence to a higher level, writers are in actuality defining spirit in terms of *emotion*—internalized and personal *feelings of* meaning, purpose, knowing, and being. Such felt emotion serves to *energize* action; thus, *spirit* is a form of energy. Feelings and emotion themselves can't be observed until they are expressed as behavior; thus, *spirituality* is the *expression* of spirit, behaviorally or cognitively. Workers *act* spiritually when their inner being believes and embraces a purpose larger than themselves. Csikszentmihalyi's (1990) notion of a "flow state" is perhaps the closest analogy to inspirited behavior. Therefore, in our view spirit represents an inner source of energy, and spirituality the outward expression of that force.

SPIRITUALITY AS EXPERIENCED IN THE WORKPLACE

Handy (1998) notes that, like people, organizations are also "hungry spirits at heart" (149). This has a significant impact in the arena of spirituality in the new workplace. How we experience our work becomes increasingly central to our lives because it serves as a "source of spiritual growth," suggesting that organizations today need to meet the meaning needs of their members (Mirvis 1997, 199). Historically, people have talked a great deal *about* their work and their work lives, but seldom did they venture below the surface to address how they actually *experienced* their work. That is changing today, likely as a result of a combination of forces including higher levels of education both attained and required to do work today. As more people pursue higher learning in college and elsewhere, their expectations similarly increase. They bring the desire to engage their acquired skills more fully and to attain a sense of fulfillment from being challenged by their work. Handy (1998) describes this in the context of the "white stone," a biblical reference to finding the "hidden self." "Life is a search for the white stone," (84) he writes, a search for meaning. Similarly, in connecting work to art, Richards (1995) observes that when "the poet does his work, he changes"(91). The experience of work in the new workplace involves the commitment of "self" in how we relate to what we do.

The underlying issue, of course, rests on the development of self-knowledge. People bring their whole selves to the workplace and seek to integrate work into their lives. This is more readily accomplished if their personal values are consistent with the organization's values. Leading spirituality consultant Richard Barrett (Dorsey 1998) proposes that both companies and people do well when there is alignment between organizational and individual beliefs and values (Dehler and Welsh 1994). Workplaces that allow people to remain true to their deepest beliefs in their daily work, he posits, provide not only an outlet for personal expression but will "become the only way for companies to make a profit," because it creates the context for creativity (Dorsey 1998, 128).

Kouzes and Posner (1995) confirm that research indicates that commitment is greater when people have greater clarity of personal and organizational values. Interestingly, however, findings suggest that people who possess greater self-knowledge about their personal values exhibit equally high levels of commitment even when organizational values are unclear! Individuals with the clearest personal values are better prepared to make choices based on principles—their own or the organization's (218–219).

There is another side to this topic, of course—a darker side—that deserves attention. Like any other management notion, spirituality does not offer the ubiquitous "solution" to coping with the complexities of organizational life. The most serious danger may be managerial attempts to exploit the emotional side of work by turning it into an instrumentality, that is, embrace people's spiritual side *because* it impacts the bottom line, rather than treating people as complete human beings as the "right" thing to do. Inevitably, there will be tension in the relationship between workers and their institutions, in part as a result of business cycles. For instance, are "responsible corporate leaders," faced with layoff decisions during economic downturns (Hammonds 1996) being true to their workers' spiritual needs? Such motives are dilemmas yet to be resolved.

There are, however, legitimate concerns about the usurpation of first the body, then the mind, and now the heart of workers by employers. The potential for spirituality to become another management fad persists. Welch (1998) warns that "there are real concerns that a boundary between the personal and the professional is being breached without any thought given to the consequences, and that the enthusiastic naïveté will do more harm than good" (33). Comments by an organizational psychologist at Birkbeck College in London raise further concerns: "There has been a huge increase in the level of emotional buy-in expected of employees—of 'you have to believe in this management' . . . Business is quite 'culty' already. So I wouldn't want to see personal values being raided for corporate ends'" (Welch 1998, 33).

Like anything else, extremes can be unhealthy. When "what you do is who you are," the potential for dysfunction is salient. Through highly insightful yet moving personal accounts, Kruger (1999) presents several cautionary tales of people—interestingly, mostly women—who felt "betrayed" (184) by allowing their work to become too personal. The dilemma, according to psychologist Ilene Philipson, is that work turned into the sole passion for her clients. It became their "primary source of self-esteem, recognition, respect" (Kruger 1999, 184).

The paradox, of course, is striking. As work consumes more of our lives and has become central to how we define ourselves, where we find meaning and purpose, "that's exactly what makes the new world of work so inspiring. It's also what makes it so treacherous" (Kruger 1999, 186). Since our "greatest sources of satisfaction in the workplace are internal and emotional" (Schwartz 2000, 400), it stands to reason that people run the risk of setting themselves up for disappointment and emotional harm. While there may be constructive coping strategies, perhaps recognizing and acknowledging the reality of the new workplace is the best place to start. Pink (2001) points out that the Organization Man's era of the "benevolent corporation" is over. And loyalty in the workplace? "Consider it dead," he says (95). In the current work environment, workers' first loyalty should be to their work as opposed to an organization. This makes them less vulnerable to toxic work situations, abusive bosses, and economic disruptions. Loyalty to profession, peers, family, friends, clients, and customers replaces devotion to an employer.

While not everyone needs to become a free agent, it is clear that a "career" has little to do any more with a long-term relationship with an employer. Instead, it has more to do with building personal competencies and connections—employability by combining talent with opportunity. Richards (1995) likens this to the artist's notion of "centering," where workers aim at "bringing the body, mind, emotion and spirit together in the workplace" (100).

The new workplace, then, becomes a place where people not only *do* work, but create an experience in the context of their work. It is a site for personal expression and fulfillment. When we bring our interior life to work, it changes us (Richards, 1995). The experience itself provides meaning and purpose—in short, the energy to pursue personal growth. In essence, this is the spirit of the new workplace—the opportunity to transcend the physical and cognitive demands into the world of emotional connection: doing *in*spirited work. And when the purposes and values of the organization are congruent with individuals, alignment provides the basis for internalization of belief systems.

In the next section we turn our attention to the evolution of "academic" treatments of spirituality and work. Our interest is in presenting some guidelines for thinking and writing about spirituality that could lead to substantive theory building.

THE STUDY OF SPIRITUALITY: THEORETICAL DEVELOPMENT

In spite of the increased attention and expanding literature on spirituality in the past few years, there has been little accompanying theory development. This is due in part to the relative newness of the topic itself as well as to the limited explication of its meaning. While it would be overly optimistic to expect definitional consensus to emerge at this early stage, definitional concerns obviously represent a critical starting point in developing a theory of spirituality in the workplace. While this section is not intended to delve deeply into theoretical and methodological concerns, a few points are worthy of considering as practitioners and academics contemplate spirituality in the workplace.

A basic starting point is the prospect of spirituality as a construct or a concept. Constructs have no objective reality, cannot be observed, and exist in people's heads only because they can be inferred from results of observable phenomena, that is, "mental abstractions designed to give meaning to ideas or interpretations" (Cameron and Whetton 1983, 7). In contrast, concepts "can be defined and exactly specified by observing objective events" (Cameron and Whetton 1983, 7). Invoking our prior work, we have proposed that, definitionally, "spirit" represents a construct, that is, an unobservable feeling or emotion analogous to motivation, and that "spirituality" is a concept, observable as behavior (Dehler and Welsh 1994). Yet, this is merely a beginning for considering a "theory" of spirituality in the workplace.

Sutton and Staw (1995) remind us that references, data, variables, diagrams, and hypotheses are *not* theory. Yet Weick (1995) counters that these five attributes may be part of the early stages of theoretical development and represent the "struggles" that complicate the "process of theorizing" (385). Indeed, that is perhaps the present stage of theoretical evolution of spirituality: an early phase of exploration in raising the prospect of a "theory of spirituality." If we review the spirituality literature, we see elements of the above—yet can make no claim that there has been much progress on true theoretical development.

In terms of references, a perusal of this chapter, as well as the entire collection in this volume, provides evidence that there has been much written on the topic. Citations in-and-of-themselves do not provide compelling arguments on a phenomenon (Sutton and Staw 1995). Turning to data, empirical studies of spirituality are sparse. Two different approaches have been advanced—one exploratory and the other definitional. Mitroff and Denton (1999a, 1999b) addressed the legitimacy of raising issues of spirituality and religion in the workplace while Ashmos and Duchon (2000) attempted to develop and empirically assess dimensions of spirituality. Each falls short, though, of explaining "*why* empirical patterns were observed or are expected to be observed" (Sutton and Staw 1995, 374).

Lists of variables, likewise, are not theory. Various scholars have related spirituality to other concepts, including empowerment (Lee 1991), leadership (Fairholm 1997, 2000), transformation (Dehler and Welsh 1994), and educational endeavors such as executive development (Delbecq 2000) and management learning (Dehler and Welsh 1997). So far, however, these treatments offer little in the way of systematic theory building. Theories need to "explain why variables or constructs come about or why they are connected" (Sutton and Staw 1995, 375). Similarly, diagrams, "by themselves, rarely constitute theory" (Sutton and Staw 1995, 376). Thus, theorizing would emerge from the table provided by Dehler and Welsh (1994) juxtaposing spirituality in organizational transformation with organizational development when accompanied by logical explanations of the suggested relationships.

Finally, hypotheses have not been developed to bridge theory and data. To be sure, there are implicit hypotheses in the literature. Ashmos and Duchon (2000) state that their approach to spirituality was explicitly grounded in understanding "how spirituality can contribute to more productive work organizations" (143). In this sense, spirituality is clearly an independent variable; the unstated hypothesis is that higher levels of spirituality will be related to higher levels of productivity. This suggests that a managerial strategy fostering spirituality will serve as a competitive advantage (Mitroff and Denton 1999b). Again, though, hypotheses represent "concise statements about *what* is expected to occur, not *why* it is expected to occur" (Sutton and Staw 1995, 377). As such, hypotheses alone do not constitute theory.

In summary, our view concerning spirituality is that it has reached a point where it is time for taking a more rigorous approach to theory building. As Weick (1995) notes, "most of what passes for theory in organizational studies consists of approximations" (385). The central issue, however, is whether the work on spirituality that has been conducted thus far represents "interim struggles in which people intentionally inch toward stronger theories" (385) in an early stage of progress along a continuum; "it is tough to judge whether something is a theory or not when only the product itself is examined. What one needs to know, instead, is more about the context in which the product lives. This is the process of theorizing" (387). The task that lies before us is to pursue consensus about what constitutes spirituality in the workplace (definition); to explore its workplace antecedents and consequences (relationships and connections); and to specify the value that consideration of spirituality has for practicing managers (rule out alternative explanations). And so, it is now up to those who invoke spirituality in their studies of the new workplace to demonstrate that their products move beyond mere theoretical "substitutes for theory (that) may result from lazy theorizing" (Weick 1995, 385).

CONCLUSION

What, then, is the place of spirituality in the new workplace as we look to the future? Where do we go from here? Is this a fad, to go the way of Total Quality Management and business process reengineering? Perhaps. But our view is more optimistic. Spirit and spirituality, per se, do not involve a set of prescriptions nor techniques. The key concerns are twofold: recognizing that people in the new workplace bring their whole selves to their jobs—including their heart and soul—and that work needs to be designed to be challenging in order to energize, or more appropriately *inspirit*, people in relating to their tasks. This suggests a fundamental employer or managerial philosophy that seeks to align workers' values with the organization's purpose *beyond the bottom line*. Acknowledging the imperative of being fiscally solvent, if spirituality is invoked only "because" it enhances the bottom line, then it will fail because talent and knowledge will walk out the door in search of meaning. On the other hand, if spirituality is invoked because it is the *right thing to do* in creating a thriving workplace where individual and organizational outcomes are integrated, then its future is promising.

Contemporary ideas and developments in organizations are largely extensions and refinements of earlier concepts. The roots of most initiatives in organizations and management thinking thread their way back to earlier concepts. For instance, Butts (2000, 37) observed that spirituality might be related to "human potential programs," for example, meditation, prayer, guided imagery (visioning). Similarly, Vaill (2000, 115) pointed out that commentators have been "noting what an organizational society we have become and how profoundly the nature of organizations affects human character, human development, and human feeling." Others focused on the impact organizations have on workers' relationship to their work. Marshall (1995) studied middle- and senior-level female managers who chose to leave successful management positions. In their case, achieving an identity they valued was not possible in the context of their work. In traditional terms, their career success led to "unbalanced" lives, that is, the more typical tension between work demands and home–family demands. Marshall notes that men leave jobs, too, but it seems "that men who choose to redirect lives do so by moving from one employed identity to another which they feel has more inherent value—the oil-executive-to-schoolteacher style of transition—rather than by challenging the assumptions of employment" (14).

Thus, today's worker is faced with both the traditional tradeoffs of balance and the realities of intermittent project-based employment consistent with free agents. In addition, economic cycles will continue to force even the most conscientious organizations to undertake periodic workforce contractions. It may become even more important, then, that individuals are able to generate and perpetuate passion for what they do by treating work as an opportunity for personal growth. More enlightened organizations will seek to create a thriving workplace where people cannot only be "productive," but connect on a cognitive, emotional, and spiritual level with the *doing* of their work. As products increasingly become commodities, organizations will need to redefine themselves as "purveyors of customer experiences" (Kirsner 2001, 50) and "compete on service and customer experience in addition to price" (54).

In conclusion, spirituality not only has a place in the new workplace, it is integral to what the new workplace represents. Contemporary organizations need to nurture employees spiritually by *sharing* the responsibility to meet their spiritual needs. Cowan (1993) reinforces this point: "Spirituality is like gravity. It must be taken into account because it is there. Ignore it and you are ignoring the most central fact of any human situation" (61).

NOTE

1. While it seems reasonable to call for clarity and a theoretical understanding of spirituality (Butts 2000), conceptual dilemmas persist because definitional consensus is easier said than done. This has been true of many constructs in organization studies. For example, as important and popular as leadership has been in the study of organizations and management, there is no agreement among scholars or practitioners on a single definition. Some may view this as a liability. But it has not constrained the proliferation of writing on the topic! In fact, it could be argued that over time such disagreement has actually enhanced the study of leadership by leading to richer descriptions and theoretical development—transformational and servant leadership being two current examples. The key point is that it is vital to *critically* explore the variety of meanings, articulate an interpretation that enhances understanding, and raise these understandings to the surface for public scrutiny and scholarly critique.

While definition of "spirituality" may therefore be problematic, conceptual clarity is not. Making distinctions between spirituality and other concepts is essential; stating meaning with clarity and precision in the context of a particular viewpoint is imperative. For example, recent *Business Week* and *Fortune* cover stories (Conlin 1999; Gunther 2001) confound spirituality with religion by using the terms interchangeably. The implication, of course, is that the two concepts have similar meaning. While for some that may be true, the authors made no attempt to address criticisms of those who might refute such a position.

On the other hand, to dodge definition by posing spirituality as a question: "What is spirituality for you?" (Rutte 2000, 32) similarly is not helpful. Of course spirituality is personal, as is "motivation"; however, that does not mean there are not common or *generalizable* aspects or dimensions that can be employed across individuals. At the other extreme, the Department of Education in the United Kingdom has declared an "official definition of spirituality: 'The valuing of the nonmaterial aspects of life, and intimations of an enduring reality'" (Handy 1998, 102). How helpful it might be to have an "official" definition is not readily evident, let alone figuring out what it means!

Other definitions dance around the term itself. Richards (1995) uses "spirit" and "soul" interchangeably. "Spiritual energy" arises from beliefs about unseen forces that shape our reality (14). Moxley (2000) notes that "spirit defines our self at the deepest levels of our being" (8). Mitroff and Denton (1999a) define spirituality primarily in terms of "connectedness"—"with one's complete self, others, and the entire universe" (83), Vaill (1998) is less concerned with "definitional precision," suggesting it may be necessary at some point, but that his interest is in what organization members mean when they talk about "spiritual aspects of life" (177–178). Handy (1998) connects spirit to "purpose." Note that these representative "definitions" focus more on deeply held personal beliefs in the *existence* of spirit and its manifestation—yet do little to actually specify a substantive definition of "spirit" or "spirituality."

Perhaps the central question is: Can one be "spiritual" without being religious? There is no ultimate answer to this. It is reasonable that people of religious faith equate spirituality with religion. But, it is also important to recognize that such expression is *value based*, that is, grounded in a particular worldview. Daniels, Franz, and Wong (2000) present a constructive framework that elaborates four distinct perspectives grounded in the "foundational context of one's worldview" (541). They describe modern, post-modern, mystical, and theistic worldviews based on the values people hold concerning the nature of reality (ontology) and ways of knowing (epistemology). Christian and other Western religious views fall within the theistic quadrant and outside the other three.

Thus, when Thompson (2000) takes issue with our (Dehler and Welsh 1994) and other views of spirituality, he is doing so from *his own* expressed worldview that "spirituality concerns the relationship between the human spirit and the divine spirit, between the human being and God" (63). The obverse position articulated by Moxley (2000) suggests that although "spirit often conjures up images of religious belief systems . . . when I talk of spirit . . . I am not talking about religion . . . I do not believe that one *has to be* religious to be spiritual" (24, emphasis added). This is a prevalent position in the organizational and management literature. Indeed, in their groundbreaking empirical study of spirituality in the workplace, Mitroff and Denton (1999a) note that respondents "differentiated strongly between religion and spirituality" (83).

If one *must be* religious in order to be spiritual, then those who are not religious *cannot be* spiritual. Our own personal value system cannot accept this exclusionary perspective, as it is inconceivable that the nonreligious cannot feel the energy of spirit and express it spiritually in behaviors and cognition. The irony, of course, is that it does not matter if there is a "correct" position as long as the author's values are made explicit. We hope our position is clear.

It should be clear from the above that definitional distinctions concerning problematic constructs are a *choice* driven by underlying personal values and cultural biases. This is particularly salient when addressing the issue of the relationship between spirituality and religion. This issue is an appropriate ongoing dialog and has been the subject of debate (e.g., Schneiders 2000). Our explicit point is that we find our own definition (Dehler and Welsh 1994) useful and employ it consistently in our work, for better or worse! This is an ongoing conversation, however, in which we welcome critique in the spirit of dialog.

REFERENCES

Ashmos, D.P., and D. Duchon. (2000). "Spirituality at Work: A Conceptualization and Measure." *Journal of Management Inquiry* 9, no. 2: 134–145.

Biberman, J., and M.D. Whitty. (2000). "A Postmodern Spiritual Future for Work." In *Work and Spirit: A Reader of New Spiritual Paradigms for Organizations*, ed. J. Biberman and M.D. Whitty. Scranton, PA: University of Scranton Press, 351–361.

Broadway, B. (2001). "Good for the Soul—and for the Bottom Line." *Washington Post*, August 19, A-1, A-15.

Butts, D. (2000). "Spirituality at Work: An Overview." In *Work and Spirit: A Reader of New Spiritual Paradigms for Organizations*, ed. J. Biberman and M.D. Whitty. Scranton, PA: University of Scranton Press, 35–39.

Cameron, K.S., and D.A. Whetton. (1983). "Organizational Effectiveness: One Model or Several?" In *Organizational Effectiveness: A Comparison of Models*, ed. K.S. Cameron and D.A. Whetten. New York: Academic Press, 1–24.

Conlin, M. (1999). "Religion in the Workplace." *Business Week* (November 1): 150–158.

Cowan, J. (1993). *The Common Table: Reflections and Meditations on Community and Spirituality in the Workplace*. New York: HarperBusiness.

Csikszentmihalyi, M. (1990). *Flow: The Psychology of Optimal Experience*. New York: Harper and Row.

Dahle, C. (2000). "Museums with a Mission." *Fast Company* 34 (May): 220–232.

Daniels, D.; R.S. Franz; and K. Wong. (2000). "A Classroom with a Worldview: Making Spiritual Assumptions Explicit in Management Education." *Journal of Management Education* 24, no. 5: 540–561.

Dehler, G., and J. Neal, eds. (2000). Special Issue: "Spirituality in Contemporary Work: Its Place, Space, and Role in Management Education." *Journal of Management Education* 24, no. 5.

Dehler, G.E., and M.A. Welsh. (1997). "Discovering the Keys: Spirit in Teaching and the Journey of Learning." *Journal of Management Education* 21, no. 4: 496–508.

———. (1994). "Spirituality and Organizational Transformation: Implications for the New Management Paradigm." *Journal of Managerial Psychology* 9, no. 6: 17–26.

Delbecq, A. (2000). "Spirituality for Business Leadership: Reporting on a Pilot Course for MBAs and CEOs." *Journal of Management Inquiry* 9, no. 2: 117–128.

Dorsey, D. (1998). "The New Spirit of Work." *Fast Company* 16 (August): 125–134.

Fairholm, G. (2000). *Perspectives on Leadership: From the Science of Management to Its Spiritual Heart*. Westport, CT: Praeger.

———. (1997). *Capturing the Heart of Leadership: Spirituality and Community in the New American Workplace*. Westport, CT: Praeger.

Fineman, S., ed. (1993). *Emotion in Organizations*. Newbury Park, CA: Sage.

Gilmore, J.H., and B.J. Pine. (1997). "The Four Faces of Mass Customization." *Harvard Business Review* (January–February): 91–101.

Gunther, M. (2001). "God and Business." *Fortune* (July 9): 58–80.

Hammonds, K.H. (1996). "Soul-searching in the Corner Office." *Business Week* (May 13): 42–43.

Handy, C. (1998). *The Hungry Spirit: Beyond Capitalism: A Quest for Purpose in the Modern World*. New York: Broadway Books.

Hochschild, A.R. (1983). *The Managed Heart: Commercialization of Human Feeling*. Berkeley: University of California Press.

Kelman, H.C. (1958). "Compliance, Identification, and Internalization: Three Processes of Attitude Change." *Journal of Conflict Resolution* 2: 51–60.

Kirsner, S. (2001). "Banking on Tomorrow." *Fast Company* 51 (October): 50–54.

———. (2000a). "Collision Course." *Fast Company* 31 (January/February): 118–144.

———. (2000b). "Experience Required." *Fast Company* 39 (October): 184–202.

Kouzes, J.M., and B.Z. Posner. (1995). *The Leadership Challenge*. San Francisco: Jossey-Bass.

Kruger, P. (1999). "Betrayed By Work." *Fast Company* 29 (November): 182–196.

Lee, M. (1991). "Spirituality and Organizations: Empowerment and Purpose." *Management Education and Development* 22: 221–226.

Lewis, M. (2001). *Next: The Future Just Happened*. New York: Norton.

Marshall, J. (1995). *Women Managers Moving on: Exploring Career and Life Choices*. London: Routledge.

McDonald, M. (1999). "Shush. The Guy in the Cubicle Is Meditating: Spirituality Is the Latest Corporate Buzzword." *U.S. News and World Report* 126, no. 17: 46–47.

Mirvis, P.H. (1997). " 'Soul Work' in Organizations." *Organization Science* 8, no. 2: 193–206.

Mitroff, I.I., and E.A. Denton. (1999a). "A Study of Spirituality in the Workplace." *Sloan Management Review* (summer): 83–92.

———. (1999b). *A Spiritual Audit of Corporate America: A Hard Look at Spirituality, Religion, and Values in the Workplace*. San Francisco: Jossey-Bass.

Mohrman, S.A.; J.R. Galbraith; E.E. Lawler; and Associates. (1998). *Tomorrow's Organization*. San Francisco: Jossey-Bass.

Moxley, R.S. (2000). *Leadership and Spirit: Breathing New Vitality and Energy into Individuals and Organizations*. San Francisco: Jossey-Bass.

Ottaway, R.N., ed. (1994). Special Issue: "Spirituality in Work Organizations." *Journal of Managerial Psychology* 9, no. 6.

Pink, D.H. (2001). *Free Agent Nation: How America's New Independent Workers Are Transforming the Way We Live*. New York: Warner Books.

Pine, B.J., and J.H. Gilmore. (1998). "Welcome to the Experience Economy." *Harvard Business Review* (July–August): 97–105.

Purser, R.E., and S. Cabana. (1998). *The Self Managing Organization: How Leading Companies Are Transforming the Work of Teams for Real Impact*. New York: Free Press.

Ray, M. and A. Rinzler. (1993). *The New Paradigm of Business*. New York: Jeremy P. Tarcher/Perigee Books.

Richards, D. (1995). *Artful Work: Awakening Joy, Meaning, and Commitment in the Workplace*. San Francisco: Barrett-Koehler.

Rutte, M. (2000). "Spirituality in the Workplace." In *Work and Spirit: A Reader of New Spiritual Paradigms for Organizations*, ed. J. Biberman and M.D. Whitty. Scranton, PA: University of Scranton Press, 29–34.

Schneiders, S.M. (2000). "Religion and Spirituality: Strangers, Rivals, or Partners?" *Santa Clara Lectures* 6, no. 2 (February 6): 1–16.

Schonfeld, E. (1998). "The Customized, Digitized, Have-It-Your-Way Economy." *Fortune* (September 28): 114–124.

Schwartz, T. (2000). "The Greatest Sources of Satisfaction in the Workplace Are Internal and Emotional." *Fast Company* 40 (November): 398–402.

Sutton, R.I., and B.M. Staw. (1995). "What Theory Is *Not*." *Administrative Science Quarterly* 40, no. 3: 371–384.

Thompson, C.M. (2000). *The Congruent Life: Following the Inward Path to Fulfilling Work and Inspired Leadership*. San Francisco: Jossey-Bass.

Vaill, P. (2000). "Introduction to Spirituality for Business Leadership." *Journal of Management Inquiry* 9, no. 2: 115–116.

Vaill, P.B. (1998). *Process Wisdom for a New Age*. San Francisco: Jossey-Bass.

———. (1989). *Managing As a Performing Art: New Ideas for a World of Chaotic Change*. San Francisco: Jossey-Bass.

Weick, K.E. (1995). "What Theory Is *Not*, Theorizing *Is*." *Administrative Science Quarterly* 40, no. 3: 385–390.

Welch, J. (1998). "Creed Is Good." *People Management* 24, no. 5: 28–33.

Whyte, W.H., Jr. (1956). *The Organization Man*. Garden City: Doubleday Anchor.

Zohar, D. (1997). *Rewiring the Corporate Brain: Using New Science to Rethink How We Structure and Lead Organizations*. San Francisco: Berrett-Koehler.

CHAPTER 8

SPIRITUAL WELL-BEING, SPIRITUAL INTELLIGENCE, AND HEALTHY WORKPLACE POLICY

RAYMOND F. PALOUTZIAN, ROBERT A. EMMONS, AND SUSAN G. KEORTGE

OVERVIEW: TRANSCENDENCE AND WORK MOTIVATION

At the level of everyday discourse, we could say that people work for a variety of obvious reasons. We need food, shelter, clothing, transportation, and social contact; and work and the money that is obtained from it is the major way in the modern world by which we get these things. For the social psychologist and the psychologist of religion, however, such "ordinary life" analyses are not sufficient. Instead, we need to know what social and mental processes regulate why people go to work, sustain it over the long haul, do or do not overcome the problems that occur therein, and find identity and meaning in it. We believe that a knowledge of these things can help us create healthier work environments and can provide the psychological model for both improving worker performance while at the same time minimizing conflict, stress, and worker dissatisfaction.

Our overriding idea is that the best performance and the greatest happiness of workers happen when they believe in what they are doing and when they feel free rather than compelled in the doing of it. That is, people are motivated to pursue transcendent goals and when they are doing this, they are more likely to continue to work, even at seemingly mundane tasks, for longer periods of time and are more likely to be content to do so. In addition, they are more likely to engage in those interpersonal behaviors that would foster trust, a sense of being part of a team, a healthy atmosphere, and that would demonstrate commitment to the employer and its goals. The employer and employee each are more likely to see the other as collaborator and coworker trying to achieve a common goal.

In order to build the argument for this idea and the rationale for our recommendations for what the features of a healthy work environment would be, it is necessary to:

1. introduce the concept of spiritual well-being, summarize research on it, and explore its implications for the workplace;
2. present the concept of spiritual intelligence, which we think is a powerful theoretical notion within which spiritual well-being and other ideas pertinent to workplace concerns can be integrated; and
3. apply the theory and research on these ideas to the practical problems of the workplace, with the purpose of stating recommendations for what would constitute an environment of optimum health.

Let us explore these three topics in the following sections of this chapter.

SPIRITUAL WELL-BEING, TRANSCENDENCE, AND WORK

It is well known that people bring to work whatever is inside their own emotional and value systems. It is nothing new that people may approach their work for reasons that might be called "spiritual." In ancient times, for example, as is evident by Judeo-Christian scriptures, those who believed in God were admonished to do good service for their employers (be the employers land owners, slave owners, or members of the Roman government) in glory to their God. Doing a good job was not merely for the sake of earning a living or only to please or avoid punishment from the master. Nor was it to be done for more "modern" concerns, such as to enhance one's self-esteem or self-actualization, nor to fulfill one's own selfish goals and purposes. Good work was to be done for a higher calling. It was imbued with spiritual meaning because it was to be performed wholeheartedly in God's service. Indeed, for Christians, because faith without works was said to be "dead" (James 2:17), the level of one's works might have been seen as an indication of the maturity of one's faith. Simply put, good work evidenced a full spiritual commitment.

Spirituality and the Need for Transcendence

Imagine the following scenario: I (RFP) spend many hours writing this chapter here in my office in beautiful Santa Barbara, California, only five minutes from my home, the ocean, a lovely café, and dolphins jumping out of the water. Why not stop writing and go enjoy the beach and sand and sunshine? Do I get more money for doing this? No. More job security? No, I am tenured. More self-esteem? I have enough. Such things are good and we need a certain amount of them, but in the end, even if all such "mundane" needs are met, a steady diet of even sweet Santa Barbara doesn't satisfy. I need something else, something meaningful to do. Writing this chapter does something for me that a steady diet of sun, surf, and a positive self-image cannot do—it fulfills a need I have to write and create and contribute to something bigger than me. I get a sense of spiritual fulfillment from it, a sense of well-being that comes no other way. This reflects a need for transcendence, a need for purpose, and a built-in tendency toward spirituality that is part of what makes a person human. Whatever else people are, we are creatures who strive to fulfill a sense of meaning for whatever we feel is important, something to which we can contribute and that will perhaps endure after we die. We begin, therefore, with the premise that human beings have this need for transcendence built into their psychological makeup. If this is so, then this idea has an important argument to offer managers, employees, academic deans, CEOs, governments, union leaders, and all those concerned with how the environments in which we work affect people (Ellison 1983).

This need for transcendence expresses itself as what is commonly called "spirituality." Spirituality is a vague term that in some circles connotes a NewAge, head-in-the-clouds mindset, although more traditional usage would focus on religion as the source and expression of "true" spirituality. More recently, the term spirituality has also come to hold a nonreligious meaning, a tendency for one to strive for those values and purposes that express whatever the individual person feels is ultimately meaningful to him or her. Overall, therefore, spirituality might be called the tendency to guide thoughts, feelings, and behavior by the gist or idea of whatever is beyond and seen as ultimately important, which can be expressed both religiously and nonreligiously (Pargament 1999; Zinnbauer, Pargament, Cole et al. 1997). Religious spirituality connotes doing something for God or a Higher Power, or whatever is seen as a derivative of God's teaching or values. Nonreligious spirituality, whether or not a person justifies it in an ultimate philosophical sense, is the striving for the fulfillment of any value, goal, or higher calling that the individual believes to be meaningful.

SPIRITUAL WELL-BEING

Within the general rubric of spirituality we can also distinguish between the expression of it, or those feelings that follow from it, and the psychological process through which it is mediated. *Spiritual well-being* (SWB) is a self-perceived state of the degree to which one feels a sense of satisfaction in relation to God (in the case of religious well-being, RWB) or a sense of purpose and direction (in the case of existential well-being, EWB) (Ellison 1983; Paloutzian and Ellison 1982). *Spiritual intelligence* (SI), on the other hand, refers to the degree to which a person has the mental and emotional properties that lead one to see an overall, guiding purpose; to see mid- and short-term tasks as subgoals that are connected to the larger purpose; and to sustain behavior in order to serve them (Emmons 1999, 2000). SWB, therefore, can be considered a psychological reflection of how much spiritual wellness one perceives, whereas SI can best be seen as a process through which SWB and other emotional and behavioral processes are regulated and sustained.

Spiritual Well-Being as a Social Indicator

Paloutzian and Ellison (1982) originally conceived of the SWB scale as a tool to assess the perceived quality of spiritual life as understood by the individual person. But it was also created to be a social indicator—a way of measuring the level at which individuals or society are functioning (Moberg 1979; Moberg and Brusek 1978). And because SWB is thought of by people in both religious and nonreligious ways, the SWB scale had both religious well-being (RWB) and existential well-being (EWB) subscales. The development of this is documented elsewhere[1] (Bufford, Paloutzian, and Ellison 1991; Ellison 1983; Paloutzian and Ellison 1982) and need not be repeated here. To be highlighted here, however, is that the same concerns that were behind people's need for transcendence or a healthy sense of well-being and functioning in society as a whole, apply to people's life on the job. Therefore, those findings that come from the general body of research on the relationships between SWB and healthy or unhealthy functioning in other life domains, are easily applicable to our understanding of what makes for a healthy or unhealthy work life.

For example, knowing that people who have low SWB have a greater probability of being depressed (Bufford, Renfroe, and Howard 1995; Ellison and Smith 1991; Fehring, Brennan, and Keller 1987; Murphy et al. 2000) means that it is to our advantage to do whatever is necessary in the employment setting to help employees recover from depressive episodes (if it is a full-blown case of clinical depression) or to respond in a healthy way to situational depression (e.g., that might be a normal response to a traumatic event such as a divorce or the death of a spouse). Accomplishing goals defined by one's job, especially when the person understands that these goals contribute to the larger purposes of the employee and employer, helps to create the sense of purpose and meaning that works against a depressive mood. Even accomplishing small steps, conceived of as subgoals en route toward the overall goals, is helpful because in order to do so the person pays attention to something outside of him- or herself and is self-reinforced with the personal satisfaction that comes from achievement.

Analogously, knowing that low SWB is associated with higher loneliness (Paloutzian and Ellison 1982) gives managers a clue to how they can socially engineer the work environment so as to increase the sense to which employees feel a sense of belonging and partnership. It is even the case that high SWB is present in people who show the greatest hardiness and hope in coping with AIDS (Carson and Green 1992; Carson et al. 1990), less anxiety in facing cancer (Kaczorowski 1989), and higher marital adjustment and intimacy (Bauman 1998; Roth 1988). Medical patients who have to adjust to the compromises of living with the long-term effects of diseases like diabetes mellitus tend to cope with it better and are less affected by the problems of uncertainty if they are higher in SWB (Landis 1996). Extending these considerations beyond the immediate, comfort-and-health benefits to the individual employee, there may also be financial benefits to the employer for implementing policies that make people feel like they are partners, that they belong, and that contribute to SWB—these reflect healthy workplace policy. For example, one important benefit may be lower costs for mental and physical health insurance, because people who work in positive environments are less likely to use such services.

Similar dilemmas occur in the workplace. There is the need for hardiness and hope in coping with problems at work. Anxiety is experienced when a person's job performance is being evaluated or when barriers to fulfilling one's responsibilities compromise performance. The need exists to adjust to changes in task assignment or people new to one's own work group. There is also the need to feel a satisfying level of interpersonal intimacy and closeness with one's coworkers. Problems may also stem from uncertainty about one's job security, safety, and (perhaps) upward mobility. Knowing this, we can establish the interpersonal climate of work environments to foster SWB, so that when problems arise (which they inevitably will) people have a greater degree of durability in facing and solving them. These examples illustrate how the general body of research on SWB can be applied to work settings.

Spirituality and Self-Esteem

There is a large volume of data that document that when people strive to accomplish goals beyond their own narrow concerns and do what they believe to be spiritual for them, there are positive personal and social outcomes (Emmons 1999; Paloutzian and Kirkpatrick 1995). The research on SWB is consistent with this—it is healthy to not be too self-focused. In addition, however, this same conclusion is suggested by research on other psychological constructs. Although space precludes an extensive review, let us briefly highlight one line of research whose conclusion is opposite to the simplified, popular notion of what gave birth to it.

One of the most important lines of research is on self-esteem. For approximately the last third of the twentieth century, school children were told to think good thoughts about themselves, to have a positive self-image, on the assumption that if they felt good about themselves, they would do better at schoolwork, display less violence, feel less angry at others, be more tolerant, and so on. Instilling a positive picture of the self was seen as the cure to many of society's ills. In fact, low self-esteem *is* associated with some negative states such as depression, use of drugs, loneliness, eating disorders, and anxiety (Murray et al. 1998; Ybarra 1999).

The data do not yield a uniformly pretty picture of high self-esteem, however. In an extensive review of the self-esteem literature, Baumeister and colleagues (Baumeister 1998; Baumeister, Smart, and Boden 1996) found that when people focus directly on enhancing how they see themselves, an artificially heightened and "dark side" of self-esteem emerges. For example, males who begin to engage in sexual activity at an "inappropriately young age" are more likely to have high, rather than low, self-esteem. Higher than average self-esteem is found among gang leaders, terrorists, and people who are high in ethnocentrism (Dawes 1994). Bushman and Baumeister (1998) found that people who had the highest opinion of themselves were also the most aggressive after being criticized for the poor quality of a written essay. Findings such as these are especially important for present concerns because accepting criticism when one's performance is evaluated is an essential part of work. The particular type of esteem that seems to be associated with such adverse effects is that which is inflated, based on a big ego rather than being genuinely earned. In one laboratory study of this (Colvin, Block, and Funder 1995) people with high esteem were more likely to irritate, interrupt, and show hostility to others, and to talk "at" instead of "with" them. Those with high self-esteem are also more likely to be antagonistic if their view of themselves is threatened, such as being told that one has failed an aptitude test (Heatherton and Vohs 2000).

In response to such findings, Baumeister (1998) and Baumeister, Smart, and Boden (1996) concluded that the claims that enhancing self-esteem was the cure to many societal ills was unsupported. This conclusion is crucial for how we design and operate our places of work because the best outcomes (e.g., increased work efficiency due to less time and effort spent trouble-shooting problems between people) for both employee and management occur when coworkers, or workers and managers, are pleasant rather than obnoxious, cordial rather than confrontational, and when they communicate openly rather than remain silent. For example, employers would be wise to communicate mutually with, rather than talk to, their employees, if they wish to foster a climate of trust and openness that will draw commitment from the employee.

Taken together, these findings on SWB and self-esteem indicate that people are better off when they are not focusing on their own narrow concerns but instead attend to a larger purpose or calling that lies outside themselves. The implications seem to have direct application to the workplace. But what we have so far is a set of static correlations—SWB and esteem associated with a variety of other attitudes, feelings, and states. What is needed is a theoretical framework that can describe how they fit into a coherent picture of the process that mediates the self-control and sustained motivation that would enable people to do their best at work and to believe in and like it.

SPIRITUAL INTELLIGENCE IN THE WORKPLACE

Research on spirituality has begun to identify the motivational and personality properties that may integrate these findings and help us describe healthy workplace policy. Toward this end, Emmons (2000) has recently proposed a "spiritual intelligence" (SI), which manifests itself through several capacities: the ability to experience transcendent states of consciousness; the ability to perceive life as sacred and hold overarching spiritual strivings that organize and integrate other life pursuits; the ability to apply a comprehensive set of religious resources flexibly and appropriately to a full range of life problems; and the ability to engage in virtuous behavior (to show forgiveness, to express gratitude, to be humble, to display compassion). Spiritual intelligence is what allows people to be sensitive to transcendent realities and perceive sacredness in everyday objects, places, relationships, and roles. It is the flexible and adaptive use of spiritual information applied to solving real life problems and thus has relevance for understanding manifestations of spirituality in workplace settings.

The ability to view or experience aspects of one's life as having sacred character or significance, as one element of SI, appears to have important consequences for individual and collective functioning. For example, personal goals and commitments can become "sanctified" or invested with spirituality as the person perceives his or her goals to reflect divine attributes (Emmons 1999; Pargament 1999). As a consequence, these goals are likely to be appraised differently than are nonsacred strivings. When work is seen as a calling rather than a job, or as an opportunity to serve God, work-related strivings take on new significance and meaning (Davidson and Caddell

1994; Novak 1996). In a study of employees with a wide range of occupations, those who character-ized their work as a "calling" reported less absenteeism than those who depicted their work as a job or career (Wrzesniewski et al. 1997). As the meaning of work is transformed to take on a sacred character, people will invest greater resources such as time and energy toward work-related goals and take more steps to protect these goals from conflicting interests. Furthermore, sanctified strivings are likely to lead to greater integration of personality, life satisfaction, emotional well-being, and sustained commitment than strivings that are viewed as simply job related.

At the same time, there might be negative consequences to sanctification of one's work. For example, such workplace difficulties as conflicts with coworkers might be appraised as more stressful for those whose identity revolves around their calling. Conflicts might arise from strained interactions with others who don't "share" the same sense of calling. Also, the increased commit-ment that comes from sanctification of work might make it more difficult to disengage from an unsatisfying employment situation and to seek more fulfilling opportunities elsewhere.

Interpersonal Virtues and Effective Organizational Functioning

One aspect of spiritual intelligence refers to the capacity to engage in virtuous behavior: to show forgiveness, to express gratitude, to be humble, to display compassion and wisdom. These virtues are included under the rubric of spiritual intelligence because of the salience of these concepts in virtually all major religious traditions. For example, gratefulness is a highly prized human dispo-sition in Jewish, Christian, Muslim, Buddhist, and Hindu thought. Conceiving of these inner qualities as virtues implies that they are sources of human strength that enable people to function effectively in the world.

Although inclusion of these virtues in a theory of intelligence is controversial (Gardner 2000; Mayer 2000), there is reason to believe that the exercise of these in daily life more often than not is the intelligent course of action. Organizational scholars are beginning to examine the dynamics of action in organizations that lead to the development of human strength, foster resiliency in employees, and produce extraordinary performance (Whitney and Cooperrider 1997). The focus is turning toward strength-building elements that go beyond effective, efficient, and reliable per-formance to those that facilitate extraordinary, excellent, and virtuous performance (Clifton and Nelson 1992). Character development, long the province of the home, school, and church, is now being emphasized in the workplace (Kloppenborg and Petrick 1999; Weaver 1999). There is some evidence that character development programs reduce absenteeism, violence, theft, dishon-esty, turnover, and compensation claims (Weaver 1999).

Several of these individual virtues or strengths have heretofore largely unacknowledged con-sequences for organizational health. For example, people with humility have been shown to be more likable, better adjusted, have fewer interpersonal conflicts, enjoy more stable personal rela-tionships, and have a lower risk of coronary heart disease (Tangney 2000). Humility has also been associated with better informational search abilities and problem-solving efficiency (Weiss and Knight 1980) and with ratings of teaching effectiveness (Bridges et al. 1971). Overall, humil-ity is characterized by an accurate assessment of one's strengths and weaknesses, thinking one-self no better or no worse than others, and being open to new ideas and new information (Tangney 2000). It is likely that humility would be a characteristic that employees would admire in their supervisors, though to our knowledge there is no research on this topic (see Meara 2001, for a similar sentiment).

Yet another spiritual strength in the workplace is forgivingness. Without the capacity to for-give, the inevitable transgressions and hurts that occur in any long-term relationship would not only make daily work unpleasant, but would also undermine the ability of coworkers to work together toward larger institutional goals. A greater organizational ethos on forgiveness is likely to be paramount in interrupting the deeply ingrained transgression-blame-retaliation cycle (Aquino, Tripp, and Bies 2001).

Gratitude as an Element of Spiritual Intelligence

Perhaps more than any other aspect of spiritual intelligence, gratitude would appear to have profound implications for individual and collective functioning in organizations. The stress physiology pioneer, Hans Selye (1956), contended that "among all emotions, there is one which, more than any other, accounts for the presence or absence of stress in human relations: that is the feeling of gratitude" (284). Gratitude is the positive recognition of benefits received, but it is also more than that. As a psychological state, gratitude is a felt sense of wonder, thankfulness and appreciation for life. It can be expressed toward others, as well as to impersonal (nature) or non-human sources (God, animals). It is considered an aspect of spiritual intelligence as some of the most profound experiences of gratitude can be religiously based or associated with reverent wonder toward an acknowledgment of the universe (Goodenough 1998).

Recent psychological research suggests that a grateful response to life circumstances may be an adaptive psychological strategy and an important process by which people positively interpret everyday experiences. The ability to notice, appreciate, and savor the elements of one's life has been viewed as a crucial determinant of well-being (Emmons and Shelton 2001). Research is under way (Emmons and McCullough in press; McCullough, Emmons, and Tsang 2002) to determine if there are measurable benefits to regularly focusing on one's blessings, and if an effective way to make one aware of benefits received is to engage in a self-guided gratitude-thought-listing procedure. In particular, we have been interested in the effect of this reflective process on psychological well-being, social relationships, and perceptions of physical health.

In one study, undergraduate participants were asked to keep gratitude journals where they wrote up to five things for which they were grateful or thankful. Those who kept gratitude journals on a *weekly* basis exercised more regularly, reported fewer physical symptoms, felt better about their lives as a whole, and were more optimistic about the upcoming week compared to those who recorded hassles or neutral life events, the two comparison groups used (Emmons and Crumpler 2000). In a second experiment, students kept *daily* gratitude journals (Emmons and McCullough in press). The gratitude condition resulted in higher reported levels of the positive states of alertness, enthusiasm, determination, attentiveness, and energy compared to a focus on hassles or a downward social comparison (ways in which participants thought they were better off than others). Participants in the daily gratitude condition were more likely to report having helped someone with a personal problem or having offered emotional support to another, relative to the hassles or social comparison conditions. This indicates that, relative to a focus on complaints, an effective strategy for producing reliably higher levels of pleasant affect is to lead people to reflect, on a daily basis, and to write about those aspects of their lives for which they are grateful.

Appreciative Inquiry in Management

Making the personal commitment to invest psychic energy in developing a personal schema, outlook, or worldview of one's life as a "gift" or one's very self as being "gifted" holds considerable sway from the standpoint of positive organizational functioning. Building up spiritual capital in the workplace has been systematized and formalized through the "appreciative inquiry" (AI) approach to management, a movement that has gained increasing momentum in recent years. Central to the AI approach to positive management are experiences and expressions of gratitude (Srivastva and Cooperrider 1990). To appreciate, in this context, is to "deliberately notice, anticipate, and heighten positive potential" (Kaczmarski and Cooperrider 1997). Its goal is to focus not on what is lacking in organizations but, rather, to seek and create the positive core of organizational life in a manner that will affirm the strengths and potentials of individuals so that they might realize their greatest good (Whitney and Cooperrider 1998). AI is based on the premise that mutual valuing and affirmation is necessary for collaborative learning and social transformation (Tenkasi 2000).

The cultivation of gratitude may be important in organizations not only because of the direct effects of improving organizational climate, but also because as a cognitive strategy, gratitude can improve individual well-being and lower toxic emotions in the workplace such as resentment and envy. A number of recent studies have demonstrated that employee happiness and well-being are positively associated with performance, morale, commitment, and negatively associated with absenteeism, turnover, and burnout (e.g. Wright and Staw 1999). As we have seen, an effective strategy for producing reliably higher levels of pleasant affect is to lead people to reflect, on a daily basis, to write about those aspects of their lives for which they are grateful. Gratitude can also be worked into employee recognition programs (Perle 1997), with predictably beneficial consequences.

Individuals who regularly practice gratitude, then, will not stagnate. Instead, they continually grow toward optimal functioning. Positive emotions generate what has been referred to as an "upward spiral" toward optimal functioning and enhanced emotional well-being (Fredrickson 2001). Positive emotions achieve these beneficial outcomes by broadening individuals' habitual modes of thinking and action. Positive emotions such as gratitude build personal (cognitive, emotional, spiritual) and interpersonal resources. For example, to the extent that positive emotions broaden the scope of cognition and enable flexible and creative thinking, they also facilitate coping with stress and adversity. Grateful people may have more psychic adaptability than the ungrateful, enabling them to be less defensive and to consciously take control of stressors by choosing to extract benefits from challenge and even adversity.

The Benefits of Gratitude in Organizations

Gratitude not only feels good for the individual, but also produces a cascade of beneficial social outcomes as it reflects, motivates, and reinforces moral social actions in both the giver and recipient of help (McCullough et al. 2001). The feeling of gratitude, McCullough and colleagues argue, reflects or identifies moral action because it surfaces when individuals acknowledge that another has been helpful to them. It motivates moral action because grateful people often feel the urge to repay in some manner those who have helped them. Finally, gratitude reinforces moral behavior because giving thanks or acknowledgment rewards help givers, making them feel appreciated and more likely to give help in the future.

By experiencing and expressing gratitude, people can transform themselves and, by extension, the larger units within which they are embedded, becoming more creative, knowledgeable, resilient, socially integrated, and healthy. The sociologist Simmel (1950) argued that gratitude was a cognitive-emotional supplement to sustain one's reciprocal obligations. Because formal social structures such as the law and social contracts are insufficient to regulate and insure reciprocity in human interaction, people are socialized to have gratitude that then serves to remind them of their need to reciprocate. Thus, during exchange of benefits, gratitude prompts one person (a benefi-ciary) to be bound to another (a benefactor) during exchange of benefits, thereby reminding beneficiaries of their reciprocity obligations. Simmel (1950) referred to gratitude as "the moral memory of mankind . . . if every grateful action . . . were suddenly eliminated, society (at least as we know it) would break apart" (388). Social and community transformation occurs because each person's positive emotions can reverberate through others. Because an individual's experiences of positive emotions can reverberate in other members of an organization and across interper-sonal transactions, positive emotions such as gratitude fuel optimal organizational functioning, helping organizations to thrive and prosper.

HEALTHY WORKPLACE POLICY

Although a number of implications of the theory and research on spiritual well-being and spiri-tual intelligence are apparent in the above reviews, it is now useful to be more explicit and prac-tical about them. Among the ways that we can understand the components of a healthy work environment, the following should be highlighted. These ideas are applications projected onto the work environment from the spiritual well-being and spiritual intelligence literatures. They are illustrations of how this application can be made.

Seamlessness Between Home and Work

There should be a greater likelihood that the processes of spiritual intelligence will be invoked and that the sense of SWB will be attained if a person's work life and home life are seen as two pieces of one puzzle, as partners that work together for a purpose bigger than each one alone. In this way, the person's ability to coordinate activities between the two includes a healthy division of time and energy that goes to "work" and "family." This reflects wisdom. On those occasions when there are conflicts between these two, the sense of seamlessness or unity between them should facilitate a sense that it is okay to make trade-offs when circumstances require it. In other words, the person should feel comfort in navigating smoothly between these two domains of life that are sometimes seen as confrontational and opposing each other.

One danger to be avoided, however, is that the person loses the sense of a healthy balance between home and work. If this should occur, the person is in danger of behaving inappropriately in both domains by, for example, exploiting the opportunities for conversation at work in order to solve problems at home, or by becoming such a "workaholic" that all the person does while physically at home is work or think about work, or fail to come home. The use of one's energy and attention for work purposes at home or for home purposes at work is apparent. In order to prevent a vicious cycle of either kind from developing, the person needs to understand that both home and work play a crucial role in fulfilling larger goals, but that a sensitive distinction be-tween the two is also necessary. Managers should communicate this clearly to employees.

Trust and Commitment

There is a relationship between the degree to which employers and managers trust their employ-ees and convey this to them, and the degree to which the employees approach what they do out of *commitment* versus out of *compliance*. This distinction can be illustrated by, for example, imag-ining two different ways that an academic dean might administrate a liberal arts college. Dean B.[2] approaches the task of administrating a college faculty out of a basic sense that they should not be trusted, that the dean is boss, and that the dean's primary agenda is to make sure that professors perform their tasks. Those who do not are made to feel threatened. There is no contrary "message" given that if one does well, one will be esteemed and rewarded. The professors do not "hear" Dean B. say "thank you." Briefly, he administrates by the stick with no carrot. Dean G., in contrast, says straightforwardly to the faculty, "I will trust you, but you should not trust me because people who are in positions of power shouldn't be trusted." Dean G. makes decisions in the faculty's favor, does not rely on inspecting their performance with the intent of administering punishment if it is not satisfactory, but instead forgives their errors (and they his). He says openly that, "We (i.e., the administration and the faculty) are in this together. Let's work as a team so that I can help you do your job better, and I will simply trust that you proceed to do so and will acknowledge and express my gratefulness to you if you do."

Two questions emerge. Which dean generates compliance from the professors and which dean draws commitment from the professors? Applying the principles discussed in this chapter is straightforward. The approach taken by Dean B. will regulate the behavior of the faculty, it will make the faculty comply and do what they are told. But that is all. It will generate neither gratefulness, nor forgiveness, nor love from the professors. What is lost is the commitment of each professor as an individual person. The intangible quality that draws the most creative energy from people, a quality that we call "spark," is compromised, and those employees with the greatest amount of it feel motivated to seek a position elsewhere. Dean B. gives no gratitude and gets no commitment. In contrast, the trust and gratitude stated by Dean G. draw commitment from the professors, so that they approach their task with vibrance, life, energy sufficient to motivate them to work hard and long beyond the minimum requirement. Dean G. gets people to love what they do out of intrinsic motivation; Dean B. only gets people to comply with the basic requirements of the job. The use of one's spiritual resources is enhanced by the approach of Dean G. and the sense of SWB is fostered as a byproduct.

Teamsmanship and Communication

The sense of being part of a team matters to all parties involved. Employees need to know that they are all working together, each doing his or her part, to accomplish a goal. This means that if management sets up a system that makes employees feel that they are in competition with each other for limited resources, in a zero-sum game—whether for money, favor in the eyes of management, a lighter workload, or other side benefits—they may be counterproductive because such a system pits worker against worker, instead of motivating worker to work with worker. Nothing could be more destructive and unhealthy than a management system built on principles that foster interpersonal conflict and negative competition because the virtues of gratitude, compassion, and humility are compromised. Because spiritual concerns are in part driven by virtues and how what one does may affect other people (in the near or short term), this social psychological dimension of workplace policy is important. For example, people feel and express gratitude when they help each other in the process of working together toward a goal, and doing this is an expression of the process of spiritual intelligence and facilitates spiritual well-being.

For workers to feel like they are part of a team, the nature of the communication among employees and between employee and management needs to be unambiguous and affirming. A worker needs to know that an employer is not being judgmental, in the negative connotation, when evaluating his or her performance, but that the employer is accepting the employee "as is" while always helping the employee to sharpen and refine performance. The key to this is that the employer communicates precisely and exactly what is meant. There should be no hidden messages or agendas.

To illustrate using concerns about gender issues in the workplace, if a female boss speaks to a male employee and says, "You look nice today," it should be understood by both parties that this is all that is meant—that the boss has no other "designs" in mind. It can take time, perhaps months or years, through trial and error, to develop this degree of purity of interpersonal communication, but when it happens, all parties know that they are on the same team, that they trust each other, and are free from the potential damage that can come from miscommunication or misinterpretation about these matters.

Helping Employees in Time of Need

One of the most important things that can interfere with someone's job performance is a crisis or a tragedy in the person's personal life. For example, someone whose wife, husband, or child recently died is not likely to be effective at doing work in the routine way, and the person is especially unlikely to find it easy to learn new tasks or to perform creative tasks requiring high-level thinking or mental manipulation. The trauma makes functioning at that level impossible. What should an employer do if its policies are guided by the principles described in this chapter? Above all else, we recommend that the employer demonstrate compassion by doing everything within his or her power to care for the employee and nurture him or her through the trauma. The employee needs to know that he or she is safe, and that even though normal work activities are to be suspended for a while, his or her position in the company is secure when it is healthy to return. This kind of response from the employer is wise for at least two reasons. First, it is in the company's self-interest to do so, so long as the employee is one that the company wanted to keep in the first place. This is because when the employer helps the worker in the face of real needs, the worker is maximally probable to respond with deep and enduring gratitude and commitment. If the company goes the extra mile to care for the employee, the employee will go the extra mile to do good service for the company. Second, responding this way is in accord with the highest level of spiritual values that a company could claim.

   To illustrate, let us take the case of a man whose wife has been diagnosed with lung cancer and is suffering through the process of chemotherapy and radiation treatments. In addition to his basic responsibilities at work (giving lectures, teaching students, editing a journal), he also is now "running frantically" in order to keep up with the demands of caring for his wife. These demands include running errands, food preparation, communication with family members and physicians, dealing with insurance companies, and so on. These must be done concurrent with facing his own trauma in response to learning that his wife will die. The healthy, compassionate way that an employer or a company should respond to this circumstance is to lighten the employee's workload as much as possible and use both the people in the organization as well as the decisions made by the management on behalf of the organization to service the needs of this employee. For example, in coordination with the management, the employee's coworkers can organize a food delivery service so that the burden of having to shop for groceries and cook is taken off of the shoulders of the employee. Also, even if it is not possible for the employer to give the employee fully paid release time, the employer can make decisions in the employee's favor. To illustrate, subordinate level responsibilities could be reduced by not assigning the employee to be on any committees for that year. This way, the employee continues to perform the tasks that comprise his basic job description while being freed from the extra "nuisance" factors that, under conditions of emergency, deplete the person's emotional resources. This example comes from the life of one of the authors of this chapter, and he now carries in his heart the deepest sense of gratitude and commitment to his employer and fellow workers.

Well-Being as a Byproduct

The argument of this chapter assumes that there is a feedback loop such that perception of spiritual well-being both feeds and flows from the attainment of goals consistent with one's spiritual values or strivings, and that these are mediated through a process within the human mind that can be called spiritual intelligence. Implicit in this idea is that the sense of well-being is not obtained by striving for it directly. It is, instead, a byproduct. This idea emerges from psychological research on individuals, but it can be extrapolated and applied to organizations. This means that an organization can be seen as having a greater or a lesser degree of spiritual intelligence embedded in its methods of treating employees, clarity of communicating goals and values with employees, and other aspects of company operation. Also, as is the case with an individual, an organization cannot experience a sense of well-being by trying to manufacture it directly. Instead, the experience of organizational well-being is a byproduct of healthy workplace policy applied in the pursuit of higher, more meaningful goals. This means that just as in the case of the proverbial butterfly that quietly sits on one's shoulder when not being chased, when a company focuses not on itself but instead implements healthy workplace policy in pursuit of spiritual goals, both the attainment of those goals and the sense of satisfaction that comes from it occur as a byproduct.

NOTES

Correspondence concerning this chapter may be addressed to Raymond F. Paloutzian, Department of Psychology, Westmont College, Santa Barbara, CA. 93108–1099 (email: paloutz@westmont.edu); or to Robert A. Emmons, Department of Psychology, University of California, Davis, CA. 95616–8686 (email: raemmons@ucdavis.edu).

   1. Information about the spiritual well-being scale is available at www.lifeadvance.com.
   2. In this example, "Dean B." refers to Dean Bad and "Dean G." refers to Dean Good.

REFERENCES

Aquino, K.; T.M. Tripp; and R.J. Bies. (2001). "How Employees Respond to Personal Offense: The Effects of Blame Attribution, Victim Status, and Offender Status on Revenge and Reconciliation in the Workplace." *Journal of Applied Psychology* 86: 52–29.

Bauman, P.J. (1998). "Marital Intimacy and Spiritual Well-Being." *Journal of Pastoral Care* 52, no. 2: 133–145.

Baumeister, R.F. (1998). "The Self." In *Handbook of Social Psychology*, 4th ed., ed. D.T. Gilbert, S.T. Fiske, and G. Lindzey. New York: McGraw-Hill, 680–740.

Baumeister, R.F.; L. Smart; and J.M. Boden. (1996). "Relation of Threatened Egotism to Violence and Aggression: The Dark Side of High Self-Esteem." *Psychological Review* 103: 5–33.

Bridges, C.M.; W.B. Ware; B.B. Brown; and G. Greenwood. (1971). "Characteristics of the Best and Worst College Teachers." *Science Education* 55: 545–553.

Bufford, R.K.; R.F. Paloutzian; and C.W. Ellison. (1991). "Norms for the Spiritual Well-Being Scale." *Journal of Psychology and Theology* 19: 56–70.

Bufford, R.K.; T.W. Renfroe; and G. Howard. (1995). "Spiritual Changes As Psychotherapy Outcomes." Paper presented at the annual meeting of the American Psychological Association, New York, August.

Bushman, B.J., and R. Baumeister. (1998). "Threatened Egotism, Narcissism, Self-esteem, and Direct and Displaced Aggression: Does Self-Love or Self-Hate Lead to Violence?" *Journal of Personality and Social Psychology* 75: 219–229.

Carson, V.B., and H. Green. (1992). "Spiritual Well-Being: A Predictor of Hardiness in Patients with Acquired Immunodeficiency Syndrome." *Journal of Professional Nursing* 8, no. 4: 209–220.

Carson, V.B.; K.L. Soeken; J. Shanty; and L. Terry. (1990). "Hope and Spiritual Well-Being: Essentials for Living with AIDS." *Perspectives in Psychiatric Care* 26, no. 2: 28–34.

Clifton, D.O., and P. Nelson. (1992). *Soar with Your Strengths*. New York: Bantam Doubleday Dell.

Colvin, C.R.; J. Block; and D.C. Funder. (1995). "Overly Positive Evaluations and Personality: Negative Implications for Mental Health." *Journal of Personality and Social Psychology* 68: 1152–1162.

Davidson, J.C., and D.P. Caddell. (1994). "Religion and the Meaning of Work." *Journal for the Scientific Study of Religion* 33: 135–147.

Dawes, R.M. (1994). *House of Cards: Psychology and Psychotherapy Built on Myth.* New York: Free Press.

Ellison, C.W. (1983). "Spiritual Well-Being: Conceptualization and Measurement." *Journal of Psychology and Theology* 11: 330–340.

Ellison, C.W., and J. Smith. (1991). "Toward an Integrative Measure of Health and Well-Being." *Journal of Psychology and Theology* 19: 35–48.

Emmons, R.A. (2000). "Is Spirituality an Intelligence? Motivation, Cognition, and the Psychology of Ultimate Concern." *The International Journal for the Psychology of Religion* 10: 3–26.

———. (1999). *The Psychology of Ultimate Concerns: Motivation and Spirituality in Personality.* New York: Guilford.

Emmons, R., and C.A. Crumpler. (2000). "Gratitude as Human Strength: Appraising the Evidence." *Journal of Social and Clinical Psychology* 19: 56–69.

Emmons, R.A., and M.E. McCullough. (in press). "Counting Blessings Versus Burdens: An Experimental Investigation of Gratitude and Subjective Well-being in Daily Life." *Journal of Personality and Social Psychology.*

Emmons, R.A., and C.S. Shelton. (2001). "Gratitude and the Science of Positive Psychology." In *Handbook of Positive Psychology,* ed. C.R. Snyder and S.J. Lopez. New York: Oxford University Press, 459–471.

Fehring, R.J.; P.F. Brennan; and M.L. Keller. (1987). "Psychological and Spiritual Well-Being in College Students." *Research in Nursing and Health* 10: 391–398.

Fredrickson, B.L. (2001). "The Role of Positive Emotions in Positive Psychology: The Broaden-and-Build Theory of Positive Emotions." *American Psychologist* 56: 218–226.

Gardner, H. (2000). "A Case Against Spiritual Intelligence." *The International Journal for the Psychology of Religion* 10: 27–34.

Goodenough, U. (1998). *The Sacred Depths of Nature.* New York: Oxford University Press.

Heatherton, T.F., and K.D. Vohs. (2000). "Personality Processes and Individual Differences—Interpersonal Evaluations Following Threats to Self: Role of Self-Esteem." *Journal of Personality and Social Psychology* 78: 725–736.

Kaczmarski, K.M., and D.L. Cooperrider. (1997). "Constructionist Leadership in the Global Relational Age." *Organization and Environment* 10: 235–258.

Kaczorowski, J.M (1989). "Spiritual Well-being and Anxiety in Adults Diagnosed with Cancer." *Hospice Journal* 5, no. 3/4: 105–115.

Kloppenborg, T.J., and J.A. Petrick. (1999). "Leadership in Project Life Cycle and Team Character Development." *Project Management Journal* 30: 8–13.

Landis, B.J. (1996). "Uncertainty, Spiritual Well-being, and Psychosocial Adjustment to Chronic Illness." *Issues in Mental Health Nursing* 17: 217–231.

Mayer, J.D. (2000). "Spiritual Intelligence or Spiritual Consciousness?" *The International Journal for the Psychology of Religion* 10: 47–56.

McCullough, M.E.; R.A. Emmons; and J. Tsang. (2002). "The Grateful Disposition: A Conceptual and Empirical Topography." *Journal of Personality and Social Psychology* 82: 112–127.

McCullough, M.E.; S. Kirkpatrick; R.A. Emmons; and D. Larson. (2001). "Is Gratitude a Moral Affect?" *Psychological Bulletin* 127: 249–266.

Meara, N.M. (2001). "Just and Virtuous Leaders and Organizations." *Journal of Vocational Behavior* 58: 227–234.

Moberg, D.O. (1979). "The Development of Social Indicators of Spiritual Well-being for Quality of Life Research." In *Spiritual Well-Being: Sociological Perspectives,* ed. D.O. Moberg. Washington DC: University Press of America, 1–13.

Moberg, D.O., and P.M. Brusek. (1978). "Spiritual Well-Being: A Neglected Subject in Quality of Life Research." *Social Indicators Research* 5: 303–323.

Murphy, P.E.; J.W. Ciarrocchi; R.L. Piedmont; S. Cheston; M. Peyrot; and G. Fitchett. (2000). "The Relation of Religious Belief and Practices, Depression, and Hopelessness in Persons with Clinical Depression." *Journal of Consulting and Clinical Psychology* 68, no. 6: 1102–1106.

Murray, S.L.; J.G. Holmes; G. MacDonald; and P.C. Ellsworth. (1998). "Through the Looking Glass Darkly? When Self-Doubts Turn into Relationship Insecurities." *Journal of Personality and Social Psychology* 75: 1459–1480.

Novak, M. (1996). *Business As a Calling: Work and the Examined Life.* New York: Free Press.

Paloutzian, R.F., and C.W. Ellison. (1982). "Loneliness, Spiritual Well-Being and the Quality of Life." In *Loneliness: A Sourcebook of Current Theory, Research and Therapy*, ed. L.A. Peplau and D. Perlman. New York: Wiley-Interscience, 224–237.

Paloutzian, R.F., and L.A. Kirkpatrick, eds. (1995). "Religious Influences on Personal and Societal Well-Being." *Journal of Social Issues* 51, no. 2: whole issue.

Pargament, K.I. (1999) "The Psychology of Religion and Spirituality? Yes and No." *The International Journal for the Psychology of Religion* 9: 3–16.

Perle, A. (1997). "Have an Attitude of Gratitude." *Workforce* 76: 77–78.

Roth, P.D. (1988). "Spiritual Well-Being and Marital Adjustment." *Journal of Psychology and Theology* 16, no. 2: 153–158.

Selye, H. (1956). *The Stress of Life*. New York: McGraw-Hill.

Simmel, G. (1950). *The Sociology of Georg Simmel*. Glencoe, IL: Free Press.

Srivastva, S., and D.L. Cooperrider. (1990). *Appreciative Management and Leadership: The Power of Positive Thought and Action in Organizations*. San Francisco: Jossey-Bass.

Tangney, J.P. (2000). "Humility: Theoretical Perspectives, Empirical Findings and Directions for Future Research." *Journal of Social and Clinical Psychology* 19: 70–82.

Tenkasi, R.V. (2000). "The Dynamics of Cultural Knowledge and Learning in Creating Viable Theories of Global Change and Action." *Organization Development Journal* 18: 74–90.

Weaver, M.A. (1999). "Influence of Character Development and Principle-Based Management on Worker Performance." Unpublished master's thesis, University of Florida.

Weiss, H.M., and P.A. Knight. (1980). "The Utility of Humility: Self-esteem, Information Search, and Problem-Solving Efficiency." *Organizational Behavior and Human Decision Processes* 25: 216–223.

Whitney, D., and D.L. Cooperrider. (1998). "The Appreciative Inquiry Summit: Overview and Applications." *Employment Relations Today* 25: 17–28.

Wright, T.A., and B.M. Staw. (1999). "Affect and Favorable Work Outcomes: Two Longitudinal Tests of the Happy-Productive Worker Thesis." *Journal of Organizational Behavior* 2: 1–23.

Wrzesniewski, A.; C. McCauley; P. Rozin; and B. Schwartz. (1997). "Jobs, Careers, and Callings: People's Relations to Their Work." *Journal of Research in Personality* 31: 21–33.

Ybarra, O. (1999). "Misanthropic Person Memory when the Need to Self-enhance Is Absent." *Personality and Social Psychology Bulletin* 25: 261–269.

Zinnbauer, B.J.; K.I. Pargament; B. Cole; M.S. Rye; E.M. Butter; T.G. Belavich; K.M. Hipp; A.B. Scott; and J.L. Kadar. (1997). "Religion and Spirituality: Unfuzzying the Fuzzy." *Journal for the Scientific Study of Religion* 36, no. 4: 549–564.

CHAPTER 9

ETHICAL CLIMATES AND SPIRITUALITY

An Exploratory Examination of Theoretical Links

K. PRAVEEN PARBOTEEAH AND JOHN B. CULLEN

Spirituality in the workplace is seen as one of the most important trends in the twenty-first century (Shellenbarger 2000) and is gaining increased attention both from corporate America and academicians as a legitimate field of study (Ashmos and Duchon 2000; Cash and Gray 2000; Jackson 1999; Mitroff and Denton 1999). This growing interest in spirituality can be explained by various factors affecting the workplace. The massive layoffs of the 1980s and various programs to boost productivity (i.e., reengineering, total quality management, downsizing) have turned the American workplace into an environment where workers are demoralized, feel alienated from their work, and generally distrust their employers (Ali and Falcone 1995; Brandt 1996). Workplace spirituality is seen as the solution to such dramatic and problematic changes. At the same time, the American workforce is continuously seeing more diversity, where one aspect of this diversity has been a dramatic increase in the various forms of formal and informal spiritual practices at the workplace. In addition, as people spend more and more time at work, and participation in such societal institutions as church and family is declining (Conger 1994), people see the workplace as their primary source of connection with other people. Increasingly, some argue that the curiosity about Pacific Rim cultures and Eastern philosophies (i.e., Buddhism, Hare Krishna movement, Confucianism) is also fueling increased acceptance of spirituality by encouraging meditation and other forms of stress reduction methods (Ashmos and Duchon 2000).

Although to date no empirical study has demonstrated a link between spirituality and organizational performance, there are nevertheless theoretical arguments and anecdotal evidence that spirituality can benefit organizations and their employees. For example, in a study of senior executives and managers, Mitroff and Denton (1999) showed that these senior managers and executives felt that spirituality, the "basic feeling of being connected with one's complete self, others, and the entire universe" (83), allowed them to become more complete at work. Spirituality, in sharp contrast with classical organizational and management theories of dealing with workers as mere ends (Taylor 1947; Weber 1947), allows human beings to go beyond material needs to find and express meaning and purpose and living in relation to others (Ashmos and Duchon 2000). Spirituality at work suggests going beyond accomplishing organizational tasks, which may have meaningless intrinsic value to the worker. Rather, it views work as necessary nourishment for workers' souls. Some have even argued that spiritual codes can provide the necessary values and principles to encourage multinationals "to follow a morality that demands more than following the minimal standards of acceptability of conventional business practices" (Jackson 1999, 61). In sum, it is strongly believed that spirituality can benefit employees by helping them deal with the realities of today's workplace, finding more meaning in their work and lives, and connecting with other people. Spirituality can also help employees "deploy more of their full creativity, emotions, and intelligence" (Mitroff and Denton 1999). Spiritual organizations also benefit because they have employees that are more satisfied and happy with their work, which can potentially enhance organizational performance.

Given the above importance of workplace spirituality, it is surprising to find that only a few studies have examined the effects of spirituality in organizations in a rigorous fashion (Gibbons 2000; Neck and Milliman 1994; Milliman, Czaplewski, and Ferguson, 2001). Most of these studies emphasized the effects of spirituality on such critical work variables as job involvement and job satisfaction. This focus on crucial organizational behavior variables is not surprising given the importance practitioners and academicians place on these variables. Lacking, however, is research that examines ways in which spirituality can be enhanced in the organization. As such, we contribute to the literature by investigating how ethics, in particular the ethical climate of an organization, can encourage spirituality in the workplace. Ethical climates are a subset of the more general array of work climates. The ethical climate construct delineates a group of prescriptive climates reflecting prevailing organizational practices with moral consequences. Ethical climates help workers solve ethical issues by giving them answers to "what should I do?" when faced with a moral dilemma (Homans 1950). In addition, ethical climates also help employees identify ethical issues within the organization. In other words, the ethical climates serve as a perceptual lens through which workers diagnose and assess situations.

SPIRITUALITY AND ETHICAL CLIMATES

Spirituality is defined as the "basic feeling of being connected with one's complete self, others, and the entire universe" (Mitroff and Denton 1999). It involves a sense of wholeness, connectedness at work, and deeper values (Gibbons 2000). A spiritual individual ponders on such fundamental questions as: Who am I? What is the purpose of life? What is it that I am supposed to do? (Block 1993; Hawley 1993).

To establish the links between ethical climates and spirituality, we rely on the recent conceptualization of spirituality by Ashmos and Duchon (2000). They developed an instrument based on the spirituality literature and tested their conceptualization with a survey of 696 respondents. Although their scale and methods are somewhat weak, their findings revealed three distinct and interesting factors reflecting spirituality: conditions for community, meaning at work, and inner life. Given the lack of other better conceptualizations, we focus our study on these three manifestations of spirituality.

The first factor, *conditions for community*, is an indication of the extent to which employees feel that there are conditions present to allow them to be part of a "community." In such a community, people can experience personal growth, can be valued as individuals, and can satisfy the important need to belong. Community at work is based on the belief that people see themselves as connected to each other and that there is some sort of connection between one's inner self and other's inner selves (Maynard 1992; Miller 1992).

The second factor, *meaning at work*, goes beyond the physical and intellectual experience of work to connote what is important, joyful, energizing, and spiritual about work. This spiritual view of work goes also beyond the human relations or Hackman and Oldham's (1976) view of work as being merely interesting, intellectual, and satisfying. The spiritual meaning at work is about "searching for deeper meaning and purpose, living one's dream, feeling good about one's work, expressing one's inner life by seeking meaningful work, and contributing to others" (Milliman et al. 2001).

Finally, *inner life* refers to "an individual's hopefulness, awareness of personal values" (Ashmos and Duchon 2000) and concern for connectedness with the universe. The inner life dimension of spirituality is based on the assumption that people have both an inner and outer life. By nourishing the inner life at work (through ways such as expressing aspects of one's being), one can lead to a more meaningful and productive outer life. As such, the recognition of an inner life at the workplace means accepting that people have both a mind and a spirit and that the development of the spirit at work is as important as the development of the mind (Ashmos and Duchon 2000).

To establish a link between ethics in organizations and these three manifestations of spirituality, we use Victor and Cullen's (1987, 1988) delineation of ethical work climates. In their studies of ethical climates, Victor and Cullen developed and tested a typology of ethical climates based on ethical philosophy and Kohlberg's (1967) theory of moral development. This typology of ethical climates has three bases of moral judgment: egoistic, benevolent, and principled. These form the three basic ethical climates. In the *egoistic climate*, company norms support the satisfaction of self-interest. In the *benevolent climate*, company norms support maximizing the interests of a particular social group. Finally, in the *principled climate*, company norms support following abstract principles independent of situational outcomes.

In addition to the three basic types of ethical climates, Victor and Cullen's typology has three levels of analysis to distinguish further the basic types of climates found in organizations. The levels of analysis range from the individual to society at large. These levels identify the referent group considered in making egoistic, benevolent, or principled moral judgments. Hence, each type of ethical criterion has three levels of reference, namely individual, local (e.g., immediate group), and cosmopolitan (e.g., the organization). Crossing the ethical criteria produces nine *possible* climate types: three egoistic; three benevolent; and three principled. According to Cullen, Victor, and Bronson (1993), ethical climate theory proposes that no one organization has all climate types operating simultaneously, although empirical evidence suggests that all exist in heterogeneous samples of organizations.

For this paper, we consider only two levels of reference (i.e., individual and local) for the three bases of moral judgment. Because the focus is on workplace spirituality, we emphasize the two levels of reference that have primary relevance to the workplace. Although equally valid, the cosmopolitan level of reference specifies "organizational sources of ethical reasoning external to the focal organization" (Victor and Cullen 1988, 106), such as a professional association or the law. While cosmopolitan sources of ethical reasoning can become part of the organization's institutionalized normative systems, it is nevertheless difficult to theoretically argue for direct links between the cosmopolitan level and workplace spirituality. This difficulty stems from the fact that cosmopolitan sources of moral reasoning are external to the organization and also vary greatly by industry. As such, we focus on two levels of reference or six possible ethical climate types that have most relevance for workplace spirituality. Table 9.1 shows an illustrative item for each ethical climate type.

Individual Level

With the individual level referent point, the bases of moral judgments for ethical climates tap into consequences of decision-making for individuals as opposed to groups. In other words, when considering individual-level ethical climates, individuals consider the consequences of the impact of their ethical decision-making for each individual's gains or benefits and losses.

Table 9.1

Ethical Climate Type and Illustrative Items

	Individual level	Local level
Egoistic	Egoistic-individual ethical climate type *Illustrative item:* In this company, people protect their own interests above other considerations.	Egoistic-local ethical climate type *Illustrative item:* People are expected to do anything to further the company's interest.
Benevolent	Benevolent-individual ethical climate type *Illustrative item:* In this company, people look out for each other's good.	Benevolent-local ethical climate type *Illustrative item:* Our major consideration is what is best for everyone in the company.
Principled	Principled-individual ethical climate type *Illustrative item:* In this company, people are expected to follow their own personal and moral beliefs.	Principled-local ethical climate type *Illustrative item:* It is very important to follow strictly the company's rules and procedures.

Egoistic-Individual Ethical Climate

An egoistic-individual ethical climate has norms, values, and expectations that promote the maximization of self-interest. It postulates that one should choose those actions that result in the maximum of good for oneself (Rosen 1978). As such, the decision-maker usually seeks the alternative with the consequences that most satisfies his/her needs, ignoring/neglecting the needs or interests of others. Within an egoistic work climate, the individual's self-interest becomes the *expected* primary source of moral reasoning for people in the organization when they make a decision (Victor and Cullen 1987; 1988). That is, the norms of the organizations support the belief that members ignore the needs and interests of others (within the same department or organization).

As such, people in egoistic-individual climates seem the least likely to develop any of the three aspects of spiritually. The emphasis on personal gains is very unlikely to contribute to a situation where individuals can feel a sense of community and ability to grow and share. A sense of community implies that members of a work group want to share and belong. However, if people continuously behave in a self-interested fashion and exclude the interest of others possibly affected adversely by the decisions, it seems unlikely that other members of the work group will identify or want to share with each other. Furthermore, continuous egoistic actions are also likely to discourage other individuals from seeking community values with the egoistic individual. Consequently, it seems plausible to argue that an egoistic-individual climate creates barriers to enhance the sense of community aspect of spirituality.

The second aspect of spirituality, meaning at work, requires that individuals want to be involved with their work, and that work gives meaning to their lives. This dimension goes beyond the traditional view of work as satisfying and connotes a higher level of connection with work. In contrast, an egoistic-individual climate creates a situation that encourages alienation from many aspects of work such as group benefits and social responsibility. As such, although the individual may be connected to his/her job, group expectations and norms of maximizing selfish interests make it improbable that such connection grows to a broad attachment to work.

Finally, the third aspect of spirituality at work is finding the inner life. This dimension "captures an individual's hopefulness, awareness of personal values, and concern for spirituality" (Ashmos and Duchon 2000, 137). Egoistic-individual climates seem unlikely to promote hopefulness and awareness of personal values. When individuals work in situations that promote a pessimistic view of people as coldly self-serving, reflective thought on personal values and hopefulness seem unlikely.

Given the above arguments, we propose the following:

> Proposal 1a: The norms, values, and expectations associated with egoistic-individual work climates make organizational members less likely to develop the sense of community aspect of spirituality.
> Proposal 1b: The norms, values, and expectations associated with egoistic-individual work climates make organizational members less likely to develop the meaning at work aspect of spirituality.
> Proposal 1c: The norms, values, and expectations associated with egoistic-individual work climates make organizational members less likely to develop the inner life aspect of spirituality.

Benevolent-Individual Ethical Climate

Benevolent climates have norm, values, and expectations promoting a concern for others (Victor and Cullen 1987, 1988). The benevolent climate encourages the decision-maker to seek the alternative that maximizes joint interests even if it means a lesser satisfaction of individual needs (Weber 1995). A benevolent climate is a context where people are most likely to make decisions that provide the greatest good for the greatest number of people. However, unlike utilitarian arguments that are used to benefit specific stakeholder groups at the expense of others, a benevolent-individual climate refers to consideration of people irrespective of organizational or specific stakeholder memberships. As such, benevolent norms encourage individuals to have a sincere interest for the well-being of everyone (Wimbush and Shepard 1994).

In contrast to the context created by the egoistic-individual climate, a benevolent climate is more likely to facilitate the development of spirituality in organizational members. By being concerned with others, individuals in benevolent climates create the necessary conditions to encourage the sense of community aspect of spirituality. Thus, a benevolent climate provides a situation of mutual caring that likely fosters people developing a deep connection and relationship with others. As such, a benevolent climate promotes the caring and well-being of others and is most likely to encourage the sense of community.

A benevolent climate is also very likely to facilitate people finding meaning at work. Consider, for example, group members helping their coworker perform a task. Through caring and help, an individual can feel more valuable and connected with his/her work. Also, assisting someone within some area is likely to make the helpers have higher levels of efficacy within that area. In turn, higher levels of efficacy can encourage people to be more satisfied with work and to find deeper meaning from their work. Caring and helping imply a sense of work connection with others and can be conducive to higher levels of spiritual meaning at work.

A benevolent climate is also very likely to foster the development of the inner life dimensions of spirituality. Benevolence, with its emphasis on friendship and caring for other people's lives, represents a noble endeavor. There have been heavy criticisms of the egoistic nature of most Western societies (Carlin and Strong 1995), and benevolence is the antidote to such selfishness. By participating in groups, departments, or organizations with more benevolent climates, people can find more meaning in their lives.

The need to find spiritual rewards in caring organizations may be illustrated by those who work in voluntary organizations. For example, the unselfish act of volunteerism is a clear benevolent act because volunteers give their time freely for the benefit of others and do not expect anything in return (Wilson and Musick 1997). As such, many individuals are seeing volunteer work as the means to achieve more meaning in their life. At the same time, organizations are finding that if they give time for their employees to engage in volunteer activities, they attract and motivate top talent (Harris 2000) and have more satisfied and committed employees (Kirchmeyer 1992). Even elected officials are reminding Americans of the need to volunteer and to be a caring people (Beebe, Snyder, and Mortimer 1994). In general, Americans seem to be highly receptive to the idea of volunteer work as representing a deeper meaning in life.

Finally, we note that benevolence is conceptually similar to one aspect of the Buddhist perspective on life. In its most rudimentary sense, Buddhism advocates a compassionate attitude that at a minimum, one should not do any harm to others and that one should be helpful to others (Gould 1995). It should be noted that Judaism also advocates this principle (Ludwig 2001). Such a view of life, as is envisioned by Buddhism, encompasses nobility and an ideal approach to life. As such, benevolence also embodies what is noble and a much deeper meaning of life relative to the selfish and shallow nature of an egoistic. Hence, based on all the above, we propose:

> Proposal 2a: The norms, values, and expectations associated with benevolent-individual work climates make organizational members more likely to develop the sense of community aspect of spirituality.
>
> Proposal 2b: The norms, values, and expectations associated with benevolent-individual work climates make organizational members more likely to develop the meaning at work aspect of spirituality.
>
> Proposal 2c: The norms, values, and expectations associated with benevolent-individual work climates make organizational members more likely to develop the inner life aspect of spirituality.

Principled-Individual Ethical Climate

Victor and Cullen's (1988) ethical criterion of principle embodies the expectation that group members guide their decision-making and behaviors by the application or interpretation of rules, laws, and standards. The principled-individual norms, values, and expectations are that group members should rely on their personal morality when making decisions that have ethical consequences. This dimension represents the independent factor most often identified in ethical climate studies and is measured through items such as "in this company, people are expected to follow their own personal and moral beliefs" and "each person in this company decides for themselves what is right and wrong." As such, one is expected to be guided by personal ethics.

Although there can be variations in personal ethics, the Victor and Cullen (1987; 1988) ethical climate development relied heavily on Kohlberg's stages of moral reasoning (Kohlberg 1984). At the principled stage, Kohlberg (1984) argues that personal ethics or self-chosen ethical principles appeal to logical comprehensiveness, universality, and consistency. In other words, a principled climate is an extension of Kantian theories where morality comes from analyzing the act rather than consequences.

Although not as evident as with a benevolent climate, working in a principled environment also seems likely to develop spiritually. An individual-principled climate implies that individuals working in this climate are expected to have gone through the various stages inherent in understanding how to approach ethical dilemmas. A principled climate implies that group members should reach a higher level of ethical maturity (Kohlberg 1984) by using one's own conclusions regarding personal ethics. In addition, a principled climate can also encourage employees to engage in considered thinking that can gradually produce Kantian universal moral judgment (Onara 1975).

Conforming to climate expectations of consistently applying personal ethics based on integrity, group members can earn the respect of others. Such respect can potentially form the base where other people feel they can trust people who belong to the group (work group, department, organization) dominated by a principled-individual climate. As such, given that a principled climate connotes an acceptance of personal morality, it seems plausible to argue that people can develop a sense of community based on this mutual acceptance and trust.

A principled-individual climate can also encourage higher spirituality through the meaning of work. Since the principled-individual climate encourages group members to face ethical decisions using their personal principles (as opposed to externally generated code), ethical decision-making requires a deeper understanding of a job and organizational issues. That is, to understand and reconcile the ethical consequences of work-related decisions, people in a principled-individual climate are encouraged to consider carefully the nature of their work as it relates to their personal morality. This climate expectation of involvement with the consequences of work likely increases the meaning work provides to a person's life.

The principled-individual climate has group members who are expected to reach higher levels of moral development, at least from the Kohlbergian perspective. As such, when climate expectations encourage people to achieve higher levels of moral maturity stage, then group members are more likely to analyze the critical questions related to the inner life (i.e., Who am I? What is my purpose in life?).

Hence, we propose:

> Proposal 3a: The norms, values, and expectations associated with principled-individual work climates make organizational members more likely to develop the sense of community aspect of spirituality.
> Proposal 3b: The norms, values, and expectations associated with principled-individual work climates make organizational members more likely to develop the meaning at work aspect of spirituality.
> Proposal 3c: The norms, values, and expectations associated with principled-individual work climates make organizational members more likely to develop the inner life aspect of spirituality.

Local Level

At the local level of reference, the important locus when making ethical decisions regardless of the basis of ethical reasoning is the work group. Depending on the nature of a company, this might be the organization or contained within the organization, such as the immediate work group or functional department (Victor and Cullen 1987; 1988). That is, when a decision has ethical consequences, the bases of ethical reasoning apply to the work group rather than the individual in general.

Egoistic-Local Ethical Climate

At the local locus of analysis, the egoistic climate takes into consideration the needs and preferences of the work group (Victor and Cullen 1987; 1988). At this level of analysis, self is the group, the team, and the organization. When people make decisions with ethical consequences, alternatives that maximize the needs and welfare of the work group at the expense of other work groups are preferred. As such, some level of conflict among groups can be expected.

To achieve the spiritual dimension of sense of community, employees have to feel a deep connection with other members of the organization (Milliman et al. 2001). Depending on the local referent for the ethical climate in an organization, egoistic-local climates may foster this community sense or inhibit it. Consider, for example, the case of Southwest Airlines where there has been a deliberate effort to infuse an organizational culture that evokes a sense of community. At Southwest Airlines, employees feel that they are all part of a larger organizational family and that employees take care of each other and customers (Freiberg and Freiberg 1996). For Southwest it seems likely that the local referent is the organization as a whole. However, with an egoistic-local climate using subunits as a referent, employees look and care for the interests of their own work groups and not the entire organization. As such, competition between work groups and potential conflicts for scarce resources make this climate less likely to foster the sense of family and community found at Southwest Airlines. Consequently, since this climate is usually found empirically at the subunit levels (Cullen et al. 1993), it can be argued that an egoistic-local climate is less likely to foster the sense of community aspect of spirituality.

We also suspect that an egoistic-local climate is unlikely to contribute to the meaning of work aspect of spirituality in spite of potential benefits from this climate that may increase a less abstract identification with work typically considered in the organizational behavior literature. With its emphasis on work unit gains, an egoistic-local climate can induce more challenging and satisfying work. However, it is unlikely that the egoistic-local climate can encourage the spirituality sense of meaning of work. The expression of spirituality at work assumes that each person is strongly interested in activities that give meaning not just to his/her job through job satisfaction and identification with the tasks. Rather meaning is related to one's life and contributions to society (Hawley 1993). As such, it seems that the most critical aspects of the meaning at work spirituality are not encouraged by working in an egoistic-local climate.

Finally, it is also unlikely that an egoistic-local climate contributes to spiritual inner life. Normative expectations that promote self-interested behaviors, even for the benefit of the immediate work group, seem unlikely to provide conditions for finding deeper meaning in one's life. The competition inherent in the egoistic climate is unlikely to evoke a deeper connection with oneself or other people or the universe. An egoistic-local climate can only promote negative aspects of work life. Therefore, we propose:

> Proposal 4a: The norms, values, and expectations associated with egoistic-local work climates make organizational members less likely to develop the sense of community aspect of spirituality.
>
> Proposal 4b: The norms, values, and expectations associated with egoistic-local work climates make organizational members less likely to develop the meaning at work aspect of spirituality.
>
> Proposal 4c: The norms, values, and expectations associated with egoistic-local work climates make organizational members less likely to develop the inner life aspect of spirituality.

Benevolent-Local Ethical Climate

In a benevolent-local ethical climate, the criterion is defined as consideration of the member's organization rather than people in general or the immediate work group (Victor and Cullen 1987; 1988). As such, the benevolent-local climate is different from the egoistic-local climate in that the benefit of the whole organization is taken into consideration as opposed to just the work group in an egoistic-local ethical climate.

Of all ethical climate types, a benevolent-local climate seems to be the most likely to result in higher sense of community. In a benevolent-local climate, each individual is concerned with the well-being of each other within the organization. Group- and organization-wide processes typical of a benevolent climate, such as cooperation, mutual personal attraction, and positive feelings about task (Wech, Mossholder, Steel and Bennett 1998) may establish the necessary conditions for a sense of community to occur. In addition, the likely benefits of a benevolent-local climate where organizational members are more sensitive and willing to help all organizational members may also produce more cohesiveness and a higher likelihood that a sense of community develops. In sum, typical situations associated with participation in a benevolent-local climate likely enhance organizational members' ability to develop deeper connections with each other.

Participation in a benevolent-local climate type is also likely to encourage organizational members to develop the meaning of work aspect of spirituality. A benevolent-local climate suggests a caring environment where people look out for each other. When organizational members look out and care for each other, they are also more likely to identify with each other and view the other members' values as similar to their own. As such, a benevolent-local climate seems to be the likely condition where cohesiveness among organizational members is enhanced. If organizational members care for each other, cooperate, and feel cohesive, they are also more likely to enjoy working with each other, take personal and group pride in achieving the organizational objectives (Wech et al. 1998). This increased enjoyment of working together and taking pride in achieving organizational goals can be the probable result of individuals finding deeper meaning in their work through their beliefs regarding the importance of their actions in the organization. In addition, by contributing to the common goal through a caring environment, organizational members can feel good about what they are doing and also contribute to others, all representing aspects of the meaning of work (Fox 1994). Finally, organizational members can also find deeper meaning at work in a benevolent-local climate through sensitiveness to others and helping others achieve the common goal.

Participation in a benevolent-local climate is also likely to enhance organizational members' inner life aspect of workplace spirituality. Because this climate creates a caring environment with an emphasis on helping and supporting each other, organizational members go beyond merely performing physical and intellectual tasks. Instead, they use work as an opportunity to express "many aspects of one's being" (Ashmos and Duchon 2000, 135). To care for each other, help each other, and cooperate, one has to be cognizant of one's actions on others and the organization. Such awareness of one's actions can only enhance reflections on one's work and one's life. As such, it is plausible to argue that in a benevolent-local climate, the caring and sensitive environment encourages organizational members to question and find deeper meanings in their work life through the consequences of their actions on others.

Based on all of the above, we propose:

> Proposal 5a: The norms, values, and expectations associated with benevolent-local work climates make organizational members more likely to develop the sense of community aspect of spirituality.
>
> Proposal 5b: The norms, values, and expectations associated with benevolent-local work climates make organizational members more likely to develop the meaning at work aspect of spirituality.
>
> Proposal 5c: The norms, values, and expectations associated with benevolent-local work

climates make organizational members more likely to develop the inner life aspect of spirituality.

Principled-Local Ethical Climate

Victor and Cullen's (1988) ethical criterion of principle embodies the application or interpretation of local (usually organizational) rules, laws and standards. In the case of the local-principled climate, the source of principles for ethical reasoning lies within the organization (e.g., rules and procedures). As such, norms, values, and expectations promote behaviors and decision-making guided by principles apart from and regardless of individual principles.

A principled-local climate seems likely to encourage all three aspects of workplace spirituality. We make this assertion based on the premise that individuals internalize principled reasoning supported in their social environment. Work climate theory (Schneider 1983) predicts that organizational members internalize climate expectations through socialization or they leave the organization. In addition, strong climates can also increase conformity pressures and induce organizational members, through cognitive dissonance, to accept organizational norms as their own (Schneider 1975).

By injecting the organization with the teachings of a principled moral reasoning and infusing the organizational culture with such values, it is expected that employees exhibit a higher degree of integrity and ethical behavior (Weber and Green 1991; Wimbush, Shepard, and Markham 1997). In addition, a principled climate also encourages employees to obey company regulations, procedures and other critical rules, thereby not emphasizing any favoritism (Joseph and Deshpande 1997). Conforming to a principled-local climate supports members moving to Kohlberg's (1984) post-conventional level, which is achieved when one is guided by inculcated principles of trust and justice. As such, it is plausible to expect individuals in such an environment to develop a sense of community. That is, an environment fostering trust, justice, and socially responsible ideals is morally rewarding and likely to bring employees more closely together. The result is a greater sense of community.

The values inherent in a principled climate can also enhance the inner life and meaning of work aspects of spirituality. Because employees know that they are operating within the confines of an ethical environment guided by rules and procedures resolving the inevitable conflicts between self, these principles can foster the development of the inner life aspects of spirituality. In addition, in an age where companies are mostly guided by profit motives, employees who work for organizations that have objective ethical guidance are probably more likely to find more meaning in their work.

Consequently, we propose:

> Proposal 6a: The norms, values, and expectations associated with principled-local work climates make organizational members more likely to develop the sense of community aspect of spirituality.
> Proposal 6b: The norms, values, and expectations associated with principled-local work climates make organizational members more likely to develop the meaning at work aspect of spirituality.
> Proposal 6c: The norms, values, and expectations associated with principled-local work climates make organizational members more likely to develop the inner life aspect of spirituality.

These propositions are summarized in Table 9.2.

Table 9.2

Summary of Propositions

	Individual level	Local level
Egoistic	P1a: The norms, values, and expectations associated with egoistic-individual work climates make organizational members less likely to develop the sense of community aspect of spirituality.	P4a: The norms, values, and expectations associated with egoistic-local work climates make organizational members less likely to develop the sense of community aspect of spirituality.
	P1b: The norms, values, and expectations associated with egoistic-individual work climates make organizational members less likely to develop the meaning at work aspect of spirituality.	P4b: The norms, values, and expectations associated with egoistic-local work climates make organizational members less likely to develop the meaning at work aspect of spirituality.
	P1c: The norms, values, and expectations associated with egoistic-individual work climates make organizational members less likely to develop the inner life aspect of spirituality.	P4c: The norms, values, and expectations associated with egoistic-local work climates make organizational members less likely to develop the inner life aspect of spirituality.
Benevolent	P2a: The norms, values, and expectations associated with benevolent-individual work climates make organizational members more likely to develop the sense of community aspect of spirituality.	P5a: The norms, values, and expectations associated with benevolent-local work climates make organizational members more likely to develop the sense of community aspect of spirituality.
	P2b: The norms, values, and expectations associated with benevolent-individual work climates make organizational members more likely to develop the meaning at work aspect of spirituality.	P5b: The norms, values, and expectations associated with benevolent-local work climates make organizational members more likely to develop the meaning at work aspect of spirituality.
	P2c: The norms, values, and expectations associated with benevolent-individual work climates make organizational members more likely to develop the inner life aspect of spirituality.	P5c: The norms, values, and expectations associated with benevolent-local work climates make organizational members more likely to develop the inner life aspect of spirituality.

(continued)

Table 9.2 *(continued)*

	Individual level	Local level
Principled	P3a: The norms, values, and expectations associated with principled-individual work climates make organizational members more likely to develop the sense of community aspect of spirituality.	P6a: The norms, values, and expectations associated with principled-local work climates make organizational members more likely to develop the sense of community aspect of spirituality.
	P3b: The norms, values, and expectations associated with principled-individual work climates make organizational members more likely to develop the meaning at work aspect of spirituality.	P6b: The norms, values, and expectations associated with principled-local work climates make organizational members more likely to develop the meaning at work aspect of spirituality.
	P3c: The norms, values, and expectations associated with principled-individual work climates make organizational members more likely to develop the inner life aspect of spirituality.	P6c: The norms, values, and expectations associated with principled-local work climates make organizational members more likely to develop the inner life aspect of spirituality.

DISCUSSION AND IMPLICATIONS FOR PRACTITIONERS

The primary objective of this chapter was to establish theoretical links between ethical climates and workplace spirituality. Our theoretical arguments suggest that the benevolent-local and principled-local ethical climate types are the most conducive to foster the development of workplace spirituality. In contrast, an egoistic ethical climate, because of its emphasis on gains at the expense of other individuals or social entities, seems to be the least desirable climate for the development of workplace spirituality.

How can companies encourage workplace spirituality through benevolent-local and principled-local ethical climates? At a basic level, companies need to establish organizational cultures that promote a sense of fellowship and community at work. Through both benevolent and principled climates, top managers can set the tone as to what is valued in the organization. By emphasizing the workplace as a family (i.e., through benevolence—caring for each other and principles—rules, mottoes, and standards), the company can create the atmosphere where organizational members feel that they belong and connect with each other. A good example is Southwest Airlines where the organizational culture includes a strong sense that employees are all part of a big family, that employees take care of each other as well as customers, and that employees' families are also part of the big Southwest Airlines family (Freiberg and Freiberg 1996).

To encourage the meaning at work aspect of spirituality, managers can emphasize and reward the norms, values, and expectations associated with benevolent and principled ethical climates to convey that the organization goes beyond merely making profits. By encouraging values and norms that support caring for each other and the organization (benevolence) and society at large (principled), a company demonstrates that they have goals other than maximizing profits. Such higher-order goals often reflect the spiritual value of contribution to society and are likely to make employees feel that their work has a higher meaning. This is consistent with Covey's (1990, 70) remarks that "the highest level of human motivation is a sense of personal contribution." Some good examples of attempts to encourage benevolent and principled climates are at Merck and Hewlett-Packard. At Merck the stated organizational purpose is to "preserve and improve human life," and at Hewlett-Packard the purpose is to make technical contributions to benefit humanity (Collins and Porras 1994).

To encourage the inner life aspect of workplace spirituality, companies can reward behaviors and decision-making consistent with both the benevolent and principled climates. Encouraging spirituality through such practices as business retreats, meditation, exercise, contemplation of the meaning of life, and encouraging community service, companies are aligned with a benevolent climate that supports expending considerable resources for everyone's benefit. Consider, for example, the corporate courses on meditation at such companies as Xerox and Motorola. Such benevolent programs provide the outlets for employees to express their spiritual being and to define their values and consistency with organization values (Cash and Gray 2000), and to question the reasons for their existence and purpose in life. Additionally, principled climates support the notion that life has a deeper meaning beyond individual or group welfare.

CONCLUSION

In an increasingly complex world filled with such changes as cross-national mergers and acquisitions and varying national and work economic conditions, companies must deal with alienated, disgruntled, unhappy, and potentially untrustworthy employees. One solace for this contemporary social situation is an increasing spirituality of the workplace. When managers seek to initiate spiritual programs to provide a relief for employees, they need practical organizational tools. In this article, we show how managers can use ethical climates to create a work context that facilitates the development of the spirituality of organizational members. In addition, we propose theoretical links between ethical climates and workplace spirituality. Future research should empirically assess the veracity of our propositions.

REFERENCES

Ali, A.J., and T. Falcone. (1995). "Work Ethic in the USA and Canada." *Journal of Management Development* 14, no. 6: 26–33.

Ashmos, D.P., and D. Duchon. (2000). "Spirituality at Work: A Conceptualization and Measure." *Journal of Management Inquiry* 9, no. 2: 134–145.

Beebe, T.; M. Snyder; and J. Mortimer. (1994). "Volunteerism in Adolescence: A Process Perspective." Paper presented at the annual meeting of the American Sociological Association, Los Angeles, August.

Block, P. (1993). *Stewardship: Choosing Service over Self-interest.* San Francisco: Berrett-Koehler.

Brandt, E. (1996). "Corporate Pioneers Explore Spirituality." *HR Magazine* 83: 82–86. (April).

Carlin, W.B., and K.C. Strong. (1995). "A Critique of Western Philosophical Ethics: Multidisciplinary Alternatives for Framing Ethical Dilemmas." *Journal of Business Ethics* 14, no. 5: 387–396.

Cash, K.C., and G.R. Gray. (2000). "A Framework for Accommodating Religion and Spirituality in the Workplace." *Academy of Management Executive* 14, no. 3: 124–134.

Collins, J., and J. Porras. (1994). *Built to Last: Successful Habits of Visionary Companies.* New York: Harper Business.

Conger, J.A. (1994). *Spirit at Work: Discovering the Spirituality in Leadership.* San Francisco: Jossey-Bass.

Covey, S.R. (1990). *Principle-Centered Leadership.* New York: Fireside.

Cullen, J.B.; B. Victor; and J.W. Bronson. (1993). "The Ethical Climate Questionnaire: An Assessment of Its Development and Validity." *Psychological Reports* 73, no. 3: 667–674.

Fox, M. (1994). *The Reinvention of Work.* San Francisco: Harper.

Freiberg, K., and J. Freiberg. (1996). *Nuts! Southwest Airlines' Crazy Recipe for Business and Personal Success.* Austin, TX: Bard Books.

Gould, S.J. (1995). "The Buddhist Perspective on Business Ethics: Experiential Exercises for Exploration and Practice." *Journal of Business Ethics* 14, no. 1: 63–70.

Gibbons, P. (2000). "Spirituality at Work: Definitions, Measures, Assumptions, and Validity Claims." Paper presented at the Academy of Management Meeting, Toronto, Canada, August.

Hackman, J.R., and G.R. Oldham. (1976). "Motivation Through the Design of Work: Test of a Theory." *Organizational Behavior and Human Performance* 16, no. 2: 250–279.

Harris, E. (2000). "Corporate Giving Goes Both Ways: Companies That Offer Volunteerism Are Attracting Top Talent and Motivating Employees." *Sales and Marketing Management* 152, no. 12: 104.

Hawley, J. (1993). *Reawakening the Spirit in Work: The Power of Dharmic Management.* San Francisco: Berrett-Koehler.

Homans, G. C. (1950). *The Human Group.* New York: Harcourt Brace.

Jackson, K.T. (1999). "Spirituality As a Foundation for Freedom and Creative Imagination in International Business Ethics." *Journal of Business Ethics* 19, no. 1: 61–70.

Joseph, J., and S.P. Deshpande. (1997). "The Impact of Ethical Climate on Job Satisfaction of Nurses." *Health Care Management Review* 22, no. 1: 76–81.

Kohlberg, L. (1967). "Moral and Religious Education and the Public Schools: A Developmental View." In *Religion and Public Education.* Boston: Houghton-Mifflin, 164–181.

———. (1984). *The Philosophy of Moral Development.* New York: Harper and Row.

Kirchmeyer, C. (1992). "Non-work Participation and Work Attitudes: A Test of Scarcity vs. Expansion Models of Personal Resources." *Human Relations* 45, no. 3: 775–798.

Ludwig, T.M. (2001). *The Sacred Paths.* Upper Saddle River, NJ: Prentice-Hall.

Maynard, H.B. (1992). "The Evaluation of Human Consciousness." In *New Traditions in Business*, ed. J. Renesch. San Francisco: Berrett-Koehler, 39–52.

Miller, W.C. (1992). "How Do We Put Our Spiritual Values to Work?" In *New Traditions in Business*, ed. J. Renesch. San Francisco: Berrett-Koehler, 69–80.

Milliman, J.; A. Czaplewski; and J. Ferguson, J. (2001). "An Exploratory Assessment of the Relationship Between Spirituality and Employee Attitudes." Paper presented at the Academy of Management Meeting, Washington, DC, August.

Mitroff, I.I., and E.A. Denton. (1999). "A Study of Spirituality in the Workplace." *Sloan Management Review* (summer): 83–92.

Neck, C., and J. Milliman. (1994). "Thought Self-leadership: Finding Spiritual Fulfillment in Organizational Life." *Journal of Managerial Psychology* 9, no. 1: 9–16.

Onara, N. (1975). *Acting on Principle: An Essay on Kantian Ethics.* New York: Columbia University Press.

Rosen, B. (1978). *Strategies of Ethics.* Boston: Houghton-Mifflin.

Schellenbarger, S. (2000). "More Relaxed Boomers, Fewer Workplace Frills and Other Job Trends." *Wall Street Journal,* December 27, B-1.

Schneider, B. (1975). "Organizational Climate: An Essay." *Personnel Psychology* 28: 447–479.

———. (1983). "Work Climates: An Interactionist Perspective." In *Environmental Psychology: Directions and Perspectives,* ed. N.W. Feimer and E. S. Geller. New York: Praeger, 106–128.

Taylor, F. (1947). *Scientific Management.* New York: Harper.

Victor, B., and J.B. Cullen. (1987). "A Theory and Measure of Ethical Climate in Organizations." In *Research in Corporate Social Performance,* ed. W.C. Frederick. Greenwich, CT: JAI Press, 57–71.

———. (1988). "The Organizational Bases of Ethical Work Climates." *Administrative Science Quarterly* 33, no. 1: 101–125.

Weber, J. (1995). "Influences Upon Organizational Ethical Subclimates: A Multi-departmental Analysis of a Single Firm." *Organization Science* 6, no. 5: 509–523.

Weber, J., and S. Green. (1991). "Principled Moral Reasoning: Is It a Viable Approach to Promote Ethical Integrity?" *Journal of Business Ethics* 10, no. 5: 325–333.

Weber, M. (1947). *The Theory of Social and Economic Organization,* trans. A.M. Henderson and T. Parsons. New York: Oxford University Press.

Wech, B.A.; K.W. Mossholder; R.P. Steel; and N. Bennett. (1998). "Does Work Group Cohesiveness Affect Individuals' Performance and Organizational Commitment? A Cross-Level Examination." *Small Group Research* 29, no. 4: 472–494.

Wilson, J., and M. Musick. (1997). "Who Cares? Toward an Integrated Theory of Volunteer Work." *American Sociological Review* 62, no. 5: 694–713.

Wimbush, J.C., and J.M. Shepard. (1994). "Towards an Understanding of Ethical Climate: Its Relationship to Ethical Behavior and Supervisory Influence." *Journal of Business Ethics* 13, no. 8: 637–647.

Wimbush, J.C.; J.M. Shepard; and S.E. Markham. (1997). "An Empirical Examination of the Relationship Between Ethical Climate and Ethical Behavior from Multiple Levels of Analysis." *Journal of Business Ethics* 16, no.16: 1705–1716.

CHAPTER 10

SPIRITUALITY, CONSUMPTION, AND BUSINESS

A Pragmatic Perspective

ROGENE A. BUCHHOLZ AND SANDRA B. ROSENTHAL

The general theme of this volume is the exploration of the issue of workplace spirituality within particular areas of expertise that the authors bring to the topic. While thus far spirituality has been related primarily to the workplace, the task of this particular article is to relate spirituality, consumption, and business in some manner that will help define this new paradigm and explore its relevance to other aspects of business and its impacts on society. Thus the article will not only explore the meaning of spirituality in relation to the workplace and production activities, but also apply it to the marketplace through a consideration of consumption activities. These activities will be examined by applying a vision of spirituality offered by classical American pragmatism, and in this manner, broader dimensions of the relevance of spirituality to business will be explored.

The Protestant Ethic (Weber 1958), which was soon secularized to become the general "work ethic," was in some sense an attempt to spiritualize the workplace and provide a moral framework for the new roles and responsibilities that were developing in newly emerging industrial societies.[1] As it originated, this ethic was a set of moral beliefs that provided meaning and purpose to the work people were doing through an emphasis on the idea of a calling. People had a primary responsibility to do their best at whatever worldly station they found themselves rather than withdraw from the world to seek perfection. They were called to engage the world and work hard and accumulate as much wealth as possible.

This ethic also contained restrictions on consumption in that whatever wealth one acquired was not to be spent in lavish consumption, but rather invested to create more wealth. The new ethic thus pressured equally toward effective production and efficient consumption, which—while sustaining maximum productivity—also maximized savings and potential investment capital. But while this ethic may have sought to bring meaning and purpose to the workplace, what it actually did was to make the production of economic wealth an end in itself, which became severed from any larger moral purpose related to the ongoing enrichment of human existence. Tied to moral justifications that were abstractions from the concreteness of existence, such an emphasis on production allowed for exploitation of both humans and nature in the interests of increasing production.

As industrial societies spread and became more successful, and as the Protestant ethic became secularized, whatever constraints it provided for consumption activities disappeared and gave way to an ever increasing demand for products that could produce pleasure and self-gratification. The idea of saving for the future gave way to instant gratification and pursuit of the good life through the creation of a consumer culture. A new approach to consumption was created where instant gratification became a cultural trait in contrast to earlier times when saving was emphasized. Thus not only production, but also consumption became an end in itself, divorced from any broader or larger moral purposes beyond the production and consumption of more goods and services themselves to increase economic growth.

THE NATURE OF SPIRITUALITY

Spirituality is a relatively new concern of business scholars and as is true of any new concept has many different definitions and is used in many different contexts. Allegretti (2000) defines spirituality as a kind of shorthand for the deepest urgings and impulses of the human self, that which gives meaning and depth to everyday life. The concept encompasses one's need for creativity, one's desire for self-expression, and a hunger for love and service. A spirituality of work refers to making work a part of spiritual life, finding opportunities for self-expression, bringing moral values into the workplace, standing up for what one believes, and developing a sense that all of life is sacred.

Guillory (2000) thinks of spirituality as referring to our inner consciousness, the source of inspiration, creativity, and wisdom. Spirituality thus comes from within and goes beyond our programmed beliefs and values. Spirituality is the life force that permeates and drives what he calls a living organization in the pursuit of its business objectives. Guillory makes a distinction between religion and spirituality. The latter is a way of being that predetermines how we respond to life's experiences, whereas religion deals with the incorporation and implementation of organized belief systems. The former is a vehicle that spirituality takes in practice, while spirituality is the source behind that form. Guillory believes that in order to be creative and innovative in today's workplace, we must reunite with our spirituality and make it a legitimate part of the working environment.

By spirituality, the editors of this book are referring to the idea that individuals hold a set of moral beliefs (distinct from religions beliefs) that inform their sense of right and wrong in the workplace. These beliefs generally center upon a desire by the individual to be their best, to help others be their best, and to feel a sense of connectedness with their work and coworkers. By acting upon these beliefs, individuals achieve a sense of sacredness in their actions and in the world. Thus beliefs involve a pervasive mode of behavior or mode of action that displays concerns with bettering oneself and others in the context of community and involves a sense of sacredness that extends to the world in general.

Explicitly connecting spirituality with moral beliefs, as the editors do, provides a starting point for the development of a perspective that will be the focus of this article. Moral beliefs that inform a sense of right and wrong are embedded in the way people act in their environment and stem from some kind of implicit assumptions about the way the world is and how it fits together. These beliefs form some kind of holistic approach to life; they constitute an implicit framework or philosophical perspective on life and its various components.

These beliefs and the assumptions they contain can be made more explicit for examination and discussion in philosophical reflection. The purpose of this paper will be to provide one such philosophical grounding by utilizing classical American pragmatism as a philosophical framework that can be used to conceptualize an understanding of the world where connectedness, growth, and sacredness are vital components.[2] The fundamental tenants of this philosophical approach can undergird these elements of spirituality in the workplace and can also be used to extend this concept to consumption activities. Classical American pragmatism contains a unique relational view of the self and community that provides a foundation for a discussion of the workplace and consumption in a different context from that of the traditional economic view of the corporation. It is to a brief development of this foundation that the ensuing discussion will first turn.

THE NATURE OF THE SELF AND COMMUNITY

The pragmatic view holds that all knowledge and experience are infused with interpretive aspects, funded with past experience, and stem from a perspective or point of view. In being inherently perspectival, experience and knowledge are at once experimental, for this perspectivalism involves a creative organization of experience that directs our anticipatory activity and that is tested by its workability in the ongoing course of experience. Within this context of experience as experimental, meaning emerges in the interactions among conscious organisms. In the adjustments and coordinations needed for cooperative action in the social context, individuals take the perspective of the other in the development of their conduct, and in this way there develops the common content that provides community of meaning.

To have a self is to have a particular type of ability, the ability to be aware of one's behavior as part of the social process of adjustment, to be aware of oneself as a social object, as an acting agent within the context of other acting agents. Not only do selves exist only in relationship to other selves, but no absolute line can be drawn between our own selves and the selves of others, since our own selves are there for and in our experience only insofar as others exist and enter into our experience. The origin and foundation of the self, like those of mind, are social or intersubjective. Pragmatism, in opposition to many entrenched positions, holds that there is no such thing as a self as an isolated, atomic unit of being.

In incorporating the perspective of the other, the developing self comes to take the perspective of others as the group as a whole. In this way the self comes to incorporate the standards and authority of the group, the organization or system of attitudes and responses that is called "the generalized other" (Mead 1934); there is a passive dimension to the self. Yet, in responding to the perspective of the other, the individual responds as a unique center of activity; there is also a creative dimension to the self. Any self thus incorporates, by its very nature, both the conformity of the group perspective and the creativity of its unique individual perspective.

Community is constituted by the dynamics of adjustment between the individual and the generalized other, which involves neither assimilation of perspectives, one to the other, nor fusion of each into an indistinguishable oneness, but an accommodation in which each creatively affects and is affected by the other through accepted organs of adjudication. Pragmatic community is constituted in its very nature by the ongoing dynamics of socializing adjustment. The social dynamic of pragmatic community lies in this continual interplay of adjustment of attitudes, aspirations, and factual perceptions between the generalized other, as the condition for the novel emergent perspective, and the novel emergent, as it conditions the generalized other. Thus, a community of any kind is a community of socializing adjustment between the free activity constitutive of the novel individual perspective and the common perspective of the generalized other, and each gains its meaning, significance, and enrichment from this process of adjustment. A community reflects the two poles of creativity and conformity, liberation and constraint, manifest above as two poles in the dynamics of selfhood.

Authentic reconstruction in cases of incompatibility must be based on the problem situation and the history within which it has emerged. Yet, reconstruction cannot be imposed by eliciting the standards of a past that does not contain the organs of resolution but must call upon a more fundamental and creative level of activity. The very relation of individual selves to the generalized other requires the openness of perspectives, and the adjustment of different perspectives through rational reconstruction requires not an imposition from "on high," but a deepening of experience to a more fundamental level of human rapport.[3] It is within this dynamic relation between the individual and the generalized other that value emerges reflecting the bipolar dynamics of adjustment.

THE CORPORATION AS A COMMUNITY

This pragmatic view of self and community has implications for the nature of the relationships within the corporation. According to classical economic theory, the corporation is considered to be an organization in which people band together as investors, employees, and so on, because of economic self-interest. By becoming part of such an organization, they are able to do things that they could not do by themselves. But the only ties that hold them together are economic in nature. This view of the corporation is in keeping with traditional social contract theories of the state as formulated by Hobbes, Locke, and so forth, but limited here to the economic realm.

If a corporation is understood solely as a organization in which people band together for self-interested reasons, as is held by traditional economic theory, such bonds cannot root them in any ongoing endeavor which is more than the sum of their separate selves, separate wills, separate egoistic desires. From a pragmatic perspective, however, the corporation is itself a community, and the individuals in the organization are what they are in part because of their membership in a corporation, while the corporation is what it is because of the people who choose to become part of the organization.

Nor are these individuals and their skills and abilities coordinated in some mechanical fashion to accomplish corporate objectives. Such a mechanistic view of the corporation is not consistent with the notion that people who work in the corporation do not sacrifice their essential humanness. Managers who treat their employees in an economic sense as just another factor of production are not treating these people as moral beings who are an essential part of the community.

Moreover, what makes a corporation efficient or inefficient is not a series of well-oiled mechanical operations, but the working interrelationships, the coordination and rivalries, the team spirit and morale of the many people who work there and are in turn shaped by the corporation. The corporation needs a certain aspect of conformity in order to operate, but at the same time needs creative input from the unique individuals who work for it in order for it to grow and remain competitive. Focusing only on the economic aspects of the relationship again abstracts out one aspect from which is in reality a rich and complex relationship that involves multiple motives and reasons for joining an organization, many of which are non-economic in nature.

THE CORPORATION IN COMMUNITY

Classical economic theory considers the corporation to be a device formed for purely economic purposes. It relates to society solely through the marketplace, and marketplace transactions make up the whole of its existence and reason for being. According to pragmatic theory, however, the corporation does not have its whole existence and reason for being in the marketplace. The corporation as understood in only its marketplace function is an abstraction from its social context and the multiple relations and relationships which this context involves. This isolated function has been allowed to take on a life of its own, detached from the social context that gives both the corporation and marketplace their existence and purpose. In the process the corporation has been given a purpose in terms of only one aspect of the fullness of its own existence. What has been lost in this process is the intrinsic moral nature of the corporation as part of a social community to which it is inextricably tied and within which it relates to and affects multiple "others," which in turn affect the corporation in a reciprocal relationship. Pragmatic theory attempts to recover its intrinsic social and moral purpose, which has been largely ignored.

The multiple relationships in which the corporation is embedded are part of the multiple relationships that are inherent in human existence. The corporation has as its major function the enrichment of the multiple environments—economic, social, cultural, and natural—in which these relationships are embedded. The production of goods and services is primarily for the flourishing of human existence, and only in this context does their production gain its concrete rationale. Growth cannot be understood only in terms of mere accumulation or mere increase of something like economic wealth but, rather, involves the ongoing reconstruction of experience to bring about the integration, expansion, and enrichment of the contexts in which human existence is embedded. Ultimately, the corporation's responsibility is for the welfare of the community, for the multiple relations in which the corporation is embedded are at once the multiple relations inherent in community life.

Several conceptual devices such as corporate social responsibility and stakeholder theory have tried to express this social aspect of the corporation and go beyond the view that the corporation exists solely to maximize the wealth of shareholders. Corporate social responsibility holds that the corporation has responsibilities to society that go beyond the making of a profit, has a broader constituency to serve than that of stockholders alone, and serves a wider range of values than economic theory implies. Stakeholder theory involves balancing the interests of various stakeholders in any given corporate decision, stockholders being only one such stakeholder. Both of these approaches embody a relational view of the firm, and their power lies in focusing management decision-making on the multiplicity and diversity of these relationships. This view involves nothing less than a redefinition of the corporation, and as Freeman (1994) insightfully notes: "Redescribing corporations means redescribing ourselves and our communities."

The multipurposes of a corporation are often lost sight of in the quest for profits as an indicator of economic well-being. But when the economic purposes of a corporation become the be-all and end-all of its existence, this artificially isolates the corporation from the social context that give it legitimacy and stagnates the relationships in which it is embedded. Profits are essential to the ongoing activity of the corporation and serve as one sign among many others that the corporation is functioning well in relationship to its environment. Profits are indeed a means to building a thriving business, but this thriving involves the thriving of the multiple environments in which the corporation is embedded.

THE SPIRITUALIZING OF CONSUMPTION

With the above background, the following discussion can now turn to the issue of consumption within a pragmatic framework. Consumption in some sense is where everything comes together, as most people work in some activity that provides a good or service to be consumed by others. The major purpose of business in society is to provide people with the good life through the production of more and more goods and services to be consumed. The economy depends on increased consumption, and when consumers cut back on expenditures, the economy is in trouble. When this happens, business must be encouraged to invest in new productive capacity through lower interest rates, and consumers must be encouraged to spend through tax relief. Consumption of more and more products, as indicated earlier, is an end in itself devoid of any larger moral purpose beyond the promotion of economic growth.

Critics of this consumer culture (Strong and Higgs 2000) argue that consumption leads to a life of disengagement, diversion, distraction, and loneliness. As consumers, according to these authors, we become disengaged from each other, and our social life becomes mediated through a commodity culture. Consumption is what most of us spend a good deal of time doing and building our lives around, but our interest in any particular commodity is short-lived and the thrills of consumption are necessarily disconnected from each other resulting in fragmentation. The irony of consumption is that we destroy the good life we are seeking when we try to enrich our lives solely through consumption.

They (Strong and Higgs 2000) argue that the culture of the table, the gathering of the family around dinner, for example, can be (and for many has been) displaced and destroyed by the use of fast food restaurants. Nature becomes packaged in a subdivision, and wilderness and the natural world are destroyed as their resources are needed for increasing levels of consumption. Attractive city streets and parks in which to walk or bike have been displaced by automobiles, freeways, and streets lined with commercial signs; in fact, these activities have been replaced by shopping at indoor malls and private entertainment. In the old days children spent most of their time playing outdoors. Today they spend most of their time watching television, playing video games, or surfing the Internet. To summarize, temporally, spatially, socially, and bodily centering activities that would give meaning and purpose to our existence have been crowded out of contemporary life by ever increasing consumption.

Instead of living the good life of creative endeavor, active citizenship, and ennobling physical adventures, we have become passive consumers, disengaged from and disburdened of those connections with the physical and social world that give substance and meaning to life. The ongoing and escalating competition to simply maintain a household's relative social status assures that these households experience material insecurity no matter what the level of affluence they have achieved. Expanded consumption is experienced as a necessity even when from a more objective point of view, the contribution that consumption is making to satisfying "needs" is trivial (Power 2000).

Some of these critics ("Treaty on Consumption and Lifestyle" 1992) suggest that we must reawaken to the reality that quality of life is based on the development of human relationships, creativity, cultural and artistic expression, spirituality, reverence for the natural world, and celebration of life, and it is not dependent upon increased consumption of nonbasic material goods. Others (Korten 1993) argue that we must be aware of the essential importance of a healthy spiritual connection to nature, place, community, and culture as fundamental to the healthy function and well-being of both individual and society and reject the contemporary economic theology that an expanding economic pie will bring universal prosperity to everyone.

Can consumption be spiritualized along with the workplace to give it a meaning and purpose beyond mere consumption itself? To deal with this question, it seems as if the idea of growth itself must be looked at and perhaps redefined. McNeill (2000) suggests that the most important idea of the twentieth century was the overarching priority of economic growth. Others argue that growth as currently defined is not itself a panacea for what ails human society. Indeed it is a major contributor to many of those ills. Yet growth dominates public policy, almost to the exclusion of other values. It is time that we shed our obsession with growth, Korten (1993) suggests, and get straight on our values and what they mean for how we choose to allocate the sustainable regenerative product of the planet's ecosystem. Real human development is neither dependent on nor well served by profligate physical consumption, for once a basic level of physical need satisfaction has been achieved, the appropriate focus is on quality of life, not quantity of consumption.

TOWARD A NEW UNDERSTANDING OF GROWTH

Rethinking growth involves a theoretical position that rejects the long held assumptions that pervade our approach to the understanding of growth, and this in turn requires a rejection of all vestiges of the atomistic understanding of humans and their relation to the world in which they live. This assumption gained its entrenchment in human thinking with the rise of modern science and the Cartesian understanding of the nature of science and of the scientific object. Such a linkage, based largely on the presuppositions of a spectator theory of knowledge, led to a naively realistic philosophic interpretation of scientific content. Scientific knowledge provided the literal description of objective fact and excluded our lived qualitative experience as providing access to the natural universe.

This world view resulted in a quantitatively characterized nature and the atomicity of discrete individual units that must be brought together through mechanistic laws or related to each other through a mechanistic process. This in turn led to the alienation of humans from nature and a radical dehumanizing of nature. Nature became a quantifiable object of value-free human manipulation. While this established a radical dualism between humans and nature, yet humans, like nature, were understood in terms of isolatable, independent, or atomic units. Moreover, rejecting dualism did not alleviate the problem, for it resulted in reducing the human in its totality to the value-free, quantifiable, mechanistic, atomistic system, which constituted physical nature.

Given the quantitative, atomistic conceptual framework of the modern world view, growth becomes quantitative accumulation of individual things, and the measurement of growth is how much has been accumulated, be it the things one owns or the total output produced by society. The wealth of the society is tied up in the goods and services it produces, and growth is measured by the increase in gross national product, which is the sum total of all the goods and services produced in society, whether these goods and services degrade the environment or enhance it in some fashion.

This view of the atomic self permeates our understanding of the economy and the functioning of the economic system (Power 2000). Economics assumes that society is nothing but the aggregation of atomistic individuals so that there are no social objectives to individual decisions. The economy and economic activity are envisioned as separate realms of human activity that can be studied outside of their social and political contexts and have an existence separate from the rest of people's existence. Economics also appeals to a mechanical model to explain how the economy functions.

Thus, one of the important accomplishments of economics has been to distinguish the economy as a separate realm of human activity and then see it as managed by an automatic mechanism that is both self-adjusting and socially rational, even though no rational thought is involved in its operation. Conscious direction of the economy is not only necessary, but also inappropriate and destructive. Through the competition among self-interested parties, the narrow self-seeking that motivates these individuals is cancelled out, and an outcome intended by none of the participants emerges. That outcome is supposedly rational in the sense of minimizing costs and using scarce resources efficiently in satisfying the aggregate preferences of the population. This reduces the determinants of individual well-being largely to the level of personal consumption achieved (Power 2000).

Pragmatism—in focusing on scientific method as the experimental activity in which the scientist engages rather than in focusing on absolutizing the results which the scientist obtains—undercuts the self-defeating frameworks and alternatives resulting from the Cartesian world view, allowing for a relational and qualitative understanding of humans and the natural universe in which they are embedded and of which they are a part. The human being is within nature, and neither human activity in general nor human knowledge can be separated from the fact that this being is a natural organism dependent upon a natural environment.

But the human organism and the nature within which it is located are both rich with the qualities and values of our everyday experience. Distinctively human traits such as mind, thinking, and self-hood are emergent characteristics of nature and part and parcel of its richness. They refer to ways in which the lived body behaves. Just as the self is essentially intertwined with other selves, so it is essentially intertwined with the body; it is a body-self that is "located," if one speaks of location, throughout the biological organism with its reflexive ability as this emerges from and opens onto the relational contexts in which it functions. Human development is ecologically connected with its biological as well as its cultural world.

From the perspective of pragmatism's understanding of self, humans and their entire environment—organic and inorganic—take on an inherently relational aspect. To speak of organism and environment in isolation from each other is never true to the situation, for no organism can exist in isolation from an environment, and an environment is what it is in relation to an organism. The properties attributed to the environment belong to it in the context of that interaction. What we have is interaction as an indivisible whole, and it is only within such an interactional context that experience and its qualities function.

Given the above framework, growth cannot be understood in terms of mere accumulation or mere increase. Rather growth involves the ongoing reconstruction of experience to bring about the integration and expansion of contexts with which self-hood is intertwined. The growth of the self is a process by which it achieves fuller, richer, more inclusive, and more complex interactions with its environment. It cannot be understood only in terms of the organization of one's own interests or the artificiality of oneself in isolation but, rather, requires growth of context as well. Growth incorporates an encompassing sympathetic understanding of varied and diverse interests—thus leading to tolerance not as a sacrifice, but as an enlargement of self; not as something totally other, but as something sympathetically incorporated as an expansion of one's self (Mead 1934).

The development of the ability both to create and to respond constructively to the creation of novel and/or other perspectives, as well as to incorporate the perspective of the other, not as something totally alien, but as something sympathetically understood, is at once growth of the self. The pragmatic understanding of growth involves reintegration of problematic situations in ways that lead to expansion of self, of community, and of the relation between the two. Moreover, though not independent of intelligent inquiry, growth is not merely a change in an intellectual perspective but, rather, is a change that affects and is affected by the individual in its total concreteness, allowing one to become more attuned to the fullness of existence in its concreteness and hence more appreciative of its qualitative richness and value-laden contexts. In this way, growth is best understood as an increase in the moral-esthetic richness of experience.

The deepening and expansion of perspective to include ever-widening horizons must extend beyond the cultural to the natural world with which we are inseparably intertwined. This receives its most intense form in Dewey's (1978) understanding of experiencing the world religiously as a way of relating one's self with the universe as the totality of conditions with which the self is connected.[4] This unity can be neither apprehended in knowledge, nor realized in reflection—for it involves such totality, not as a literal content of the intellect, but as an imaginative extension of the self; not an intellectual grasp, but a deepened attunement. This is the reason poets get at nature so well. This would seem to provide a concrete sense of the "holistic approach for the common good, understood beyond Plato's model, as both a communitarian and a universal but nonanthropocentric goal," which Westra (1995, 20) considers a requirement for establishing "guidelines of ecosystem integrity."

Such an experience brings about not a change in the intellect alone, but a change in moral consciousness. It allows one to "rise above" the divisiveness we impose through arbitrary and illusory in-group/out-group distinctions by "delving beneath" to the sense of the possibilities of a deep-seated harmonizing of the self with the totality of the conditions to which it relates. And, for all the pragmatists, this involves the entire universe, for their emphasis on continuity reveals that at no time can we separate our developing selves from any part of the universe and claim that it is irrelevant. Indeed, while one may seek to describe "objective" relationships among interacting individuals—human, nonhuman, organic, and inorganic—that make up the biosphere, the properties attributed to the individuals are not possessed by them independently of the interactions in which they exhibit themselves. Nature cannot be dehumanized, nor can humans be denaturalized. Humans exist within and are part of nature, and any part of nature provides a conceivable relational context for the emergence of value.

Whatever the relational contexts involved in specific situations, the sense of value is an immediately experienced quality of our ongoing concrete existence, but cannot be located either "in" us or "there" in an independently ordered universe. Rather, value is a relational, emergent quality of concrete contexts, and our abstract "oughts" are not rules handed down from on high but, rather, are experimental hypotheses for the organization of valuing experiences that lead to the enhancement of value for all. The conflict of value, like all conflicts, requires a deepening to a more fundamental level of rapport, to a sense of the concrete richness of humans and the diversity of valuings that must be harmonized, to a sense of one's openness to a deeper community and the possibilities contained therein.

Our normative claims are about the experience of value, and unless one is attuned to the sense of concrete existence and the value qualities contained therein, our normative claims become sterile and empty. If individuals remain oblivious to the value dimension pervasive of concrete human existence, then artificial values will be substituted. The consumerism of today is partially the product of a desperate substitute for the experience of felt value and the demands of concrete human existence for ongoing growth. When consumerism becomes such a substitute, then the holistic skills needed for the reconstruction and expansion of value-laden self-community growth cannot occur.

It was stressed earlier that the Protestant work ethic provided a moral frame for early stages of industrialization. However, the moral vision itself eventually became production/consumption in the interests of ever increasing economic growth. There is needed a new moral vision in which to place production and consumption, and the vision offered by pragmatism is that of concrete growth as inherently moral and qualitative. Economic growth is an abstraction from a concrete situation, and when it stifles rather than furthers concrete growth, it is an abstraction that forgets the concrete reality it is intended to serve, a fallacy similar to that operative in the modern world view understanding of the quantification of nature. Moreover, to separate economic growth from its moral soil is a remnant of the fact-value distinction rooted in the dichotomies of that era.

Quality of life is often understood as enhanced through economic production rather than through ongoing concrete growth. But, ongoing concrete growth as inherently moral requires integration of ever widening contexts of the environments of which we are culturally and naturally a part. To speak of economic development as enhancing quality of life while destroying any of the multiple environments within which ongoing growth is achieved shows the abstract and nonrelational understanding of quality of life incorporated in the concept of economic development. As has been noted (Wackernagel and Rees 1996, 135–136), "Once material sufficiency is secured," there is no longer a correlation of quality of life "with national or personal income," and the thought that there is involves a misguided understanding of "quality of life." The protection of all our multiple environments in which we are embedded and the enhancement of quality of life are inextricably joined through their inextricable dependency on the moral nature of concrete growth as involving the ongoing integration and expansion of concrete contexts in their qualitative richness in workable ways. This leads directly to the issue of workability. First, workability cannot be taken in the sense of workable for oneself only, for the entire discussion has stressed that the self is inextricably tied to the community of which it is a part, and growth of self is intertwined with growth of community. Second, workability cannot be taken in terms of the short-range expedient, for actions and their consequences extend into an indefinite future and determine the possibilities in that future. Finally, workability cannot be taken in terms of some abstract aspect of life, such as economic workability, for workability as normative involves the ongoing development of the concrete richness of human experience in its entirety. It was seen above that community life in general involves the functioning of humans in their concrete fullness, and this functioning embodies moral dimensions throughout. Workability within community in general, then, must ultimately concern the enrichment of concrete human existence in its entirety. Workability in the ongoing dynamics of community life has, like growth, an inherently moral quality.

The significance of workable consequences involved in the choice among values is encapsulated in Dewey's (1983, 216–217) assertion that, "In short, the thing actually at stake in any serious deliberation is not a difference of quantity, but what kind of person one is to become, what sort of self is in the making, what kind of a world is in the making." What is needed for responsibility in directing the course of growth in the most workable ways is the development of the reorganizing and ordering capabilities of creative intelligence, the imaginative grasp of authentic possibilities, the vitality of motivation and, undergirding it all, a deepened attunement to the sense of concrete human existence in its richness, diversity, and multiple types of interrelatedness with the social, cultural, political, and natural environments of which it is a part.[5] It is this attunement that will give vitality to the diverse and changing experimental courses of action that we develop to guide the direction of ongoing growth for individuals, corporations, and the totality of environments in which they are relationally embedded.

CONCLUSION

This chapter has argued that there is a need for a new concept of growth to be promoted in society, a reeducation of the American consumer to realize that growth can mean more than mere accumulation of more and more things and that wealth means more than just material wealth as measured by an ever-increasing gross national product. Consumer culture with its emphasis on ever-increasing consumption to promote continued economic growth is not sustainable into the future. Spiritualizing of the workplace and the marketplace both involve a new understanding of the self and community, as it is within community that concrete growth of the individual human being takes place. But mere pleading of this case is not enough. As Albert Borgmann (2000, 363) has pointed out:

> In all of these cases of exhortation, pleading does not come merely to emotional appeals of persistent haranguing. There are facts that people need to be reminded of, connections and

implications that must be clarified, and deceptions and fallacies that have to be exposed. But none of this will do much good as long as most people remain enthralled by consumption. To dislodge them from that persuasion, they need to be presented with or reminded of an alternative vision of life.

This chapter has attempted to provide that vision by offering a novel philosophic approach, one in which spirituality and a new, richer understanding of growth are inseparably intertwined and in which spirituality in any limited context, such as the workplace or the marketplace, extends by its very nature into all the relational contexts within which human existence is located. While individuals may take on many roles, such as the role of consumer or the role of worker, these are abstractions from the concreteness of their existence that underlies all the various roles we play in society, and from the multiple environments in which this existence is embedded.

The dynamics of adjustment that are constitutive of community life, provide the means by which the particular activities of production and consumption, as two dimensions of an ever-adjusting social process, can mutually affect each other for ongoing enriching growth of community life in the concrete. These activities must be understood in terms of their contribution to concrete growth of the human being and the multiple environments in which they function, to the enrichment of human existence in its totality. Production and consumption are not ends in themselves, but must be made to serve a larger moral purpose. The spiritualizing of the workplace and the marketplace, based on a philosophic approach such as that described in this article, can present a new vision that may wean both workers and consumers off the meaningless treadmill of ever-continuing economic growth as the ultimate goal of society. Implementation of this vision would certainly mean that companies must evaluate their products in terms of how they contribute to concrete growth, how they enrich the lives of consumers, not just whether money can be made through their sale on the marketplace.

NOTES

1. For an extensive discussion of this ethic and its cultural significance, see our other works (Buchholz 1998; Rosenthal and Buchholz 2000).
2. By pragmatism in this essay is intended classical American pragmatism, that movement incorporating the writings of its five major contributors, Charles Peirce, William James, John Dewey, G.H. Mead, and C.I. Lewis. That these philosophers provide a unified perspective is assumed in this essay, but this claim is defended at some length in Rosenthal (1986).
3. The use of flextime by many organizations provides a concrete example of the socializing adjustment that an organization can make to accommodate the needs of employees. In this case, the situation was reconstructed by allowing employees greater freedom to choose their hours of work in order to accommodate their needs, and yet meet organizational needs by having all employees at work for a core period of time.
4. And thus, James holds that the broadest forms of moral commitment are held by those who appreciate the religious dimension of existence. Similarly, Mead (1934, 275) claims that the religious is an attitude that carries the "extension of the social attitude to the universe at large."
5. The importance of this attunement cannot be overstressed. In Dewey's (1990, 76) words, "A problem must be felt before it can be stated. If the unique quality of the situation is had immediately, then there is something that regulates the selection and the weighing of observed facts and their conceptual ordering."

REFERENCES

Allegretti, J.G. (2000). *Loving Your Job, Finding Your Passion: Work and the Spiritual Life.* New York: Paulist Press.

Borgmann, A. (2000). "Reply to My Critics." *In Technology and the Good Life*, ed. Eric S. Higgs, Andrew Light, and David Strong. Chicago: University of Chicago Press.

Buchholz, R. (1998). "The Ethics of Consumption Activities: A Future Paradigm?" *Journal of Business Ethics* 17: 871–882.

Dewey J. (1978). "Ethics." In *The Middle Works*, vol. 5, ed. J. Boydston. Carbondale and Edwardsville: Southern Illinois University Press.

———. (1983). "Human Nature and Conduct." In *The Middle Works*, vol. 14, ed. J. Boydston. Carbondale and Edwardsville: University of Southern Illinois Press.

———. (1990). "The Theory of Inquiry." *The Later Works*, vol. 12. Carbondale and Edwardsville: Southern Illinois University Press.

Guillory, W.A. (2000). *Spirituality in the Workplace*. Salt Lake City, UT: Innovations International.

Freeman, R.E. (1994). "The Politics of Stakeholder Theory: Some Future Directions." *Business Ethics Quarterly* 4: 414–427.

Korten, D. (1993). "Economy, Ecology and Spirituality: Toward a Theory and Practice of Sustainability." Available at: http://iisd.ca/pcdf/1993/orgprin.htm.

McNeill, J.R. (2000). *Something New Under the Sun: An Environmental History of the Twentieth-Century World*. New York: Norton.

Mead, G.H. (1934). *Mind, Self, and Society*, ed. C. Morris. Chicago: University of Chicago Press.

Power, T.M. (2000). "Trapped in Consumption: Modern Social Structure and the Entrenchment of the Device." In T*echnology and the Good Life*, ed. Eric S. Higgs, Andrew Light, and David Strong. Chicago: University of Chicago Press.

Rosenthal, S. (1986). *Speculative Pragmatism*. Amherst: University of Massachusetts Press.

Rosenthal, S.B., and R.A. Buchholz. (2000). *Rethinking Business Ethics: A Pragmatic Approach*. New York: Oxford University Press.

Strong, D., and E. Higgs. (2000). "Borgmann's Philosophy of Technology." In *Technology and the Good Life*, ed. Eric S. Higgs, Andrew Light, and David Strong. Chicago: University of Chicago Press.

"Treaty on Consumption and Lifestyle." (1992). Available at: http://www.prosus.uio.no/bu/alternativ-agenda/Consumption-Lifestyle.html.

Wackernagel M., and W.E. Rees. (1996). *Our Ecological Footprint: Reducing Human Impact on the Earth*. Philadelphia: New Society.

Weber, M. (1958). *The Protestant Ethic and the Spirit of Capitalism*. New York: Scribner's.

Westra, L. (1995). "Ecosystem Integrity and Sustainability: The Foundational Value of the Wild." In *Perspectives on Ecological Integrity*, ed. L. Westra and J. Lemons. Dordrecht, Netherlands: Kluwer, 12–33.

CHAPTER 11

EMBRACING WORKPLACE SPIRITUALITY AND MANAGING ORGANIZATIONAL POLITICS

Servant Leadership and Political Skill for Volatile Times

ROBERT W. KOLODINSKY, MICHAEL G. BOWEN, AND GERALD R. FERRIS

> I'm talking about her (mankind's) mysterious inner life, the fertile invisible realm that is the wellspring for our species' creativity and morality. . . . For want of a better term, one could call it the spirit-led or spiritual life of our species. . . . And yet, as a student of the American psyche, at no time in my life can I remember our culture being so estranged from this essential part of itself. One can see it in the loss of faith in leaders and institutions—the cynicism, selfishness, and erosion of civility—and the hunger for connectedness that stalks our nation today.
>
> —*Norman Lear 1992*

> Something very, very profound is going on. It is a true metamorphosis inside our society. I haven't any question about it at all. People have had it with giving their whole lives to a business. I'm sensing a lot of imbalance, an awareness of a hollowness in people's lives.
>
> —*Stephen R. Covey, in Lee and Zemke 1993, 23*

INTRODUCTION

As described throughout this book, the growing spiritual revival in today's society (see Ali 2001; Gunther 2001; Woodward 2001) is having profound effects in many organizational settings. Whether it be lunchtime meetings of executives discussing how to "listen to their hearts," CEOs who have dedicated their businesses to serving a higher power, or business school conferences organized to debate the role of God in the workplace, the sentiments embodied in television writer/producer Norman Lear's and in popular author Stephen Covey's comments above are apparently widespread, and reflect how many of us feel about the current state of organizational life. In fact, there is ample evidence to suggest that the needs for connectedness, purpose, and meaning are so pervasive and so deeply felt that the actions taken by individuals at every organizational level to address these needs are changing how we think about the ways we work, do business, and lead the organizations we create.

Despite the growing attention given to spirituality in the workplace, the effects of this emergent phenomenon on our business organizations are oftentimes overshadowed by frenetic efforts made by organizational members just to keep up with the typically rapid pace of change in today's organizations. This can be especially true in situations marked by the struggle to survive, a situation that too often results in tough, harsh, and perhaps even unethical decisions. For example, the dot-com that is burning through cash at a rate that threatens exhaustion of funds within a few months, with no additional funding in sight, will likely find its leaders in a difficult decision-making position, having to choose between product/market forces and the very people needed to do the work necessary to get the firm back on its feet. When such decisions are made solely by management without apparent regard for, or involvement of, nonmanagement workers, the lack of understanding by workers about such decisions—along with corollary feelings of uncertainty and insecurity—can fuel the negative effects associated with perceptions of organizational politics.

For purposes of clarification, given that the "reality" of organizational politics is largely perceptual in nature (Ferris, Russ, and Fandt 1989; Ferris, Harrell-Cook, and Dulebohn 2000), in this chapter we view organizational politics and one's perceptions of organizational politics synonymously (and different from power; see Bacharach and Lawler 1980), and thus use them interchangeably in the text. In addition, while we recognize that some researchers believe organizational politics to be a necessary and even functional part of organizational life (e.g., Bacharach and Lawler 1980; Pfeffer 1992; Weber 1947), research during the past dozen or so years has shown it to have primarily detrimental effects (e.g., Kacmar and Baron 1999; Valle and Perrewé 2000; Zhou and Ferris 1995). Given this recent evidence, we are taking the view in this chapter that organizational politics and political perceptions have adverse effects on important intra-organizational outcomes. Furthermore, as described in greater depth later in this chapter, political skill and organizational politics are separate constructs. Whereas organizational politics is viewed here as self-serving behavior with largely detrimental effects, political skill is essentially an ability to navigate political environments and effectively influence others. We see political skill as a critical ability of effective leaders and a key characteristic that can promote spirituality and neutralize the dysfunctional consequences of organizational politics.

The purpose of this chapter is to explore the interplay between leadership, organizational politics, and workplace spirituality. Specifically, we suggest two emerging areas of leadership as most appropriate to the development of more spirit-based organizations, while concurrently helpful in reducing the negative effects brought on by organizational politics. Leaders who are servant-oriented and politically skilled inspire trust and confidence in both internal and external stakeholders, enabling organizations with such leaders not only to be effective competitors in the marketplace, but also better vehicles for allowing organizational workers to achieve the sense of balance, meaning, and personal fulfillment lacking in many of today's politically charged workplaces. It is our belief that organizational politics and spirituality coexist in most organizations. However, we also believe that the most effective organizations actively seek to minimize those factors (e.g., uncertainty, ambiguity, insecurity) that give rise to organizational politics and concurrently try to encourage spiritual practices at work.

BACKGROUND ISSUES AND LITERATURE

The growth in interest in organizational politics and workplace spirituality has not occurred without cause. Unprecedented and ever-increasing volatility in organizational environments (Mitroff, Mason, and Pearson 1994), caused by a variety of factors, have trickle-down effects that are wide-ranging and deeply felt by nearly all workers (Pfeffer 1998). For example, the monumental change from an industrial to an information society—brought on in part by extraordinary technological advances in such areas as computers and telecommunications—has enabled many organizations to decentralize and more effectively reach stakeholders virtually anywhere in the world. The global reach enabled by such technologies has helped many organizations grow and gain market share, but often results in increased worker travel and a blurring of work–life boundaries, pulling workers away from their established community ties and out of their comfort zones. Furthermore, the increasingly fast pace of change and intensely competitive business environment, along with highly disruptive organizational events, such as downsizing, restructurings, mergers and acquisitions, have not only contributed to job insecurity and feelings of detachment, but also to an increased cynicism toward management and organizations, and a search for meaning at work (e.g., Moxley 2000; Noer 1993).

The volatility resulting from such changes has implications both intra- and inter-organizationally, but some issues are simply much less well understood than others. Our focus in this chapter is on the intra-organizational factors of workplace spirituality and organizational politics, and how certain leadership attributes may be most effective in addressing these issues. We first briefly explore the issue of spirituality: what it is and why it might be emerging as a workplace issue at this time. We then examine current thinking on organizational politics in this context, and we follow it with a discussion of servant leadership and political skill whereby we suggest how politically skilled leaders with a servant-first orientation might best foster spirituality in the workplace, while concurrently helping to reduce organizational politics and its negative effects. The chapter concludes with sections on implications for both theory and practice.

Spirituality in Organizations

Discussions of workplace spirituality have taken many forms in the scholarly and business literatures, reflecting the high level of interest in today's society. For example, there are numerous books and articles on the inner life and corporate soul (DePree 1992; Palmer 1998; Whyte 1994), spiritual leadership (Fairholm 1998), servant leadership (Greenleaf 1977, 1978; Spears 1997), stewardship (Block 1993), "followership" (Kelley 1998), spiritual laws of success (Chopra 1994), work–life balance (Laabs 1995; O'Neil 1995), and values-based leadership (Bolman and Deal 2001; Vaill 1998; Williams and Houck 1992), among many others.

There are also various ideas about how to define workplace spirituality. Some authors (e.g., Gunther 2001) have viewed it primarily in religious terms, whereby the central issue is how to better incorporate religious values and activities in the everyday operations of organizations. Others, such as Ashmos and Duchon (2000), have argued that spirituality is not necessarily religious but, rather, involves "finding and expressing meaning and purpose and living in relation to others and to something bigger than oneself" (135). In a study of organizational executives, managers, and human resources professionals, Mitroff and Denton (1999) found that survey respondents differentiated between spiritual and religious expression in the workplace, reporting that spirituality was "essential" and "appropriate" for workplace discussion, whereas religion was seen as a highly inappropriate form of workplace expression. Some viewed religion as "organized, close-minded, and intolerant" (90), whereas spirituality largely was seen as highly individualized, tolerant, and open-minded. From the findings of their study, the authors suggested that the key elements of spirituality include an individualistically defined sense of informality, unstructuredness, inclusivity, universality, timelessness, meaning, purpose in life, interconnectedness, and inner peace and calm (89). Like many other authors (e.g., Conger 1994; Judge 1999; Moxley 2000), we view religion as part of the much broader spirituality construct. Though religion clearly plays an important role in the spiritual lives of most Americans (Judge

1999), our focus here in the organizational context is on the larger, broader, and perhaps less controversial construct.

There are many ideas about why interest in workplace spirituality has emerged and grown so widely in recent years. Burack (1999), for example, has argued that two mainstream business developments are responsible for this. He described the first as the "economic-technological imperative," the notion that impersonal economic and technological change forces have historically been responsible for the growth and development of corporations on the modern business scene. Unfortunately, these change forces also help contribute to greater worker uncertainty, ambiguity, and insecurity, factors that contribute to organizational politics and undesirable outcomes for the individual workers and, ultimately, for the organization. Burack referred to the second development as the "people centered imperative," a phenomenon that is occurring because of the declining competitive advantage and personnel backlash wrought by the economic–technological imperative. Other ideas that have been proposed to explain the emergence of workplace spirituality include the feeling that workplaces have become insecure, even terrifying, environments for many workers (Brandt 1996). Moreover, due to the declining influence of many of the groups that have traditionally provided reliable community support (e.g., neighborhoods, churches, the extended family), the workplace provides the only consistent link to other people and to the basic human needs for connection (Conger 1994; Jurkiewicz, Massey, Jr., and Brown 1998).

Given the growing belief that people make the primary difference in today's organizations (e.g., Pfeffer 1998), factors that will improve the experience of workers, contributing to greater meaning and purpose in the workplace and filling the need for connection, are thus naturally assuming more fundamental importance. This need for connection manifests in a desire for community, and the synergism resulting from community-oriented work settings often results in achievements far greater than we can achieve through "rugged individualism" (e.g., Jackson 1995; Moxley 2000). Whereas some leaders take the attitude that "eagles don't flock" (Moxley 2000, 16), a ruggedly individualistic leadership stance tends to manifest in hierarchical and autocratic forms of decision-making, thereby serving to fuel negative political perceptions and erode rather than build a sense of community and spirituality, ultimately resulting in reduced worker productivity. The fact is, according to Weisbord (1991), "We hunger for community and are a great deal more productive when we find it" (xiv).

Furthermore, the exploration of spiritual issues at work can result in greater self-discovery and the building of an increased sense of personal security (Anderson 2000), which can help combat the insecure feelings workers typically have about their work, particularly work environments perceived as political. This might contribute to individuals personally feeling more secure in a holistic sense even if the workplace itself is not secure. The nature of organizational politics in work environments as they relate to spirituality issues is addressed in the following section.

Organizational Politics, Work Environments, and Spirituality

As described above, organizational volatility and constant change has resulted in increased uncertainty, ambiguity, and insecurity in the workplace, conditions that are ripe for the increased experience of organizational politics (e.g., Ferris, Russ, and Fandt 1989). Given these factors, it is no wonder that there has been a corollary rise in interest in the scientific study of organizational politics, its antecedents, and its consequences.

Organizational politics has been defined as unsanctioned and typically self-serving activities that are seen as detrimental to organizational functioning (Ferris et al. 1994; Mintzberg 1983).

According to Ferris, Harrell-Cook, and Dulebohn (2000), perceptions of organizational politics involve ". . . an individual's attribution to behaviors of self-serving intent and is defined as an individual's subjective evaluation about the extent to which the work environment is characterized by coworkers and supervisors who demonstrate such self-serving behavior" (90). Important aspects of this definition are that perceptions of politics involve an attribution of intent regarding the behavior of other organizational members, that these behaviors are interpreted as self-serving, and that such perceptions usually involve negative subjective feelings regarding political behavior in the work environment.

Increasingly studied during the last two decades, organizational political perceptions consistently have been found to be associated with a variety of undesirable organizational outcomes, including lower job satisfaction (e.g., Ferris and Kacmar 1992; Valle and Perrewé 2000), higher job tension and stress (e.g., Cropanzano et al. 1997; Ferris et al. 1996), higher intent to turnover (e.g., Harrell-Cook, Ferris, and Dulebohn 1999; Hochwarter et al. 1999), and lower commitment (e.g., Maslyn and Fedor 1998; Witt 1998). As proposed in the original political perceptions model (Ferris et al. 1989), worker understanding of organizational decisions and events has been found to reduce the negative effects that political perceptions typically have on valued organizational outcomes (e.g., Gilmore et al. 1996; Kacmar et al. 1999). Likewise, when workers perceive they have control over work situations, negative outcomes associated with political perceptions tend to be ameliorated (e.g., Ferris et al. 1993; Witt, Andrews, and Kacmar 2000).

Leaders who cultivate organizational environments characterized by openness and sharing of information help workers to feel that they have greater understanding of decisions and events. Coupled with today's increasingly more empowered work environments, the increased understanding and control workers gain from such participatory environments should also help to reduce threatening reactions (e.g., lower job satisfaction; higher job tension) brought on by political perceptions. In the current context, we believe that leaders who pay increasing attention to spirituality in the workplace may also help to promote a climate that enables workers to experience greater feelings of personal security and understanding, leading to more favorable work outcomes. Leadership that embraces openness and individually defined spiritual practices in the workplace will help workers feel more valued and connected and may ultimately result in more fulfilled, more committed, more satisfied, and more productive workers. In essence, leaders should strive to develop spiritually-rich workplaces. A spiritually-rich workplace is one that values and encourages openness and spiritual diversity in the workplace, particularly in the context of reducing the negative effects associated with organizational politics. The crucial role leaders play in fostering such environments is the subject of the following section.

Leadership, Spirituality, and Organizational Politics

Behavioral scientists have been studying leadership for decades in efforts to develop a more generalizable understanding of the qualities, characteristics, and behaviors of effective leaders. Though it is well beyond the scope of this chapter to comprehensively review the leadership literature, we offer several characteristics of two increasingly studied leadership areas that we believe have important implications for the spirituality-enhancing capacity of leaders in organizations today. Furthermore, we examine how certain leadership characteristics can lead to a more spirit-filled workplace, while simultaneously reducing the negative effects of political perceptions.

Before we discuss leadership characteristics, it is important to initially consider the current nature of leadership. One can surmise from the constant deluge of leadership-related books and articles that this area of study has been, and will continue to be, ripe for exploration. We believe that the steady flow of leadership writings is due, in part, to a failure on the part of organizational leaders to understand the needs of the workers they are supposed to be leading. The failure to connect with workers, to understand their needs, and to proactively engage them in ways that are meaningful all contribute to an all-too-common spiritless workplace. According to Moxley (2000):

> Americans are a dispirited lot . . . [in part because] their work does not engage all their energies, does not provide them the sense of meaning and purpose for which they long, and does not call forth the best they have within them. . . . Too often, [the] practices of leadership suffocate spirit. . . . Organizations, and how we understand and practice leadership in them, are killing our spirit. (Moxley 2000, xiii, 7, 8)

Recognition by leaders of the sad state of spirituality in today's organizations may be an important first step, because "leadership can liberate and elevate spirit and thus enliven people" (Moxley 2000, 8). For example, spirit clearly matters at some highly successful organizations like Southwest Airlines. Herb Kelleher, Southwest's founder and chairman, stated, "We look for people who are unselfish and altruistic and who enjoy life. The focus is on the intangibles, the spiritual qualities, not an individual's educational experience. We can train anybody to do a job, from a technical standpoint. We are looking for people with an esprit de corps, an attitude" (in Verespej 1995, 22).

According to Palmer (1998), a leader is an individual with "an unusual degree of power to create the conditions under which other people must live and move and have their being" (200). In the current context, good leadership involves valuing diversity and individual differences, proactively enabling empowerment of workers at all levels, setting clear vision and fair (and ethical) guidelines for performance expectations and reward systems, and monitoring and taking steps to reduce uncertainty and ambiguity that have been shown to lead to higher perceptions of organizational politics. Today's leaders also benefit from encouraging workers to discover their true potential as workers and human beings (Kouzes and Posner 1999; Pfeffer 1998); that is, to "be all they can be." Leaders who openly embrace alternative viewpoints, who accept failure as learning experiences and teaching tools, and who empower workers to grow and take on greater responsibility, are much more likely to have workers who find greater meaning in their work. The inner security and self-discovery that can come from exploring one's spirituality can serve to reduce the negative effects of politics as well.

In our view, leaders need certain attributes to foster a spiritually-rich workplace and manage negative outcomes commonly associated with organizational politics. Leaders who are both servant-oriented and politically skilled may be in the best position to lead spiritually-rich workplaces and diminish perceptions of organizational politics. These leader types and their respective attributes are explained next in the current context of workplace spirituality and organizational politics.

SERVANT LEADERSHIP

From its beginnings in the writings of the late Robert Greenleaf in the 1970s, principles of servant leadership have been embraced by such notable writers and consultants as Warren Bennis (2001), Ken Blanchard (1995), Stephen Covey (1994), Peter Drucker (1996), Peter Senge (1994), and Meg Wheatley (1992), and by leaders in such organizations as Herman Miller, Ritz-Carlton, Saturn, ServiceMaster, Toro, and Wal-Mart. According to Greenleaf, servant leadership is grounded in the notion that the best leadership is provided not by those who seek leadership roles but, rather, by those with a compelling vision or goal and a desire to serve others first (e.g., Greenleaf 1977, 1978; Spears 1998). Similar to the notion of stewardship (e.g., Block 1993) and based on Christian principles, this servant-first attitude differs substantially from the traditional leader mindset; one that is too often control-oriented and paternalistic (Doyle 1997). Gilbert Fairholm, in his book, *Perspectives on Leadership: From the Science of Management to its Spiritual Heart*, described five levels of leadership along a continuum ". . . from managerial control to spiritual holism" (1998, xix). According to Fairholm (1998), the more leaders value workers and attempt to meet and address the needs and values of workers, the further they move away from the management control end of the continuum and the closer they come to the most effective type of leadership, that which is based on spiritual holism, where "Leaders are first servants of those they lead" (118).

A behavior we tend to associate with leadership is the clear articulation of a vision through which workers are inspired. The creation of a compelling vision by the leader is at least as important as the ability of the leader to inspire followers to accept, believe in, and embrace the essence of this vision. As Bennis and Nanus (1985) noted, ". . . by focusing attention on a vision, the leader operates on the emotional and spiritual resources of the organization, on its values, commitment, and aspirations" (92). Hence, one key challenge for an effective servant leader is to cocreate (with those being served) and articulate a vision that is sufficiently clear and focused, yet flexible enough to reconcile the organization's need for effectiveness (i.e., profitability and efficiency) with its employees' needs for personal growth, purpose, and richer meaning in their work.

Servant leadership also has substantial conceptual overlap with the principles of *transformational* leadership (e.g., Bass 1985; Burns 1978). Compared to *transactional* leadership, which focuses on a simple exchange (e.g., work for pay) relationship (e.g., Yukl 1998), transformational leadership occurs "when one or more persons engage with others in such a way that leaders and followers raise one another to higher levels of motivation and morality" (Burns 1978, 20). As with servant leadership, transformational leadership involves personal identification with the leader, shared vision, and going beyond the self-interested exchange of rewards for compliance, resulting in followers being motivated to do more than originally expected (Hater and Bass 1988). The four dimensions of transformational leadership—individualized consideration, idealized influence, inspirational motivation, and intellectual stimulation (Bass and Avolio 1994)—also mesh well with tenets of servant leadership. Indeed, the transforming nature of the servant-led workplace (e.g., Greenleaf 1977, 1978; Rinehart 1998) is now a powerful cultural element in such organizations as Ritz-Carlton, ServiceMaster, and Wal-Mart.

According to former Herman Miller CEO Max DePree in his book *Leadership Jazz* (1992), the twelve characteristics of servant leaders are:

1. integrity,
2. vulnerability,
3. discernment,
4. awareness of the human spirit,
5. courage in relationships,
6. sense of humor,
7. intellectual energy and curiosity,
8. respect for the future,
9. predictability,

10. breadth,
11. comfort with ambiguity, and
12. presence.

Furthermore, servant leaders articulate goals, inspire trust, know how to listen, are masters of positive feedback, and emphasize personal development (Lee and Zemke 1993). Servant leadership is an ideal type of leadership for embracing workplace spirituality, particularly since a main premise of this approach focuses on listening and understanding (i.e., listening to and understanding each individual worker's needs, values, desires, and issues; Greenleaf 1977). Furthermore, the integrity and vulnerability attributes of servant leadership, in particular, are signals to workers that the servant leader is honest, trustworthy, and willing to admit they are not perfect or all-knowing. In order for servant leadership to be effective in today's chaotic times, there needs to be a common vision and purpose, free information flow, and a helper mentality (Wheatley 1992). This natural instinct of a servant leader to freely and readily provide information to workers helps create a work climate based on inclusivity and partnership, which are key facets of a spiritually-rich workplace. Moreover, the clarity and improved understanding that should come from such sharing of information, coupled with a partnership mentality that encourages and values worker participation in organizational decisions, will likely result in reduced perceptions of politics as uncertainty, ambiguity, and, likely, worker insecurity are reduced.

Political Skill

If organizations are political arenas (Mintzberg 1983), and inherently social in nature (Pfeffer 1992; Rousseau 1997), then organizational members need both political and social skills in order to effectively interact with others and to navigate organizational politics. While the term political skill has been in the management literature for nearly two decades (Mintzberg 1983), it was not until Ferris and colleagues (e.g., Ferris, Fedor, and King 1994; Ferris et al. 1999; Perrewé et al. 2000) reintroduced the term that it came to be more mainstream as a research topic. Mintzberg (1983) viewed political skill as effectively exercising influence through persuasion, manipulation, and negotiation. Ferris and colleagues have defined political skill as an interpersonal style construct that combines interpersonal perceptiveness and social astuteness with the capacity to adjust one's behavior to different situational demands in a manner that inspires confidence, trust, sincerity, and genuineness, resulting in the building of social capital and in the effective influence and control of the responses of others (Ferris et al. in press; Ferris et al. 2001). A summary of the characteristics of both politically skilled leaders and servant leaders is shown in Table 11.1.

Politically skilled leaders have strong social (e.g., Thorndike 1920) and emotional intelligence (e.g., George 2000; Goleman 1995, 1998), as high degrees of both are necessary in order for organizational leaders to effectively and consistently influence workers to achieve organizational goals. Regulation of emotional expression may be particularly important in learning how to deal effectively with the apparent rise of spiritual expression in the workplace. Except in spiritually homogeneous organizational settings (e.g., a Christian bookstore), most leaders will encounter and need to come to grips with the growing diversity of spiritual expression that most workplaces appear to be experiencing (e.g., Ashmos and Duchon 2000). Organizational leaders who are rigid and unaccepting in their views of alternative spiritual expression during work hours may be substantially less likely to see the potentially positive connection between workplace spirituality and effective organizational functioning (Mitroff and Denton 1999), reacting from an emotional base rather than from a rational one. Leaders who exhibit negative emotional reactions when faced

Table 11.1

Characteristics of Servant Leaders and Politically Skilled Leaders

Characteristics of servant leaders[a]	Characteristics of politically skilled leaders[b]
Integrity	Sincerity*
Vulnerability	Genuineness*
Discernment	Honesty*
Awareness of the human spirit	Integrity*
Courage in relationships	Trustworthy*
Sense of humor	Self-awareness
Intellectual energy and curiosity	Social intelligence/social astuteness
Respect for the future	Emotional intelligence
Predictability	Network building
Breadth	Social capital
Comfort with ambiguity	Influence and control of others
Presence	

Sources: [a]DePree, M. (1992).
           [b]Ferris et al. (2001).
*Actual and/or perceived by others as so.

with alternative spiritual viewpoints are more likely to lose the trust and respect of the very subordinates needed to help them reach organizational goals. Hence, high emotional intelligence, characteristic of those with political skill, is seen as an important attribute of spiritually flexible and effective organizational leaders.

In addition to its strong relationship with social and emotional intelligence, political skill is related to various other dimensions of social skill, including ego-resiliency, social self-efficacy, self-monitoring, tacit knowledge, and practical intelligence, and is "critical to performance and success in a broad array of jobs at all levels of organizations" (Ferris et al. 2000, 33). It should be noted that political skill is not typically used to become *more* political but, rather, represents a set of abilities that one can draw on to navigate political environments and to influence others. In fact, Ferris and colleagues (Ferris et al. 2001) recently found political skill to be a multidimensional construct, consisting of (1) social astuteness, (2) genuineness and sincerity, (3) social capital and networking, and (4) social influence and control. Socially astute organizational leaders accurately observe the behaviors of others and are keenly attuned to diverse social situations in organizational settings (Ferris et al. 1999, 2001). As with socially and emotionally intelligent people, they have strong powers of discernment and are keenly aware of their own behavior and that of others in their environment. They comprehend social interactions easily and are typically moderate to high self-monitors (e.g., Snyder 1974), able to appropriately adapt their behavior and interactive manner to each situation.

Beyond being socially astute, politically skilled people are seen as genuine and sincere in their social interactions. Those possessing political skill appear to others as having high integrity, authenticity, and sincerity. They are, or appear to be, honest, ethical, fair, genuine, just, open, forthright, and trustworthy. Because their actions are never seen as manipulative or coercive, politically skilled individuals consistently inspire trust and confidence in and from those around them.

With their genuine manner and strong social awareness, politically skilled leaders are adept at building networks and using the social capital from these networks in appropriate ways. Such individuals enjoy a favorable social identity (Ashforth and Kreiner 1999) and reputation (Fombrun and Shanley 1990) among those in their network, resulting in significant and tangible benefits, such as gaining favorable reactions to one's ideas, enhanced access to important information, and increased cooperation and trust (e.g., Baron and Markman 2000). They know when to call on others for favors and are perceived as willing to reciprocate in kind. In addition, they inspire commitment and personal obligation from those around them.

Importantly, politically skilled leaders know how to effectively influence and, if necessary, control the behavior of others. Their strong and convincing personal style and social skill tends to exert a powerful influence on those around them. They know how to recognize and use influence tactics in each appropriate context and effectively use the social capital from the wide networks they've built to influence those around them. Masters of the quid pro quo, they often are highly skilled negotiators and dealmakers and are typically adept at conflict management. Although these individuals are not always overtly political, they are seen as competent leaders who play the political game fairly and effortlessly. Seen as expert, attractive, and trustworthy (e.g., Strong 1968), their facile political style is seen as a positive, rather than a negative, force within the organization.

Based on these attributes, leaders high in political skill are well positioned to facilitate the development of spiritually-rich workplaces and, further, combat the negative effects that high political perceptions can bring about. With their keenly tuned sense of social interaction and genuine manner, such politically skilled leaders as Herb Kelleher of Southwest Airlines have been able to create legions of loyal and productive workers who have found work to be a fun and spiritually-rich experience. Highly socially astute, the politically skilled leader is very much aware of the needs and values of his or her workforce and strives to create an organizational climate that addresses these needs and values.

Along with strong social awareness and a facile ability to communicate, the genuine and sincere manner with which the politically skilled leader operates provides an encouraging environment in which workers can share their complaints and concerns. This "open-door" environment can help to suppress perceptions of organizational politics and thus reduce the potentially devastating effects of politics in the workplace. In addition, the ease with which politically skilled leaders build networks enables them to make connections and create the type of organizational community characteristic of spiritually-rich workplaces.

Lastly, because such leaders are skilled at social interaction and exert powerful influence over their workers, the referent power typically attributed to such leaders makes it easier for followers to embrace the leader's notion of a spiritually-rich workplace. Politically skilled leaders may even choose to model spiritual practices, such as attending voluntary Bible studies or taking part in yoga exercises run by coworkers. They can also call on their social networks and use the social capital from such networks to provide information and training on spiritual issues, enabling even the most nonspiritual workers to consider exploring the benefits of spiritual practices at work.

The Politically Skilled Servant Leader

Can a leader be both servant-oriented and politically skilled? We believe that the answer is yes; it is a powerful combination leaders should strive to achieve. The two types of leadership share much in common. For example, for potential followers to believe that a leader is truly putting their needs first and serving them, the leader must be authentic, genuine, sincere, and trustworthy, which are all hallmarks of political skill and critical to building a spiritual environment and in helping workers feel valued. Furthermore, in order to build networks and use accrued social capital to influence others, a leader must have presence and integrity—key attributes of servant leadership. Both types of leaders inspire trust and have great facility at making connections, important for building a sense of community that is characteristic of a spiritual workplace. Both types tend to be socially and emotionally intelligent, being skilled listeners with the ability to astutely discern worker needs and concerns, which are attributes that can help workers feel connected and understood.

Additionally, both leadership types have been described as having other attributes that are valuable in the current context. Among other characteristics, servant leaders have been described as being excellent communicators of their leadership vision, willing and able to provide feedback when warranted, and proactive about helping workers to develop personally and professionally. Politically skilled leaders are able to build powerful networks and take advantage of the social capital in those networks for the good of all in the organization. Furthermore, when necessary, they can use their skill to influence and control worker behavior, for instance, when a crisis occurs requiring fast action and decision-making. In sum, leaders who are both servant-oriented and politically skilled have the attributes required and are best positioned to develop a spiritually-rich workplace and to take action to help reduce organizational politics. Perhaps most importantly, workplaces that are rich in spirituality and low in politics should enjoy more positive work outcomes, such as reduced job tension, lower employee cynicism and turnover, and increased job satisfaction and commitment to the organization.

DISCUSSION

Implications for Theory and Research

Whereas workplace spirituality and leadership is a relatively new topic area, and while a literature base has developed in this area, it has tended to be mostly anecdotal and conceptual in nature, with "no hard [empirical] evidence suggesting that companies that weave together spirit and leadership are more profitable" (Moxley 2000, 19). Before a sound program of theory-driven empirical research can be undertaken in this area, measures need to be developed that assess workplace spirituality and worker spiritual need fulfillment. Then, initial efforts should be made to test the notions that certain leader types (e.g., political skill, servant-orientation) and characteristics demonstrate positive relationships with the capacity of workers to see their spiritual needs fulfilled, including worker realization of a greater sense of meaning and purpose through their work and workplace experiences.

A second phase of research in this area would be to demonstrate that spirituality mediates the relationship between leaders' characteristics and important outcomes such as cynicism, turnover, and organizational commitment. Our arguments above have proposed that spirituality at work, through leader efforts, can help to reduce employee political behavior, cynicism, and turnover, and increase attachment and commitment to the organization. If that is the case, then we should find that spirituality serves as a mediating variable between leadership and outcomes.

A third stream of research could productively attempt to sort out precisely what spirituality contributes to leader effectiveness in creating work environments with the potential for workers to achieve greater security, higher-order meaning, purpose, and whether all of this translates into more effective organizations. Although we have already specified certain attributes of political skill and of servant leadership as key characteristics, a more specific and well-formulated theory of leadership needs to be articulated which incorporates key leader characteristics and behaviors, along with appropriate moderators and mediators, before an initial "spiritual leader" program of research can be developed. Interestingly, we might find that such a theory closely resembles what

House and others (Ahearn et al. 2001; House and Aditya 1997) outlined in their appeal for a political theory of leadership.

Another area of needed research is to assess exactly what it means for workers to realize greater meaning, purpose, and a sense of spirituality at work. While Mitroff and Denton's (1999) study is a step in the right direction, more comprehensive multi-method empirical work needs to be performed before a better understanding of the emerging workplace spirituality phenomenon can be reached. For example, some combination of quantitative and qualitative research methods might be used to better examine the central themes and issues in this paper. We need to further ascertain the extent to which spirituality at work is associated with critical intrapersonal outcomes for workers, like greater job satisfaction, job tension, cynicism, commitment, and other attitudinal and affective outcomes. From a behavioral perspective, we need to determine whether workers in spiritually-rich workplaces behave in more organizationally productive ways. Furthermore, scientific efforts need to be made to explore whether leader efforts to embrace workplace spirituality also reduce, as suggested, organizational politics (i.e., both perceptions of politics and actual political behavior). These represent just a few directions for future theory and research in this new and important area of inquiry.

Implications for Practice

In "Radical Surgery: What Will Tomorrow's Organizations Look Like?" Mitroff and colleagues (Mitroff, Mason, and Pearson 1994) proposed that organizations need to "... be structured around five new organizational entities: (1) a knowledge/learning center, (2) a recovery/development center, (3) a world service/spiritual center, (4) a world class operations center, and (5) a leadership institute" (11). In their view, older established organizations have failed to adapt to new problems, resulting in "... one quick-fix and band-aid approach after another" (11). Moreover, too often these organizations focused primarily on operations, to the detriment of workers and worker development. The ideas contained in the current manuscript should not be taken as a proposition to ignore operations and other management issues but, rather, as a call to move to styles of leadership that also embrace knowledge and learning, recovery and development, and service and spirituality.

Leaders who foster spiritually-rich workplaces characterized by openness and sharing of information will help workers feel that they have greater understanding of decisions and events. Coupled with today's increasingly more empowered work environments, the increased understanding and control workers have from such environments should also help to reduce threatening feelings and negative reactions brought on by political perceptions. Leader-led spirituality can thus help to reduce uncertainty, ambiguity, and insecurity in the workplace and help to provide workers with a greater sense of meaning, purpose, connectedness, and understanding—all factors that can contribute to the feeling of community that so many workers seek from their employers (Conger 1994; Jurkiewicz et al. 1998; Weisbord 1991).

So, too, involvement in such spiritual activities as meditation, contemplative prayer, bible studies, and yoga appear to help at least some individuals foster a sense of inner peace and security that can help to combat the negative effects of organizational politics. Organizational leaders that encourage spiritual activities in the workplace will find that workers may be more likely to be relaxed, rested, and clear-thinking than in workplaces that fail to encourage such activities. Moreover, when organizational leaders show that they welcome spiritual exploration, they are also telling workers that management trusts them; that is, despite the seemingly unproductive nature of spiritual activities as they take place, management trusts that workers will get their work done satisfactorily. Coupled with greater sharing of information and decision-making power, the embrace of spiritual activities enables greater worker understanding and control resulting in lessening the negative effects of political perceptions. Although vacations can help workers to renew their energy while away from work, spiritual activities that take place in the workplace and during work hours can serve to reenergize workers on a daily basis. With a servant-first attitude and political skill, leaders can offer the kind of attention that shows workers that their idiosyncratic needs are valued.

One work environment characteristic that leaders might strive for is based on Csikszentmihalyi's (1990) notion of "flow." Also referred to as optimal experience, flow is the state whereby "people are so involved in an activity that nothing else seems to matter; the experience itself is so enjoyable that people will do it at even a great cost, for the sheer sake of doing it" (4). Leaders can contribute to this process by creating work environments that shift the rewards, punishments, and control over behavior from the external social/work environment to workers themselves, enabling workers to ". . . develop the ability to find enjoyment and purpose regardless of external circumstances" (16). A fundamental issue for the flow experience, therefore, is the nature of control and shifting the source of control from the external (e.g., management, formalized structures) to the internal (e.g., the individual). Workers who perceive that they are in control of their work are more likely to experience flow. Given the evidence that perceived control has shown in reducing the negative effects of political perceptions (Ferris et al. 1993; Witt et al. 2000), leaders who foster work environments characterized by greater worker control (i.e., more empowered workplaces) will likely find that the workplace will be viewed as less political and result in more favorable worker outcomes, such as higher job satisfaction and commitment and lower job tension and turnover intentions. As such, we believe the politically skilled servant leader may best be qualified to create "flow environments" by staying in tune with the spiritual heartbeat of the workplace—by listening, understanding, serving, and empowering workers.

Finally, because spirituality is such a sensitive and deeply felt issue for many individuals, perhaps the crucial responsibility of leaders, underlying any attempt to create a more spirit-based workplace, is to demonstrate their genuine and sincere interest in their workers and in their commitment to the spiritual development process. As in any change process, without authentic commitment to that process and its ideals, leaders' efforts may instead produce cynicism and mistrust rather than the intended effects.

CONCLUSION

There is no doubt that workplace spirituality has emerged in recent years as a topic of considerable interest and importance for the organizational sciences. As we see this interest grow, we as scholars need to provide better theory and research on the precise nature of workplace spirituality and its antecedents and consequences. This chapter sought to demonstrate how leadership, with particular reference to political skill and servant leader characteristics, can serve to facilitate the process of creating work environments whereby workers can achieve a greater sense of meaning, purpose, and experience, while also helping to reduce organizational politics.

Leaders who embrace a spiritually-rich workplace also embrace a workplace characterized by sharing (i.e., sharing of information, power, decision-making). Such sharing will serve to reduce uncertainty and ambiguity, key factors contributing to political perceptions. Leaders who develop spiritually-rich workplaces will concurrently be developing organizational climates and cultures whereby workers feel involved, connected, and important. As stated by Moxley (2000),

"Spirit works within us . . . [but] also works between and among us. It connects us to everything that exists. It is because of the work of the spirit that we experience deep communion with others, experience ourselves as part of something much larger, experience connectedness to all of life" (23). Furthermore, when leadership becomes collaborative and partner-oriented and accepting of demographic and spiritual diversity, lower perceptions of organizational politics should be a natural effect. This should result in part because reductions in uncertainty and ambiguity occur through, for example, improved information sharing, but also because empowered workers come to believe that they are very much involved in cocreating with management the very organizational climate and reward systems that can give rise to organizational politics.

Peter Drucker wrote that "Bob [Greenleaf] was a moralist and I am a pragmatist. . . . The world needs both types of people" (in Frick and Spears 1996). Organizations need them as well, as we believe that these qualities are not mutually exclusive. With a servant-leadership mentality and political skill, the moral, idealistic, pragmatic, and inspirational aspects of leading an organization are well covered. In many respects, we believe that we may have raised more questions than we have answered in this chapter. But, if this stimulates further thought as well as research activity in this important area, then we will feel that we have accomplished our objectives.

REFERENCES

Ahearn, K.K.; J. Poertner; G.R. Ferris; W.A. Hochwarter; A.P. Ammeter; and C. Douglas. (2001). "Leader Political Skill and Team Performance in a State Public Welfare System." Paper presented at the Academy of Management, Sixty-first Annual National Meeting, Washington, DC, August.

Ali, L. (2001). "The Glorious Rise of Christian Pop." *Newsweek*, July 16, 38–44.

Anderson, P. (2000). "This Place Hurts My Spirit!" *Journal for Quality and Participation* (fall): 16–17.

Ashforth, B.E., and G.E. Kreiner. (1999). "How Can You Do It?: Dirty Work and the Challenge of Constructing a Positive Identity." *Academy of Management Review* 24, no. 3: 413–434.

Ashmos, D.P., and D. Duchon. (2000). "Spirituality at Work: A Conceptualization and Measure." *Journal of Management Inquiry* 2: 134–145.

Bacharach, S.B., and E.J. Lawler. (1980). *Power and Politics in Organizations: The Social Psychology of Conflict, Coalitions, and Bargaining.* San Francisco: Jossey-Bass.

Baron, R.A., and G.D. Markman. (2000). "Beyond Social Capital: How Social Skills Can Enhance Entrepreneurs' Success." *Academy of Management Executive* 14: 101–116.

Bass, B.M. (1985). *Leadership Performance Beyond Expectations.* New York: Academic Press.

Bass, B.M., and B. Avolio. (1994). *Improving Organizational Effectiveness Through Transformational Leadership.* Thousands Oaks, CA: Sage.

Bennis, W. (2001). "Become a Tomorrow Leader." In *Focus on Leadership: Servant-leadership for the 21st Century,* ed. L.C. Spears and M. Lawrence. San Francisco: Jossey-Bass.

Bennis, W., and B. Nanus. (1985). *Leaders.* New York: Harper and Row.

Blanchard, K. (1995). "Servant Leadership." *Executive Excellence* (October): 12.

Block, P. (1993). *Stewardship: Choosing Service over Self-interest.* San Francisco: Berrett-Koehler.

Bolman, L.G., and T.E. Deal. (2001). *Leading with Soul: An Uncommon Journey of the Spirit Revisited.* New York: Wiley.

Brandt, E. (1996). "Corporate Pioneers Explore Spirituality." *HR Magazine* 41, no. 4: 82–87.

Burack, E.H. (1999). "Spirituality in the Workplace." *Journal of Change Management* 12: 280–291.

Burns, J.M. (1978). *Leadership.* New York: Harper and Row.

Chopra, D. (1994). *The Seven Spiritual Laws of Success.* San Rafael, CA: Amber-Allen.

Conger, J.A. (1994). "Introduction: Our Search for Spiritual Community." In *Spirit at Work: Discovering the Spirituality in Leadership,* ed. J.A. Conger. San Francisco: Jossey-Bass, 1–18.

Covey, S.R. (1994). "New Wine, Old Bottles." *Executive Excellence* (December): 3–4.

Cropanzano, R.; J.C. Howes; A.A. Grandey; and P. Toth. (1997). "The Relationship of Organizational Politics and Support to Work Behaviors, Attitudes, and Stress." *Journal of Organizational Behavior* 18: 159–180.

Csikszentmihalyi, M. (1990). *Flow: The Psychology of Optimal Experience.* New York: Harper and Row.

DePree, M. (1992). *Leadership Jazz.* New York: Dell.

Doyle, R.J. (1997). "The Case of a Servant Leader." In *Leadership: Understanding the Dynamics of Power and Influence in Organizations,* ed. R.P. Vecchio. South Bend, IN: University of Notre Dame Press, 439–457.

Drucker, P.F. (1996). "Foreword." In *On Becoming a Servant Leader: The Private Writings of Robert K. Greenleaf,* ed. D.M. Frick and L.C. Spears. San Francisco: Jossey-Bass, ix–xxii.

Fairholm, G.W. (1998). *Perspectives on Leadership: From the Science of Management to Its Spiritual Heart.* Westport, CT: Quorum Books.

Ferris, G.R.; W.P. Anthony; R.W. Kolodinsky; D.C. Gilmore; and M.G. Harvey. (in press) "Development of Political Skill." In *Research in Management Education and Development,* ed. C. Wankel and R. DeFillippi (1st vol.—Rethinking Management Education). Greenwich, CT: Information Age.

Ferris, G.R.; H.M. Berkson; D.M. Kaplan; D.C. Gilmore; M.R. Buckley; W.A. Hochwarter; and L.A. Witt. (1999). "Development and Initial Validation of the Political Skill Inventory." Paper presented to the Academy of Management at the Fifty-ninth Annual National Meeting, Chicago.

Ferris, G.R.; J.F. Brand; S. Brand; K.M. Rowland; D.C. Gilmore; T.R. King; K.M. Kacmar; and C.A. Burton. (1993). "Politics and Control in Organizations." In *Advances in Group Processes,* ed. E.J. Lawler, B. Markovsky, J. O'Brien, and K. Heimer, vol. 10. Greenwich, CT: JAI Press, 83–111.

Ferris, G.R.; D.D. Frink; D.P.S. Bhawuk; J. Zhou; and D.C. Gilmore. (1996). "Reactions of Diverse Groups to Politics in the Workplace." *Journal of Management* 22: 23–44.

Ferris, G.R.; D.D. Frink; D.C. Gilmore; and K.M. Kacmar. (1994). "Understanding As an Antidote for the Dysfunctional Consequences of Organizational Politics As a Stressor." *Journal of Applied Social Psychology* 24: 1204–1220.

Ferris, G.R.; G. Harrell-Cook; and J.H. Dulebohn. (2000). "Organizational Politics: The Nature of the Relationship Between Politics Perceptions and Political Behavior." In *Research in the Sociology of Organizations,* ed. S.B. Bacharach and E.J. Lawler, vol. 17. Stamford, CT: JAI Press, 89–130.

Ferris, G.R., and K.M. Kacmar. (1992). "Perceptions of Organizational Politics." *Journal of Management* 18: 93–116.

Ferris, G.R.; R.W. Kolodinsky; W.A. Hochwarter; and D.D. Frink. (2001). "Conceptualization, Measurement, and Validation of the Political Skill Construct." Paper presented to the Academy of Management at the Sixty-first Annual National Meeting, Washington, DC.

Ferris, G.R.; P.L. Perrewé; W.P. Anthony; and D.C. Gilmore. (2000). "Political Skill at Work." *Organizational Dynamics* 28: 25–37.

Ferris, G.R.; G.S. Russ; and P.M. Fandt. (1989). "Politics in Organizations." In *Impression Management in the Organization,* ed. R.A. Giacalone and P. Rosenfeld. Hillsdale, NJ: Erlbaum, 143–170.

Fombrun, C., and M. Shanley. (1990). "What's in a Name? Reputation Building and Corporate Strategy." *Academy of Management Journal* 33, no. 2: 233–258.

Frick, D.M., and L.C. Spears, eds. (1996). *On Becoming a Servant Leader: The Private Writings of Robert K. Greenleaf.* San Francisco: Jossey-Bass.

George, J.M. (2000). "Emotions and Leadership: The Role of Emotional Intelligence." *Human Relations* 53: 1027–1056.

Gilmore, D.C.; G.R. Ferris; J.H. Dulebohn; and G. Harrell-Cook. (1996). "Organizational Politics and Employee Attendance." *Group and Organization Management* 21: 481–494.

Goleman, D. (1995). *Emotional Intelligence.* New York: Bantam Books.

———. (1998). *Working with Emotional Intelligence.* New York: Bantam Books.

Greenleaf, R.K. (1977). *Servant Leadership: A Journey into the Nature of Legitimate Power and Greatness.* New York: Paulist Press.

———. (1978). *Servant, Leader and Follower.* New York: Paulist Press.

Gunther, M. (2001). "God and Business." *Fortune.com* (July 9).

Harrell-Cook, G.; G.R. Ferris; and J.H. Dulebohn. (1999). "Political Behaviors As Moderators of the Perceptions of Organizational Politics—Work Outcomes Relationships." *Journal of Organizational Behavior* 20: 1093–1106.

Hater, J.J., and B.M. Bass. (1988). "Superiors' Evaluations and Subordinates' Perceptions of Transformational and Transactional Leadership." *Journal of Applied Psychology* 73: 695–702.

Hochwarter, W.A.; P.L. Perrewé; G.R. Ferris; and R. Guercio. (1999). "Commitment As an Antidote to the Tension and Turnover Consequences of Organizational Politics." *Journal of Vocational Behavior* 55: 277–297.

House, R.J., and R.N. Aditya. (1997). "The Social Scientific Study of Leadership: Quo Vadis?" *Journal of Management* 23: 409–473.

Jackson, P. (1995). *Sacred Hoops*. New York: Hyperion.

Judge, W.Q. (1999). *The Leader's Shadow: Exploring and Developing Executive Character*. Thousand Oaks, CA: Sage.

Jurkiewicz, C.L.; T.K. Massey, Jr.; and R.G. Brown. (1998). "Motivation in Public and Private Organizations: A Comparative Study." *Public Productivity and Management Review* 21, no. 3: 230–250.

Kacmar, K.M., and R.A. Baron. (1999). "Organizational Politics: The State of the Field, Links to Related Processes, and an Agenda for Future Research." In *Research in Personnel and Human Resources Management*, ed. G.R. Ferris, vol. 17. Stamford, CT: JAI Press, 1–39.

Kacmar, K.M.; D.P. Bozeman; D.S. Carlson; and W.P. Anthony. (1999). "A Partial Test of the Perceptions of Organizational Politics Model." *Human Relations* 52: 383–416.

Kelley, R. (1998). "Followership in a Leadership World." In *Insights on Leadership: Service, Stewardship, Spirit, and Servant-Leadership*, ed. L.C. Spears. New York: Wiley.

Kouzes, J.M., and B.Z. Posner. (1999). *Encouraging the Heart: A Leader's Guide to Rewarding and Recognizing Others*. San Francisco: Jossey-Bass.

Laabs, J.J. (1995). "Balancing Spirituality and Work." *Personnel Journal* (September): 61–76.

Lear, N. (1992). "Social Responsibility: A Cure for the Loneliness in Our Time." Remarks at a joint faculty seminar of the Harvard Divinity School and the Harvard Business School, Cambridge, MA, April.

Lee, C., and R. Zemke. (1993). "The Search for Spirit in the Workplace." *Training* (June): 21–26.

Maslyn, J., and D.B. Fedor. (1998). "Perceptions of Politics: Does Measuring Different Foci Matter?" *Journal of Applied Psychology* 84: 645–653.

Mintzberg, H. (1983). *Power in and Around Organizations*. Englewood Cliffs, NJ: Prentice-Hall.

Mitroff, I.I., and E.A. Denton. (1999). "A Study of Spirituality in the Workplace." *Sloan Management Review* 40: 83–84.

Mitroff, I.I.; R. Mason; and C. Pearson. (1994). "Radical Surgery: What Will Tomorrow's Organizations Look Like?" *Academy of Management Executive* 8, no. 2: 11–21.

Moxley, R. (2000). *Leadership and Spirit*. San Francisco: Jossey-Bass.

Noer, D. (1993). *Healing the Wounds*. San Francisco: Jossey-Bass.

O'Neil, J.R. (1995). *The Paradox of Success: When Winning at Work Means Losing at Life*. New York: Putnam's.

Palmer, P.J. (1998). "Leading from Within." In *Insights on Leadership: Service, Stewardship, Spirit, and Servant Leadership*, ed. L.C. Spears. New York: Wiley, 97–208.

Perrewé, P.L.; G.R. Ferris; D.D. Frink; and W.P. Anthony. (2000). "Political Skill: An Antidote for Workplace Stressors." *Academy of Management Executive* 14: 115–123.

Pfeffer, J. (1992). *Managing with Power: Politics and Influence in Organizations*. Boston: Harvard Business School Press.

———. (1998). *The Human Equation: Building Profits by Putting People First*. Boston: Harvard Business School Press.

Rinehart, S. (1998). *Upside Down: The Paradox of Servant Leadership*. Colorado Springs: NavPress.

Rousseau, D.M. (1997). "Organizational Behavior in the New Organizational Era." *Annual Review of Psychology* 48: 515–546.

Senge, P.M. (1994). "Creating Quality Communities." *Executive Excellence* (June): 11.

Snyder, M. (1974). "Self-monitoring of Expressive Behavior." *Journal of Personality and Social Psychology* 4: 526–537.

Spears, L.C., ed. (1997). *Insights on Leadership: Service, Stewardship, Spirit, and Servant Leadership*. New York: Wiley.

Strong, S.R. (1968). "Counseling: An Interpersonal Influence Process." *Journal of Counseling Psychology* 15, no. 3: 215–224.

Thorndike, E.L. (1920). "Intelligence and Its Use." *Harper's Magazine* 140: 227–235.

Vaill, P.B. (1998). *Spirited Leading and Learning*. San Francisco: Jossey-Bass.

Valle, M.P., and P.L. Perrewé. (2000). "Do Politics Perceptions Relate to Political Behaviors?" *Human Relations* 53: 359–386.

Verespej, M. (1995). "Flying His Own Course." *Industry Week* 20 (November): 22–24.

Weber, M. (1947). *The Theory of Social and Economic Organization*, trans. and ed. A.R. Henderson and T. Parsons. New York: Oxford University Press.

Weisbord, M. (1991). *Productive Workplaces: Organization and Managing for Dignity, Meaning, and Community.* San Francisco: Jossey-Bass.

Wheatley, M.J. (1992). *Leadership and the New Science: Learning About Organization from an Orderly Universe.* San Francisco: Berrett-Koehler.

Whyte, D. (1994). *The Heart Aroused: Poetry and the Preservation of the Soul in Corporate America.* New York: Currency-Doubleday.

Williams, O.F., and J.W. Houck. (1992). *A Virtuous Life in Business.* Lanham, MD: Rowman and Littlefield.

Witt, L.A. (1998). "Enhancing Organizational Goal Congruence: A Solution to Organizational Politics." *Journal of Applied Psychology* 83: 666–674.

Witt, L.A.; M.C. Andrews; and K.M. Kacmar. (2000). "The Role of Participation in Decision Making in the Organizational Politics—Job Satisfaction Relationship." *Human Relations* 53: 341–358.

Woodward, K.L. (2001). "Platitudes or Prophecy?" *Newsweek*, August 27.

Yukl, G. (1998). *Leadership in Organizations*, 4th ed. Upper Saddle River, NJ: Prentice-Hall.

Zhou, J., and G.R. Ferris. (1995). "The Dimensions and Consequences of Organizational Politics Perceptions: A Confirmatory Analysis." *Journal of Applied Social Psychology* 25: 1747–1764.

CHAPTER 12

ORGANIZATIONAL CITIZENSHIP BEHAVIOR AND THE SPIRITUAL EMPLOYEE

BENNETT J. TEPPER

> You know what the scariest thing is? To not know your place in the world.
> To not know why you're here. That's just an awful feeling.
>
> —*excerpt from M. Night Shyamalan's (2000) film,* Unbreakable

Almost twenty-five years ago, Dennis Organ laid the foundation for what would become one of the most influential streams of management research. In a pioneering conceptual work, Organ (1977) offered an intriguing answer to a conundrum that had baffled scholars and practitioners for decades—why is the relationship between employees' attitudes and performance weaker than conventional wisdom might predict? Intuitively, it would seem that happy workers should be more productive. Yet the research evidence suggested a rather modest, positive correlation between employees' affective liking for the job (i.e., job satisfaction) and performance (see Brayfield and Crockett 1955; Iaffaldano and Muchinsky 1977 for meta-analyses of the satisfaction-performance relationship).

Organ (1977) attributed these findings to the *kind* of performance contribution early research emphasized; these studies focused on objective performance measures and ratings of in-role activities, contributions that tend to be constrained by employees' ability, technology, and work-flow processes. Consequently, though employees may be motivated to bring their attitudes in line with their performance by modifying their in-role behavior upward when they feel satisfied, and downward when they feel dissatisfied, the constraints on their ability to do so attenuate the satisfaction-performance correlation. This line of reasoning led to a novel prediction, that individual attitudes are more likely to be expressed in performance contributions over which employees have some discretion, and the emergence of a new construct, organizational citizenship behavior, discretionary actions not formally rewarded, but which in the aggregate promote organizational effectiveness (Organ 1988a; 1988b; 1990). Consistent with these ideas, Organ and his colleagues found that employees who were more satisfied with their jobs performed organizational citizenship behaviors (e.g., helping colleagues, not complaining about trivial problems, and speaking favorably of the organization to outsiders) with greater frequency (Bateman and Organ 1983; Smith, Organ, and Near 1983).

In the years since the organization citizenship behavior (OCB) construct was introduced, researchers have compiled an impressive empirical literature. Podsakoff et al.'s (2000) recent review of the OCB literature suggests that over 200 articles on the topic have been published in the last seventeen years, and that the rate of publishing in the area is on the upswing. Moreover, most of this research has explored the antecedents of OCB. Two themes underlie extant theory and research regarding the motivational bases for OCB: that employees perform these behaviors to (1) reciprocate their organization for fair treatment and (2) manage favorable impressions.

In this chapter, I propose a third antecedent to employees' OCB—that employees perform OCB with greater frequency when they are motivated to find sacred meaning and purpose to their existence, what the literature refers to as spirituality. In the following sections I review extant conceptualizations of the motivational bases for OCB, describe the means by which spirituality influences OCB, and outline an agenda for future research.

EXTANT CONCEPTUALIZATIONS OF THE MOTIVATIONAL BASES FOR OCB

Social Exchange and OCB

Most studies of the antecedents of OCB have invoked Organ's (1990) social exchange–based explanation of OCB performance. Organ argued that employees perform OCB when they believe that the relationship with their employer is one of social exchange (i.e., relationships that exist outside formal contracts such that the participants' contributions are unspecified) rather than economic exchange (i.e., relationships in which each party's contribution is contractually speci-fied; Blau 1964). Compared to economic exchanges, social exchanges consist of diffuse informal agreements in which the party's contributions are open to individual interpretation. Organ (1990) argued that organizational practices that engender favorable attitudes incur a sense of obligation to recompense the organization in a manner befitting a social exchange relationship. Moreover, employees will reciprocate using OCBs, contributions that lie outside formal role requirements and reward structures and are therefore structurally similar to the social rewards afforded by a fair system (e.g., feelings of trust, support, and good faith). Consistent with Organ's (1990) conten-tion that OCB performance should be based on conditions of social exchange, research suggests that employees perform OCB with greater frequency when they experience psychological states indicative of social exchange such as trust (Konovsky and Pugh 1994), organizational support (Moorman, Blakely, and Niehoff 1998), and leader-member exchange (Manogran, Stauffer, and Conlon 1994).

Impression Management and OCB

More recent contributions to the literature suggest that OCB may be motivated by impression management concerns as well as the social exchange motivations identified in previous research (Bolino 1999). Performing OCB can achieve a number of impression management objectives outlined by Jones and Pittman (1982), including being seen as likable, dedicated, and competent (Schnake 1991). Consequently, some employees may perform citizenship behaviors in order to influence the image others have of them (Eastman 1994; Fandt and Ferris 1990; Ferris et al. 1995). Consistent with these ideas, empirical studies suggest that observers evaluate coworkers more favorably when they performs OCBs (Podsakoff and MacKenzie 1994), observers may attribute actors' OCB to image enhancement (Allen and Rush 1998), and employees who are motivated to manage impressions perform OCBs with greater frequency (Blakely, Fuller, and Smith 1996; Zellars et al. 2001).

Summary

The research to date supports the idea that employees perform OCB in order to fulfill their social exchange obligations *and* to manage favorable impressions. Both involve instrumental reasons for performing OCB. From the social exchange perspective, OCB reflects the employees' input to an ongoing, psychological contract with their employer; failure to perform OCB could constitute a contract breach and put the relationship between employer and employee at risk of eroding into one based solely on economic exchange (Rousseau 1995). From the impression management perspective, OCB performance reflects efforts to portray oneself in favorable terms, presumably because doing so is instrumental in receiving valued outcomes from resource allocators.

Interestingly, however, no research has explored the possibility that individuals perform OCB for noninstrumental reasons despite the fact that early work characterized OCB as involving self-sacrifice and an expression of a prosocial value orientation (Organ 1988a). For example, in the first investigation of OCB performance, Smith et al. (1983) labeled one OCB dimension, "altruism," implying that individuals perform these behaviors without the expectation that doing so produces valued outcomes. Hence, the notion that individuals perform OCB for noninstrumental reasons is not without precedent, though the idea has not been well developed or empirically studied. In the section that follows, I develop the idea that OCB represents a contribution that can fulfill one's spiritual strivings, thus forming the basis for expecting relationships between spirituality and OCB.

SPIRITUALITY

Any attempt to model linkages between two constructs must begin with good definitions of the constructs involved (Pedhauzer and Schmelkin 1991). Though the OCB definition is not without its shortcomings (Fandt and Ferris 1990; Morrison 1994; Van Dyne, Cummings, and Parks 1995), efforts to refine how OCB is conceptualized have produced defensible construct definitions that provide a sound basis for theoretical development and empirical inquiry (Organ 1997; Tepper, Lockhart, and Hoobler 2001; Van Dyne, Graham, and Dienesch 1994).

In this chapter, I define spirituality as *the extent to which an individual is motivated to find sacred meaning and purpose to his or her existence.* There are several aspects of this definition that warrant some elaboration. First, as a motivating force, spirituality refers neither to the actions in which individuals engage in their pursuit of meaning and purpose, nor to the perceptual, attitudinal, and well-being end-states that may ensue. Hence, a belief in a higher being is not spirituality, though a belief in God and regular attendance at church may be consequent to spiritual strivings. Spirituality may be regarded as an acquired need, not unlike the learned needs McClelland (1971) described. Individuals acquire the need to have meaningfulness and purpose from their environment, learning from their experiences.

Second, individuals' spirituality should be regarded as falling on a continuum ranging from very low to very high rather than an "either-or" motivating force. Low levels of spirituality would be reflected in a complete lack of concern with the importance of one's life; high levels of spirituality would be characterized by an obsession with whether each and every aspect of a person's life contributes to the quest for meaning and purpose. Anecdotal evidence suggests that as they approach death, people generally become more concerned with their life's importance—"I have tended to many people in the last moments of their lives. Most were not afraid of dying. The ones who had the most trouble with death were the people who felt that they had never done anything truly worthwhile in their lives. It was not death that frightened them. It was insignificance—the fear that they would die and have left no mark in the world" (Kushner 2001, 3). It may be expected, however, that long before death is imminent, individuals differ in the extent to which they experience a striving to see their life as meaningful.

Third, by "sacred" I mean worthy of reverence or respect rather than necessarily divine or holy. Religion is one of many avenues through which individuals may find meaning and purpose (I will argue later that work itself may provide a path for spiritual expression). Individuals differ in terms of what they revere and may include saving whales, curing diseases, or reclaiming land taken from one's ancestors. Hence, I do not equate religion and spirituality. I see spirituality as a higher-order construct, one that influences religiosity, but that can be expressed in a variety of ways having nothing to do with a belief in, or connection with, the divine.

Fourth, I do not view spirituality as an inherently "good" thing. The car-bombing, religious zealot may be no less spiritual than the individual whose search for meaning in life drives him or her to organize walks for AIDS victims. Whether or not these strivings are functional or dysfunctional depends on one's perspective. The car-bomber may be revered by his compatriots—the AIDS crusader may be reviled by anti-gay groups. The observer's perspective determines how they regard the radical environmentalist—even if I do not care one way or the other about the disposition of the spotted owl, it would be disingenuous of me to deny the spirituality of the people who commit themselves to saving the species by lying in the path of bulldozers, strapping themselves to trees, and generally spending most of their waking hours strategizing on the owl's behalf. The point is that if we constrain spirituality to reflect that which is "good," the construct comes to have no meaning because there are no causes everyone embraces as "good."

To illustrate how one's spiritual strivings may derive from wildly divergent sources, consider the quote with which I began this essay. The line comes from M. Night Shyamalan's (2000), *Unbreakable,* a film that focuses on two fictional characters, David Dunn, an embodiment of heroism who can achieve meaningfulness only by doing good, and Elijah Prince, an embodiment of destruction who can achieve meaningfulness only by rendering evil. As the story unfolds, we come to learn that the characters have something in common, that their spiritual strivings have been blocked, that they cannot achieve meaningfulness without the other or at least not without what the other represents. The hero cannot fight evil if there is no evil to fight, and the embodiment of evil can best achieve his quest for meaningfulness if he has a nemesis of his own. Few moviegoers would regard the villain's strivings as functional, but they give his life meaning and, in an ironic twist, give meaning and purpose to the hero's life.

A final elaboration on my definition is that spiritual strivings need not be grand; individuals may achieve meaning and purpose in tasks others might regard as mundane (e.g., raising bees, laying brick, planting trees). The goal of the spiritual person is to see his or her life and contributions as meaningful; how this is achieved is less important than the degree of commitment to that objective the individual is willing to exhibit.

Spirituality and OCB

I turn now to a discussion of the relationship between spirituality and OCB. Figure 12.1 depicts the linkages guiding this conceptual analysis. Spirituality influences OCB through three mediating psychological states: gratefulness, sensitivity to the needs of others, and tolerance for inequity. Figure 12.1 also shows that the strength of these relationships depends on the values held by the intended target of OCB. Finally, spirituality moderates the relationship between the motivations investigated in previous research (social exchange and impression management) and OCB. In the sections that follow, I describe these linkages in greater detail.

Figure 12.1   **Model Depicting Mediators and Moderators of the Relationship Between Spirituality and Organizational Citizenship Behavior**

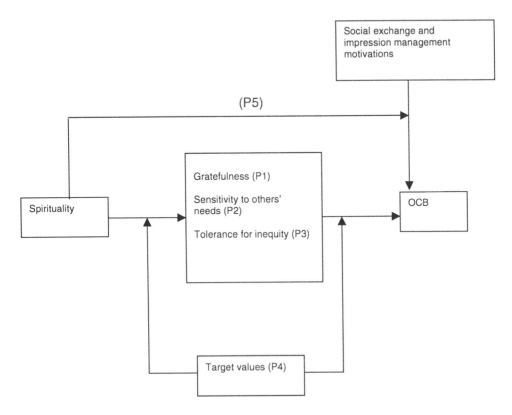

Mediating Effects of Gratefulness

As I noted above, spiritual individuals are more likely to look for and find meaning and significance in what nonspiritual individuals might regard as mundane events. For example, whereas the nonspiritual person might regard a trip to the grocery store as a burdensome time-killer, the spiritual person should be more likely to experience the trip as a unique and special event. Consequently, the pursuit of meaningfulness puts spiritual individuals in a unique position to appreciate their life experiences, and, more so than their nonspiritual counterparts, spiritual individuals should be more likely to experience gratefulness, a sense of appreciation derived from having received cherished gifts or from having witnessed favorable events. This is not to say that spiritual people find all life experiences to be special and important or that nonspiritual individuals fail to experience meaningfulness in their lives. Some activities are inherently meaningful (e.g., looking out over the Grand Canyon), whereas others are not (e.g., mopping a floor). However, spiritual individuals have the ability to elevate routine experiences such that they are more likely to experience gratefulness for the meaning and reverence others (i.e., nonspiritual individuals) cannot find in ordinary events.

One way individuals can express their gratitude is by performing behaviors that benefit other people. Consequently, spirituality should translate into the psychological state of gratefulness, which should, in turn, produce OCBs, behaviors that benefit one's coworkers and employer.

Experienced gratefulness should influence OCB in a manner not unlike the social exchange–based interpretation Organ (1990) described. Grateful individuals should be motivated to express their appreciation in some fashion, one of which is OCB. However, whereas the well-treated individual in Organ's social exchange framework is expected to express his or her gratefulness by reciprocating the source of his or her favorable treatment (i.e., paying back the organization), the spiritual individual may express his or her gratefulness toward a variety of targets. Taken together, these arguments suggest the following research proposition: Employees' gratefulness will mediate the relationship between spirituality and OCB; employees who are more spiritual will be more grateful, which will, in turn, cause them to perform OCB with greater frequency (Proposition 1).

Mediating Effects of Sensitivity to Others' Needs

The motivation to find meaning in one's existence is not accomplished in isolation. Individuals use the perceptions, attitudes, and behaviors of others as signals as to whether their spiritual strivings are appropriate and efficacious. Of course this implies that the process of validating individuals' spiritual strivings involves significant interdependencies. Individuals look to others to validate their own strivings and serve as a source of validation for others' spiritual strivings. To validate their own strivings, the spiritual person must be sensitive to what others think, but in order to serve as a source of validation for others, he or she must also be sensitive to what others need. Moreover, an obvious source of feedback is others whose spiritual strivings are similar. Consequently, we would expect that individuals are especially sensitive to those who share their spiritual strivings.

The spiritual person's sensitivity to the needs of others should, in turn, translate into OCB. OCB in the form of helping others when they require assistance, showing courtesy by informing people of decisions or policies that will affect them, and encouraging others to do their best, allows spiritual individuals to demonstrate concern for the well-being of others. Taken together, these arguments suggest a second research proposition: Employees' sensitivity to the needs of others will mediate the relationship between spirituality and OCB; employees who are more spiritual will be more sensitive to others' needs, which will, in turn, cause them to perform OCB with greater frequency (Proposition 2).

Mediating Effects of Tolerance for Inequity

Spirituality is not easy. In fact, a defining feature of the quest for meaning in one's existence is that it involves overcoming significant obstacles. Individuals place less value on easily accomplished tasks; consequently, spiritual strivings typically require diligence and continuous effort. Part of the satisfaction derived from the spiritual journey comes from the knowledge that doing so challenges one's commitment. Moreover, not only do minor inequities make the striving more meaningful, but they also condition the person to expect that the road to fulfilling one's search for meaning will be fraught with challenges. More so than their nonspiritual counterparts, spiritual individuals should develop a willingness to accept experiences that fall short of expectations, to persist in the face of negative turns, and to forgive organizations and fellow coworkers for mistakes or minor indiscretions. That is, spiritual persons should develop a high tolerance for inequity, a capacity to accept less-than-ideal outcomes.

Tolerance for inequity should, in turn, produce greater OCB. To the extent fairness perceptions are related to OCB (i.e., the social exchange–based interpretation of OCB; Organ 1990), individuals who have a high tolerance for inequity should perform OCB with greater frequency because, all other things equal, they are more likely to experience fairness. That is, even in the face of what might be viewed as objectively unfair allocations or unfair decision-making processes, individuals with a high tolerance for inequity should be more forgiving and willing to behave as if outcomes and procedures are just. Taken together, these arguments suggest the third research proposition: Employees' tolerance for inequity will mediate the relationship between spirituality and OCB; employees who are more spiritual will have a higher tolerance for inequity, which will, in turn, cause them to perform OCB with greater frequency (Proposition 3).

Moderating Effects of Target Values

Figure 12.1 shows that the mediating effects suggested in Propositions 1, 2, and 3 depend on the level of convergence between the person's spiritual strivings and the values of the target for OCB. Targets for OCB may be specific coworkers or the organization itself (Williams and Anderson 1991), and I predict that the extent to which spirituality influences OCB depends on whether the OCB target's values and goals conflict with the individual's spiritual strivings. For example, the spiritual employee's gratefulness will manifest in OCB performance toward the organization, so long as the employee sees convergence between the emphasis of his or her spiritual striving and the organization's objectives. For example, an individual may bring meaning to his or her own life by taking a teaching position with a university whose mission involves inexpensive undergraduate education for a large segment of the population. We can expect this employee to perform OCB, so long as the university stays true to that mission. However, should the university modify its mission to become more research-oriented and abandon its primary commitment to undergraduate education, we can expect that employee to withhold OCB. Even if he or she experiences tremendous gratefulness owing to his or her spiritual orientation, he or she will be less inclined to perform OCB on behalf of his or her employer, preferring to express gratitude in some other context or toward some other target. By the same token, an individual whose spiritual strivings involve finding meaning in the legacy of research he or she produces can be expected to perform OCB on behalf of the university only after it changes its mission to one that converges (or at least does not conflict) with his or her spiritual striving.

Regarding OCB directed at specific individuals, it may be expected that the spiritual person's sensitivity to the needs of others will translate into OCB, so long as his or her strivings are not contradictory. The Kamikaze pilot may see a suicide run as the highest form of commitment to his or her spiritual leanings. This implies some insensitivity to those likely to be injured or killed in the explosion. Yet it is the bomber's sensitivity to the needs of his comrades that compels him to take his own life. In this case, the pilot experiences a sense of commitment to his comrades and no such commitment to those who will be hurt by his actions. Whether the spiritual person experiences sensitivity to the needs of others and performs OCB on behalf of others depends on the convergence between his or her spiritual strivings and others' values.

Taken together, these arguments suggest that the extent to which the spiritual person's gratefulness, sensitivity to others, and tolerance for inequity produce OCB will depend on the target's values, be it the employer or a specific person—these mediating relationships will be stronger when there is greater convergence between the employees' spiritual strivings and the target's values (Proposition 4).

Moderating Effects of Spirituality

Figure 12.1 shows that spirituality is expected to moderate the effects of social exchange and impression management motivations on OCB. Employees who have a stronger spiritual orientation should perform OCB, whether or not the relationship with their organization is one of social exchange and whether or not they are motivated to manage impressions. For spiritual individuals, the search for meaningfulness represents an obsession that influences their willingness to perform desired work behaviors, irrespective of the individuals' relationship with the organization and irrespective of their desire to manage favorable impressions. However, among employees who are less spiritual, social exchange and impression management motivations should play more significant roles in OCB performance. Nonspiritual individuals, who are less concerned about performing OCB as a way of achieving a sense of meaningfulness, should be more keenly aware of the roles played by social exchange and impression management motivations. These arguments suggest that the extent to which social exchange and impression management motivations produce OCB will depend on the employees' spirituality; these relationships will be stronger when spirituality is lower (Proposition 5).

CONCLUSION

From both practical and scholarly perspectives, the OCB literature represents one of the most promising and useful domains of management inquiry. Organizational survival is dependent on, among other things, employees' willingness to perform behaviors akin to OCB (Katz and Kahn 1978). Consequently, understanding the factors that contribute to OCB performance has serious implications for organization effectiveness (Podsakoff and MacKenzie 1994).

But despite this promise, the OCB literature has evolved little since early work revealed reliable relationships between employees' attitudes and OCB. As I said earlier, research on the antecedents of OCB have focused on employees' attitudes and, more recently, some work has explored the effects of impression management motivations on OCB. Simply put, the OCB construct warrants new lines of inquiry, and a well-defined and articulated spirituality construct could prove useful in the pursuit of knowledge about the antecedents of OCB performance.

This chapter takes a first step toward that end. I have proposed that spirituality indirectly influences employees' OCB through three psychological states: gratefulness, sensitivity to others' needs, and tolerance for inequity. My framework accounts for the notion that spirituality does not always translate into OCB; the spiritual person's gratefulness, sensitivity, and tolerance for inequity are more likely to produce OCB when the target's values are not inconsistent with the individual's spiritual strivings. I have also argued that spirituality moderates the effects of social exchange and impression management motivations on OCB such that spirituality magnifies these effects.

Future research should proceed along several fronts. First, psychometrically sound measures of spirituality should be developed. Extant measures conflate spirituality with religiosity or the consequences of spiritual strivings (Elkins et al. 1988; Kass et al. 1991; Maltby and Day 2001; Paloutzian and Ellison 1982; Piedmont 1999). Consequently, these measures are of little use to researchers who seek to explore the antecedents and consequences of spirituality in any context, work-related or otherwise.

Second, theoretical conceptions of spirituality must distinguish between spirituality and constructs related to it. For example, rather than using the terms *spirituality* and *religiosity* interchangeably, it would be more useful to develop models that explain under what circumstances spirituality translates into religious involvement and when it does not. With respect to this chapter's concerns for workplace behavior, models should be developed that explain whether the consequences of spirituality involve a spillover effect (e.g., individuals who seek religion as a way of fulfilling their spiritual strivings are more likely to perform OCB compared to nonreligious individuals), a compensatory model (e.g., spiritual individuals who perform OCB are less likely to seek meaningfulness through religion, and vice versa), or independence (e.g., the consequences of spirituality are unrelated to one another).

Finally, the effects of spirituality on workplace phenomena besides OCB should be investigated. Some questions that could be answered include: how does spirituality affect individuals' perceptions of and behavior toward coworkers (e.g., do spiritual supervisors rate subordinates more favorably than nonspiritual supervisors, all other things equal); is individual spirituality related to individual, group, or organizational effectiveness (e.g., are spiritual individuals more reliable employees); and do spiritual employees cope better with organizational stressors than nonspiritual employees? These and many other important research questions warrant investigation, though conceptual and measurement issues will have to be addressed as first steps in the making of a viable spirituality construct.

REFERENCES

Allen, T.A., and M.C. Rush. (1998). "The Effects of Organizational Citizenship Behavior on Performance Judgments: A Field Study and a Laboratory Experiment." *Journal of Applied Psychology* 83: 247–260.

Bateman, T., and D. Organ. (1983). "Job Satisfaction and the Good Soldier: The Relationship Between Affect and Employee 'Citizenship.'" *Academy of Management Journal* 26: 587–595.

Blakely, G.L.; J. Fuller; and D. Smith. (1996). "Are Chameleons Good Citizens? The Relationship Between Self-Monitoring and Organizational Citizenship Behavior." Paper presented at the annual meeting of the Southern Management Association, New Orleans, November.

Blau, P. (1964). *Exchange and Power in Social Life.* New York: Wiley.

Bolino, M.C. (1999). "Citizenship and Impression Management: Good Soldiers or Good Actors?" *Academy of Management Review* 24: 82–98.

Brayfield, A.H., and W.H. Crockett. (1955). "Employee Attitudes and Employee Performance." *Psychological Bulletin* 52: 396–424.

Eastman, K.K. (1994). "In the Eyes of the Beholder: An Attributional Approach to Ingratiation and Organizational Citizenship Behavior." *Academy of Management Journal* 37: 1379–1391.

Elkins, D.N.; L.J. Hedstrom; L.L. Hughes; J.A. Leaf; and C. Saunders. (1988). "Toward a Humanistic-Phenomenological Spirituality: Definition, Description, and Measurement." *Journal of Humanistic Psychology* 28: 5–18.

Fandt, P.M., and G.R. Ferris. (1990). "The Management of Information and Impressions: When Employees Behave Opportunistically." *Organizational Behavior and Human Decision Processes* 45: 140–158.

Ferris, G.R.; D.P.S. Bhawuk; D.B. Fedor; and T.A. Judge. (1995). "Organizational Politics and Citizenship: Attributions of Intentionality and Construct Definition." In *Attribution Theory: An Organizational Perspective,* ed. M.J. Martinko. Delray Beach, FL: St. Lucie Press, 231–252.

Iaffaldano, M.T., and P.M. Muchinsky. (1977). "Job Satisfaction and Job Performance: A Meta-Analysis." *Psychological Bulletin* 97: 251–273.

Jones, E.E., and T.S. Pittman. (1982). "Toward a General Theory of Strategic Self-presentation." In *Psychological Perspectives on the Self,* ed. J. Suls. Hillsdale, NJ: Erlbaum, 231–263.

Kass, J.D.; R. Friedman; J. Leserman; P.C. Zuttermeister; and H. Benson. (1991). "Health Outcomes and a New Index of Spiritual Experience." *Journal for the Scientific Study of Religion* 30: 203–211.

Katz, D., and R.L. Kahn. (1978). *The Social Psychology of Organizations,* 2d ed. New York: Wiley.

Konovsky, M.A., and S.D. Pugh. (1994). "Citizenship and Social Exchange." *Academy of Management Journal* 37: 656–669.

Kushner, H.S. (2001). *Living a Life That Matters.* New York: Random House.

Maltby, J., and L. Day. (2001). "Spiritual Involvement and Belief: The Relationship Between Spirituality and Eysenck's Personality Dimensions." *Personality and Individual Differences* 30: 187–192.

Manogran, P.; J. Stauffer; and E.J. Conlon. (1994). "Leader-Member Exchange As a Key Mediating Variable Between Employees' Perceptions of Fairness and Organizational Citizenship Behavior." In *Academy of Management Best Paper Proceedings,* ed. D.P. Moore. Dallas, TX: Academy of Management, 249–252.

McClelland, D.C. (1971). *Assessing Human Motivation.* New York: General Learning Press.

Moorman, R.H.; G.L. Blakely; and B.P. Niehoff. (1998). "Does Perceived Organizational Support Mediate the Relationship Between Procedural Justice and Organizational Citizenship Behavior?" *Academy of Management Journal* 41: 351–357.

Morrison, E.W. (1994). "Role Definitions and Organizational Citizenship Behaviors: The Importance of the Employees' Perspective." *Academy of Management Journal* 37: 1543–1567.

Organ, D.W. (1977). "A Reappraisal and Reinterpretation of the Satisfaction-Causes-Performance Hypothesis." *Academy of Management Review* 2: 46–53.

———. (1988a). *Organizational Citizenship Behavior: The "Good-Soldier" Syndrome.* Lexington, MA: Lexington Books.

———. (1988b). "A Restatement of the Satisfaction-Performance Hypothesis." *Journal of Management* 14: 547–557.

———. (1990). "The Motivational Basis for Organizational Citizenship Behavior." In *Research in Organizational Behavior,* ed. B. Staw and L. Cummings, vol. 12. Greenwich, CT: JAI Press, 43–72.

———. (1997). "Organizational Citizenship Behavior: It's Construct Clean-up Time." *Human Performance* 10: 85–97.

Paloutzian, R., and C. Ellison. (1982). "Loneliness, Spiritual Well-being, and the Quality of Life." In *Loneliness: A Sourcebook of Current Theory, Research, and Therapy,* ed. L. Peplan and D. Perlman. New York: Wiley, 224–236.

Pedhauzer, E.J., and L. Schmelkin. (1991). *Measurement, Design, and Analysis: An Integrated Approach.* Hillsdale, NJ: Erlbaum.

Piedmont, R.L. (1999). "Does Spirituality Represent the Sixth Factor of Personality? Spiritual Transcendence and the Five-Factor Model." *Journal of Personality* 67: 985–1013.

Podsakoff, P.M., and S.B. MacKenzie. (1994). "Organizational Citizenship Behavior and Sales Unit Effectiveness." *Journal of Marketing Research* 31: 351–363.

Podsakoff, P.; S. MacKenzie; J. Paine; and D. Bacharach. (2000). "Organizational Citizenship Behaviors: A Critical Review of the Theoretical and Empirical Literature and Suggestions for Future Research." *Journal of Management* 26: 513–563.

Rousseau, D.M. (1995). *Psychological Contracts in Organizations: Understanding Written and Unwritten Agreements.* Thousand Oaks, CA: Sage.

Schnake, M. (1991). "Organizational Citizenship: A Review, Proposed Model, and Research Agenda." *Human Relations* 44: 735–759.

Shyamalan, M.N. (2000). *Unbreakable.* Blinding Edge Pictures.

Smith, C.A.; D.O. Organ; and J.P. Near. (1983). "Organizational Citizenship Behavior: Its Nature and Antecedents." *Journal of Applied Psychology* 68: 653–663.

Tepper, B.J.; D. Lockhart; and J. Hoobler. (2001). "Justice, Citizenship, and Role Definition Effects." *Journal of Applied Psychology* 86: 789–796.

Van Dyne, L.; L.L. Cummings; and J.M. Parks. (1995). "Extra-role Voice Behaviors: In Pursuit of Construct and Definitional Clarity (A Bridge over Muddied Waters)." In *Research in Organizational Behavior,* ed. B. M. Shaw and L.L. Cummings, vol. 17. Greenwich, CT: JAI Press, 215–285.

Van Dyne, L.; J.W. Graham; and R.M. Dienesch. (1994). "Organizational Citizenship Behavior: Construct Redefinition, Measurement, and Validation." *Academy of Management Journal* 37: 765–802.

Williams, L.J., and S.E. Anderson. (1991). "Job Satisfaction and Organizational Commitment As Predictors of Organizational Citizenship and In-Role Behavior." *Journal of Management* 17: 601–617.

Zellars, K.; B.J. Tepper; R.A. Giacalone; and D. Lockhart. (2001). "Social Exchange, Impression Management, and Organizational Citizenship Behavior." Paper presented at the Annual Meeting of the Academy of Management, Washington, DC, August.

CONCEPTUALIZING
WORKPLACE SPIRITUALITY

CHAPTER 13

RECONCILING PROFESSIONAL AND PERSONAL VALUE SYSTEMS

The Spiritually Motivated Manager as Organizational Entrepreneur

ANDREW J. HOFFMAN

Consider the following statistics. Nearly three-quarters of Americans label themselves as environmentalists. Twenty-one percent identify with the description of "active environmentalist" while another 51 percent identify with the category of "sympathetic toward environmental concerns" (*The Environmental Two Step* 1995). Now consider that many of these same people also work within business. And business is at the root of most environmental problems. Does a natural tension thus exist between an individual's values and the values held by his or her employer? What effect does this have on individual and organizational performance? How can individuals reconcile their personal values related to environmental protection with their workplace values implicitly tied to environmental destruction? For many, the answers to these questions lie in the realm of the growing phenomenon of workplace spirituality. Many employees are finding a call to a spiritual purpose by bringing social values, such as environmental protection, into the workplace in order to serve the greater good of society. And many employers are recognizing this shift and attempting to channel this energy toward the mutual gain of employer and employee.

Normally, dissonant relations between personal and professional values produce tensions that people generally tend to avoid or reduce. If such tensions exist, a person can choose to either: (a) behave in ways that are inconsistent with their personal characteristics but consistent with the organization's culture, (b) leave the organization, or (c) exert influence on organizational characteristics in order to make them congruent with their own characteristics (Hirschman 1972; Chatman 1991). The deciding factor behind an individual's decision to conform, leave, or alter is based on the relative priority given to the conflicting values. If the need for a job is an individual's overriding value above all others, conformance is the likely response to the detriment of the individual's personal value system (Jackall 1988). If deeply embedded values are under attack from incongruent and inflexible organizational values, theory predicts that departure is the likely response.

Yet today, increasing numbers of managers are choosing to remain within organizations whose professional values clash with their personal values. Rather than succumb to these pressures, they are seeking to change the organization's culture in ways that fit their personal beliefs (Hall and Richter 1990). And in the process, they are striving to "express and develop their complete self at work" (Mitroff and Denton 1999) by bringing their personal values, used here as synonymous with spiritual beliefs, into the workplace (McDonald 1999). These individuals derive a sense of self-actualization through their actions, a sense of sacredness and purpose through their work that allows them to feel more genuine and authentic in resolving conflicted value systems and shaping new ones (Ray and Anderson 2000).

There are many reasons proposed as to why this is happening at this point in time. First, people are spending significantly more time at work than did previous generations. Therefore, the workplace is where many social phenomena are likely to emerge (Conlin 1999). Second, society has advanced in terms of leisure time such that people are searching for more meaning in the work realm of their lives (Neck and Milliman 1994). Third, many people in the present generation are reaching a stage in their development where they feel secure in their basic needs such that they are striving for the highest stage of human development, self-actualization (Maslow 1954). Fourth, much of the current workforce is made up of baby boomers who grew up in the idealistic 1960s and 1970s and are trying to maintain their idealistic roots (Hall and Richter 1990; Cash, Gray, and Rood 2000). And fifth, fewer people today identify themselves with a career path within a single company. Instead their career path represents a more personal journey of self-discovery and direction (Hall and Mirvis 1996).

For these and other reasons, many managers are seeking a sense of meaning in their work lives by merging their personal and professional values. In so doing, they search for ways to "leave a legacy," to achieve satisfaction in knowing that their lives made the world a better place (Covey 1995). For some, this involves a religious connotation (Vaughan 1989), while for others it does not (Ray 1992). The critical factor is that individuals within the workplace become guided by a set of deeply personal and highly individual values that are larger than themselves, hence spiritual in nature. These values drive them to experience a higher sense of service in making a difference and contributing to society as a whole (Block 1993). As a result, the nature of their work changes from a career in which they earn a living to a vocation in which they express themselves and make a difference (Neal 2000).

One area in which such personal values are becoming increasingly prominent in the workplace is environmental protection. Today, many hold a personal set of moral beliefs about the proper role of the corporation toward the natural environment. These beliefs are held at the level of the individual and are formed through personal reflection, professional development, and association with other environmentally oriented individuals or cultural groups. The values underlying these beliefs inform an individualized sense of right and wrong that may be at odds with the dominant values in the workplace. Rather than acquiesce to the organization's values or leave, many of today's managers choose to stay within the organization, acting as change agents, or organizational entrepreneurs, trying to alter the firm's cultural values.

This chapter will consider why and how this is happening. First, it will consider how social institutions (Scott 1995) are changing on the subject of environmental protection, thereby changing individual beliefs and creating a clash with the dominant economic institutions that exist. Second, it will consider the tactics used by managers who respond to this clash by acting as organizational entrepreneurs and bring these values into the workplace. It will conclude with a prognosis for the future of this phenomenon and what it means for organizational competencies and performance.

CONFLICTING ECONOMIC AND ENVIRONMENTAL VALUES

The past century has witnessed unprecedented economic growth and human prosperity. Global per capita income has tripled (World Business Council on Sustainable Development 1997), average life expectancy has increased by almost two-thirds (World Resources Institute 1994), and people are significantly more literate than their predecessors. But, many individuals and organizations are also beginning to question the methods by which this economic growth has been achieved. They are spurred to action by mounting evidence of the environmental damage caused by industrial processes.

The U.S. industrial system alone creates 2.5 million metric tons of toxic chemicals (U.S. Environmental Protection Agency 1992), 7 billion metric tons of solid waste, and 120 million metric tons of conventional air pollutants (World Resources Institute 1994). Worldwide, the emission of greenhouse gases has increased from 1.6 billion tons in 1995 to 7.0 billion tons in 1997, causing some scientific models to predict an increase in the earth's temperature of 1.5–4.5°F in the next one hundred years (U.S. Office of Science and Technology Policy 1997). According to the UN Food and Agriculture Organization, four of the world's seventeen major fisheries are commercially depleted and nine more are in serious decline (Nickerson 1994). Each year, an estimated 27,000 species of flora and fauna are estimated to be going extinct (Wilson 1992). Scientists estimate that another 4 to 8 percent of tropical forest species may face extinction over the next twenty-five years (Reid 1988).

Some see these statistics as evidence of immoral or unethical behavior. Others see them as a lamentable but unavoidable consequence of human existence. The former see the negative effects of material development on the world's natural ecosystems, both as individuals and as a society, as suggestive of a need to alter social, political, and economic institutions. The latter see attempts to "green" economic institutions as tantamount to placing the value of natural ecosystems over that of human beings (Sirico 1994), and believe such attempts will serve only to inhibit economic growth that is necessary for the betterment of all humankind (Stone 1998). This debate is taking place at the level of broad institutional regimes (e.g., as it relates to attempts to reduce greenhouse gas emissions under the Kyoto Protocol), specific organizational contexts, and the value sets of individual managers.

Those who see the clash as indicative of a need to change institutions and organizations argue that much environmentally destructive behavior is supported by some very basic taken-for-granted beliefs of modern society and modern capitalism (Allenby 1998; Bazerman and Hoffman 1999). For example, capitalistic society has as one of its fundamental assumptions the human-centered view that unlimited progress is possible through the exploitation of nature's infinite resources. In the pursuit of that progress, organizations and individuals are perceived as independent, existing in a free market where resource extraction and development are the right of the property-owner to the exclusion of other social interests. Present management theory has been criticized for supporting these beliefs by promoting several basic assumptions: an uncritical belief in the necessity of increasing economic growth, the perception of nature as a limitless sink for wastes and a limitless source for materials, the supremacy of technological development for controlling natural systems, the social and physical autonomy of the firm, and the profit motive as a singular objective of the firm (Daly and Cobb 1994; Daly 1991; Gladwin, Kennelly and Krause 1995; Capra 1982).

In the pursuit of a spiritual element to their work, environmentalists in the workplace are challenging these dominant beliefs, attempting to reconcile them with their own personal value systems. They see their attempts to bring environmental sustainability into the core values of the organization as a spiritual cause and purpose both for maintaining their personal identity and for positively impacting society.

ORGANIZATIONAL LIFE: RECONCILING MULTIPLE CULTURAL VALUE SYSTEMS

While managerial action is internally directed, it is also strongly guided by organizational cultures and social institutions in which individuals reside. A large literature in social psychology suggests that people identify themselves with particular groups and, hence, define their identities via their social relationships with other groups and institutions (Tajfel and Turner 1986; Kramer 1993). In this way, individuals seek to construct their own identities and communicate or project these identities to others through these groups (Thompson and Gonzalez 1997; Tetlock et al. 2000).

Organizational and social cultures become filters through which the external world is viewed and information is developed, interpreted, disseminated, and acted upon (March 1981). Cultures shape individual consciousness, imposing routines that reflect socially approved, purposive action (Jackall 1988). They guide the perception and behavior of all members (Schein 1985) and present cultural and contextual constraints that alter individual and organizational perspectives on social issues. They give collective meaning and value to particular events and activities (Meyer, Boli, and Thomas 1987), among them the state of the environment (Hoffman and Ventresca 1999).

But managers are members of multiple social groups—professions, religion, social activist groups, political affiliation, socioeconomic class, education, and so forth—each of which possesses its own particular value sets that influence individual beliefs and behavior (Schein 1996). Thus, managerial action becomes a choice among a set of legitimate options determined by multiple groups within society at large (Scott 1991). The form of this influence is manifested in cultural institutions: rules, norms, and beliefs that create descriptions of reality for the individual; explanations of what is and what is not, what can be acted upon and what cannot—in short, how social choices are shaped, mediated, and channeled.

For the individual manager then, organizational life becomes an attempt to mediate between the competing cultural demands of multiple social groups. As shown in Figure 13.1, they are committed to their professional workplace values, seeking career success within the workplace. And they are also committed to their personal social values, seeking to remain true and genuine to their social ideology. But they may find themselves committed to a multiplicity of value sets that are internally consistent within their own settings but clash within the individual (Jurkiewicz 1994, 1999). Professional values may be supported by institutions embedded within places of employment, professional training, and the market environment. Social values may be supported by institutions embedded within activist groups, religious organizations, government agencies, and the educational environment. But, since the dawn of the environmental movement in the 1970s, these two sets of values have been increasingly in conflict within the common domain of the workplace.

In the face of such value conflict, there is a tendency for the individual to change those cultural elements that are easiest to change (Jones, Hendrick, and Epstein 1979). At first, in the 1970s and 1980s, the clash between environmental and workplace values was so severe as to warrant that an individual change his or her personal values to fit the workplace (Hoffman 1997). Business values were simply too rigidly established to change and personal values were subsumed for the sake of employment. At this time, environmental groups were the primary institutional drivers of environmental issues within the workplace. They articulated values about the role of corporations

Figure 13.1 **Mediating Between Competing Value Sets**

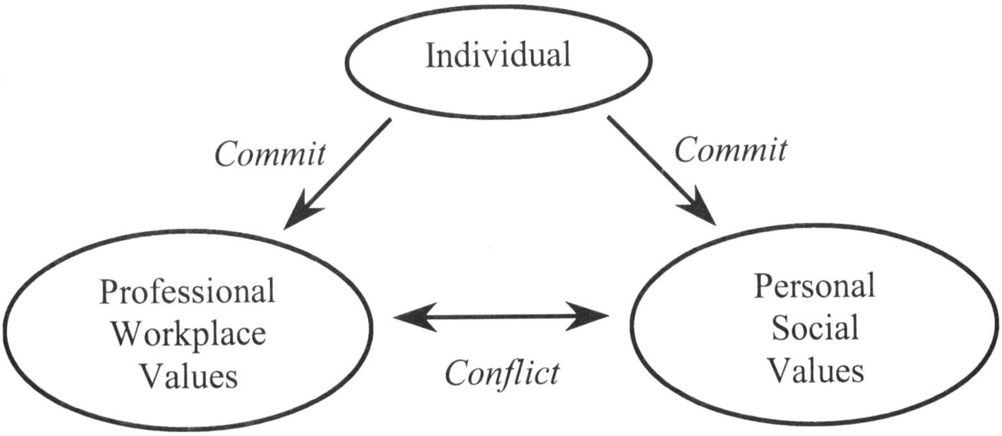

with respect to the environment and drove change primarily through policy pressure and social protest, both of which are sources *external* to the firm.

But since the 1990s, social institutions have changed in ways to make environmental issues more of a direct influence on managerial action (Hoffman 2000). The drivers of environmental responsibility emerged from sources *internal* to the corporation "as younger managers and their families began making demands on top management that previous generations would never have dared to do" (Morrison 1991, 18). These managers emerged as a new workforce demographic that questioned authority, held a strong concern for basic values, and felt a strong sense of freedom to act on those values (Hall and Richter 1990). And since the early 1990s, historically traditional acts of conformity have become increasingly less acceptable as environmental values have become more pervasive in the institutional environment. Managers have since begun to search for ways to mutually satisfy environmental and economic objectives. Representative of this shift, 70 percent of Americans now think that there is no tension between environmental protection and economic development, and that the two can work together (*The Environmental Two Step* 1995).

From where do such new social values emerge? Clearly, environmental groups continue to exert social influence within the belief systems of contemporary managers. But, two other social institutions—education and religion—are now creating a more powerful link between personal and environmental values, one that is harder to subsume in the workplace as it relates more directly to the identity of the individual. These institutions occupy an important place within society, shaping norms, values, and beliefs of individuals directly. They alter beliefs at the core of individual identity—what people believe about the reality of the world, how the world behaves, what fundamental rights people have, notions of justice, and what is right and wrong.

Educational institutions indoctrinate the young on the appropriate ways to think and act within society. They teach the right and wrong of living within modern society. And interest and involvement in ecological issues is strong in today's colleges and universities (Dembner 1994). Tomorrow's workforce is being influenced by a growing number of environmental courses being offered at schools of business, engineering, science, journalism, law and public policy (Makower 1993; Mangan 1994; Pham 1994; Friedman 1996; Wagner 1994; Finlay, Bunch, and Neubert 1998). Today's youth are being educated on the environment in ways that are far different from the ways previous generations were taught. Academia is becoming an important force in shaping the future evolution of environmentalism and, in particular, its integration into the practices and objectives of the contemporary workforce.

This growing concern for environmental awareness has gone well beyond postsecondary education, suggestive of a more fundamental shift in personal beliefs taking place at more formative levels of the education system. For example, thirty-one states require school systems to incorporate environmental concepts into courses on most grade levels. Some even go so far as to require special training in environmentalism for teachers. Some high schools are teaching courses in ecology, for which students can receive college credit. From 1992 until 1997, the EPA spent $13 million on environmental education, giving grants to about 1,200 school projects (Cushman 1997). The U.S. federal government's Global Environmental Education Initiative is designed to involve children throughout the world in monitoring environmental quality, thereby teaching them about global environmental issues while using scientific instrumentation to gather and analyze data (U.S. National Science and Technology Council 1994). Supporting such initiatives, environmental groups like the World Resources Institute and Environmental Defense are developing curriculum packages to help high schools integrate environmental education into their programs (Cushman 1997).

Religious institutions, more so than education, can alter people's behaviors by directly affecting their values and beliefs. Issues defined as religious values can be viewed as "sacred," such that people are more likely to defend them when challenged (Tetlock et al. 2000) and more willing to express them to others. Indeed, with today's changing context of species extinction and global environmental change, many religions are changing their views on the morality of behavior toward the environment.

In 1991, the Presbyterian Church decided to place environmental concerns directly into the church canon, thus making it a sin to "threaten death to the planet entrusted to our care" (Associated Press 1991). In 1992, the Roman Catholic Church equated environmental degradation with theft from future generations in its new catechism (Woodward and Nordland 1992)—"The seventh commandment (Thou shalt not steal) enjoins respect for the integrity of creation. Animals, like plants and inanimate beings, are by nature destined for the common good of past, present, and future humanity. Use of the mineral, vegetable, and animal resources of the universe cannot be divorced from respect for moral imperatives. Man's dominion over inanimate and other living beings granted by the Creator is not absolute; it is limited by concern for the quality of life of his neighbor, including generations to come; it requires a religious respect for the integrity of creation" (*Catechism of the Catholic Church* 1994, 580).

In 1997, His All Holiness Bartholomew I, spiritual leader of the world's 300 million Orthodox Christians, equated specific ecological problems with sinful behavior. He announced that "For humans to cause species to become extinct and to destroy the biological diversity of God's creation, for humans to degrade the integrity of the Earth by causing changes in its climate, water, its land, its air, and its life with poisonous substances—these are sins" (Stammer 1997, 1A). Pointing out that "Excessive consumption may be understood from a world view of estrangement from self, from land, from life and from God," he used his comments to specifically target the issue of climate change. "Many are arguing that someone else should address the problem, or that they should not have to take serious action unless everyone else does. . . .This self-centered behavior is a symptom of our alienation from one another and from the context of our common existence" (Stammer 1997, 1A).

The first of the basic Buddhist precepts counsels those pursuing the path toward liberation to avoid destroying life, while the religion as a whole fosters a worldview that emphasizes the interdependence of all beings. According to the Dalai Lama, relations with one's fellow human beings, animals, and insects, "should be based on the awareness that all of them seek happiness. . . . All are interdependent in creating our joy and happiness" (Tenzin 1992, 115). In 1988, Shomrei Adamah, Keepers of the Earth, was founded, the first institution dedicated to cultivating the ecological think- ing and practices integral to Jewish life (Bernstein 2000). Many spiritual groups that are not affili- ated with any particular denomination, such as existentialists, secular humanists, and communitarians, are seeking to change social norms on environmental protection (among other issues) as connected with a higher purpose of creating a better society (*Businessline* 1999).

Changes in religious thought are also being mobilized into social and political action. In 1996, evangelical groups rallied support for Endangered Species Act reauthorization, calling it "the Noah's ark of our day," while questioning Congress's apparent attempt to "sink it" (Steinfels 1996, C19). Buoyed by surveys that showed that 78 percent of Americans believed that "because God created the natural world, it is wrong to abuse it" (*Greenline* 1995), the winter 1996 issue of *Green Cross,* a Christian environmental quarterly, focused on the "implications of Christian re- sponsibility to protect species" (*Greenline* 1996). In 1998, twenty-two members of the National Council of Churches—a coalition of Protestant, Greek Orthodox, Catholic, and Jewish religious leaders—rallied to support the Kyoto Treaty on climate change, sending a letter to President Clinton pledging to work to get the treaty implemented because it is "an important move toward protecting God's children and God's creation" (Cushman 1998, A10). The National Religious Partnership for the Environment—a coalition of the National Council of Churches, the U.S. Catholic Conference, and the Coalition on the Environment and Jewish Life—also vowed to lobby sena- tors to support the treaty (Cushman 1998).

Even applying religious pressure to shift consumer behavior, the Episcopal Diocese of Cali- fornia adopted a resolution in 1998 instructing all eighty-seven Episcopal churches in California to buy clean, renewable energy. In 1999, Commonwealth Energy Corp. and the North American Coalition on Religion and Ecology (NACRE) announced the formation of the "Greensmart Re- newable Energy Project" to promote the benefits of green power. NACRE encouraged the more than thirty thousand religious organizations and other nonprofit organizations in California to demonstrate their environmental commitment by switching to electricity generated by renewable energy sources.

In the end, religious values toward the environment are changing. Environmental protection is being adopted as a religious and moral issue as religious leaders in many faiths are searching to individually and jointly find ways for society to live in the natural world that promote sus- tainable development (Rockefeller and Elder 1992). And with this process of change comes an alteration in the beliefs and identity of individuals who are members of those faiths. Religious values—in combination with changes in educational values—form a potent force in shifting social thought and values of individual managers. With changes in such values come changes in conceptions of right and wrong in workplace behavior that impacts the environment as well as the role of the manager in setting those conceptions. Many managers now see that role as spiritually motivated.

TACTICS OF THE SPIRITUALLY MOTIVATED MANAGER

As educational experience and religious doctrine increasingly support the social ideology regard- ing the environment, it becomes more tightly tied to individual identity and becomes an important motivator of managerial action. Yet, managers also seek to accomplish managerial success within their chosen profession through traditional metrics. And so, they find themselves in the middle, mediating between conflicting value sets. To resolve this tension, they seek to "fit" within both cultural domains. This can be done to varying degrees. On one end of the spectrum, the manager may simply act in locally genuine ways by working to fit within the workplace and carefully remaining true to his or her ideals. These managers succeed by the rules, protocols, and reward systems of the organization, but they act in ways that are authentic with their personal beliefs. Through discrete visible actions that reflect individualized motivations, they model new beliefs about appropriate behavior in the workplace. On the other end of the spectrum, the manager may act as a change agent, trying to alter workplace cultural elements and align them with his or her personal set of cultural values. These managers look like what the organization determines to be valid and appropriate, but they are also entrepreneurial in that they are trying to drive change. In this way, the spiritually motivated manager becomes an organizational entrepreneur, or what Meyerson and Scully (1995) refer to as a "tempered radical" (Hammonds 2000). This balancing of competing demands and expectations can bring vitality to the organization and spiritual satisfaction to the individual. But it can also create hazards for the individual who chooses to play this role (Meyerson and Scully 1995).

For the organization, entrepreneurs who remain connected to multiple identities act as boundary spanners, linking the organization to external constituencies that may provide important information for the organization's success. Through these network ties, they can access demographic market segments and gather information about changing external conditions. Further, by thinking differently than the organizational norm, they can be critics of the status quo, identifying opportunities for change that may be overlooked (Hasenfeld and Chesler 1989). Thus, they can act as important sources of energy and creativity for the organization.

But for individuals there may exist perceptions of hypocrisy (Goffman 1969), leading to feelings of isolation from either side of their identity groups, workplace and social or environmental. They must withstand pressures for co-optation to forfeit one side or the other. Concomitant with these perceptions and pressures may come emotional burdens of guilt or self-doubt about their effectiveness and importance (Kolb and Williams 1993).

But spiritually motivated managers also derive "sustenance from artfully working the system to make changes" (Meyerson and Scully 1995, 594). They draw personal satisfaction by injecting environmental values into the workplace as representative of meeting their spiritual objectives. Success in reconciling their spiritual selves with their managerial selves becomes tied to their ability to transform the organization and make it more consistent with their beliefs about what is right and wrong in the workplace.

Two purposive tactics are available for the spiritually motivated manager turned organizational entrepreneur. The first is to learn to be "multilingual," adopting the insider language in order to gain legitimacy while remaining conversant in the languages of his or her other constituencies (Meyerson and Scully 1995). The second is to use this ability to maintain multiple affiliations with people who represent both sides of his or her identity. This section will discuss each tactic in turn.

BECOMING MULTILINGUAL

For many managers, religion is an inappropriate topic for the workplace. In surveys, most report hesitancy at expressing religious or even spiritual beliefs for fear of, at the least, offending their peers (Mitroff and Denton 1999) or, at the worst, violating the law by being construed as promoting religion in the workplace (Brandt 1996). In practical terms, an appeal for organizational action that employs individualistic and highly personal values will lack the power to persuade others of the merits of an argument. To be effective at triggering change, spiritually motivated managers must employ the professional language, metrics, and rhetoric of the workplace.

A survey by Arthur D. Little identified that differences in language, rhetoric, and metrics limited efforts at environmental change within many corporations (Shelton and Shopley 1995). Environmental managers often took for granted that the value of their strategic environmental programs was apparent. So, they failed to adopt the business metrics and lexicon that were employed by other parts of the organization in communicating that value. Return on investment (ROI) and earnings per share (EPS) remain the most common business validation metrics, yet most environmental managers did not provide such economic cost-benefit analyses on environmental initiatives when attempting to gain budgetary approval. Instead, they used nonbusiness metrics such as pounds of toxics, biological oxygen demand (BOD), notice of deficiency (NOD), environmental impact statement (EIS), and life-cycle assessment (LCA), which were familiar to their external constituency but served to distance other business managers from environmental matters (Shelton and Shopley 1995).

By reframing environmental issues in the terms, language, and rhetoric of the workplace culture, spiritually motivated managers translate their spiritually motivated beliefs about what the firm should rightly be doing into terms that are more able to gain broad support. Several business groups have identified six basic frames to justify corporate environmental practice (Aspen Institute 1998; GEMI 1999; Hoffman 2001). These include opportunities to:

1. *Improve operational efficiency.* By reducing the input of total or hazardous materials or by minimizing the output of wastes, some argue that it is possible to lower the costs of production.
2. *Reduce risk management costs.* By limiting environmental exposures to employees, contractors, and customers, the firm can directly lower corporate insurance premiums and contingent emergency preparedness costs.
3. *Reduce costs of capital.* Integrating environmental considerations into the capital acquisition and change processes may reduce the uncertainty of corporate transactions, uncover hidden environmental liabilities, and gain more favorable terms with financial institutions.
4. *Increase market demand.* Companies may enhance the market share for products and services by appealing to environmentally conscious end-use customers or buyers and up-front suppliers or vendors.
5. *Improve strategic direction.* Environmental protection is argued to expose important information and insights for guiding new strategic directions by entering newly emerging markets and exiting increasingly risky ones.
6. *Improve human resource management.* Improved environmental performance is framed as an opportunity to increase workplace productivity, attract higher-caliber applicants, and reduce replacement costs by retaining such workers.

However, spiritual values may not always fit so easily with the accepted notions of business purpose. In such cases, the task of the spiritually motivated manager may become even more entrepreneurial in seeking to change the very metrics and measures of success within the organization. Performance metrics act as an articulation of values about what is important and unimportant, what is right and wrong within the organization. When social and professional values irreconcilably collide, existing metrics must be altered to reflect new sets of values consistent with the manager's personal set of environmental values.

In just one example, some organizational entrepreneurs have attempted to change the fore-most economic indicator of national economic progress, the Gross Domestic Product (GDP). This is a metric of financial well-being as measured by all financial transactions for products and services. But it does not acknowledge (or value) a distinction between those transactions that add to the social and environmental well-being of a country and those that actually dimin-ish it. Any productive activity in which money changes hands will register as GDP growth. This creates perverse economic signals that promote shortsighted economic activity at the ex-pense of environmental objectives (Redefining Progress 1996). For example, GDP treats the cleanup costs from natural or man-made disasters as economic gain. GDP increases with pol-luting activities and then again with pollution cleanup. GDP treats the depletion of natural capital as income, rather than the depreciation of a capital asset even if such extraction is occurring at rates faster than the resource can be replenished, such that the net resource pool is diminished for the use of future generations. Economic calculations encourage environmental degradation over environmental conservation.

Some are promoting a redefinition of traditional GDP formulae. Rather than measuring the quantity of economic activity, new measures could replace GDP to measure the quality of economic activity. New values could establish the measurement of true progress, not only how much money is being spent, but also what it is being spent on (Rowe and Silverstein 1999). It could measure the physical change in (or level of) environmental quality and how this change is valued when there is no market price as a guide (Atkinson 1995). To challenge the underly-ing values of GDP calculations more directly, some suggest redefining the concept of growth or, more importantly, ending the assumption that anything called growth is automatically good. GDP is just one example of attempts to change business metrics. Others include attempts to change the metrics of loan payback calculations, reward and bonus schemes, and corporate investor reports.

MAINTAINING MULTIPLE AFFILIATIONS

By becoming multilingual, spiritually motivated managers maintain ties with critical con-stituencies both inside and outside the workplace. Outside the workplace, they remain firmly connected to the environmental, educational, and religious groups through which they derive their individual identity. This is necessary for remaining true to their personal ideals and resisting the pressures for co-optation. It is also necessary for deepening conviction, com-mitment, and understanding of the issues and events that are important to the ideological value system. On the issue of environmental protection, new issues and information are con-stantly emerging on global climate change, species habitat endangerment, ozone depletion, acid rain, material toxicity, and a host of other environmental hazards. To remain a true source of vitality, the network ties and the information those ties provide are the manager's source of personal strength and professional value. On the issue of the environment, these constituencies include not only social constituencies but also key business constituencies with an interest in the environment that include investors, insurance companies, banks, buy-ers, and suppliers (Hoffman 2000).

Inside the workplace, the spiritually motivated manager establishes networks with key con-stituents who are necessary for making change happen. By framing environmental issues into multiple languages, spiritually motivated managers link their change efforts to important internal constituencies from other functions. For example, framed as market demand, environmental is-sues draw the attention of the marketing staff. Framed as operational efficiency, they appeal to the engineering group. Similar framing effects draw in other departments such as finance, strategy, human resources, executive planning, accounting, and others. Astute organizational entrepreneurs understand the politics of change within the organization and are able to draw resources (in the form of people, information, and capital) to support their objectives (Kanter 1982).

CONCLUSION: SPIRITUALLY MOTIVATED MANAGEMENT AND SUSTAINABLE CHANGE

Managers faced with conflicting value sets in their personal and professional lives are challenged with the decision to conform, leave, or alter the organization (Hirschman 1972; Chatman 1991). In today's business environment, more managers are choosing the latter, seeking self-actualization through their work lives by acting as change agents. They are not willing to compromise their personal values for the sake of their professional careers, nor willing to do the reverse. And more important, they are willing to work to make their work environments consistent with their personal values about what is right and wrong.

This chapter has presented the forces by which environmental issues are becoming spiritually motivated, both through educational and religious institutions, and are thus becoming deeply embedded within the personal identities of individual managers. Further, it presented the tactics by which these spiritually motivated managers act as organizational entrepreneurs, expressing their identity by fomenting change within their organizations. In so doing, they act as radicals or subversives, altering the dominant logics, metrics, and values of the organization through localized and discrete efforts at change. In an attempt to resolve the tension between their own personal and professional values, they promote change within their broader social settings.

This phenomenon is not lost in today's management world. Companies are finding that employees who act on their personal sense of workplace spirituality are more creative, self-directed, committed, and desirable employees, and are therefore highly sought after (DeFoore and Renesch 1995). Further, companies are finding that the importance of a congruent fit between an individual's values and that of the organization's culture is tied to organizational success. When a greater fit exists between personal characteristics and organizational values, a variety of potentially desirable behaviors and attitudes ensues, including longer tenure, better performance, and greater satisfaction (Chatman 1991). Values make a difference in how people feel about themselves and about their work and company. Fundamentally, values affect an employee's willingness to commit to organizational goals and responsibilities (Posner and Schmidt 1992).

Empirical evidence shows that environmental values are finding their way into the workplace. Executives from corporations such as Dow, Monsanto, DuPont, Union Carbide, and others have actively espoused the benefits of proactive environmental management in the name of increasing corporate competitiveness and shareholder equity (Hoffman 1997). Forty percent of American companies have a formal environmental policy statement in place, and another 11 percent have added environmental responsibility to their existing company ethics statements (Berenbeim 1992). Seventy-six percent of American companies felt that environmental standards were reasonable or technically feasible and that "there was general agreement that, philosophically, pollution must be controlled" (Morrison 1991, 11). More than seventy-seven percent of companies had a formal system in place for identifying key environmental issues (Morrison 1991).

But, is this move toward reconciling environmental and economic values sustainable? The central premise of the organizational entrepreneur described in this chapter is that environmental issues can be compatible with business management. But, this is not a universally held opinion. Many believe that business management, as it is now fundamentally defined, is completely incompatible with the goals of environmental protection, and that attempts to integrate these goals into business management disregard their complexity and the inability of present social structures to resolve them (Schnaiberg 1980).

Some argue that environmental considerations call for a complete restructuring of the capitalist system, arguing that the integration of environmentalism into present-day capitalism does not fundamentally change the social rules that are causing the environmental problem and therefore will not affect their ultimate result. In corporate environmentalism, they argue, the environment remains external to the economy, internalized through the application of norms and rules based principally on human utility and not ecological stability. Neil Evernden (1985, 128) writes, "the crisis is not simply something we can examine and resolve. We are the environmental crisis. The crisis is a visible manifestation of our very being, like territory revealing the self at its center. The environmental crisis is inherent in everything we believe and do; it is inherent in the context of our lives."

One might reasonably infer from this assessment that the tension between workplace and environmental values will not likely go away. In fact, new concerns and new awareness of environmental problems are continually emerging—global climate change, endocrine disrupters, ozone depletion—and exposing further tensions in the workplace. It is fair to say that there may never be a static definition of a "green" company. There will only be notions of how companies are changing in response to an evolving economic, social, and political environment (Hoffman 2000). The underlying tension remains the same, but it is manifested in different and evolving terms.

For example, in 1906 John Muir opposed the damming of the Hetch-Hetchy Valley in Yosemite National Park as a violation against the deep moral value that nature has worth beyond its material resources. He wrote, "Hetch-Hetchy valley is a grand landscaped garden, one of nature's rarest and most precious mountain temples. Dam Hetch-Hetchy, as well dam for water tanks the people's cathedrals and churches. For no holier temple has ever been consecrated by the heart of man" (Hott and Garey 1989). He railed against dam supporters (which he called "Satan and company"), writing, "These temple destroyers, devotees of ravaging commercialism, seem to have a perfect contempt for nature. And instead of lifting their eyes to the God of the Mountain, lift them to the almighty dollar" (Hott and Garey 1989).

Gifford Pinchot, the first head of the U.S. Forest Service, could not fathom the idea that utilitarian values should not drive our land-use policies. To him, nature represented material resources for human use and questioned the notion that it possessed inherent or innate value. He wrote, "As for me, I have always regarded the sentimental horror of some good citizens at the idea of using natural resources as unintelligent, misdirected and short-sighted. . . . The question is so clear that I cannot understand why there's been so much fuss about it. The turning of the Hetch-Hetchy into a lake will not be a calamity. In fact, it will be a blessing. It is simply a question of the greatest good to the greatest number of people" (Hott and Garey 1989).

In the end, the Hetch-Hetchy dam was granted final approval for its construction in 1913. But today, while the context has changed, the inherent tension remains. The debate over whether to allow oil companies to drill in the Alaska National Wildlife Refuge (ANWR) triggers the same questions as Hetch-Hetchy. Should we place the value of a pristine ecosystem such as ANWR—one that almost no human will ever see—over the utilitarian needs of the United States for energy security? Should we challenge the notion that the environment is an unlimited source of resources destined for human use through technological exploitation? Should the spiritual value of nature held by some take precedence over the utilitarian values held by others? And when both sets of values are held within the same individual, how will they be resolved to the satisfaction of both the individual and the organization that employs him or her? The tension between professional and social values continues albeit in different forms and in different contexts. The reconciliation of these competing value systems will continue as a challenge within the workplace.

In meeting this challenge, organizations must devote resources toward helping employees resolve internal tensions between personal and professional values. In many cases, the tension is not between clearly "good" and "bad" choices but rather between two "goods." Thus, organizations will find it in their interests to participate in this process. Unresolved tensions inhibit individual commitment to workplace goals, thereby reducing organizational performance. But resolving these tensions can enhance productivity by channeling action toward activities that benefit both the individual and the organization. Organizations must develop new proficiencies to understand the basic motivations behind an employee's decision to act as an organizational entrepreneur. When does an employee identify an internal clash in values? Once that clash is identified, why does an employee decide to turn it into action within the workplace? What factors fit into the process through which this decision is reached? In assisting in the resolution of these types of questions, organizations also transform themselves, concerning themselves with the improvement of an employee's developmental skills, not just rational skills. In this way, organizations and employees work together toward creating the most committed of possible workforces by actively seeking to align professional and personal values.

NOTE

I'd like to thank Tim Hall and Robert Giacalone for helpful comments and suggestions for the development of this chapter.

REFERENCES

Allenby, B. (1998). "USA vs. SD: Can American Values and Sustainable Development Live Together in Peace?" *Tomorrow* 4, no. 8: 61.
Aspen Institute. (1998). *Uncovering Value: Integrating Environmental and Financial Performance.* Washington, DC: Aspen Institute.
Associated Press. (1991). "Presbyterians Ratify Teaching on Sex, Ecology." *Boston Globe*, June 9, 4.
Atkinson, G. (1995). "Greening the National Accounts." *Environment* 37: 25–28.
Bazerman, M., and A. Hoffman. (1999). "Sources of Environmentally Destructive Behavior: Individual, Organizational and Institutional Perspectives." *Research in Organizational Behavior* 21: 39–79.
Berenbeim, R. (1992). *Corporate Ethics Practices.* New York: Conference Board.
Bernstein, E. (2000). *Ecology and the Jewish Spirit: Where Nature and the Sacred Meet.* Woodstock, VT: Jewish Lights Publications.
Block, P. (1993). *Stewardship: Choosing Service Over Self-interest.* San Francisco: Berrett-Koehler.
Brandt, E. (1996). "Corporate Pioneers Explore Spirituality." *HR Magazine* 41: 82–88.
Businessline. (1999). "Lifewatch." (February): 1.
Capra, F. (1982). *The Turning Point.* New York: Bantam Books.
Cash, K.; G. Gray; and S. Rood. (2000). "A Framework for Accommodating Religion and Spirituality in the Workplace." *Academy of Management Executive* 14: 124–134.
Catechism of the Catholic Church. (1994). Liguori, MO: Liguori Publications.
Chatman, J. (1991). "Matching People and Organizations: Selection and Socialization in Public Accounting Firms." *Administrative Science Quarterly* 36: 459–484.
Conlin, M. (1999). "Religion in the Workplace." *Business Week* 3653: 151–158.
Covey, S. (1995). *First Things First.* New York: Simon and Schuster.
Cushman, J. (1997). "Critics Rise Up Against Environmental Education." *New York Times*, April 22, A-8.
———. (1998). "Religious Groups Mount a Campaign to Support Pact on Global Warming." *New York Times*, August 15, A-10.
Daly, H. (1991). *Steady-State Economics.* Washington, DC: Island Press.

Daly, H., and J. Cobb. (1994). *For the Common Good.* Boston: Beacon Press.

DeFoore, B., and J. Renesch. (1995). *Rediscovering the Soul of Business: A Renaissance of Values.* San Francisco: New Leader Press.

Dembner, A. (1994). "Movement Is Strong on Campus." *Boston Globe,* November 12, 28.

The Environmental Two Step: Looking Forward, Moving Backward. (1995). New York: Times Mirror.

Evernden, N. (1985). *The Natural Alien.* Toronto: University of Toronto Press.

Finlay, J.; R. Bunch; and B. Neubert. (1998). *Grey Pinstripes with Green Ties: MBA Programs Where the Environment Matters.* Washington, DC: World Resources Institute.

Friedman, S. (1996). "Teaching the Beat: Rising Interest in E-Journalism Reflected in Academic Option." *SE Journal* 6: 1, 7.

Gladwin, T.; J. Kennelly; and T. Krause. (1995). "Shifting Paradigms for Sustainable Development: Implications for Management Theory and Research." *Academy of Management Review* 20: 874–907.

Global Environmental Management Initiative (GEMI). (1999). *Environment: Value to Business.* Washington, DC: Global Environmental Management Initiative.

Goffman, E. (1969). *The Presentation of Self in Everyday Life.* New York: Doubleday.

Greenline. (1995). "Mainstream." *Greenline,* no. 15 (December 11): 1.

———. (1996). "Green Cross." *Greenline,* no. 48 (January 31): 1.

Hall, D.T., and P. Mirvis. (1996). "The New Protean Career: Psychological Success and the Path with a Heart." In *The Career Is Dead, Long Live the Career: A Relational Approach to Careers,* ed. D.T. Hall. San Francisco: Jossey-Bass, 15–45.

Hall, D.T., and J. Richter. (1990). "Career Gridlock: Baby Boomers Hit the Wall." *Academy of Management Executive* 4: 7–22.

Hammonds, K. (2000). "Practical Radicals." *Fast Company* (September): 162–174.

Hasenfeld, Y., and M. Chesler. (1989). "Client Empowerment in Human Services: Personal and Professional Agenda." *Journal of Applied Behavioral Science* 25: 499–521.

Hirschman, A. (1972). *Exit Voice and Loyalty: Responses to Decline in Firms, Organizations, and States.* Cambridge: Harvard University Press.

Hoffman, A. (1997). *From Heresy to Dogma: An Institutional History of Corporate Environmentalism.* San Francisco: New Lexington.

———. (2000). *Competitive Environmental Strategy: A Guide to the Changing Business Landscape.* Washington, DC: Island Press.

———. (2001). "Linking Organizational and Field Level Analyses: The Diffusion of Corporate Environmental Practice." *Organization and Environment* 14: 133–156.

Hoffman, A., and M. Ventresca. (1999). "The Institutional Framing of Policy Debates: Economics versus the Environment." *American Behavioral Scientist* 42: 1368–1392.

Hott, L., and D. Garey. (1989). *The Wilderness Idea: John Muir, Gifford Pinchot and the First Great Battle for Wilderness.* Video documentary. Santa Monica, CA: Direct Cinema Ltd.

Jackall, R. (1988). *Moral Mazes: The World of Corporate Managers.* New York: Oxford University Press.

Jones, R.; C. Hendrick; and Y. Epstein. (1979). *Introduction to Social Psychology.* Sunderland, MA: Sinaver.

Jurkiewicz, C.L. (1994). "The Case for Ethical Multiplicity: Let Reformers Beware." Proceedings from the International Conference of the Academy of Business Administration, London, July.

———. (1999). "The Phantom Code of Ethics vs. the Formal Code of Ethics: The Battle for Right and Wrong Amidst a Culture of Reform." Proceedings from the International Conference of the International Institute of Administrative Sciences, July, Sunningdale, UK.

Kanter, R. (1982). "The Middle Manager as Innovator." *Harvard Business Review* (July–August): 95–106.

Kolb, D., and S. Williams. (1993). "Professional Women in Conversation: Where Have We Been and Where Are We Going?" *Journal of Management Inquiry* 2: 14–26.

Kramer, R. (1993). "Cooperation and Organizational Identification." In *Social Psychology in Organizations,* ed. J.K. Murningham. Englewood Cliffs, NJ: Prentice Hall, 244–268.

Makower, J. (1993). "Business Schools Get in Line." *Tomorrow* 3, no. 3: 50–53.

Mangan, K. (1994). "The Greening of the MBA." *Chronicle of Higher Education* (November 2): A-19–A-20.

March, J. (1981). "Footnotes to Organization Change." *Administrative Science Quarterly* 26: 563–577.

Maslow, A. (1954). *Motivation and Personality.* New York: HarperCollins.

McDonald, M. (1999). "Shush. The Guy in the Next Cubicle Is Meditating." *U.S. News and World Report* 126, no. 7: 46.

Meyer, J.; J. Boli; and G. Thomas. (1987). "Ontology and Rationalization in Western Cultural Account." In *Institutional Structure: Constituting State, Society, and the Individual*, ed. G. Thomas et al. Newbury Park, CA: Sage, 12–38.

Meyerson, D., and M. Scully (1995). "Tempered Radicalism and the Politics of Ambivalence and Change." *Organization Science* 6: 585–600.

Mitroff, I., and E. Denton (1999). "A Study of Spirituality in the Workplace." *Sloan Management Review* 40 (summer): 83–92.

Morrison, C. (1991). *Managing Environmental Affairs: Corporate Practices in the U.S., Canada and Europe.* New York: Conference Board.

Neal, J. (2000). "Work As Service to the Divine." *American Behavioral Scientist* 43: 1316–1334.

Neck, C., and J. Milliman. (1994). "Thought Self-leadership: Finding Spiritual Fulfillment in Organizational Life." *Journal of Managerial Psychology* 9: 9–16.

Nickerson, C. (1994). "Stripping the Sea's Life." *Boston Globe*, April 17, 1, 24, 25.

Pham, A. (1994). "Business Schools See Green." *Boston Globe*, June 28, 35.

Posner, B., and W. Schmidt. (1992). "Values and the American Manager: An Update Updated." *California Management Review* 34: 80–94.

Ray, M. (1992). "The Emerging New Paradigm in Business." In *New Traditions in Business*, ed. J. Rensch. San Francisco: Berrett-Koehler, 25–38.

Ray, P., and S. Anderson. (2000). *The Cultural Creatives.* New York: Harmony.

Redefining Progress. (1996). *What's Wrong with GDP?* San Francisco: Redefining Progress.

Reid, W. (1988). "How Many Species Will There Be?" In *Evolution and Coadaptation in Biotic Communities*, ed. S. Kawano, J.H. Connell, and T. Hidaka. Japan: University of Tokyo Press, 17.

Rockefeller, S., and J. Elder. (1992). *Spirit and Nature: Why the Environment Is a Religious Issue.* Boston: Beacon.

Rowe, J., and J. Silverstein. (1999). "The GDP Myth: Why 'Growth' Isn't Always a Good Thing." *Washington Monthly* (March): 17–21.

Schein, E. (1985). *Organizational Culture and Leadership.* San Francisco: Jossey-Bass.

_____. (1996). "Three Cultures of Management: The Key to Organizational Learning." *Sloan Management Review* (fall): 9–20.

Schnaiberg, A. (1980). *The Environment: From Surplus to Scarcity.* New York: Oxford University Press.

Scott, W.R. (1991). "Unpacking Institutional Arguments." In *The New Institutionalism in Organizational Analysis*, ed. W. Powell and P. DiMaggio. Chicago: University of Chicago Press, pp. 164–182.

_____. (1995). *Institutions and Organizations.* London: Sage.

Shelton, R., and J. Shopley. (1995). "Hitting the Green Wall." In *Perspectives.* Cambridge: Arthur D. Little.

Sirico, R. (1994). "The Greening of American Faith." *National Review*, August 29, 47.

Stammer, L. (1997). "Harming the Environment Is Sinful, Prelate Says." *Los Angeles Times*, November 9, A-1.

Steinfels, P. (1996). "Evangelical Group Defends Endangered-Species Laws As a Modern Noah's Ark." *New York Times*, January 31, C-19.

Stone, R. (1998). "A Call for Common Sense: The Potential Impact of Climate Change Legislation on the U.S. Pulp and Paper Industry." In *Global Climate Change: A Senior Level Dialogue*, ed. A. Hoffman. San Francisco: New Lexington, 49–52.

Tajfel, H., and J. Turner. (1986). "The Social Identity Theory of Intergroup Behavior." In *Psychology of Intergroup Relations*, ed. S. Worchel and W. Austin. Chicago: Nelson-Hall, 7–24.

Tenzin, G., His Holiness the 14th Dalai Lama. (1992). "A Tibetan Buddhist Perspective on Spirit in Nature." In *Spirit and Nature: Why the Environment Is a Religious Issue*, ed. S. Rockefeller and J. Elder. Boston: Beacon Press, 109–124.

Tetlock, P.; O. Kristel; S. Elson; M. Green; and J. Lerner. (2000). "The Psychology of the Unthinkable: Taboo Trade-offs, Forbidden Base Rates, and Heretical Counterfactuals." *Journal of Personality and Social Psychology* 78: 853–870.

Thompson, L.L., and R. Gonzalez. (1997). "Environmental Disputes: Competition for Scarce Resources and Clashing of Values." In *Environment, Ethics and Behavior*, ed. M. Bazerman, D. Messick, A. Tenbrunsel, and K. Wade-Benzoni. San Francisco: New Lexington Press, 75–104.

U.S. Environmental Protection Agency. (1992). "1990 Toxic Release Inventory." Report No. 700–S-92–002. Washington, DC: U.S. Environmental Protection Agency.

U.S. National Science and Technology Council. (1994). "Technology for a Sustainable Future." Washington, DC: Office of Science and Technology Policy.

U.S. Office of Science and Technology Policy. (1997). "Climate Change: State of Knowledge." Washington, DC: Executive Office of the President.

Vaughn, F. (1989). "Varieties of Intuitive Experience." In *Intuition in Organizations*, ed. W. Agor. Newbury Park, CA: Sage, 40–61.

Wagner, B. (1994). "The Greening of the Engineer." *US News and World Report* (March 21): 90–91.

Wilson, E. (1992). *The Diversity of Life.* Cambridge: Harvard University Press.

Woodward, K., and R. Nordland. (1992). "New Rules for an Old Faith." *Newsweek* (November 30): 71.

World Business Council on Sustainable Development. (1997). *Exploring Sustainable Development: WBCSD Global Scenarios.* London: World Business Council on Sustainable Development.

World Resources Institute. (1994). *World Resources 1994–1995.* New York: Oxford University Press.

CHAPTER 14

A STUDY OF QUALITY OF WORK LIFE, SPIRITUAL WELL-BEING, AND LIFE SATISFACTION

DONG-JIN LEE, M. JOSEPH SIRGY, DAVID EFRATY, AND PHILLIP SIEGEL

According to spillover theory in quality-of-life studies, satisfaction in one life domain influences life satisfaction and satisfaction in other life domains (e.g., Wilensky 1960; Diener 1984). There are two types of spillover—vertical spillover and horizontal spillover. Vertical spillover refers to the notion that satisfaction or dissatisfaction in a life domain vertically spills over to the most superordinate domain, life satisfaction. For example, studies have identified that *spiritual well-being*, or satisfaction in the spiritual life domain, has a positive influence on life satisfaction (e.g., Paloutzian 1996, 1997; Reed 1991; Ventis 1995). This is because spiritual well-being provides meaningful goals in life, positive affect, and social support (e.g., Emmons 1999; Paloutzian 1997; Schumaker 1992; Scott, Agresti, and Fitchett 1998). The positive relationship between spiritual well-being and life satisfaction is stronger especially for those who are intrinsically religious (e.g., Delbridge, Headley, and Wearing 1994; Genia 1996), and for those who are strongly affiliated with religious groups (e.g., Reed 1991; Ventis 1995).

In contrast, horizontal spillover refers to the notion that satisfaction with one life domain influences satisfaction of neighboring life domains (e.g., Diener 1984; Rice, Near, and Hunt 1980; Sirgy 2001; Wilensky 1960). For example, one can argue that spiritual well-being has a positive influence on job satisfaction. This is because spirituality injects meaning into work (Emmons 1999). In addition, spiritual well-being is affected by satisfaction with other life domains (e.g., Diener 1984; Rice, Near, and Hunt 1980; Sirgy 2001; Wilensky 1960). For example, a person's job satisfaction may cause one to feel more satisfied with social and other spiritual activities.

This chapter focuses on the relationship between quality of work life (QWL) and spiritual well-being. In this chapter, QWL is defined as the degree of satisfaction with various needs at work (e.g., Loscocco and Roschelle 1991; Sirgy et al. 2001), and spiritual well-being refers to satisfaction in the spiritual life domain. It should be noted that QWL is not job satisfaction. QWL refers to need satisfaction from social and financial resources provided to the individual through work (Danna and Griffin 1999; Sirgy et al. 2001). QWL has been shown to affect job satisfaction (Sirgy et al. 2001), which has a positive effect on job performance (Bagozzi 1980).

Much research has been conducted on the vertical relationship between spiritual well-being and life satisfaction (e.g., Chamberlain and Zika 1992; Delbridge, Headley, and Wearing 1994; Emmons 1999; Genia 1996; Levin and Tobin 1995; Moberg 1972; Paloutzian 1997; Reed 1991; Ventis 1995). However, limited research has been done on horizontal spillover—the relationship between spiritual well-being and satisfaction with other life domains. As such, there are still many research questions that remain to be answered, such as: How does QWL affect spiritual well-being? How do job satisfaction and spiritual well-being interact with each other and affect overall life satisfaction?

In order to answer these questions, this chapter develops and tests a model that explains interrelationships among QWL, spiritual well-being, and life satisfaction. The conceptual model of this study is guided by vertical and horizontal spillover theories (e.g., Diener 1984; Near, Rice, and Hunt 1980; Wilensky 1960). The goal is to provide managers with a better understanding related to the horizontal spillover between spiritual well-being and job satisfaction as well as their vertical spillover into life satisfaction. The findings of this study should provide managers and policy makers with suggestions on how to enhance spiritual well-being effectively through the enhancement of QWL, and ultimately shed more light on public policies that effectively enhance subjective well-being.

QWL AND LIFE SATISFACTION

Historically, research in QWL has been the turf of organizational behavior scientists and management scholars (O'Brien 1990). QWL is a topic that was motivated by McGregor's Theory Y in management. Marketing scholars also became interested in studying QWL issues mostly from the perspective of sales management and retailing (e.g., how managers of sales organizations and retailing firms can enhance the QWL of their employees). This movement has been referred to as *internal marketing* (e.g., Popovich-Hill and Hubbard 1995), and internal marketing is becoming a subdiscipline of marketing. The idea is that management has to cater to the needs of the employees in the same manner marketers cater to the needs of consumers.

In this section, we will describe selected findings from studies on QWL. We will organize this discussion by the following questions:

- What is QWL?
- Does QWL contribute significantly to overall quality of life (QOL)?
- How does QWL contribute to overall QOL?
- What are other consequences of QWL?
- What are the factors affecting QWL?

WHAT IS QWL?

Although there are many definitions and conceptualizations of QWL, most industrial psychologists and management scholars agree in general that QWL is a construct that deals with the well-being of employees, and that QWL differs from job satisfaction (e.g., Champoux 1981; Davis and Cherns 1975; Efraty and Sirgy 1990a; Hackman and Suttle 1977; Kabanoff 1980; Kahn 1981; Lawler 1982; Near et al. 1980; Quinn and Shephard 1974; Quinn and Staines 1979; Staines 1980). QWL differs from job satisfaction in that job satisfaction is construed as one of many outcomes of QWL. QWL affects not only job satisfaction but also satisfaction in other life domains such as family life, leisure life, social life, financial life, and so on.

There are many definitions and conceptualizations of QWL. For example, Lane (1991) defined QWL as meaningful work, and argued that QWL contributes to self-esteem, sense of control over one's environment, and happiness in life. Danna and Griffin (1999) viewed QWL as a hierarchy of concepts that includes life satisfaction (top of the hierarchy), job satisfaction (middle of the hierarchy), and work-specific need satisfaction such as satisfaction with pay, coworkers, and supervisor, among others (bottom of the hierarchy).

Ostrognay et al. (1997) defined QWL as *a positive affective response toward the work environment.* They made a distinction between job satisfaction and QWL. They argued that specific features of the work environment determine job satisfaction, whereas QWL is determined by employees' affective responses to their work environment. Based on this distinction, they hypothesized that job satisfaction is related more strongly to perceptions of organizational climate, whereas QWL is related more strongly to individual affect. Staats and Partlo (1992) have defined QWL in terms of *job uplifts and hassles.* In other words, high QWL of an employee is the job situation in which s/he experiences plenty of job uplifts and few job hassles. They have conducted a study showing that job uplifts are more predictive of older employees' QWL than job hassles. Those hassles and uplifts are somewhat independent, comparable to the notion of satisfiers and dissatisfiers (Herzberg 1968).

In this chapter, we define QWL as *employees' satisfaction of various needs through resources, activities, and outcomes stemming from participation in the workplace.* Thus, need satisfaction resulting from the workplace contributes to job satisfaction and satisfaction in other life domains (Sirgy et al. 2001). Satisfaction in the major life domains (e.g., work life, family life, home life, and leisure life) contributes directly to overall life satisfaction.

DOES QWL CONTRIBUTE SIGNIFICANTLY TO OVERALL QOL?

Andrews and Withey's (1976) measure of QWL, the Efficacy Index, was found to be significant and a very strong predictor of life satisfaction. The study controlled for the effects of satisfaction with family, money, amount of fun one is having, house/apartment, things done with family, time to do things, spare-time activities, recreation, national government, and consumer life. Campbell, Converse, and Rodgers (1976) showed that satisfaction with work contributes approximately 18 percent of variance in life satisfaction, controlling for the effects of satisfaction with nonworking activities, family life, standard of living, savings and investments, marriage, friendship, and housing. In most QOL studies, attitude toward work is closely linked to life satisfaction (e.g., Schmitt and Bedian 1982; Shaver and Freedman 1976).

HOW DOES QWL CONTRIBUTE TO OVERALL QOL?

There are a number of psychological strategies that people use to maximize satisfaction (and minimize dissatisfaction) across a variety of life domains. These are spillover, segmentation, and compensation (e.g., Near et al. 1980; Quinn and Staines 1979; Staines 1980). The *spillover effect* refers to the process by which affective experiences in one life domain influence affect experienced in other life domains. Hence, it explains the influence of affective experiences in the work life domain on affect experienced in other life domains and overall life.

The *segmentation effect* refers to the method by which people isolate experiences and affect in one life domain, thus preventing affect transfer between life domains. For example, people are said to "segment" when they manage to leave their work troubles and concerns at the office and do not bring these home. They say to themselves, "Work is work and home is home. I don't think about work when I'm away from my office. And I don't bring my family troubles to work either." Thus, affect experienced in one life domain becomes independent from affect experienced in other life domains. This independence may account for the lack of correlation between work and family satisfaction.

The *compensation effect* refers to the method by which people attempt to balance their affect across life domains. For example, people who feel quite dissatisfied with their jobs may try to channel much of their energy to feel good in other areas of their lives. Doing so "compensates" for the dissatisfaction they experience on their job. Thus, people attempt to create balance in affect across life domains. If a person experiences negative affect in one life domain, the person becomes motivated to engage in activities to increase positive affect in other domains to ensure a certain level of overall life satisfaction.

Evans and Ondrack (1990) hypothesized that the extent to which workers experience spillover, segmentation, and compensation between work and leisure may be dependent on individual differences such as growth need, locus of control, and self-monitoring. For example, employees with high growth need who find themselves in impoverished jobs are likely to experience compensation by immersing themselves in satisfying leisure activities. However, their study involving 1,193 male blue-collar, full-time workers did not bear this out (Evans and Ondrack 1990).

Efraty and Sirgy (1990a, 1990b, 1992) have examined the effect of occupational prestige and bureaucratization on the spillover between job satisfaction and life satisfaction. They have shown that, compared to employees with low-prestige occupations, employees with high-prestige occupations tend to experience higher levels of job satisfaction, higher levels of life satisfaction, and higher levels of spillover between job satisfaction and life satisfaction. In addition, employees working in decentralized bureaucracies were found to experience higher levels of job satisfaction, higher levels of life satisfaction, and higher levels of spillover between job satisfaction and life satisfaction. The managerial implications of this research are that managers should make a concerted effort to decentralize their organizations and treat all occupations with value and respect. Doing so is likely to decrease job dissatisfaction and life dissatisfaction among employees in general, especially those with low-prestige occupations.

Yet another study conducted by Efraty, Sirgy, and Siegel (1997) has shown that the spillover of job satisfaction to life satisfaction is moderated by organizational commitment. That is, employees with a higher level of organizational commitment experienced a greater spillover effect than those with a lower level of organizational commitment. The authors explained this finding using the saliency-bias hypothesis. That is, spillover of affect from one life domain to another is more likely to occur when that domain is considered highly salient in the mind of that individual than when that domain is not considered salient.

WHAT ARE OTHER CONSEQUENCES OF QWL?

Much research has shown that QWL has a significant impact on employee behavioral responses such as job satisfaction, job involvement, job performance, intention to quit, organizational turnover, and organizational identification (e.g., Carter et al. 1990; Efraty and Sirgy 1990a; Efraty, Sirgy, and Claiborne 1991; Greenhaus, Bedian, and Mossholder 1987; Lewellyn and Wibker 1990).

Efraty et al. (1991) found that low QWL resulting from personal alienation decreases job satisfaction and organizational identification. Specifically, their study revealed that personal alienation increases need deprivation (lowers QWL), which in turn decreases job satisfaction, which in turn decreases job involvement, which ultimately decreases organizational identification. Based on the study's findings, the authors recommended that managers should reduce employees' level of alienation, satisfy as many of their needs as possible, and increase their job satisfaction and job involvement. Doing so will increase the likelihood of organizational identification and commitment.

Tse and Jackson (1990) have shown that low QWL is related to alcohol abuse in the hospitality industry. Lack of need satisfaction within the hospitality industry (e.g., stress, time pressure, and low pay) is conducive of alcohol abuse, especially for the young and low-income people. The authors recommended employee assistance programs (EAPs) that provide medical treatment and various help for employees. Besides reducing health costs, employee assistance programs serve to improve productivity, decrease absenteeism, decrease employee turnover, and increase job satisfaction (Tse and Jackson 1990).

Cooper and Davis's (1997) study indicates that enhancement of QWL can increase safety at work. They report the results of a QWL program designed to reduce workers' personal injuries at nursing homes (e.g., injuries from lifting of nursing home patients, transfer practices, and incidents with combative patients). The program entailed the formation of worker teams that were empowered to select a specific safety concern and develop short-term manageable strategies. An elected worker led each team. Team members regularly attended brief meetings, and were encouraged to communicate openly with each other. The QWL program resulted in a significant reduction of workers' personal injuries.

WHAT ARE THE FACTORS AFFECTING QWL?

Much research has been done in this area, especially in relation to job satisfaction (for excellent reviews of the research literature on job satisfaction, see Locke 1976 and Jayarante 1993).[1] We classify factors affecting QWL into four groups: (1) social environment at work, (2) job facet, (3) information technology, and (4) others (see Gallie 1996).

Social Environment at Work

Social environment at work affects QWL. For example, *teamwork* is a social environment at work that enhances QWL for its employees (e.g., Nandan and Nandan 1995; Qvale and Hanssen-Bauer 1990). Teamwork is a form of collaboration in which team members confer with each other on issues relevant to the team (Brill 1976). Effective teamwork is characterized by reciprocal trust and respect among team members. There is a certain degree of felt interdependence of functions, tasks, and decision-making. In addition, social support from coworkers and supervisory behaviors also influence QWL of employees (Sirgy et al. 2001).

To ensure that team members work as a team and therefore enhance the QWL and job performance, Nandan and Nandan (1995) suggested the following strategies: (1) role clarity—clarify and negotiate the role expectations of each team member, (2) problem solving—educate team members on how to solve problems, (3) goal clarity and priority—develop clear and measurable performance goals and prioritize these goals, and (4) conflict resolution—resolve conflicts through an established process and with open communication.

Job Facet

Job facet is an important factor affecting QWL. Examples of job facet include salary, job requirements, freedom to do work one's own way, learning opportunities, opportunities to suggest work procedures, promotion opportunities, performance feedback, and contact with customers (e.g., Loscocco and Roschelle 1991; McFarlin and Rice 1991; Sirgy et al. 2001).

A study by McFarlin and Rice (1991) supported the hypothesis that job facet satisfaction is a function of three basic determinants: (1) facet amount, (2) facet wanted, and (3) facet importance. Specifically, facet satisfaction was highest when employees wanted a large amount of a job facet, were currently receiving a large amount of the facet, and felt that facet was personally important (see Rice et al. 1991). The managerial implications of the study are as follows. Before undertaking any action to enhance QWL among employees, managers should first assess employees' perceptions about the job facets that they currently experience, their wants of these facets, and their perceived importance of these facets. Managers should make an effort to close have-want gaps especially on the important facets. For example, if a manager finds out that "opportunity to take action" is regarded as a very important facet by an employee, but notes that there is a significant gap between have and want along that facet, the manager should create conditions that can reduce the have-want gap for that employee.

Information Technology

Meeting informational needs of employees can enhance their QWL (Welsh and Parr 1990). For example, Sherman and Sanders (1997a) have argued that *satisfaction with information systems* does play a significant role in QWL. Sherman and Sanders (1997b) have hypothesized that information technology does impact QWL through three dimensions—(1) task environment, (2) perceived equity in information system resources, and (3) health and safety. They found that the first two dimensions significantly contribute to user satisfaction with information systems. The third dimension, health and safety, failed to predict user satisfaction with information systems.

Other Factors

Studies also have shown that several other factors affect QWL. Examples include physical work environment, job design, and meaningfulness of work (e.g., Cummings and Malloy 1977; Glaser 1980; Lawler 1986; Quinn and Staines 1979; Sheppard and Herrick 1972; Simmons and Mares 1985; Susman 1976). In addition, need satisfaction from flexible work time and location enhances QWL (Sirgy et al. 2001).

SPIRITUAL WELL-BEING AND LIFE SATISFACTION

In this section, we will describe selected findings from QOL research dealing with spiritual well-being. We will organize this discussion around the following questions:

- What is spiritual well-being?
- Does spiritual well-being contribute significantly to overall QOL?
- How does spiritual well-being contribute to overall QOL?
- What are other consequences of spiritual well-being?
- What are the factors affecting spiritual well-being?

WHAT IS SPIRITUAL WELL-BEING?

Paloutzian and Ellison (1982) developed a scale of spiritual well-being composed of two major dimensions—religious well-being and existential well-being. *Religious well-being* refers to the degree to which individuals experience a satisfying relationship with God, while *existential well-being* is related to a sense of life satisfaction and purpose.

Scott, Agresti, and Fitchett (1998) identified spiritual well-being as having three major dimensions—affiliation, alienation, and dissatisfaction with life. *Affiliation* refers to a person's belief that s/he is loved and cared for by God and that the person experiences a positive relationship with God. *Alienation* is an individual's sense of distance from God. *Dissatisfaction with life* refers to the negative existential aspects of people's lives.

We conceptualize *spiritual well-being* as satisfaction with one's spiritual life domain, and maintain that spiritual well-being influences life satisfaction. A person's spiritual life domain is composed of various subdomains, including satisfaction with various religious beliefs, religious affiliations, religious orientations, religious participation, social relationships with other religious members, and other spiritual activities (e.g., Emmons, Cheung, and Tehrani 1998; Paloutzian 1997; Reed 1991; Ventis 1995). We define spiritual well-being as overall satisfaction in one's spiritual life domain, and conceptualize spiritual well-being and life satisfaction as two separate constructs.

DOES SPIRITUAL WELL-BEING CONTRIBUTE SIGNIFICANTLY TO OVERALL QOL?

Paloutzian (1997) argued that spiritual well-being does play a significant and positive role in life satisfaction. However, much of the research literature does not deal with the direct effect of spiritual well-being on life satisfaction. Instead, there is much evidence showing surrogates or related constructs of spiritual well-being affect life satisfaction and happiness.

Studies have demonstrated the effect of *strength of religious affiliation* on life satisfaction (e.g., Chamberlain and Zika 1992; Diener 1984; Levin and Tobin 1995; Moberg 1972; Reed 1991). Specifically, those who are strongly affiliated with religious groups are likely to be more satisfied with life than those who are weakly affiliated with religious groups.

Religiosity was also found as another factor that affects happiness. Robbins and Francis (1996) found a significant association between scores on the Francis Scale of Attitude toward Christianity and scores on the Oxford Happiness Inventory. Poloma and Pendleton (1990) provided a comprehensive critique of the research literature on religiosity and general well-being. These authors found that religiosity was an important predictor of life satisfaction, existential well-being, and happiness. However, replication of this study by Lewis and Joseph (1996) failed to demonstrate this relationship.

Ventis (1995) reviewed over 100 studies and reported that only *intrinsics* tend to experience life satisfaction and happiness, not extrinsics. The study argued that those who exhibit high strength of religious affiliation or religiosity should be further distinguished in terms of intrinsic versus extrinsic religiosity. Those with intrinsic religiosity practice their religion as a way of life, while those with extrinsic religiosity use religion as an instrumental tool for personal goals and gains. Efforts to achieve the intrinsic spiritual goals, or spiritual striving, include (1) increasing one's knowledge of a higher power (e.g., "learn about God's creation in the world"), (2) developing or maintaining a relationship with a higher power (e.g., "learn to tune in to a higher power throughout the day"), and (3) attempting to exercise one's spiritual principles in daily life (e.g., "treat others with compassion") (Emmons, Cheung, and Tehrani 1998).

HOW DOES SPIRITUAL WELL-BEING CONTRIBUTE TO OVERALL QOL?

Emmons (1999) has put forth a theory that shows how spiritual strivings contribute to overall well-being. These spiritual strivings "sanctify" important goals in other life domains (e.g., work life, leisure life, family life, and community life) and elevate the importance of the goals. Goal sanctification refers to the process by which personal goals are "made holy." When personal goals embedded in many domains of life become "sanctified," they take precedence over other competing goals. Hence, the attainment of those "sanctified" goals contributes to overall well-being. Spiritual well-being contributes to overall QOL as it provides meaningful goals in life and positive affect (Emmons 1999; Paloutzian 1997; Schumaker 1992; Scott, Agresti, and Fitchett 1998).

WHAT ARE OTHER CONSEQUENCES OF SPIRITUAL WELL-BEING?

A literature review of studies in this area reveals that spiritual well-being is positively related to better coping with terminal illness, physical well-being, sense of hope, and social support (Emmons 1999; Scott, Agresti, and Fitchett 1998). Spiritual well-being is negatively related to anxiety, depression, prejudice and right-wing authoritarianism, feelings of loneliness, and other risky behaviors (e.g., alcohol and substance abuse, unsafe sex, and driving under influence) (Pargament 1997; Paloutzian 1997).

WHAT ARE THE FACTORS AFFECTING SPIRITUAL WELL-BEING?

Spiritual well-being is affected by several factors, including strength of religious belief and religious affiliations. In addition, QOL research in spiritual well-being has found that *intrinsics* tend to score higher on measures of spiritual well-being than *extrinsics* (e.g., Bassett et al. 1991; Chamberlain and Zika 1992; Delbridge, Headley, and Wearing 1994; Donahue 1985; Ellison 1983; Genia 1996). Intrinsically religious people are those who are genuinely committed to their faith (Reed 1991; Ventis 1995). In this study, we argue that need satisfaction at work (QWL) also has a positive influence on spiritual well-being. This is because both satisfaction of higher-order needs and spiritual well-being share similar goals, and thus spillover between them is likely to occur. We also argue that a person's job satisfaction causes him or her to feel more satisfied with spiritual activities. The next section develops a testable model that shows how QWL, job satisfaction, and spiritual well-being are interrelated and how these interrelationships contribute to life satisfaction.

TOWARD A MODEL OF QWL, SPIRITUAL WELL-BEING, AND LIFE SATISFACTION

The conceptual model of this study is depicted in Figure 14.1. The model posits that overall life satisfaction is influenced positively by spiritual well-being and job satisfaction. Job satisfaction is influenced by satisfaction of both higher- and lower-order needs, whereas spiritual well-being is influenced by satisfaction of higher-order needs only. Spiritual well-being and job satisfaction are reciprocally interrelated.

QWL and Spiritual Well-being

The *need satisfaction* approach to QWL is based on need satisfaction models developed by Maslow (1954), McClelland (1961), Herzberg (1966), and Alderfer (1972). The basic tenet of this approach to QWL is that employees derive satisfaction from their jobs to the extent that their jobs provide satisfaction of various needs (e.g., Cohen, Chang, and Ledford, 1997; Golembiewski and

Figure 14.1 **Conceptual Model**

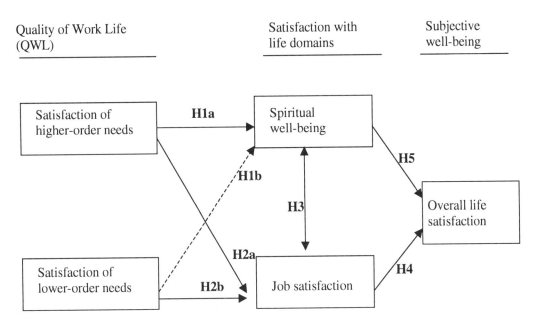

Sun 1988, 1989; Hall, Schneider, and Nygren 1970; Porter 1961; Sirgy et al. 2001). Based on this notion, Porter (1961) developed a QWL measure to gauge need satisfaction in an organizational context. Porter's Need Satisfaction Questionnaire (NSQ) was used to assess the level of employee needs that are pursued on the job, the level of organizational resources relevant to the needs experienced by the employee, and the congruence between a person's needs and organizational resources—with greater congruence reflecting increased need fulfillment by the organization. Four need categories, including seven needs based on Maslow's hierarchy, were covered by the NSQ measure. These are (1) survival needs (security need and pay), (2) social needs (need for interpersonal interactions and friendships and need for membership and being-in-the-know in a significant social group), (3) ego needs (need for self-esteem and need for autonomy), and (4) self-actualization needs.

The basic premise of our QWL construct is reflected in the measure we used (Sirgy et al. 2001). This new measure builds on Porter's (1961) NSQ in the way that it employs a comparable taxonomy of needs in an organizational context. Unlike the NSQ, however, the new measure used in this study does not rely on computing a difference score between actual state and "need levels." Specifically, we conceptualize QWL in terms of satisfaction of two sets of needs, namely satisfaction of lower-order needs (health and safety needs, economic and family needs) and satisfaction of higher-order ones (social needs, esteem needs, self-actualization needs, knowledge needs, and aesthetics needs). Mathematically stated,

$$QWL = NS_{hs} + NS_{ef} + NS_s + NS_t + NS_a + NS_k + NS_{cs}.$$

Where,

NS_{hs} = satisfaction of *health and safety needs*, which involves three need dimensions:

- Protection from ill health and injury at work
- Protection from ill health and injury outside of work
- Enhancement of good health

NS_{ef} = satisfaction of *economic and family needs*, which involves three need dimensions:

- Pay
- Job security
- Other family needs

NS_s = satisfaction of *social needs*, which involves two dimensions:

- Collegiality at work
- Leisure time off work

NS_t = satisfaction of *esteem needs*, which involves two dimensions:

- Recognition and appreciation of one's work within the organization
- Recognition and appreciation of one's work outside the organization

Ns_a = satisfaction of *actualization needs*, which involves two dimensions:

- Realization of one's potential within the organization
- Realization of one's potential as a professional

NS_k = satisfaction of *knowledge needs*, which involves two dimensions:

- Learning to enhance job skills
- Learning to enhance professional skills

NS_{cs} = satisfaction of *aesthetics needs*, which involves two dimensions:

- Creativity at work
- Personal creativity and general aesthetics

Our model posits that QWL positively influences spiritual well-being. Specifically, we believe that satisfaction with higher-order needs at work (e.g., social needs, esteem needs, self-actualization needs, knowledge needs, and aesthetics needs) is likely to contribute to spiritual well-being. This is because there is a high degree of overlap between goals of satisfaction of higher-order needs and goals of spiritual well-being. Both higher-order need satisfaction and spiritual well-being are related to high-level personal goals, a sense of purpose in life, and end states that reflect the meaning of life (Delbridge, Headley, and Wearing 1994; Lane 1991). When the goals of two individual life domains are compatible and overlap each other, spillover between them is likely to occur (Staines 1980).

Satisfaction of lower-order needs (health and safety needs, economic and family needs), however, is not likely to spill over to spiritual well-being because the goals in satisfaction of lower-order needs are less compatible with the goals in the spiritual life domain. Hence, we hypothesize that spiritual well-being is likely to be more influenced through higher- than lower-order need satisfaction. Based on the discussion, we propose the following:

H1: QWL has a positive influence on spiritual well-being.

H1a: Satisfaction of higher-order needs positively influences spiritual well-being.

H1b: Satisfaction of lower-order needs does not influence spiritual well-being.

QWL and Job Satisfaction

One can easily argue that QWL affects job satisfaction (e.g., Danna and Griffin 1999; Hall, Schneider, and Nygren 1970; Porter 1961). Employees whose QWL is high are likely to feel satisfied with their jobs. That is, the individual who experiences a higher level of need satisfaction is likely to experience a higher level of job satisfaction.

According to spillover theory (Wilensky 1960), affect is segmented in a variety of life domains (e.g., family life, leisure life, community life, and work life). The work life domain is considered to be a psychological space in which all affective experiences related to work are stored. Affective experience in the work life domain (e.g., job satisfaction) stems from satisfaction of the employee's various needs as manifested at work. That is, need satisfaction at work has a positive impact on job satisfaction (Danna and Griffin 1999; Efraty, Sirgy, and Siegel 1997; Sirgy et al. 2001). As both higher-order needs and lower-order needs are located within the psychological space of the work life domain, we propose that job satisfaction is positively influenced by satisfaction of higher-order needs as well as satisfaction of lower-order needs (cf. Loscocco and Roschelle 1991; Sirgy et al. 2001). Based on the discussion, we propose the following:

H2: QWL has a positive influence on job satisfaction.

H2a: Satisfaction of higher-order needs positively influences job satisfaction.

H2b: Satisfaction of lower-order needs positively influences job satisfaction.

Job Satisfaction and Spiritual Well-being

Horizontal spillover theory (Wilensky 1960) posits that satisfaction with one life domain affects satisfaction with other life domains. *Horizontal spillover* is the influence of affect in one life domain on a neighboring life domain. Based on horizontal spillover theory, we propose that job satisfaction and spiritual well-being are positively related.

Job satisfaction may influence satisfaction in other life domains such as family, leisure, social, health, financial, and so forth (e.g., Andrisani and Shapiro 1978; Bromet, Dew, and Parkinson 1990; Crohan et al. 1989; Crouter 1984; George and Brief 1990; Kabanoff 1980; Kavanagh and Halpern 1977; Leiter and Durup 1996; Levitin and Quinn 1974; Loscocco 1989; Orpen 1978; Rice, Near, and Hunt 1980; Schmitt and Bedian 1982; Schmitt and Mellon 1980; Staines 1980; Steiner and Truxillo 1989). We believe that job satisfaction and spiritual well-being are positively related. This is because a person's job satisfaction may cause him or her to feel more satisfied with social and other spiritual activities. The spillover effect from job satisfaction to spiritual well-being is likely to be high when the person has a high level of organizational commitment (Efraty, Sirgy, and Siegel 1997) and has a prestigious job (Efraty and Sirgy 1990a, 1992).

Those with high spiritual well-being are likely to exercise their moral principles in their daily lives by treating others with compassion (Emmons, Cheung, and Tehrani 1998). Thus, spiritual well-being is likely to enhance collaboration and citizenship behaviors in the workplace (Nandan and Nandan 1995; Organ 1988), reduce feelings of personal alienation (Efraty and Sirgy 1990a), and increase organizational identification (Efraty, Sirgy, and Claiborne 1991). All these factors contribute to the enhancement of job satisfaction.

Based on the discussion, we propose the following:

H3: Job satisfaction and spiritual well-being are positively related.

Job Satisfaction and Overall Life Satisfaction

The notion of life domain hierarchy indicates that life domains are organized hierarchically in people's minds (e.g., Andrews and Withey 1976; Campbell et al. 1976; Danna and Griffin 1999; Rice, Near, and Hunt 1980). At the top of the hierarchy is the most superordinate domain, namely overall life. Feelings in this most superordinate domain reflect what QOL researchers call life satisfaction, personal happiness, or subjective well-being. Subordinate to the most superordinate life domain are the major life domains such as family, job, leisure, community, spiritual life, and so on.

Vertical spillover theory suggests a positive relationship between work and overall life satisfaction. Comprehensive reviews of the research literature (Kabanoff 1980; Liu, Sylvia, and Brunk 1990; Tait, Padgett, and Baldwin 1989; Rice, Near, and Hunt 1980; Rain, Lane, and Steiner 1991) show a consistent positive relationship between job satisfaction and life satisfaction across a variety of settings and individuals. Some studies (e.g., Schmitt and Bedian 1982; Schmitt and Mellon 1980) reported findings suggesting a reciprocal relationship between job and life satisfaction, as originally proposed by Rice, Near, and Hunt (1980). Based on vertical spillover theory, we believe that job satisfaction contributes positively to overall life satisfaction.

H4: Job satisfaction positively influences overall life satisfaction.

Spiritual Well-being and Overall Life Satisfaction

Our model also posits that spiritual well-being vertically spills over to life satisfaction. It has been found that religious commitment and participation contribute to overall life satisfaction (Chamberlain and Zika 1992; Delbridge, Headley, and Wearing 1994; Levin and Tobin 1995; Ventis 1995). Specifically, overall life satisfaction was found to be higher for those who are strongly affiliated with religion (Moberg 1972; Reed 1991) and for those with intrinsic religiosity and spiritual goals (Emmons, Cheung, and Tehrani 1998; Ventis 1995).

We believe that spiritual well-being has a positive impact on overall life satisfaction. Spiritual well-being is positively related to meaningful goals in life, positive affect, and social support (Emmons 1999; Pargament 1997; Schumaker 1992). In addition, spiritual well-being is negatively related to substance abuse, anxiety, depression, and other malfunctional behaviors (Paloutzian 1997). Based on the discussion, we proposed the following:

H5: Satisfaction with spiritual well-being positively influences overall life satisfaction.

METHOD

Sampling and Method of Data Collection

Survey data were collected from three samples for this study—two samples involved employees of universities, and the third sample involved employees of various accounting firms. The respondents involved in sample 1 were selected from the directory of a southwestern urban university in the United States. Data collection was done through 490 questionnaires mailed out to faculty and staff. Twenty questionnaires were returned because of change in status; 180 questionnaires were returned completed. From those, seven incomplete questionnaires were discarded. The net response rate was 41 percent.

The respondents involved in sample 2 were selected from the directory of a Mid-Atlantic rural university in the United States. One thousand employees were randomly selected from the university directory and a survey questionnaire was mailed to them. Forty-six survey questionnaires were returned because of changes in address; 310 completed questionnaires were returned. The final response rate was 32.5 percent.

The respondents involved in sample 3 were selected from several accounting firms located in the United States. Two hundred questionnaires were mailed out to employees of accounting firms; fifteen questionnaires were returned because of changes in status or address; and seventy-three questionnaires were returned completed. The net response rate was 44 percent.

We collected three samples from various organizations for the purpose of ensuring high variance in the study variables. No attempt was made in this study to generalize these results to the populations from which the samples were derived because our main goal in this study is to test certain hypotheses related to QWL and spiritual well-being. The respondents were almost equally divided between men and women. Respondents were mostly middle age, had some college education, had a median income in the range of $30,000 to $39,000. Their average tenure at work was sixteen years with eleven years with the current employer. The educational level and median income were quite low as many respondents in the sample held secretarial and administrative positions at the universities and accounting firms. Yet, the demographic characteristics of each sample are quite similar across three samples, and thus data analyses were conducted using the pooled sample.

The Survey Questionnaire

Respondents were introduced to the survey questionnaire via a cover letter from the principal investigators describing study objectives. Respondents were assured that their responses would remain confidential and anonymous. The questionnaire consisted of several major parts. The first part of the questionnaire was related to QWL, or satisfaction with seven categories of needs at work. The second part of the questionnaire included measures of job satisfaction, spiritual well-being, satisfaction with other life domains, and overall life satisfaction. The last part of the questionnaire contained demographic questions related to gender, age, educational level, salary, years of service in current type of work, and years of service.

Measures

The model involved the following constructs: employee satisfaction of lower-order needs, employee satisfaction of higher-order needs, job satisfaction, spiritual well-being, and life satisfaction.

The measure of *employee satisfaction of lower-order needs* consisted of six items related to two dimensions of lower-order needs—satisfaction with health and safety needs and satisfaction with economic and family needs. Satisfaction from *health and safety needs* involves three items, including (a) satisfaction with protection from ill health and injury at work, (b) satisfaction with protection from ill health and injury outside of work, and (c) satisfaction with enhancement of good health. Satisfaction of *economic and family needs* involves three items, including (a) satisfaction with pay, (b) satisfaction with job security, and (c) satisfaction with other family needs. Responses are captured on a seven-point scale ranging from "very untrue" to "very true." The overall score of employee satisfaction of lower-order needs was computed as an average composite of the individual scores from the various single-item indicators. Reliability and predictive validity of these measures are established by Sirgy et al. (2001).

The measure of *employee satisfaction of higher-order n*eeds was similarly constructed. That is, the measure consisted of ten items relating to the five dimensions of higher-order needs. Higher-order needs include social needs, esteem needs, actualization needs, knowledge needs, and aesthetics needs. Satisfaction with *social needs* involves two items, including (a) satisfaction with collegiality at work and (b) satisfaction with leisure time at work. Satisfaction with *esteem needs* includes (a) satisfaction with recognition and appreciation of work within the organization and (b) satisfaction with recognition and appreciation outside of the organization. Satisfaction with *actualization needs* include (a) satisfaction with realization of one's potential within the organization and (b) satisfaction with realization of one's potential as a professional. Satisfaction with *knowledge needs* includes (a) satisfaction with learning to enhance job skills and (b) satisfaction with learning to enhance professional skills. Satisfaction with *aesthetics needs* includes (a) satisfaction with creativity at work and (b) satisfaction with personal creativity and general aesthetics. Responses are captured on a seven-point scale ranging from "very untrue" to "very true." The overall score of employee satisfaction of lower-order needs was computed as an average composite of the individual scores from various single-item indicators. For more information about this measure's reliability and validity, see Sirgy et al. (2001).

Job satisfaction was measured using a single-indicator measure, commonly used in QOL studies (e.g., Andrews and Withey 1976; Efraty and Sirgy 1990a, 1992; Efraty, Sirgy, and Siegel 1997). The measure involved asking subjects "How do you feel about your present job in general?" Responses were captured on five-point rating scales ranging from "very dissatisfied" to "very satisfied."

We similarly measured *spiritual well-being* and *satisfaction with other life domains* such as family, leisure, health, among others—the latter were used as covariates in the analysis. That is, satisfaction/dissatisfaction in spiritual life and other life domains were measured using single-indicator items in the same manner that job satisfaction was measured. These measures were borrowed from past QOL studies (e.g., Andrews and Withey 1976; Efraty and Sirgy 1990a, 1992; Efraty, Sirgy, and Siegel 1997). The measure involved asking subjects "How do you feel about your (particular life domain, e.g., spiritual life in general)?" Responses were captured on five-point rating scales ranging from "very dissatisfied" to "very satisfied."

We also measured life satisfaction using a single-item indicator in the same manner satisfaction with other life domains was measured. Again, we borrowed this measure from past QOL studies (e.g., Andrews and Withey 1976; Efraty and Sirgy 1990a, 1992; Efraty, Sirgy, and Siegel 1997). The measure involved asking subjects "How satisfied are you with your life as a whole?" Responses were captured on five-point rating scales ranging from "very dissatisfied" to "very satisfied."

Table 14.1

Path Analysis Results

Dependent variable	Independent variable	Estimate	T-value	Error variance	R^2
Spiritual	High	0.14**	4.31	0.66	0.036
	Low	0.051	1.27		
Job	High	0.42**	11.50	0.58	0.40
	Low	0.26**	6.87		
Overall	Job	0.32**	11.23	0.43	0.26
	Spiritual	0.24**	7.04		

Notes:
Model Fit [$\chi^2 = 6.39$, $df = 3$, $p = 0.0$; GFI = 0.99; AGFI = 0.98; NFI = 0.99; NNFI = 0.98; CFI = 0.99; RMSEA = 0.045].
Correlation between work life domain and spiritual well-being ($r = 0.138$,** $p < 0.05$).
Low = Satisfaction with lower-order needs at work; High = Satisfaction with higher-order needs at work; Job = Job satisfaction; Spiritual = Satisfaction with spiritual life; Overall = Overall life satisfaction.

RESULTS

We tested the proposed model (Figure 14.1) as a whole using path analysis. The model provided an acceptable fit ($\chi^2 = 639$; $df = 3$; $p = 0.0$; GFI = 0.99; NFI = 0.99; NNFI = 0.98; CFI = 0.99; RMSEA = 0.045). The results of path analysis are shown in Table 14.1. We will discuss these results in relation to each hypothesis.

H1 posits that QWL has a positive impact on spiritual well-being. The results indicate that employees' higher-order need satisfaction has a positive impact on spiritual well-being ($\beta = 0.14$, $p < 0.01$), and employee's satisfaction with lower-order needs indeed does not have a positive impact on spiritual well-being ($\beta = 0.051$, $p > 0.05$). These results provide support for both H1a and H1b.

H2 states that QWL has a positive impact on job satisfaction. The results indicate that employees' satisfaction with higher-order needs has a positive influence on job satisfaction ($\beta = 0.42$, $p < 0.01$), and similarly, satisfaction with lower-order needs has a positive impact on job satisfaction ($\beta = 0.26$, $p < 0.01$). These results provide support for both H2a and H2b.

H3 posits a positive relationship between job satisfaction and spiritual well-being. The result indicates that satisfactions with these two life domains are indeed positively related ($r = 0.138$, $p < 0.05$).

H4 and H5 state that job satisfaction and spiritual well-being positively influence overall life satisfaction. The results indicate that overall life satisfaction is a positive function of satisfaction with spiritual life ($\beta = 0.32$, $p < 0.05$) and spiritual well-being ($\beta = 0.24$, $p < 0.05$), also supporting H4 and H5.

In order to control the effects of satisfaction with various other life domains, a regression analysis was conducted (Table 14.2). The regression results indicate that job satisfaction still has a significant influence on overall life satisfaction ($\beta = 0.268$, $p < 0.00$), and spiritual satisfaction also has a marginally significant influence on life satisfaction ($\beta = 0.068$, $p < 0.10$) when satisfactions with all other life domains are controlled. The results also indicate that satisfaction with

Table 14.2

Regression Results (dependent variable = overall life satisfaction)

Independent variable	Beta coefficient	T-value	P
Satisfaction with work life (job satisfaction)	0.268**	6.79	0.000
Satisfaction with spiritual life (spiritual well-being)	0.068**	1.922	0.055
Satisfaction with family life	0.36	9.69	0.000
Satisfaction with leisure life	0.136**	3.75	0.000
Satisfaction with financial life	0.056*	1.446	0.149
Satisfaction with health life	0.114**	3.39	0.001
Satisfaction with education life	0.026	0.797	0.426
Satisfaction with friends	0.096**	2.648	0.008
Satisfaction with neighborhood	0.023	−0.531	0.596
Satisfaction with community	0.040	0.935	0.350
Satisfaction with environment	−0.008	−0.214	0.831
Satisfaction with housing	0.051	1.303	0.193
Satisfaction with cultural life	−0.036	−0.0906	0.365
Satisfaction with social life	−0.011	−0.365	0.791
Satisfaction of lower-order needs at work	0.02	0.513	0.608
Satisfaction of higher-order needs at work	−0.041	−1.015	0.310

Notes:
**$p < 0.05$; *$p < 0.10$.
Model Fit: $R = 0.734$, $R^2 = 0.538$, Adjusted $R^2 = 0.524$; F-value = 38, $p < 0.00$.

lower-order needs does not have a significant influence on life satisfaction ($\beta = 0.02$, $p > 0.10$), and also satisfaction with higher-order needs does not have a significant influence on life satisfaction ($\beta = -0.041$, $p > 0.10$). That is, QWL does not have a direct influence on life satisfaction. Instead, QWL influences overall life satisfaction through the mediation effect of job satisfaction and spiritual well-being.

DISCUSSION

The study findings provide evidence that QWL influences life satisfaction through the mediation effect of spiritual well-being and job satisfaction. The study results confirmed that employees' higher-order needs satisfaction has a positive influence on both job satisfaction and spiritual well-being. Yet, satisfaction with lower-order needs has a positive influence only on job satisfaction, not on spiritual well-being. Satisfaction with higher-order needs represents satisfaction with social needs, pursuit of the ideal self, and self-actualization (Sirgy et al. 2001). Because spiritual well-being is related to satisfaction with one's spiritual life domain, satisfaction with higher-order needs and spiritual well-being are understandably related to each other. Spiritual well-being, however, is not related to satisfaction with lower-order needs.

In addition, the findings of this study provide evidence of horizontal and vertical spillover. That is, the results indicate that job satisfaction and spiritual well-being are positively related (horizontal spillover), and at the same time, satisfactions with these two life domains influence overall life satisfaction (vertical spillover).

Managerial Implications

To the best of our knowledge, this is the first study to examine the effect of QWL on spiritual well-being. The findings of this study suggest that managers can enhance employees' spiritual well-being and job satisfaction by meeting the employees' higher-order needs (e.g., social needs, self-esteem needs, self-actualization needs, knowledge needs, and aesthetics needs). Enhancing job satisfaction and spiritual well-being will boost the employees' morale, facilitate organizational citizenship behaviors, and enhance work performance (cf. MacKenzie, Podsakoff, and Paine 1999). Managers can enhance satisfaction with higher-order needs by ensuring that the work environment is collegial, helping employees learn more about their jobs, and helping employees realize their potential. At the same time, managers should also make every effort possible to meet employees' lower-order needs. Doing so should enhance job satisfaction.

To enhance employees' life satisfaction, the findings of this study suggest that managers should give a higher priority to satisfaction of higher-order needs than satisfaction of lower-order needs. This is because satisfaction of higher-order needs enhances job satisfaction as well as spiritual well-being, both of which have a synergistic effect on life satisfaction. That is, satisfaction of higher-order needs has a positive impact on life satisfaction mediated both by spiritual well-being and job satisfaction. In contrast, satisfaction of lower-order needs positively influences life satisfaction mediated only by job satisfaction.

Study Limitations and Future Research

This study has several limitations. This study focuses on the QWL and spiritual well-being relationship. Spiritual well-being interacts with satisfaction with other life domains (e.g., family, financial, and health). Future studies should examine the dynamics between spiritual well-being and other life domains.

This study suggests that QWL indeed influences spiritual well-being. The study has demonstrated a horizontal spillover effect between the spiritual and work life domains. However, the cause-effect relationship has not been established by this study. Future research may attempt to establish causation through either experimental or longitudinal designs.

Future studies can also examine under what conditions segmentation and compensation effects between job satisfaction and spiritual well-being are likely to occur. One possible situation can be when employees experience a sense of value incompatibility with the values of the firm (e.g., a devout Christian who is working for a cigarette company promoting the use of cigarette products; a devout Muslim who is obligated to work around the clock with no time for prayers).

This study has focused on the QWL effect on spiritual well-being. One can argue that the relationship is moderated by a host of individual factors (religious orientation, self-concept, organizational commitment, job prestige, personality type, and growth need) and situational factors (economic conditions and cultural pressure). Future research should uncover moderator effects.

Although limited in scope, we believe that this study makes an important contribution to the literature. This study examines the interrelationships between two seemingly unrelated life domains and explains their interrelationships and effects on subjective well-being. We hope this study stimulates future research in this area.

NOTE

1. Jayarante (1993), based on a review of the literature, concluded that organizational determinants such as pay and status are significant and robust determinants of job satisfaction. Job dissatisfaction is directly related to job stress and is an important determinant to employee general well-being. Furthermore, evidence suggests that job dissatisfaction is related to work-related fatigue and injury at work, theft, sabotage, turnover, and absenteeism.

REFERENCES

Alderfer, C.P (1972). *Existence, Relatedness, and Growth: Human Needs in Organizational Settings.* New York: Free Press.

Andrews, Frank M., and S.B. Withey. (1976). *Social Indicators of Well-Being: America's Perception of Quality of Life.* New York: Plenum.

Andrisani, P., and M. Shapiro. (1978). "Women's Attitudes Towards Their Jobs: Some Longitudinal Data on a National Sample." *Personnel Psychology* 31: 15–34.

Bagozzi, Richard P. (1980). "Performance and Satisfaction in an Industrial Salesforce: An Examination of Their Antecedents and Similarity." *Journal of Marketing* 44: 65–77.

Bassett, R.; W. Champlin; D. Humphrey; C. Durr; S. Briggs; R. Distaffen; M. Flahrty; P. Hinsberger; R. Pnage; and H. Thompason. (1991). "Measuring Christian Maturity: A Comparison of Several Scales." *Journal of Psychology and Theology* 19: 84–93.

Brill, N.I. (1976). *Teamwork: Working Together in the Human Services.* Philadelphia: Lippincott.

Bromet, E.J.; A. Dew; and D.K. Parkinson. (1990). "Spillover Between Work and Family: A Study of Blue-Collar Working Wives." In *Stress Between Work and Family*, ed. J. Eckenrode and S. Gore. New York: Plenum, 133–151.

Campbell, Angus C.; Philip E. Converse; and W.L. Rodgers. (1976). *The Quality of American Life.* New York: Russell Sage.

Carter, Carolyn G.; Diana G. Pounder; Frances G. Lawrence; and Patricia J. Wozniak. (1990). "Factors Related to Organizational Turnover Intentions of Louisiana Extension Service Agents." In *Quality-of-Life Studies in Marketing and Management*, ed. H. Lee Meadow and M. Joseph Sirgy. Blacksburg: Virginia Tech, Center for Strategy and Marketing Studies, 170–181.

Chamberlain, K., and S. Zika. (1992). "Religiosity, Meaning in Life, and Psychological Well-being." In *Religion and Mental Health*, ed. J.F. Schumaker. New York: Oxford University Press, 104–134.

Champoux, J.E. (1981). "A Sociological Perspective on Work Involvement." *International Review of Applied Psychology* 30: 65–86.

Cohen, S.G.; L. Chang; and G.E. Ledford, Jr. (1997). "A Hierarchical Construct of Self-Management Leadership and Its Relationship to Quality of Work Life and Perceived Work Group Effectiveness." *Personnel Psychology* 50: 275–308.

Cooper, Jack, and Glenn Davis. (1997). "Improving Management-Labor Relations and Employee and Patient Well Being Through Quality-of-Work-Life Programs." In *Developments in Quality-of-Life Studies*, ed. H. Lee Meadow. Blacksburg, VA: International Society for Quality-of-Life Studies, 15.

Crohan, S.E.; T.C. Antonucci; P.K. Adelmann; and L.M. Coleman. (1989). "Job Characteristics and Well Being at Midlife: Ethnic and Gender Comparisons." *Psychology of Women Quarterly* 13: 223–235.

Crouter, A.C. (1984). "Spillover from Family to Work: The Neglected Side of the Work-Family Interface." *Human Relations* 37: 425–442.

Cummings, Thomas G., and Edmund S. Malloy. (1977). *Improving Productivity and the Quality of Work Life.* New York: Praeger.

Danna, K., and R.W. Griffin. (1999). "Health and Well-being in the Workplace: A Review and Synthesis of the Literature." *Journal of Management* 25, no. 3: 357–384.

Davis, L.E., and A.B. Cherns. (1975). *The Quality of Working Life: Problems, Prospects, and the State of the Art.* New York: Free Press.

Delbridge, J.; B. Headley; and A.J. Wearing. (1994). "Happiness and Religious Belief." In *Religion, Personality, and Mental Health*, ed. Laurence B. Brown. New York: Springer-Verlag, 50–68.

Diener, E. (1984). "Subjective Well-Being." *Psychological Bulletin* 95: 542–575.

Donahue, M.J. (1985). "Intrinsic and Extrinsic Religiousness: Review and Meta-Analysis." *Journal of Personality and Social Psychology* 48: 400–419.

Efraty, David, and M. Joseph Sirgy. (1990a). "The Effects of Quality of Working Life (QWL) on Employee Behavioral Responses." *Social Indicators Research* 22, no. 1: 31–47.

———. (1990b). "Job Satisfaction and Life Satisfaction Among Professionals and Paraprofessionals." In *Quality-of-Life Studies in Marketing and Management*, ed. H. Lee Meadow and M. Joseph Sirgy. Blacksburg: Virginia Tech, Center for Strategy and Marketing Studies, 157–169.

———. (1992). "Occupational Prestige and Bureaucratization Effects on the Spillover Between Job Satisfaction and Life Satisfaction." In *Developments in Quality-of-Life Studies in Marketing*, vol. 4, ed. M. Joseph Sirgy, H. Lee Meadow, Don Rahtz, and A.C. Samli. Blacksburg, VA: Academy of Marketing Science, 115–119.

Efraty, David; M. Joseph Sirgy; and C.B. Claiborne. (1991). "The Effects of Personal Alienation on Organizational Identification: A Quality-of-Work Life Model." *Journal of Business and Psychology* 6 (fall): 57–78.

Efraty, David; M. Joseph Sirgy; and Philip H. Siegel. (1997). "The Job Satisfaction/Life Satisfaction Relationship for Professional Accountants: The Moderating Effect of Organizational Commitment." In *Developments in Quality-of-Life Studies*, vol. 1, ed. H. Lee Meadow. Blacksburg, VA: International Society for Quality-of-Life Studies, 25.

Ellison, C. (1983). "Spiritual Well-Being: Conceptualization and Measurement." *Journal of Psychology and Theology* 11: 330–340.

Emmons, R.A. (1999). *The Psychology of Ultimate Concerns: Motivation and Spirituality in Personality.* New York: Guilford Press.

Emmons, R.A.; C. Cheung; and K. Tehrani. (1998). "Assessing Spirituality Through Personal Goals: Implications for Research on Religion and Subjective Well Being." *Social Indicators Research* 45: 391–422.

Evans, Martin G., and Daniel A. Ondrack. (1990). "Individual Differences in the Accommodation to Work and Leisure." In *Quality-of-Life Studies in Marketing and Management*, ed. H. Lee Meadow and M. Joseph Sirgy. Blacksburg: Virginia Tech, Center for Strategy and Marketing Studies, 125–139.

Gallie, Duncan. (1996). "The Quality of Employment: Perspectives and Problems." In *The Pursuit of the Quality of Life*, ed. Avner Offer. New York: Oxford University Press, 163–187.

Genia, Vicky. (1996). "I, E, Quest, and Fundamentalism as Predictors of Psychological and Spiritual Well-Being." *Journal of the Scientific Study of Religion* 35, no. 1: 56–59.

George, J.M., and A.P. Brief. (1990). "The Economic Instrumentality of Work: An Examination of the Moderating Effects of Financial Requirements and Sex on the Pay-Life Satisfaction Relationship." *Journal of Vocational Behavior* 37: 357–368.

Glaser, Edward M. (1980). "Productivity Gains Through Work Life Improvement." *Personnel Journal* 59 (January): 71–77.

Golembiewski, R.T., and B.C. Sun. (1988). "QWL, One More Time." *Healthcare Human Resource Forum* 1: 1–2.

———. (1989). "QWL Improves Worksite Quality." *Human Resource Development Quarterly* 1: 35–44.

Greenhaus, Jeffrey H.; Arthur G. Bedian; and Kevin W. Mossholder. (1987). "Work Experiences, Job Performances, and Feelings of Personal and Family Well Being." *Journal of Vocational Behavior* 31: 200–215.

Hackman, J.R., and J.L. Suttle. (1977). *Improving Life at Work.* Glenview, IL: Scott, Foresman.

Hall, D.H.; B. Schneider; and H.T. Nygren. (1970). "Personal Factors in Organizational Identification." *Administrative Science Quarterly* 15: 176–190.

Herzberg, F. (1966). *Work and the Nature of Man.* Cleveland, OH: World.

———. (1968). "One More Time: How Do You Motivate Employees?" *Harvard Business Review* 46: 53–62.

Jayarante, Srinika. (1993). "The Antecedents, Consequences, and Correlates of Job Satisfaction." In *Handbook of Organizational Behavior*, ed. Robert T. Golembiewski. New York: Marcel Dekker, 111–141.

Kabanoff, B. (1980). "Work and Nonwork: A Review of Models, Methods, and Findings." *Psychological Bulletin* 88: 60–77.

Kahn, R. (1981). *Work and Health.* New York: Wiley.

Kavanagh, M.J., and M. Halpern. (1977). "The Impact of Job Level Sex Differences on the Relationship Between Life and Job Satisfaction." *Academy of Management Journal* 20: 66–73.

Lane, Robert E. (1991). *The Market Experience.* Cambridge: Cambridge University Press.

Lawler, Edward E., III. (1982). "Strategies for Improving the Quality of Work Life." *American Psychologist* 37: 486–493.

———. (1986). *High Involvement Management.* San Francisco: Jossey-Bass.

Leiter, M.P., and M.J. Durup. (1996). "Work, Home, and In-between: A Longitudinal Study of Spillover." *Journal of Applied Behavioral Science* 32, no. 1: 29–47.

Levin, J.S., and S.S. Tobin. (1995). "Religion and Psychological Well-Being." In *Aging, Spirituality, and Religion: A Handbook*, ed. M.A. Kimble, S.H. McFadden, J.W. Ellor, and J.J. Seeber. Minneapolis, MN: Fortress Press, 30–46.

Levitin, T.E., and R.P. Quinn. (1974). "Changes in Sex Roles and Attitude Toward Work." Paper presented at the 1974 Conference of the American Association for Public Research.

Lewellyn, Patsy A., and Elizabeth A Wibker. (1990). "Significance of Quality of Life on Turnover Intentions of Certified Public Accountants." In *Quality-of-Life Studies in Marketing and Management*, ed. H. Lee Meadow and M. Joseph Sirgy. Blacksburg: Virginia Tech, Center for Strategy and Marketing Studies, 182–193.

Lewis, Christopher A., and Stephen Joseph. (1996). "Is Religiosity Associated with Life Satisfaction?" *Psychological Reports* 79: 429–430.

Liu, K.T.; R.D. Sylvia; and D. Brunk. (1990). "Non-work Factors and Job-Satisfaction Revisited." *Human Relations* 43, no. 1: 77–86.

Locke, E.A. (1976). "The Nature and Causes of Job Satisfaction." In *Handbook of Industrial and Organizational Psychology*, ed. M.D. Dunnettee. Chicago: Rand McNally.

Loscocco, K.A. (1989). "The Interplay of Personal and Job Characteristics in Determining Work Commitment." *Social Science Research* 18: 370–394.

Loscocco, K.A., and A.R. Roschelle. (1991). "Influences on the Quality of Work and Nonwork Life: Two Decades in Review." *Journal of Vocational Behavior* 39: 182–225.

MacKenzie, Scott B.; Philip M. Podsakoff; and Julie B. Paine. (1999). "Do Citizenship Behaviors Matter More for Managers than for Salespeople?" *Journal of the Academy of Marketing Science* 27, no. 4: 396–410.

Maslow, A.H. (1954). *Motivation and Personality*. New York: Harper.

McClelland, D.C. (1961). *The Achieving Society*. New York: Free Press.

McFarlin, Dean B., and Robert W. Rice. (1991). "Determinants of Satisfaction with Specific Job Facets: A Test of Locke's Model." *Journal of Business and Psychology* 6: 25–38.

Moberg, David O. (1972). "Religion and the Aging Family." *Family Coordinator* 21: 47–60.

Nandan, Shiva, and Monica Nandan. (1995). "Improving Quality of Care and Quality of Work Life Through Interdisciplinary Health Care Teams." In *Developments in Quality-of-Life Studies in Marketing*, vol. 5, ed. H.L. Meadow, M. Joseph Sirgy, and Don Rahtz. DeKalb, IL: Academy of Marketing Science and the International Society for Quality-of-Life Studies, 80–86.

Near, J.P.; R.W. Rice; and R.G. Hunt. (1980). "The Relationship Between Work and Nonwork Domains: A Review of Empirical Research." *Academy of Management Review* 5: 415–429.

O'Brien, Edward J. (1990). "Business and Public Administration: Synergistic Combination for Quality of Life Enhancement." In *Quality-of-Life Studies in Marketing and Management*, ed. H. Lee Meadow and M. Joseph Sirgy. Blacksburg, VA: Center for Strategy and Marketing Studies, 597–604.

Organ, Dennis W. (1988). *Organizational Citizenship Behavior: The Good Soldier Syndrome*. Lexington, MA: Lexington Books.

Orpen, C. (1978). "Work and Nonwork Satisfaction: A Causal Correlational Analysis." *Journal of Applied Psychology* 63: 530–532.

Ostrognay, Gabrielle M.; Peter M. Hart; Mark A. Griffin; Melinda J. Norris; and Alexander J. Wearing. (1997). "Quality of Work Life and Job Satisfaction: Similarities and Differences." In *Developments in Quality-of-Life Studies*, vol. 1, ed. H. Lee Meadow. Blacksburg, VA: International Society for Quality-of-Life Studies, 67.

Paloutzian, Raymond F. (1996). *Invitation to the Psychology of Religion*, 2d ed. Needham Heights, MA: Allyn and Bacon.

———. (1997). "Religious and Spiritual Factors in Individual and Societal Well Being: Positive and Negative Contributions." In *Developments in Quality-of-Life Studies*, vol. 1, ed. H. Lee Meadow. Blacksburg, VA: International Society for Quality-of-Life Studies, 68.

Paloutzian, Raymond F., and C.W. Ellison. (1982). "Loneliness, Spiritual Well-Being, and the Quality of Life." In *Loneliness: A Sourcebook of Current Theory, Research, and Therapy*, ed. L.A. Peplau and D. Perlman. New York: Wiley, 224–237.

Pargament, K.I. (1997). *The Psychology of Religion and Coping: Theory, Research, Practice*. New York: Guilford Press.

Poloma, M.M., and B.F. Pendleton. (1990). "Religious Domains and General Well-being." *Social Indicators Research* 22: 255–276.

Popovich-Hill, Paulette, and Susan S. Hubbard. (1995). "Quality of Life in the Workplace: The Role of Internal Marketing." In *Developments in Quality-of-Life Studies in Marketing*, vol. 5, ed. H. Lee Meadow, M. Joseph Sirgy, and Don Rahtz. DeKalb, IL: Academy of Marketing Science and the International Society for Quality-of-Life Studies, 133–137.

Porter, L.W. (1961). "A Study of Perceived Need Satisfaction in Bottom and Middle Management Jobs." *Journal of Applied Psychology* 45: 1–10.

Quinn, R.P., and Graham L. Shephard. (1974). *The 1972–1973 Quality of Employment Survey*. Ann Arbor: Institute for Social Research, University of Michigan.

Quinn, Robert P., and Graham L. Staines. (1979). *The 1977 Quality of Employment Survey*. Ann Arbor: Institute for Social Research, University of Michigan.

Qvale, Thoralf Ulrik, and Jon Hanssen-Bauer. (1990). "Implementing QWL in Large Scale Project Organizations: 'Blue Water' Site Design in the Norwegian Offshore Oil Industry." In *Quality-of-Life Studies in Marketing and Management*, ed. H. Lee Meadow and M. Joseph Sirgy. Blacksburg: Virginia Tech, Center for Strategy and Marketing Studies, 529–535.

Rain, J.S.; I.M. Lane; and D.D. Steiner. (1991). "A Current Look at the Job Satisfaction/Life Satisfaction Relationship: Review and Future Considerations." *Human Relations* 44 (March): 287–307.

Reed, Kimberly. (1991). "Strength of Religious Affiliation and Life Satisfaction." *Sociological Analysis* 52, no. 2: 205–210.

Rice, R.W.; J. Near; and R.G. Hunt. (1980). "The Job-Satisfaction/Life-Satisfaction Relationship: A Review of Empirical Research." *Basic and Applied Social Psychology* 1: 37–64.

Rice, Robert W.; Robert S. Pierce; Reed P. Moyer; and Dean B. McFarlin. (1991). "Using Discrepancies to Predict the Perceived Quality of Work Life." *Journal of Business and Psychology* 6 (fall): 39–56.

Robbins, M., and L.J. Francis. (1996). "Are Religious People Happier? A Study Among Undergraduates." In *Research in Religious Education*, ed. L.J. Francis, W.K. Kay, and W.S. Cambell. Herefordshire, UK: Gracewing, 207–217.

Schmitt, N., and A.G. Bedian. (1982). "A Comparison of LISREL and Two-Stage Least Squares Analysis of a Hypothesized Life-Job Satisfaction Reciprocal Relationship." *Journal of Applied Psychology* 67: 806–817.

Schmitt, N., and P.A. Mellon. (1980). "Life and Job Satisfaction: Is the Job Central?" *Journal of Vocational Behavior* 16: 51–58.

Schumaker, J.F., ed. (1992). *Religion and Mental Health*. New York: Oxford.

Scott, Eric R.; Albert A. Agresti; and George Fitchett. (1998). "Factor Analysis of the 'Spiritual Well-Being Scale' and its Clinical Utility with Psychiatric Inpatients." *Journal for the Scientific Study of Religion* 37, no. 2: 314–318.

Shaver, Philip, and Jonathan Freedman. (1976). "Your Pursuit of Happiness." *Psychology Today* 10 (August): 27–29.

Sheppard, Harold L., and Neal O. Herrick. (1972). *Where Have All the Robots Gone? Worker Dissatisfaction in the 70's*. New York: Free Press.

Sherman, Barbara A., and G. Lawrence Sanders. (1997a). "The Assessment of Technology Impact on Quality of Work Life and User Representation in the Context of User Information Systems Satisfaction." In *Developments in Quality-of-Life Studies*, vol. 1, ed. H. Lee Meadow. Blacksburg, VA: International Society for Quality-of-Life Studies, 88.

———. (1997b). "The Development of Constructs to Measure Technology Impacts on Quality of Work Life." In *Developments in Quality-of-Life Studies*, vol. 1, ed. H. Lee Meadow. Blacksburg, VA: International Society for Quality-of-Life Studies, 89.

Simmons, John, and William Mares. (1985). *Working Together: Employee Participation in Action*. New York: New York University Press.

Sirgy, M. Joseph. (2001). *Handbook of Quality of Life Research: An Ethical Marketing Perspective*. Netherlands: Kluwer.

Sirgy, M. Joseph; David Efraty; Phillip Siegel; and Dong-Jin Lee. (2001). "A New Measure of Quality-of-Work Life (QWL) Based on Need Satisfaction and Spillover Theories." *Social Indicators Research* 55: 241–302.

Staats, Sara, and Christie Partlo. (1992). "Uplifts, Hassles, and Quality of Life in Workers over 50 Years of Age." In *Developments in Quality-of-Life Studies in Marketing*, vol. 4, ed. M. Joseph Sirgy, H. Lee Meadow, Don Rahtz, and A.C. Samli. Blacksburg, VA: Academy of Marketing Science, 101–106.

Staines, G. (1980). "Spillover versus Compensation: A Review of the Literature on the Relationship Between Work and Nonwork." *Human Relations* 33: 111–129.

Steiner, D.D., and D.M. Truxillo. (1989). "An Improved Test of the Disaggregation Hypothesis of Job and Life Satisfaction." *Journal of Occupational Psychology* 62: 33–39.

Susman, Gerald I. (1976). *Autonomy at Work: A Socio-Technical Analysis of Participative Management*. New York: Praeger.

Tait, Marianne; Margaret Y. Padgett; and Timothy T. Baldwin. (1989). "Job and Life Satisfaction: A Reevaluation of the Strength of the Relationship and Gender Effects As a Function of the Date of the Study." *Journal of Applied Psychology* 74: 502–507.

Tse, Eliza Ching-Yick, and Giles A. Jackson. (1990). "Alcohol Abuse in the Workplace: Challenges and

Strategic Implications for the Hospitality Industry." In *Quality-of-Life Studies in Marketing and Management*, ed. H. Lee Meadow and M. Joseph Sirgy. Blacksburg: Virginia Tech, Center for Strategy and Marketing Studies, 215–226.

Ventis, W.L. (1995). "The Relationships Between Religion and Mental Health." *Journal of Social Issues* 51: 33–48.

Welsh, Dianne H.B., and June Parr. (1990). "The Social Information Processing Approach and Climate: Toward Improving Salesforce Work Life." In *Quality-of-Life Studies in Marketing and Management*, ed. H. Lee Meadow and M. Joseph Sirgy. Blacksburg: Virginia Tech, Center for Strategy and Marketing Studies, 204–214.

Wilensky, H. (1960). "Work, Careers, and Social Integration." *International Social Science* 12: 543–560.

CHAPTER 15

COMING TO TERMS WITH SPIRITUALITY AND RELIGION IN THE WORKPLACE

PETER C. HILL AND GARY S. SMITH

Two of the most central and defining features of life for many people are their religion and spirituality (RS)[1] and their work. Few accounts of life's experiences would be complete without a consideration of both features. The primary purpose of this chapter is to analyze one of these components of human experience (RS) in the context of the other (the workplace), with a special focus on how religion and spirituality in the workplace are distinct from, yet similar to, each other. While it is often a useful heuristic to identify characteristics that distinguish spirituality from religion, the two experiences frequently overlap and affect individuals in similar ways.

We will present an overview and analysis of how RS can be conceptualized in a manner that will help explain how they operate in the lives of working people. Some commonalities and differences between religion and spirituality will be noted, and we will recommend that religion and spirituality be viewed primarily as different ways of searching for that which is sacred. This conceptualization will not only help us better understand how RS are similar to, yet different from, each other, but it should also help provide direction for future systematic research on RS in the workplace. Finally, in light of our discussion about how each construct should be conceptualized, we will consider the role of RS belief and practice in the workplace.

RELIGION AND SPIRITUALITY'S PERSISTENT AND PERVASIVE NATURE

The vast majority of the North American populace report that RS are integral parts of their life experience. Surveys (e.g., Gallup 1994; Gallup and Castelli 1989; also see Greeley 1989 and Hoge 1996) have found repeatedly that RS in the United States and many other Western societies are alive and well. Hoge (1996) reports that though the numbers vary slightly from survey to survey, they consistently show, for example, that around 95 percent of the population believe in God, close to 90 percent report that religion is at least fairly important in their lives, around 75 percent believe in the divinity of Christ and in a personal afterlife, and about 67 percent claim that prayer is an important part of their daily life. Furthermore, levels of general RS belief in the United States have remained consistent since the 1940s (Greeley 1989; Hoge 1996). In most of Europe, participation in religious practices has declined, but at least one leading researcher (Hoge 1996) maintains that the global picture of overall religious involvement suggests that modern Europe, not North America, is the exception. Religion, according to Hoge, "is a human universal, here to stay in one form or another" (24).

Secularization Theory

RS's tenacious nature contradicts a dominant theory held by many social scientists since the late 1800s. Secularization theory posits that modern scientific truth supersedes all previous belief systems, including forms of superstition and mysticism, many of which can be categorized as "religious." Some classical social theorists such as Auguste Comte, for example, argued that though societies have long used religious teachings to provide cohesion and a framework for moral living, the triumphant rise of science and rational enlightenment are sure signs of social progress. Yet the persistent commitment of the populace in the United States—a scientifically dominated Western culture—to a viable and personally relevant RS has caused many contemporary social scientists to question the adequacy of the secularization thesis (see Hammond 1985). The puzzle itself is easy to articulate: Why does a society remain committed to its religious heritage in the face of the onslaught of science and secular education? Solving this puzzle, however, is an ongoing and difficult task.

Revising the Secularization Thesis

While religion continues to provide an important function in contemporary society, it does not function in its traditional role. Indeed, the religious landscape is changing, with institutional religion losing much of its influence over people. The secularization model has been necessarily revised (e.g., Hunter 1983; Luckmann 1967; Stark and Bainbridge 1996), suggesting that in an age of science and rational enlightenment, religion has not been eliminated, but rather has been transformed. Hunter (1983) contends that this transformation is best described as a process of privatization or a "deinstitutionalization of religious reality" (14). He cites three characteristics of modern society that contribute to this privatization. First, he argues that today's worldview places rational controls on all of human experience. Second, contemporary society is increasingly pluralistic, in part due to technological advances, which undercut the support of monopolistic worldviews. Third, contemporary society contains a structural pluralism that divides human experience into private and public spheres. In premodern society, the distinction between the public and private spheres was far more blurred; one's identity was at least partially defined through the community, including the institutions that helped define the individual's sense of community. In contrast, modern society not only allows, but indeed imposes, on its people the distinction between the public and the private, or what Newbigin (1989) differentiates as the realm of "knowing"—that which can be publicly verified (to which culture suggests that science, but not religion, can speak), from "believing"—that which is a matter of personal decision (to which culture suggests that religion, but not science, can speak). In modern society, this structural pluralism dictates that institutional religion can exist and make public pronouncements, but it can legitimately speak with authority only in the realm of private experience.

> At the subjective level of people's world views, the privatization of religion is internalized. Among other things this means that religious symbols and meanings tend to be relevant only within certain contexts of the modern person's everyday life, the moments spent in the private sphere. The highly rational character of the public sphere and the inutility and implausibility of religious definitions of reality in that context make it less likely that a person's religious beliefs will be relevant to him in such settings. Religion will seem much more viable in ordering his personal affairs. (Hunter 1983, 14)

So, according to Hunter (1983), to remain viable, religion cannot directly contradict rational explanations, must acknowledge the possible legitimacy of other truth claims or at least be willing to call into question any exclusive claim of moral superiority, and must speak with authority only in the private sphere of personal experience. Bellah and his associates argue that this cultural context, unique to contemporary society, has fostered a new approach to religion now identified by others as "Sheilaism," derived from a young nurse "Sheila Larson," a pseudonym they gave to one of the individuals studied in depth in *Habits of the Heart* (1985). They contend that many contemporary Westerners adhere to "Sheilaism": "I believe in God. I'm not a religious fanatic. I can't remember the last time I went to church. My faith has carried me a long way. It's Sheilaism. Just my own little voice" (221).

What the Sheila Larsons of the world (including some researchers) may fail to realize is that this emphasis on a personal experiential spirituality is not new. A century ago, William James (1902/1961) distinguished what he called a "firsthand" experiential religion that is direct and immediate and something over which the individual assumes ownership from a "secondhand" institutional religion as an inherited tradition. For James, both first- and secondhand RS experiences fell under the purview of religion. Wulff (1997) rightly points out that the "new spirituality," which stresses an emergent model of a journey or quest with the goal of actualizing some variously conceived human capacity, has such deep roots in historical faith traditions that, for example, "the classic Christian mystics would find every element in the model familiar" (7).

However, in the context of religious individualism and privatization of experience, new spiritual understandings, motivations, orientations, and practices are evolving to the point that many believe they deserve a label different than *religion* and *religiousness. Spirituality* has now become the favored term to describe the privatization of religion, and with it are identified such internal experiences as supraconscious activity, personal transcendence, mystical union, and personal meaningfulness (Spilka and McIntosh 1996). These components, which were once commonly understood as part of one's religious experience and practice, are now applied to a spirituality that helps, as Hunter (1983) states it, order one's personal affairs. Reserving the term *spirituality* for this "loftier/functional side of life" (Pargament 1999, 6), many see religion as a more rigid, formally structured, institutional side of life that may even inhibit or restrict human potential (Pargament 1997).

Common Concerns Between Spirituality and Religion

Social scientists interested in investigating R and S also seem to accept this conceptual distinction. For example, Koenig, McCullough, and Larson (2001), leading researchers of how RS relate to physical and mental health, provide a number of contrasts between religion and spirituality that fit well with this distinction: religion is more community focused while spirituality tends to be more individualistic; religion is more observable, measurable, and objective while spirituality is less visible and quantifiable and more subjective; religion is more formal, orthodox, and organized while spirituality is less formal, less orthodox, and less systematic; religion tends to be behavior-oriented with an emphasis on outward practices while spirituality tends to be more emotionally oriented and inwardly directed; religion is more authoritarian, especially in terms of behaviors, while spirituality is less authoritarian and has little external accountability; and religion is more oriented toward doctrine, especially that which distinguishes good from evil while spirituality stresses harmony and unity and is less concerned with doctrine. This emphasis on the different and largely contrasting characteristics of spirituality and religion has now been so widely accepted that some people, including many researchers, even seem to view the two constructs as opposites (see Bibby 1995; Roof 1993, 1999; Roof, Carroll, and Roozen 1995 for discussions of this tendency).

Overlapping Identities

While the distinctions between R and S identified by Koenig et al. (2001) may be accurate to some degree, such an emphasis on contrasts may overlook many functional and substantive commonalities. First, empirical research (Bibby 1995; Zinnbauer et al. 1997) has found that the experience of spirituality for many, indeed most, people remains embedded within a religious context and, therefore, they experience a good deal of commonality between R and S (see Hill et al. 2000). For example, Zinnbauer et al. 1997 found that about three out of four people in their diverse sample prefer to identify themselves as both spiritual and religious, however the terms are defined. The researchers found that these people tend to participate in traditional forms of worship and prayer and view religion in a positive light. They are not likely to endorse nontraditional (e.g., New Age) beliefs or to conceptually differentiate spirituality from religiousness.

A Sacred Core

Second, both R and S are interested in the sacred dimension of life, though their understanding of what constitutes the sacred often varies. Ignoring the sacred strips both R and S of the very characteristic that distinguishes them from other areas of study. Pargament (1997, 1999) maintains that what is sacred or divine cannot be confused with something simply important or even integrative in a person's life. For example, one's spirituality would likely not be enhanced through watching pro football, even though the behavior of millions on any given Sunday afternoon in the fall suggests that it is highly important and even (for some) connected to their sense of identity. People often find great pleasure or even a sense of comfort (if their team is doing well) in their enthusiastic support of a favorite team. But, by definition, however, the sacred should provide more than just a sense of pleasure or comfort.

One of the key characteristics of the sacred is its quality of transcendence (Hill et al. 2000; Thoresen 1998); that is, the sacred is capable of producing some sort of transcendent (beyond the self) experience. Enjoying music or gardening, for example, fails to be a religious or spiritual experience unless it is somehow related to a perception of the sacred (e.g., the experience of music causes one to contemplate the majesty and power of God or the beauty and order of the universe; the caring for nature is motivated by one's sense of stewardship or accountability to a Creator, etc.). Sacred objects must provide meaning beyond the self and mundane concerns.

A Sense of Meaning

Both religion and spirituality involve questions of meaning and purpose. Social theorist Max Weber (1922/1964) concurred with Comte that the rise of secularization would undermine religion, but disagreed that a culture dominated by science would be a suitable replacement. Weber argued that any culture based primarily on science and rational explanation will be impoverished, in part because of its limited capacity to fulfill the human search for meaning. Psychologists are just beginning to study the centrality and importance of meaning to human experience (Baumeister 1991; Emmons 1999; Klinger 1977; Wong and Fry 1998).

Despite their benefits, science and rational analysis frequently fail to fulfill people's needs for meaning. Though science has done much to provide a sense of personal control over events (consider, for example, the plight of the farmer in primitive cultures who has to rely only on the mercies of nature for water compared with the contemporary farmer in Western culture who can utilize the technology of modern irrigation systems), many aspects of life still appear to defy science and human understanding. And while science has done much to describe what heretofore were considered the mysteries of the universe, it has not discovered the purpose behind such ordered intricacies. Baumeister (1991) contends that for many people religion is best able to answer many life questions. Those who turn away from religion may not experience through any other means "the powerful consolations, ecstasies, and moral certainties that religion can offer" (183).

DWELLING AND SEEKING SPIRITUAL ORIENTATIONS

Yet another approach that we find quite helpful in describing contemporary changes in religious and spiritual understandings, and one that will guide our discussion through the rest of this chapter, is Wuthnow's (1998) distinction between a "dwelling" and "seeking" orientation to spirituality. Wuthnow maintains that many Americans have shifted from a spirituality of dwelling, which dominated RS experience and understanding until recently, to a spirituality of seeking.

> A spirituality of dwelling emphasizes *habitation*: God occupies a definite place in the universe and creates a sacred space in which humans too can dwell; to inhabit sacred space is to know its territory and to feel secure. A spirituality of seeking emphasizes *negotiation*: individuals search for sacred moments that reinforce their conviction that the divine exists, but these moments are fleeting; rather than knowing their territory, people explore new spiritual vistas, and they may have to negotiate among complex and confusing meanings of spirituality. (4–5; emphasis in the original)

Wuthnow (1998) explains that a dwelling spirituality stresses security, provides clear distinctions between the sacred and the profane, promotes a sense of community and interrelatedness, and emphasizes a spiritual home. A seeking spirituality, by contrast, stresses faith as a quest, makes fewer distinctions between the sacred and the ordinary, and offers individuals greater freedom from the restraints of community expectations. Characterizing religion as a dwelling spirituality and contemporary spirituality as the seeking variety is overly simplistic. It is fair to say, however, that traditional religions tend to emphasize a dwelling approach whereas contemporary spirituality stresses Wuthnow's seeking orientation. Wuthnow maintains that both dwelling and seeking is part of what it means to be human and that a rigid insistence that either a dwelling or a seeking spirituality is superior or more authentic is a dubious, hard to defend, position. In fact, what might best distinguish between these two forms of RS experience are people's underlying needs and motivations.

The Attraction to a Dwelling Spirituality

Moral Certainty and Stability

A dwelling RS orientation carries with it important psychological benefits. Chief among them is a sense of certainty and stability that reduces chaos and confusion. Psychologists have long studied how a sense of personal control contributes to well-being. Such control (or lack thereof) is, however, interpretive in nature; that is, personal control often stems from one's belief system and is enhanced by a supportive environment (see Peterson 2000). Believing that one is in a special relationship with God, which is reinforced through others who reside in the same dwelling place, can provide a great sense of control. Accepting the "rules of the house" as definitions of what is good or bad, right or wrong, provides standards that define a sense of orderliness. Those with a dwelling mentality can look to God as a safe haven, much as children look to their parents for protection. In the safety of the dwelling, God offers care and protection in times of danger and stress. Pargament and his associates (Pargament 1996; Pargament et al. 1998) supply considerable evidence that RS offers people a variety of coping strategies by enhancing their sense of control (paradoxically as they defer or surrender that control to God).

Social Support

People's sense of control can be strengthened by the support they receive from others. Such social support may be a feature that attracts some to a dwelling RS. RS groups can also help *legitimate* an individual's search for the sacred. Legitimation provides a socially established explanation that both attributes ontological validity to the object of the search and assures that the experience of the sacred is "real," thus providing a sense of comfort and assurance. Research (see chapter 15 in Koenig, McCullough, and Larson 2001) has also shown that people who are well connected to others, especially in a setting such as a church, synagogue, or mosque where great care or concern is frequently demonstrated, generally display less loneliness, depression, and anxiety.

The Attraction to a Seeking Spirituality

Experiential Freedom

A seeking RS orientation also furnishes important psychological benefits. First and perhaps foremost, a person's seeking orientation provides a perceived sense of freedom. Contemporary Western culture emphasizes individual freedom, and most people find meaning independent of their relation to permanent groups; that is, the self is perceived as a bounded, unique center of thought, feeling, and behavior independent of others. In contrast, in many non-Western cultures, people find meaning predominantly through relationships; that is, the self is perceived through a normative interdependence or fundamental connectedness with others. Of course, in some cultures such interdependence need not be social or even tangible—human relationships may also be understood spiritually or metaphysically. Nevertheless, given Western values of freedom and independence, it is not surprising that contemporary Western culture is fertile ground for an individually focused seeking spirituality.

Triandis and his associates (Triandis et al. 1988) suggest that individualistic cultures, relative to collectivistic cultures, subordinate group goals to personal goals, place less emphasis on social norms and duties, see a consensual belief system shared with a group as less essential, are less ready to cooperate with a group, and deemphasize emotional attachment to a group. Individualistic cultures may help foster a seeking orientation and a reliance on the individual's own interiorized ability to define truth. Wuthnow (1998) believes that the 1960s was a key decade for many to switch to a seeking orientation. He states:

> If my argument is correct, then, the 1960s did not simply introduce new religions that encouraged Americans to be more eclectic in their spirituality; rather, during the 1960s the nature of freedom itself was contested and redefined. The freedom that living in a secure community of

like-minded individuals offered was gradually replaced by a freedom to exercise choice in a marketplace of ideas and life-styles. . . . In spirituality, freedom of conscience thus came to mean paying attention to the inner voices of feelings, and freedom of choice meant exposing oneself to alternative experiences that would help develop those voices. (83)

Exploring the Inner Life

Roof (1999) discusses a number of themes from his 1988–1989 survey of spiritual-seeking baby boomers who were then in their late thirties and early forties. Central among his themes is their willingness to explore the inner life in search of personal empowerment—"a need for finding a spiritual centering and for the strength that might come with it" (82). Whether "outsiders" looking in on established religious traditions to see what they may or may not have to offer, or "insiders" striving to use the resources of their faith tradition to express deep spiritual longings, what they were primarily seeking was some form of personal transformation. For these seekers, Roof explains, religion "had to arise out of their own experiences and encounters; anything less failed to grab their attention" (82). Indeed, a seeker's willingness to explore the inner life is frequently motivated by a desire to achieve self-authenticity. Of course, those with a dwelling orientation may also wish to explore the inner life. Such exploration, however, will be guided by the teachings of the institutional dwelling place.

    When Roof (1999) asked "Is it good to explore many different religious teachings or should one stick more to a particular faith?" over twice as many (60 percent vs. 29 percent) of his seekers preferred to explore rather than to stick to a particular faith tradition. Furthermore, over half of Roof's respondents agreed that churches and synagogues have lost the spiritual vitality of religion, and a third agreed that "people have God within them, so churches aren't really necessary."

Subjective Determination of Truth

Spiritual seekers, Roof (1999) found, are also likely to stress spiritual benefits in terms of personal growth or inner development. Thus, phrases like "you discover things about yourself you never knew" were common open-ended responses in his survey. The fact that nearly half (48 percent) of his respondents agreed with the statement "all the religions of the world are equally true and good" suggests that for many the criterion of truth is subjectively determined. Furthermore, for seekers, the sacred is to be individually experienced. Though many felt that both a private and public worship experience could be authentic, Roof's respondents reported a clear preference for a spiritual style that stresses meditation and solitude.

    These results may reflect Roof's (1999) sample more than the U.S. population as a whole. Still, however, it is clear that the RS landscape is undergoing a radical shift and that such change may have important implications for the workplace. Before we consider these implications, we will briefly discuss how a shift, albeit over a longer period of time, has also occurred in our culture's understanding of the meaning of work and vocation and what role might RS experience play in this change.

CHANGING CONCEPTIONS OF WORK AND VOCATION

The Protestant Reformers Martin Luther and John Calvin argued for the sacralization of all vocations; that is, all vocations are of equal value in God's sight and can be used to glorify God. Such teachings helped elevate the status of work "from a distasteful and degrading activity, to be avoided if possible, to a dignified and glorious means of affirming God and the world he created" (McGrath 1990, 245). As Ryken (1995) explains, "In the original Protestant ethic, the doctrine of vocation or calling combined a cluster of related ideas: the providence of God in arranging human work, work as the response of a steward to God, and contentment in one's tasks" (106). For the Puritans in both England and America, the rewards of work were primarily perceived as spiritual and moral. They insisted that work should glorify God, benefit society, and help others.

After 1750, however, the combination of Enlightenment humanism and the Industrial Revolution reshaped the meaning of work for many in Western nations. Secular ideologies portrayed people as "merely a part of nature, driven by self-interest and expediency. As a result, many sought to separate the Protestant work ethic from its Christian context of stewardship and service and recast it as a creed of personal success" (Colson and Pearcey 1999, 389). At the same time, leading cultural arbiters reduced vocation to an alternative word for work and reconceptualized occupations as directed by people's duties and roles in society rather than by the commands of God. Consequently, as Western life became increasingly secularized, demystified, and rationalized, for many work was severed from any spiritual meaning and became primarily a way to earn a living and perhaps find personal fulfillment.

This interpretation of the meaning of work led work to become a source of frustration for many. Furthermore, with the continued increase of industrialization and secularization, much work has become more mechanized, routine, and repetitive, and workers have experienced a lack of creativity, control, and fulfillment. Many people's attitude toward their job is somewhere between grudging acceptance and active dislike (Terkel 1974), leading some to yearn for greater meaning and fulfillment in their work. Yet, despite such yearning, many researchers contend that few people connect religion and spirituality with their jobs. Wuthnow (1993), for example, reports that most of the people he interviewed, whether involved in institutional religion or not, said that their religious beliefs did not influence their choice of career, the way they did their work, or their views of money. Furthermore, they did not think of their work as a calling nor did they understand the concept of stewardship. Hunter (1987) claims that even for many evangelical Protestants, work has lost its spiritual and eternal significance and is important only as a means of fostering certain personal qualities. Pierce (2001) agrees that many people see no connection between work and spirituality; to them work seems to be the opposite of spirituality. He contends that few people are able to adapt the contemplative spiritual disciplines to the activist workplace and those who do attempt to practice spirituality in the workplace have not developed a distinctive set of disciplines to help others to do so.

Despite these assessments, significant numbers of Americans appear to be reevaluating the relationship between RS and their work. Especially important are a burgeoning literature on the subject, companies that are taking a greater interest in this issue, and organizations that have been created to encourage RS in the workplace. Numerous companies have established more relaxed work environments, family-friendly and flexible policies, and team-building activities (Hochschild 1997; Levering and Moskowitz 1993; Morgan and Tucker 1991). They seek to respect each individual as unique and to create a place where people enjoy working and can use their gifts effectively, enthusiastically give their best, and experience psychological and spiritual as well as material rewards.

SPIRITUAL DWELLERS AND SEEKERS IN THE WORKPLACE

This resurgence of interest in how RS relate to work is evident among Protestants, Catholics, New Agers, and proponents of Eastern pantheism. However, how individuals view the connection of

RS and work will be influenced by their understandings of the RS experience itself—in Wuthnow's (1998) terminology, a dwelling versus seeking RS orientation.

A Dwelling Spirituality

In his encyclical *On Human Work* (1981), Pope John Paul II presents a dweller approach to RS and work. He maintains that work is a fundamental part of human existence that should express and increase human dignity and provide fulfillment. People must work because God commanded them to and made them in such a way that they would find satisfaction and meaning through their labor. Pointing to the many references to work in Genesis 1–3, other Old Testament books, and the parables of Jesus, the pope emphasizes that all work is important in God's sight, which endows it with purpose and dignity. The encyclical seeks to construct a "spirituality of work" by discussing the connection between work and people's personal relationship to God. For work to achieve its full meaning, an "inner effort on the part of the human spirit, guided by faith, hope and charity" is necessary, and the church should "help all people to come closer, through work, to God" (56).

Spiritual dwellers, though they focus more on the theological and spiritual basis of work than do seekers, also argue that work should offer meaning and fulfillment by providing people the opportunity to give a legitimate account of themselves (Wuthnow 1996). Dwellers often find meaning in their work when they do a conscientious job, provide high-quality goods or services, furnish the needs of their families, achieve pleasing results, or feel they have fulfilled their duty as taught by their faith tradition.

Like spiritual seekers, dwellers may see work as a form of worship. Shelly (1985), for example, suggests that Christians should seek to glorify God through considering their work as a service to God and others and therefore as a means of worship. Mark D. Hostetter, CEO of Vinik Asset Management, a large money-management firm in New York City, asks: "How, in my day-to-day life . . . can I reflect the unconditional and inclusive and reconciling love of God in the lives of the people I encounter; how can I integrate the values of my faith into my workaday life?" (Pierce 2001, x).

A view such as Hostetter's reflects the cherished notion, common among spiritual dwellers, of work as a "calling"; that is, one's primary calling is to serve and love God with vocations and career aspirations as complementary secondary callings (Guinness 1998; Hill 1997; Ryken 1995). For the spiritual dweller, "Neither work nor career can be fully satisfying without a deeper sense of calling—but 'calling' itself is empty and indistinguishable from work unless there is Someone who calls" (Guinness 1998, 38). Catholic theologian Michael Novak (1996) insists that a calling involves four characteristics: each calling is unique to each individual; a calling requires certain preconditions, most notably talent; a true calling reveals its presence by the enjoyment and sense of renewed energies its practice yields us; and callings are not usually easy to discover. Such an emphasis on calling may also encourage dwellers to pursue excellence in their work. If vocation is a "calling" that complements one's primary calling of service to God and others, then dwellers may become motivated to use their skills and talents more fully.

Given their desire for social support, those with a dwelling RS orientation often join like-minded individuals in the workplace to discuss spiritual issues, help each other cope with job-related pressures, or study the Scriptures or some other sacred writings. These "fellowship" groups often provide a support network that encourages individuals to express their faith through their style of work, their concern for others, their spoken words, and the ways they help to shape the workplace to reflect more fully principles of love, justice, and shalom (Bernbaum and Steer 1986; Shelly 1985).

Most of those with a dwelling RS orientation find their safe haven, security, and stability in a church, synagogue, mosque, or other distinctively religious community. For some, however, the workplace itself has become a quasi-spiritual home, a comfortable place. As ties to family and church have weakened in contemporary society, coworkers have become the new family, the tribe, the social community, or the spiritual fellowship (Colson and Pearcey 1999).

In summary, those more inclined to a dwelling spirituality stress several major themes in their views of work. They insist that God commands people to work and that attitudes toward work should reflect, at least in part, one's relationship with God. Work is both a form of worship and a calling that demands excellence. People's faith traditions provide a supportive social network and help them handle the pressures and demands of work.

A Seeking Spirituality

Those who view RS through the lens of a seeker orientation are more inclined to focus on the process of work, the personal benefits to be achieved through work, and the way work affects the inner life. Conventional measures of success such as making money or achieving fame or status, long considered primary reasons for devotion to work, "figure surprisingly little in the accounts people give of why they are committed to their work" (Wuthnow 1987, 124), especially among spiritual seekers. Those who seek to experience RS in their work, no matter whether they are oriented to dwelling or seeking spirituality, may be more likely than others to resist the pressures of materialism and commodification, the process whereby money becomes so dominant in society that everything and everyone is seen and treated as a commodity to be bought and sold. Spiritual seekers (and dwellers) often substitute a service ethic for the traditional view of success (Wuthnow 1996).

Seekers prize freedom and individuality. Thus they tend to enjoy work that gives them a sense of freedom, allows them to express their individuality, and provides them with a sense of personal fulfillment (Wuthnow 1996). A sense of accomplishment in one's work may motivate seekers more than salary, fringe benefits, time off, and other extrinsic factors. For many workers, pride of performance becomes an end in itself, but for those with a seeker mentality, it is usually a "part of the quest for beauty, truth, or goodness" (115).

Seekers typically believe that people are spiritual beings and that all human behaviors are inherently spiritual. All aspects of people's lives are potentially spiritual, whether they acknowledge it or not (Pierce 2001). Consequently appreciating, affirming, and capitalizing on the RS dimensions of work require focusing and centering, consciously striving to be in touch with cosmic forces.

Often, but not always, rejecting institutionalized religion as creed bound and stifling, seekers typically follow their own unique spiritual journeys. Saks (1998), for example, maintains that improving their inner selves can increase people's satisfaction and success in their work. Enhanced spirituality enables people to reach a relaxed centeredness, heighten their awareness, get along more effectively with others, and make better business decisions. Saks urges individuals to align themselves with the flow of the life force—the "intelligent current of Universal Knowledge" (79)—and "move in the most gracious way through life" (125).

The Organizational Response

What can organizations do to respond to the RS needs of both dwellers and seekers? As discussed, dwellers and seekers have quite different RS motivations and any organizational attempt to meet RS needs must be flexible and inclusive. Thus, on the one hand, a company should respect dwellers' sense of moral order and the social support that like-minded individuals within the workplace can provide. At the same time, however, the organization must guard against a narrow sectarian approach and recognize seekers' need for experiential freedom from prescribed RS programs that may be viewed as too legalistic and constraining. Companies need to support people's attempts to find meaning in their work, especially in a technological age where many workers report a lack of vocational creativity and fulfillment.

Organizations can actively encourage their employees, whether they are dwellers or seekers, to view their work as a vocation and not just a means of earning a living. Although it is easier in some types of work than others, organizations can better educate their workers about how their products or services benefit society and help them to understand their crucial role in the development of that product or service. Organizations may also consider establishing an ecumenical office of spiritual development whose work could parallel or complement that of the organizational psychologist. Similarly, companies could establish special facilities at the workplace where employees, individually or collectively, could meet on their own time (e.g., at lunch or before/after work) to meditate, pray, read sacred writings, or hold special meetings. These facilities might also be especially useful for individuals who are undergoing personal crises or for workplace communities that experience a tragic loss.

CONCLUSION

Recent social trends indicate that increasing numbers of people are searching for greater meaning and purpose in their work. At the same time, the religious landscape will likely continue to undergo substantial change with privatized religion gaining increased influence at the expense of institutional religion. Still, however, many people consider themselves both religious and spiritual and will approach RS experience from both a dweller and a seeker orientation. Thus, the implications of each RS view for the workplace should be considered. Future research should consider not only how these two orientations may or may not differ in the workplace, but also how each may impact such variables as how people evaluate their work; how much time they spend working; the type of jobs they desire and accept; the way they do their work; and how they relate to work routine, coworkers, customers, and products.

NOTE

1. The acronym "RS" will denote when the terms *religion* and *spirituality* could be used interchangeably (i.e., "religion and spirituality" or "religion or spirituality"). There are times, however, when the two terms are meant to be distinct from each other; under these circumstances, either the word *religion* or *spirituality* will be used.

REFERENCES

Baumeister, R.F. (1991). *Meanings of Life.* New York: Guilford Press.
Bellah, R.N.; R. Madsen; W.M. Sullivan; A. Swidler; and S.M. Tipton. (1985). *Habits of the Heart: Individualism and Commitment in American Life.* New York: Harper and Row.
Bernbaum, J., and S.M. Steer. (1986). *Why Work? Careers and Employment in Biblical Perspective.* Grand Rapids, MI: Baker.
Bibby, R.W. (1995). "Beyond Headlines, Hype and Hope: Shedding Some Light on Spirituality." Paper presented at the meeting of the Society for Scientific Study of Religion, St. Louis, MO, November.
Colson, C., and N. Pearcey. (1999). *How Now Shall We Live?* Wheaton, IL: Tyndale.

Emmons, R.A. (1999). *The Psychology of Ultimate Concerns: Motivation and Spirituality in Personality.* New York: Guilford.

Gallup, G., Jr. (1994). *The Gallup Poll: Public Opinion in 1993.* Wilmington, DE: Scholarly Resources.

Gallup, G., Jr., and J. Castelli. (1989). *The People's Religion: American Faith in the 90's.* New York: Macmillan.

Greeley, A.W. (1989). *Religious Change in America.* Cambridge: Harvard University Press.

Guiness, O. (1998). *The Call: Finding and Fulfilling the Central Purpose of Your Life.* Nashville, TN: Word.

Hammond, P.E., ed. (1985). *The Sacred in a Secular Age: Toward Revision in the Scientific Study of Religion.* Berkeley: University of California Press.

Hill, A. (1997). *Just Business: Christian Ethics for the Marketplace.* Downers Grove, IL: InterVarsity Press.

Hill, P.C.; K.I. Pargament; R.W. Hood, Jr.; M.E. McCullough; J.P. Swyers; D.B. Larson; and B.J. Zinnbauer. (2000). "Conceptualizing Religion and Spirituality: Points of Commonality, Points of Departure." *Journal for the Theory of Social Behaviour* 30: 51–77.

Hochschild, A.R. (1997). *The Time Bind: When Work Becomes Home and Home Becomes Work.* New York: Henry Holt.

Hoge, D.R. (1996). "Religion in America: The Demographics of Belief and Affiliation." In *Religion and the Clinical Practice of Psychology,* ed. E.P. Shafranske. Washington, DC: American Psychological Association, 21–41.

Hunter, J.D. (1983). *American Evangelism: Conservative Religion and the Quandary of Modernity.* New Brunswick, NJ: Rutgers University Press.

———. (1987). *Evangelicalism: The Coming Generation.* Chicago: University of Chicago Press.

James, W. [1902] (1961). *The Varieties of Religious Experience.* New York: Collier Books.

John Paul II. (1981). *On Human Work.* Washington, DC: Catholic Conference.

Klinger, E. (1977). *Meaning and Void: Inner Experience and the Incentives in People's Lives.* Minneapolis, MN: University of Minneapolis Press.

Koenig, H.G.; M.E. McCullough; and D.B. Larson. (2001). *Handbook of Religion and Health.* New York: Oxford University Press.

Levering, R., and M. Moskowitz. (1993). *The 100 Best Companies to Work for in America.* New York: Penguin.

Luckmann, T. (1967). *The Invisible Religion.* New York: Praeger.

McGrath, A.E. (1990). *The Life of John Calvin: A Study in the Shaping of Western Culture.* Cambridge, MA: Basil Blackwell.

Morgan, H., and K. Tucker. (1991). *Companies That Care: The Most Family-Friendly Companies in America—What They Offer and How They Got That Way.* New York: Simon and Schuster.

Newbigin, L. (1989). *The Gospel in a Pluralist Society.* Grand Rapids, MI: Eerdmans.

Novak, M. (1996). *Business As a Calling: Work and the Examined Life.* New York: Free Press.

Pargament, K.I. (1996). "Religious Methods of Coping: Resources for the Conservation and Transformation of Significance." In *Religion and the Clinical Practice of Psychology,* ed. E.P. Shafranske. Washington, DC: American Psychological Association, 215–239.

———. (1997). *The Psychology of Religion and Coping: Theory, Research, Practice.* New York: Guilford.

———. (1999). "The Psychology of Religion *and* Spirituality? Yes and No." *International Journal for the Psychology of Religion* 9: 3–16.

Pargament, K.I.; B.W. Smith; H.G. Koenig; and L. Perez. (1998). "Positive and Negative Religious Coping with Major Life Stressors." *Journal for the Scientific Study of Religion* 37: 710–724.

Peterson, C. (2000). "Personal Control and Well-Being." In *Well-Being: The Foundations of Hedonic Psychology,* ed. D. Kahneman, E. Diener, and N. Schwarz. New York: Russell Sage Foundation, 288–301.

Pierce, G. (2001). *Spirituality at Work: Ten Ways to Balance Your Life on the Job.* Chicago: Loyola.

Roof, W.C. (1993). *A Generation of Seekers: The Spiritual Journeys of the Baby Boom Generation.* San Francisco: Harper.

———. (1999). *Spiritual Marketplace: Baby Boomers and the Remaking of American Religion.* Princeton, NJ: Princeton University Press.

Roof, W.C.; J.W. Carroll; and D.A. Roozen, eds. (1995). *The Post-War Generation and Establishment Religion: Cross-Cultural Perspectives.* Boulder, CO: Westview.

Ryken, L. (1995). *Redeeming the Time: A Christian Approach to Work and Leisure.* Grand Rapids, MI: Baker.

Saks, C. (1998). *Spirituality for the Business Person: Inner Practices for Success.* Santa Fe, NM: Heartsfire.

Shelly, J.A. (1985). *Not Just a Job: Serving Christ in Your Work.* Downers Grove, IL: InterVarsity Press.

Spilka, B., and D.N. McIntosh. (1996). "Religion and Spirituality: The Known and Unknown." Paper presented at the meeting of the American Psychological Association, Toronto, Ontario, August.

Stark, R., and W.S. Bainbridge. (1996). *A Theory of Religion.* New Brunswick, NJ: Rutgers University Press.

Terkel, S. (1974). *Working People Talk About What They Do All Day and How They Feel About What They Do.* New York: Pantheon.

Thoresen, C.E. (1998). "Spirituality, Health and Science: The Coming Revival?" In *The Emerging Role of Counseling Psychology in Health Care*, ed. S. Roth-Roemer, S. Kurpius Robinson, and C. Carmin. New York: Norton, 409–431.

Triandis, H.C.; R. Bontempo; M.J. Villareal; M. Asai; and N. Lucca. (1988). "Individualism and Collectivism: Cross-Cultural Perspectives on Self-Ingroup Relationships." *Journal of Personality and Social Psychology* 54: 323–338.

Weber, M. [1922] (1964). *The Sociology of Religion.* Boston: Beacon Press.

Wong, P.T.P., and P.S. Fry, eds. (1998). *The Human Quest for Meaning: A Handbook of Psychological Research and Clinical Applications.* Mahwah, NJ: Erlbaum.

Wulff, D.M. (1997). "The Psychology of Religion: An Overview." In *Religion and the Clinical Practice of Psychology*, ed. E.P. Shafranske. Washington, DC: American Psychological Association, 43–70.

Wuthnow, R. (1987). *Meaning and Moral Order: Explorations in Cultural Analysis.* Berkeley: University of California Press.

———. (1993). *Christianity in the 21st Century: Reflecting on the Challenges Ahead.* New York: Oxford University Press.

———. (1996). *Poor Richard's Principle: Recovering the American Dream Through the Moral Dimension of Work, Business, and Money.* Princeton, NJ: Princeton University Press.

———. (1998). *After Heaven: Spirituality in America Since the 1950s.* Berkeley: University of California Press.

Zinnbauer, B.J.; K.I. Pargament; B.C. Cole; M.S. Rye; E.M. Butter; T.G. Belavich; K.M. Hipp; A.B. Scott; and J.L. Kadar. (1997). "Religion and Spirituality: Unfuzzying the Fuzzy." *Journal for the Scientific Study of Religion* 36: 549–564.

CHAPTER 16

DRAWING THE LINE

Religion and Spirituality in the Workplace

RICHARD D. WHITE, JR.

Successful leaders recognize that a spiritually healthy workplace positively influences employee and organizational performance. Spiritual health leads people to experience consciousness at a deeper level, improves their intuitive skills, encourages teamwork, develops more purposeful and compelling organizational vision, and boosts innovation. Organizations that offer spirituality-oriented work goals offer opportunities for their employees to feel a higher sense of commitment and greater personal growth.

There are limitations, however, on encouraging workplace spirituality. When spiritual beliefs develop into actual behavior, conflicts in the workplace often arise. Values can, and do, collide. This becomes especially true when the line between secular and sectarian beliefs becomes blurred and fuzzy. New Age convictions and expanding, divergent meanings of spirituality have confused many as to where spiritual belief ends and religious belief begins, if indeed such a demarcation exists. Traditional definitions no longer suffice. While some people access their spirituality through secular exploration, others meet their spiritual needs through sectarian beliefs (Rosner 2001, 2). Because of the potential benefits of workplace spirituality, a key challenge for both business executives and public managers is how they can empower employees to envision and implement more spiritual values into the workplace, while at the same time minimizing conflicts (Neck and Milliman 1994, 9).

People tap into their spirituality in many ways. Some turn to secular methods to enrich their lives and make their workplace experience more productive, rewarding, and enjoyable. They might do yoga exercises during their lunch hour, join Toastmasters, or simply meditate to release the stresses built up in today's hectic work environment. Many others turn to religion to bring spirituality into their work. Those who turn to religion often must behave in particular ways to uphold their faith. Sikhs may have a religious responsibility to wear a turban at work, male Muslims to wear a beard, Wiccans may want to work on a Christian holiday in exchange for having their Sabbath off work, Jews might want to leave work early on Friday night to attend services by working overtime earlier in the week, and Christians, employed on rotating shifts, might wish to have every Sunday off. When employees begin to transform their spiritual thoughts into observable behavior, especially when it entails religious observances, conflicts can arise between an employee's right to practice his or her religion and an employer's right to efficiently conduct a business and not be burdened by excess cost due to employee religious needs. How can leaders minimize, and manage, the conflicts that can arise when spirituality, especially in the form of religious behavior, collides in the workplace?

In the public workplace, where religious conflict can often ignite a particularly heated firestorm of controversy, government officials must be sensitive to potential conflicts between secular and sectarian beliefs. When does the spiritual behavior of public employees become sectarian? When spiritual behavior does verge on the sectarian, when is it allowed and condoned as free expression of religion? When is religious exercise at work prohibited as an illegal conflict between church and state?

At the crossroads of secular and sectarian behavior are substantial legal and constitutional rights of public employees to speak, act, and associate in conformity with their inner beliefs. These freedoms are not necessarily absolute and lie between two significant but conflicting constitutional protections guaranteed by the U.S. Constitution. The First Amendment maintains: "Congress shall make no law respecting an *establishment* of religion, or prohibiting the *free exercise* thereof." The Supreme Court construes the *establishment* clause as prohibiting a state or the federal government from either creating a church or passing laws that aid one, or all, religions, or giving preference to one religion, or forcing belief or disbelief in any particular religion. By contrast, the Court construes the *free exercise* clause to protect persons from control or intervention by civil authorities over religious belief or activity.

The inherent contradiction between the establishment and free exercise clauses generates a persistent tension when attempting to locate the boundary between church and state. Inflaming real passions, religious controversy has become increasingly political and creates intense public interest. Pressures have mounted to allow prayers in public schools, to support sectarian education through tax revenues and vouchers, and to provide public funding to faith-based public welfare programs. In the public sector, religious protections exert massive pressures on the government as employer. Federal and state constitutions outlaw government's infringement on the free exercise of religion. At some point, however, the freedom given to an individual by a public employer can become a de facto establishment of religion. When does appropriate accommodation of spiritual thought and behavior develop into improper aid to, and thus the establishment of, religion? When does accommodation of the majority religion become discriminatory toward religious minorities?

Confusing and contradictory court decisions, statutes, and executive orders unfortunately hamper the resolution of conflicts involving spiritual and/or religious values. Another complication is an increasingly diverse and pluralistic society where the freedoms of expression guaranteed to one person can run afoul of the freedoms guaranteed to another. The last twenty years have seen an increase in religious diversity within America. Buddhists and Hindus have grown into significant minorities, while Muslims have quadrupled. At the same time, the number of nonreligious has risen from 2 percent in 1952 to 10 percent today (Thiemann 1996, 3). Because of the increasing size and influence of religious minorities, the once tight grip of the traditional Christian hegemony has lessened significantly.

No definitive guidelines exist for deciding constitutionally appropriate standards for sectarian speech in the public workplace. However, an assessment of current research can provide a framework to better understand the diverse interests that this controversial issue creates. As such, this assessment examines the considerations inherent in any personnel decision regarding religious expression, traces the historical and legal evolution of the separation of church and state, offers a framework that helps define the more important issues, and suggests recommendations for the public employer who faces the controversies created by the clash between the secular and the sectarian.

THE EVOLUTION OF RELIGIOUS RIGHTS AND SEPARATION OF CHURCH AND STATE

The argument over the limits of religious freedom predates the republic. One of the main reasons for colonization of America was tolerance of minority Christian religions. In the 1640s, the Maryland colony enacted (but later rescinded) the Act of Toleration guaranteeing "no person . . . professing to believe in Jesus Christ shall from henceforth be in any ways troubled, molested, or discountenanced for or in respect to his or her religion, nor in the free exercise thereof within this province" (Audi 1989, 260). After the Revolution, the Framers feared a predominant religion and memories of the Anglican Church of England's influence in colonial Virginia were fresh in their minds. They also recognized the dilemma of ensuring religious expression and yet limiting the influence of any specific religion. Among the endeavors to guarantee religious liberty, the contributions of James Madison are truly exceptional.

As early as 1776, Madison argued that freedom of worship is a natural right that no majority can curtail. In debating George Mason's *Declaration of Rights* he insisted that the word *entitlement* be substituted for *toleration* in the article protecting freedom of worship (Leibiger 1993, 449). With this change in wording, Madison recast religious liberty from a privilege to a natural and absolute right, a remarkable modification that would be highlighted in the constitutional amendments, and would shape America's philosophy of religious freedom for generations to come. In 1785 Madison captured the complexity of his views on religion when he wrote the "Memorial and Remonstrance Against Religious Assessments." In "Remonstrance," he challenges Virginia's use of public funds to pay teachers in Christian schools. Madison feared Christianity becoming the official religion of the commonwealth and possible discrimination against minority beliefs. His fears of religious hegemony are clear when he wrote, "Who does not see the same authority which can establish Christianity, in exclusion of all other Religions, may establish with the same ease any particular sect of Christians, in exclusion of all other Sects?" (Madison 1973).

Madison also defended the nontheist and argued that freedom implicitly guarantees the right to have *no* religious beliefs (Audi 1989, 261). He protested unsuccessfully against laws prohibiting clergy from holding public office, urging such prohibition punishes a religious profession by denying a basic civil right. Madison led the fight for Virginia's *Statute for Religious Freedom* to separate church and state and to remove an individual's right of religious belief from government control. Evocative of Locke and composed by Jefferson, the *Statute* remains a timeless affirmation of intellectual and religious freedom (Knoles 1943, 194). By the time the Framers amended the Constitution, the deliberations in Virginia had established a precedent that helped ensure the passage of an otherwise controversial First Amendment. To the Framers, ensuring religious expression was paramount, as reflected in both the free exercise and establishment clauses, as well as the symbolism of highlighting religious freedom in the first clause of the First Amendment.

DEVELOPMENT OF WORKPLACE RELIGIOUS POLICY

Religious freedom continues to evoke great controversy and constantly undergoes a subtle evolution caused by social changes and, more specifically, court decisions. The modern development of workplace religious policy falls within three distinct periods, with each period marked by a different emphasis. The first period, which ran from the nation's formation to the 1950s, stresses the rights of the employer; the second period, running from the 1950s through the 1960s, shifts the emphasis to the employee; and the third period, beginning in the 1960s and continuing to the present, focuses on balancing the rights of the employer, the employee, and the public interest.

During the pre-1950s period, the constitutional rights of government employees were substantially restricted as the *doctrine of privilege* prevailed. The dominant view maintained by the government as employer and the judiciary as arbitrator of employment disputes was that, because a government employee has no right to public employment, the employer may "condition employment on any reasonable terms, including the employee's surrender of certain constitutional rights" (Harvard 1984, 1743). Under the doctrine of privilege an employee could be fired because of religious belief with no regard for due process. Before World War II, the courts began to distinguish between religious thought and religious behavior, ruling that while the freedom to act on one's belief could be restricted, the freedom to believe what one will "is absolute" (*Cantwell v. Connecticut*, 310 US 296, 1940).

During the early period, many states restricted the freedoms of religious minorities and nonbelievers, and despite constitutional protections, antiquated statutes remain. Christian teachings dictated decisions concerning religion in the workplace. When attempts were made to liberalize religious freedom, it was usually for Christian beliefs. At best, non-Christian beliefs were tolerated and at worst, discriminated against. Seven states still define atheists, secular humanists, and other freethinkers as second-class citizens. The constitutions of Arkansas, Maryland, North Carolina, Pennsylvania, South Carolina, Tennessee, and Texas retain historic provisions that prohibit unbelievers and minority religionists from holding public office. Fortunately, states have seldom enforced clauses establishing these restrictions (Flynn 1999, 13). However, the Arkansas anti-atheist statute survived a court challenge as late as 1982, and only Maryland's provision has been overturned by the Supreme Court (*Torcaso v. Watkins*, 367 US 488, 1961).

A SHIFT TOWARD EMPLOYEE RIGHTS

By the mid-1950s, a more proemployee view of religious rights in the workplace began to emerge. This was the era of the Warren Court (1953–1969) and landmark decisions guaranteeing individual rights and equality. In cases involving religious freedom, the Court's dramatic shift was significant, as when it declared school prayer unconstitutional (*Engel v. Vitale*, 370 US 421, 1962). The Court also ruled that Maryland could not require applicants for public office to swear that they believed in the existence of God and ruled unanimously that religious tests violate the establishment clause (*Torcaso v. Watkins*, 367 US 488, 1961). In 1963 the Court issued the landmark *Sherbert v. Verner* (374 US 398, 1963) involving a Seventh-Day Adventist who would not work on a Saturday, that religion's Sabbath. After being fired, the employee applied for unemployment benefits but was denied on the grounds that suitable employment was available. The Supreme Court reversed in favor of the employee and, more broadly, forced states to recognize the unique requirements of various religious traditions.

The Warren Court clearly decided that, even as an employer, the government remains subject to constitutional limitations. The Court ruled that government can restrict the religious rights of employees only if such action is narrowly tailored and serves a compelling state interest. In effect, the Warren Court shifted the burden of proof in religious workplace disputes from the employee to the employer and ultimately altered the balance of power toward the employee. Government no longer could condition employment upon an individual's willingness to sacrifice fundamental constitutional rights.

The third period in the development of employee constitutional rights began in the 1960s and continues to this day. This period focuses on balancing three concerns: (1) ensuring the constitutional rights of the employee; (2) the government's responsibility to function in an efficient, effective, and economical manner; and (3) the impact on the public interest. The connection between these three concerns represents what often is referred to as the public service model. The courts recently have adopted balancing tests that create criteria and case law that help to determine which of the three concerns takes precedent at a particular time.

The public service model becomes particularly relevant when resolving conflicts concerning religion in the workplace. The issues surrounding religion in the workplace fall within two categories created by the tension of the First Amendment: expression and establishment. Freedom of religious expression is the less controversial of the two, for it falls within the guidelines guaranteeing freedom of speech, press, etc., that are protected by the Constitution and civil rights legislation. The establishment of religion category is more complicated, for it is a unique set of case law that has no legal counterpart, while the court decisions involving government establishment of religion are more inconsistent and contradictory than decisions resolving freedom of expression.

RELIGIOUS EXPRESSION IN THE PUBLIC WORKPLACE

The landmark Supreme Court decision involving religious expression in the workplace is *Pickering v. Board of Education* (391 US 563, 1968). *Pickering* held that when a government employer restricts a constitutionally protected right of its employees, the court must balance the gravity of the burden on employees against the government's interests in providing the efficient delivery of public services (Richards 1998, 758). Among many important governmental interests inherent in the "efficient delivery of public services" is the government's responsibility to maintain order within the workplace, to provide social services, stabilize the economy, and to preserve democracy. The public sector employer maintains a constitutional obligation to eliminate employee actions that are disruptive, controversial, or detrimental to efficiency, even when the employee believes such actions to be constitutionally protected (Richards 1998, 758).

Pickering involved a teacher fired for criticizing his school board. While *Pickering* focuses on freedom of speech, the courts apply its provisions to the broad spectrum of constitutionally protected individual rights, including religious expression. Two Supreme Court cases further illustrate *Pickering*. *Connick v. Meyers* (461 US 138, 1983) involved an assistant district attorney fired for distributing a questionnaire to other attorneys concerning office morale, the need for a grievance committee, the level of confidence in supervisors, and whether employees felt pressured to work in political campaigns. Lower courts ruled in the plaintiff's favor and decided that her firing violated her constitutional right of free expression. The Supreme Court reversed, determining that her actions endangered the efficient functioning of the government office and that there was "a compelling governmental interest" in maintaining morale within the district attorney's office. The Court again balanced an employee's individual rights against the government's responsibility to operate efficiently and in the public interest, falling this time on the side of government.

In another Supreme Court case (*Rankin v. McPherson*, 483 US 378, 1987), a county constable fired a clerk for remarking to a coworker, after hearing of an attempt on the president's life, "if they go for him again, I hope they get him." The courts ruled in favor of the clerk and determined that the governmental interest in maintaining efficiency and discipline did not outweigh society's First Amendment interest in protecting an individual's freedom of speech. *Connick* and *Rankin* illustrate the fine line separating constitutionally protected First Amendment rights and the responsibility of government to operate efficiently and serve the public interest.

Recent cases demonstrate the application of *Pickering*. In *Brown v. Polk City, Iowa* (61 F.3d 650, 8th Cir. 1995), a city government ordered an employee to cease activities that could be interpreted as religious proselytizing on the job. Other city workers complained that the employee, an evangelical Christian, had his secretary type Bible study notes, said prayers with employees during official meetings, and scolded his employees using biblical passages on laziness. The Eighth Circuit held these actions did not constitute a disruption of government efficiency, the limitation was not narrowly tailored, and the government displayed unwarranted hostility toward religion. In a similar case, a government computer programmer labeled all of the programs he wrote with the acronym SOTLJC, standing for "servant of the Lord Jesus Christ." Again, the court struck down state strictures because it found no substantial disruption to government efficiency and found no establishment clause violation. Merely allowing religious expression did not equate to endorsement of the expression (Richards 1998, 764).

In the above cases, the decisive factor for allowing religious expression in the public workplace is whether an employee's remark is a matter of public concern. An employee praying in a cafeteria would not be of public concern, while placing "servant of the Lord Jesus Christ" on official documents may be of public concern and not protected by the First Amendment. Proselytizing is a more difficult issue. When does preaching to coworkers become a matter of public concern? Again, *Pickering* and the public service model help to clarify competing concerns: a person's right to exercise religious expression; the government's responsibility to maintain efficiency and morale within the office; and the public interest, which in this case is other workers, especially those of another religion, who may regard proselytizing as an infringement upon their religious freedom. If the government agency allows proselytizing at work, is it indeed an unlawful governmental establishment of religion? When does proselytizing create a "hostile work environment"?

PREVENTING ESTABLISHMENT OF RELIGION

The Supreme Court provides guidelines for preventing government establishment of religion. In *Lemon v. Kurtzman* (403 US 602, 1971), the Court declared state supplements to the salary of Catholic schoolteachers to be unconstitutional. The *Lemon* test declares that to prevent establishment of religion, any government action must first, have a secular purpose; second, can neither advance nor inhibit religion; and third, cannot foster an excessive entanglement between government and religion.

Unfortunately, since World War II court decisions regarding governmental establishment of religion have been confusing and contradictory. The confusion was inevitable due to the natural contradiction between the establishment and free exercise clauses. But the Supreme Court and lower courts have fostered the religious aporia by interpreting inconsistent opinions. In *Everson v. Board of Education* (330 US 1, 1947) the Court ruled that, on one hand, the First Amendment creates a wall between church and state that must be kept high and impregnable. The Court determined that no tax may be levied to support religious activities. On the other hand, the Court contradicted itself in *Everson* and found no fault with a New Jersey school board using public funds to reimburse bus fares of children attending Catholic schools.

In a recent, deeply divided case, the Court rendered a bizarre Solomonic decision when it found, in a single case, that a crèche on government property violated the First Amendment but a menorah in similar circumstances did not (*Allegheny County v. Greater Pittsburgh ACLU*, 492 US 573, 1989). The crèche sat on the grand staircase of the Allegheny County Courthouse, a very prominent position and readily visible by all who entered, and therefore an unconstitutional endorsement of religion. The menorah, located in a building owned jointly by the city and county, was allowed because, unlike the crèche, it did "not have an exclusively religious message." The menorah stood beside a Christmas tree and a sign saluting liberty, a setting that the Court ruled neither endorsed nor disapproved any religious group.

Since *Everson*, there have been several similarly perplexing decisions by the Supreme Court and lower courts. Characterized by questionable logic and contradictory opinions, the religious case law has become little more than an assortment of ad hoc and confusing judgments. Even when Supreme Court justices agree on a verdict, they provide little guidance to lower courts as they often use vastly different criteria to render their individual opinions. Cases involving religious freedom are often polarized, with decisions made by bare, five-to-four majorities. Passions of the justices enter the findings and dissents contain some of the most vituperative language seen on the docket.

RELIGIOUS CONTROVERSY AND THE PUBLIC FORUM TEST

The Seventh and Ninth Circuits, departing somewhat from their colleagues, created the public forum test to resolve First Amendment conflicts in the workplace. The public forum test judges government restrictions on constitutional rights according to *where* these restrictions occur. The Supreme Court, in *Cornelius v. NAACP Legal Defense and Educational Fund* (473 US 788, 1985), decided that a governmental workplace is not an open forum when the premises are used for government business. On government property designated as a public forum and places where government allows free access by the public, restraints on religious expression are allowed only where there exists a compelling state interest that is narrowly tailored to serve that particular purpose (Richards 1998, 749).

Meanwhile, locations where government does not allow unlimited public access, government may limit individual rights in pursuance of any reasonable objective so long as there exists no intent to discriminate against any one particular viewpoint. In *Kelly v. Municipal Court of Marion County* (F.3d———, 1996 WL 559941) a county government dismissed a bailiff for preaching to prisoners (Richards 1998, 771). The Ninth Circuit dismissed the bailiff's free exercise claim, ruling that a courtroom is not a public forum and the government's desire to maintain a neutral religious posture in judicial proceedings constitutes a reasonable purpose (Richards 1998, 771). The public forum rationale presumes the First Amendment does not require that a public office become a roundtable for purely private speech and actions of its employees. Instead, there is a tendency on the part of the judiciary to defer to the judgment of the government employer in order to guarantee efficient public service (Harvard 1984, 1748).

While courts seldom turn to the public forum test, the guidelines nevertheless are useful in stressing the importance of location in freedom of expression controversies. Most jurists favor the *Pickering* test over the public forum test and conclude that *Pickering* proves fairer to the employee, the employer, and the public interest because it is necessarily more fact-specific, better resolves the tension between the free exercise and establishment clauses, and its wide application in First Amendment issues makes it more acceptable in the context of religious expression in the public arena (Richards 1998, 750). However, as long as circuit courts use different approaches to resolve religious freedom cases, continued confusion, inconsistency, and increased litigation will besiege the subject.

ACCOMMODATING RELIGIOUS EXPRESSION

Along with the Constitution and court decisions are numerous statutory and administrative initiatives that provide guidelines for appropriate religious activity. The Civil Rights Act of 1964 and presidential executive orders define the boundaries of religious liberty for many government workers. Congress modified the Civil Rights Act in 1972 to require religious accommodation for employees except where the cost would be prohibitive. The Act bans employment discrimination based on religion and requires employers to "reasonably accommodate" employees' religious beliefs. Congress interprets reasonable accommodation to mean any action that does not impose an "undue hardship" on the employer (McIntosh 1996, 354). However, despite the language of the Act, there remains substantial confusion on the definitions of reasonable accommodation and undue hardship and whether the Civil Rights Act actually gives an advantage to either the employer or the employee. In essence, the Act supplies little concrete guidance for determining the level of accommodation required by an employer or what creates an undue hardship.

The Supreme Court aggravated workplace religious controversy with inconsistent interpretations of Title VII of the Civil Rights Act. In *Trans World Airlines v. Hardison* (432 US 63, 1977), an employee was dismissed because, as a Seventh-Day Adventist, he refused to work on his Sabbath. The airline attempted to allow him to swap shifts to avoid Saturday work, but the worker did not have sufficient seniority under union rules to swap shifts at will. The Supreme Court decided that Title VII does not require employers to bear more than a *de minimis* cost to accommodate religious observances. The Court also ruled that allowing an employee to work only four days per week or breaching a collective bargaining agreement with the airline's unions constituted a significant economic cost which was held more than *de minimis* (McIntosh 1996, 354). While the Court ruled in the airline's favor, it also declared that the burden of proof rests on the employer to prove that reasonable accommodations allow for religious freedom and the accommodations do not cause undue hardship to the employer. *Trans World* is generally regarded as a proemployee decision, but some analysts conclude the finding aids employers who need only link efforts at accommodation to any diminution in efficiency.

Since *Trans World,* Civil Rights Act interpretations have swung back and forth between the employer and employee. The Eighth Circuit, in *Brown v. General Motors Corporation* (601 F.2d 956, 1979), decided in favor of employee rights in mandating that employers must demonstrate a real, and not merely abstract, hardship when accommodating religious practices (McIntosh 1996, 355). General Motors argued that if it allowed one employee to change shifts, it would cause chaos among other employees who might want to alter their schedules. However, this argument was overruled. According to the Court, employers must tolerate religious activities by their employees "to the extent that these activities do not disrupt the work environment and force employers to sustain real, non-hypothetical costs."

The Supreme Court further expanded employee rights in *Thomas v. Review Board of the Indiana Employment Security Division* (450 US 707, 1981). Thomas, a Jehovah's Witness who worked in a steel foundry that closed, was transferred to another foundry that built military tanks. With no other departments available for transfer, Thomas requested to be laid off due to his pacifist religion. Denied the layoff, he quit, arguing his religious beliefs forbade him from producing weapons. The state of Indiana denied unemployment compensation, saying he was ineligible because his termination was voluntary. The Court reversed, finding that the state improperly burdened Thomas's right to the free exercise of his religion.

The pendulum shifted somewhat toward the employer in *Ansonia Board of Education v. Phillbrook* (479 US 60, 1986). The Court held Title VII of the Civil Rights Act does not direct an employer to consider the accommodation suggested by an employee. Rather, once an employer demonstrates it furnished *any* reasonable accommodation, the inquiry ends (Epperson 1996, 739). The Court found that providing an employee with unpaid leave to observe religious holidays was reasonable and dismissed the argument that an employer had to accept the employee's accommodation unless it would impose an undue hardship. Nothing in the law requires an employer to select any particular reasonable accommodation. The Court rendered a proemployer decision when it sustained an Air Force regulation prohibiting a Jewish psychologist from wearing a religious skullcap. The Court declared, in a five-to-four decision, that the military is not required to accommodate religion when it would detract from the uniformity sought by dress regulations and found the need for military uniformity to be compelling (*Goldman v. Weinberger*, 475 US 503, 1986).

Brown v. Polk County (61 F.3d 650, 1995) provides another example of the diverse and contradictory opinions whereby a lower court takes another proplaintiff stance (Koral 1986, 95). A pious supervisor defended his open prayer at work not because his faith forced him to pray, but rather because the government policy was "oppressive and vexatious." The Eighth Circuit ignored whether the individual's beliefs required such religious expressions, ruling an employee need only show that he is sufficiently annoyed by an employer's antireligious policies without ever showing that the egregious policy forced him to stop religious behavior (McIntosh 1996, 362).

Collectively, court decisions over past years have muddled the boundaries of religious freedom, and neither proemployee nor proemployer groups are satisfied with the current state of religious freedom rulings. Neither the statutes nor the courts define undue hardship clearly and some critics conclude that Title VII guarantees only minimal protection to employees because its standards are ambiguous, confusing, and controversial.

PRESIDENTIAL EXECUTIVE ORDERS AND RELIGIOUS EXPRESSION

Presidential executive orders also provide guidelines for defining the limits of appropriate religious expression within the government workplace. However, these guidelines also contribute to the confusion over workplace religious policy. In August 1997, President Clinton issued "Guidelines on Religious Exercise and Religious Expression in the Federal Workplace" that prohibit federal employees from activities that could be interpreted as a government endorsement or disparagement of religion. The guidelines allow agencies to restrict religious expression only when the employee's interest is outweighed by the government's efficient provision of public services, or where the expression intrudes on the rights of other employees, or where the expression appears to be an official endorsement of religion. To some critics, the executive order signals a shift back toward the employer, exceeds the scope of the president's authority, fosters worker coercion by supervisors, and contains unconstitutional standards (Hayes 1997; Kao 1999, 251). Other critics argue the president's guidelines emphasize establishment clause prohibitions and fail to refer to the reasonable accommodation standard (Kao 1999, 256). If a religious practice violates the standards, the practice must cease without regard for possible reasonable accommodation as required under Title VII of the Civil Rights Act.

Others, nevertheless, defend the guidelines because of their detail and specificity. Regulations do not require agencies to allow employees to use work time to pursue religious agendas, for "federal employees are paid to perform official work, not to engage in personal religious or ideological campaigns during work hours." Employees can satisfy their religious obligations by such behavior as keeping a Bible or Koran on a private desk and reading during breaks, as long as the expression does "not interfere with workplace efficiency." The guidelines suggest when and where religious proselytizing is permitted. Generally, proselytizing is "as entitled to constitutional protection as any other form of speech," as long as one would not interpret the expression as government endorsement of religion. Employees must abstain from such expression when another employee asks that it stop and, when proselytizing becomes excessive or harassing, it may constitute a hostile work environment. Proselytizing should not be treated more harshly than nonreligious expression solely because of its content.

Created by a coalition of religious organizations, the federal executive order contains a loose amalgam of religious policies, some contradictory, and with little relationship to legislation or court decisions. Throughout the document, the interest of the government in "promoting effi- ciency" supersedes an employee's freedom of religious expression. Only at the end of the execu- tive order is a stricter and legally grounded test specified, declaring that government action "that substantially burdens a private party's exercise of religion can be enforced only if it is justified by a compelling interest and is narrowly tailored to advance that interest."

SUGGESTIONS FOR THE PUBLIC EMPLOYER

How does the public employer balance the often conflicting religious rights of individuals, the public interest, and government efficiency? How can the public employer safely navigate the often sensitive, conflicting, and confusing laws and court decisions embracing religious behav- ior? Deciding the propriety and legality of various forms of religious expression by employees in the public sector remains difficult. The potential for litigation remains high. A government agency must assure that its personnel policies do not create either a disparate impact on, or an endorsement of, religious expression. Meanwhile, the primary assets for any public agency is its employees, and employees, whether in the public or private sector, cannot be separated from their deeply held religious convictions. Where these convictions can reasonably be accommo- dated with little financial expenditure or loss in efficiency or infringement on the rights of other employees, religious expression must be positively endorsed. Beyond this point, the gov- ernment as an employer must balance the delicate and often divisive interests. The rights of the individual must be evaluated according to the overarching principles of efficiency and effec- tiveness in the delivery of public services to the people. The final decision as to which interest dominates remains a sensitive deliberation that may unfortunately resort to litigation in lieu of more definitive legal standards.

In most situations, the public employer should take positive steps that will prevent religious controversies from reaching the courts. According to the Equal Employment Opportunity Com- mission, religious discrimination cases increased 31 percent between 1990 and 1994, with 2,900 filed in 1994 (Jacobs 1995). Religious cases will continue to increase as minority religions mul- tiply, turnover in a more dynamic workforce rises, and society becomes increasingly litigious. When cases involving religious behavior reach the courts, they lead to a no-win situation, with high costs borne by all and bitter animosities left festering. The public employer must walk a fine line to meet the religious obligations of the employee, prevent litigation, and provide efficient service to the public.

The employer should ensure that policies governing free expression, including religious ex- pression, in the public workplace should be "content neutral." Religious expression should not be handled any differently than any other type of expression. Leaders must be careful not to treat employees differently based on religion and should be cautious about their own religious expres- sion (Zachary 1996, 6). Questions regarding a job applicant's religion are not permissible. An employer can ask only if an employee will be able to perform the job requirements when told of the regular days, hours, and shifts for the job.

At the same time, leaders must base decisions involving religious behavior in the workplace primarily on the job. A religious skullcap, or a content-neutral Yankees ball cap for that matter, will seldom interfere with an employee's job duties. However, a worker might be fired from a job when he refuses to shave a beard that renders him unable to wear a required facemask or respirator. If the wearing of religious—or nonreligious—jewelry or head wear does not influence an employee's ability to perform his official job, then the chosen dress is generally beyond the control of the employer.

While dealing with religious expression at work is often complicated, a knowledgeable and perceptive supervisor can lessen the potential for legal liability and emotional conflicts (Zachary 1996, 6). Training is necessary for both employers and employees. Supervisors must know that the law protects religious expression. For employees, diversity training should include tolerance of religious beliefs. Training in this area is not a one-shot practice but should be incorporated into a long-term, recurring training program.

The potential for lawsuits in the workplace creates an increasingly important need for carefully written policies across a wide range of areas, and employee expression in the workplace is no exception. Clear, straightforward guidelines are necessary for employers and employees alike to understand what is, and is not, permissible in the workplace. Policies should be reviewed carefully by the legal staff and updated with the latest rulings. Some analysts propose a policy on workplace spirituality be drafted based on the requirements of the ADA, since the laws regarding religious freedom and accommodations of disability have many similarities (Ettorre 1996, 15). With clear policies in place, supervisors no longer must worry so much about the literal interpretation of the statutes or what constitutes an undue hardship to the employer or *de minimis* accommodation of employee needs. Instead, if in doubt, follow the written policies, while at the same time become flexible and err on the side of the employee (Frierson 1988, 60). Examples of possible accommodation without causing undue hardship include voluntary substitutions, swaps, flexible scheduling, lateral transfers, and change of job assignments. The federal government permits federal employees to work compensatory overtime when their religious beliefs require absence from work. A creative employer and a cooperative employee will have more success at resolving a conflict than a host of attorneys.

Employees also have a responsibility. Those seeking to observe their spiritual beliefs are obligated to resolve conflicts in the workplace before they do serious harm. An employee must indicate a potential problem arising from a religious commitment, such as not working on Saturdays, at the time the employee accepts the job or immediately on becoming observant when employed. Union members should disclose their religious observance to their union steward if they perceive a problem. When relevant, unions should be involved in resolving workplace conflicts that may affect the entire workforce. When writing a policy on workplace spirituality, management should include employee representation in the process.

Finally, intolerance of an employee's internal belief is illegal, immoral, fosters long-term inefficiency, and is anathema in a democratic society. The government employer has a distinct responsibility to ensure religious freedom. The public workplace should be the model workplace for the private sector to follow and must uphold the highest legal and moral standards. Whether it be providing on-site day care facilities, wheelchair access to all work areas, or a liberal toleration of all employees' religious beliefs, it is government actions to which the public first looks for setting examples of progress in a spiritually healthy workplace.

As another aspect of diversity, spirituality, including religious expression, should not merely be tolerated but, when appropriate, celebrated (Ettorre 1996, 15). An employer's open commitment to improving spiritual health can improve employee morale by demonstrating that the organization is sensitive to both its religious and nonreligious employees' needs. By accommodating spiritual health in the workplace, the employer acknowledges and values its most important asset—its employees.

NOTE

Portions of this chapter are adapted from Richard D. White and Jeffrey D. Jeter (2002). "Separating Church and State or Guaranteeing Religious Expression? Resolving Religious Conflict in the Public Workplace." *Review of Public Personnel Administration* 22: 4. Copyright © 2002 Sage Publications.

REFERENCES

Audi, R. (1989). "The Separation of Church and State and the Obligations of Citizenship." *Philosophy and Public Affairs* 18: 259–296.

Epperson, R.F. (1996). "Protecting the Rights of Public Employees Under Title VII and the Free Exercise Clause." *Missouri Law Review* 61: 719–742.

Ettorre, B. (1996). "Religion in the Workplace: Implications for Managers." *Management Review* 85: 15–20.

Flynn, T. (1999). "Outlawing Unbelief." *Free Inquiry* 20: 13–18.

Frierson, J.G. (1988). "Religion in the Workplace: Dealing in Good Faith." *Personnel Journal* 67: 60–68.

Harvard Law Review Association. (1984). "The Constitutional Rights of Public Employees." *Harvard Law Review* 97: 1738–1800.

Hayes, A.S. (1997). "Clinton Puts Faiths in Fed Workplace: Religious Rights Lawyers Say Secular Workplace Is Next." *National Law Journal* 19: 1.

Jacobs, M.D. (1995). "Courts Wrestle with Religion in Workplace." *Wall Street Journal*, B-1.

Kao, S.S. (1999). "The President's Guidelines on Religious Exercise and Religious Expression in the Federal Workplace: A Restatement or Reinterpretation of Law?" *Boston University Public Interest Law Journal* 8: 251–267.

Knoles, G.H. (1943). "The Religious Ideas of Thomas Jefferson." *Mississippi Valley Historical Review* 30: 187–204.

Koral, A.M. (1986). "Religion in the Workplace: Mixed Signals from the Courts." *Employment Relations Today* 95–104.

Leibiger, S. (1993). "James Madison and the Amendments to the Constitution, 1787–1789: Parchment Barriers." *Journal of Southern History* 59: 441–468.

Madison, J. (1973). *The Mind of the Founder: Sources of the Political Thought of James Madison.* Indianapolis, IN: Bobbs-Merrill.

McIntosh, D. (1996). "Expanding the Public Employer's Duty to Accommodate Employee's Religious Practices Under Title VII and the First Amendment." *Boston College Law Review* 37: 353–363.

Neck, Christopher P., and John F. Milliman. (1994). "Thought Self-leadership: Finding Spiritual Fulfillment in Organizational Life." *Journal of Managerial Psychology* 9, no. 6: 9–18.

Richards, B. (1998). "The Boundaries of Religious Speech in the Government Workplace." *Journal of Labor and Employment Law* 1: 745–788.

Rosner, Bob (2001). "Is There Room for the Soul at Work?" *Workforce* 80, no. 2: 82–83.

Thiemann, R.F. (1996). *Religion in Public Life: A Dilemma for Democracy.* Washington, DC: Georgetown University Press.

White, Richard D., and Jeffrey D. Jeter. (2002). "Separating Church and State or Guaranteeing Religious Expression? Resolving Religious Conflict in the Public Workplace." *Review of Public Personnel Administration* 22: 4.

Zachary, M.C. (1996). "Handling Religious Expression in the Workplace." *Supervision* 57: 5–12.

COURT DECISIONS

Allegheny County v. Greater Pittsburgh ACLU, 492 US 573,1989.
Ansonia Board of Education v. Phillbrook, 479 US 60, 1986.
Braunfield v. Brown, 366 US 599, 1961.
Brown v. General Motors Corporation, 601 F.2d 956, 1979.
Brown v. Polk City, Iowa, 61 F.3d 650, 8th Cir., 1995.
Cantwell v. Connecticut, 310 US 296, 1940.
Connick v. Meyers, 461 US 138, 1983.
Cornelius v. NAACP Legal Defense and Educational Fund, 473 US 788, 1985.

Engel v. Vitale, 370 US 421, 1962.
Everson v. Board of Education, 330 US 1, 1947.
Goldman v. Weinberger, 475 US 503, 1986.
Kelly v. Municipal Court of Marion County, F.3d——, 1996 WL 559941.
Lemon v. Kurtzman, 403 US 602, 1971.
Pickering v. Board of Education, 391 US 563, 1968.
Rankin v. McPherson, 483 US 378, 1987.
Sherbert v. Verner, 374 US 398, 1963.
Thomas v. Review Board, 450 US 707, 1981.
Torcaso v. Watkins, 367 US 488, 1961.
Trans World Airlines v. Hardison, 432 US 63, 1977.

CHAPTER 17

ETHICS AT WORK

Money, Spirituality, and Happiness

ADRIAN FURNHAM

Work is often dedicated to material advancement and productivity. Work is a social activity; spirituality often a personal endeavor. Work has mainly extrinsic rewards; spirituality mainly intrinsic rewards. But spirituality is not just about business ethics and morality: it extends much further than that and has often been associated with a particular faith and religious condition. However, it is possible to have secular spirituality of the sort of people who feel spirituality in nature or even in poetry. The arts, particularly music, can have both short-term and enduring effects on the spiritual outlook of individuals.

The concept of spirituality at work has returned to capture the imagination of many in the West. It is clear that this is a very old concept and it remains a socio-historical question why its demise and reappearance occurs. Some argue that it is due to downsizing, globalization, and greater work insecurity.

In Great Britain there was a great deal of surprise at the outpouring of the public grief over the death of Diana, Princess of Wales. Social commentators, church leaders as well as academics attempt to explain the acute and chronic grief reaction of so many, as well as many public manifestations of private mourning. Britain was considered a post-Christian, postmodern, secular society famous for its skepticism and stoicism. Yet this event alerted people to the fact that there are powerful wells of spirituality in the nation that one only really sees in times of personal and national crisis.

This response can also be seen during times of economic crisis: when a company goes out of business or lays off staff. As well as anger there is often a remarkable spiritual change in the management and employees, often to their own surprise. Moreover, increasing talk about the work-life balance is couched in the language of spirituality. The contrast is between the material and the spiritual; stress-inducer and stress-releasor; short-term and long-term; meaningless and meaningful work; less important, more important to the job holder. An increasing interest in workplace spirituality may be seen as a reaction to the demands of the modern workplace, which insists on the total commitment of individuals but without addressing some of their fundamental needs.

More recently for social scientists the concept of spirituality at work has surfaced in the concept of spiritual intelligence: the idea that spirituality is an ability as well as a preference. It is considered an individual difference factor that predicts how people behave in the workplace and elsewhere.

SPIRITUAL INTELLIGENCE

Emmons (2000) believes the core of the concept of spiritual intelligence is fourfold: the capacity for transcendence; the ability to enter into heightened spiritual states of consciousness; the ability to invest everyday activities, events, and relationships with a sense of the sacred or divine; and an ability to utilize spiritual resonance to solve problems in everyday living. Mayer (2000) preferred the term *spiritual consciousness*, which involves (1) attending to the unity of the world and transcending one's existence; (2) consciously entering into heightened spiritual states; (3) attending to the sacred in everyday activities, events, and relationships; (4) structuring consciousness so that problems in living are seen in the context of life's ultimate concerns; and (5) desiring to act, and, consequently, acting in virtuous ways (to show forgiveness, to express gratitude, to be humble, to display compassion).

Gardner (1999) has written about existential, as opposed to spiritual, intelligence, though there is clearly overlap between the two concepts. He agues that it is "a concern with 'ultimate issues' (and) seems the most unambiguously cognitive strand of the spiritual" (60). It is the "capacity to locate oneself with respect to such existential features of the human condition as the significance of life, the meaning of death, the ultimate fate of the physical and the psychological worlds, and such profound experiences as love of another person or total immersion in a work of art."

For Gardner (1999) existential intelligence is a cognitive ability acquired through learning and personal experience. He notes in a very personal section of his book that he is frightened and intrigued by spiritual individuals—fearing both the strangeness of their ideas but also fascinated by the power of charismatic leaders over hapless followers. He points out the effects of music on himself: ". . . lose track of mundane concerns, alter my perceptions of space and time, and occasionally, feel in touch with issues of cosmic import. . . . I feel enriched, ennobled and humbled by the encounter" (65).

From the ability perspective, spiritual or existential intelligence is being sensitive to spiritual issues. Presumably people are normally distributed on this ability so that people may score from very low to very high ability. The intriguing question of course is where that intelligence comes from: that is, its genetic/biological versus environmental determinants. Equally interesting is the attitudinal, cognitive, and behavioral correlates of spiritual intelligence. Are people with more spiritual intelligence happier at work, more money conscious, more stressed by work adversity? These remain important empirical questions for those who conceive of spirituality in this way.

WORK SPIRITUALITY

A cursory "surfing of the Web" indicates a proliferation of Web sites, newsletters, and conferences all on the topic. However, it is very apparent that the concept has multiple meanings. These include: Acting with honesty and integrity in all aspects of work; treating employees, suppliers, shareholders, and customers in a responsible, caring way; having social, environmental, and ecological responsibility by serving the "wider social community"; holding religious study groups and/or prayer/meditation meetings at work; and being able to discuss values without the dogmatism and overstructuring of organized religion.

Certainly there is a range of values that seems to fall under the umbrella of spirituality: accountability, caring, cooperativeness, honesty, integrity, justice, respect, service, and trustworthiness. Spirituality is a means, not an end. It encourages questions like: Are our business decisions based exclusively on profit? Are employees required to sacrifice private/family time to be successful? Are we self-centered and forgetting the principles of service to others in the wider community? But also, do employees get a sense of wonder at work? Do they have a sense of community?

Another theme rediscovered within the rubric of workplace spirituality is the concept of vocation: to work consciously and to celebrate all aspects of work's purpose. Indeed the word *vocation* has always had both secular and spiritual significance: it can mean both a divine call to religious life and also the work in which a person is regularly employed. It implies that the fit is right between person and organization, that they suit each other in terms of preferences, values, and lifestyles.

Sceptics and cynics of the workplace spirituality concept have such concerns as the imposition of religious concepts or ethics of a particular religious group on everyone. Others are concerned by the superficiality and trivialization of religious and spiritual belief. Some are worried about cost, time wasting, and the potential harassment of the "nonspiritual." It has been suggested that the movement is in fact led by the baby-boomer generation who is now postmaterialist and much more aware of its mortality. But it does seem to have "struck a nerve." Further there has been considerable multidisciplinary academic interest, and this book is testament to that.

A focus on workplace spirituality makes the workplace somewhere to express and fulfill one's deeper purpose. Work is an integral part of life and one does not disengage heart or brain at the factory door or office. People bring to work their attitudes, beliefs, and values about both material and spiritual affairs. Even within more formal religious beliefs, historically there has not been a clear distinction between work and nonwork. One does not suspend faith and values on entering the workplace. Personal ethics and values are relevant in nearly all aspects of work: from the very choice of vocation itself to the treatment of colleagues and customers.

MONEY AND HAPPINESS

Does happiness come with being financially well-off? When asked what would improve the quality of our lives, for most people the first answer would be "More money." Yet researchers in the area have showed only a modest correlation between income and happiness. Money and happiness is akin to the issue of materialism and spirituality. Can material goods (e.g., art) increase spiritual experiences? If so, when and how? To many people these are either antithetical or unrelated concepts. There is, however, a relatively recent and often counterintuitive literature on the relationship between money and happiness.

The central issue for researchers is whether increasing personal and national wealth lead to increasing happiness and contentment. Longitudinal data collected over seventy years in the West shows first a linear rise in personal income (such that it doubles every thirty years) but second a flat, horizontal line for self-reported happiness/well-being suggests little or no difference over time (Myers 1992). The results seem to suggest that, at least after a certain point, there is no relationship between personal wealth and happiness.

However, aggregated data such as this may easily obscure important differences between individuals, between organizations, and between countries. At the individual difference level there is considerably accumulating evidence that happiness is related to stable, biologically based personality traits (extraversion and stability). This suggests that happiness is stable over the lifetime in part because people with particular personality profiles seek out and change situations to fit their personality. A more intriguing and salient question is whether there are similar links between personality and spirituality; are certain people more prone to spirituality and others not? This raises the interesting possibility of personality as an intervening or moderating variable. Is it possible that personality is related both to spirituality and happiness and that the observed relationship between the two is simply epiphenomenal? Also it is possible that people with particular "spirituality-prone" profiles seek out particular work settings (while avoiding others) with other like-minded people and experience strong spirituality there.

Personality and differential psychologists emphasize the important role of traits as causal factors. However organizational and work psychologists are equally happy to focus on work group, company, and organizational differences as possible causes of different levels of both (or either) happiness and spirituality. Organizations differ widely in structure, process, and product as well as culture, mission, and vision. Over the last twenty years organizations were encouraged to focus on the philosophic nature of their business and consider their vision and mission. In many instances these were expressed in almost spiritual terminology. While certain cynics saw these as little more than "advertorials" for the business (Anderson 2000), others saw these as expressing the beliefs and values of many who worked in the business. Further, they had the effect of attracting particular people to the business. For many they came to be seen as an acknowledgment of at least the nonmaterial nature of the business.

Certainly those interested in corporate culture have noted dramatic differences between organizations in what they do, believe, and value (Furnham and Gunter 1993). Because corporate culture is an implicit but powerful force, it can have an effect on the manifestations or suppression of spirituality in the workplace. Some organizations seem happy to acknowledge the spiritual dimension to life while others find it faintly embarrassing.

At the third level—namely cultural/national—there are also interesting differences. Some cultures seem more spiritual than others, though, of course, the spirituality is manifested quite differently. History, geography, language, and religion as well as economic development all have a part to play in the quality and quantity of spirituality in a culture. Countries differ most obviously in their wealth, which has been linked to a national feeling of well-being. However it is never clear in cross-cultural correlational studies whether wealth leads to happiness, vice versa, or the relationship (or lack of it) is moderated by a third variable.

In a review, Diener (1984) summarizes the data thus: "There is an overwhelming amount of evidence that shows a positive relationship between income and SWB (subjective well-being) within countries. . . . This relationship exists even when other variables such as education are controlled. . . . Although the effect of income is often small when other factors are controlled, these other factors may be ones through which income could produce its effects . . ." (571).

There are also consistent national differences in happiness. Inglehart (1990) reported an extensive study with representative samples of 170,000 people in sixteen nations. Results indicated that first, there are genuine national differences. For example, the Danes, Swiss, Irish, and Dutch feel happier and more satisfied with life than do French, Greeks, Italians, and West Germans. Second, the nations' well-being differences correlate modestly with national affluence, but the link between national affluence and well-being is not consistent. In fact there is no clear statistical relationship or trend. For instance, for the French, the average income was almost doubled the Irish, but the Irish were happier.

However, there is more than one fact that makes the nations differ in self-reported happiness. For instance, the most prosperous nations have enjoyed stable democratic governments, and there is a strong link between a history of democracy and national well-being. Moreover, countries that have both democracy and a free press also tend to have happier people. Further, the freedom in choosing type of jobs, the workplace, and one's own lifestyle, which are associated with democracy, may also be the contributors of individual SWB.

From another point of view, within any country are the richest the happiest? Some surveys have shown that here again, there is a modest link between SWB and being financially well-off.

Those who live in affluent countries yet have low incomes, clearly live with less joy and more stress than do those who live with the comfort and security of higher incomes (Easterlin 1995).

In a cross-cultural study, Diener and Suh (1999) surveyed forty-one nations and found that there are substantial differences between nations in reported SBW. People in wealthier nations tend to report greater SWB than people in poor nations. However the causal factors relating wealth to well-being are not yet understood. The wealth of nations strongly correlates with human rights, equality between people, the fulfillment of basic biological needs, and individualism. Another variable that also correlated with higher SWB in nations is political stability and a related variable, interpersonal trust. Unfortunately, because of the high intercorrelations of predictor variables and the relatively small sample sizes of nations, the various potential national factors that cause SWB could not be disentangled. For example, Diener, Diener, and Diener (1995) reported that income correlated with human rights and with the equality within nations .80 and .84, respectively. Besides, individualism is a cultural variable that correlates across nations with both higher reported SWB and higher suicide rates. With sample sizes of nations that rarely exceed forty in number, the effects of such overlapping variables cannot be statistically disentangled and larger samples and longitudinal designs are needed to ascertain the causal influence on SWB of the variables that tend to occur together with the national affluence.

In a longitudinal study, intended to test the most fundamental idea in economics that money makes people happy, Gardner and Oswald (2001) examined approximately 9,000 randomly chosen people. Results showed that those in the panel who receive windfalls (by winning lottery money or receiving an inheritance) have higher mental well-being in the following year. Specifically, a windfall of £50,000 ($75,000) is associated with a rise in well-being of between 0.1 and 0.3 standard deviations.

In another study, Kasser and Sheldon (2000) examined the connection between feelings of insecurity and materialistic behavior by experimentally inducing feelings of insecurity. Results showed that participants exposed to death (by writing short essays about death) became greedier and consumed more resources in a forest-management game. They conclude, ". . . people's tendencies toward materialism and consumption stem in part from a source unlikely to disappear: the fear of death. It remains to be seen whether psychological research can discover effective ways of helping people find more adaptive and beneficial means of coping with their insecurities. . ." (351).

In a review of family and economic well-being, White and Rogers (2000) found that women showed stronger income growth than men in the decade, and two-earner households became increasingly associated with advantage. In particular, they reviewed four dimensions of family outcomes: family formation, divorce, marital quality, and child well-being. The review supports the expectation that both men's and women's economic advantage is associated with more marriage, less divorce, more marital happiness, and greater child well-being.

But having more than enough provides little additional boost to SWB. One plausible reason is that low income is a strong predictor of negative affect but not positive affect. Since positive and negative affect, contrary to common belief, are found to be fairly independent (Bradburn 1969), the scales designed to measure happiness or SWB (normally contain positive affect but not negative affect) do not readily detect the causes (predictors) of negative affect, thus fail to obtain substantial associations between income and SWB. However, as the best predictor of happiness or SWB is the balance of positive and negative affect as Bradburn and many other researchers have indicated, both the causes of positive and negative affect should be examined before a conclusion as to what are the causes of full human functioning can be drawn.

Theoretically speaking, it might be true that human needs can be arranged on different levels, like the famous hierarchy formulated by the founder of humanistic psychology, Abraham Maslow

(1954). It states that human beings have a set of different kinds of needs, which starts at the biological level such as food, water, and air followed by security needs such as shelter, clothes, and basic belongings; next is the love needs (family, children); then the esteem needs (self-esteem and the esteem from others); and finally the highest needs: the needs for self-actualization (self-fulfilling, develop one's potential, etc.). Once the lower level of needs is gratified, a higher one would become more urgent. From this point of view, it is likely that the lower levels of needs such as the biological and security needs are mainly associated with negative affect and mental illness, and the deprivation of these needs would lead to the presence of negative affect and mental distress; whereas the higher levels of needs such as self-actualization and esteem needs are more strongly associated with positive affect and mental health such as happiness or SWB, and satisfying these needs would lead to the presence of positive affect and psychological well-being. No doubt the deprivation of biological needs would cause the extinction of the life of any living being, and the lack of the security needs, such as low income, would lead to various psychological as well as physical dysfunction such as stress-related illness and emotional disorder, which is in line with the previous findings. On the other hand, various studies have shown that self-esteem is one of the most powerful predictors of happiness and SWB. Moreover, the well-established happiness measure, the Oxford Happiness Inventory (Argyle, Martin, and Crossland 1989), which has psychometrically sound properties, contains one principal factor, named satisfaction from achievement (Furnham and Brewin 1990).

The strongest predictors of happiness are found to be personality traits such as stability and extraversion (e.g., Argyle and Lu 1990; Brebner, Donaldson, Kirby, and Ward 1995; Francis 1999; Furnham and Brewin 1990; Furnham and Cheng 1999), agreeableness (Furnham and Cheng 1997), and high self-esteem (Campbell 1981; Campbell, Converse, and Rodgers 1976; Furnham and Cheng 2000; Rosenberg 1965), which account for more than two-thirds of the variance of psychological well-being and mental health.

However, there is much evidence for the moderate association between wealth and happiness (Brickman, Coates, and Janoff-Bulman 1978; Csikszentmihalyi 1999; Eysenck 1990). There are many sound theoretical reasons why this may be so (Furnham and Argyle 1998): these include adaptation level theory (one soon adapts to wealth at any level), social comparison theory (one's comparison group changes, so that one never feels rich), and the marginal declining utility of money. Yet the idea that money brings happiness remains pervasive.

Those interested in spirituality at work are not necessarily antimaterialists (or anticapitalists). However, many would not be surprised by the psychological data that finds no relationship between income and happiness. For many, they already know that it is nonmaterial things like social support, empathy, and integrity at home and work that lead to real and continuing happiness.

It could be that how people actually perceive their money is important to individual happiness. Thus, there may be a spiritual-material dimension with the former or sacred-profane. For the economist money is almost profane: it is not treated irreverently or disregarded but it is commonplace and not special. It has no spiritual significance. However, money can be sacred—it is feared, revered, and worshiped. Belk and Wallendorf (1990) point out that it is the myth, mystery, and ritual associated with the acquisition and use of money that defines its sacredness and spirituality.

For all religions, certain persons, places, things, times, and social groups are collectively defined as sacred and spiritual. Sacred things are extraordinary, totally unique, set apart from, and opposed to, the profane world. Sacred objects and people can have powers of good or evil. "Gifts, vacation travel, souvenirs, family photographs, pets, collections, heirlooms, homes, art, antiques and objects associated with famous people can be regarded as existing in the realm of the sacred by many people" (Belk and Wallendorf 1990, 39). They are safeguarded and considered special and of spiritual value. Art and other collections become for many people sacred personal icons. Equally, heirlooms serve as mystical and fragile connections to those who are deceased. They can have more than "sentimental value" and some believe that a neglected or damaged heirloom could unleash bad luck or evil forces.

Unlike sacred objects, profane objects are interchangeable. They are valued primarily for their mundane use value. Sacred objects often lack functional use and cannot, through exchange, be converted into profane objects. Further, exchange of sacred objects for money violates their sacred status, because it brings them into inappropriate contact with the profane realm.

Money can be too sterile and ordinary to be used on special occasions. In Western societies money cannot buy brides, expiation from crimes, or (ideally) political offices. The Judeo-Christian ethic is paradoxical on money. People with money acquired honestly may be seen as superior, even virtuous, and removing the desire to accumulate money is condemned. Believers are called on to be altruistic, ascetic, and selfless, while simultaneously being hard-working, acquisitional, and, frankly, capitalistic. The sacred and profane can get easily mixed up (Furnham 1995).

Belk and Wallendorf (1990) also believed that the sacred meaning of money is gender and class linked. They argue that women think of money in terms of the things into which it can be converted, while men think of it in terms of the power its possession implies. The money women deal with is profane (unless used for personal pleasure, in which case it is evil), while some of the use of money by men is sacred. Similarly, in working-class homes men traditionally gave over their wages to their wife for the management of profane household needs with a small allowance given back for individual personal pleasures, most of which were far from sacred. Yet in a middle-class house, men typically gave, and indeed sometimes still give, their wife an allowance (being a small part of their income) for collective household expenditure.

Money (an income) obtained from work that is not a source of intrinsic delight is ultimately profane, but an income derived from one's passion can be sacred. An artist can do commercial work for profane money and the work of the soul for sacred money. From ancient Greece to twentieth-century Europe, the business of making money is tainted. It is the activity of the nouveau riche, not honorable "old money." Thus, volunteer work is sacred, while the identical job that is paid is profane. The idea of paying somebody to be a mother or home-keeper may be preposterous for some because it renders the sacred duty profane. But the acts of prostitutes transform a sacred act into a formal business exchange. Some crafts people and artists do sell their services but at a "modest," almost not going-rate, price because their aim is not to accumulate wealth but to make a reasonable income and not become burdened by their work.

Belk (1991) considered the sacred uses of money. A sacred use—for example, a gift—can be "desacralized" if a person is too concerned with price. Sacralizing mechanisms usually involve the purchase of gifts and souvenirs, donations to charity, as well as the purchase of a previously sacralized object. The aim is to transform money into objects with special significance or meaning. Money-as-sacrifice and money-as-gift are clearly more sacred than money-as-commodity. Charity giving is a sacred gift only when it involves personal sacrifice and not when there is personal gain through publicity or tax relief. Money used to redeem and restore special objects (e.g., rare works of art, religious objects) also renders it sacred.

Thus, to retain all money for personal use is considered antisocial, selfish, miserly, and evil. To transform sacred money (a gift) into profane money (by selling it) is considered especially evil. Many people refuse to turn certain objects into money, preferring to give them away. Money violates the sacredness of objects and commodifies them. Equally, people refuse money when offered by those who have been voluntarily helped. The "good Samaritans" thereby assign their assistance to the area of the gift rather than a profane exchange. Thus, a gift of help may be reciprocated by another gift.

The argument is thus: the dominant view of money concentrates on its profane meaning. It is a utilitarian view that sees money transactions as impersonal and devoid of sacred money. But it becomes clear when considering the illogical behavior of collectors, gift-givers, and charity donors that money can and does have sacred meanings, both good and evil. Further, it is these sacred meanings that so powerfully influence our attitudes to money.

ETHICS AT WORK

The idea that religious/spiritual values may be important at work goes back a long way. Perhaps the most well known theory of the effect of spirituality at work is referred to as the Protestant Work Ethic (Furnham 1995). It embodied the idea that work is not merely an economic activity but a spiritual end in, and of, itself.

The Protestant Ethic and the Spirit of Capitalism was published, in German, nearly 100 years ago by Max Weber as a two-part article in the 1904–1905 issue of the journal *Archive für Sozialwissenschaft und Sozialpolitik.* Some fifteen years later it was revised and published as a single volume with rebuttals to criticism of the earlier work. It was the revised edition that was first translated into English by Talcott Parson in 1930.

For Weber the central problem was explaining the fact that people pursue wealth and material gain (the achievement of profit) for its own sake, not because of necessity. The aim of obtaining, accumulating, and storing money/capital is an end in itself, not a means to an end. Weber located the answer to this problem in Puritan asceticism and spirituality and the concept of calling for the individual to fulfill his or her duty in this (rather than the other) world. Weber maintained that Puritans felt obliged to be regarded as chosen by God to perform good works. Success in a calling (occupational rewards) thus came to be seen as a sign of being the elect. Puritans thus sought to achieve salvation through economic activity.

There were four elements in Weber's scheme:

1. "The Doctrine of Calling," according to which the believer is called by God to work for His glory, and hence work itself was virtuous and had to be excellently and honestly done. However, this aspect is least central to Weber's argument and serves merely as an introduction to the PWE concept itself.
2. A second theme was "The Doctrine of Predestination," which suggested that signs of God's grace, such as occupational success, could be seen in this life, and hence successful people could see themselves as among the elect. Because one has only limited time to grasp God and make sure of one's election by attaining that quiet self-confidence of salvation that is the fruit of true faith and of proving one's regeneration in the conduct of one's daily life, then every moment spent in idleness, leisure, gambling, or hedonism is worthy of moral condemnation and is a sign of imperfect grace.
3. Strong asceticism is another crucial cornerstone of the theory that stressed saving, investment, the systematic use of the amassing of capital and the reduction of expenditure on vices and luxuries.
4. Finally, "The Doctrine of Sanctification," which, by rejecting the mystical sacramental system of Catholicism, stressed rational control over all aspects of life. Rationalization was a common theme in Weber's work, and he argued that in Calvinism each individual had to make his or her own moral decisions and that all actions had to be considered in terms of their ethical consequences.

Weber explained the origin of capitalism by arguing that the acquisitive motive was transformed from personal eccentricity into a moral order, which destroyed reliance on traditional forms of economic satisfaction and replaced it with the rational calculus of returns coming from the investment of given amounts of capital and labor.

Hampden-Turner (1981) has attempted to summarize and contrast PWE beliefs and what he calls Anglo-Catholic organicism (see Table 17.1). Relying heavily on the work of Koestler, among others, Hampden-Turner (1981) argued that PWE beliefs have informed scientific epistemology. He notes: "It is my contention that modern doctrines of scientism and behaviorism, so far from having escaped from religion, 'superstition,' and a priori beliefs, are steeped in Calvanistic ideology, having borrowed even its most objectionable characteristic, a devastating lack of self-awareness" (36).

There are relatively few clear statements on the actual constituents of the PWE. Innumerable writers have tried to define or elucidate the components of the PWE. Oates (1971) noted:

> The so-called Protestant Work Ethic can be summarized as follows: a universal taboo is placed on idleness, and industriousness is considered a religious ideal; waste is a vice, and frugality a virtue; complacency and failure are outlawed, and ambition and success are taken as sure signs of God's favour; the universal sign of sin is poverty, and the crowning sign of God's favour is wealth. (84)

Cherrington (1980) listed eight attributes of the PWE. The broader meaning of the work ethic typically refers to one or more of the following beliefs:

1. People have a normal and religious obligation to fill their lives with heavy physical toil. For some, this means that hard work, effort, and drudgery are to be valued for their own sake; physical pleasures and enjoyments are to be shunned; and an ascetic existence of methodical rigor is the only acceptable way to live.
2. Men and women are expected to spend long hours at work, with little or no time for personal recreation and leisure.
3. A worker should have a dependable attendance record, with low absenteeism and tardiness.
4. Workers should be highly productive and produce a large quantity of goods or service.
5. Workers should take pride in their work and do their jobs well.
6. Employees should have feelings of commitment and loyalty to their profession, their company, and their work group.
7. Workers should be achievement-orientated and constantly strive for promotions and advancement. High-status jobs with prestige and the respect of others are important indicators of a "good" person.
8. People should acquire wealth through honest labor and retain it through thrift and wise investments. Frugality is desirable; extravagance and waste should be avoided. (20)

Ditz (1980), in an interesting essay on the PWE and the market economy, has described the PWE idea of profit making as a calling, "the sacramentalization of acquisition." He explains in lay economic terms how the PWE beliefs and spirituality affected the market economy (what Marx called capitalism) over the last few hundred years. Ditz (1980) believed that various features

Table 17.1

Anglo-Catholic Organicism Versus the Protestant Work Ethic

Anglo-Catholic organicism

The person is part of an organic hierarchy, a great chain of being, rooted in kinship, feudal loyalties, neighborhood, animals, and land.

Communal mediated relationships

Salvation is in communal faith, with access to God mediated by kings, bishops, judges, and lords.

Intercessionist God

God is ever-present, interceding in human affairs in miraculous and supernatural ways.

Salvation through communion

Man is saved less by his own efforts than by faith and partaking of the passion, mercy, forgiveness, and indulgence of the crucified God in the family of believers.

God experienced with many senses

God is experienced as mystery in many dimensions, inritual, community, sacrament, awe, asceticism, and participation, by way of Mary and the saints.

Other worldliness

In this vale of tears the greatest respect belongs to those who prepare us for the world to come.

Human personality cultivated

Virtue is personified by self-cultivation, courtliness, wit, charm, and the flamboyant manners of the cavalier.

Puritan atomistic individualism:

The person is alone, a saintly outcast from corrupt feudalism but can enter holy leagues or covenants with other upright persons.

Private direct relationships

Salvation is a private matter between God and His agents on earth, who have direct access to His will.

Delegating God

God is distant and delegates His power to chosen human instruments and the laws of nature.

Salvation through work

God is the taskmaster to His earthly agents, a state of grace they can demonstrate but not alter. Interpersonal emotions are indulgences of a corrupt order.

The Word read, heard, enacted

God gives ambiguous instructions to man's reason by way of His objective words. Mystery, magic, and speculation are vain, when compared with active obedience.

This worldliness

God's kingdom will be founded in this world by the saints doing the work to which God calls them.

Personality submerged in work

Virtue is achieved by self-effacement, and becoming the mere agent of God's objective order (e.g., the Roundhead).

would inevitably lead to a decline in the PWE. These included: the waning of religious faith and with it the moral justifications for the market economy; the fact that excessive individualism loosened kinship and ethnic community ties, so leading to a weakening of the overall social structure; the emergence of unionism, monopolies, and other anti-PWE ethics; hedonism replacing asceticism; institutional minimal risk taking replacing individual risk taking; indifference and disrespect for rationality and the "calculating" professions; desacramentalization of property, erosion of property rights, and indifference to crimes of property; taxation and inflation causing a waning of consumer sovereignty; an increase in egalitarianism that inhibits innovation, entrepreneurship, and risk taking.

Debate about the work ethic has continued for a century. The spiritual values of the Puritans, the Protestants, and others have been examined in detail. Indeed it probably represents the best study of spirituality at work.

ALTERNATIVE ETHICS

Scholars, in their attempt to define and delineate the work ethic have suggested the existence of many other ethics, some of which coexisted with the work ethic (Furnham 1995). Maccoby and Terzi (1981) found that the term *PWE* was being used very loosely and actually contained few overlapping ethics including the *Puritan ethic* supporting a highly individualistic character, oriented to self-discipline, saving, and deferred rewards and antagonistic to sensuous culture; the *craft ethic* emphasizing pride in work, self-reliance, independence, modernization, mobility, and thrift; the *entrepreneurial ethic*, which emphasized merchandising not manufacture, the organization and control of craftsmen, growth, and zeal to succeed; and the *career ethic* that emphasizes meritocracy, talent, and hard work within organizations leading to success and promotion.

There are alternatives to the work ethic, each with its own distinctive values and type of emphasis on spirituality. These alternatives have been espoused by different groups at different times, often in reaction to other dominant ethics. The following are briefly described and an attempt is made to be comprehensive, at least from a Western perspective.

We shall consider seven work-related ethics that are all forms of ethics. They have very different ideas about the part of work, money, and spirituality in the workplace.

The Wealth Ethic

Kelvin and Jarrett (1985) dismiss the PWE thesis as a wholly false account of the past (in fact a myth) whose function is more to inspire the present than explain the past. They are adamant that the PWE is an explanatory concept of our time, invented to explain the past. But Kelvin and Jarrett (1985) are not content to dismiss the PWE as a historically incorrect self-fulfilling prophecy. They suggest that what has been incorrectly historically perceived as the work ethic was in fact the wealth ethic.

> When one looks at the situation from the very historical perspective that ostensibly gave rise to it, explanations in terms of the Protestant Ethic emerge as little more than an invention of twentieth-century social science, with unwarranted pretensions to an ancient lineage. The "ethic" which has truly been predominant and pervasive is not a work ethic but, for want of a better term, a wealth ethic. Wealth is (quite correctly) perceived as the basis of economic independence: that is the key issue, and has been so for centuries. The "ethic" is to make or to have sufficient wealth not to have to depend on others; work is only one means to that end, and certainly not the only one universally most esteemed: not in any class. Provided that one has money enough to be independent, there is no great moral obligation to work, certainly not in the sense of gainful, productive employment. (Kelvin and Jarrett 1985, 104)

Work is normative and not an ethic and that moral significance does not attach to work, but to not living off others. In other words, not only are Kelvin and Jarrett (1985) disputing the historical, or indeed current, existence of the PWE, they believe that the essence of the PWE is the accumulation of wealth in order to ensure independence and, to a lesser extent, freedom and leisure. Work is only one, and presumably a moderately unpleasant or at least effortful, way of accumulating wealth.

For Kelvin and Jarrett (1985) all people gain numerous satisfactions from work, as well as money and things that money enables them to have and to do. The wealth ethic adherent then condemns the unemployed not for being idle, but for being poor. Spirituality that derives from this perspective is aimed at acquiring wealth honestly because of its obvious and manifest benefits.

The Welfare Ethic

Furnham and Rose (1987) have argued that the rise of the welfare state, particularly in Western Europe, has seen the emergence of what may be called the welfare ethic. This belief system is based on the idea of a cunning claimant of welfare, who believes that because welfare is so easy to obtain (and to some extent one's right), one should enjoy the good life (without work) by living off payments received from the welfare system. People who do this have become known somewhat pejoratively as "super-scroungers." The "laxness, excessive generosity, inefficiency and vulnerability to exploitation of the welfare system" (Golding and Middleton 1983, 109) makes it open to less-than-honest people. There has been quite a lot of research on attitudes toward social security claimants (Furnham 1985) that, in fact, suggests that many people not on welfare payments believe those who are, are both idle and dishonest. Although there is considerable research to show that this view is misplaced, there is anecdotal evidence of people who thrive on welfare and exploit the welfare ethic.

However, Taylor-Gooby (1983) has pointed out that whereas people are in favor of some aspects of welfare they are against others. More importantly perhaps, Taylor-Gooby (1983) found evidence for various values associated with welfare payments. These include a reduction in self-help; a more integrated, caring society; an increased tax burden; a reduction in the work ethic; and a reduction in the family ethic. Still, spirituality associated with the welfare ethic often stresses interdependence and the necessity of mutual support.

The Leisure Ethic

Many writers have talked about the new leisure ethic that states that "to leisure" is by far the greatest virtue, namely to develop one's potential in discretionary time. Although it is not entirely clear what this new ethic stands for, some empirical work has to be done in this field. Thus Buchholz (1976) attempted to measure what he termed the leisure ethic, which regards work as a means to personal fulfillment through primarily its provision of the means to pursue leisure activities. According to Buchholz (1976), the leisure ethic is defined thus:

> Work has no meaning in itself, but only finds meaning in leisure. Jobs cannot be made meaningful or fulfilling, but work is a human necessity to produce goods and services and enable one to earn the money to buy them. Human fulfillment is found in leisure activities where one has a choice regarding the use of his time, and can find pleasure in pursuing activities of interest to him personally. This is where a person can be creative and involved.

Thus the less hours [time] one can spend working and the more leisure time one has available, the better. (1180)

Studies using the leisure ethic have found it to be related to occupational status (high status people endorse it less than low status), age (leisure ethic beliefs decline with age), and nationality (Americans endorse it more than Scots [Dickson and Buchholz 1977]). The leisure ethic has also been shown to be significantly negatively correlated with general conservative beliefs, the PWE, and measures of job involvement (Furnham 1984a). The leisure ethic may be seen as the positive opposite of the work ethic. People who do not endorse the PWE may or may not endorse the leisure ethic, but it is unlikely that people endorse both the PWE and the leisure ethic. The leisure ethic spirituality emphasizes that it is through leisure rather than work that one recreates, refreshes, and renews oneself. Thus, the more work approaches the idea of leisure, the better.

The Sports Ethic

Ritzer, Kammeyer, and Yelman (1982) have implied that the norms that govern sport are not dissimilar from those of the PWE. Sport is thought of in many countries as an important and healthy socialization experience for young people, and it is assumed that they learn many important lessons.

Sporting norms have "become a conservative force functioning to maintain and reinforce certain of the traditional American values, beliefs and practices while countering others" (Ritzer et al. 1982, 18). These include sportsmanship, competition, success, universalism (open to all and evaluated according to performance), diligence, self-discipline, and teamwork.

However, as it is quite apparent, some of these values are in conflict. Individualism conflicts with teamwork, self-discipline with accepting orders. Nevertheless, the outward portrayal of the sporting ethic, which may be seen in lockers and slogans, in postsuccess sporting speeches, and in sports commentators, is remarkably similar to that of the PWE. No doubt the above are largely the values espoused by sports-oriented organizations.

Some sports stress more of a spiritual component than others. Thus, some sports like mountaineering and orienteering find the former panentheism in nature. Fast, highly competitive sports like squash have little spiritual component though nearly all team sports put strong emphasis on team spirit and cooperation that is often expressed in spiritual terms.

The Narcissistic Ethic

Many commentators on contemporary culture have attempted to discern trends and patterns that trace the waxing and waning of movements, ethics, or cults. Lasch (1985) argued that the dominant current American culture of competitive individualism has changed into the pursuit of happiness and a narcissistic preoccupation with self.

Lasch (1985) argued that PWE values no longer excite enthusiasm or command respect for a variety of reasons: inflation erodes investments/savings; the society is now fearfully, rather than confidently, future-oriented; self-preservation has become self-improvement; moral codes have changed. But this change has been graduated over the centuries. The Puritan gave way to the Yankee, who secularized the PWE and stressed self-improvement (instead of socially useful work) that consisted of the cultivation of reason, wisdom, and insight as well as money. Wealth was valued because it allowed for a program of self-improvement and was one of the necessary preconditions of moral and intellectual advancement. The nineteenth century saw the rise of the "cult of compulsive industry" that was obsessed with the "art of money-getting," as all values would be expressed or operationalized in money terms. Further, there became more emphasis on competition.

The spirit and spirituality of self-improvement, according to Lasch (1985), was debased into self-culture—the care and training of the mind and body through reading great books and healthy living. Self-help books taught self-confidence, initiative, and other qualities of success. "The management of interpersonal relations came to be seen as the essence of self advancement. . . . Young men were told that they had to sell themselves in order to succeed" (58). The new prophets of positive thinking discarded the moral overtones of Protestantism that were attached to the pursuit of wealth, save that it contributed to the total human good. The pursuit of economic success now accepted the need to exploit and intimidate others and to ostentatiously show the winning image of success.

The new ethic meant that people preferred admiration, envy, and the excitement of celebration, to being respected and esteemed. People were less interested in how people acquired success—defined by riches, fame, and power—than in that they had "made it." Success had to be ratified and verified by publicity. The quest for a good public image leads to a confusion of successful completion of the task with rhetoric that is aimed to impress or persuade others. Thus impressions overshadow achievements and the images and symbols of success are more important than the actual achievements.

For Lasch (1985) the cult or ethic of narcissism has a number of quite distinct features:

- The waning of the sense of historical time. The idea that things are coming to an end means that people have a very limited time perspective, neither confidently forward nor romantically backward. The narcissist lives only in, and for, the present.
- The therapeutic sensibility. Narcissists seek therapy for personal well-being, health and psychic security. The rise in the human potential movement and the decline in self-help tradition has made people dependent on experts and organizations to validate self-esteem and develop competence. Therapists are used excessively to help develop composure, meaning, and health.
- From politics to self-examination. Political theories, issues, and conflicts have been trivialized. The debate has moved from the veridical nature of political propositions to the personal and autobiographical factors that lead proponents to make such suppositions.
- Confession and anti-confession. Writers and others attempt single self-disclosure, rather than critical reflection, to gain insight into the psycho-historical forces that lead to personal development. But these confessions are paradoxical and do not lead to greater, but lesser, insights into the inner life. People disclose not to provide an objective account of reality, but to seduce others to give attention, acclaim, or sympathy and, by doing so, foster the perpetual, faltering sense of self.
- The void within. Without psychological peace, meaning, or commitment, people experience an inner emptiness that they try to avoid by living vicariously through the lives of others, or seeking spiritual masters.
- The progressive critique of privatism. Self-absorption, which dreams of fame, avoidance of failure, and quests for spiritual panacea means that people define social problems as personal ones. The cult suggests a limited investment in life and friendship, avoidance of dependence, and living for the moment.

In fact it could be argued that current interest in spirituality is a direct reaction to the self-obsessed, narcissistic ethic.

The Romantic Ethic

Campbell (1987) proposed that a cultural, anti-Puritan force—the romantic ethic—was responsible for the rise of the modern consumer ethic. He attempted to identify an autonomous, imaginative, pleasure-seeking force—the romantic ethic—which created and justified consumer hedonism at the onset of the Industrial Revolution. He argued that one should distinguish between traditional and modern hedonism—the former concerned with sensory experience and discrete, standardized pleasures while the latter is envisaged as a potential quality in all experience.

Campbell (1987) attempted to explain the high growth of consumerism in the middle classes, supposedly ascetic, puritanical bearers of the PWE. He argued that, after the seventeenth century, Calvinist Christianity changed to allow emotional sentimentalism. Concern with aesthetics was inherited from the aristocratic ethic, and taste became a sign of moral and spiritual worth. Taste allowed people to take genuine pleasure in the beautiful and respond with tears to the pitiable. In this romantic movement pleasure becomes the crucial means of recognizing that ideal truth and beauty that imagination reveals and that become the means by which art encourages moral enlightenment. The romantics assured that people could be morally improved through the provision of cultural products that yielded pleasure and that helped people dream about a more perfect world.

It is also suggested that both individuals and society have a compatible "purito"-romantic personality system when the values of puritan-utilitarianism and romantic sentimentalism occur compatibly, but are conveniently compartmentalized in time and space, allowing both to exist. He quotes evidence as wide-ranging as Victorian sentimentalism and utilitarianism, as well as lifestyle of the bourgeois individual that passes from youthful romanticism to adult bureaucracy. It is further suggested that Puritanism is primarily socialized into males and romanticism into females; hence the stress on science for males, arts for females.

The Being Ethic

Many religious and philosophic systems have distinguished between two strong opposing beliefs or "ways of existence." First there is the having model of modern industrialist societies, which concentrates on material possession and power. The second is the being model of many postmodern groups, which puts greater stress on shared experience and the affirmation of living. There are many ways to contrast these two approaches: acquisitiveness versus existence, pleasure versus joy.

Fromm (1980) argued persuasively for the being model. This may be best illustrated in his description of "the new man," which is in a sense a blueprint for the being model. This model is summarized in Table 17.2.

Though he recognized the theme in many other Western and Eastern writers, Fromm (1980) has exposed this new ethic of being. The argument is predicated on the assumption that the materialistic way of having has failed. Economic and technical progress that at any rate has remained restricted to richer nations is not conducive to well-being. This ethic is based on two erroneous principles: that the aim of life is to maximize pleasure and happiness; and that egoism, selfishness, and greed lead to harmony and peace. Though rather crudely stated, these two assumptions of the way of having are thought to have the seeds of destruction within them.

Thus one needs a new ethic—that of being. Whereas the having mode is characterized by possessing and owning, for which the dictum is I am equal to what I have and what I consume, the being mode is characterized not by greed, envy, and aggressiveness but love, joy, and ascendancy

Table 17.2

The New Man and the Philosophy of Being According to Fromm

1. Willingness to give up all forms of having, in order to fully be.

2. Security, sense of identity, and confidence based on faith in what one is, on one's need for relatedness, interest, love, solidarity with the world around one, instead of on one's desire to have, to possess, to control the world, and thus become the slave of one's possessions.

3. Acceptance of the fact that nobody and nothing outside oneself give meaning to life, but that this radical independence and no-thingness can become the condition for the fullest activity devoted to caring and sharing.

4. Being fully present where one is.

5. Joy that comes from giving and sharing, not from hoarding and exploiting.

6. Love and respect for life in all its manifestations, in the knowledge that not things, power, all that is dead, but life and everything that pertains to its growth are sacred.

7. Trying to reduce greed, hate, and illusions as much as one is capable.

8. Living without worshipping idols and without illusions, because one has reached a state that does not require illusions.

9. Developing one's capacity for love, together with one's capacity for critical, unsentimental thought.

10. Shedding one's narcissism and accepting the tragic limitations inherent in human existence.

11. Making the full growth of oneself and of one's fellow beings the supreme goal of living.

12. Knowing that to reach this goal, discipline and respect for reality are necessary. Knowing also, that no growth is healthy that does not occur in a structure, but knowing, too, the difference between structure as an attribute of life and "order" as an attribute of no-life, of the dead.

13. Developing one's imagination, not as an escape from intolerable circumstances but as the anticipation of real possibilities, as a means to do away with intolerable circumstances.

14. Not deceiving others, but also not being deceived by others; one may be called innocent, not naïve.

15. Knowing oneself, not only the self one knows, but also the self one does not know—even though one has a slumbering knowledge of what one does not know.

16. Sensing one's oneness with all life, hence giving up the aim of conquering nature, subduing it, exploiting it, raping it, destroying it, but trying, rather, to understand and cooperate with nature.

17. Freedom that is not arbitrariness but the possibility to be oneself, not as a bundle of greedy desires, but as a delicately balanced structure that at any moment is confronted with the alternative of growth or decay, life or death.

18. Knowing that evil and destructiveness are necessary consequences of failure to grow.

19. Knowing that only a few have reached perfection in all these qualities, but being without the ambition to "reach the goal," in the knowledge that such ambition is only another form of greed, of having.

20. Happiness, in the process of ever-growing aliveness, whatever the further point is that fate permits one to reach, for living as fully as one can is so satisfactory that the concern for what one might or might not attain has little chance to develop.

Source: Fromm 1980.

over our material values. Perhaps because it is difficult to elucidate the concept of having—which is rejected and described in straw-man terms—it is described in detail and it is for the reader to infer that the opposite is desirable.

Fromm (1980) reports a change in the PWE character described as authoritarian, obsessive, and hoarding, to what he calls a marketing character. This character type is based on experiencing oneself as a commodity and one's value as exchange value.

Success depends largely on how they get their "personality" across, how nice a "package" they are; whether they are "cheerful," "sound," "aggressive," "reliable," "ambitious"; furthermore, what their family background is, what clubs they belong to, and whether they know the "right" people. The type of personality required depends to some degree on the special field in which a person may choose to work. A stockbroker, a salesperson, a secretary, a railroad executive, a college professor, or a hotel manager each offers a much different kind of personality that, regardless of their differences, must fulfill one condition: to be in demand. What shapes one's attitudes toward oneself is the fact that skill and equipment for performing a given task are not sufficient; one must win in competition with many others in order to have success. But since success depends largely on how one sells one's personality, one experiences oneself as a commodity or, rather, simultaneously as the seller and the commodity to be sold. A person is not concerned with his or her life and happiness, but with becoming saleable.

Fromm (1980) goes on to describe the new type, occasionally loosely distinguishing his contempt for it, and indeed its connection with the PWE. This new ethic of being is spelled out in a number of points such as: Security, sense of identity, and confidence based on faith in what one is, in one's need for relatedness, interest, love, solidarity with the world around one instead of one's desire to have, to possess, to control the world, and thus become a slave of one's possessions.

This new ethic of being is in accordance with many other spiritual and religious teachings. It is pantheistic, amaterialist, and humanist. Directly opposed to PWE values on some accounts, it is tangential at others. Certainly there is nothing new in this ethic and it is uncertain how widely it is held.

CONCLUSION

Table 17.3 shows the emphases of the different ethics.

In this chapter it has been suggested that there are many different spiritual beliefs in the workplace. There is, in a sense, nothing new about the idea of workplace spirituality as beliefs about and experiences at work, leisure, and money are all integrated and certainly set out specifically in all of the world's major religions as well as ethical systems. Special attention was paid to the topic of money in the workplace and the curious lack of relationship between money and happiness in aggregated figures. It was suggested that money carries different meanings for different individuals and that if this is taken into consideration, maybe the relationship would become clearer. It was suggested one could distinguish between the spiritual/sacred and materialistic/profane attitude to money, possessions, and work. However, almost no empirical work has been done in this area.

To some extent spirituality stands in contrast to materialism. However, it must be acknowledged that there may be various (superficially) different forms of both spirituality and materialism. To be anti- or amaterialist, however, does not necessarily imply the presence of a spiritual approach. The two phenomena may be unrelated one to another.

In a related vein, the study of business ethics shows that there are contrasting positions to

Table 17.3

Comparing the Eight Ethics and Their Emphasis on Seven Factors

Ethic	Work	Success	Development	Emphasis on Money	Happiness	Spirituality	Competitiveness
Work	+++	+++	+	++			++
Wealth	-	++		+++		+	+++
Welfare	--			+	+		
Leisure	---			++	+		
Sports	++	+++	++		++	+	-
Narcissistic		+++	+++	+	+		+++
Romantic		+	++		+++	++	+
Being	+		+++		+++	++	--

Scale: +++ ++ + strong positive emphasis; - --- strong negative emphasis.

recommendations of how one should behave at work. There is no agreed standard. Indeed if one looks at the work ethic it is clear there are many alternative ethics as proposed and followed by different groups. Some of these ethics are clearly spiritual (e.g., the being ethic) while others are not (e.g., the wealth ethic). Each represents a way of understanding the role of work in one's life and the most appropriate conduct in the workplace. These alternative ethics may be related: thus, there is an overlap between the wealth and narcissistic ethic and between the welfare and leisure ethic, though each is conceptually distinct. Some would see the role of spirituality at work much more clearly than others, particularly whose who endorse the romantic and being ethic.

REFERENCES

Anderson, D. (2000). *Good Companies Don't Have Missions*. London: Social Affairs Unit.

Argyle, M. (1987). *The Psychology of Happiness*. London: Routledge.

Argyle, M., and L. Lu. (1990). "The Happiness of Extraverts." *Personality and Individual Differences* 11: 1011–1017.

Argyle, M.; M. Martin; and J. Crossland. (1989). "Happiness As a Function of Personality and Social Encounters." In *Recent Advances in Social Psychology: An International Perspective*, ed. J.P. Forgas, and J.M. Innes. North Holland: Elsevier.

Belk, R. (1991). "The Ineluctable Mysteries of Possessions." *Journal of Social Behavior and Personality* 6: 17–55.

Belk, R., and M. Wallendorf. (1990). "The Sacred Meaning of Money." *Journal of Economic Psychology* 11: 35–67.

Bradburn, N.M. (1969). *The Structure of Psychological Well-being*. Chicago: Aldine.

Brebner, J., J. Donaldson, N. Kirby, and L. Ward. (1995). "Relationships Between Personality and Happiness." *Personality and Individual Differences* 19: 251–258.

Brickman, P.; D. Coates; and R. Janoff-Bulman. (1978). "Lottery Winners and Accident Victims: Is Happiness Relative?" *Journal of Personality and Social Psychology* 36: 917–927.

Buchholz, R. (1976). "Measurement of Beliefs." *Human Relations* 29: 1177–1198.

Campbell, A. (1981). *The Sense of Well-being in America: Recent Patterns and Trends*. New York: McGraw-Hill.

Campbell, A.; P.E. Converse; and W.L. Rodgers. (1976). *The Quality of American Life*. New York: Sage.

Campbell, C. (1987). "The Romantic Ethic and the Spirit of Modern Consumerism." Oxford: Blackwell.

Cherrington, D. (1980). *The Work Ethic: Working Values and Values That Work*. New York: AMACOM.

Csikszentmihalyi, M. (1999). "If We Are So Rich, Why Aren't We Happy?" *American Psychologist* 54: 821–827.

Dickson, J., and R. Buchholz. (1977). "Differences in Beliefs About Work Between Managers and Blue-Collar Workers." *Journal of Management Studies* 16: 235–251.

Diener, E. (1984). "Subjective Well-being." *Psychological Bulletin* 95: 542–575.

Diener, E., and E.M. Suh. (1999). "National Differences in Subjective Well-Being." In *Well-Being: The Foundations of Hedonic Psychology*, ed. D. Kahneman and E. Diener. New York: Russell Sage Foundation, 434–450.

Diener, E.; M. Diener; and C. Diener. (1995). "Factors Predicting the Subjective Well-being of Nations." *Journal of Personality and Social Psychology* 69: 851–864.

Ditz, G. (1980). "The Protestant Ethic and the Market Economy." *Kyklos* 33: 623–657.

Easterlin, R.A. (1995). "Will Raising the Incomes of All Increase the Happiness of All?" *Journal of Economic Behavior and Organization* 27: 35–47.

Emmons, R. (2000). "Spirituality and Intelligence: Problems and Prospects." *International Journal for the Psychology of Religion* 10: 57–64.

Eysenck, M. (1990). *Happiness, Facts and Myths*. London: Erlbaum.

Francis, L. (1999). "Happiness Is a Thing Called Stable Extraversion." *Personality and Individual Differences* 26: 5–11.

Fromm, E. (1980). *To Have or to Be*. London: Abacus.

Furnham, A. (1984a). "The Protestant Work Ethic, Voting Behaviour, and Attitudes to the Trade Unions." *Political Studies* 32: 420–436.

————. (1984b). "Many Sides of the Coin: The Psychology of Money Usage." *Personality and Individual Differences* 5: 501–509.

————. (1985). "The Determinants of Attitudes Towards Social Security Benefits." *British Journal of Social Psychology* 25: 19–27.

————. (1995). *The Protestant Work Ethic.* London: Routledge.

Furnham, A., and M. Argyle. (1998). *The Psychology of Money.* London: Routledge.

Furnham, A., and C. Brewin. (1990). "Personality and Happiness." *Personality and Individual Differences* 11: 1093–1096.

Furnham, A., and H. Cheng. (1997). "Personality and Happiness." *Psychological Reports* 80: 761–762.

————. (1999). "Personality As Predictors of Mental Health and Happiness in the East and West." *Personality and Individual Differences* 27: 395–403.

————. (2000). "Lay Theories of Happiness." *Journal of Happiness Studies* 1: 227–246.

Furnham, A., and B. Gunter. (1993). *Corporate Assessment: Auditing a Company's Personality.* London: Routledge.

Furnham, A., and M. Rose. (1987). "Alternative Ethics: The Relationship Between the Wealth, Work and Leisure Ethic." *Human Relations* 40: 561–574.

Gardner, H. (1999). *Intelligence Reframed.* New York: Basic Books.

Gardner, J., and A. Oswald. (2001). "Does Money Buy Happiness? A Longitudinal Study Using Data on Windfalls." Unpublished manuscript, University of Warwick, UK.

Golding, P., and S. Middleton. (1983). *Images of Welfare.* Oxford: Martin Robertson.

Hampden-Turner, C. (1981). *Maps of the Mind.* New York: Collier Books.

Inglehart, R. (1990). *Culture Shift in Advanced Industrial Society.* Princeton, NJ: Princeton University Press.

Kasser, T., and K.M. Sheldon. (2000). "Materialism, Mortality Salience, and Consumption Behaviour." *Psychological Science* 11: 348–351.

Kelvin, P., and J. Jarrett. (1985). *Unemployment: Its Social Psychological Effects.* Cambridge: Cambridge University Press.

Lasch, C. (1985). *The Culture of Narcissism.* Glasgow: Collins.

Maccoby, M., and R. Terzi. (1981). "What Happened to the Work Ethic?" In *The Work Ethic in Business*, ed. W. Hoffman and T. Wyly. Cambridge, MA: Oelgeschlager, Gunn & Hain.

Maslow, A.H. (1954). *Motivation and Personality.* New York: Harper and Row.

Mayer, J. (2000). "Spiritual Intelligence or Spiritual Consciousness." *International Journal for the Psychology of Religion* 10: 47–56.

Myers, D. (1992). *The Pursuit of Happiness.* New York: Avon Books.

Oates, W. (1971). *Confessions of a Workaholic: The Facts About Work Addiction.* New York: World Publishing.

Ritzer, G.; C. Kammeyer; and N. Yelman. (1982). *Sociology: Experiencing a Changing Society.* Boston: Allyn and Bacon.

Rosenberg, M. (1965). *Society and the Adolescent Self-image.* Princeton, NJ: Princeton University Press.

Taylor-Gooby, P. (1983). "Legitimation Deficit, Public Opinion and the Welfare State." *Sociology* 17: 165–184.

White, L., and S.J. Rogers. (2000). "Economic Circumstances and Family Outcomes: A Review of the 1990s." *Journal of Marriage and the Family* 62: 1035–1151.

CHAPTER 18

HONESTY, SPIRITUALITY, AND PERFORMANCE AT WORK

DAWN R. ELM

In the last ten years, there has been an increasing trend in the workplace and in research regarding the workplace to create a more complete and fulfilling space in our organizations. This trend has taken many forms and is widely represented in streams of research and practice in organizational studies (Andrews 1989; Collins and Porras 1997; Dobson and White 1995; Friedman, Christensen and DeGroot 1998; Liedtka 1996; Velasquez 2002; Waddock 2002). My efforts here will be focused on the continued development and the implications of a particular stream in this trend: the impact of honesty on spirituality at work. To accomplish this, I would first like to provide a definition of honesty and an overview of research on this topic. Following this, I will discuss the relationship between honesty and spirituality in work organizations, and attempt to elicit a useful model for practicing managers to promote spirituality at work.

HONESTY

Honesty is a term that has been bandied around a multitude of theoretical and empirical studies of organizational and ethical behavior, as well as one that has supplied the foundation for a number of practically oriented tests that can be administered to employees to assess their integrity.

In the research regarding this concept, much of it in the fields of moral philosophy and business ethics, the concept of honesty is not well defined, nor is it well understood. In previous work (Elm and Teplensky 1998), I have pointed out this deficiency. If we cannot define the concept of honesty, how can we conduct valid research into its impact on employee behavior in the workplace? I have argued that a clear definition of the concept is required for further usefulness in either research or practice. In order to further our understanding of honest and dishonest behavior, we need to be clear about the conceptual foundations of such behavior. Much of the research has assumed a common understanding of the term and has focused on either the justification for dishonest behavior, or the desirability of honesty (see Bhide and Stevenson 1990; Bok 1978; Brenkert 1998; Velasquez 2002; Werner, Jones, and Steffy 1989; Messick and Bazerman 1996; Cramton and Dees 1993).

Common definitions of honesty are often confounded with truth telling, respectful property ownership, and integrity. In fact, if you were to ask several people you know what it means to be honest, you will likely receive varying answers. However, the answers may share some common elements. The first will be that honesty is a value or characteristic that is *good*. This is consistent with a large number of works in moral philosophy, business ethics, and organizational theory and behavior as well as everyday interactions between individuals in society (Brenkert 1998; Bok

1978; Etzioni 1994; Hosmer 1994; Messick and Bazerman 1996). Thus, there is widely held agreement that the characteristic of honesty, or engaging in honest behavior, is desirable, and the literature in the field of business ethics consistently supports this perspective (Bok 1978; Bhide and Stevenson 1990; Cramton and Dees 1993; Hosmer 1994; Singhapaki, Rao, and Vitell 1996; Strong, Ringer, and Taylor 2001). In fact, in describing undesirable and unethical examples of behavior in organizations, dishonest behaviors are typically cited. Cheating in academia, covering up incidents, lying about sick days, lying to customers, and stealing from employers are used to describe unethical actions (Desruisseaux 1999; Hefter 1986; Werner, Jones, and Steffy 1989). Further, in the past fifteen years, several articles and books have been written to help organizations assess the integrity of their employees by conducting honesty tests (Dalton and Metzger 1993; Jones 1991; Steiner 1990).

The second common element will likely be recognition that honesty involves some form of being open and true to fellow human beings. This is probably the most common definition of honesty—that is, to tell the truth (Bok 1978; Brenkert 1998; Bhide and Stevenson 1990; Messick and Bazerman 1996). The degree to which human beings are open and tell the truth, and thus, the justification of honesty, differs depending on the characteristics of the individuals involved, and the potential harm from telling the whole truth. I will discuss this further later in this chapter.

The third common element will likely be recognition of respect of property ownership. Stealing, in all its various forms, is typically considered dishonest since it involves violation of ownership rights. For example, issues regarding cheating in academia (Desruisseaux 1999; Stevens and Stevens 1987) are about stealing. The recent concern regarding intellectual property and computer theft is also a reflection of the undesirability of stealing. Velasquez (2002) notes that information technologies have raised ethical issues about property rights when the property is information. For example, he notes the difficulties associated with determining the ethical implications of copying computer software, codes, or data, as well as the implications of computer "hacking." While it is undesirable to obtain such property without ownership, there are also implications for larger societal issues regarding the creation and generation of such property.

The responses you receive will also intertwine the characteristics of integrity and honesty with trust. This is reflected in our actions, conversations, popular press, and literature (Brenkert 1998; Dobson and White 1995; Waddock 2002; Strong, Ringer, and Taylor 2001). Pick up any article or book that mentions honesty and you will find integrity and trust discussed as well. You may also find other values (or virtues) such as courage, prudence, or temperance, but the frequency with which honesty, integrity, and trust are linked, is quite astounding. For example, Fukuyama (1995) discussed the lack of trust in American business. He described a world devoid of trust that involved an endless effort to keep oneself from being *cheated*. He then argued that trust is, in fact, a function of honest behavior: "As a general rule, trust arises when a community shares a set of moral values in such a way as to create expectations of regular and honest behavior" (Fukuyama 1995, 153).

Becker (2000) studied employees' perceptions of integrity in organizations and found one of the hallmarks of high integrity was trustworthiness. In his study trust, positive working relationships, and positive business outcomes were consequences of integrity. Strong, Ringer, and Taylor (2001) use honesty and integrity together to build trust as a key element in positive relationships with stakeholders. Regardless of our consensual understanding about the linkages between these concepts, there has been little writing that systematically defines these terms and their relationships with each other.

This confusion led to a study I conducted with a colleague in the 1990s. As an initial attempt to clarify the concept of honesty, we empirically assessed the definitions of honesty used by a sample of college students (Elm and Teplensky 1998). We found that honesty is, in fact, a multidimensional construct. Furthermore, we found significant support for three substantively different dimensions, which coincide with the everyday elements of honesty I described above. Each of the dimensions is defined in terms of the *lack of honesty,* since our subjects used these definitions. The first dimension involved telling the truth—we called this *commission.* It is comprised of intentionally telling a lie, or misrepresenting information in an untruthful way. The second dimension also involved telling the truth, and some might argue is a form of lying, but it was distinct in our research. It involved the omission of information in relating to others—we called the dimension *omission* for this reason. This is consistent with keeping secrets and relates more closely to the common belief that being honest involves being open with others. Omission is dishonest by lack of openness and sharing all information. The third dimension was very distinct from the first two, because it involved stealing. We called this dimension *possession,* since it related to the obtainment of property without ownership.

Later research (Scott 2001) supported the existence of these dimensions and broadened our understanding of what it means to be honest in the workplace. In her study, Scott examined the effect of employee dishonesty on the reputation of the firm in the airline industry. She noted that some organizations actually promote dishonesty to increase customer satisfaction. On the other hand, Maclean (2001) assumed that honesty was the desired outcome in her study of rule breaking in organizations. She found that dishonest behaviors ("churning") in the life insurance industry were a direct function of the social relationships of the participants. Similarly, Lewicki, Dineen, and Tomlinson (2001) investigated the effects of supervisor modeling on creation of a dishonest or honest climate at work. They found that supervisors who modeled dishonest behaviors helped create a dishonest climate, and vice versa for supervisors who modeled honest behaviors.

Even before we undertook our study of the dimensions of honesty, work in the fields of psychology and psychiatry suggested that honesty is central to our well-being. In his book, *To Thine Own Self Be True*, Andrews (1989) discussed the resurgence of ethical therapy in the field of psychology. Ethical therapy is based on the treatment of emotional/mental illnesses by removing or correcting unethical values and behaviors. Andrews argued that deception/lying has negative psychological and physiological consequences, as demonstrated by a number of studies cited in his book. Not the least of those is the large study on the physiological consequences of lying conducted by Hartshorne and May (1928). He lamented the rise of "value-free" therapy and suggested that more and more practicing therapists are basing their treatments on breaking unethical habits or behaviors to create emotional health. He also linked this directly to reaching a higher spiritual place. This perspective is echoed by recent work on the role of emotion in organizational life and the resurgence of virtue ethics in our studies of unethical and ethical behavior. For example, Gaudine and Thorne (2001) argue that emotion is not antithetical to a rational, ethical decision-making process; while Whetstone (2001) suggested that honesty is one virtue that supports a virtuous, or moral, choice. He noted that a virtuous (moral) action is a rational action based on a wise and careful assessment of the situation and a choice that reflects the character of the individual. A person who is honest (as well as possessing other virtues) will likely make good moral choices.

SPIRITUALITY AT WORK

Interestingly, while we were working on defining honesty for better research and understanding in business ethics, colleagues in our field were researching two concepts related to our work: meaningful work and spirituality at work. The research in meaningful work was centered on the concept of wholeness in the workplace. The work of Collins and Porras (1997); Friedman, Christensen, and DeGroot (1998); and many others suggested that organizations had become sterile places where individuals were not encouraged to be themselves. The wildly popular work of David Whyte (1994) using poetry to express the need to "bring one's whole self to work" was built on the recognition that meaning in work could not be achieved without true engagement of the entire person.

In a very similar fashion, research on spirituality in the workplace also began to garner more attention during this time. This research was related to the work being done on meaningful work, since there was also an explicit recognition that being more fully engaged in the workplace required more of the entire human psyche at work. In all of the research, an increase in meaning in work or in workplace spirituality is suggested as a desirable outcome (Ashmos and Duchon 2000; Collins and Porras 1997; Mitroff and Denton 1999). Research on spirituality at work has paralleled that on meaningful work with some, but not overwhelming, overlap. In fact, many authors have suggested that meaningful work is a dimension of spirituality. Bell and Taylor (2001) describe the definition of spirituality at work this way:

> From within the overall frame of reference, attempts have been made to define workplace spirituality as based on three main components (Ashmos and Duchon 2000). First, it relies on recognition that employees have an inner life related to the soul and accessed through practices such as meditation, self-reflection and prayer. Second, there is an underpinning assumption that employees need to find work meaningful, and third, a spiritually informed company provides the context or community within which spiritual growth can take place. This final element is perhaps the most significant. Writers on workplace spirituality often portray the organization as a communal center, in which individuals are able to explore the meaning of work as a source of spiritual growth, and means of connection to a larger purpose. (Bell and Taylor 2001, 2)

Recent work done by Milliman, Czaplewski and Ferguson (2001) built on Ashmos and Duchon's (2000) conceptualization of spirituality at work comprised of these three dimensions. They measured their impact on employee attitudes at work such as organizational commitment, intention to quit, job satisfaction, and organizationally based self-esteem, and found that community and meaningful work related significantly to the employee attitudes in their study. In addition, Mitroff and Denton (1999) have suggested that spirituality is a cultural phenomenon that has significant potential to enhance human life in organizations. In fact, Leider and Shapiro (2001) in their practical advice book, *Whistle While You Work,* describe spirituality as a source of strength and force in identifying our special calling in life:

> In order to flourish, we need to discover and internalize an authentic reason for living that is bigger than we are. . . . This energy, emanating from our very essence, tells us we are dialed into the right number, if we only listen. Our inner spirit, God within, provides us with the surest guidance for finding our true passions. Communicating with our inner spirit is the source and insight into our special calling in life. (Leider and Shapiro 2001, 79)

While Leider and Shapiro (2001) specifically link spirituality with religion (in the form of God or a higher power), this is not necessarily a prerequisite for spirituality at work. In fact, a substantial amount of research on creating "caring organizations" that are based on and focus on human relationships (Liedtka 1996; Dobson and White 1995; White 1992) has emerged from feminist ethics. I believe there is significant conceptual overlap between research on workplace spiritual-ity, meaningful work, and caring organizations. From very different foundations, the desired result is more human space in organizations.

HONESTY AND SPIRITUALITY AT WORK

When I was asked if I would contribute a chapter to this volume, I was very excited to have a forum to extend some of the research noted above. I have been teaching and conducting research in business ethics for the past twenty years. In that time, I have come to believe that work organi-zations are changing, and are, in fact, vehicles for continued human growth and enlightenment. What is required for this to occur? We need to make our organizations the reflection of our-selves—our whole selves. That means being honest and attempting to maintain full human rela-tionships in the workplace. This is consistent with creating a "caring organization" (Liedtka 1996; Dobson and White 1995) and, in essence, would provide greater spirituality, productivity, and *life* in organizations. I believe we should do this because greater spirituality in the workplace can provide more fulfilling lives and more productive organizations. Velasquez (2002) explicitly argues for ethical behavior as the best long-term strategy for a business. As part of this ethical behavior, spirituality at work, defined as connectedness and wholeness in the organization, should be desirable for better performance as well. This is consistent with the previously mentioned research that argues to promote spirituality at work (Mitroff and Denton 1999; Ashmos and Duchon 2000). Further, Dobson and White (1995) have argued that a caring organization will have better economic performance than a rational or political organization. In order to increase spirituality in the workplace, I would like to present a model that relates the concepts of hon-esty and workplace spirituality. The model suggests that honesty is a component of integrity, which leads to trust. Trust is the foundation for building and maintaining human relationships, and it is these relationships that provide the foundation for spirituality at work. The model is outlined below in Figure 18.1.

Let me return to my discussion of the intertwining of three critical concepts in honesty re-search: honesty, integrity, and trust. I believe all three of these are elements in the process of creating spirituality in the workplace. It is not an accident that the terms are used together often. Whether in casual conversation or academic literature, honesty, integrity, and trust are fundamen-tal to achieving a more desirable state of being. I believe this begins with the concept of honesty. I would like to suggest that honesty is a *component* of integrity. This is consistent with the defini-tion of integrity used by Waddock (2002) in her recent work on corporate citizenship. She sug-gests that integrity comprises the elements of wholeness and honesty. She considers integrity as one of the foundational pillars of corporate citizenship, which she defines as "Relationships with stakeholders constitute the essence of corporate citizenship" (Waddock 2002, 4).

Acting with integrity is highly desirable in virtually all cultures and organizational venues. Webster's dictionary (1973, 600) defines integrity as "firm adherence to a code of values, especially moral or artistic." Exactly what is this code of values? Virtue-based moral philoso-phers would likely suggest it is the cardinal virtues that comprise the code (Whetstone 2001), but I will limit composition of the characteristic to three underpinning concepts: *honesty, respect,* and *courage.* Some might argue there are other concepts crucial to the establishment of integrity, but I would suggest that these three are the most critical. These three values are critical to the characteristic of integrity because they are necessary for building and maintain-ing *trust.* Trust is, as Fukuyama (1995), Brenkert (1998), Dobson and White (1995), and oth-ers have noted, key for creating *relationships* with others. This is the pinnacle of my argument.

Figure 18.1 **The Relationship Between Honesty, Integrity, and Workplace Spirituality**

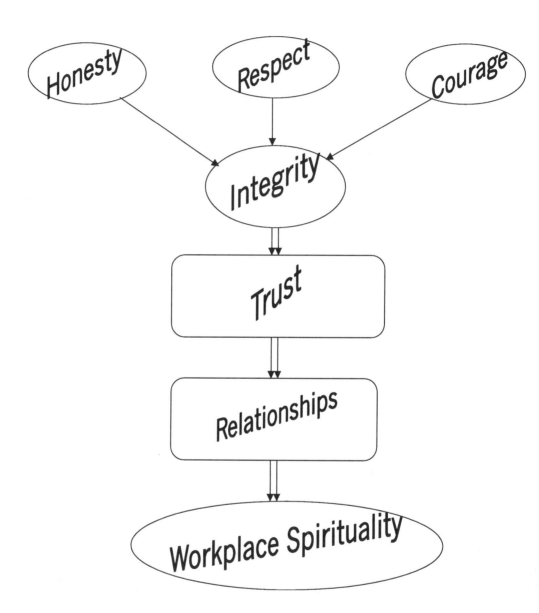

I believe it is our relationships with each other that allow us to bring all of ourselves to work and find meaning and community in the workplace. This cannot be achieved without trust. We must trust each other to be capable of taking risks and sharing our innermost thoughts. This is echoed in the research on caring organizations. Liedtka (1996) describes a caring organization as one in which networks of ongoing personal relationships are formed by "connected selves." Basing her argument on concepts in feminist ethics, she suggests that caring organizations are ones that focus on persons, are ends in themselves instead of a means to profits, are essentially personal, and are growth enhancing for the members by developing people to their full capacities. Liedtka (1996) and others (White 1992; Dobson and White 1995) suggest that business organizations that exhibit these caring tendencies will have better economic performance than organizations based on other foundations. Dobson and White (1995) specifically suggest that a caring organization will be a place where trust will flourish because trust is required for personal relationships: "One needs to be trusting if one sees oneself as interdependent and connected" (Dobson and White 1995, 466).

Brenkert (1998) argued that trust is important for sustaining the social, economic, and moral systems in which we conduct business. He also suggests that at least two of the relevant features of trust are mutual understanding, which involves openness, and willingness to expose one's vulnerabilities to others. This trust cannot be achieved if the individuals involved do not act with integrity. At great length I have already discussed honesty, so let me explain the inclusion of respect and courage as components of integrity.

Respect refers to the open and forthright consideration of others as whole human beings. I am not referring to respect as the moral duty associated with age or accomplishment. Rather, I mean the recognition that other individuals have multiple roles, emotions, and intelligence that are worthy of consideration. This reflects bringing our "whole self" into the workplace. As Friedman et al. (1998) note, successful managers who promote "win-win" with work-life balance do three things: clarify what's important, recognize and support their employees as "whole people," and experiment with the way work is done. They suggest this allows interactions to be tempered by the ongoing realization that we are more alike than different, and to thoughtfully consider other perspectives. This is the cloak of integrity. Respect must be present in order to be honest and courageous.

Courage, of course, means the fortitude to act when there is considerable risk to self. David Whyte (1994) talks eloquently of courage in his poetry regarding the pressure to "go along" with the boss even when you disagree. He assumes (as many others do as well) that work organizations do not promote courage. The person who disagrees, and says so, may well be passed over for the next promotion. I argue that courage is essential to acting with integrity because doing the right thing may mean disagreement with others, and this can only be accomplished with courage, respect, and honesty.

Acting with integrity, and therefore being honest, respectful, and courageous, is required to create trust. Without this, we cannot maintain or build relationships with each other. Even from an economic perspective, Fukuyama (1995) describes how empty our relationships would be:

> It is perhaps easier to appreciate the economic value of trust if we consider what a world devoid of trust would look like. If we had to approach every contract with the assumption that our partners would try to cheat us if they could, then we would have to spend a considerable amount of time bulletproofing the document to make sure that there were no legal loopholes by which we could be taken advantage of. Contracts would be endlessly long and detailed, spelling out every possible contingency and defining every conceivable obligation. We would never offer to do more than we were legally obligated to in a joint venture, for fear of being exploited, and we would regard new and possibly innovative proposals from our partners as tricks designed to get the better of us. Moreover, we would expect that, despite our best efforts in the negotiations, a certain number of people would succeed in cheating us or default on their obligations. We would not be able to resort to arbitration, because we would not trust third-party arbitrators sufficiently. Everything would have to be referred to the legal

system for resolution, with all of its cumbersome rules and methods, or potentially even to the criminal courts. (Fukuyama 1995, 152)

Trust makes it possible, and in fact, desirable to maintain our human relationships. Without these relationships we cannot have community or meaningful work. Etzioni (1994) argues that the relationships we have with each other are the very fabric of community. He suggests that the lack of these relationships leads to fragmentation of the community, culture, and consensus of moral values. If we actively attempt to build and maintain our relationships with others, we can find ways to positively influence the creation of community and meaningful work. We can create caring organizations that promote meaning in work by being focused on our relationships with each other. This can only be accomplished if we are honest, respectful, and courageous. We need to be honest not only with others, but also with ourselves as suggested by both virtue ethics (Whetstone 2001) and ethical therapy (Andrews 1989). We need to be respectful of others, and we need to be strong enough to act when we are afraid. If we do this, we can create trust and strong relationships with each other that form the fabric of community in our organizations.

Now, how might we accomplish this so we can promote spirituality in our work organizations? I suggest there are four steps we can take to promote acting with integrity in work organizations to create trust: understanding ourselves, and practicing honesty, respect, and courage.

UNDERSTANDING OURSELVES

First, we need to *understand ourselves*. This entails engaging in significant self-reflection to discover that internal essence described by Leider and Shapiro (2001). This is necessary not only to begin the connection with our spirit, but also to facilitate acting with integrity. Thoughtful actions begin with an understanding of oneself. We cannot act honestly toward others if we are not first honest with ourselves. This is a formidable step toward becoming a person with greater happiness and integrity. We need to take time to *honestly* reflect on our recent interactions with others. Have I lied? Have I stolen? Have I allowed others to believe things I knew were not true or accurate? How often have I done that? Why? Can I justify my dishonesty? What about respect—have I been respectful of others' views and values? We need to think about how often we interrupt another speaker or discount their point of view. Finally, how courageous am I? Have I taken any risks lately? Why or why not? There are other processes that can be used to aid in self-reflection, but the key is to engage in this process honestly, so self-understanding is the result.

PRACTICE HONESTY

To create trust, we must act with integrity. We can accomplish this by practicing the three components of this characteristic. First, we can try to practice honesty. Try to fully engage in the process of interacting with others at work, and be cognizant of our tendency to be honest or dishonest in our behavior.

We need to respect the property of others. Stealing anyone's ideas, their physical property, or credit for work they have done is dishonest. This means we need to consider our own interests in conjunction with the interests of other employees to be sure that we are not taking property that does not belong to us. The next time we are working with a colleague on a project, we could actively encourage that person to take credit for his or her ideas and contributions.

We need to tell the truth. This must be tempered with the justification for not telling the truth I mentioned at the outset of this chapter. That is, to tell the truth is a desirable thing, but there are times when a "white lie" (Bok 1978) can be justified. This is based on the concept of respect, and refers to the omission of information based on the potential for harm. Telling the truth, then, becomes a behavior that presents information in a forthright manner, but not in a destructive manner. If the truth of your opinion will harm another, a white lie is justifiable (Velasquez 2002). This is because the relationship with that person is important. In order to maintain the relationship, telling the truth in a destructive manner is harmful and not desirable. We can practice telling the truth when it is not personally harmful in all of our interactions with others at work.

We need to correct others when they are operating under false assumptions or information. This can be difficult when we are in a managerial role. Often, there is information available to upper-level executives that is not appropriate for subordinates to have. However, if we practice giving information that is appropriate, we can also at least stop others from acting on the basis of incorrect information. When we cannot share additional information, at least we can tell that the information being used, or assumed, is incorrect. This worked very effectively for an executive at a large midwestern bank during a recent acquisition process. His managers were not aware of the activities taking place in the beginning of the process, and rumors and innuendoes began circulating regularly around the office. Since he couldn't tell his managers what was happening due to proprietary information constraints, he called everyone together and told them that he couldn't tell them what was happening, but he could correct some of the inaccurate information circulating. This allows our relationships and trust to be maintained because we have respected people and been open about what information can and cannot be shared.

PRACTICE RESPECT

As I noted earlier, being respectful is tightly linked with behaving honestly. We can see from our discussion above that practicing honesty involves respecting others' needs in the workplace. We need to pay attention to the whole person when we are interacting at work. One of the things that contributes to the difficulty to do this is it takes *time*. Being respectful of others means taking the time and effort to learn about the others we are interacting with. There is increasing pressure in organizations today to move very quickly through our work tasks and lives. For example, there is often an implicit pressure to respond to e-mail as soon as it's received. I have had colleagues chastise me for responding a few days later. This doesn't bode well for taking time to learn about the people you are working with (never mind time to reflect on that learning). We must take the time because we need to see our coworkers as more than just their role in the organization. We need to build relationships with them that are based on human characteristics, not just task orientation. We need to encourage bringing all of our self to work, so we can be full human beings at work. Some might argue that we shouldn't do this because work has so much of us, we should save a little for outside the office. I would suggest that without being fully present at work, we cannot build trust and relationships that are meaningful. There can be no community if we are not willing to engage in those relationships. The validity is there—look at the enthusiasm that surrounds the beginning and end of meetings at work. Most often these conversations are about personal or social activities. These are the connections of whole human beings in the community. We need to pay attention to, and nurture, these relationships by learning about and respecting our coworkers.

PRACTICE COURAGE

We need to become more courageous at work. We have become very fearful in work organizations today (Whyte 1994; Friedman, Christensen, and DeGroot 1998). The economic climate is not all that positive and it can imply that taking a risk at work can mean a loss of livelihood. We cannot act with integrity if we don't practice courage. The value of our relationships with others should outweigh the fear we have about fitting in, or losing our next promotion. This might be accomplished by taking the risk next time. When it is the right thing to do, even if it is unpopular, consider the courageous choice. The most likely test will be linked to our discussion about honesty. Telling the truth when it's not what the boss wants to hear, requires courage. Experimenting with different ways to work and different patterns of interaction requires courage. If we practice taking the risk and keep our relationships in mind, we will be able to take more and more courageous actions because we find that we will not be ostracized or criticized—instead, we will be trusted because we acted with integrity.

FINDING SPIRITUALITY AT WORK

How will we know when we have accomplished this? I believe we will know that greater spirituality at work has been achieved when we fully know our coworkers, when our experience in the organization is one that revolves around the relationships we have with our coworkers. These relationships will be full—that is, they will involve *all* of who we are. This requires bringing our whole self to work and interacting with others from that basis. We can achieve this if we trust each other. We can trust each other only if we act with integrity, and doing so requires honesty, respect, and courage. The tangible results will be seen in more experimentation with the ways work is accomplished, more risk-taking by organizational members, and by less physiological and psychological stress and illness. In addition, we will see more productive organizations because we *want* to be a part of them. Organizations based on our relationships can provide the forum for human growth and enlightenment that will be demonstrated by our individual actions and the actions of others, because we will be a community.

CONCLUSION

In this chapter I have attempted to promote the relationship of honesty, as a component of integrity, to spirituality at work. I believe integrity forms the foundation for building trust, which is the key element in creating and maintaining relationships with our fellow human beings. These relationships are what enable us to have community at work and find meaning in our work. This is what spirituality at work is all about—creating fulfilling space in our work organizations. We must nurture these relationships with care and hard work. If we are successful, our organizational communities will enable us to have greater growth and enlightenment because we are sharing our whole selves with each other.

REFERENCES

Andrews, L.M. (1989). *To Thine Own Self Be True—The Relationship Between Spiritual Values and Emotional Health*. New York: Doubleday.
Ashmos, D.R., and D. Duchon. (2000). "Spirituality at Work: A Conceptualization and Measure." *Journal of Management Inquiry* 9, no. 2: 134–145.

Becker, T. (2000). "Hallmarks and Consequences of Integrity in Organizations: The Employees' Perspective." Paper presented at the Academy of Management Conference, Toronto, Ontario, August.

Bell, E., and S. Taylor. (2001). "A Rumor of Angels: Researching Spirituality and Work Organizations." Academy of Management Proceedings, Washington, DC.

Bhide, A., and J.J. Stevenson. (1990). "Why Be Honest If Honesty Doesn't Pay?" *Harvard Business Review* (September–October): 317–325.

Bok, S. (1978). *Lying*. New York: Random House.

Brenkert, G.C. (1998). "Trust, Morality and International Business." *Business Ethics Quarterly* 8, no. 2: 254–266.

Collins, J.C., and J.I. Porras. (1997). *Built to Last: Successful Habits of Visionary Companies*. New York: Harper.

Cramton, P.C., and J.G. Dees. (1993). "Promoting Honesty in Negotiation: An Exercise in Practical Ethics." *Business Ethics Quarterly* 4, no. 3: 359–394.

Dalton, D.R., and M.B. Metzger. (1993). "Integrity Testing for Personnel Selection: An Unsparing Perspective." *Journal of Business Ethics* 12, no. 2: 147–156.

Desruisseaux, P. (1999). "Cheating Is Reaching Epidemic Proportions Worldwide, Researchers Say." *Chronicle of Higher Education* 45, no. 34: A-45.

Dobson, J., and J. White. (1995). "Toward the Feminine Firm." *Business Ethics Quarterly* 5, no. 3: 463–478.

Elm, D.R., and J.G. Teplensky. (1998). "The Three Faces of Honesty: A Confirmatory Factor Analysis." In *Research in Corporate Social Performance and Policy*, vol. 5, ed. J. Post. New York: JAI Press, 107–123.

Etzioni, A. (1994). "America's Victim Culture Lacks Moral Values." In *Taking Sides*, 3d ed., ed. L. Newton and M. Ford. Guilford, CT: Dushkin, 29–35.

Friedman, S.; P. Christensen; and J. DeGroot. (1998). "Work and Life: The End of the Zero-Sum Game." *Harvard Business Review* (November): 22–31.

Fukuyama, F. (1995). *Trust—the Social Virtues and the Creation of Prosperity*. New York: Simon and Schuster.

Gaudine, A., and L. Thorne. (2001). "Emotion and Ethical Decision-Making in Organizations." *Journal of Business Ethics* 31, no. 2: 175–187.

Hartshorne, H., and M. May. (1928). *Studies in Deceit*. New York: Macmillan.

Hefter, R. (1986). "The Crippling Crime." *Security World* 23: 36–38.

Hosmer, L.T. (1994). "Why Be Moral? A Different Rationale for Managers." *Business Ethics Quarterly* 4, no. 2: 191–204.

Jones, J. (1991). *Pre-Employment Honesty Testing: Current Research and Future Directions*. New York: Quorum.

Leider, R.J., and D.A. Shapiro. (2001). *Whistle While You Work*. San Francisco: Berrett-Koehler.

Lewicki, R.; B. Dineen; and E. Tomlinson. (2001). "Coaching Versus Modeling: Examining Supervisory Impact on Climate and Attitudinal Outcomes at the Branch Level of Analysis." Paper presented at the Academy of Management Conference, Washington, DC, August.

Liedtka, J.M. (1996). "Feminist Morality and Competitive Reality: A Role of an Ethic of Care?" *Business Ethics Quarterly* 6, no. 2: 182–194.

Maclean, T.L. (2001). "Thick As Thieves: A Social Embeddedness Model of Rule Breaking in Organizations." *Business and Society* 40, no. 2: 167–196.

Messick, D.M., and M.H. Bazerman. (1996). "Ethical Leadership and the Psychology of Decision-Making." *Sloan Management Review* (winter): 9–22.

Milliman, J.F.; A.J. Czaplewski; and J.M. Ferguson. (2001). "An Exploratory Empirical Assessment of the Relationship Between Spirituality and Employee Work Attitudes." Academy of Management Proceedings, Washington DC, August.

Mitroff, I., and E.A. Denton. (1999). A *Spiritual Audit of Corporate America: A Hard Look at Spirituality, Religion, and Values in the Workplace*. San Francisco: Jossey-Bass.

Scott, E. (2001). "The View from the Passenger's Seat: A Multimethod Assessment of Passengers' Perceptions of Employee Dishonesty in the Airline Industry." Paper presented at the Academy of Management Conference, Washington, DC, August.

Singhapaki, A.; C.P. Rao; and S.J. Vitell. (1996). "Ethical Decision-Making: An Investigation of Services Marketing Professionals." *Journal of Business Ethics* 15, no. 6: 635–644.

Steiner, J. (1990). "Honesty Testing." *Business Forum* 15, no. 2: 31–33.

Stevens, G., and F. Stevens. (1987). "Ethical Inclinations of Tomorrow's Managers Revisited: How and Why Students Cheat." *Journal of Education for Business* 63, no. 1: 24–29.

Strong, K.C.; R.C. Ringer; and S.A. Taylor. (2001). "THE* Rules of Stakeholder Satisfaction (*Timeliness, Honesty, Empathy)." *Journal of Business Ethics* 32, no. 3: 219–230.

Velasquez, M.G. (2002). *Business Ethics: Concepts and Cases*, 5th ed. New York: Prentice-Hall.

Waddock, S. (2002). "Integrity and Mindfulness: Foundations of Corporate Citizenship." *Journal of Corporate Citizenship* 1, no. 1: 12–23.

Webster's Collegiate Dictionary. (1973). Springfield, MA: G&C Merriam Company.

Werner, S.H.; J.W. Jones; and B.D. Steffy. (1989). "The Relations Between Intelligence, Honesty, and Theft Admissions." *Educational and Psychological Measurement* 49: 921–927.

Whetstone, J.T. (2001). "How Virtue Fits Within Business Ethics." *Journal of Business Ethics* 33, no. 2: 101–114.

White, T.I. (1992). "Business Ethics and Carol Gilligan's Two Voices." *Business Ethics Quarterly* 2, no. 1: 51–61.

Whyte, D. (1994). *The Heart Aroused*. New York: Doubleday.

CHAPTER 19

SPIRITUAL WELLNESS IN THE WORKPLACE

R. Elliott Ingersoll

Everywhere I go it seems that people are killing themselves with work. . . .
—Diane Fassel

They all attain perfection when they find joy in their work.
—Bhagavad Gita

There can be no joy in living without joy in work.
—Thomas Aquinas

You can't do good unless you feel good.
—Timothy Leary

The four quotes above may be construed as pointing to work as an avenue to the sacred aspects of life. The etymological roots of the word "sacred" point to something that can be blessed or cursed and our work lives can certainly be either of those. As blessing, the sacred aspects of work may enliven our spirit; as curse these aspects may dash our spirit against stone. We may kill ourselves with it or find joy in it. In this chapter I will discuss how work can be a place where one may enliven one's spirit by applying ten dimensions of spiritual wellness (Ingersoll 1998).

In the past thirty years there has been an increased interest in spirituality as evidenced by polls (Caplow, Chadwick, and Hoover 1983; Gallup and Castelli 1989), psychological studies of the topic (Richards and Bergin 2000; Shafranske 1996), and popular writing (Ram Dass 2000). Paralleling this interest are efforts by social scientists to operationalize spirituality resulting in such constructs as spiritual well-being (Moberg 1979; Ellison 1983) and spiritual wellness (Ingersoll 1994, 1998). In addition to making the notion of spirituality more accessible, these constructs are directly applicable in the workplace.

Health and wellness are positively correlated with both religious and spiritual involvement (George et al. 2000). Employee wellness programs designed to offset rising health care costs (Bubin and Campbell 1994) may include activities like yoga or meditation since wellness includes supporting spirituality (Galemore 2000). This, however, is just the beginning. Employers may find that incorporating dimensions of spiritual wellness into their company mission further enhances employee wellness as well as the health of the organization in general (Castle 1999).

Spiritual wellness and spiritual well-being have been pioneered by researchers in sociology and psychology over the past thirty years (e.g., Moberg and Brusek 1978; Ellison 1983; and Ingersoll 1998). These constructs provide ways to talk about spirituality, and, as such, provide a vocabulary to point toward that which is best within us. Certainly such a construct is useful in the workplace where most of us spend a great deal, perhaps even a majority, of our waking time. This chapter aims to describe dimensions of spiritual wellness and some roles they can play in work. Hopefully the reader will come away with a way of thinking and talking about spirituality in the workplace that is useful while being sensitive to the diversity of spiritual expressions and traditions. Before beginning that discussion though, it is important to touch on the strengths and weaknesses of constructs in general.

YOUR FRIEND THE CONSTRUCT OR WHY CAN'T JOHNNY OPERATIONALIZE?

A construct is a complex image or idea formed from simpler images or ideas. Constructs serve the paradoxical purpose of defining or describing things that are difficult to define or describe. Just like the word implies, constructs are mentally constructed or put together by individuals and then referred to (or ignored) by larger groups the individuals are part of. As such, constructs are tiny maps, but as Alfred Korzybski pointed out, human beings have a habit of confusing their maps with the territory toward which they point. This tendency and the somewhat variable nature of constructs in general must be kept in mind in any discussion of spirituality.

It should also be noted that there is a political dynamic to constructs since numerous people (including researchers) may have their own version of a construct and a personal agenda to promote it. One hopes that constructs are tested or validated to make them more than just personal preferences but this process is ongoing and one can never be certain that a construct totally and accurately reflects that which it is pointing to. The reader should know that my personal agenda has been to explore ways to discuss spirituality that honor various traditions without necessarily being wed to those traditions.

CONSTRUCTS DESCRIBING SPIRITUALITY

Spirituality has been said to be intrinsic to all people (Ingersoll 1994; Vaughan 1995) and an important component of mental health (Payne 1990; Worthington 1989; Westgate 1996). Spirituality is a word that defies an absolute, operational definition (Ingersoll 1994), so social scientists have attempted to develop constructs that point to spiritual health without pretending to be able to define spirituality. Following are examples of related constructs.

RELIGIOSITY

One construct that has been used to operationalize spirituality has been religiosity (Allport 1950). Religiosity left some social scientists uncomfortable due to its connection to the institutions of organized religion (Moberg 1971). More recently, many researchers prefer using constructs related more directly to spirituality because more and more U.S. citizens polled describe themselves more often as "spiritual" than "religious" (Hoge 1996). Early attempts to develop a construct that was more reflective of spirituality than religion included Pahnke and Richards's (1966) focus on mystical experience as one manifestation of spirituality in both peak experiences and LSD psychotherapy sessions.

SPIRITUAL WELL-BEING

Another construct developed to operationalize spirituality was spiritual well-being, which grew out of the Social Indicators Movement (Ellison 1983). This movement emphasized the inclusion

Table 19.1

Ingersoll's 1998 Dimensions of Spiritual Wellness

Conception of the absolute or divine	Spiritual freedom
Meaning	Forgiveness
Connectedness	Hope
Mystery	Knowledge/Learning
Present-Centeredness	Experience/Ritual

of subjective measures when trying to assess satisfaction with quality of life (Campbell 1976). Moberg and Brusek (1978) noted that quality of life indicators could be individualistic (focused on personal achievement) or transcendental (focused on meaning in a larger interpersonal context). The idea of the spiritual well-being as one such transcendental construct was that it would include dimensions or components that pointed to spiritual wellness much the same as certain physical indicators (e.g., blood pressure) point to physical wellness.

Moberg (1971) hoped that a spiritual well-being construct could, when necessary, differentiate "spiritual" from "religious." Moberg (1984) identified seven components of spiritual well-being including Christian Faith, Self-Satisfaction, Personal Piety, Subjective Spiritual Well-Being, Optimism, Religious Cynicism, and Elitism. Many members of Moberg's sample had a Christian religious affiliation resulting in more religious language in the components than may have resulted from a different sample. Moberg's work was elaborated on by Ellison and Paloutzian (1982) who developed only two dimensions of spiritual well-being, the existential dimension and the religious dimension. Other spiritual well-being constructs were developed by Tubesing (1980) and Hungelmann et al. (1989).

SPIRITUAL WELLNESS

Spiritual wellness is another construct developed to operationalize spirituality. According to Westgate (1996), this term has its origins in the medical wellness movement where wellness is summarized as the optimum integration of the various dimensions of human functioning including spirituality (Bensley 1993). Spiritual wellness has been operationalized by Banks (1980); Chandler, Holden, and Kolander (1992); Hinterkopf (1997); Ingersoll (1994, 1998); and Myers (1988). Each of the latter researchers described dimensions to spiritual wellness. While each took a different approach, there were some common dimensions, including meaning or purpose and transcendent beliefs/experiences.

My dimensions of spiritual wellness (Ingersoll 1998) and their relationship to the workplace are focused on in this chapter because the dimensions were developed using a panel of experts from eleven different spiritual traditions, thus giving them some cross-traditional validation. These dimensions are summarized in Table 19.1 and details about their development can be found in Ingersoll (1998). Each of these will be discussed in the context of the workplace.

Conception of the Absolute or Divine

There are many ways that human beings describe their sense of the ultimate source of life. Some may speak of a god or goddess, others a higher power, and some may simply use a notion of a life force pervading all things. People will typically describe their conception of divinity as helping them develop ethically and guiding their actions in a variety of ways. The point is not so much how different people describe this ultimate force but what effect it has on how they conceptualize work and working.

Many traditions focus on how honest work is a manifestation of one's commitment to God or the life force. In Eastern traditions this is often referred to as "right livelihood" and includes concepts like honesty in one's business dealings with others and promoting practices that have a positive impact on communities and society in general. Managers and administrators may want to examine these two ethical principles that derive from a sense of an absolute or divine force. Does the atmosphere of the workplace promote honest interactions? Can the product of labor be viewed as having a growth-oriented or healing impact on society in general? Obviously these can be challenging questions and they require the capacity for honest dialogue at the top of the organization.

Since many people's ethical sense derives from their conception of an absolute or divine higher power, a healthy organization can view the workplace as an arena where the employee can practice these ethics. A company that is comfortable acknowledging a spiritual worldview may find that it helps foster a healthy work environment. Sadly, as Peck (1987) noted, organizations that would most benefit from such an acknowledgment are frequently the least likely to make it. As a species, there is no limit to the ways in which we rationalize our own destructive tendencies and avoid confronting our ethical shortcomings. Managers and administrators who want to honor the type of ethical living that derives from a connection to a higher spiritual force or power will find there is no substitute for practicing their own spiritual path and modeling the ethics that derive from their own sense of the absolute.

Meaning

Meaning is the individual sense that life is worth living. Certainly it can be an overwhelming question in times of crisis but is also a component of everyday life. Meaning in one's work is the personal sense that the hours of life traded for wages serve purposes beyond physical existence. Meaning may be related to a worker's sense of the divine but may simply reflect what that particular worker holds most dear. Many clients enter counseling or psychotherapy with acute crises of meaning that are centered on their work life. One client told me, "I practically live at work. I am up by 5 A.M. every day and don't return home until after 6 P.M. I am even starting to work on Saturdays. I have no life." I noted that if he equated his work life with no life that was certainly something we needed to explore. This particular client was also a visual artist and, although he liked earning money, his work had nothing to do with his art. His artistic abilities in this sense were a blessing and a curse that had in part precipitated his crisis of meaning. He was faced with the challenge of what the existentialists call authentic living. He needed to be responsible for his choices, recognizing that every choice is expensive in that it costs all the alternatives.

Managers and administrators would do well to explore the meaning they derive from their work. Afterward, they may wish to explore with their employees the meaning the work has for them. Again, the capacity for honest dialogue is essential to such exploration. If the climate of the company is one where honesty is punished, little of value will result from such dialogue. Many companies interpret meaning as the key values of the company. This is fine as long as it is recognized that meaning-making is an individual exercise. Knowing the key values of those running the company can certainly go a long way in helping individual employees decide if they can find meaning working in such a company.

Connectedness

Connectedness is a broad concept that in the spiritual sense may refer to a person's connectedness to their sense of the divine, other people, the natural world, or perhaps all of the above. The extent to which a workplace can foster connectedness is certainly a marker of its ability to be spiritually well. One of our greatest shortages currently is healthy communities. Fewer and fewer people live near their work and may commute 40–80 miles just to go to and from work each day. The result is that they don't spend as much time with their neighbors and they are less likely to socialize with coworkers. This increases the value of connectedness in the workplace.

Managers and administrators may wonder if competitiveness and connectedness are mutually exclusive. I don't believe so, but a company certainly needs to know what it hopes to gain from a competitive work environment. Competition in and of itself is nothing more than a force that requires direction. Valuing competition blindly in the hopes that it will, undirected, bring out the best in workers is akin to rolling one's car into the street driverless in the hope that it will get to an appointed destination. Many companies are able to manage competition between coworkers in a growth-oriented manner. Having a sense of how the competition relates to the higher goals of the company regarding climate and product is a start. One company tied bonuses to performance within units that had different functions but quantifiable goals. While all units competed with one another for the fewest errors across categories like marketing, sales, and distribution, management continually reinforced the connection between quality performance and the profit margin that provided the bonuses.

A sense of connectedness also promotes awareness of the needs of others and may result in things like compassion and a desire for justice for others. Within a work setting, compassion is particularly important. It may grow from a sense of connectedness and manifest as an ability to empathize with others. In this sense it is particularly valuable to those in management positions.

Mystery

Mystery is a dimension of spiritual wellness that relates to how a person deals with ambiguity and uncertainty. This may also be thought of as a person's capacity for awe and wonder and is certainly related to a person's ability to be present-centered (discussed below). It seems a paradox of the human condition that we seek security through predictability but the nature of life is change and flux. In the work setting, times of uncertainty are often times of risk and, in unhealthy work settings, may be interpreted by management as times to assign blame. If this is the case, workers will seek concrete explanations, minimize risk, and struggle to resist change—all behaviors that will likely increase anxiety and decrease performance.

Being able to dwell in mystery does not guarantee particular outcomes but it does increase the probability that employees are able to take care of themselves as well as focus their energies on the task at hand. On a related note, being able to tolerate uncertainty frees energy for focusing on the here and now with all its attendant risks and challenges.

Present-Centeredness

This is the ability to focus on and respond to each moment as it unfolds. It, too, is somewhat of a paradox in that the focusing shouldn't be thought of as "trying hard to concentrate." As the philosopher Alan Watts has written, the past is just a memory and, as such, a thought. The future, too, is just a fantasy of what may come—also a thought or a series of thoughts. The ability to be present-centered is a valuable skill in any discipline. In counseling and psychotherapy, it is the ability to be present with our clients, picking up their nuances and subtleties while letting go of our "agenda" or "theory" about what might be wrong with them. Our clinical skills are only as good as our ability to be in the present with our client. It is in the present that our experience of the client occurs and guides us in how exactly we should apply our clinical skills.

Present-centeredness has also been described as a type of attention. Numerous studies have documented how techniques like mindfulness meditation and concentration meditation can improve attention (Arnold 2001; Jhansi and Rao 2000; Valentine and Sweet 1999). Present-centeredness manifesting as attention is a useful tool in the workplace. In consulting with business leaders in Northeast Ohio, the willingness to work with others and the ability to sustain attention to a task are among the most desirable characteristics in potential employees.

As noted, various forms of concentration or mindfulness meditation may serve to enhance attention as well as spiritual wellness. Meditation is one of the oldest practices on the spiritual path but also one that has received considerable attention from Western science. Since Wallace's (1970) article on the physiological effects of Transcendental Meditation, the scientific world has joined the spiritual/religious world in affirming that something "real" is happening during meditation. This ever-increasing scientific base supporting both psychological and physiological benefits of meditation (as well as the nondenominational nature of the practice) make it easy to support in the workplace.

Spiritual Freedom

The dimension of spiritual freedom began as a dimension of playfulness. Spiritual freedom is a concept devised by St. Ignatius of the Roman Catholic Church. For Ignatius, spiritual freedom was not being overly coerced from within or without. By coercion, I mean distracted and perhaps moved toward a course of action for the wrong reason. The person who is spiritually free feels safe in the world. This relates to playfulness in that one cannot be playful if one feels unsafe. When we are coerced from within or without we tend to feel less safe as we are always vigilant regarding the source of our coercion.

One client whose suffering illustrated this had lost a job as CEO of a prominent firm. He was in that netherworld of severance pay and job hunting. He and his family had grown accustomed to a fairly high standard of living and the man was practically crippled with anxiety over the thought of not being able to find employment that would allow them to continue their standard of living. His coercion was primarily internal as he mentally replayed scenarios daily about what his friends and family would think of him were he to take a cut in pay, buy a smaller house, lease a less expensive car, etc.

Certainly some people may criticize the man's material priorities from a "spiritual" perspective, but this does not ease his suffering and misses the point. The point being, that so much energy was going into his anxiety that it decreased the available energy for his job search and distracted him from what was truly the most important thing to him—his family. Our work together was to address this coercion to enhance his spiritual freedom. From that point he was able to realize his priorities, which were far more about his family than the style of living to which they had been accustomed. The client did eventually decide to take a lower-paying position because he realized it would allow him to spend more time with his family.

Forgiveness

Despite being encouraged for thousands of years by major world religions (Rye et al. 2000), forgiveness has received scant attention in the social sciences (McCullough 2000). In the context of our fast-paced, quick-fix society, forgiveness is often misconstrued as simply "moving on" from a difficult situation. From a purely psychological perspective it has been described as a prosocial, motivational construct that has positive correlations with health and wellness (McCullough 2000). From a broader perspective I think of it as a way of approaching life as a journey of learning and healing. The path of forgiveness is not about forgetting but simply working through the negative emotions that accompany feeling hurt by another.

The stages of trauma are helpful in conceptualizing the path of forgiveness. The three characteristic stages following a trauma are numbness, anger, and integration. In interactions involving forgiveness where the hurt inflicted is substantial, these stages seem to follow. The person hurt (the *victim* for lack of a better word) is initially stunned physically and/or psychologically. As the nature of what has been done to her or him dawns in her or his awareness, the person typically gets justifiably angry. It is in the integration stage that the person hurt may activate forgiveness. Typically at this point the victim realizes that her or his anger actually keeps her or him tied to the situation and, at least psychologically, to the person who hurt her or him. In this sense forgiving may initially be motivated by not wanting one's life ruled by the memory of the incident any longer.

In less severe types of offenses, the first reaction of the hurt person may be anger. Often it is the conscious commitment to forgiveness that stops the person from retaliating in anger. As one client said, "Forgiveness is a path I walk to deal with anger. When I feel angry with a coworker, I pause and tell myself that if I feel the same way tomorrow, I can tell him/her off then. Then, later in the day when I am less angry, I try to put myself in the shoes of the person I feel hurt me. More often than not this leads me to re-evaluate the situation by the next day. At that point, instead of telling the person off, I either confront them and tell them my reaction to what they did or I just move on."

Like any of these dimensions, the workplace provides ample opportunity for the practice of forgiveness. Some people may misinterpret forgiveness as reinforcing inappropriate behavior by "turning the other cheek." This is not the meaning intended here. The client described in the last paragraph stated that for him, the path of forgiveness freed him from being overly attached to feelings of anger whether they were justifiable or not. This, in turn, freed him to redirect his energies elsewhere. In this context the client's efforts at forgiveness were really a form of self-care.

Hope

Huston Smith (1976) noted that hope was like a mountain-climbing pick that helps the climber chin herself to the next peak to see a new horizon. As the simile implies, hope is indispensable to navigating the terrain of life, including life in the workplace. On one level, many of us work with the hope of a better life for our loved ones and ourselves. While each person has the choice to cultivate or give up hope, the workplace itself may be a source of hope or a place to lose it.

Psychological descriptions of hope have ranged from "positive expectation" (Stotland 1969), to what Snyder (2000) called "hopeful thought." Hopeful thought was comprised of goals, agency, and pathways. The goals anchor Snyder's hope theory and always include some ambiguity because goals that one is 100 percent certain of meeting require no hopeful thought. To attain goals, Snyder noted that people required pathways from which to pursue goals and the agency or motivation to make the journey down the pathways.

One client I recall worked as a short-order cook for slightly above the minimum wage. She was in counseling for symptoms of depression and alcohol dependence. Having done short-order cooking myself, I projected my own negative experiences onto her and stated, "it must be hard doing that work." She responded that it wasn't something she wanted to do forever but she really enjoyed the people she worked with. She noted "I think everyone there has something or someone in their life that they really love. It is exciting to be around and sort of helps me believe that maybe I'll find that someday." Indeed, this client learned a great deal from the time spent with her coworkers that helped her through a very difficult period in her life. In listening to her coworkers' stories, this woman said she realized new courses of action she had not thought of before. In Snyder's terms, this woman refined her goals about what was possible through her contact with coworkers, found their stories motivating, and experimented with new pathways for attaining goals based on her coworkers' experiences.

What can managers do to foster hope? First they may assess how employee goals relate to the workplace and whether the workplace provides pathways for employees to attain their goals. Clearly this can help employers screen potential employees for goodness of fit but also may help employers clarify their own expectations. Perhaps most importantly employers can do small things well. In behavioral terms this means emphasizing reinforcers over punishers. In humanistic terms it means to remember that each employee comes to the job with her or his own hopes, dreams, and a sense of where work fits into those. And, as with every dimension in this chapter, managers and employers should be aware of what they do to foster hope as well as where they turn when hope is ebbing.

Knowledge/Learning

This dimension of spiritual wellness developed out of discussions I had with the panelists from different spiritual traditions who helped create the dimensions. The idea behind this is that a person who is spiritually well is often inherently interested in their life and life in general. They are less likely to be bored or boring and more likely to engage new things with interest and curiosity. This can have distinct advantages in the workplace even when the work is of a repetitive nature.

This dimension also reflects what in education is referred to as lifelong learning. Granted, the learning is not necessarily academic in nature or job related. This brings up the subject of time and workload. As Schor (1993) has documented, Americans in particular have fewer and fewer long periods of leisure time. Many Americans are working such long hours and their only "downtime" comes in front of the television set. As a quality of life issue, workers must balance their financial needs and their need for personal time. With longer periods of free time employees may pursue the things that inherently interest them. Even if these things are not directly work related, the positive benefits on the employee will generalize to the workplace.

Experience/Ritual

This dimension refers to the rituals clients engage in that are related to their spiritual practices or worldview. One could define ritual narrowly as relating only to corporate worship or very broadly including more secular activities. I prefer the latter as it more accurately reflects reality. In terms of spiritual wellness, we may think of a ritual as a regular activity that directs a person's mind and/or body to the transcendent (however they define that).

How might this relate to the workplace? It could be directly related as in the case of one company that provides meditation and yoga sessions twice a week for employees, or it may be indirectly such as in the positive benefits a private practitioner of meditation or yoga would bring to the work environment. We should also mention the power that the ritual of going to work has on people in general. This can be positive or negative.

Having grown up in Youngstown, Ohio, watching the effects of steel mill closure on family and friends, I am acutely aware of how people can come to identify almost exclusively with their jobs and how devastating it can be when the job is suddenly gone and the person is plunged into despair. The positive side of looking at working in general as a ritual is that it does connect the individual to something larger than her- or himself, something he or she feels a part of that helps him or her make meaning in life. Ideally that meaning includes more than work.

SUMMING UP

There is no doubt that spirituality plays an increasingly important role for more and more Americans. Addressing spirituality, let alone spirituality in the workplace, is a daunting task. Trying to capture something in words that by its very definition defies verbal description, forces us to rely on constructs that point to spirituality without pretending to be able to define it. As one such construct, spiritual wellness can provide us a vocabulary with which to speak about spirituality without being bound by the words or phrases of one particular spiritual tradition.

There is still much research that needs to be done. While the social sciences have just begun exploring relevant constructs in general, we have yet to conduct systematic research on how these constructs may be used or manifested in the workplace. Every one of the ten dimensions I have touched on in this chapter can be an area of focused research as well as the umbrella concept of spiritual wellness that they are part of. It is my hope that such research will increase. It is hard to say whether more global research like that on the spiritual wellness construct or more focused research (such as research on each dimension) is more valuable at this point in time. They both have a place, and the choice of which direction to go in should be left to the temperament and interests of the researcher.

While further research is necessary, a genuine application of spiritual wellness principles in the workplace need not wait for published studies. Anecdotal and clinical evidence points toward the efficacy of this area to enhance human functioning both inside and outside of the workplace. An application of spiritual wellness principles requires honesty and courage, but the potential benefits are worth the risk. The uses of these dimensions of spiritual wellness in the work setting are limited only by the imaginations of managers and employers.

REFERENCES

Allport, G. (1950). *The Individual and His Religion.* New York: Macmillan.

Arnold, L.E. (2001). "Alternative Treatments for Adults with Attention Deficit Hyperactivity Disorder." In *Adult Attention Deficit Disorder: Brain Mechanisms and Life Outcomes*, ed. J. Wasserstein and E. Lorraine. New York: New York Academy of Sciences, 113–142.

Banks, R. (1980). "Health and the Spiritual Dimension: Implications for Professional Preparation Programs." *Journal of School Health* 50: 195–205.

Bensley, R. J. (1993). "The Relationship Between Mind and Soul Characteristics and Job Satisfaction." *Dissertation Abstracts International* 54: 1686.

Bubin, J.W., and D.P. Campbell. (1994). "Employee Wellness Programs: A Strategy for Increasing Participation." In *Health Care Marketing: A Foundation for Managed Quality*, ed. P.D. Cooper, 3d ed. Gaithersburg, MD: Aspen Publications, 282–294.

Campbell, A. (1976). "Subjective Measures of Well Being." *American Psychologist* (February): 117–124.

Caplow, T., H.M. Bohr, B.A. Chadwick, and D.W. Hoover. (1983). *All Faithful People: Change and Continuity in Middletown's Religion.* Minneapolis: University of Minnesota Press.

Castle, A. (1999). *There Is Wealth in Wellness.* Available at: www.herald-sun.com/cchamber/magz/1198/bt119808.html.

Chandler, C.K.; J.M. Holden; and C.A. Kolander. (1992). "Counseling for Spiritual Wellness: Theory and Practice." *Journal of Counseling and Development* 71: 168–176.

Ellison, C.W. (1983). "Spiritual Well-Being: Conceptualization and Measurement." *Journal of Psychology and Theology* 11: 330–340.

Ellison, C.W., and R.F. Paloutzian. (1982). "Loneliness, Spiritual Well-Being, and Quality of Life." In *Loneliness: A Sourcebook of Current Theory, Research, and Therapy*, ed. L.A. Peplar and D. Perlman. New York: Wiley.

Galemore, C.A. (2000). "Worksite Wellness in the School Setting." *Journal of School Nursing* 16: 42–45.

Gallup, G., and J. Castelli. (1989). *The People's Religion: American Faith in the 90's.* New York: Macmillan.

George, L.K.; D.B. Larson; H.G. Koenig; and M.E. McCullough. (2000). "Spirituality and Health: What We Know, What We Need to Know." *Journal of Social and Clinical Psychology* 19: 102–116.

Hinterkopf, E. (1997). *Integrating Spirituality in Counseling: A Manual for Using the Experiential Focusing Method.* Alexandria, VA: American Counseling Association.

Hoge, D.R. (1996). "Religion in America: The Demographics of Belief and Affiliation." In *Religion and the Clinical Practice of Psychology*, ed. E.P. Shafranske. Washington, DC: American Psychological Association, 21–42.

Hungelmann, J.; E. Kenkel-Rossi; L. Klassen; and R. Stollenwerk. (1989). "Development of the JAREL Spiritual Well Being Scale." In *Classification of Nursing Diagnosis: Proceedings of the Eighth Conference Held in St. Louis, MO*, ed. E. Lippincott. New York: Carroll-Johnson.

Ingersoll, R.E. (1994). "Spirituality, Religion, and Counseling: Dimensions and Relationships." *Counseling and Values* 38: 98–112.

———. (1998). "Refining Dimensions of Spiritual Wellness: A Cross-Traditional Approach." *Counseling and Values* 42: 156–165.

Jhansi, R.N., and P.V. Krishna Rao. (2000). "Effects of Meditation of Attention Processes." *Journal of Indian Psychology* 18: 52–60.

McCullough, M.E. (2000). "Forgiveness As Human Strength: Theory, Measurement, and Links to Well-Being." *Journal of Social and Clinical Psychology* 19: 43–55.

Moberg, D.O. (1971). *Spiritual Well-Being: Background.* Washington, DC: University Press of America.

Moberg, D.O., ed. (1979). *Spiritual Well-Being: Sociological Perspectives.* Washington, DC: University Press of America.

———. (1984). "Subjective Measures of Spiritual Well-Being." *Review of Religious Research* 25: 351–364.

Moberg, D.O., and P.M. Brusek. (1978). "Spiritual Well-Being: A Neglected Area in Quality of Life Research." *Social Indicators Research* 5: 303–323.

Myers. L. (1988). *Optimal Psychology: An Afrocentric Perspective.* New York: Kendall Hall.

Pahnke, W.N., and W.A. Richards. (1966). "Implications of LSD and Experimental Mysticism." *Journal of Religion and Health* 5: 175–185.

Payne, B.P. (1990). "Research and Theoretical Approaches to Aging." *Generations* 14: 11–14.

Peck, M.S. (1987). *A Different Drum: Community Making and Peace.* New York: Touchstone.

Ram Dass. (2000). *Still Here: Embracing Aging, Changing, and Dying.* New York: Riverhead Books.

Richards, P.S., and A.E. Bergin, eds. (2000). *The Handbook of Counseling and Religious Diversity.* Washington, DC: American Psychological Association.

Rye, M.S.; K.I. Pargament; M.A. Ali; G.L. Beck; E.N. Dorff; C. Hallisey; V. Narayanan; and J.G. Williams. (2000). "Religious Perspectives on Forgiveness." In *Forgiveness: Theory, Research, and Practice*, ed. M.E. McCullough, K.I. Pargament, and C.E. Thorsen. New York: Guilford.

Shafranske, E.P., ed. (1996). *Religion and the Clinical Practice of Psychology.* Washington, DC: American Psychological Association.

Schor, J.B. (1993). *The Overworked American: The Unexpected Decline of Leisure.* San Francisco: Harper.

Smith, H. (1976). *Forgotten Truth: The Common Vision of the World's Religions.* San Francisco: Harper.

Snyder, C.R. (2000). "The Past and Possible Futures of Hope." *Journal of Social and Clinical Psychology* 19: 11–28.
Stotland, E. (1969). *The Psychology of Hope.* San Francisco: Jossey Bass.
Tubesing, D.A. (1980). "Stress, Spiritual Outlook, and Health." *Specialized Pastoral Care Journal* 3: 17–23.
Valentine, E.R., and P.L.G. Sweet (1999). "Meditation and Attention: A Comparison of the Effects of Concentrative and Mindfulness Meditation on Sustained Attention." *Mental Health, Religion, and Culture* 2: 59–70.
Vaughan, F. (1995). *Shadows of the Sacred: Seeing Through Spiritual Illusions.* Wheaton, IL: Quest.
Wallace, R. (1970). "The Physiological Effects of Transcendental Meditation." *Science* 167: 1751–1754.
Westgate, C.E. (1996). "Spiritual Wellness and Depression." *Journal of Counseling and Development* 75: 26–35.
Worthington, E.L. (1989). "Religious Faith Across the Lifespan: Implications for Counseling and Research." *Counseling Psychologist* 17: 555–612.

CHAPTER 20

THE ROLE OF SPIRITUALITY
IN OCCUPATIONAL STRESS AND WELL-BEING

KELLY L. ZELLARS AND PAMELA L. PERREWÉ

As evidenced throughout the chapters in this book, spirituality and the need for meaning, purpose, and connectedness are important issues currently being examined within the organizational sciences. One goal of this research is to explore the effects of spirituality on the everyday functioning of the business organization and on the well-being of employees. Throughout this chapter we examine the role of spirituality on employee well-being by focusing on the occupational stress process.

OCCUPATIONAL STRESS

A survey of 700 American workers found that 79 percent felt that 1995 was one of the most stressful years ever, and that work was the primary cause of that stress ("Speaking of Stress" 1996). Surveys of managers reported that 88 percent are experiencing elevated levels of stress (Tilson 1997), and most report feeling more stress now than in the past (Cohen 1997). Numerous studies in the psychological and medical literature support a relationship between stress and negative outcomes (for reviews, see Kahn and Byosiere 1992; Matteson and Ivancevich 1987), and the estimated financial costs associated with job stress are staggering. For example, depression-related absenteeism costs businesses $11.7 billion annually (Greenberg, Finkelstein, and Berndt 1995), and stress-related disability claims are the most rapidly growing from of occupational illness within the worker's compensation system (King 1995). Karasek and Theorell (1990) cite data indicating that the total costs of stress to U.S. companies resulting from absenteeism, reduced productivity, compensation suits, health insurance claims, and direct medical expenses exceeds $150 billion annually. In short, work stress continues to plague workers, and organizations are seeing mounting costs.

It is difficult to identify all of the sources of stress and the exact conditions under which job stress will occur. Individuals within the same organization and position may experience and/or perceive environmental stimuli differently (Perrewé and Zellars 1999). Job stress generally refers to the physiological and psychological reactions of individuals to conditions encountered at work (Kahn and Byosiere 1992). Years of conceptual and empirical research have identified a wide variety of job and organizational stressors, including long hours, high workloads (Fox, Dwyer, and Ganster 1993), conflicting or ambiguous demands (Katz and Kahn 1978), work and family conflict (Frone 2000), and even organizational politics (Perrewé et al. 2000).

Our aim is not to review all of the antecedents and consequences to stress within organizations, but to explore how a worker's spirituality influences the experience of job stress and strain. Lazarus and his colleagues have proposed a transactional model of the stress process (Lazarus 1968, 1999; Lazarus and Folkman 1984) that includes both a primary appraisal of the stressor and a secondary appraisal of the coping mechanisms available. An extensive attribution literature argues that the causal attributions individuals assign to events in their lives affect the responses to those events. In our discussion of how individuals cope with job stress (Perrewé and Zellars 1999), we integrated the transactional analysis model, attributional theory, and resulting emotions to propose a model of the job stress process. In this chapter, we extend our earlier work to incorporate the role of spirituality in coping with job stress. First, because there have been numerous definitions of spirituality, it is important to define our use of the term. Then, we discuss how spirituality may impact a traditional view of the organizational stress and coping processes.

SPIRITUALITY IN ORGANIZATIONAL RESEARCH

In this chapter, we define spirituality as the search and experience of the sacred (Pargament 1997; Vaughan 1991). By focusing on "the paths people take in their efforts to find, conserve, and transform the sacred in their lives" (Zinnbauer, Pargament, and Scott 1999, 909), spirituality reflects "the presence of a relationship with a Higher Power that affects the way in which one operates in the world" (Armstrong 1995, 3). It also includes a yearning to find one's place in the world (Benner 1989; Soeken and Carson 1987), and a quest for meaning in one's existence (Shafranske and Gorsuch 1984). Under this definition, spirituality is broader than any single formal or organized religion with its prescribed tenets, doctrines, or practices. Instead, spirituality is reflected in the search for meaning in one's life, insight into oneself and the world, a sense of interconnectedness with the other living things, and spiritual disciplines (e.g., yoga, meditation) (Zinnbauer 1997). Our definition emphasizes a search process that is dynamic (Wulff 1996). Individuals seeking greater spirituality purposefully seek to discover their potential, an ultimate purpose, and a personal relationship with God (Tart 1975) or Higher Being. We recognize that not all of those who advocate spirituality believe in a Higher Being (e.g., existentialists). For the parameters of this paper, however, our definition is consistent with scholars such as Tart (1975) and Elkins (1995) in that spirituality does involve a search and a belief in a Higher Being. In this search, spirituality emerges through "awareness of a transcendent dimension," and specific "values in regard to self, others, nature, life, and whatever one considers the Ultimate" (Elkins 1995, 10) are exhibited. Although individuals can experience spirituality quite differently, the construct of spirituality reflects several themes: "a selfless sense of love and compassion for others, respect and concern for well being and life, and reverence for the universe, and its creation" (Conger 1994, 12).

Outside the organizational sciences, a large body of research has examined the role of spirituality on individual health outcomes. The power of spirituality in maintaining health has achieved greater recognition in mainstream medical research during the last twenty years (Quick et al. 1997). Some have even argued that the "experience of spiritual support may form the core of the spirituality-health connection" (Mackenzie et al. 2000). Spiritual well-being has been shown to be negatively correlated with anxiety arising from a cancer diagnosis (Kaczorowski 1989). Overall, in a review of existing research on the relationship between spirituality and physical health, researchers have reported a strong positive relationship (Matthews, Larson, and Barry 1994). Beyond the possible physical and psychological health consequences related to spirituality, Emmons (1999) reported that individuals who reported more efforts to become spiritual had more purpose in life, and higher marital and life satisfaction.

Although still in its infancy, the role of spirituality in the workplace has begun to receive some attention (e.g., Conger 1994; Fairholm 1998). Zinnbauer et al. (1999) recently proposed that employees who view their work as a sacred vocation are likely to approach their role quite differently from employees who see their work as means to pay bills. Even if a worker does not consider his or her job a sacred vocation, spirituality may influence job-relevant behaviors. Specifically, this chapter examines spirituality in job-related coping. Figure 20.1 depicts how spirituality may influence an employee's experience of job stress. In the following sections, we integrate organizational stress literature and spiritual studies to discuss coping with job stressors. First, we briefly review traditional features of job stress research.

TRADITIONAL ANTECEDENTS OF JOB STRAIN

Job stress "is the subjective feeling that work demands exceed the individual's belief in his or her capacity to cope" (Cropanzano, Howes, Grandey, and Toth 1997, 164). Feelings of job stress produce job strain, physiological and psychological reactions such as headaches, ulcers, anxiety, sleeplessness, and, in some cases, job burnout, reflected in feelings of complete exhaustion and personal failures. Researchers have generally looked at two categories of antecedents to job stress: personality characteristics and job/organizational conditions.

PERSONALITY CHARACTERISTICS

The work of Lazarus and Folkman (1984) has largely influenced the proposition that person variables influence the stress-strain relationship. They argue that the degree of fit of the person to his (her) environment is a significant determinant of the amount of stress experienced. Focusing on significant person characteristics in experiences of strain, Watson, David, and Suls (1999) have proposed that the personality traits of neuroticism and extraversion need to become a central focus within stress and coping research. Research substantiates that negative affect (neuroticism) and positive affect (a component of extraversion) have significant influences on the experience of job stress and job burnout (e.g., Spector and O'Connell 1994; Zellars, Perrewé, and Hochwarter 2000). In our model we included negative and positive affectivity as well as locus of control, which have been shown to influence the amount of job strain reported by workers.

Negative Affectivity

Negative affectivity (NA) is probably the most frequently examined personality characteristic in the job stress literature (Cooper 2000). Individuals high in NA report pervasive feelings of anxiety, fear, or depression (Tellegen 1982; Watson and Pennebaker 1989). The link between high NA and greater levels of felt stress has been attributed to a variety of causes: the tendency of high NA individuals to enact more stressful situations (Depue and Monroe 1986); cope less effectively (Bolger 1990); generate more negative interpretations of ambiguous stimuli (Watson and Clark 1984); or simply overreport stressors and strains because they selectively focus on negative aspects of situations (Brief et al. 1988). Regardless of the underlying reasons, over time, workers higher in NA report greater levels of work-related stress. The role of negative affectivity in job stress research as substance or bias, and how researchers should measure or control for its effects, are the subjects of ongoing debate (Spector et al. 2000; Payne 2000; Judge, Erez, and Thorsen 2000).

303

Figure 20.1   **The Role of Spirituality in Occupational Stress and Well-Being**

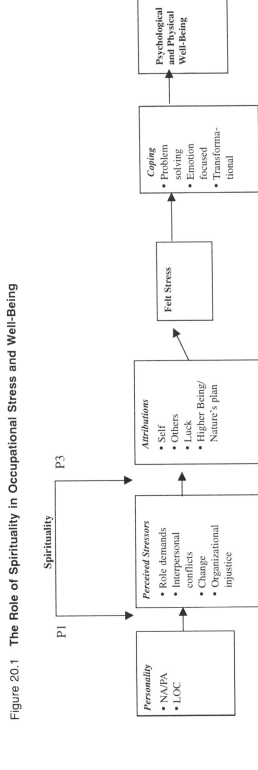

Notes: P1 = proposition 1, P2 = proposition 2, etc.; NA = negative affectivity; PA = positive affectivity; LOC = locus of control.

Positive Affectivity

Individuals high in positive affectivity (PA) exhibit a positive sense of well-being and also perceive stimuli, think, and behave in a manner that encourages positive emotions (George 1992). Their inherent optimistic outlook likely provides such individuals with a stronger sense of well-being about themselves and others. Evidence suggests that individuals who have a strong sense of well-being are less likely to experience work exhaustion and perform better (Wright and Cropanzano 1998; 2000).

Locus of Control

Locus of control refers to the degree to which an individual perceives he (she) can control the outcomes he (she) experiences in life. Workers who believe they control their fate are labeled "internals" and workers who perceive their lives as largely controlled by others or outside forces are "externals." An extensive literature indicates that internals compared to externals are more satisfied with their jobs, more involved in their work, and report less job stress (Blau 1987; Spector 1982).

JOB AND ORGANIZATIONAL CONDITIONS

Years of research and numerous studies have identified a wide variety of job demands contributing to strain, including long hours, high workloads, conflicting or ambiguous requests, and, more recently, work-family conflicts. Research has shown role ambiguity and conflict to be linked with a number of dysfunctional outcomes, including uncertainty, job dissatisfaction, psychological strain, intentions to leave the organization (Jackson 1993; Schaubroeck, Cotton, and Jennings 1989), and burnout (Jackson, Turner, and Brief 1987; Zellars and Perrewé 2001). Work-family conflict has been associated with a number of dysfunctional outcomes, including decreased family and occupational well-being (Kinnunen and Mauno 1998), psychological costs and physical complaints (Frone 2000; Frone, Russell, and Cooper 1992), and job and life dissatisfaction (Netemeyer, Boles, and McMurrian 1996; Kossek and Ozeki 1998; Perrewé, Hochwarter, and Kiewitz 1999). In addition to stressors related to a specific job, individuals encounter organizational stressors, including job insecurity; interpersonal conflicts; structure, personnel, and technology changes; and procedural (i.e., organizational policy), distributive (work outcomes), and interactional (interpersonal) injustices. Overall, research indicates that the greater number of stressors present on the job, the higher level of work stress.

THE TRANSACTIONAL MODEL AND SPIRITUALITY

A fundamental proposition of the transactional model (Lazarus 1968; Lazarus and Folkman 1984) is that it is the interaction of the person and environment that creates a felt stress for the individual. In the model, an individual engages in a primary appraisal to determine if "there is any personal stake in the encounter" (Lazarus 1993, 6) and whether the transaction thwarts or facilitates the individual's goals (Smith and Lazarus 1990). An encounter can be deemed to be irrelevant, beneficial, or threatening (Lazarus 1994; Peacock, Wong, and Reker 1993). Research suggests that the existence of stress may be less important to an individual's well-being than how the individual appraises and copes with stress (for review see Aldwin and Revenson 1987). Not all potential stressors actually cause stress for an individual. In Lazarus's transactional model, individuals differ in their assessment of motivational relevance of a potential stressor, and, hence, in what they appraise as being stressful.

We propose that an additional reason that individuals differ in their assessment of potential stressors is their sense of spirituality, based on experiences that are highly personalized and therefore subjective (Conger 1994). Specifically, Figure 20.1 indicates that in the initial appraisal of a work situation, spirituality will moderate the relationship between personality characteristics of the worker and perceived job stressors. For example, compared to externals, an individual with an internal locus of control (LOC) is more likely to downgrade or minimize the perceived threat of a job stressor since they anticipate having control over their outcomes; however, this relationship may be moderated by a sense of spirituality. Although an individual with an external LOC is more likely to perceive events as beyond her (his) control and therefore more stressful, if he (she) also has a strong sense of spirituality, he (she) may minimize the threat from a potential stressor since he (she) is guided by a sense of purpose surrounding his (her) life; that is, there is meaning or a reason for the events that occur. If true, spirituality may act as the means by which individuals maintain their sense of coherence (Antovnosky 1987).

Similarly, spirituality may moderate the relationship between negative affectivity and perceptions of stressors. Those high in NA, who would normally perceive events as more stressful than those high in PA, may not perceive events as stressful if coupled with a strong sense of spirituality. Spirituality may minimize the perceived threat arising from job and organizational demands—particularly for those high in NA. Spirituality can help give individuals a sense of coherence and control that reduces the likelihood that environmental stimuli will be perceived as stressful. Hence,

> Proposition 1: Spirituality moderates the relationship between personality and perceptions of stressors such that spirituality will reduce the likelihood that events will be perceived stressful for those most likely to perceive their environment as stressful (e.g., those with an external LOC and those high in NA).

We note that some (e.g., Piedmont 1999) have argued that spirituality can be considered a dimension of personality. However, our view of spirituality is that it is a dynamic process rather than a stable trait. Although personality traits are generally considered stable, spirituality is more dynamic and can change. Throughout their lives, individuals may be strongly or weakly guided by the influence of spirituality. The dynamic nature of spirituality suggests that its influence on predispositional tendencies and/or perceptions may grow or weaken over time.

ATTRIBUTIONS IN THE STRESS PROCESS AND SPIRITUALITY

A second way that spirituality may influence the stress process is through its influence on the attributions made for the source of the stress. Attribution theorists (e.g., Kelley and Michela 1980; Weiner 1979, 1985, 1995) have argued that the causal attributions individuals assign to certain events in their lives affect the manner in which they respond to those events. Perceived causes are analyzed over three dimensions: internal/external causality, stability (individual's perception that the cause will continue over time), and controllability (Weiner 1979). The causality and controllability dimensions have the highest priority in the attributional search (Wong and Weiner 1981). Individuals engage in a causal analysis when encountering an outcome that is unexpected or challenging. Experienced stress is such an outcome. Specifically, when individuals experience or feel stress, they will attempt to assign a cause to their felt stress.

In the expanded transactional model of organizational stress proposed by Perrewé and Zellars (1999), following the primary appraisal, an individual searches for causes of the felt stress along the locus of causality (internal and external) and controllability dimensions. Consistent with Weiner, we propose that the attributional search generates an affective response (e.g., anger, shame, guilt, frustration). In the current model, we expand our earlier model to indicate that in considering the cause of stress, an individual either accepts or rejects the cause as legitimate which influences the amount of stress felt. For example, when a subordinate perceives a supervisor's actions as legitimate and not arbitrary, the stress reaction is less severe (Tyler 1994). Consistent with Weiner's (1985, 1986) attribution theory of achievement, we propose that individuals will seek to determine the causes of felt stress following the primary appraisal of a situation as challenging (or threatening), anxiety provoking, and motivationally relevant to personal goals. Figure 20.1 extends the original model to include the work of a Higher Being as a cause of one's current circumstances, in addition to internal (self) and external (others or luck) sources. Spirituality differs from other external categories in that it is nonspecific—that is, it does not focus on a specific person or event. We also distinguish it from "luck" in that spirituality conveys a sense of order and purpose while "luck" is serendipity or happenstance. In Weiner's terms, spirituality is deemed to be stable in that it is an ongoing state within the individual. The perceived stability of a cause affects the expectancies of the individual and magnitude of emotions, thereby directing motivated behavior (Weiner 1985; Weiner, Graham, and Chandler 1982). An attribution based on a sense of spirituality affects the individual's acceptance of a situation and reduces the felt stress. Hence,

> Proposition 2: Attributing stressful events to a Higher Being will reduce felt stress. We also propose that spirituality moderates the relationship between perceived stressors and the search for causes (i.e., attributions made). A strong sense of spirituality may influence the efforts to search for causes. For example, an individual with a weaker sense of spirituality may only look for causes that are more immediate in nature (people present, current task undertaken, time) and select an internal or external cause from the salient characteristics of the current situation. Alternatively, if obvious causes for stressful events are not perceived, an individual with a stronger sense of spirituality may focus on a broader view of the current situation and accept a stressful event as one of life's experiences. Specifically, individuals with a strong sense of spirituality may be better able to accept an unexplainable stressful situation as purposeful and part of a greater scenario of events. Consistent with Heider's (1958) attribution model, spirituality becomes a means by which the individual regains some sense of control over her (his) environment and makes it more predictable. Hence,

> Proposition 3: Spirituality moderates the relationship between perceptions of stressors and attributions such that spirituality reduces the likelihood that stressful events without obvious causes will be perceived as random and unlucky, and increases the likelihood that those stressful events will be perceived as having coherence and purposefulness.

Spirituality may also influence whether the individual perceives the stressor as "challenge related" or "hindrance-related" (Cavanaugh et al. 2000). If true, it may help explain why the managerial development literature reports that executives, while recognizing some job demands to be pressure-laden and stressful, also derive rewarding experiences from their work (McCall, Lombardo, and Morrison 1988). Spirituality may also encourage transformational coping, which is discussed in the next section.

SPIRITUALITY AND COPING WITH OCCUPATIONAL STRESS

As stated earlier, not every potential stressor becomes a source of felt stress for an individual. However, when a threat to well-being is identified, felt stress results when a person feels unable to adequately cope (Lazarus 1981, 1991; Lazarus and Folkman 1984). In numerous studies, styles of coping fall into one of two categories: emotion-focused or problem-focused coping. Emotion coping efforts focus on improving the feelings experienced while problem focused efforts center on altering the source of the stress. Running five miles after work or doing yoga may improve the emotional reactions to a long day at the office (emotion coping). Individuals seeking a greater spirituality may engage in other emotion-focused efforts such as prayer, meditation, or similar rituals in order to gain a better understanding of their current situation and its place in a larger plan of their life or destiny. Time spent in such coping activities may offer the opportunity to contemplate how one's job, and the accompanying opportunities and strain, fits into one's overall life and goals.

Some evidence for the possible benefits of using spirituality in one's coping efforts can be found in the Transcendental Meditation (TM) literature. While we are not promoting the TM practice of two 20-minute periods daily of repeating a mantra, meditation practices have been linked to positive outcomes. For example, Frew (1974) concluded that businessmen who practiced TM exhibited higher productivity, greater job satisfaction, and better interpersonal relationships with their supervisors and coworkers. However, Frew's results are weakened by the retrospective nature of the study and the failure to examine individual characteristics encouraging an employee to meditate (Quick et al. 1997). Some additional evidence for the benefits of meditation is reported in a more recent study of TM. In a controlled study comparing two groups of employees, Alexander et al. (1993) reported that those who practiced TM twice daily for three months showed greater improvements in job satisfaction, general health, productivity, and working relationships. These employees also reported a greater decrease in fatigue and job tension. In summary, studies on the effects of meditation suggest that deliberation and reflection as part of one's spirituality may reduce felt job stress and improve psychological and physical well-being.

Problem-focused coping reflects efforts of an individual to alter or change the source of stress. For example, if work overload is the stressor, an employee may attempt to set priorities or delegate as a means to reduce the felt stress. Alternatively, spirituality may encourage an employee to perceive her (his) job in the larger context of their life's purpose, thereby renewing their sense of direction and restoring energy to "attack the problem." Treadgold (1999) reported that engagement in meaningful work is positively correlated with problem-focused coping and negatively correlated with avoidance coping. Individuals who perceived their work as related to an "inner calling" or transcendent vocation were more likely to respond to stressful experiences by attempting to alter the source of strain. In this study, the level of engagement in meaningful work was also positively related to clarity of self-concept, suggesting that workers with a more transcendent view of their work have a strong sense of self.

Some suggest that the most beneficial results of coping can be realized when both emotion-focused and problem-solving methods are used (Koeske, Kirk, and Koeske 1993), such as in transformational coping. In regard to transformational coping (Maddi 1995), a worker gains perspective and understanding in order to be able to take actions in managing stressful events. "Transformation coping involves actively changing a stressful event by viewing it in a broader life perspective, thus reducing the emotional power and impact of the event. It also involves achieving a greater understanding of the process of the event, which enables one to alter the course and outcome of the event through appropriate action" (Quick et al. 1997, 214). In this light, transformational coping appears to involve both emotion-focused efforts and problem-focused efforts. Spirituality appears to be closely linked to transformational coping efforts in that it alters the view of an event and provides perspective and also gives an individual direction for altering the source of stress. Quick et al. (1997) suggest that individuals who engage in transformational coping are more likely to interpret stressors as challenges rather than threats and perceive themselves to be in control of a situation. They provide the example of the student who engages in transformational coping and thereby interprets a test as a challenge and exerts control through preparation and study. Such an explanation may explain why soldiers derive meaning from harsh work under stressful conditions (Britt, Adler, and Bartone 2001) and executives derive fulfillment from jobs containing numerous stressors (McCall, Lombardo, and Morrison 1988). Spirituality may be the motivation that encourages adequate preparation and the decisiveness necessary to take action when information is incomplete or ambiguous or outcomes uncertain. In sum, spirituality may enhance a sense of control over trying situations and allow one to cope. Hence,

> Proposition 4: Spirituality increases the likelihood that transformational coping (both emotion focused and problem solving) will be utilized to reduce felt stress rather than using only emotion-focused or problem-solving coping mechanisms alone.

An extensive amount of research has examined the impact of perceived control on the consequences of felt stress. In a process he described as the General Adaptation Syndrome (GAS), Selye (1976) was among the first to posit that under stress, an individual senses alarm, resistance, and either flees or adapts to a situation. One means by which individuals adapt to a stressful situation is to place it in the larger context of one's overall goals. A strong sense of spirituality may be the means by which an individual can cope with the numerous stressors that arise on a job—that is, if an employee senses an overriding purpose in one's life, small or trivial stressors will not generate too much concern. Spirituality may therefore increase an individual's sense of control over a stressful job situation, possibly because the transitory nature of some stressors becomes clearer. Employees in a community health facility who felt in control were less likely to react to organizational frustration with counterproductive behaviors than those who did not feel in control (Storms and Spector 1987). By relying on spiritual beliefs, an individual can respond to the environment—that is, assert oneself in such a way as to alter the response to the stressor even when the conditions causing the strain cannot be altered. Rather than striking back at the supervisor either verbally or physically, he (she) may be able to reframe the negative emotions arising in the current situation in light of the rewarding aspects of the overall job.

Organizational researchers have reported that perceived control over work demands has important positive consequences for the individual. Fox and her colleagues (1993) found that the interaction of workload demands and perceived control predicted physiological measures of strain, including blood pressure effects several hours after the workday had ended. In a recent review of the control literature, Terry and Jimmieson (1999) concluded that high levels of control were directly associated with a variety of positive outcomes including decreased anxiety and depression (Carayon 1993; Mullarkey et al. 1997). In the context of workplace violence, Schat and Kelloway (2000) reported that perceptions of control are associated with reduced fear and enhanced emotional well-being.

In our literature search we did not find any organizational studies that have examined the effects of spirituality on perceived control over one's job. However, findings from the clinical psychology literature suggest that individuals who are more spiritual report a greater sense of control in their lives when faced with serious or long-term physical health problems (e.g., Mackenzie et al. 2000). Organizational research can be expanded by examining how spirituality influences perceived control over job stressors and the resulting coping behaviors. One possible explanation is that a deeper sense of spirituality creates a sense of harmonious interconnectedness with others (Hungelmann et al. 1985). This sense of interconnectedness may enhance one's sense of control through trusting a Higher Being that things will work out or even just trusting others at work to help. Mistrust of coworkers has been linked to poor psychological well-being (see Cooper and Cartwright 1994). Some (Quick et al. 1997) have suggested "that faith and spirituality constitute the highest form of secure attachment" (244). Therefore, if spirituality enhances one's sense of security, it may encourage an ability to trust others at work and improve workers' psychological and physical health. We argue that spirituality and the sense of interconnectedness with others serves to guide coping choices and enhances individuals' psychological and physical well-being. Hence,

> Proposition 5: Under stressful conditions, spirituality increases psychological and physical well-being through transformational coping.

DISCUSSION

Our review of the relevant literature leads us to conclude that spirituality can be an effective coping tool for employees working in stressful jobs. It is important to reiterate that we separate specific religious practices from the construct of spirituality. Issues of religious accommodations are addressed in the legal arena under Equal Employment Opportunity laws. Our focus here is on the belief in a Higher Being and on the personal search for sacredness and meaning in one's existence.

Much of the research on workplace spirituality has tended to be anecdotal and conceptual in nature, with little empirical evidence suggesting that organizations that encourage spirituality are more profitable (Moxley 2000). However, we believe the time has come to begin a more systematic and empirical examination of the relationship between workplace spirituality and stress on employee and organizational outcomes. Perhaps one of the primary challenges for organizational scientists is the development of a valid measure of workplace spirituality. Once researchers have developed a measure that adequately assesses workplace spirituality, efforts can then be made to test relationships within the proposed occupational stress model.

Encouraging spirituality goals among workers may improve self-understanding. Organizational managers who encourage spiritual activities in the workplace may find that this promotes more psychological and physiological well-being than in workplaces that fail to encourage such activities. However, much empirical research is needed before these propositions can be used to guide managers and provide sound practical implications.

REFERENCES

Aldwin, C.M., and T.A. Revenson. (1987). "Does Coping Help? A Reexamination of the Relation Between Coping and Mental Health." *Journal of Personality and Social Psychology* 53: 337–348.

Alexander, C.N.; G.C. Swanson; M.V. Rainforth; and T.W. Carlisle. (1993). "Effects of the Transcendental Meditation Program on Stress Reduction, Health, and Employee Development: A Prospective Study in Two Occupational Settings." *Anxiety, Stress and Coping: An International Journal* 6: 245–262.

Antovnosky, A. (1987). *Unraveling the Mystery of Health: How People Manage Stress and Stay Well.* San Francisco: Jossey-Bass.

Armstrong, T.D. (1995). "Exploring Spirituality: The Development of the Armstrong Measure of Spiritual-ity." Paper presented at the annual convention of the American Psychological Association, New York.

Benner, D.G. (1989). "Toward a Psychology of Spirituality: Implication for Personality and Psychotherapy." *Journal of Psychology and Christianity* 5: 19–30.

Blau, G.J. (1987). "Locus of Control As a Potential Moderator of the Turnover Process." *Journal of Occupational Psychology* 60: 21–29.

Bolger, N. (1990). "Coping As a Personality Process: A Prospective Study." *Journal of Personality and Social Psychology* 59: 525–537.

Brief, A.P.; M.J. Burke; J.M. George; B.S. Robinson; and J. Webster. (1988). "Should Negative Affectiv-ity Remain an Unmeasured Variable in the Study of Job Stress?" *Journal of Applied Psychology* 73: 193–198.

Britt, T.W.; A.B. Adler; and P.T. Bartone. (2001). "Deriving Benefits from Stressful Events: The Role of Engagement in Meaningful Work and Hardiness." *Journal of Occupational Health Psychology* 6: 53–63.

Carayon, P. (1993). "A Longitudinal Test of Karasek's Job Strain Model Among Office Workers." *Work and Stress* 7: 299–314.

Cavanaugh, M.C.; W.R. Boswell; M.V. Roehling; and J.W. Boudreau. (2000). "An Empirical Exami-nation of Self-Reported Work Stress Among U.S. Managers." *Journal of Applied Psychology* 85: 65–74.

Cohen, A. (1997). "Facing Pressure." *Sales and Marketing Management* 149: 30–38.

Conger, J.A. (1994). "Introduction. Our Search for Spiritual Community." In *Spirit at Work*, ed. J.A. Conger and Associates. San Francisco: Jossey-Bass, 1–18.

Cooper, C.L. (2000). "Introduction: A Discussion About the Role of Negative Affectivity in Job Stress Research." *Journal of Organizational Behavior* 21: 77.

Cooper, C.L., and S. Cartwright. (1994). "Healthy Mind: Healthy Organizations." *Human Relations* 47: 455–471.

Cropanzano, R.; Howes, J.C.; Grandey, A.A.; and Toth, P. (1997). "The Relationship of Organizational Politics and Support to Work Behaviors, Attitudes, and Stress." *Journal of Organizational Behavior* 18: 159–180.

Depue, R.A., and S.M. Monroe. (1986). "Conceptualization and Measurement of Human Disorder in Life Stress Research: The Problem of Chronic Disturbance." *Psychological Bulletin* 99: 36–51.

Elkins, D.N. (1995). "Psychotherapy and Spirituality: Toward Theory of the Soul." *Journal of Humanistic Psychology* 35: 78–98.

Emmons, R.A. (1999). *The Psychology of Ultimate Concerns: Motivation and Spirituality in Personality.* New York: Guilford Press.

Fairholm, G.W. (1998). *Perspectives on Leadership.* Westport, CT: Quorum Books.

Fox, M.L.; D.J. Dwyer; and D.C. Ganster. (1993). "Effects of Stressful Job Demands and Control on Physiological and Attitudinal Outcomes in a Hospital Setting." *Academy of Management Journal* 36: 289–318.

Frew, D.R. (1974). "Transcendental Meditation and Productivity." *Academy of Management Journal* 17: 362–368.

Frone, M. (2000). "Work-Family Conflict and Employee Psychiatric Disorders: The National Comorbidity Survey." *Journal of Applied Psychology* 85: 888–895.

Frone, M.; M. Russell; and M.L. Cooper. (1992). "Antecedents and Outcomes of Work-Family Conflict: Testing a Model of the Work-Family Interface." *Journal of Applied Psychology* 77: 65–75.

George, J.M. (1992). "Feeling Good—Doing Good: A Conceptual Analysis of the Mood at Work-Organiza-tional Spontaneity Relationship." *Psychological Bulletin* 18: 185–213.

Greenberg, P.F.; S.N. Finkelstein; and E.R. Berndt. (1995). "Economic Consequences of Illness in the Work-place." *Sloan Management Review* 36: 26–39.

Heider, F. (1958). *The Psychology of Interpersonal Relations.* New York: Wiley.

Hungelmann, J.; E. Kenkel-Rossi; L. Klassen; and R.M. Stollenwerk. (1985). "Spiritual Well Being in Older Adults: Harmonious Interconnectedness." *Journal of Religion and Health* 24: 147–152.

Jackson, S.E. 1993. "Participation in Decision Making As a Strategy for Reducing Job-Related Strain." *Journal of Applied Psychology* 68: 3–193.

Jackson, S.E.; J.A. Turner; and A.P. Brief. (1987). "Correlates of Burnout Among Public Service Lawyers." *Journal of Occupational Behavior* 8: 339–349.

Judge, T.; A. Erez; and C.J. Thorsen. (2000). "Why Negative Affectivity (and Self-Deception) Should Be

Included in Job Stress Research: Bathing the Baby with the Bath Water." *Journal of Organizational Behavior* 21: 101–111.

Kaczorowski, J.M. (1989). "Spiritual Well Being and Anxiety in Adults Diagnosed with Cancer." *Hospice Journal* 5: 105–116.

Kahn, R.L., and P. Byosiere. (1992). "Stress in Organizations." In *Handbook of Industrial and Organizational Psychology*, 2d ed., vol. 3, ed. M.D. Dunnette and L.M. Hugh. Palo Alto, CA: Consulting Psychologists Press, 571–650.

Karasek, R., and T. Theorell. (1990). *Health Work: Stress, Productivity, and the Reconstruction of Working Life.* New York: Basic Books.

Katz, D., and R. Kahn. 1978. *The Social Psychology of Organizations*, 2d ed. New York: Wiley.

Kelley, H.H., and J.L. Michela. (1980). "Attribution Theory and Research." *Annual Review of Psychology* 31: 457–501.

King, P.M. (1995). "The Psychosocial Work Environment: Implications for Workplace Safety and Health." *Professional Safety* 40: 36–39.

Kinnunen, U., and S. Mauno. (1998). "Antecedents and Outcomes of Work-Family Conflict Among Employed Women and Men in Finland." *Human Relations* 51: 157–177.

Koeske, G.F.; S.A. Kirk; and R.D. Koeske. (1993). "Coping with Job Stress: Which Strategies Work Best?" *Journal of Occupational and Organizational Psychology* 66: 319–335.

Kossek, E., and C. Ozeki. (1998). "Work-Family Conflict, Policies, and the Job-Life Satisfaction Relationship: A Review and Directions for Organizational Behavior-Human Resources Research." *Journal of Applied Psychology* 83: 139–149.

Lazarus, R.S. (1968). "Emotions and Adaptation: Conceptual and Empirical Relations." In *Nebraska Symposium on Motivation*, ed. W.J. Arnold. Lincoln: University of Nebraska Press, 175–266.

———. (1981). "The Stress and Coping Paradigm." In *Models of Clinical Psychopathology*, ed. C. Eisdorfer, D. Cohen, A. Kleinman, and P. Maxim. New York: Spectrum, 177–214.

———. (1991). *Emotion and Adaptation.* New York: Oxford University Press.

———. (1993). "From Psychological Stress to the Emotions: A History of Changing Outlooks." *Annual Review of Psychology* 44: 1–21.

———. (1994). "Psychological Stress in the Workplace." In *Occupational Stress: A Handbook*, ed. R. Crandall and P.L. Perrewé. New York: Taylor and Francis, 3–14.

———. (1999). *Stress and Emotion.* New York: Springer.

Lazarus, R.S., and S. Folkman. (1984). *Stress, Appraisal, and Coping.* New York: Springer.

Mackenzie, E.R.; D.E. Rajagopal; M. Meibohm; and R. Lavizzo-Mourey. (2000). "Spiritual Support and Psychological Well Being: Older Adults' Perceptions of the Religion and Health Connection." *Alternative Therapies* 6: 37–45.

Maddi, S.R. (1995). "Workplace Hardiness for These Turbulent Times." Paper presented at the annual meeting of the Academy of Management, Vancouver, Canada.

Matteson, M.T., and J.M. Ivancevich. (1987). *Controlling Work Stress: Effective Human Resource and Management Strategies.* San Franscisco: Jossey-Bass.

Matthews, D.A.; D.B. Larson; and C.P. Barry. (1994). *The Faith Factor: An Annotated Bibliography of Clinical Research on Spiritual Subjects.* Rockville, MD: John Templeton Foundation, National Institute for Healthcare Research.

McCall, M.W.; M.M. Lombardo; and A.M. Morrison. (1988). *The Lessons of Experience: How Successful Executives Develop on the Job.* Lexington, MA: Lexington Books.

Moxley, R. (2000). *Leadership and Spirit.* San Francisco: Jossey-Bass.

Mullarkey, S.; P.R. Jackson; T.D. Wall; J.R. Wilson; and S.M. Grey-Taylor. (1997). "The Impact of Technology Characteristics and Job Control on Worker Mental Health." *Journal of Organizational Behavior* 18: 471–489.

Netemeyer, R.G.; J.S. Boles; and R. McMurrian. (1996). "Development and Validation of Work-Family Conflict and Family-Work Conflict Scales." *Journal of Applied Psychology* 81: 400–410.

Pargament, K.I. (1997). *The Psychology of Religion and Coping: Theory, Research, and Practice.* New York: Guilford.

Payne, R. (2000). Comments on "Why Negative Affectivity Should Not Be Controlled in Job Stress Research: Don't Throw Out the Baby with the Bath Water." *Journal of Organizational Behavior* 21: 97–99.

Peacock, E.J.; P.T. Wong; and G.T. Reker. (1993). "Relations Between Appraisals and Coping Schemas: Support for the Congruence Model." *Canadian Journal of Behavioural Science* 25: 64–80.

Perrewé, P.L.; G.R. Ferris; D.D. Frink; and W.P. Anthony. (2000). "Political Skill: An Antidote for Work-place Stressors." *Academy of Management Executive* 14: 115–123.

Perrewé, P.L.; W.A. Hochwarter; and C. Kiewitz. (1999). "Value Attainment: An Explanation for the Negative Effects of Work-Family Conflict on Job and Life Satisfaction." *Journal of Occupational Health Psychology* 4: 318–326.

Perrewé, P.L., and K.L. Zellars. (1999). "An Examination of Attributions and Emotions in the Transactional Approach to the Organizational Stress Process." *Journal of Organizational Behavior* 20: 739–752.

Piedmont, R.L. (1999). "Does Spirituality Represent the Sixth Factor of Personality? Spiritual Transcendence and the Five-Factor Model." *Journal of Personality* 67: 985–1013.

Quick, J.C.; J.D. Quick; D.L. Nelson; and J.J. Hurrell, Jr. (1997). *Preventive Stress Management in Organizations.* Washington, DC: American Psychological Association.

Schat, A.C., and E.K. Kelloway. (2000). "Effects of Perceived Control on the Outcomes of Workplace Aggression and Violence." *Journal of Occupational and Health Psychology* 5: 386–402.

Schaubroeck, J.; J.L. Cotton; and K.R. Jennings. (1989). "Antecedents and Consequences of Role Stress: A Covariance Structure Analysis." *Journal of Organizational Behavior* 10: 35–58.

Selye, H. (1976). *The Stress of Life,* 2d ed. New York: McGraw-Hill.

Shafranske, E.P., and R.L. Gorsuch. (1984). "Factors Associated with the Perception of Spirituality in Psychotherapy." *Journal of Transpersonal Psychology* 16: 231–241.

Smith, C., and R.S. Lazarus. (1990). "Emotion and Adaptation." In *Handbook of Personality: Theory and Research,* ed. L.A. Pervin. New York: Guilford Press, 609–637.

Soeken, K.L., and V.J. Carson. (1987). "Responding to the Spiritual Needs of the Chronically Ill." *Nursing Clinics of North America* 22: 603–611.

Spector, P.E. (1982). "Behavior in Organizations As a Function of Employee's Locus of Control." *Psychological Bulletin* 91: 482–497.

Spector, P.E., and B.J. O'Connell. 1994. "The Contribution of Personality Traits, Negative Affectivity, Locus of Control and Type A to the Subsequent Reports of Job Stressors and Job Strains." *Journal of Occupational and Organizational Psychology* 67: 1–11.

Spector, P.; D. Zapf; P.Y. Chen; and M. Frese. (2000). "Why Negative Affectivity Should Not Be Controlled in Job Stress Research: Don't Throw Out the Baby with the Bath Water." *Journal of Organizational Behavior* 21: 79–95.

"Speaking of Stress." (1996). *HR Focus* (May): 12.

Storms, P.L., and P.E. Spector. (1987). "Relationships of Organizational Frustration with Reported Behavioural Reactions: The Moderating Effect of Locus of Control." *Journal of Occuapational Psychology* 60: 227–234.

Tart, C. (1975). "Introduction." In *Transpersonal Psychologies,* ed. C.T. Tart. New York: Harper and Row, 3–7.

Tellegen, A. (1982). "Brief Manual for the Differential Personality Questionnaire." Unpublished manuscript, University of Minnesota, Minneapolis.

Terry, D.J., and N.L. Jimmieson. (1999). "Work Control and Employee Well Being: A Decade in Review." In *International Review of Industrial and Organizational Psychology,* vol. 14, ed. C.L. Cooper and I.T. Robertson. Chichester, UK: Wiley, 95–148.

Tilson, T. (1997). "Is Your Career Killing You?" *Canadian Business* 70: 78–84.

Treadgold, R. (1999). "Transcendent Vocations: Their Relationship to Stress, Depression, and Clarity of Self-Concept." *Journal of Humanistic Psychology* 39: 81–105.

Tyler, T.R. (1994). "Psychological Models of the Justice Motive: Antecedents of Distributive and Procedural Justice." *Journal of Personality and Social Psychology* 67: 850–863.

Vaughan, F. (1991). "Spiritual Issues in Psychotherapy." *Journal of Transpersonal Psychology* 23: 105–119.

Watson, D., and L.A. Clark. (1984). "Negative Affectivity: The Disposition to Experience Aversive Emotional States." *Psychological Bulletin* 96: 465–490.

Watson, D., and J.W. Pennebaker. (1989). "Health Complaints, Stress, and Distress: Exploring the Central Role of Negative Affectivity." *Psychological Review* 96: 234–254.

Watson, D.; J.P. David; and J. Suls. (1999). "Personality, Affectivity, and Coping." In *Coping: The Psychology of What Works,* ed. C.R. Snyder. Oxford, UK: Oxford University Press, 119–140.

Weiner, B. (1979). "A Theory of Motivation for Some Classroom Experiences." *Journal of Educational Psychology* 71: 3–25.

———. (1985). "An Attributional Theory of Achievement-Related Emotion and Motivation." *Psychological Review* 29: 548–573.

————. (1986). *An Attributional Theory of Motivation and Emotion.* New York: Springer-Verlag.

————. (1995). *Judgments of Responsibility.* New York: Guilford Press.

Weiner, B.; S. Graham; and C.C. Chandler. (1982). "Pity, Anger, and Guilt: An Attributional Analysis." *Personality and Social Psychology Bulletin* 8: 226–232.

Wong, P., and B. Weiner. (1981). "When People Ask 'Why': Questions and the Heuristics of Attributional Search." *Journal of Personality and Social Psychology* 40: 650–663.

Wright, T.A., and R. Cropanzano. (1998). "Emotional Exhaustion As a Predictor of Job Performance and Voluntary Turnover." *Journal of Applied Psychology* 83: 486–493.

————. (2000). "Psychological Well Being and Job Satisfaction As Predictors of Job Performance." *Journal of Occupational Health Psychology* 5: 84–94.

Wulff, D.M. (1996). *Psychology of Religion: Classic and Contemporary.* New York: Wiley.

Zellars, K.L., and P.L. Perrewé. (2001). "Affective Personality and the Content of Emotional Social Support: Coping in Organizations." *Journal of Applied Psychology* 86: 459–467.

Zellars, K.L.; P.L. Perrewé; and W.A. Hochwarter. (2000). "Burnout in Healthcare: The Role of the Five Factors of Personality." *Journal of Applied Social Psychology* 30: 1570–1598.

Zinnbauer, B. (1997). "Capturing the Meanings of Religiousness and Spirituality: One Way Down from a Definitional Tower of Babel." Unpublished doctoral dissertation, Bowling Green State University, Ohio.

Zinnbauer, B.J.; K.I. Pargament; and A.B. Scott. (1999). "The Emerging Meanings of Religiousness and Spirituality: Problems and Prospects." *Journal of Personality* 67: 889–919.

CHAPTER 21

WORKPLACE SPIRITUALITY IN THE UNITED STATES AND THE FORMER EAST GERMANY

JEAN-CLAUDE GARCIA-ZAMOR

There is a spiritual awakening in many countries around the world. In the United States, this spirituality has manifested itself more visibly in the behavior of Americans in the workplace. Many corporations are encouraging the development of this new trend because they think that a humanistic work environment creates a win-win situation for both the employees and the organization. If the members of the organization are happy, they will be more productive, more creative, and will enjoy a greater sense of fulfillment. Personal fulfillment and high morale are closely linked to outstanding performance and, therefore, have a direct impact on an organization's financial success. On the other hand, a dispirited workplace can manifest itself in low morale, high turnover, burnout, frequent stress-related illness, and rising absenteeism. The events of September 11, 2001, in New York City have further contributed to a reexamination of the nature and meaning of work by many Americans and to the emergence of both a more personal and widespread spirituality.

This spiritual awakening is also occurring in the former German Democratic Republic (GDR) but its manifestation is not focused in the workplace. It is occurring in the new way that the East Germans are interacting in the society at large. Under the socialist regime that prevailed during the forty years that preceded the demolition of the Berlin Wall in 1989, people mistrusted each other in many ways. The infamous East German state security service known as *Stasi* had so many informants that people were afraid to confide to close friends and even to the members of their family. But after 1990, a full and public analysis of the post-totalitarian society was considered a fundamental condition for a new beginning. Most East Germans felt that the conspiratorial fabric of the socialist regime needed to be recognized and understood in order to move forward. They felt so strongly about this point that a few days before reunification, on October 3, 1990, the East German parliament, the *Volkskammer,* and the government of the newly democratized GDR even played a last, very risky card, by threatening to reject the reunification treaty if there were no guarantees for a controlled opening of *Stasi* files (Schuller 2000). The files made plain how painful the snooping into personal lives could be. But they also showed how much determination, good sense, solidarity, and willingness to take risks was necessary to remain capable of acting in the face of adversity. The wiretaps documented not only the typically human foibles of the opposition but also how they surmounted those weaknesses (Schuller 2000). The consequences of the opening of these files had some negative impacts on family and friendship ties. Despite the fact that each file was read before being

314

released and the names of any *Stasi* informers were deleted, the circumstances surrounding the reports were so specific that their identity could easily be guessed.

In the Soviet Union, where the spirit was officially shut down for some seventy years, an explosion of spiritual manifestations occurred when Communism fell. Spirituality had been repressed under Communist rule. This was not the case in the GDR probably because spiritual manifestations were never totally suppressed. The churches were allowed to function and until the late 1980s they collaborated with the government. It was an odd balancing act where the government was trying to glorify atheism while not alienating the churches to a point where they might openly agitate against the status quo. On the other hand, the churches were trying to ensure their survival in the midst of the socialist regime. During the forty years of the Soviet domination, East Germans suppressed only any open manifestations of spirituality but never allowed their spiritual souls to be crushed. This was evident in Leipzig in 1989 when they held massive nonviolent peace marches to overthrow the government. However, during the post-unification years, the attitude of the eastern Germans reflected a certain restraint toward spirituality. The tradition in Western countries that tends to define the identity and worth of individuals in terms of their useful work had extended to the former East Germany. All kinds of personal and social stress and the problem of a low self-esteem arose in part because most eastern Germans had strongly identified themselves with their jobs. Unemployment practically did not exist before 1989. After the new social reality set in, some eastern Germans rejected certain values. That was true of those they had associated with Western and Christian cultures.

Despite a definite linkage that exists between spirituality, religion, and ethics, they are still different. A clear definition of the boundaries of spirituality has been elusive. This is why this chapter will first review the literature on spirituality in both the United States and the former East Germany. Then it will look at spirituality in a historical context and compare it first to religious beliefs and then to ethics. Finally, the chapter will look at spirituality in the workplace and suggest ways in which workplace spirituality could be used by managers and administrators in both the public and private sectors of the two countries to increase performance and develop ethical organizations. Starting from the anthropologic assumption that apparently each individual seems to have a certain, constant need for answers to transcendent or metaphysic questions—which arose from the "infinite regress" of philosophy, where "God" or any other transcendent construct represents a final authority—and the role of work and the workplace as one center of today's life, two different levels are examined: the individual one, analyzing the importance of spirituality, and the level of businesses, which use that need as a tool to increase productivity.

SPIRITUALITY: A DEFINITIONAL MESS

Spurred by years of downsizing and job insecurity, employees in the United States are at the forefront of a grassroots movement that is quietly creating a spiritual revival in the workplace. Religion and spirituality, normally taboo in corporate America, are suddenly on the agenda as some employees search for more meaning at work and as some business leaders seek more socially responsible approaches to business and new ways to motivate and inspire workers. The spirituality movement seems to be a reaction to the corporate greed of the 1980s. The environment, corporate responsibility, and spiritual movements all got a big boost after the 1980s because people were unhappy. They were making money but their personal values had to be checked at the door. Some left the corporate world. Others stayed and said that they will bring their values to work. Statistics from the Gallup Organization in New York appear to support such claims. In 1998, when Gallup asked 800 Americans whether their jobs had influenced their spiritual lives,

33 percent credited work with "greatly improving" or "improving" their spirituality, suggesting that the nation's interest in matters of faith has transcended church and home and entered the workplace (Lewis 2001).

Those who write about spirituality in the workplace do not always agree on what the term means. Many authors associate it with religion. Webster's defines spirituality as: "of, relating to, consisting of, or affecting the spirit; of or relating to sacred matters; ecclesiastical rather than lay or temporal; concern with religious values; of, related to, or joined in spirit" (Laabs 1995, 60). Even the dictionary definition is cryptic. And translating it to the workplace is even trickier. Those who are encircled in the spirit-at-work movement often have trouble defining it. According to another definition, spirituality is that which comes from within, beyond the survival instincts of the mind.

> It means engaging the world from a foundation of meaning and values. It pertains to our hopes and dreams, our patterns of thought, our emotions, feelings and behaviors. As with love, spirituality is multidimensional, and some of its meaning is inevitably lost when attempts are made to capture it in a few words. (Turner 1999, 41)

The very thin line between superstition and spirituality has become increasingly difficult to negotiate in today's workplace. Ironically, just as management and workers are being called on to be more rational and productive, basic human nature suggests that issues of faith and nonrational ritual will assume a far greater presence in the workplace. For example, Feng shui, a design scheme of Chinese origin, is now becoming very popular in the United States. It gives an ordinary office an unexpected touch of character by placing a desk in the corner with an odd angle and unusual exposure to natural light. But it is more than just interior design. Many people believe that such rearrangement of their physical space helps in their quest for spirituality in the workplace. In many cases, photographs of family members and close friends may suffice to create an "altar" arrangement that foments spiritual moments at work. Regardless, managers will have to spend more time and ingenuity balancing the spirituality that people bring into the workplace and the culture the firm itself is trying to create. Should a line be drawn between gestures that affirm one's commitment to family values, and other acts that are mostly associated with one's faith?

The theory that personal issues should be left at home is simply not realistic, especially when so many people link their personal self-image with who they are in the professional world. Spirituality seems to be working well where the motivation industry has failed. That multibillion-dollar business in which top gurus command fees of up to $65,000 for a speech has been declining recently. Billions of dollars of rewards were sold to companies—from T-shirts to exotic vacations—to be dangled in front of workers to boost performance. However, there has been exhaustive academic research trying to find out what motivates workers, and it has turned up almost no evidence that motivational spending makes any difference (Jones 2001). Increasingly major corporations, retailers, and advertisers are seeking out trend spotters for information that might give them an edge in shaping strategic planning. Professional trend spotters are a growing breed who spend their working days gathering information—through surveys, interviews, and observation. Marian Salzman, a professional trend spotter who has made a career of predicting market trends and how they will impact the economy, observed:

> We are living in a very antisocial time. Divorce is keeping people apart. Families are not spending time with each other. And to a large degree, telecommunications has become a barrier for people to interact face to face. (Daidone 2000, 1)

She thinks that we are becoming a barrier culture and as a result, more and more people are seeking out things of a spiritual nature to find solace or to fill some void (Daidone 2000).

In the GDR, the political system encouraged close family ties. People needed to find some support from individuals they could trust. This phenomenon can also be found in other countries that have a totalitarian regime. The indicators of "quality of life" in the GDR, such as school experience, family life, peer group culture, and informal networks, were reviewed by a German scholar and showed that these experiences were all part of a political learning process. The State was advocating personal behavior that resembles the one of spiritual individuals in the United States by shaping a Communist goal culture where people would have a "socialist personality." Christiane Lemke wrote:

> The basic goal of political socialization in the GDR is the socialist personality. By defini-
> tion this personality follows the precepts of socialist morality, such as community spirit,
> feelings of duty and responsibility toward the state and society, and an optimistic outlook
> on life and the aims of socialism. Moreover, the socialist personality is willing to put his or
> her knowledge, capability, and talents to full use in the cause of the socialist society, and is
> willing to learn and acquire skills needed to master the scientific-technical revolution and to
> help increase productivity. (1989, 60)

Socialism and capitalism have at least this point in common: they both share the same goal—increased productivity. Both in the United States and in East Germany, the main motive behind motivational spending from the organization's perspective is the idea that only happy workers are productive workers.

The following are some of the direct results of the spiritual vacuum left behind by the Socialist regime in East Germany:

- *A Hardened Atheism.* Despite the fact that the churches were allowed to function in the GDR, very few young people frequented them. Thus, young East Germans who have grown up under Communism had really little or no framework to understand Christianity. One of his students at Leipzig University once told the author of this chapter that he was sixteen when he realized that Christmas had something to do with Jesus. To East Germans, trusting in anything "spiritual" was absurd;
- *A Hunger for Material Possessions.* As soon as the Wall came down, East Germans started playing catch-up with the West. For years they lived without many of the commodities the West enjoyed. The quest for material possessions became one of the main distractions competing against spiritual life;
- *A Rise in the Occult.* Rooted in its Nazi past, the occult was once again popular in East Germany. It provided an alternative spirituality for many undiscerning youth. Also Satanism and the very popular Gothic Society played a big role. The Society took its name from a literary style of fiction, the gothic novel, involving mystery and horror in a medieval setting. Europe's largest meeting of that group with ten of thousands of attendees is still held every May in Leipzig. It is a spectacular event with all women dressed entirely in black baroque garments. Their Gothic personality includes individualism, an interest in the darker side of life and the supernatural, a focus on beauty and dark aesthetics, art, emotion, creativity, intellectualism, mystery, drama, and music. The author of this chapter witnessed this gathering on several occasions; and
- *A Prevalent Suspicion and Disillusionment.* East Germans are generally quite suspicious

toward new ideas and systems, especially if they sound too good to be true. They had been lied to about the glory of Communism. As a result, even though the Berlin Wall fell in 1989, it still exists culturally. East Germans do not like the feeling of being invaded and swallowed up by the deals of Western capitalism. The German discussion on the reunification often emphasizes the fact that the process is characterized by a problematic structure because initial success was followed by disillusionment. Initial "gratifications" (new rights and freedom, consumption) remained a singular event, followed by massive problems and structural changes (unemployment, deindustrialization) (Wiesenthal 1995). In contrast to other Eastern European countries, the best came first in East Germany, whereas in Poland, for example, people started to feel pride because of their growing economy only in the late 1990s. This structure has a certain impact on the legitimacy of the new system, but a vast majority of eastern Germans does not necessarily want the old system back. They desire a new identity of their own.

Spirituality was kept alive in the GDR through rituals and indoctrination. The most important of these rituals was the *Jugendweihe* (youth dedication). This old ritual was first performed in Germany in the mid-1800s. It was reintroduced by Communist officials in 1954 as the official ceremony marking the entry of the youth into adulthood. They actually used that ritual to indoctrinate fourteen-year-olds into Communist principles. But it was also a communal event, where families came together and celebrated their children. It was a rite of passage that corresponds to the Christian confirmation or the Jewish bar mitzvah. The child received political ideological instruction before his/her formal initiation, which included a vow of loyalty to the socialist state. Almost all eligible East German youths had participated in the *Jugendweihe*. Participation was a virtual necessity for any young person who wished to secure a higher education or a good job. When the Berlin Wall fell and Communism disappeared, they stopped doing it. The families and the kids reported that they were missing the ritual and that something had been really valuable about the ceremony. And so the people in the former GDR created a new ceremony that is less about indoctrination and more about just what it means to be a responsible adult. Two factors, culture and gender, have been found to have an impact on the way spirituality is manifested.

Culture and Spirituality

Several historians acknowledge spirituality and trace its interconnection with culture. Katharine Massam thinks that in doing so, they are simply pointing to the mutability and diversity that characterize the relationship of individuals and groups with their God. She argues that within the wide diversity of Catholic spiritualities there were two distinct approaches to the divine:

> In broad terms, lay Catholic spirituality in the forty years before the Second Vatican Council was characterized on the one hand by a passive and highly emotive piety centered on personal holiness for the next world and, on the other hand, by an active apostolic spirit which called for an analytical understanding of this world in order that it might be transformed. (1996, 3)

She also states that these two strands of passive and active spirituality tugged against each other and were woven together and their priorities and concerns threaded through the choices that ordinary people made about the way they expressed their faith (Massam 1996). Another intellectual historian sees spiritualism as a fundamental doctrine of mainline Protestantism in America (Conkin 1995). Carmody and Carmody (1991) studied the manifestation of spirituality in many religions from the religions of oral peoples to Hinduism, Buddhism, Chinese and Japanese religions, Judaism, and Islam. They offer a balanced view of world religions by tracing elements in the varied religious traditions: respect for the sacred, love for beauty, the interaction of the divine in human destiny. They found that key aspects of Christian spirituality are reflected in these world religions. They equated Christian spirituality with Catholic spirituality and observed that it has two major concerns: prayers and actions to improve the world, to increase social justice. As a companion to a public television series, three other authors edited interviews with twenty-eight spiritual leaders from around the world who also described the close link between spirituality and the various world religions (Tobias, Morrison, and Gray 1995).

Cultures definitely affect the manifestation of spirituality. In one culture the natural attributes for spirituality may be enhanced while in another they may be denigrated. North American culture tolerates a great range of diversity, enabling a variety of spiritualities to come into creation. It also values action—quick thinking, fast pace, utilitarianism, achievement, competition (Finn 1990). American culture has countless examples of diverse manifestations of belief in a higher power that are regularly proclaimed not from church pews, but in Alcoholics Anonymous meetings, in books, in magazine articles, at weekend retreats, in hotel seminar rooms (Taylor 1999). A voluminous reader published in 2001 by a university press documents the variety of approaches to spirituality in America. It traces the concepts and presence of spirituality in America's past and explains the strong attraction to spiritual themes in the present, with attention to questions of definition, historical usage, and connection to religion (Albanese 2001). A missionary who worked with the indigenous Indians in the Peruvian Amazon observed that in developing countries uneducated peasants who might not be familiar with the word "spirituality" still might express their spirituality in words and actions (Laur 1987). The author of this chapter had the same experience during a lengthy trip throughout numerous small towns and villages in India. It was often possible to discuss spiritual matters in depth with individuals who had very little formal education.

But interestingly enough, one sometimes may encounter different cultural trends within a single location. This is particularly true in the United States, which is, in fact, a nation made up of a multitude of immigrants, some very anxious to be integrated, others more willing to keep their ties to their origin. African-American spirituality for example has played a vital role in the formation and practice of black freedom in America. African-Americans have managed to create a unique experience of freedom that embraces African-American spirituality and culture as essential elements for building personal identity, consolidating community, and determining their values and destiny. According to an African-American scholar, African-American spirituality affirms, negates, and transcends aspects of Anglo-American culture, creates and sustains African-American culture, and establishes psychological and spiritual relocation in response to oppression and various systems of devaluation in American society (Stewart 1999). Along the same line, another African-American scholar wrote that African-American religion and spirituality influenced and informed the framework of social norms and values by which the people ordered their lives and their relationship to others (Bridges 2001). Good expressions of African-American spirituality can be found in Martin Luther King's famous speech: "I have a dream" (Sterba 2000) and in the lengthy letter that he wrote to fellow clergymen from a Birmingham jail. He challenged the conventional morality of Anglo-American society by stating the following:

> One who breaks an unjust law must do so openly, lovingly, and with a willingness to accept the Penalty. I submit that an individual who breaks a law that conscience tells him is unjust, and who willingly accepts the penalty of imprisonment in order to arouse the conscience of the community over its injustice, is in reality expressing the highest respect for law. (King 2001, 354)

Ironically, while Native American culture had impacted very little on young Americans, it fascinated young Germans because of its spiritual content. They became acquainted with it through the writing of a German author, Karl May, who had published numerous novels dealing with the post–Civil War American West. One of these novels involving the Apache Chief Winnetou and a young German immigrant christened Old Shatterhand presented a uniquely Teutonic view of that time and region. May's ennoblement of Native Americans and admiration for Indian culture and customs was an early (1870s to 1890s) call for racial justice and tolerance. May's books enchanted young Germans with their description of reservation life, politics, and spiritual beliefs.

Gender and Spirituality

Several authors have written about the distinctive ways that men and women express their spirituality in the United States. These works are quite relevant here since both genders are well represented in the workplace. One of these authors, David C. James, thinks that there is a hunger on the part of men to understand the potential of their masculine spirit and to be able to answer questions of identification, empowerment, connection, development, and relationship. He wrote that "the scope of men's deliberation is not limited to issues related to personal gain, but rather embraces communitarian, familial and societal renovation. In other words, men are interested in appropriate uses of masculine power to contribute to the advancement of humankind" (1996, 5). Another author, Carol Ochs, writes that a woman can bring a unique perspective to spiritual questions based on experiences that are unique to her, such as insights she derives from her capacity to bear and nurture children. "What is required is a consciousness that will reflect on an experience and not let go until its value has been understood. Many experiences undergone only by women can be quite ordinary, yet nonetheless reveal the nature of reality and shed lights upon the questions of meaning and value" (1983, 27–28).

In Germany, spiritual women have learned from Americans because several of the earlier spiritual women in America were of European, German-Jewish origins. But by now, German spiritual women have developed their own knowledge in their own language. One of them wrote that:

> We do not only come together to help each other, but for some "higher" or "other" purpose which is not easily explainable—we call it "the Goddess." Everyone of us feels that the spirit of the Goddess is with her, or even that she is the Goddess. We feel connected with nature around us, with stones and rocks, with plants, animals, other human beings, with the whole cosmos. In the spirit of the Goddess, we accept and respect who and how we are, and we respect the other in her way of being. We may not always like how we or the others are, but knowing that the Goddess is with us, we feel that we have the responsibility for our "constructing" ourselves and our world in a meaningful way. (Krüll 1995, 3)

The founding of the GDR demonstrated to millions of women that they were needed by the new society. Even then it was clear that socialism could not be established without the women's experience and initiative, or without their enterprise and ideas (Statkowa 1976). While West Germany solved the labor shortage by importing *Gastarbeiter* (guest workers) to support its postwar *Wirtschaftswunder* (economic miracle), East Germany brought women into the workforce in unprecedented numbers during the reconstruction period following World War II (Frink 2001). Article 20 of the GDR's Constitution stipulated that: "Men and women shall have equal rights and shall be equal before the law in all spheres of social, civic and private life. All organs of government, indeed the whole society, shall be responsible for the advancement of women, especially in acquiring and improving their professional qualifications" (Arnold 1976, 45–46). However, managerial positions in business and public administration remain today the preserve of men in Germany. According to a Federal Statistics Office survey taken in 2000, only 1.6 million of some 5.1 million managers were women (Fickinger 2001). Two American scholars interviewed twenty-six East Berlin women after the German reunification and their book made a valuable contribution to the discussion of the role of women in German society (Dodds and Allen-Thompson 1994). But women were the first victims of the transition. They were the first to be made redundant. The majority of unemployed East Germans were women. They generally had to bring up their children alone (the divorce rate was already very high in the GDR, nearing 50 percent). Under the socialist regime, there was a very sophisticated system of kindergartens and other institutions that took care of children, enabling women to work all day. That system is still considered to be one of the best things achieved in East Germany under Communism. In the United States for example, the lack of adequate kindergartens is a big issue since more and more American women have full-time jobs, a stable trend that started in the 1970s. Used to going to work, East German women much like American women after World War II hated being sent back to the kitchen. However, despite their setback, they showed a remarkable spirit during the years following reunification.

SPIRITUALITY VERSUS RELIGION

The concept of spirituality refers more generally to transcendent matters and universal principles or struggles, for instance the search for truth and morals. But it is hard to separate those questions from religious models, which provide answers to the individual—especially in an environment like the American society. Thus, the spiritual revival in the workplace in the United States reflects, in part, a broader religious reawakening in America, which remains one of the world's most observant nations. Recent polls have shown, for example, that six in ten Americans feel religion is "very important" in their lives and even more (63 percent) say religion can answer all or most of today's problems, including those that intrude on, or arise in, the workplace (*EAP Association Exchange* 2001). Depending on how the question is asked, as many as 95 percent of Americans say they believe in God; in much of Western Europe, the figure is closer to 50 percent. The Princeton Religious Research Index, which has tracked the strength of organized religion in America since World War II, reports a sharp increase in religious beliefs and practices since the mid-1990s (Gunther 2001). When the Gallup Poll asked Americans in 1999 if they felt a need to experience spiritual growth, 78 percent said yes, up from 20 percent in 1994; nearly half said they'd had occasion to talk about their faith in the workplace in the past twenty-four hours. Sales of Bibles and prayer books, inspirational volumes, and books about philosophy and Eastern religions are growing faster than any other category, with the market expanding from $1.69 billion to $2.24 billion from 1995 to 2000, according to the Book Industry Study Group. Literally hundreds of those titles address spirituality at work, from Christian, Jewish, Buddhist, and nondenominational perspectives (Gunther 2001).

Some businesses openly advocate religious practices such as prayer in the conference room. An increasing number of business owners and chief executive officers are bringing their Christian faith to work. *Business Week*'s November 1, 1999, cover story on religion in the workplace speaks to this growing trend. The article details the increased acceptance of corporate prayer groups, and mentions the fact that more than ten thousand groups meet weekly to pray. In Jacksonville, Florida, a monthly luncheon meeting for Christian business professionals that started in

1994 with twelve men was drawing up to 500 people seven years later. But legal experts think that mixing business with religion means walking a fine line. Forcing an employee to join a prayer session or Bible study is clearly illegal. But even when employers make it optional, they could be exposing themselves to liability. It could be perceived as a form of favoritism that could easily lead to discrimination. Some companies affiliated with the Atlanta-based Fellowship of Companies for Christ have been sued for discrimination. However, none has lost a case. They have learned to be careful and treat everyone the same. No one is required to participate and they are sensitive to nonbelievers as well. If morning meetings are to begin with prayer, employers tell those who wish to be excluded to come five to ten minutes late (Maraghy 2001). But in a study released in June 2001, the Society for Human Resource Management in Virginia reported that complaints of religious bias have jump 40 percent since 1992. Moreover, damages associated with such legal claims have increased to $5.5 million, up from $1.4 million in 1997 (Lewis 2001). The group noted that bias may take many forms, ranging from jokes about a coworker's spirituality or denying a worker break time for prayer, to outright firings. Some companies shy away from using the words "religion" or "spirituality" to describe their gatherings. Others stress that workplace prayer, religious study, or other meetings do not favor any denomination or belief. And at most companies, proselytizing is prohibited (Lewis 2001).

Several workers in the United States and Canada have access to a full-time corporate chaplain. The Rev. Diana Dale of Houston, who heads the National Institute of Business and Industrial Chaplains, estimates that there are about four thousand corporate chaplains in the United States. Some of them are full-time employees of one organization; others are involved in individual workplaces as outside contractors. Marketplace Ministries, based in Dallas, provides chaplaincy teams to 148 companies in 35 different states. The company has a resource staff of one thousand, representing Protestantism, Roman Catholicism, Judaism, and Buddhism. In addition to these formally trained chaplains is another group of in-house consultants—no one knows how large—who see their work as having a specifically spiritual element. Anything that resembles religion in the workplace makes some people nervous. But there is widespread consensus among corporate chaplains that they are there to present spiritually based alternatives, not to push religion (Walker 1998).

Michael Schrage wrote that the expanding quest for corporate meaning recalls Emile Durkheim's landmark work *The Elementary Forms of Religious Life.* At the core of the French sociologist's work almost a century ago was his belief that there is something valuable in fervent religious experiences even if one does not necessarily believe in the existence of a Supreme Being. Instead of studying the main religions such as Judaism, Christianity, or Islam, Durkheim looked at primitive religions that used totems. Under totemism a clan or tribe had a sacred object or totem— usually something found in nature. Durkheim found out that the tribe usually valued the image of the totem more than the totemic item itself. The totem was not sacred because of any intrinsic properties it possessed but because of the role it played in the community. It provided a sense of unity—of oneness—among the tribe. The totem was both the symbol of the community and an expression of what it found sacred (Schrage 2000).

Spirituality and religious belief are compatible though not identical; they may or may not coexist. In office settings, it is absolutely crucial to understand the difference between these two. A study of spirituality in the workplace published in the *Sloan Management Review* describes spirituality as "the basic feeling of being connected with one's complete self, others, and the entire universe. If a single word best captures the meaning of spirituality and the vital role that it plays in people's lives, that word is interconnectedness" (Mitroff and Denton 1999a, 83). The two authors published a larger study of spirituality, religion, and values in the workplace after conducting surveys and more than ninety interviews with high-level managers and executives. Among their findings: people differentiate strongly between religion and spirituality; religion is viewed as intolerant and divisive; and spirituality is seen as universal and broadly inclusive (Mitroff and Denton 1999b). Another study, in *The Academy of Management Executive,* clarifies that advocates of spirituality in the work environment often view spirituality and religion as very different concepts; while they generally oppose the promotion of formal religion in the workplace, they openly defend spirituality as a workplace practice. They assert that spirituality looks inward to an awareness of universal values while formal religion looks outward, using formal rites and scripture (Cash and Gray 2000). Spirituality is not exclusively about religion.

> It's not about converting people. It's not about making people believe a belief system or a thought system or a religious system. It's about knowing that we're all spiritual beings having a human experience. It's about knowing that every person has within him or herself a level of truth and integrity, and that we all have our own divine power. (Laabs 1995, 60)

The former East Germany was an atheistic state that had no interest in religious and independent-minded individuals who might place the state at risk and make it unstable. Christians were often denied higher education, making it impossible for them to achieve positions of leadership in the government. They were discriminated in career and chosen profession and there were restrictions on travel, publications, assembly, vacation to spas and inexpensive resorts. Despite vehement protests from the churches, the government compelled children to join Communist youth organizations (Allison 2000). In a discussion on moral obligations and values in an individualized society, Bertram (2000) points out that in present-day Germany the "generation contract," which comprises the solidarity between the older generation, the adult generation, and children and young people, is being called into question not only in politics, but also in the media and by scholars. Because religion played an immense role in resistance to Communism, when the Soviet Empire collapsed, many people assumed East Germany would witness a new religious renaissance.

The Evangelical-Lutheran Church had long represented a key element in civil society in the GDR, and in 1989, it became a key actor in political change. The local churches became the cradle of the revolution, as demonstrated most vividly by the Nikolai Church in Leipzig. The Monday prayer services for peace became the catalysts for public protest. These peaceful gatherings formed the core around which the peaceful protest demonstrations grew. The "New Forum," founded on September 9, 1989, was a loose coalition of Christians and environmentalists, "Green" type thinkers who wanted simply to open the possibility of free discussions about aspects of life in the GDR that were generally "off limits" to debate. Throughout the entire period, the churches kept advocating nonviolence and dialogue. The individual congregations provided shelter from the police in certain cases and when the government collapsed, church officials often provided a semblance of order in turbulent and frustrating conditions.

However, Western observers may have underestimated the intellectual heritage of Communism and the impact of a half-century of atheism as the official ideology. In reality, Communism has stifled religion in the former East Germany. Interest in religion largely failed to boom in eastern Germany. After the reunification, there was neither a major trend back to the church, nor a turn toward alternative religious practices (Smith 1998). Yet spirituality boomed as discussed earlier in this chapter. By providing a protected forum where free discussion was possible, the Church has had a catalytic function in the peaceful change in the country but it was eclipsed after the reunification and had little influence in the eastern part of Germany. According to Henkys and

Schweitzer (1994), it can be assumed that in 1949, the founding year of postwar German states, the percentage of church members from the whole population on both sides of the border was the same. In 1950, approximately 94 percent of the population in the newly formed GDR belonged to a Christian church. In 1990, at the end of the GDR, only about 25 percent were members. At the same time the percentage of church members in West Germany was approximately 83 percent. One of the reasons pointed out by the two authors for this dramatic drop in membership in the former East Germany was the refusal of payment of the so-called church tax. An agreement between the churches and the GDR government allowed church employees to solicit and collect membership fees from churchgoers. Continuous refusal to pay resulted in an informal withdrawal from the church. There is no doubt that the introduction of the church tax had damaged the churches there.

Another study (Allen 1999) found that atheists form a majority in East Germany—62 percent of the population, and that an additional 13 percent are agnostics. Data from the European Values Study between 1990 and 1998 show that the younger generation is increasingly alienated from the churches. Catholics in Germany decreased from 51 percent in 1950 to 43 percent in 1965, and to 22 percent in 1989 (Allen 1999). Islam is presently the fastest-growing religion in reunified Germany, with 3 million mainly Turkish adherents. There are some 500 mosque associations in the country. While making a deliberate effort to avoid the impression of open indoctrination so as to bond with young people, they offer programs in all areas of life and try to restrict their contact with Germans. An Arab scholar thinks that this "creeping Islamization" is the responsible element for the disintegration dynamics of West European societies (Luft 2001). Buddhism is also expanding, mostly Asian immigrants, though it is also attracting some German practitioners. Due to immigration from the former Soviet Union, the Jewish community is also growing. Several new synagogues and Jewish Community Centers were recently opened or are being built.

Allen (1999) quoted a research study that shows that while religious faith—as measured by variables such as belief in life after death and belief in miracles—is increasing somewhat in Eastern Europe, religious practice is not. The church was healthier and more vigorous when it was officially suppressed because in the Socialist era Christians would seek each other out. In a society where the government spies were everywhere, they trusted each other. But by the end of the year 1990, two generations of East Germans have undergone the anti-God indoctrination of the Communist government. And in practice, at least, the new order is echoing the old. As pointed out by Maynard (1998, 1), "Marx's dialectical materialism was exchanged for run-of-the-mill materialism. The former is more hate-filled than the latter, but neither philosophy is friendly to God."

Despite the decline of organized religions all over Europe, there seem to be at the same time a strong new wave of spiritual interest. According to the Turin-based Center for the Study of New Religions, 90 percent of Europeans think there is a God—up an astonishing 20 percent in the last decade. The growth of esoteric and New Age movements is rapid enough that the European Parliament recently voted to create an "observatory" to keep tabs on these groups. Therefore, the actual religious phenomenon in Europe, including East Germany, is not secularization, but deinstitutionalization of spirituality. Most Europeans maintain vestigial ties to a church—95 percent of European funerals are religious—but few turn to it for nourishment. Instead, they look to new movements and to an eclectic blend of spiritual practices (Allen 1999).

An international survey by the World Values Surveys of the University of Michigan's Institute for Social Research also found that the percentage of churchgoing had dropped in East Germany. Investigators on five continents surveyed sixty countries representing 70 percent of the world's population to study the shift in human values. Questions in the enormous survey, translated into thirty-one languages, were designed and tested to have the same basic meaning from one culture to the next. Its findings showed that while allegiance to religious institutions declined, spiritual concerns remained strong. Church attendance and belief (which represent outside authority) dropped. But at the same time people became more trusting and tolerant of strangers and individual spirituality soared. One of the authors of the survey stated: "The established churches today may be on the wrong wavelength for most people in industrial societies, but new theologies such as the theology of environmentalism, or New Age beliefs, are emerging to fill an expanding gap" (*Charisma News Service* 2000, 1). Rossiter (2000) writes that many young people in Eastern Europe wondered why there was any need to have a religious identity at all. Many appeared to be searching for a spirituality that was more independent of their own traditional religion. It was one of a variety of sources (both religious and secular) that these young people drew on for their eclectic spirituality. Even under the Communist rule, East German spirituality was vibrant. Faith meant a lot to people there. It cost them to be Christian then, and people seemed more committed.

In contemporary German politics religious beliefs play a much smaller role and religious institutions a much greater one than in American politics. Church and state are not strictly separated in Germany. Whereas the American Constitution forbids any law "respecting the establishment of religion," the German maintains a traditional *Staatskirchenrecht* that gives the Protestant and Roman Catholic Church exceptional legal privileges at every level of government (Edinger and Nacos 1998). The German church-state cooperation dates from the Reformation. In exchange for their support, the churches are granted a variety of special privileges (tax-free lands, bishops' residences, salaries), many of which are still in effect. Certainly the most important privilege, and one that makes German churches among the most affluent in the world, is the church tax. This is computed as a percentage (about 9 percent) of an employee's income tax, automatically withheld from paychecks, and then transferred to the churches. To avoid paying the tax, a citizen has to officially "contract out" of his church by signing the appropriate documents with state officials (Conradt 2001). This dependence on state authorities makes the churches essentially conservative institutions oriented to the status quo. This attitude was sealed in 1978 in a historic meeting between General Secretary Erich Honecker and leaders of the Evangelical Church that laid the basis for a new understanding between church and state. They agreed to a strict separation between the two, meaning that the state would not interfere with the right to practice religion freely and the church was not to interfere with politics (Olivo 2001). However, this agreement may not have changed much the prior relation between state and church in the GDR, especially in terms of control by the *Stasi*.

Spirituality Versus Ethics

A growing body of literature that deals with spirituality and the workplace has been emerging and has become part of some ethics courses in the United States. But like spirituality and religion, spirituality and ethics are also different. Spirituality encompasses the same topic that is so important in ethics: character, and how to live life well. There are many spiritual practices that are practically lifted from prominent ethical theories and moral principles, such as the discipline of "dealing with others as you would have them deal with you"; the discipline of "balancing our work, personal, family, community, and church responsibilities"; the discipline of "working to make the system work"; and the discipline of "engaging in personal and professional development" (Pierce 1999). Behaving ethically is a necessary but not sufficient component of integrating faith and work. Ethics, or moral philosophy, aims to explain the nature of good and evil. It is important because the human world is dominated by ideas about right and wrong and good and bad. Most ordinary conversation consists of value judgments (Teichman 1996; Bond 1996).

Ethics is primarily concerned with shedding light on the question of what should count as morally good behavior, of what is the good life, and providing the justification of the sort of rules and principles that may help to assure morally good decisions. To this end it employs arguments and theories in order to convince others that certain claims are the best ones to hold (Liszka 1999). Thus, ethics is viewed as a way of behaving that can be prescribed and imposed by the work environment. It is often presented as a Code of Conduct that new employees have to accept before being hired. But candidates for employment are not asked how they will handle ethical dilemmas. It is understood in the workplace that each individual has a basic understanding of what kind of behavior is morally acceptable and sometimes obligatory and what is considered morally inadmissible. But within this broad framework lie a multitude of variables that quite often have their roots in the individual's own spirituality. An individual's spirituality will be a determinant factor in that person's understanding and interpretation of ethical behavior. This is why some employers think that ethical commitments are personal. They believe that some employees have it and others don't and do not consider ethical behavior as a skill to be learned. However, several books have been written to provide a framework that allows for the clear identification and implementation of strategies to improve the ethical climate of the workplace (Costa 1998; Clark and Lattal 1993; Lewis 1991; Hitt 1990).

The U.S. federal government requires a yearly ethics refresher for most employees, with more rigorous training for employees involved in contracting. In several county and city governments throughout the United States, "ethics awareness training" has been initiated. In Miami-Dade County, the mayor mandated ethics training for all county employees in 1998 after a series of corruption scandals at the seaport and elsewhere rattled county government, prompting outcry from business and civic leaders (Garcia-Zamor 2001). Ethics training there includes explanations about rules pertaining to communication with lobbyists, receiving gifts from vendors, conflicts of interest, outside employment, the policies that regulate the procurement and contracting process. The ethics manuals distributed in the training serve as a resource guide for employees concerned about possible misconduct by their colleagues. They list telephone numbers for the state attorney's office, Miami-Dade Police, and a hotline for the county's Office of the Inspector General. One of the loudest advocates of mandatory ethics training for county employees was the Greater Miami Chamber of Commerce. Business leaders were worrying that the bad image of a city plagued by constant ethical scandals might cause new investors to shy away. This is a good example to illustrate the various functions that ethics can have. Not only do they provide a framework for meaningful human behavior, but on a lower theoretical level they can also be good instruments to protect material interests.

There is little doubt that it is very difficult to change people's character in term of personality traits. It is not sufficient for employers to point out the benefits of behavioral change. Some employees might not be willing to do the hard work required for ethical change. Their individual greed and flawed characters might dispose them to behave unethically. But organizational culture might also play a role as well. In their Multimedia Course, Robert Mertzman and Peter Madsen pointed out that:

> If the opportunity presents itself, and the risk of not getting caught is low, and if the organization does not foster an ethical climate, then chances are fairly good that corruption will take place. This organizational explanation of governmental mischief, then, sees such conduct as less the function of individual, psychological disposition and more the result of institutional dysfunction. (1992, 86)

Therefore, the organization should conduct an "ethics audit" to redesign work settings, create proper incentive systems, and modify patterns of interaction among employees. Such an "ethics audit" would identify sensitive situations that might tempt an individual to act unethically.

In the United States, in addition to or in lieu of ethical training, some companies now offer training courses in spirituality in the workplace. In 1997, helicopter manufacturer Sikorsky Aircraft began offering a professional development program designed to boost retention and productivity among women. During the two-day course, participants explored their personal and professional goals, on the premise that success in one area strengthens the other. After the course, many felt renewed and ready to tackle challenges—with retention rates rising accordingly. Some participants felt that after the course they had a new sense of contributing more in the job, at home, and in the community. Values have begun to be part of the workday. The movement has spawned a push for managerial concession, as well as programs that help redefine life goals. After the demoralizing downsizing of the early 1990s, some businesses are recognizing that cultivating employee fulfillment is important to the bottom line. In addition to Sikorsky, companies such as GE Industrial Systems said that development courses have helped raise productivity by increasing job satisfaction (Hua 1999).

The trends in today's Christian spirituality are quite different from the concept of ethics. Like ethics, these trends have evolved over time and are different from the trends expressed in other times. A scholar on Christian spirituality wrote that it is now oriented toward four trends: (a) it responds to life, to its beauty and its injustices and leads to action; (b) it looks to the universe—the whole world becomes a part of the spiritual person; (c) it is responsive and responsible to the poor and oppressed; and (d) it is social oriented. Not only the persons (e.g., coworkers), but also the society in which a person is living (e.g., the organization), are important in a relationship with God (Missinne 1990). The relationship between work and the spiritual life is more complex than just good ethical behavior. Seeing work as more than a livelihood, and surely more than a means of amassing wealth, can bring peace to the many who must work at apparently unsatisfying jobs. In this view their work becomes a part of the vision of the whole of humanity co-operating, one with all the others, in the common pilgrimage through this world. Father Dominic Hoffman warns that many of us waste our lives trying to be something we cannot be and ought not be. "We eat ourselves up with envy and die a thousand deaths of frustration. But from the doctrine of the Mystical Body we see that we all have our place, that we are useful in some way, perhaps mysteriously hidden from us, to the whole of God's plan" (1976, 299–300).

In Germany, the difference between ethics and spirituality is best illustrated in the questions of value that are addressed in the feminist inquiry of two Australian scholars. They surveyed many issues of concern to German feminists, including feminine aesthetics, theology, ethics and spirituality, women's social and political responsibilities, and feminist critiques of the Enlightenment. One of the chapters of their book discusses the difference between feminist ethics and spirituality (Beinssen and Rigby 1996). The concept of "social justice" is another area where the difference between spirituality and ethics is clearly illustrated. East Germans who had to deal with the Federal German bureaucracy after 1989 experienced the "culture shock" of German unification. When an East Berlin writer applied in 1990 for the restitution of a villa that had belonged to his parents, Jews who had disappeared in the Nazi camps, he was told that it was too late. He had missed the deadline. The law was framed in such a way that 2.2 million applications for restitution from West German citizens had been allowed, while not a single East German application had been considered. And as for compensation to former prisoners, "One month of incarceration in GDR prisons was worth 550 marks, while a month in the Nazi camps was only worth 150 marks." There were also two different yardsticks for assessing pension rights: a Wehrmacht soldier, even a former SS member, was entitled to the full pension while GDR officials got only a reduced pension (Pätzold 1997). Other compelling legal battles were the trials that arose from shootings at the Wall. Where did responsibility lie? What retrospective justice should be sought? (Maier 1997). Thus, despite the fact that the East Germans appreciated their new freedoms, they were more interested in seeing ethical theories and moral principles applied equally to them. They were primarily interested in Justice: 77 percent regarded justice as more important than freedom. The kind of justice meant here is social justice, which is another term for (material) equality, which opens the classical front line between personal freedom (promoted by the liberal model) and the problem of material resources in a society (equality). For East Germans, the pressure of money had replaced the pressure of politics and many thought that despite everything, they were freer as they were before 1989. Coming from a society with a very high level of social homogeneity, in which university professors, workers, and managers often lived in the same block of flats, they did not much care for this individualistic system in which they had to elbow their way to the top of a social pyramid that was becoming increasingly remote from the base. Faced with the postunification crisis, the East Germans at least had one advantage over their West German compatriots. They were more flexible, more resourceful, and they displayed more solidarity.

SPIRITUALITY IN THE WORKPLACE AND ORGANIZATIONAL PERFORMANCE

A fundamental tension between rational goals and spiritual fulfillment now haunts workplaces in the United States. It is not enough that workers feel productive and effective. Survey after management survey affirms that a majority wants to find meaning in its work. For a long time, employers compartmentalized workers, carefully separating business concerns from personal identities. But productivity waned because people's personal lives do affect their work. That's why in the United States companies increasingly have added work-and-family programs and a variety of other benefits aimed at helping employees achieve balanced lives (Laabs 1995). Lewis Richmond, a former Buddhist monk turned catalog software tycoon and author of *Work as a Spiritual Practice*, points out that Buddha himself found enlightenment out of a "serious case of job dissatisfaction" as an Indian prince twenty-five hundred years ago (McDonald1999). Spirituality is about acknowledging that people come to work with more than their bodies and minds; they bring individual talents and unique spirits. For most of the twentieth century, traditionally run companies have ignored that basic fact of human nature. Now, they explore spiritual concepts such as trust, harmony, values, and honesty for their power to help achieve business goals. Spiritual needs are fulfilled by a recognition and acceptance of individual responsibility for the common good, by understanding the interconnectedness of all life, and by serving humanity and the planet. Therefore, when one speaks about bringing spirituality into the workplace, he/she is talking about changing organizational culture through the transformation of leadership and employees so that humanistic practices and policies become an integral part of an organization's day-to-day function. A humanistic work environment would create a win-win situation for both the employees and the organization (Turner 1999).

The Industrial Age concept of "a day's pay for a day's work" is yielding to the postindustrial perception that work itself should be a medium for self-expression and self-discovery. People are entitled, encouraged, and even expected to find meaning in their work (Schrage 2000). Among recent factors that have increased the apprehension in the workplace are the massive corporate downsizing; a series of mergers that reduced the workforce of many large corporations; more work has been moving offshore; and more recently the terrorist attacks of September 11, 2001. The uncertainty in the workplace was magnified by the fact that some successful companies were laying people off. As Rutte pointed out, that's never happened before: "The understanding used to be that when a company was in fiscal trouble, it would lay off people and when the company was successful, it would keep and even hire people. But with re-engineering and new advanced technology, there is a need for less people, so successful companies are downsizing" (1996, 1).

Spirituality in the workplace can be manifested in several ways but at two different levels, the personal one and the organizational one. At the first level, the people involved are spiritual ones who might have had some concerns about the adequacy of their workplace for their spiritual life even before accepting employment. John Cowan (1993) wrote that the Latin word *spiritus* means "breath." He defined a spiritual person as one who is conscious, aware of the special breath of life in all creation, particularly in humans and certainly in oneself, and acts accordingly. These individuals, according to Cowan, would ask questions such as these when entering the workplace:

> Is this work worthy of the human spirit? Is this the work that expresses my spirit? Am I respectful of the spirit within my fellow workers? Do I assent to and assist their call? Is this place beautiful enough to be worthy of the presence of the human spirit? Do I make my work a worthy expression of my spirit? (1993, 60)

This type of spirituality does not necessarily have to be associated with a specific religion. Some workplaces could be less productive only because people cannot find a way to breathe their spirituality into work. But when spiritual people join a workplace that fits their expectations, they will support their colleagues. They will seek quality. They will do good work. Cowan admits that these results can be achieved without a sense of spirituality. But they are not seeking these results in themselves. They believe in the spirit and see these as ways the spirit expresses itself. In his hierarchy of being, "the spirit does not exist as the servant of the workplace; rather the workplace exists as the playground of the spirit" (Cowan 1993, 60).

At the second level, the organization emphasizes spirituality in order to improve productivity. Most workplaces understand well that employees bring with them to the job personal moral core values that are linked to their cultural backgrounds and their religions. They try to connect faith and work ethics. A growing literature reveals that this practice already exists in the business sector. A recent questionnaire surveying the interests of members of the Council for Ethics in Economics in Columbus, Ohio, asked: "How do you view the role of your personal religious belief and heritage as you make business decisions?" Virtually all the businesspeople responding circled "very important" (Childs 1995). This might explain the proliferation in the 1990s of books on stories and strategies for building self-esteem and reawakening the soul at work (Bracey et al. 1990; Canfield and Miller 1996; Chappell 1993; Walsh 1999; Ulrich, Zenger, and Smallwood 1999; Bennis 2000; and many others).

When two thousand global powerbrokers gathered for the elite World Economic Forum in Davos, Switzerland, in the spring of 1999, the agenda included confabs on "spiritual anchors for the new millennium" and "the future of meditation in a networked economy." Indeed, thirty MBA programs now offer courses on the issue and it was the focus of a 1999 issue of the *Harvard Business School Bulletin* (McDonald1999). In the first four months of his presidency, few of George W. Bush's proposals have generated as much controversy as his decision to establish the Office of Faith-Based and Community Initiatives. Critics have complained that this move blurs, if not completely erases, the line between church and state and injects religion into areas of life from which it should remain distinct. Such criticisms ignore the fact that spiritual and religious beliefs are not easily compartmentalized; they shape attitudes toward, and actions in, all aspects and spheres of daily life.

Workplace spirituality is more difficult to detect in East Germany. For one thing, years of indoctrination into atheism have made spiritual manifestations uncommon. The presence of a large number of foreign workers complicates further the workplace situation because of increased violence against them by right-wing orientated fellow workers. The Cologne-based federal *Verfassungsschutz* (the Office for the Protection of the Constitution), which monitors political extremism in Germany, estimated there were about 350 extreme right-wing Internet sites being operated in Germany in 2000 (Burger 2000). The Environmental Research Center (ERC) located in Leipzig sees this trend as a threat to the State of Saxony's economic and research bases. ERC pointed out it is already difficult to get foreign academics to go to eastern German universities such as the renowned Leipzig University (Finsterbusch 2000). Many companies are considering taking legal action against right-wing employees. Several major corporations, including the German automaker Volkswagen, have adopted work agreements laying down specific sanctions for employees who disrupt peace in the workplace. The state government of Magdeburg has drafted a program for "more civil courage in the workplace" together with chambers of commerce and business associations. But xenophobic attitudes are not the only problem in the eastern German workplace. Harassment takes place for a variety of other reasons including age and gender discrimination. In 2000, opinion pollsters *Emnid* conducted a survey and found that nearly one in two German workers feels subjected to psychological pressure from colleagues or managers. As many as 51 percent of respondents who changed jobs cited harassment as the reason for doing so (Groschl 2001). Victims of workplace harassment cost business a great deal of money because of absenteeism, fluctuating moods, and poor performance. Experts acknowledge that many German managers are incapable of solving a conflict, preferring to avoid confrontation whenever possible, and leave their staff to sort out the difficult situation themselves.

An American scholar wrote that when he was in Germany in the summer of 1994, he had a hard time because after unification, the Germans have become enemies of themselves. The body politic had gone back to the 1950s and the 1960s. People were again mistrusting each other. He found that the differences between West and East were no more easily detectable in terms of economics or urban planning but in the opinions that people voiced. There was dissatisfaction all over. The reason: they have been promised to be as wealthy as the West Germans within three to, at least, five years. Of course, that did not happen (Wenzel 1994). Such an observation might seem to indicate that spirituality has taken a step backward in the 1990s. But it has to be placed in the context of the new socioeconomic reality that the East Germans were facing during the years that followed the end of socialism. After reunification a painful truth emerged. Despite Stalinist discipline, its workers were not used to hard work when compared to their West German counterparts who worked for wage incentives. Work discipline had to be built up slowly, and it may take a full generation before habits of hard work are ingrained. This point of view is a very controversial one in eastern Germany because it contains a moral judgment and reminds the East Germans of the old prejudices of the West about them being lazy. It will also take massive new investments, or migration westward, before East Germany can be equal to the West. Meanwhile, East has dragged down West into stagnation, and there were social tensions, with right-wing fanaticism appearing all over the country, especially in East Germany where frustrated unemployed youths targeted nonwhite immigrants and foreigners for assaults. Although such aggressive acts received wide coverage in the world media, they did not represent the opinion of the majority of East Germans on the way their society should be structured.

A retired East German engineer who had worked all his life in a large GDR *Kombinat*—a term describing a usually huge cluster of firms involved in the economic sector—related to one of my Leipzig University students his work experience in the research and development department there (Mücklisch 2001). New inventions were always blocked both by political decisions and resource shortages. When writing about East German workplaces, one has to deal with these system-related problems: A controlled economy based on centralized planning had fundamentally different mechanisms than a capitalistic system. The lack of efficiency compared to Western standards had an impact on workplace spirituality. Everything took longer in East Germany. The smallest public work took several years to be completed. The work had to be stopped often due to all kinds of shortages. East German construction workers who had moved to the West and have found new jobs in the construction sector there could not handle it at the beginning. They were not used to a situation where working materials were always available, and they could not take continuous breaks because of shortages. "Will it never stop?" one worker reportedly asked when seeing the continuing flow of trucks bringing cement blocks to a construction site.

Working in East Germany was a political activity. There were propaganda slogans and posters everywhere ("Our work creates a better world"; "My workplace—the place where I fight for justice and peace!"). And since it was a socialist country, East German society was focused on the production process, in contrast to society after reunification, which is focused on consuming. Uniformity and control were also important. The workplace presented the best opportunity to influence people. It was also militarized—the largest companies created "Company Battle Troops" consisting of company workers who received military training regularly. The valuing of the individual as a person was important in East Germany. It is rather ironic that a government that legitimized destruction, violence, and discrimination was also capable of creating and upholding ethical and cultural values. In present-day eastern Germany the actual societal circumstances play a very important role in individuals' behavior in the workplace. Many young people show a special flexibility and willingness to work hard in order to achieve a good social status. They have realized that by changing some of their values they might be better prepared to succeed in a dynamic global economy.

A SUMMING UP

How does spirituality affect the goal of every business, which is to make a profit? A Harvard Business School study examined ten U.S. companies with strong corporate cultures (spirited workplaces) and ten with weak corporate cultures, drawn from a list of 207 leading corporations. In an eleven-year period, the researchers found a dramatic correlation between the strength of an organization's corporate culture and its profitability. In some cases, the more-spirited companies outperformed the others by 400 to 500 percent in terms of net earnings, return-on-investment, and shareholder value. A Vanderbilt University Business School study resulted in similar findings, using the Fortune listing of "The 100 Best Companies to Work For" (Thompson 2000). CEOs, now and in the future, must realize that they need to focus on the individual. Corporations also need to attempt to establish themselves as worthy organizations—that is, organizations with a higher sense of business purpose.

There has been ample empirical evidence that spirituality in the workplace creates a new organizational culture where employees feel happier and perform better. Bringing together the motivation for work and the meaning in work increases retention. Employees may also feel that belonging to a work community, which is an important aspect of spirituality, will help them when things get rough in the future. Furthermore, a culture of sharing and caring will eventually reach all the stakeholders of the organization: suppliers, customers, and shareholders. In such a humanistic work environment, employees are usually more creative and have high morale, two factors that are closely linked to good organizational performance. In the case of the former East Germany, Klaus Blech (1995) pointed out that one did not have to identify with the Communist system to be part of it. He wrote that one became part of it simply by living in it:

> Adopting the techniques and compromises of co-existence and accommodation with the system was inevitable. This was humiliating, and it was meant to be so by a regime that used humiliation as an instrument of domination and manipulation. These were the unpleasant rules of the games, and everybody had to live by them. But those in the same boat did not have to be ashamed before each other. One could even be proud of one's own work, accomplishments, and personal decency. (3)

Unification brought a lack of understanding and sympathy for the East Germans from their western countrymen who taught that there was nothing to be proud of in the old system. The disparaging feelings toward the East expressed by some westerners have been antispiritual. One of the fundamental aims of spiritual practice has been to extend human identities, to overcome feelings of separateness with the rest of mankind and nature. As a consequence of the rift between East and West, further light was shed by an examination of the level and nature of East German pride in their nation. According to Flockton, Kolinsky, and Pritchard (2000), pride in being German was especially high among East Germans in 1980 to 1990 (74 percent) but fell by 16 percent in 1995 under the impact of economic realities and the reconfiguration of Germany's international role.

Both in the United States and in eastern Germany, many people feel disconnected. Some of them might be atheists, but for those who are not, their faith does not seem part of what they are doing in their day-to-day life, no matter if they are Christian, Jewish, or Muslim. In the United States, numerous managers have been focusing on the spirituality of individuals to create a humanistic workplace environment. But this approach underlies cyclic dynamics. In times of recession it is likely that such an approach might be quickly forgotten (e.g., mergers, massive lay-offs, etc.), because the fundamental principle of a capitalist economy opposes it. The American drive for profit above all is a well-known characteristic of corporate America. But profit maximization requires the permanent implementation of even more rational and efficient processes. On an individual level that might result in various forms of stress: more speed, more pressure, and so forth. In order to work, the concept of a human workplace definitely needs long-range market certainty. Managers could then interpret the time spent on the well-being of employees as an investment. But in times of trouble, managers might not be able to resist the temptation of short-term profits by using that time for activities that are productive immediately. Maybe that separates successful from unsuccessful companies. In the first case, the corporate culture of the organization might encourage managers to have a long-term perspective that might eventually bring higher profits. Still, the needs of short-term profits to satisfy investors and shareholders may be in some cases a major obstacle for the implementation of the concept of workplace spirituality. But independently of the policies of an organization, people in the United States will continue to bring their own spirituality into their workplace. The events of September 11, 2001, in New York have brought an even more real openness. People are showing that they want to be spiritually connected. In the case of East Germany, the use of "spirituality" in the workplace illustrates how ideological indoctrination can be used successfully in a centralized system without free markets and, most importantly, without competition and means of economic competition. Other incentives such as medals, and so forth, combined with Communist ideology were used to achieve high productivity rates. When discussing that relation theoretically, one can see that in a capitalist system spirituality plays a similar role from the perspective of business leaders.

REFERENCES

Albanese, C.L. (2001). *American Spiritualities. A Reader.* Bloomington: University of Indiana Press.

Allen, J.L. (1999). "European Synod." *National Catholic Reporter*, September 24.

Allison, M. (2000). *Politics and Popular Opinion in East Germany 1945–68.* Manchester, UK: Manchester University Press.

Arnold, K.H. (1976). *Policies Which Put People First. Life and Social Welfare in the GDR.* Dresden, GDR: Panorama DDR.

Beinssen, H., and K. Rigby. (1996). *Out of the Shadows. Contemporary German Feminism.* Melbourne, Australia: Melbourne University Press.

Bennis, W. (2000). *Managing the Dream. Reflections on Leadership and Change.* Cambridge, MA: Perseus.

Bertram, H. (2000). "Moral Obligations and Values in an Individualized Society." In *Adversity and Challenge in Life in the New Germany and in England*, ed. J. Bynner and R.K. Silbereisen. New York: St. Martin's, 193–211.

Blech, K. (1995). *Germany Between East and West*: http://www.press.jhu.edu/demo/sais_review/ 15.3blech.html (December 31, 2001).

Bond, E.J. (1996). *Ethics and Human Well-Being.* Cambridge, MA: Blackwell.

Bracey, H.; J. Rosenblum; A. Sanford; and R. Trueblood. (1990). *Managing from the Heart.* New York: Delacorte.

Bridges, F.W. (2001). *Resurrection Song. African-American Spirituality.* Maryknoll, NY: Orbis Books.

Burger, R. (2000). "Far-Right Makes Increasing Use of Internet." *Frankfurter Allgemeine*, August 2: http:// www.faz.com (January 18, 2002).

Canfield, J., and J. Miller. (1996). *Heart at Work.* New York: McGraw-Hill.

Carmody, J.T., and D.L. Carmody. (1991). *Catholic Spirituality and the History of Religions.* Mahwah, NJ: Paulist Press.

Cash, K., and G.R. Gray. (2000). "A Framework for Accommodating Religion and Spirituality in the Workplace." *Academy of Management Executive* 14, no. 3: 124.

Chappell, T. (1993). *The Soul of a Business. Managing for Profit and the Common Good.* New York: Bantam Books.

Charisma News Service. (2000). *Study: Fewer Americans Seek Spiritual Answers From Church*: http:// www.mcjonline.com (January 7, 2002).

Childs, J.M. (1995). *Ethics in Business: Faith at Work.* Minneapolis: Fortress.

Clark, R.W., and A.D. Lattal. (1993). *Workplace Ethics: Winning the Integrity Revolution.* Lanham, MD: Rowman and Littlefield.

Conkin, P.K. (1995). *The Uneasy Center: Reformed Christianity in Antebellum America.* Chapel Hill: University of North Carolina Press.

Conradt, D.P. (2001). *The German Polity*, 7th ed. New York: Addison-Wesley Longman.

Costa, J.D. (1998). *The Ethical Imperative. Why Moral Leadership Is Good Business.* Reading, MA: Addison-Wesley.

Cowan, J. (1993). *The Common Table. Reflections and Meditations on Community and Spirituality in the Workplace.* New York: HarperCollins.

Daidone, A. (2000). "Trend Spotters See Spirituality Getting Hot." *Record*, August 25.

Dodds, D., and P. Allen-Thompson, eds. (1994). *The Wall in My Backyard. East German Women in Transition.* Amherst: University of Massachusetts Press.

EAP Association Exchange 31, no. 3 (May 2001): 11.

Edinger, L.J., and B.L. Nacos. (1998). *From Bonn to Berlin. German Politics in Transition.* New York: Columbia University Press.

Fickinger, N. (2001). "Men Have It Better Than Women, Survey Finds." *Frankfurter Allgemeine*, April 19: http://www.faz.com (January 18, 2002).

Finn, V.S. (1990). *Pilgrims in This World. A Lay Spirituality.* Mahwah, NJ: Paulist Press.

Finsterbusch, S. (2000). "Racism May Deter Investors in Saxony-Anhalt." *Frankfurter Allgemeine*, August 23: http://www.faz.com (January 18, 2002).

Flockton, C.; E. Kolinsky; and R. Pritchard. (2000). *The New Germany in the East. Policy Agendas and Social Developments Since Unification.* London: Frank Cass.

Frink, H.H. (2001). *Women After Communism. The East German Experience.* New York: University Press of America.

Garcia-Zamor, J-C. (2001). *Administrative Ethics and Development Administration.* New York: University Press of America.

Groschl, J. (2001). "When a Promising New Job Turns Into Hell on Earth." *Frankfurter Allgemeine*, November 19: http://www.faz.com (January 18, 2002).

Gunther, M. (2001). "God and Business." *Fortune* 144, no. 1 (July 9).

Henkys, J., and F. Schweitzer. (1994). *Atheism, Religion, Indifference: Issues for Religious Education in Germany*: http://www.acu.edu.au/ren/isrev401.htm (December 31, 2001).

Hitt, W.D. (1990). *Ethics and Leadership. Putting Theory Into Practice.* Columbus, OH: Batelle.

Hoffman, D.M. (1976). *Beginnings in Spiritual Life.* Boston: St. Paul Editions.

Hua, V. (1999). "Profiting the Heart Programs Help Workers Define Goals, Be More Productive." *Hartford Courant*, September 23.

James, D.C. (1996). *What Are They Saying About Masculine Spirituality?* Mahwah, NJ: Paulist Press.

Jones, D. (2001). "Firms Spend Billions to Fire Up Workers—with Little Luck." Arlington, VA: *USA Today*, May 10.

King, M.L. (2001). "Letter from Birmingham Jail." In *American Spiritualities. A Reader*, ed. Catherine L. Albanese. Bloomington: University of Indiana Press, 349–362.

Krüll, M. (1995). *Women's Spirituality and Healing in Germany*: http://www.mariannekruell.de (December 31, 2001).

Laabs, J.J. (1995). "Balancing Spirituality and Work." *Personnel Journal* 74 (September): 60–62.

Laur, P.P. (1987). *Cerca del corazón del pueblo. En el umbral de la espiritualidad del Pueblo Amazónico.* Iquitos, Peru: Centro de Estudios Teológicos de la Amazonia (CETA).

Lemke, C. (1989). "Political Socialization and the 'Micromilieu.' Toward a Political Sociology of GDR Society." In *The Quality of Life in the German Democratic Republic. Changes and Developments in a State Socialist Society*, ed. M.Rueschemeyer and C. Lemke. Armonk, NY: M.E. Sharpe, 59–73.

Lewis, C.W. (1991). *The Ethics Challenge in Public Service. A Problem-Solving Guide.* San Francisco: Jossey-Bass.

Lewis, D.E. (2001). "Workplace Spirituality Moves Up on Agenda." *Boston Globe*, December 16.

Liszka, J.J. (1999). *Moral Competence. An Integrated Approach to the Study of Ethics.* Upper Saddle River, NJ: Prentice Hall.

Luft, S. (2001). "Parallel Lives: Germans, Foreigners Look for Common Ground." *Frankfurter Allgemeine*, November 15: http://www.faz.com (January 18, 2002).

Maier, C. (1997). *Dissolution. The Crisis of Communism and the End of East Germany.* Princeton, NJ: Princeton University Press.

Maraghy, M. (2001). "God CEOs Bringing Faith into the Workplace and Finding Solace." *Florida Times-Union*, May 9, 1.

Massam, K. (1996). *Sacred Threads. Catholic Spirituality in Australia: 1922–1962.* Sydney: University of New South Wales Press.

Maynard, R. (1998). "Berlin's Remaining Walls." *World on the Web* 13: 47.

McDonald, M. (1999). "Shush. The Guy in the Cubicle Is Meditating." *U.S. News and World Report* 126, no. 17 (May 3): 46.

Mertzman, R., and P. Madsen. (1992). *Ethical Issues in Professional Life: A Multimedia Course.* Lincoln: University of Nebraska-Lincoln.

Missinne, L.E. (1990). "Christian Perspectives on Spiritual Needs of a Human Being." In *Spiritual Maturity in the Later Years*, ed. James J. Seeber. Binghamton, NY: Haworth Press, 143–152.

Mitroff, I.I., and E.A. Denton. (1999a). "A Study of Spirituality in the Workplace." *Sloan Management Review*, 40, no. 14: 83.

———. (1999b). *A Spiritual Audit of Corporate America; A Hard Look at Spirituality, Religion, and Values in the Workplace.* San Francisco: Jossey-Bass/Pfeiffer.

Mücklisch, R. (2001). E-mail from Leipzig. (November 6, 2001).

Ochs, C. (1983). *Women and Spirituality.* Totowa, NJ: Rowman and Allanheld.

Olivo, C. (2001). *Creating a Democratic Civil Society in Eastern Germany. The Case of the Citizen Movements and Alliance 90.* New York: Palgrave.

Pätzold, B. (1997). "Face to Face with Reunification. East Germans Hold Up Their Heads Again." *Le Monde Diplomatique*, February.

Pierce, G. (1999). "Let's Create a Spirituality of Work That Works." *U.S. Catholic* 64, no. 9: 24–28.

Rossiter, G. (2001). "Taking Down the Iron Curtain: Religion and Culture in a Changing Europe, An International Response": http://www.acu.edu.au/ren/goslar.htm (December 31, 2001).

Rutte, M. (1996). *Spirituality in the Workplace*: www.martinrutte.com/heart.html (December 31, 2001).

Schrage, M. (2000). "Sorry About the Profits. My Feng Shui Is Off." *Fortune* 142, no. 27 (November 27).

Schuller, K. (2000). "Many Private Lives Exposed By Opening of Stasi Files." *Frankfurter Allgemeine*, December 18: http://www.faz.com (January 18, 2002).

Smith, P.J. (1998). *After the Wall. Eastern Germany Since 1989.* Boulder, CO: Westview.

Statkowa, S. (1976). *Women and Socialism. Facts, Figures and Information on Equality for Women in the GDR*, 2d ed. Dresden, GDR: Panorama DDR.

Sterba, J.P. (2000). *Ethics. Classical Western Texts in Feminist and Multicultural Perspectives.* Oxford: Oxford University Press.

Stewart, C.F. (1999). *Black Spirituality and Black Consciousness. Soul Force, Culture and Freedom in the African-American Experience.* Trenton, NJ: Africa World Press.

Taylor, E. (1999). *Shadow Culture. Psychology and Spirituality in America.* Washington, DC: Counterpoint.

Teichman, J. (1996). *Social Ethics. A Student's Guide.* Cambridge, MA: Blackwell.

Thompson, W.D. (2000). "Can You Train People to Be Spiritual?" *Training and Development* 54, no. 12: 18–19.

Tobias, M.; J. Morrison; and B. Gray. (1995). *A Parliament of Souls. In Search of Global Spirituality.* San Francisco: KQED Books and Tapes.

Turner, J. (1999). "Spirituality in the Workplace." *CA Magazine* 132, no. 10: 41–42.

Ulrich, D.; J. Zenger; and N. Smallwood. (1999). *Results-Based Leadership.* Boston: Harvard Business School Press.

Walker, R. (1998). "Preachers on the Payroll." *Christian Science Monitor*, June 25.

Walsh, R. (1999). *Essential Spirituality. The 7 Central Practices to Awaken Heart and Mind.* New York: Wiley.

Wenzel, E. (1994). "Body in Time—Timeless Body. A Patchwork of Thoughts." *Annual Review of Health Social Sciences* 4: 121–151.

Wiesenthal, H. (1995). *Die Transformation Ostdeutschlands.* In *Transformation sozialistischer Gesellschaften: Am Ende des Anfangs*, ed. H. Wollmann, H. Wiesenthal, and F. Bönker. Opladen, Germany: Westdeutscher Verlag, 134–159.

CHAPTER 22

SPIRITUALITY AND INFORMATION

RICHARD O. MASON

I,
The song,
I walk here!
—*Soens 1999*

Experience the shaman's sacred song of the Modoc Indians from Northern California. The ceremony unites the song, the singer, the Holy Person who gave the vision, and the vision from which the song itself sprang into one. In earlier civilizations information was sung, making it attuned with the grander cosmos in which they lived. Spirituality was a process in which information was active—walking, singing, healing, dancing, and speaking. Information presupposes action in these civilizations. It is not to be read or seen. It is instead to be experienced.

SPIRITUALITY AND INFORMATION IN THE WORKPLACE

In early societies much of this experiencing took place out of the workplace. Work is the application of human and physical resources, such as people, equipment, time, effort, and money, to generate outputs desired or needed by society (Alter 1996). It consists of three fundamental components: people, technology, and information.

For the ancient Greeks work was ignoble. Indeed trade and commerce were considered beneath the dignity of full-fledged citizens. Work was carried out by slaves who were excluded from citizenship and held in low esteem. Such work was largely manual—physical labor pitted against material and technology—and drew on little in the way of information. Such spirituality as the slaves had, and they may have experienced their work-a-day world deeply and sought to understand it cosmically, was not related to the information they handled. It was the citizens who practiced the information-based activities of art, literature, language, and drama. These practices may have been, in part, spiritual, but they were not considered work.

The advent of capitalism changed these relationships. Max Weber observed that one of the profound implications of Martin Luther's reformation was the notion that a worker could have a "calling"—fulfilling the obligations imposed on him by his world (Weber [1905] 1958). Worldly affairs became a high form of moral activity for the worker. It gives the performing of one's earthly duties religious significance and sanction. Every person's work became a calling and all callings were legitimate in the eyes of God. One engaged in work because it was divine will. During this era spirituality and work were closely connected although the information component of work was still rather minimal. During the Industrial Revolution, however, the demand for information in the workplace increased and the information sought became more objectified. But, what did this do for spirituality?

THE RISE OF OBJECTIVE INFORMATION

Information in the modern world threatens the shaman's fundamental notion of spirituality. In the long march of history, information—as we currently conceive of it—has become almost antithetical to spirituality. Beginning at least with the Cro-Magnon cave dwellers of the Dordogne River valley in modern-day France, humans have sought to extract a piece of the spirit and objectify it. When some innovative soul descended into a dark limestone cave, powdered some nearby clay, and using a bone for a stylus began to paint marks on the walls, he or she was trying to secularize experience. These marvelous depictions of ibexes, bulls, horses, and deer were intended for day-to-day use. They were more profane than sacred. Such symbols might inspire a spiritual response or even be intended to remind one of or stimulate spiritual experience. But information merely serves as a prop toward spirituality; it is not its essence. The spirit is grasped only in the process—feeling, thinking, using. It does not inhere in the package of symbols that constitute an item of information. It follows, then, that growth in the quantity of information—an explosion in bits and packets—constitutes a potential threat to humans experiencing spirituality. Under conditions of information overload the prop overwhelms the process. It replaces the vital subjective with the objective.

Arguably, the social expansion of the use of printing, following Johannes Gutenberg's application of movable type to print the *Mazarin Bible* (circa 1455), resulted in a major leap toward the objectification of information. Ideas were abstracted from the ongoing subjective flux and frozen into atemporal packages of symbols. Ironically, many of the early uses of information celebrated religious causes. The traditional, active process of chanting—reaching for the spirit through direct, vocal experience—was replaced by the more passive process of reading. Consequently, one might read an objective, spiritual text as a kind of provocation to reach beyond it or as a reminder for a ceremony; but the text itself was flat. The reader must wring any spirituality out of it herself. Motivational information must strike a responsive cord in the mind of the beholder. That is, motivational information is experienced first as an intellectual process that might subsequently evoke a feeling as a response.

The Enlightenment exacerbated the break between subjective and objective information. One outcome of the new emphasis on rationality was operationally and philosophically to forge a rather decisive separation between subjective information and objective—between singer and song. A greater faith in human reason and empirical observation as the principal source of truth emerged. These beliefs also reinforced reason as the means to improve society's physical and social environment. This faith had been espoused earlier during the Renaissance by Francis Bacon and was bolstered by scientific discoveries, uncovered mostly in spite of theological opposition, such as Galileo's forced retraction in 1633. This set the stage a few years later for Rene Descartes's rationalistic approach, modeled on geometry, to discovering "self-evident" truths as a foundation of knowledge. "I think, therefore I am." Sir Issac Newton subsequently emphasized induction from experimental observation. Spinoza developed a systematic rationalistic philosophy in his classic work *Ethics,* published in 1677. All in all, this was heady stuff because it reified the individual and promised human beings the hope of power to exercise control over their environment.

The intellectual scene moved to the continent during the eighteenth century as French philosophers assumed the leadership. Montesquieu used British history to support his notions of limited government. Voltaire wrote diaries and novels of his travels to encourage a stronger intellectual movement toward secular ethics and relativism. Rousseau developed the radical concept of a social contract in which members of a community negotiate for their rights and duties rather than receiving them from on high. The *Encyclopedia,* which was largely devoted to practical technology, was edited by Diderot and d'Alembert to serve as a monument to the accomplishments of reason and objective information.

The science and political systems that emerged during this period, especially the presupposition of human freedom, served also to disengage people from their spiritual roots. God's role was to assure a rational world. One, then, had only to use reason to live effectively in it. One's work in a rational institution—a government agency or market-oriented business—became the new basis of personal identity. Objectified information became a necessary ingredient for maintaining rationality.

INDUSTRIALIZING INFORMATION

The Industrial Revolution expanded the demand for objectified information. James Scott's (1998) *Seeing Like a State: How Certain Schemes to Improve the Human Condition Have Failed* and James Beninger's (1986) *The Control Revolution: Technological and Economic Origins of the Information Society* describe how, during the nineteenth century, governments and businesses turned to objective information in order to discharge their new responsibilities. Railroads, for example, needed information and communication systems to manage their increased scope and scale of operations, to keep their schedules on time, and to avoid accidents. These books' common theme is simple: institutional power is enhanced by the collection and use of objective information. They also focus on the same underlying problem that information was devised to solve: an increase in entropy in the system—a government sovereign or business market area—with respect to the systems users' safety or production needs. Both authors acknowledge the great strides made by better organization, science, and technology in improving the systems clients' power. Both argue that the process of innovation must continue and will keep humankind in control, although Scott addresses some negative outcomes as well. Thus, these books report on the Zeitgeist that shaped the twentieth century.

These are the motivational underpinnings of the Information Age. To wit: in a rational world information is used by governments, business, and individuals to pursue their individual goals. The drive behind this motivating force was captured by Friedrich Nietzsche in *The Will to Power,* published in 1901 shortly after his death. Nietzsche's theme soon emerged as the characteristic outlook of our times. Humanity's most basic need is power; power confers the ability to bring perfect fruition to all of human capabilities and desires. "It is only a question of power," he said, "to have all the morbid [and, especially ascetic] traits of the [19th] century, but to balance them by means of overflowing, plastic, and rejuvenating power" (Nietzsche 1924, 132). Human beings, Nietzsche thought, have a "love affair" with power—be it the raw power of a Napoleon or the aesthetic power of a Leonardo da Vinci. The prospect of losing our power, consequently, is humankind's most pervasive source of fear and anxiety. That is why we continue to buy and use computers, telecommunications, and such interactive networked technologies as the Internet and the World Wide Web. They provide the objective information we need to maintain or amplify our power.

INFORMATION'S SHADOW

But what is the end result? Arguably, human beings have benefited, for the most part, from the freedom and power made possible by the objectification of information as it first oozed forth for the Cro-Magnon until it exploded globally affecting all of us entering the twenty-first century.

Yet, taken to its limit, this trend leads to an unbridgeable social chasm. Objective material—stuff that is representational, symbolic, expandable, compressible, substitutable, transportable, diffusive, hard to contain, and shareable among people speaking a common language—is separated from the human subjective person who experiences it. The "song"—a string of symbols, now digitized, careening in packets over fiber, wires or airways, through routers and servers, to a personal computer to be displayed on a screen or broadcast on speakers—has been disembodied from the "singer." In the process something very fundamental is lost.

What would happen if all of our experience came from the "tube"—TV or PC? One gets a glimpse into the possibilities at *010101: Art in Technological Times* showing at the San Francisco Museum of Modern Art (March 3 to July 8, 2001), presented by Intel. The exhibition certainly meets its objective, which was to demonstrate "that technology is enabling a whole new range of expression for artists working in all media" based on the observation "that digital technology, like photography and video before it, offers a new and vital means of creative expression and communication." In an essay entitled "Beyond the Saturation Point: The Zeitgeist in the Machine," author John Weber observes that the "dramatic emergence of video technologies as a mainstream art medium is only one byproduct of a more encompassing shift in contemporary culture. E-mail; cell phones; DVD movies; CD audio disks; MP3 files; desktop, laptop, and palmtop computers; the World Wide Web; digital cameras; and video camcorders—communication, by image or word, occurs more and more along networked digital pathways, via digital devices, aggressively marketed by a global economy. Like it or not," he concludes, "high tech has arrived as a component of everyday life . . ." (*010101* 2001, 15–16).

All of this is captured, at least in part, by the term *cyberspace*. Modern society is steadfastly replacing physical space—a world of atoms—and all of the visceral sensations that inhabiting it entails with this new world of bits. In his foreword to the catalogue, director David Ross reaches for the meaning of this change.

> As we slip past the border delineating the end of the age of mechanical reproduction and find ourselves in a new territory, we sense that things have changed in ways we cannot fully express. For one thing, we are still quite unsure of the nature of this new space we inhabit. It's not that we aren't trying, or that there are insufficient clues to the nature of the era in which we find ourselves. For the past decade, poets, pundits, and academics alike have been trying with only limited success to name or describe this new thing. (*010101* 2001, 3)

Whatever it is called—and novelist William Gibson's "cyberspace" seems as good as any name—it is clear that it is encompassing a great deal of human activity: art, business, government, and personal living.

One painting in the exhibition alerts us to the ultimate result. It is called "System Almighty" and is presented by Droog Design from Amsterdam. The painting depicts a woman who is seated in a curved-backed swivel office chair mounted on casters situated in front of a computer table. She faces a large computer monitor. There she sits dressed in pink shoes and a light colored, rather short skirt, knees spread out, legs akimbo, left limb forward, right splayed back, both feet resting loosely on their sides rather than planted firmly. She wears a coal black sweater starting an inch or so above her skirt, so that it reveals her lower midriff. The sweater flows upward, engulfing her breasts, arms, neck, and head, hiding them from the viewer's sight, while subliminally raising the question as to whether these normal body parts exist at all. Like a large tube, the black sweater swoops back, forming a giant sickle-shaped arc that thrusts forward so that its neck is pulled down over and engulfs the monitor. Woman and monitor become one.

THE THREAD TO SPIRITUALITY

The metaphor is clear: human beings are being totally consumed, addicted, and depersonalized by their technology. "System Almighty" is in control. If spirituality is, as Mitroff describes it, "the basic desire to find ultimate meaning and purpose in one's life and to live an integrated life" (Mitroff and Denton 1999), then the woman in the black sweater makes a disturbing statement. She either finds spiritual meaning in the most mundane (which is unlikely) or she is devoid of it altogether. Her total absorption into the technology raises a fundamental question: Is spirituality compatible with a complete surrender to technology?

There are many reasons to answer no to this question. The route to one's personal spirituality involves the integration of mind, body, and spirit. The woman in "System Almighty" is ingesting large amounts of objective information; some of it may prompt mental activities of a somewhat spiritual sort. But no matter how inspirational the bits she is consuming are for her, no matter how much they stimulate her mental processes, she is not engaging atoms. Her body is not participating as the flaccid way she is depicted conveys.

William James (1927) in his *Principles of Psychology* observed that all human beings have an instinctive concern with their bodily selves. For James, the knower and the known were inseparable components of any experience. Thus, to be fully human one has to come to terms with one's body. It is the sensations of the body transmitted through a "reflex arch" that triggers the mind and gives it wholeness. The woman in "System Almighty" is excluding a great range of tactile and other sensations from her experience. She cannot, therefore, be fully human.

Almost all approaches to achieving spirituality actively involve the body.

- Chanting—Chanting is a more direct route to the spiritual than the words or sounds uttered.
- Yoga—Yoga seeks to reach the spiritual through position and postures that energize the body in new ways. It seeks the source of strength, mental clarity, and peace that is within all humans. Doing yoga, the person breaks away from the objective stream of thought that holds his or her attention and reaches deeper within him- or herself. Practicing yoga, people have experienced the Real, the Self, the Source, Being, Brahman, Allah, God, or Awareness. They have tasted spirituality.
- Breathing—Breathing and breathing exercises are an essential component in many spiritual practices. The breath connects the body and the mind. Breathing exercises not only increase one's energy, they also open up a person to greater spiritual awareness.

"What we feel and think and are," Aldous Huxley (1931, 27) opined, "is to a great extent determined by the state of our ductless glands and viscera." All of this is a very personal, subjective process, and not founded essentially on objectified information.

CODA

Objective information is the source and sustainer of many of the things we call modern or progressive in our twenty-first-century world. Our lives depend on it. Pull the plug and we would be stalemated if not dead. But we are also enamored with the material power it brings us and this obsession sublimates subjective information, inner experience, and body awareness. This means that the dominant tools of our information age tend to work counter to the requirements of spirituality. They restrict the full immersion of the body, perhaps also parts of the mind, in the quest.

So constrained, a complete experience of the spirit is precluded. It may be that another generation of information technology and systems can be designed to overcome this barrier. This would be a great human achievement. But, as the woman in the black sweater illustrates, current interactive, networked technology is a long way from this goal. Designers who are inclined to take on this monumental task may start their inquiry by seeking to operationalize a simple traditional triplet:

> I walk here!
> The song,
> I

REFERENCES

Alter, Steven. (1996). *Information Systems: A Management Perspective*, 2d ed. Menlo Park, CA: Benjamin/ Cummings.
010101: Art in Technological Times. (2001). A catalogue published by the San Francisco Museum of Modern Art (ISBN 0–918471–63–X), 15–16.
Beninger, J.R. (1986). *The Control Revolution: Technological and Economic Origins of the Information Society*. Cambridge: Harvard University Press.
Huxley, A. (1931). In *Music at Night and Other Essays*. London/Garden City, NY: Chatto and Windus/ Doubleday, Doran.
James, W. [1890] (1927). *The Principles of Psychology*. New York: Henry Holt.
Mitroff, I.I., and E.A. Denton. (1999). *A Spiritual Audit of Corporate America*. San Francisco: Jossey-Bass.
Nietzsche, F. (1924). "The Will to Power." In *The Complete Works of Friedrich Nietzsche*, trans. A.M. Ludovici, ed. O. Levy. New York: Macmillan, 132.
Scott, J.C. (1998). *Seeing Like a State: How Certain Schemes to Improve the Human Condition Have Failed*. New Haven: Yale University Press.
Soens, A.L. (1999). *I, the Song: Classical Poetry of Native North America*. Salt Lake City: University of Utah Press.
Weber, Max. [1905](1958). *Protestant Ethic and the Spirit of Capitalism*, trans. Talcott Parsons. New York: Scribner.

APPLIED THEORY
IN WORKPLACE SPIRITUALITY

CHAPTER 23

CULTURE AND CONSCIOUSNESS

Measuring Spirituality in the Workplace by Mapping Values

RICHARD BARRETT

OVERVIEW

The purpose of this chapter is to explore the interface between organizational culture, corporate consciousness, and workplace spirituality. I propose to address three questions. First, how does spirituality manifest itself in a business context? In other words, what does spirituality look like and how would you recognize it in a corporate setting? Second, how do you measure culture and spirituality in organizations? And third, what is the relationship between the different levels of organizational consciousness, spirituality, and financial success? I propose to explore this last topic by referencing two case studies.

I place emphasis on the topic of measurement for two reasons. First, measurement allows organizations to map progress in the development of cultural capital, and second, it provides an opportunity to explore the link between financial performance and workplace spirituality. If a strong positive link can be established, then the incentive for organizations to pursue workplace spirituality will be compelling. In order to measure workplace spirituality, we must first develop a model of consciousness that includes spirituality.

A MODEL OF CONSCIOUSNESS

Abraham Maslow was one of the first psychologists to make the link between motivation and spirituality. In *Motivation and Personality* (1954) and *Toward a Psychology of Being* (1968), Maslow proposed that humans operate as if they have a hierarchy of needs. The primary human need concerns survival. When the necessary conditions for survival are met, individuals shift their focus to belonging. When they have established satisfying emotional relationships, they shift their focus to self-esteem. When they have developed a healthy sense of their own self-worth, they shift their focus to self-actualization. During self-actualization the sense of "self" expands so that an individual no longer considers *only* their own needs, but also considers the needs of others—a shift from pure self-interest to the common good. This is the state of consciousness that I call "transformation." It is at this level of consciousness that we begin to encounter an individual's spiritual motivations. The term *transformation* corresponds to Carl Jung's *individuation*, and Roberto Assagioli's *psychosynthesis*.

In *Liberating the Corporate Soul* (Barrett 1998), I proposed that each level of Maslow's hierarchy of needs can be thought of as a state of consciousness, and that the state of consciousness that Maslow labeled self-actualization could be expanded to include four distinct stages in the development of spiritual awareness—transformation, cohesion, inclusion, and unity. By expanding Maslow's concept of self-actualization, I was able to develop a model of motivation based on seven levels of consciousness. Each level of consciousness corresponds to an existential life theme that is inherent to the human condition. Associated with each life theme are specific states of psychological functioning, each with its own motivations, beliefs, and behaviors. The seven life themes that constitute the seven stages in the development of personal consciousness are shown in Figure 23.1.

The first three stages in the development of personal consciousness focus on self-interest. Stage 1 deals with safety, security, and survival. It is about learning to create the physical and financial conditions that are necessary for the continuance of existence. The second stage deals with belonging. It is about learning to develop relationships that give an individual a sense of emotional connectedness. The third stage deals with self-esteem. It is about learning to feel good about yourself as an individual through the development of self-worth and pride.

The focus of the fourth stage in the development of personal consciousness is transformation. It involves learning to balance one's own needs with needs of others.

The last three stages in the development of personal consciousness focus on collective-interest. Stage 5 deals with internal cohesion. It is about developing a personal sense of mission that brings meaning to an individual's life. The sixth stage deals with inclusion. It is about actualizing an individual's sense of meaning by making a difference in the world. It also involves deepening an individual's sense of internal cohesion, as well as building external connectedness with other like-minded individuals. The seventh stage deals with unity. It is about fully integrating the concept of service to others into an individual's way of life. It also involves a further deepening of an individual's sense of internal cohesion, as well as extending the sense of external connectedness to include all humanity and the planet.

From a psychological perspective, the first three stages in the development of personal consciousness represent stages in the development of the human ego, and the last three stages represent stages in the development (or unfolding) of the human soul. Between the last stage in the development of the human ego and the first stage in the development of the human soul, lies the fourth stage in the development of human consciousness (transformation). This is the stage where the individual learns to align the needs of the ego with the needs of the soul.

The motivating forces that correspond to the first three stages in the development of the human ego are:

- Physical survival—meeting the individual's basic physical needs so that he or she can survive into the future.
- Belonging—meeting the individual's basic emotional needs for mutually supportive interpersonal relationships.
- Self-esteem—meeting the individual's basic operational needs so that he or she can function effectively in the world with a sense of self-worth and pride.

The motivating forces that correspond to the first three stages in the development or unfolding of the human soul are:

- Meaning—understanding and integrating the motivations of the soul into the consciousness of the individual.
- Making a difference or making a contribution—acting out the soul's motivation to create beneficial outcomes for other individuals or groups.

347

Figure 23.1 **The Seven Stages in the Development of Personal Consciousness**

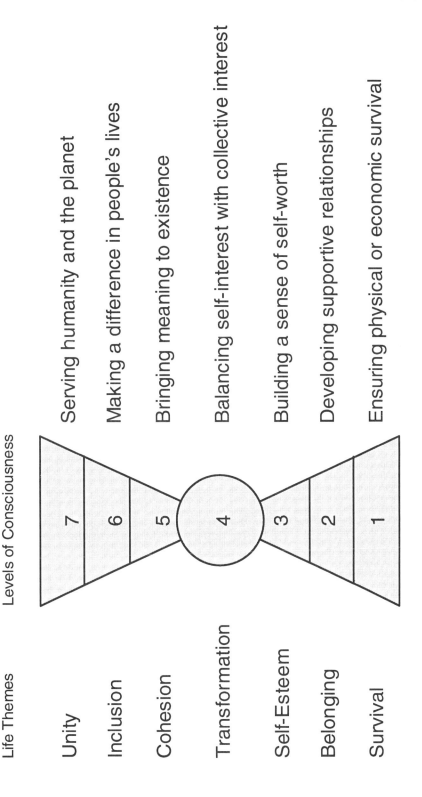

Life Themes	Levels of Consciousness	
Unity	7	Serving humanity and the planet
Inclusion	6	Making a difference in people's lives
Cohesion	5	Bringing meaning to existence
Transformation	4	Balancing self-interest with collective interest
Self-Esteem	3	Building a sense of self-worth
Belonging	2	Developing supportive relationships
Survival	1	Ensuring physical or economic survival

- Self-less service—becoming one with the world so that serving others becomes synonymous with serving self. When individuals operate from this level of consciousness, making a difference becomes a permanent way of life.

When the motivations of an individual's ego conflict with the motivations of the individual's soul, then the individual must decide which has precedence. The process of learning how to balance the needs of the ego with the needs of the soul is called personal transformation. Personal transformation occurs when the individual learns how to align the beliefs of the ego with the beliefs of the soul.

One of the most frequently occurring ego-soul conflicts individuals encounter has to do with work. It is the conflict between survival and self-esteem on the one hand, and meaning and making a difference on the other. Many people, through various circumstances, find themselves in jobs or careers that provide them with a decent living but hold no meaning for them. They cannot wait to retire. Without being aware of it, they have chosen ego gratification over soul gratification. Very often the realization that they are in the wrong job occurs when they have significant financial commitments such as a mortgage and school fees. The thought of leaving their chosen career to do something they are passionate about is too scary to consider. They believe that they will have to sacrifice their living standards to what they love to do. To successfully resolve situations of this type we must openly recognize the beliefs that are at the root of our fears and replace them with beliefs that support us in making the transition to what we love to do.

Personal transformation is never a singular event. It is an ongoing series of encounters between the fear-based beliefs of the ego and the love-based beliefs of the soul. At each encounter the individual must learn how to blend the needs of the ego with the needs of the soul. Whereas the ego is hard and dominant and wants to control, the soul is patient and persistent and yearns for meaning and connectedness. Normally the soul does not usurp the ego. It makes its presence felt through subtle means. When the needs of the soul are ignored over long periods of time, depression and physical sickness result. Regular bouts of anger, emotional upset, and rage are sure signs that the ego is out of alignment with the soul. The process of alignment is often painful. The individual must confront and overcome the fears of the ego. This requires courage, and a willingness to work through the unresolved pain that is at the root of the individual's fear-based beliefs.

THE SEVEN LEVELS OF PERSONAL CONSCIOUSNESS AND ORGANIZATIONAL CONSCIOUSNESS

Based on the framework of consciousness described above, I was able to develop a model of the Seven Levels of Personal Consciousness and Seven Levels of Organizational Consciousness. These are summarized in Table 23.1 and described in detail below.

The Seven Levels of Personal Consciousness

The Survival Level of Personal Consciousness

The first stage in the development of personal consciousness is concerned with physical survival. We need clean air, food, and water to keep our bodies alive and healthy. We also need to keep ourselves safe from harm and injury. Our basic motivation at this level of consciousness is self-preservation. When we feel threatened or insecure physically or economically, we shift into survival consciousness. How we deal with this situation in later life will depend on how well we

Table 23.1

The Seven Levels of Personal and Organizational Consciousness

Level	Life theme	Personal consciousness	Organizational consciousness
7	Unity	Self-less service, wisdom, and forgiveness	Social responsibility, long-term perspective
6	Inclusion	Focus on making a difference at work or in society	Strategic alliances with like-minded partners
5	Cohesion	Focus on meaning, purpose, vision, and values	Strong culture based on shared vision and values
4	Transfor-mation	Learning to balance self-interest with collective interest	Continuous renewal and employee participation
3	Self-esteem	Search for recognition through expression of individualism	Organizational effectiveness and being the best
2	Belonging	Development of relationships that provide emotional comfort	Harmonious customer and employee relationships
1	Survival	Physical survival and security	Financial stability

integrated this level of consciousness as a child. If in our early childhood there was a lot of anxiety in our family group about survival or money, then we will replay these tapes in our mind when we encounter survival situations later in life. The survival situation we encounter triggers our repressed fears, causing us to "react" emotionally rather than "respond" rationally to the situation. When an individual holds deep insecurities about survival, this mode of consciousness can become a way of life. Such individuals easily get angry. Whenever something goes wrong they see it as a personal threat. They believe they live in a hostile environment. They are always on guard and feel that if they don't look out for themselves, no one else will. Consequently, to feel safe they feel they must control everything around them. They have great difficulty in trusting. The focus of this stage of consciousness is physical survival in the external world.

The Belonging Level of Personal Consciousness

The second stage in the development of human consciousness is concerned with emotional survival. We need to experience love and nurturing if we are to develop a healthy emotional life. We also need an environment where there is mutual caring and support. If in our early childhood we did not develop a sense of belonging by being nurtured and loved, then we may develop fears that we are not liked or not worthy of love. In such situations relationship consciousness may become a way of life. Such individuals are constantly looking for signs of affection or inclusion. They desperately want to be loved. They will avoid telling the truth if they think it may prevent them from getting the love they want. They will be dutiful to their families and excessively loyal. They may resort to emotional blackmail or manipulation to get the attention they crave.

When we have a healthy relationship consciousness, we like ourselves. We like ourselves because we grew up feeling loved. If we have an unhealthy relationship consciousness, somewhere in our unconscious we hold the belief that we are not lovable or not liked. We spend our time trying to get others to like us to prove to ourselves that we are lovable. When we do this we give away our emotional power. In this state, how we are feeling is dependent on our perception of how others are feeling about us. We may even tolerate verbal and physical abuse to get the love we crave. Alternatively we may have had a role model that causes us to be the abuser. Such people demand loyalty, require submission and obedience, and may also be disciplinarians. They are prepared to use force to get and maintain harmonious relations. They get very angry whenever there is any sign of disloyalty. The source of many gender relationship issues originates at this level of consciousness. Ultimately, all emotional reactions, both positive and negative, are concerned with being loved, being liked, being nurtured, or being cared for in some way. The focus of this stage of consciousness is developing a sense of belonging through loving relationships—emotional survival in the external world. We need to know we are loved if we are to develop a healthy relationship consciousness.

The Self-Esteem Level of Personal Consciousness

The third stage in the development of personal consciousness is concerned with self-esteem and self-worth. We need to feel good about ourselves and respected by others, not just in our immediate family but also among our peers. Self-esteem is built by successfully performing physical or mental tasks in such a way that it draws praise or commendation from other people. During this stage of the development of consciousness we use our minds to improve ourselves in the external world. We focus on what the latest science is telling us, because we want to be the best. We become enamored with logic and reason. Rules become important because they create order.

If, as a child, we are praised for our physical and mental efforts, then we develop a healthy sense of internal self-esteem. We do not need to be the best. We just need to be praised for doing the best we can. If we do not receive this praise or we are only praised when we "win," then we may develop fears about our worthiness or we may develop an exaggerated sense of competitiveness. When this happens, self-esteem consciousness can become a way of life. Such individuals seek to gain the respect of others through power, status, wealth, or beauty. They want to stand out from the crowd. They become very competitive. They want to be the best, not just to feel good about themselves, but to gain the adulation of others and bask in fame.

Sometimes such individuals mask their sense of inferiority by becoming arrogant. They are trying to cover up the fact that at some level of their unconscious they feel inferior. They are telling us, "Look how great I am" in the hope that we will agree. They see the world not as it is, but how they want it to be. If we have a healthy self-esteem, we do not feel the need to seek the approval of others. We operate on the basis of self-referral. If we have an unhealthy self-esteem, we are constantly trying to measure our self-worth through the approval of others. We operate on the basis of object-referral. When we do this, we give away our personal power.

The focus of this stage of consciousness is about using our minds to successfully navigate the external world—ultimately it is about performance and efficiency. To build performance and efficiency we need to create order. This leads to the need for rules. The danger at this level of consciousness is too become too focused on rules. When this happens we develop an exaggerated sense of right and wrong. We become dogmatic and judgmental. Transgressors of the rules are severely punished. The rules that were designed to enhance performance become liabilities preventing us from exploring new opportunities. We become inflexible and rigid. Stuck in our own beliefs, we are incapable of seeing things differently. Ultimately we may suffer the pain of failure.

Up to this point, the focus of our consciousness has been on the development of our "self" as an individual human being separate from other human beings. By the time we reach the fourth stage of the development of our consciousness, we have a fully developed ego. If the ego is reasonably healthy, then we will be able to proceed with the fourth stage of the development of consciousness. If it is unhealthy—if we hold significant unconscious fear-based beliefs that cause us to have a victim mentality—then we may find it difficult to move forward.

The Transformation Level of Personal Consciousness

The fourth stage of the development consciousness is the stage where we begin to activate soul consciousness. It is the first stage in the development of an expanded identity that is inclusive of others. During this stage of consciousness, we open ourselves up to three possibilities that had been previously suppressed:

- The possibility of fully expressing our inner self (who we really are, including our suppressed emotions) without fear of what others may think of us,
- The possibility of seeing ourselves and the world through the eyes of others, and
- The possibility of expanding our sense of identity.

All three possibilities are significant departures from our previous modes of consciousness and require courage and self-knowledge.

Fully expressing who we are without fear of what others think, particularly our parents and peers, gives us the opportunity to make choices. Instead of reacting to situations or responding in ways that suppress how we really feel, or ways that we believe will minimize unpleasant reactions, we develop the ability to choose responses that are more authentic and affirming of who we really are. We need courage to face the pain that working with these fears might cause. Unless we take this step, we will remain slaves to our perceptions of the wishes of others and we will never find or express our true self. This step is a precursor to the step of seeing ourselves through the eyes of others.

The possibility of seeing the world and ourselves through the eyes of others also requires courage. We must be willing to suspend judgment, to actively listen, and to make compromises—even to change our beliefs. We must also become willing to receive feedback. To be successful at this stage of the development of consciousness, we must get to a place of "no fear"—a place where we actively encourage the opinions of others. We must open up the darkest recesses of our unconscious mind and be willing to discuss the content with others. This is particularly scary for someone who has not developed a healthy sense of self-esteem. The ego is afraid that others will discover those things that it has taken great pains to hide from our "self" and from "others." The words that run through our mind are, "If you find out who I really am, you may not love me." What the ego doesn't realize is that true relationship is built on intimacy. If we are unable to be authentic with ourselves then we will be unable to be authentic with others. If we are not authentic with others then our relationships will not last. The one thing we require above all others from a relationship is intimacy. We cannot get intimacy without authenticity.

The main focus at this stage of consciousness is self-knowledge and the recovery of the soul. It is the first stage of soul awareness. At this stage of consciousness we are constantly asking the question "Why?" Asking "Why?" takes us deeper and deeper into understanding. Who asks "Why?" more than anyone else on the planet? Children! They ask "Why?" because they are growing and developing. They need clarity. So often, by the time we reach midlife we stop asking "Why?" Our beliefs become fixed and rigid. We develop a belief system that seems to work for us, and we are unwilling to change it. "Why?" frees us from this rigidity. It opens up our minds. We can re-evaluate life from a new perspective—not just ours, but others' as well. We become adaptable—more willing to explore others' points of view.

The Cohesion Level of Personal Consciousness

The fifth stage in the development of personal consciousness is concerned with personal meaning. The biggest questions we have on our minds as we pass into the second stage of soul awareness are "Why am I here?" and "What is the purpose of my life?" Having uncovered the soul at Stage 4, and learned the benefits that a deeper sense of connectedness can bring us, we begin to look for the meaning of this connectedness. What is our role in the big scheme of things? We need to know that our life has meaning. The main focus of this stage of consciousness is uncovering that meaning—discovering our soul purpose. It may be something small, it may be something large. We will know when we have found it because it will feel right. We will feel a sense of resonance with the activities associated with our purpose and we will feel a sense of passion. This generates commitment and enthusiasm. It brings us joy. Because of the connectedness we feel to our soul purpose we are able to tap into the higher states of consciousness and streams of creativity.

As I sit here writing this paragraph, I am strongly aware of my soul purpose and of the creativity that is pouring through me into the words on the computer screen. The work of writing this book feels like play. It is not a chore. It is a way of expressing my soul consciousness. And, as I write these words, I feel close to my soul. Discovering your soul purpose can take time. Some people know from a young age what it is they will be doing for the rest of their lives. Others discover it later in life. I did not actively work on discovering my soul purpose until I was forty-five. Even then, it took about four to five years to fully comprehend my soul mission. Some people never get a clear picture of their soul mission. They spend different parts of their lives following different paths. Each path resonates with them and brings them joy. Accompanying the sense of mission, we also feel the need to develop a sense of vision. What is it that we are trying to achieve? What is the big goal? A mission motivates the soul. A vision gives us direction and inspires others to contribute to our cause.

The Inclusion Level of Personal Consciousness

The sixth stage in the development of personal consciousness addresses our need to interact with the world by making a difference. It is at this level of conscious that we demonstrate our purpose through our actions. It is frustrating to discover your soul purpose and then feel that you are unable to do anything about it. Finding the right avenue to express your purpose may not be straightforward. It may mean giving up a whole way of life that you have become used to. It may mean moving location, giving up friends and financial stability. You may have to confront more of your fears. When I fully understood the scope of what I was being asked to do and its importance to the future of the evolution of humanity, I knew that I had to leave my job at the World Bank. This was not easy. A generous pension was awaiting me if stayed for another ten years. It would mean giving up a tax-free salary. It would mean stepping into a situation with no financial stability. It would mean starting a completely new business in a completely new field. Was it scary? Yes! Was it something that I could avoid? No! I knew I could not be at ease with myself if I did not follow my passion. There was simply no alternative. That's how it is when the mission possesses you. You either follow or waste away. You either confront your fears or you give in to them. Personal growth demands that we confront them.

The Unity Level of Personal Consciousness

The seventh stage in the development of personal consciousness concerns service. At this level of consciousness we learn to let go of the last vestiges of any personal agenda we may have with regard to our mission. We learn that any belief we might hold about our "work" could limit our impact on the world. We develop the wisdom to know that at this level of consciousness we are operating from a place of infinite connectedness. We learn that we have no needs. What ever is necessary for us to successfully complete our mission will be provided. There is nothing to do but to follow the path in front of us. Everyone we develop a connection with is part of the mission. They are there for us. We are there for them. There is no us and them. There is only us and there is only me. We are one and the same. What I do for you, I do for myself. Service to others becomes an expression of self-love. What I need to do, and the means by which to do it, magically appears in front of me. My only contribution is to hold the vision of the future, believe that it is possible to achieve, stay aware of the opportunities as they present themselves, and keep in touch with my soul. My service is to a higher purpose and that purpose knows how to unfold.

The Seven Levels of Organizational Consciousness

The Survival Level of Organizational Consciousness

The first level of organizational consciousness focuses on two basic issues—the survival of the organization and the safety of employees. Survival issues are usually linked to issues of financial stability, financial prudence, and shareholder value. An organization's capacity to increase its shareholder value depends on its profitability. Profitability, in turn, depends on the ability of the organization to expand and grow. Fears about survival can lead to caution, control, and a myopic preoccupation with short-term results. When the fears around survival are strong and deep, exploitation and greed often result. The key to the success at Level 1 is financial performance. Without profits, companies cannot invest in their employees, research new products, or build strong relationships with their customers and the local community. Financial stability is the first basic essential for all organizations.

The Belonging Level of Organizational Consciousness

The second level of organizational consciousness focuses on interpersonal relationships and communication. The critical survival issue at this level of consciousness is to create a sense of belonging amongst employees, and a sense of caring and connection between the organization and its customers. Preconditions for belonging are friendship, open communication, and mutual respect. Preconditions for caring are friendliness, responsiveness, and listening. When these are in place, loyalty and satisfaction among both customers and employees will be high. Happy employees generate happy customers. The best publicity an organization can have is employees speaking highly of their organization. Fears about belonging can lead to dissension, dishonesty, and disloyalty. When leaders meet behind closed doors, or fail to communicate openly, employees suspect the worst. Cliques form and gossip becomes rife. When fears about belonging occur at the same time as fears about survival, employees will leave. When issues of belonging are linked to issues of diversity, then serious internal conflicts can arise. To move beyond Level 2, organizations must bring order and efficiency to their business. They need to introduce administrative systems and control procedures that build or improve organizational effectiveness. The focus must shift from relationships to organizational performance.

The Self-Esteem Level of Organizational Consciousness

The focus of the third level of organizational consciousness is on results. It is about the organization being the best it can be. The critical survival issues at this level of consciousness are order, productivity, and efficiency. Attention is given to best practice and quality. Results are measured through performance management systems. Preconditions for strengthening performance include systems and processes that build efficiency, enhance productivity. Reengineering, cost reduction, and Total Quality Management are typical Level 3 responses to issues of performance. Organizations at this level of consciousness are structured hierarchically for the purposes of central control. The hierarchical structure also provides promotional opportunities for rewarding individuals who themselves are focused on self-esteem. To maintain central control, Level 3 organizations develop rules to regulate all aspects of their business.

Mature Level 3 organizations tend to suffer from the creeping cancer of bureaucracy—a form of institutionalized control that drains the spontaneity and entrepreneurial spirit from organizations. Bureaucracy is a sign that the organization has become too inward looking. Inward looking organizations tend toward complacency and pay little attention to their customers' needs. The principal fears at this level of consciousness are about image and status. These fears create a shift in focus from being the best that you can be, to being better than everyone else. Organizations who are focused at this level of consciousness tend to be very competitive and have vision statements such as "to be the leading supplier of . . . ," or "to be the number one provider of. . . ." Such statements inspire only employees who themselves are focused at Level 3. Most employees are not. These statements do nothing to inspire customers because they are organization focused (inward looking), rather than customer focused (outward looking). The key to success at Level 3 is to build a lean but effective administration that allows the organization to operate with speed. Without systems and processes to manage organizational effectiveness, the organization will not be efficient or productive. To move beyond Level 3, organizations must develop new products, new services, and new businesses. They must be willing to reinvent themselves by learning from the past and focusing on the future. The emphasis must shift from organizational performance to continuous renewal.

The Transformation Level of Organizational Consciousness

The fourth level of organizational consciousness focuses on continuous renewal. The critical survival issue at this level of consciousness is the development of new products and services that respond to market opportunities. This requires the organization to be adaptable and take risks. To fully respond to the challenges of this level of consciousness the organization must actively garner employees' ideas and opinions. This is the level where the leaders and managers admit they don't have all the answers, and invite employee participation.

The key to organizational success at Level 4 is adaptability, continuous renewal, and a balanced approach to measuring performance. A precondition for success at this level is encouraging all employees to think and act like entrepreneurs. Self-interest must give way to the good of the whole. To move beyond Level 4, the organization's leaders must create a company vision that gives meaning to the lives of employees. The focus must shift from continuous renewal to collective purpose. The organization must have a cause that inspires all employees.

The Cohesion Level of Organizational Consciousness

The fifth level of organizational consciousness focuses on the development of a unique cultural identity that differentiates the organization from its competitors. The critical survival issue at this level of consciousness is creating a strong sense of community. It is not just a matter of giving employees a voice, but giving them a future—a sense of hope and a sense of direction. To do this the leader must create an inspiring vision—a cause that resonates with the souls of all employees.

The cause (vision) generates commitment, because it gives meaning to employees' lives. The commitment generates enthusiasm, and the enthusiasm generates passion. Passion fosters creativity. Humor and fun support the creativity and engender a sense of community. The inspiring cause must have an internal and external dimension. The internal dimension of the vision should focus on the needs of employees. It should describe how the organization will grow and develop, and what the organization will look like in the future. It must give employees a sense of their collective destiny. The external dimension of the vision should focus on the needs of customers and society. It should indicate how the company contributes to the success of its clients, and should be very specific about the contribution that the company intends to make to the development of a safe, equitable, and environmentally sustainable society. The keys to success at Level 5 are shared vision and shared values—the creation of a unique culture that inspires and encourages every individual to grow and develop so that they can become all they can become. There must be a sense of openness, trust, and transparency. The culture of the organization must allow every individual to align his or her personal sense of mission with the organization's sense of vision. The ultimate goal is to make employees feel passionate about their work. To move beyond Level 5, the organization's leaders must deepen the sense of community inside the organization and form strategic alliances and partnerships with like-minded companies.

The Inclusion Level of Organizational Consciousness

The sixth level of organizational consciousness focuses on the deepening and expanding of both internal and external relationships. The leaders of the organization must take community building to a new level. The critical survival issue internally, is to support all employees in finding personal fulfillment in their work. Employees find personal fulfillment by taking part in activities that make a difference. These activities may be part of their normal work, or they may be activities that involve working in the local community. What is important is that the company supports the employee in these activities. Providing time off for employees to do volunteer work and making a financial contribution to the charities that employees are involved in are two of the ways that companies can support their employees in finding personal fulfillment. The critical survival issue externally, is to build mutually supportive relationships with other companies and the local community. Level 6 leaders develop strategic alliances with like-minded partners and they get involved in their local communities. They recognize that the organization is a part of the local community and has a role to play in creating a sustainable future. Level 6 organizations are environmentally aware and make sure they do not pollute the land, water, or air. Level 6 companies choose to work with suppliers and partners that support their values. To be successful at Level 6, organizations must actively support their employees in making a difference. They must make a meaningful ongoing contribution to the local community, and they must develop mutually supportive relationships with other organizations that share their values. To move beyond Level 6, organizations must continue to deepen the sense of community within the organization and fully embrace social responsibility.

The Unity Level of Organizational Consciousness

The seventh level of organizational consciousness focuses on the deepening of the sense of community within the organization and the expansion of the external sense of connection to society. The leaders of level 7 organizations display the deepest levels of compassion and forgiveness. They recognize that their organization is part of the global society and actively support causes that improve social justice and human rights. Level 7 organizations care about the global environment and the well-being of the planet. Social responsibility and ethical behavior is very high on a Level 7 organization's agenda. To be successful at Level 7, organizations must embrace the highest ethical standards in all their interactions with employees, suppliers, customers, shareholders, and the local community. They must act with compassion at all times. They must actively work toward building a world free from corruption, injustice, and pollution. They must care about humanity and the planet.

ALIGNMENT OF VALUES

Two conditions need to be met for organizations to achieve long-term success. First, there must be a strong alignment (high number of value matches) between the Personal Values of employees, the values of the Current Culture of the organization, and the values that employees consider necessary for a high-performance organization (Desired Culture Values). Second, the top ten values of the Current Culture of the organization should cover the full spectrum of consciousness. There should be one or two values at every level. Our research[1] shows that highly aligned, full-spectrum organizations give emphasis to employee fulfillment and customer satisfaction, and are highly profitable.

The following case studies illustrate the relationship between values alignment, full-spectrum consciousness, and profitability.

A COMPARISON OF A SUCCESSFUL COMPANY AND A FAILED COMPANY

The culture assessment instrument we use to map the values of individuals and organizations has three questions:

- Which of the following values and behaviors most represent who you are, not what you desire to become? (Personal Values)
- Which of the following values and behaviors most represent how your company operates? (Current Culture Values)
- Which of the following values and behaviors most represent for you an ideal, high-performance organization? (Desired Culture Values)

Employees pick ten values from a list of ninety to one hundred values. Every value on the list is related to one of the Seven Levels of Consciousness. The template of Personal Values is different from the template of organizational values (used in the second two questions) in that it does not contain values such as customer satisfaction or employee fulfillment. These are organizational values and are used only in the organizational templates. The templates of values are customized for each organization to ensure that they include values that are particular to the type of business the company is in and values that are included in the company's mission, vision, and values statements.

A Successful Company

As I mentioned already, the most successful organizations are those that are able to operate from the full spectrum of consciousness and have a high degree of values alignment. Sterling Bank, located in Houston, Texas, is an example of such an organization. Sterling leaders recognized from the start that if they could outperform the market in employee fulfillment and customer satisfaction, then they would be able to outperform the market in shareholder value. Their results suggest they have achieved this objective.

Sterling Bank opened it doors for business in 1974 with seven employees and $3 million in assets. In 2001 it was present in thirty-three locations throughout Texas with one thousand employees and $2 billion in assets. Sterling has had record annual earnings over the past thirteen years and 680 percent growth since going public in 1993. Every member of staff at Sterling shares in the success. They receive salaries that are 18.5 percent more than the average for commercial banks, and have consistently received 9.5 percent salary bonuses. The average annual return over the past five years was 32 percent.

There is a high level of trust and respect in Sterling Bank. The Bank transformed its "tellers" into "front line managers" and provided professional training programs for them at Sterling University. "Front line managers" are empowered to make decisions that directly impact their customers. Sterling University also offers a course on "Creating the Life You Want" and supports their staff in achieving their life-long dreams. To keep track on how well the bank is doing in the area of employee fulfillment, Sterling Bank carries out a quarterly survey of a sample of staff.

In 1999 Sterling Bank commissioned Richard Barrett and Associates to measure the culture of Sterling Bank using the Corporate Transformation Tools. The results are displayed in Figures 23.2 and 23.3. Figure 23.2 shows the *top ten* Personal Values, Current Culture Values, and Desired Culture Values of the 453 employees who participated in the survey. Figure 23.2 shows the *distribution* across the seven levels of consciousness of all the values that were voted for by the 453 employees.

The results show an extraordinary degree of values alignment (see Figure 23.2):

- There are three matching values between the employee's personal values and the Current Culture of the organization. These are commitment, integrity, and friendliness.
- There are no potentially limiting values in the Current Culture. These are values that are fear-based.
- There are eight matching values between the Current Culture and Desired Culture.
- Together the top ten values in the Current Culture cover every level of organizational consciousness—a full-spectrum organization.

These results support the central thesis of *Liberating the Corporate Soul*—*that the most successful individuals and the most successful groups operate from all levels of consciousness.* Out of the 200 organizational culture assessments we have completed during the past four years, we have encountered only a handful of organizations that show the same level of alignment and full-spectrum consciousness as Sterling Bank. In every case however, these organizations have displayed sustained financial success.

A Failed Company

marchFirst was created from the merger of an Internet technology company and an Internet design company in March 2000 to become one of the first global Internet professional services companies in the world. The combined company had seventy offices in fourteen countries, and employed close to eight thousand people. The vision of the company was to be the "one-stop-shop" for a Fortune 500's Internet development needs. The company was positioned to perform

Figure 23.2   Values Assessment for Sterling Bank (453 people)

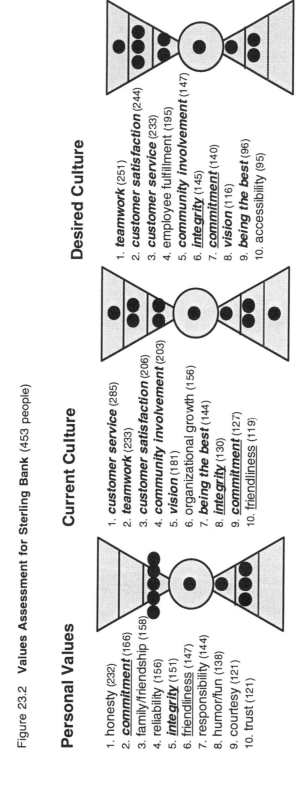

Personal Values

1. honesty (232)
2. _**commitment**_ (166)
3. family/friendship (158)
4. reliability (156)
5. _**integrity**_ (151)
6. friendliness (147)
7. responsibility (144)
8. humor/fun (138)
9. courtesy (121)
10. trust (121)

Current Culture

1. **customer service** (285)
2. **teamwork** (233)
3. **customer satisfaction** (206)
4. **community involvement** (203)
5. **vision** (181)
6. organizational growth (156)
7. **being the best** (144)
8. _**integrity**_ (130)
9. _**commitment**_ (127)
10. friendliness (119)

Desired Culture

1. _**teamwork**_ (251)
2. **customer satisfaction** (244)
3. **customer service** (233)
4. employee fulfillment (195)
5. **community involvement** (147)
6. _integrity_ (145)
7. _**commitment**_ (140)
8. **vision** (116)
9. **being the best** (96)
10. accessibility (95)

359

Figure 23.3 **Values Histogram for Sterling Bank** (453 people)

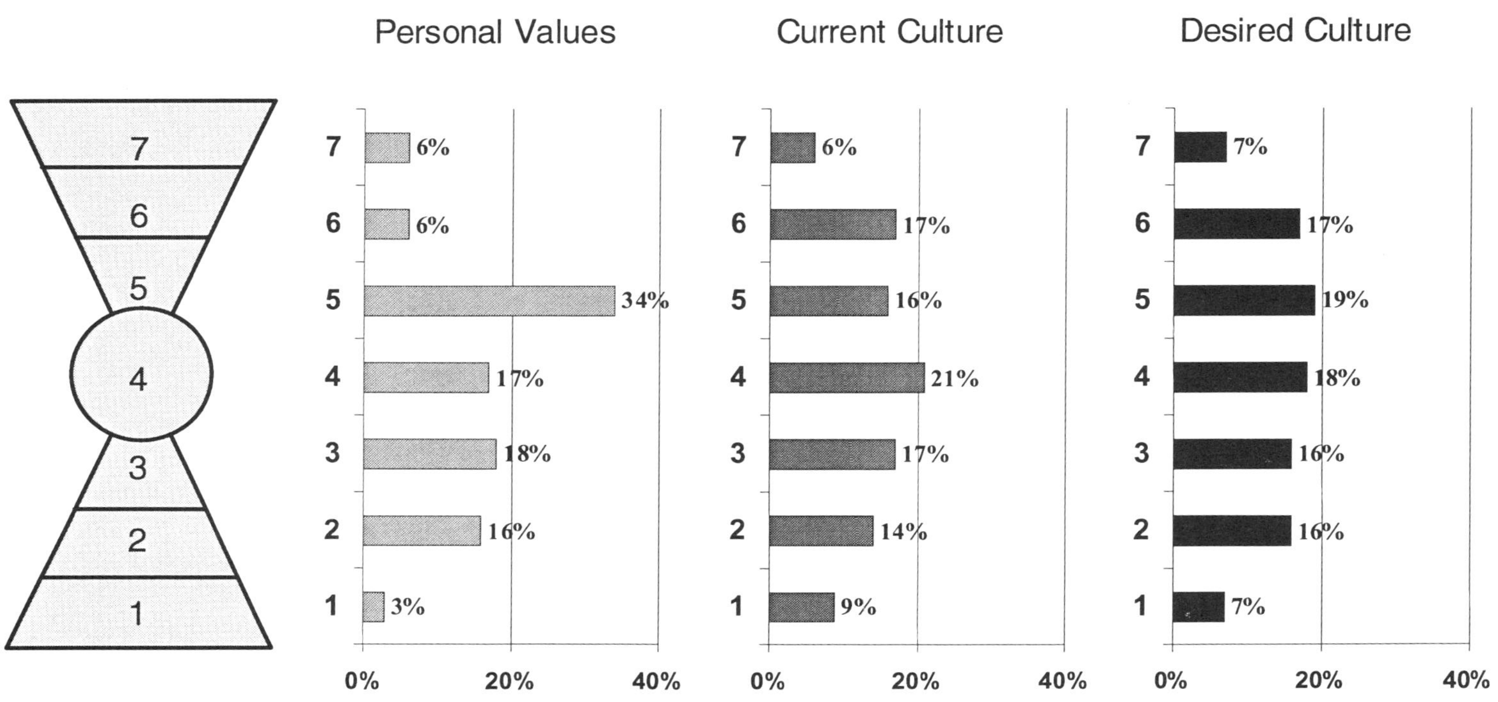

Personal Values

7	6%
6	6%
5	34%
4	17%
3	18%
2	16%
1	3%

Current Culture

7	6%
6	17%
5	16%
4	21%
3	17%
2	14%
1	9%

Desired Culture

7	7%
6	17%
5	19%
4	18%
3	16%
2	16%
1	7%

services ranging from "front end" Web design through "back end" system integration. This was a revolutionary vision at the time that promised marchFirst would be the leader in a "new economy" fueled by the Internet.

Prior to the merger both companies were doing well and both were "Wall Street Darlings." However, on the announcement of the merger, both companies' stock dropped significantly. The reason, Wall Street was extremely concerned about the newly formed Senior Management Team's ability to effectively integrate very diverse systems, processes, and mindsets. While marchFirst leadership assured investors that plans were in place for a common technology platform and redefined processes, they were silent about how the "technology minds" and "creative minds" would coexist and gel into a high-performing team.

Sadly, a year later the new company had lost 90 percent of its value and was on the verge of becoming another Internet dot.bomb. The downward slide ended in April 2001 when the company declared bankruptcy. A significant factor in the demise of the company was the bursting of the dot.com bubble. However, as can be seen from the results of the culture assessment, even in July 2000, the company was not in a strongly sustainable situation.

The Culture Assessment survey was carried out at one of the main offices of marchFirst in July 2000. The number of employees responding to the survey was 188. While only one office participated in the assessment, most employees agreed that the results were typical of the company as a whole. The results are shown in Figures 23.4 and 23.5.

The results show a significant lack of values alignment (see Figure 23.4):

- There are no matching values between the employee's personal values and the Current Culture of the organization.
- There are four potentially limiting values in the Current Culture—bureaucracy, short-term focus, internal competition, and control.

Bureaucracy is a form of institutionalized control. Too much bureaucracy can block employee creativity and entrepreneurial spirit, and takes away accountability and trust. Bureaucratic organizations tend to lose their competitive edge.

Short-term focus is potentially limiting when it sacrifices long-term growth for short-term gain.

Internal competition is potentially limiting when it prevents open communication and the sharing of information, resources, or ideas. The focus is on self-interest rather than the common good.

Control implies a lack of trust in others. Control can block innovation, creativity, accountability, and entrepreneurship. It is usually a sign of deep-seated fears.

- There is only one matching value between the Current Culture and Desired Culture—client partnerships.
- There are significant gaps in the Seven Levels of Consciousness model in the Current Culture. There are no positive values at Level 2—the level of relationships and communications. There are no values at Level 4—the level of continuous improvement and learning. There are no values at Level 5—the level of internal cohesion—shared vision and shared values. There are no values at Level 7—the level of social responsibility. There are values at Level 6—client partnerships and community service.

In Figure 23.5 we see a significant difference between the distribution of Current Culture Values and Desired Culture Values.

Figure 23.4 Values Assessment for marchFirst (188 people)

Personal Values

1. family (93)
2. **integrity** (78)
3. honesty (74)
4. **commitment** (62)
5. **trust** (61)
6. **balance (home/work)** (58)
7. humor/fun (53)
8. responsibility (51)
9. **accountability** (50)
10. ethics (48)
11. respect (48)

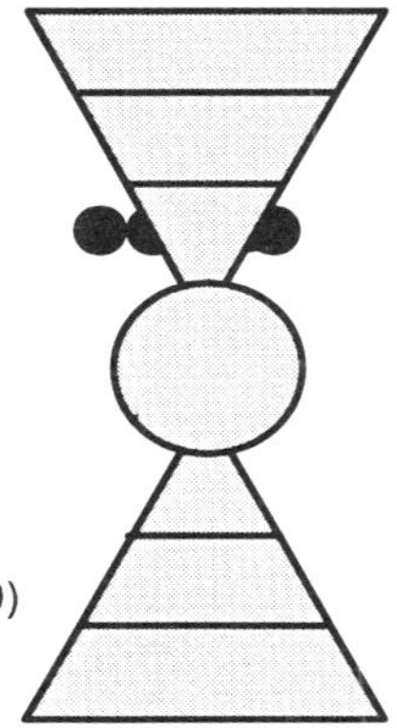

Current Culture Values

1. brand image (75)
2. profit (74)
3. bureaucracy (62) (L)
4. short-term focus (59) (L)
5. corporate growth (52)
6. being the best (47)
7. internal competition (46) (L)
8. community service (45)
9. *client partnerships* (44)
10. control (42) (L)
11. market focus (42)

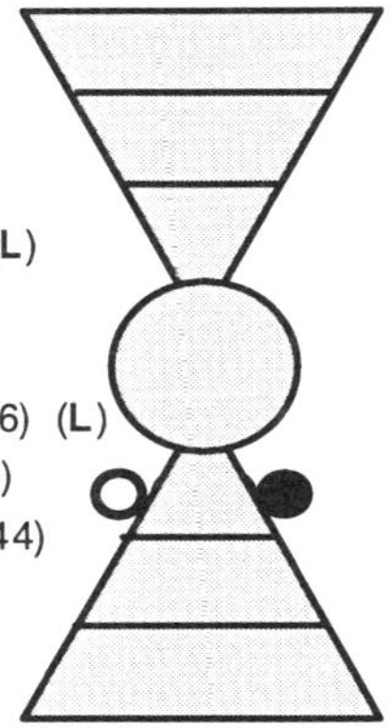

Desired Culture Values

1. **balance (home/work)** (72)
2. **accountability** (71)
3. teamwork (68)
4. employee fulfillment (65)
5. *client partnerships* (59)
6. customer focus (59)
7. customer satisfaction (58)
8. **commitment** (52)
9. **integrity** (48)
10. open communication (44)
11. **trust** (44)

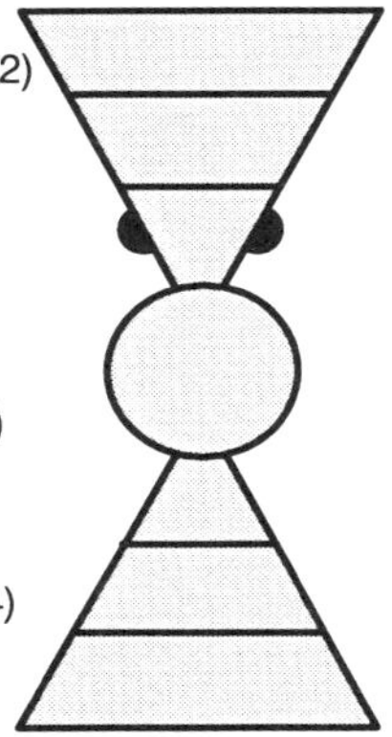

362

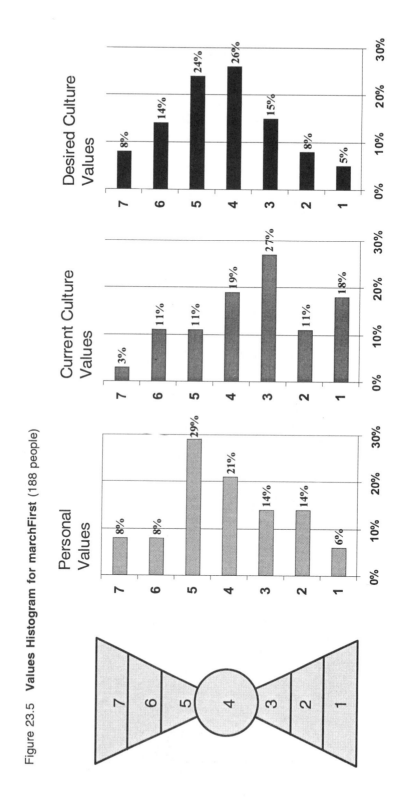

Figure 23.5 **Values Histogram for marchFirst** (188 people)

- The personal values of marchFirst are typical of people working in the service industries—a strong focus at Level 5—the level of meaning and community.
- The distribution of the Current Culture and Desired Culture Values is very different. The Current Culture is heavily focused at levels 1 and 3. The Desired Culture is focused at levels 4 and 5.
- Only 25 percent of the Current Culture Values are in the upper three levels of consciousness and 56 percent in the lower three levels.

WHY ORGANIZATIONS DIE

The case study of marchFirst provides us with an interesting example of why companies die. In terms of the Seven Levels Model, marchFirst failed to achieve a consciousness of continuous renewal, and had significant value gaps in the lower three levels of consciousness.

Basically, organizations die for two reasons: either they are unable to meet the simple financial condition that *over the long term, income exceeds expenditure,* or they are absorbed into another organization. The reasons why organizations are unable to sustain a positive cash flow are manifold. They either fail to master the first four levels of organizational consciousness or they do not pay sufficient attention to the upper three levels of organizational consciousness.

Organizations are taken over or get absorbed into other organizations because they are unable to realize their full potential. They lack the talent or ability to shift to a higher level of performance. To be successful over the long term, organizations need to be able to operate from every level of consciousness. The beliefs and behaviors associated with each level must be integrated into the organization's culture for long-term success. Starting at Level 1 and moving upward, the mastery of each level of consciousness increases the organization's sustainability.

Success and Failure at the Survival Level

Organizations can successfully operate from the survival level of consciousness providing they have a unique product or service in the territory that defines their market place. In other words, they have created a niche or a monopoly. However, the risks and costs of operating from survival consciousness are high. Because the organization does not care about its employees or its customers (Level 2), it may have a high turnover in both categories. This is expensive in terms of hiring and marketing. The company must continue to find new employees and new customers. As soon as an organization loses its niche or monopoly and begins to face stiff competition, it must shift its focus or die. It must build customer loyalty (Level 2) or reduce costs by increasing productivity (Level 3). If it jumps directly to Level 3—the productivity strategy—it may maintain its market share because of price. Eventually, however, some of its competitors will be able to match that price. It could then try to jump to Level 4—the new products and services strategy—but this will be difficult. Because the organization did not spend time building open communications (it skipped Level 2), there will be no employee loyalty. People will take their ideas for new products and services, leave the company, and set up competing companies. A company that is highly focused on survival consciousness will lose its intellectual capital because talented people want more from life than just making money.

Success and Failure at Belonging Level

Organizations can successfully operate from the level of belonging consciousness provided also they have mastered the lessons of Level 1 (maintaining a positive cash flow). Level 2 companies develop strong positive relationships with employees and between employees and customers. Because Level 2 organizations are not concerned about productivity and organizational effectiveness (Level 3), they may find it difficult to grow. They will be unable to develop the systems and processes that are necessary for expansion. Level 2 companies are built around relationships. Typically, they are small family-run businesses. If they are successful, they will usually be taken over by a larger organization. If they try to expand without developing a consciousness of organizational effectiveness, they will become increasingly ineffective and fall apart. They will be unable to streamline their systems and process to manage the expenditures that are required for expansion. Companies that are focused at Level 2 fail for two reasons: either they are unable to match marketplace prices or quality, or they do not have the talent within the family to successfully build a Level 3 organization.

Success and Failure at Self-Esteem Level

Organizations can successfully operate from the level of organizational effectiveness providing they can develop a positive cash flow (Level 1); maintain employee and customer loyalty (Level 2); and constantly improve productivity, quality, and organizational effectiveness (Level 3). Because a Level 3 organization is not concerned about the development of new products and services (Level 4), it may find it difficult to maintain its growth over a long period. Level 3 organizations are well-managed production machines. If they are to remain successful over the long term, they must reinvest a significant part of their profits in research and development of new products and services (Level 4). Level 3 organizations fail because they are unable to develop the entrepreneurial spirit that will allow them to adapt to the changing marketplace. They either develop a short-term focus, milking their cash cow for all it is worth, or they develop an internal focus and fall into the trap of taking organizational effectiveness to the level of bureaucracy.

Success and Failure at the Level of Continuous Renewal

Organizations can successfully operate from a consciousness of continuous renewal providing they can develop a positive cash flow (Level 1); maintain employee and customer loyalty (Level 2); improve productivity, quality, and organizational effectiveness (Level 3); and constantly adapt their products and services to the changing marketplace (Level 4). Because Level 4 organizations focus their attention on learning and adapting to the external marketplace, they may not be concerned about internal cohesion (Level 5). Without internal cohesion in the form of shared vision and shared values, they will fail to tap into the commitment, passion, and enthusiasm of employees. Level 4 organizations are focused on innovation, learning, and knowledge management. Because they know how to adapt to a changing marketplace, they can remain successful for long periods of time. If they want to become market leaders they must develop an inspiring vision for the organization, one that builds the commitment and enthusiasm of employees. Level 4 companies do not generally fail unless they invest heavily in a product for which there is no demand. Level 4 organizations that are unable to develop the commitment and enthusiasm of their employees (Level 5) are like racehorses that always come in second or third. They never quite make it to the winner's enclosure.

Success and Failure at the Level of Internal Cohesion

Organizations can successfully operate from a consciousness of internal cohesion if they can develop a positive cash flow (Level 1); maintain employee and customer loyalty (Level 2); improve productivity, quality, and organizational effectiveness (Level 3); constantly adapt their products and services to the changing marketplace (Level 4); and develop the commitment and enthusiasm of employees by creating a strong culture. Because the organization is focused on developing strong internal cohesion, it may not devote enough attention to developing external alliances and partnerships (Level 6). Level 5 organizations are great places to work. They are full of enthusiasm and creativity. Employees are aligned with the organization's vision and share the same values. If a Level 5 organization wants to consolidate its position as a market leader, it will need to develop external partnerships and strategic alliances. Level 5 organizations do not generally fail. Their biggest danger is that they lose their vitality or their sense of vision and fall back to Level 4.

Success and Failure at the Level of Inclusion

Organizations can successfully operate from the level of inclusion consciousness providing they can develop a positive cash flow (Level 1); maintain employee and customer loyalty (Level 2); improve productivity, quality, and organizational effectiveness (Level 3); constantly adapt their products and services to the changing marketplace (Level 4); develop the commitment and enthusiasm of employees by creating a strong culture; and build mutually beneficial strategic alliances with like-minded partners and the local community (Level 6). Level 6 organizations are not just great places to work, they provide opportunities for all employees to find personal fulfillment. Level 6 organizations want their employees to be successful at everything they do. For a Level 6 company to consolidate its position and become a global market leader, it needs to focus on ethics and social responsibility. Level 6 organizations do not generally fail. Their biggest danger is that they do not build alliances that are strong enough to support them during difficult market conditions.

Success and Failure at the Level of Unity

Organizations can successfully operate from the level of unity consciousness providing they can develop a positive cash flow (Level 1); maintain employee and customer loyalty (Level 2); improve productivity, quality, and organizational effectiveness (Level 3); constantly adapt their products and services to the changing marketplace (Level 4); develop the commitment and enthusiasm of employees by creating a strong culture (Level 5); build mutually beneficial strategic alliances with like-minded partners and the local community (Level 6); and take a strong stand on ethical standards and social responsibility. Level 7 organizations are successful because they protect their long-term interests by being good global citizens. They are recognized as being exemplary organizations. Employees, customers, and partners support them because they care about people, the planet, and society. They want to create a better world for all. Unity consciousness organizations never fail. They simply regress to Level 6 or 5. Their biggest danger is that they are unable to sustain their social vision.

For more information on the model of the seven levels of consciousness and its application to business, government agencies, not-for-profits, schools, communities, and nations, go to *www.corptools.com* or *www.richardbarrett.net.*

NOTE

1. Between 1997 and 2001 we conducted over 200 organizational assessments and several hundred individual assessments in fifteen countries.

REFERENCES

Barrett, R. (1998). *Liberating the Corporate Soul*. Boston: Butterworth-Heinemann.
Maslow, A.H. (1954). *Motivation and Personality*. New York: Harper and Row.
———. (1968). *Toward a Psychology of Being*. New York: Van Nostrand Reinhold.

CHAPTER 24

HOPE IN THE WORKPLACE

Virgil H. Adams III, C.R. Snyder, Kevin L. Rand, Elisa A. King, David R. Sigmon, Kim M. Pulvers

THE AMERICAN WORKER TODAY

"Beep, beep, beep . . ." Ron reaches out to silence his 5:30 A.M. wake-up call. Blinking, he stares up at the ceiling and mentally walks himself through his day. Wondering how he will fit everything in, he pulls himself out of bed. Ron typically feels as though his job is beyond his skills, almost as if there is no way to accomplish the tasks at hand. Indeed, he all too frequently can't visualize the goals of his efforts. He quickly goes through the motions of his morning routine, dreading the commuter traffic ahead. As a mid-level manager for a large insurance company, Ron must arrive at the office before 7:00 A.M. to ensure that his team is at work on time. Lately, he has been feeling more like a watchdog than a manager, and getting results from his team feels like pulling teeth. Ron has been with the company for eleven years, and he already dreams of his retirement although it is many years off.

Across the city, Anthea, a single mother, awakens to her infant daughter's crying. She often gets up an hour earlier than her alarm clock is set. The extra time seems to disappear while she wakes her other two children, deals with the usual conflicts over what should be worn and eaten, and tries to pile everyone into the van by 8:00 A.M. She must be to work by 8:30 A.M., which is a challenge because she must first drop off her infant daughter at day care and her two other children at school. Anthea has been a receptionist at a small law firm for just six months, having returned to the workforce two weeks after the birth of her third child. Anthea frequently finds herself struggling for energy, feeling lethargic and unmotivated.

Ron and Anthea are part of the estimated 140 million Americans who make up the civilian labor force (approximately 67 percent of the civilian noninstitutionalized population; U.S. Bureau of the Census 2001). They are fortunate, however, because they are employed. Currently, 4 percent of the labor force is classified as "unemployed yet actively seeking employment." Worse off are the many others who have left the workforce, in essence having given up hope of finding employment.

The U.S. workplace has seen many changes over the past several decades. The American economy has shifted from a manufacturing to a service base. This shift has resulted in a decline of high-paying, long-tenure jobs and single careers. Instead, today we have increasing part-time and contingent employment (Turner, Barling, and Zacharatos 2002). Thus, today's employees often work in uncertainty—they live with the knowledge that the next downsizing or corporate restructuring could mean that their jobs have disappeared. This uncertainly can undermine their hopes of achieving work and life goals.

Media portrayals of the disgruntled employee who returns to a former place of employment to kill coworkers and supervisors suggest that violent, work-related incidents are becoming more prevalent. In actuality, there has been a decrease in the overall number of fatal work injuries (U.S. Bureau of the Census 2001). Most job fatalities are related to travel on highways, as well as to falls. Of note, however, workplace homicides are the third leading cause of death. Indeed, next to robbery, violence by coworkers and customers or clients is the leading cause of workplace homicides. To compound matters, many of these incidents involve multiple fatalities. For example, in 1999, 235 incidents resulted in 617 job-related deaths (U.S. Bureau of the Census 2001).

As millions of Americans arrive at their place of employment, the unfortunate reality is that many see their work environment not as an opportunity, but as a place of mundane misery. This mentality seems to be in stark contrast to the work environments of older generations. As noted by Turner, Barling, and Zacharatos (2002), the attempt to create lean productive companies has had a negative effect on most employer/employee relations (see Landsbergis, Cahill, and Schnall, 1999; and Sennett 1998 for reviews). We argue that such people have lost hope for a better future—such is the case for Ron and Anthea. Ron doesn't visualize himself as being capable of finding routes to his work goals (i.e., he lacks pathways thought). Anthea, on the other hand, is unmotivated (i.e., she lacks agentic thought).

How individuals will choose one work environment over another is important for understanding hope. It also is crucial to understand how some work environments promote employee growth and others do not. What are the implications for employees who are low in hope? These questions form the impetus for this chapter. In the following pages, we outline a theory of hope and its application to the work setting. Further, we examine how hope can be established so as to bring greater happiness to the workplace.

DEFINING HOPE

Hope (Snyder et al. 1991) has been defined as "a cognitive set that is based on a reciprocally-derived sense of successful agency (goal-directed determination) and pathways (planning to meet goals)" (571). Thus, hope is composed of pathways and agency thoughts.

Pathways thinking reflects the perceived capacity to produce cognitive routes to desired goals (Snyder, Cheavens, and Michael 1999). It should be emphasized, however, that pathways thought is the perception that effective routes to goals can be developed, rather than having concrete plans per se. Ron is a good example of someone who is low in pathways thought; he is unable to visualize ways to accomplish his tasks. More importantly, he also lacks the perception that he can generate the necessary routes to his goals.

Agentic thinking (agency) is "the thoughts that people have regarding their ability to begin and continue movement on selected pathways toward goals" (Snyder et al. 1999, 180). Thus, agency thought is the motivational component that propels people along their imagined routes to goals (Snyder 2000). As such, agency taps the perceptions that people can *begin* and *sustain* goal-directed movements. Anthea's feeling of apathy and lethargy are an example of someone low in agentic thought. She is not motivated to seek change, nor will she be likely to sustain any changes she does make.

Pathways and agency thinking act in concert so as to help people to reach their goals. If either component is lacking, then the likelihood of goal attainment is impaired or blocked. Pathways and agency are the two primary components of hopeful thinking. In our studies substantial reliability has been established for both components (alphas of .76 to .95 for pathways, and .59 to .93 for agency) (see Snyder 2000; Snyder et al. 1991, 1996). As noted later in this chapter, there are characteristics specific to high-hope workplaces. High-hope workplaces have positive atmospheres, and they generally give employees the feeling that goals can be achieved.

Inherent in hope theory is the idea of goals (the mental targets of hope). Whereas some individuals actually may have visual images of their desired goals, it is not necessary for the goals to be "pictures in our minds." For example, verbal descriptions suffice for some people (Pylyshyn 1973). Goals may vary in their vagueness, although high-hope people typically are quite lucid in their goals. Importantly, a goal also must be sufficiently highly valued so as to warrant sustained cognitive attention. Therefore, the goals toward which people persistently strive to achieve are important and within conscious attention. Looking back on Ron and Anthea, it becomes apparent that Ron has some sense of what needs to be done, but he lacks the ability to generate routes to those goals. Anthea's goals are a bit more vague, and she is lacking the ability to clearly visualize her goals.

Research on Hope and the Workplace

We now turn to the empirical work performed on the role of hope in the workplace. We follow this section with a brief discussion of employee stress and burnout, as well as self-esteem. We then conclude with findings from a recent survey of high-hope companies.

Schulman (1999) found that ability and motivation are not always enough in the absence of positive expectations, particularly in situations that require persistence to overcome adverse situations—such as sales. Hope, as we define it, is a positive mental state in which motivation (agency) energizes employees to persist in their particular goal achievements. It also should be the case that high-hope employees would be readily able to find alternative routes to attain their work-related goals when their normal routes are blocked. This may include changing jobs if necessary for goal achievement. For instance, Salzmann (1997) found that optimistic as compared to nonoptimistic employees were significantly more likely to thrive when facing organizational changes that resulted in blockages to previously successful routes to goal attainment (which is hopeful thought in action). More specifically, these optimistic employees generated new pathways (including learning new skills and more efficient ways of achieving organizational goals) when encountering corporate restructuring.

There also is evidence that building hope among employees enhances the organizations' missions. For instance, Lovallo (1997) found that when employees had high levels of optimism, they were more likely to "scale up" from cognitive operations to group behavior. In other words, employees invested more cognitive energy in individual tasks that contributed to larger unit or group goals within the organization. In short, such positive, hope-related thoughts enhanced the task completion climates of the organizations.

Friedman, Kane, and Cornfield (1998) demonstrated that forming managers into cohesive work groups with shared tasks and goals led to an increased sense of social support and career optimism. In hope theory terms, these managers began to perceive that they had more agency and pathways available because of their social contacts. These findings have important implications for the workplace because management often sets the tone for employee interactions. As demonstrated later, there are leadership characteristics common for successful employers. Under the conditions of shared goals and tasks, the frontline employees may internalize a sense of hope. As Wagner (1996) has noted, optimistic managers see more organizational interventions as being available, they report specific change occurring because of elevated optimism, and they focus on the positive aspects of change in the workplace settings.

It also has been shown that there are stable patterns of individual differences in satisfaction/

happiness as they relate to the workplace. For instance, Diener and Larson (1984) reported that the average levels of pleasant affect experienced in work situations were highly correlated with the average levels of pleasant affect experienced in recreation situations. Simply stated, if people are happy at work they are more likely to also report being happy away from the work setting, and vice versa. This makes sense, and we already know from our research, for instance, that meaning or purpose in life is highly related to hope (Feldman and Snyder 2001). In the search for meaning in life, it is common to find that many individuals find a sense of purpose through work. Thus, high-hope employees also are likely to be hopeful in their personal lives.

As we have noted earlier, the workplace has changed over recent years. Unlike previous decades, employees today are not likely to remain with one company or even within one career throughout their working lives (Turner, Barling, and Zacharatos 2002). This has caused some employers to be fearful of divulging company "secrets." Accordingly, these managers parse tasks among several employees, none of whom knows the entire process of a job task; moreover, such employers may strive to make certain that employees are not privy to the ultimate outcomes of their particular job tasks. This ambiguity of job purpose can make the work environment become more stressful. As we will describe subsequently, such stress itself is detrimental to employee satisfaction and self-esteem.

Job Stress Findings and Implications on Hopeful Work Environments

One of the most widely researched workplace subjects relates to job stress. The findings of this research demonstrate the importance of creating hopeful working environments, because hopeful environments lead to hopeful employees. Within hope theory, job stress would be conceptualized as resulting from impeded goal pursuits (Snyder, in press; see also Lazarus, Deese, and Osler 1952). As barriers to goals remain in place, feelings of stress give way to negative emotions. High—relative to low—hope people, however, are less likely to view obstacles as stressful (Snyder, in press). In addition, the high—in comparison to low—hope individuals reduce stress by initiating and sustaining thoughts and actions in the face of goal-blockages. This process reflects what others have referred to as coping (Lazarus 1999, 2000). Hence, hopeful employees are more productive and happier, and, as we will show later, it is likely that their companies also will be more profitable.

The literature on job stress also provides insights into how to create hopeful work environments. One of the key factors in reducing job stress is to create an altruistic versus a cutthroat corporate climate. McGregor (1960) made this distinction by labeling traditional bureaucratic models of business as Theory X, and the supportive, participative, and engaging business environment as Theory Y; moreover, McGregor theorized that Theory Y would produce more motivated employees. Similarly, Maslow (1965) argued that the role of work was not just to meet the basic food and shelter needs (i.e., goals) of employees, but that it also should fill higher goals such as creativity, meaning, and human participation. Likewise, Argyris (1958) predicted that traditional, paternalistic companies would grow only in noncompetitive markets because they keep their employees apathetic, detached, and uninvolved.

This distinction between working climates becomes increasingly important as workers become a more valuable resource, and as our economy shifts from a production to a service and information emphasis (Jaffe 1995). Healthy companies will foster hope among their employees by being concerned with their individuation and creativity (Maccoby 1988). Thus, business success in the twenty-first century will come from balancing the needs of the employees, executives, and stockholders (e.g., Beer, Eisenstat, and Spector 1990; Kotter and Heskett 1993).

A key aspect of a hopeful work environment is social support. During times of stress, high-hope people rely on their friends and family for help and reassurance (Snyder, in press). It follows then, that hopeful workers will need to rely on their peers and supervisors for guidance, assistance, and emotional support. In this regard, research shows that social support is a key variable in assuaging job stress (Karasek and Theorell 1990). In addition, whereas threatening environments produce rigid and simple-minded thinking, supportive and open relationships with co-workers foster productivity and creativity (Karasek and Theorell 1990).

Another job characteristic that has been shown to influence job stress is worker control (Karasek and Theorell 1990). Given that the pursuit of goals is dependent on the effective use of pathways to those goals, it is not surprising that workers who have little control over their work experience greater stress. In fact, severe limitations on worker control can directly lead to job burnout, which is tantamount to a loss of hope in the workplace (Snyder 1994). As a result, hopelessness and burnout at work not only happen to individual workers, but also to entire work teams (see Golembiewski, Munzenrider, and Stevenson 1986).

By giving employees control over their work, companies not only are fostering higher hope, but they also are engendering trust between the workers and the corporation. Demonstrating that the company is interested in the employees' personal growth also can foster this trust. As previously mentioned, the worker is the most precious "commodity" in the new economy. Hence, companies are well advised to put their employees' personal goals at the top of their priority list. Companies that foster the personal growth of their employees (e.g., through education) are more productive than companies where such personal growth is not encouraged (Lawler 1986). Likewise, as shown in research on the "Prisoner's Dilemma" paradigm, trust between two parties (i.e., employee and employer) is essential for working together to achieve the most beneficial outcome. In fact, the evidence suggests that "nice" (i.e., cooperative) companies outperform "nasty" (i.e., hostile) companies by an average of 86 percent (Lloyd 1990). In addition, "nice" companies grow faster, are more profitable, and get higher returns on their investments (Lloyd 1990).

One final note on stress in the workplace is worth making here. Namely, hope theory and research suggest that higher-hope people are invigorated by challenges, whereas lower-hope people feel overwhelmed and stressed by their goals (Snyder, in press). Research in working environments has shown that cognitive variables such as hope can have important impacts on the response to stress. For example, a hopeful cognitive interpretation of stressors can lead to better coping behavior and physical health (Edwards and Cooper 1988). Thus, it is not the stress per se in the work setting that is harmful, but rather how one interprets that stress that is crucial to subsequent coping. Related to this perspective, theorists have begun to make the distinction between *eustress* (i.e., the perception of challenges and opportunities) and *distress* (i.e., the perception of threats) as responses to stressors (Simmons and Nelson 2001).

Self-Esteem and the Workplace

Self-esteem reflects the self-referential emotions that result from people's appraisals of their overall effectiveness in the conduct of their lives (Hewitt 1998). It should be noted that many self-esteem models are built implicitly upon goal-directed thinking. Within hope theory, the focus is on the goal pursuit process as causally eliciting subsequent emotion and esteem. Self-esteem correlates about .45 with hope (Barnum et al. 1998; Munoz-Dunbar 1993; Snyder et al. 1991; Sympson 1993), but the evidence supports the assumption that goal-pursuit thinking (i.e., hope) causally drives esteem and not vice versa. Furthermore, hope enhances the prediction of positive outcomes beyond predictions made from self-esteem alone (Curry et al. 1997; Snyder, Cheavens, and Michael 1999).

·In hope theory, we have theorized that people feel good about themselves (i.e., high self-esteem) when they perceive themselves as being successful in goal pursuits. Conversely, low self-esteem results when individuals perceive themselves as being blocked or unsuccessful in reaching life goals (Snyder 1994). Within this framework, teaching children ways of reaching goals and sustaining motivation in the pursuit of goals will produce higher self-esteem (Snyder et al. 2000). Using hope theory, therefore, we would posit that increases in job performance should enhance job satisfaction, as well as increase self-esteem. Presumably, people feel more satisfied with their jobs if they perceive that they are pursuing or meeting goals. As noted earlier, the goals must be important enough to hold an individual's attention, and high-hope people tend to have clearly defined goals. This leads to positive feelings about themselves, thereby increasing self-esteem. As such, level of hope should be a better predictor of work performance than self-esteem, given that hope is viewed as the source of self-esteem.

Self-esteem obviously is linked to individuals' well-being in their workplaces. For example, self-esteem is thought to be closely associated with the career that a person chooses. Korman (1966, 1967) has drawn the following conclusions about the link between self-esteem and occupational choice: (1) people with high self-esteem believe that their chosen career is likely to satisfy their desires to a greater extent than do people with low self-esteem; (2) people with high self-esteem believe that they possess more of the ability necessary to succeed; and (3) there is a weaker, though typically still significant, relationship between self-esteem and perceived possession of ability. Using the language of hope, people with high self-esteem, or more fundamentally high hope, believe that their chosen career is a suitable pathway for reaching their higher goals, and they also believe that they have the necessary agency to succeed. This reasoning would suggest that employers should stress the ways in which employment at their company would enhance workers' abilities to reach their goals. By following such a course, employers would attract applicants with high hope and self-esteem.

High self-esteem individuals respond better to stressful or challenging tasks than do people with low self-esteem, with high self-esteem people increasing and low self-esteem people decreasing their efforts (Brockner 1985; Sigall and Gould 1977, in Brockner 1988). Such findings are consistent with the idea that high-hopers, when faced with difficult challenges, are able to generate more pathways to reach their goals; low-hopers, on the other hand, see only impenetrable or unchanging obstacles.

Another important area of research in the workplace centers on job satisfaction. Low job satisfaction has been related to increases in job turnover, absenteeism, less desire to unionize, and shorter longevity (Feldman and Arnold 1983, in Brockner 1988). People with high self-esteem are more satisfied with their jobs than are people with low self-esteem (Tharenou 1979, in Brockner 1988). In a parallel manner, it follows that high-hopers are likely to be absent less and to stay with the company longer.

It is important for workplaces to understand the potential impact of worker self-esteem and hope. Individuals with high hope are more likely to view their careers as pathways toward their higher goals, and to feel that they have the ability to succeed. They also are more likely to accomplish challenging tasks and stay with a company over the years. As companies focus on increasing the hope of their employees, they will see improved performance and job satisfaction.

HOPE IN AMERICAN BUSINESSES

In the spring of 2000, *Success* magazine contacted C.R. Snyder about doing a yearly survey of hopefulness in the work climates of U.S. companies. This project was launched in early 2001 and

Table 24.1

Characteristics of High-Hope Organizations

No one, including management, is greatly feared by employees.
There is a level playing field where everyone has an equal chance to succeed.
Advancement and benefits are linked to effort expended.
Lowest person in the organization is treated with the same respect as every other employee,
    including management.
Management sees its first priority as helping the employees to do the best job possible.
There are open, two-way communications between employees and management.
Employee feedback is solicited and is seen as a source of making the company better.
When possible, decisions are given to the employees performing that particular task.
Employees are included in making company goals.
Employees are given responsibility for finding solutions to problems.
Whether it is solving problems or trying new ideas, employees are given the responsibility for
    implementing the changes.
Enduring relationships with customers are encouraged rather than a given sale or objective.

the first wave of results is now available. Snyder developed a brief self-report questionnaire that asked the respondents to rate their company on several dimensions that have been found to relate to hopeful thinking in previous research. The questionnaire was available in *Success* magazine, as well as on a special Web site. There was no control over what companies answered the questionnaire, and the only requirement was that the chief executive officer, a person from middle management, and an employee from the lower echelon of the company complete the questionnaire and return it to the magazine. Employees did not identify themselves. Part of the questionnaire was the Hope Scale, which is an eight-item self-report index of hope that has been developed and validated by Snyder and colleagues (Snyder et al. 1991). If all three questionnaires were returned, the company was included in the results. One hundred and twenty-five companies fulfilled the criterion, and these companies ranged in size from eight to forty thousand employees. Of note, the size of the company did not relate to the hope levels of the employees. The top ten companies in terms of employee hope were identified, and their other responses were then examined in order to ascertain the characteristics of high-hope businesses.

What are the commonalities across these top ten hopeful companies? First, the hopeful companies were profitable (shown in Table 24.1). They reported financial success, along with projected growth. Thus, in terms of the "bottom line" monetary analysis, the high-hope companies appeared to be prospering.

Additionally, the top ten companies all anchored hope to concrete goals. The company CEOs reported that sharing ownership of goals between management and employees seemed to increase creativity and pride in their companies. For example, Tage Inns, an East Coast hotel chain, incorporates daily meetings in which the tasks for the day are shared with all levels of the company—from housekeeping to the kitchen, from the front desk to the porters. Thus, all employees are aware of what must be done in order to bring clients the best experience possible.

Another shared characteristic in the top ten hopeful companies is that CEOs do not run dictatorships. The CEOs instead work hard to create trust, respect, and genuine affection among their employees. In turn, this creates loyalty. For instance, TechTarget.com has continued to grow and be successful while many other .coms have disappeared. TechTarget.com CEO Greg Strakosch tells the story of an employee who came to him with resignation in hand because he wanted to try out for the U.S. rowing team. Rather than accept the resignation, Mr. Strakosch developed a plan that allowed the employee to take the needed time off for tryouts, as well as to meet the deadlines on his work projects.

Equally amazing is TeleChoice, a privately held telecommunications company. The employees go months without seeing each other because they are spread out across eleven different states, and their clients often offer employees job opportunities that would take them away from TeleChoice. In one instance, when an employee wanted to return to the corporate workforce, TeleChoice worked out a program where the employee spent three months working for a potential client who carried part of the cost. At the end of the three months, the employee decided that she was crazy to leave a company that cared so much for their employees that it would give her the opportunity to explore other options. This high-hope approach to employees contrasts with the heavy-handed "This is what you will do" tactics seen in some companies.

Almost all of the high-hope companies mentioned being innovative as a key to recruiting and keeping good employees. Innovations included casual attire, group outings and traditions, and team performance–based awards. The actual form of the innovation mattered less, however, than did the managers showing respect and care about employee job performance, *as well as their personal lives*. In essence, this is creating hope by extending the notion of family to include the corporate family. For example, Xilinx, a computer chip manufacturer in the top ten hopeful companies, has been quite successful despite the problems in the computer chip industry. Based in Silicon Valley, Xilinx interviews employees with an eye on team playing skills, as well as individual technical skills. Peg Wynn, vice president of human resources, says that employees work hard, but give even more. Their company regularly participates in community activities by serving as tutors, volunteering at children's shelters, or donating stock to help a nearby school. The mutual respect and care taken in the hiring process has paid off handsomely for the company. Not only are profits up (revenues of $1.6 billion), but they also boast a turnover rate of less than 6 percent—in Silicon Valley, which is known for its "job hopping."

The Top 10 Hopeful Companies all hold high the goal of strong communication. All the companies constantly work at creating and maintaining an environment in which independent thought and discourse are encouraged. Employees are given the opportunity to communicate across various levels of the corporation and to be creative in problem solving. For instance, Landec Computer Corporation recently awarded its employees by taking the entire company on a cruise. This Dallas-based company never works on weekends, and even salaried employees are limited to no more than forty-five hours per week. All of this leads to an impressive profit margin in which the company is on target to gross $6 million this year. Employees seem to know that they can always approach the Landec CEO Chuck Lande if they have a problem. Moreover, this company gives back to the community—including Internet services, computers, and the sponsoring of community teen activities.

Collectively, these companies illustrate the power of hope in the workplace. They have demonstrated that actively investing in employees is a key goal for financial success, and this "investment" apparently takes the form of caring about the employee in and out of the office. The positive and hopeful cultures at these companies make people want to go to work and to perform well. Value and integrity also appear to be important in creating a hopeful workplace. Secrets are discouraged, and some of these companies even eliminated the doors separating offices. They pay close attention to their hiring processes, they are protective of their corporate cultures, and they do not allow anyone to undermine the work atmospheres that they have nurtured. Employees are given opportunities and authority to make decisions—and mistakes. These are workplaces of growth and happiness that are built on foundations of hope.

In conclusion, there are several direct lessons that can be taken from our work on hope as they pertain specifically to the workplace. At the organizational level, high-hope organizations exist on a level playing field in which every employee has an equal chance of succeeding. Consistent with the idea of a level playing field is the respect that is accorded everyone within the organization, from employees in the lowest echelon to those in upper management. Management views its first priority as helping employees achieve the highest level of performance. High-hope organizations also maintain open, two-way communication between employees and management. Employees not only are given a clear conception of company goals, but they also are included in the process of defining those goals. Advancement and benefits are linked to the effort expended so that hard work is rewarded. Further, employees are given responsibility for finding solutions to problems. Whether it is solving problems or trying a new idea, employees are given responsibility for implementing changes. Collectively, everyone in the organization works to build enduring relationships between everyone in the organization and its clients.

High-hope employees set clear work goals and are conscientious about their job performance. They maintain a helping attitude toward others within the organization and the surrounding community. When difficult times arise, high-hope employees do not seek to assign blame to others; instead, they double their efforts to find solutions. High-hope employees motivate themselves, especially during difficult times. High-hope employees are not resentful of fellow employees who receive awards (raises, advancement, recognition, etc.), conceivably because they understand that as their fellow employee succeeds they also succeed. Perhaps most importantly, high-hope employees are constantly seeking good and multiple routes to desired goals, both as they relate to their work, and for life in general. High-hope employees understand that their sense of meaning flows both at work and at home. They maintain a balance within the various aspects of their lives.

We began this chapter with a description of the lives of two employees who were either low in hope and/or they worked in environments that were not hopeful. With the suggestions that we have previously made, their lives can become more hopeful. The following vignettes show how this can happen.

"*Beep, beep, beep . . .*" Ron reaches over and silences his 6:00 A.M. wake-up call. Following a company poll about employee satisfaction and beliefs, his company instigated a number of changes. Ron feels comfortable sleeping in because he no longer doubts his team's dependability and motivation. He now leads weekly team meetings to discuss team progress and goals, and participates in monthly meetings with other teams. The company also holds banquets every few months to recognize team accomplishments, including updates on the standings of the company's new sports teams. Because he feels more active and valued in the company, Ron no longer views retirement as an escape from work dissatisfaction.

Across the city, Anthea is watching out the window for the neighborhood car pool. Several families on her block now take turns driving their children to school. She realized that changes were needed after the law firm had requested that she write down her personal and work goals. One of her work goals had been to start her workday at 8:00 rather than 8:30 so that she could be home before her children got home from school; this also fit her personal goal of spending more time with her children. She had gotten information about the day care located in the building that the law firm rented from, so now she was able to visit her infant daughter during her lunch break. Anthea was especially happy that the law firm encouraged and would pay for continuing education classes, and she was optimistic about future employment opportunities within the firm and perhaps outside of it.

NOTE

For further information about hope as applied to various populations, contact the senior author, c/o Psychology Dept. 1415 Jayhawk Blvd., University of Kansas, Lawrence 66045, or e-mail to vhadams@ku.edu. For information about hope theory, contact C.R. Snyder at the same address, or e-mail to crsnyder@ku.edu.

REFERENCES

Argyris, C. (1958). "The Organization: What Makes It Healthy?" *Harvard Business Review.*
Barnum, D.D.; C.R. Snyder; M.A. Rapoff; M.M. Mani; and R. Thompson. (1998). "Hope and Social Support in the Psychological Adjustment of Pediatric Burn Survivors and Matched Controls." *Children's Health Care* 27: 15–30.
Beer, M.; R.A. Eisenstat; and B. Spector. (1990). *The Critical Path for Corporate Renewal.* Boston: Harvard Business School Press.
Brockner, J. (1985). "The Relation of Self-esteem and Positive Inequity to Productivity." *Journal of Personality* 53: 517–529.
———. (1988). *Self-esteem at Work: Research, Theory, and Practice.* Lexington, MA: Lexington Books.
Curry, L.A.; C.R. Snyder; D.L. Cook; B.C. Ruby; and M. Rehm. (1997). "The Role of Hope in Student-Athlete Academic and Sport Achievement." *Journal of Personality and Social Psychology* 73: 1257–1267.
Diener, E., and R.J. Larsen. (1984). "Temporal Stability and Cross-Situational Consistency of Affective, Behavioral, and Cognitive Processes." *Journal of Personality and Social Psychology* 47: 580–592.
Edwards, J.R., and C.L. Cooper. (1988). "Research in Stress, Coping, and Health: Theoretical and Methodological Issues." *Psychological Medicine* 18, no. 1: 15–20.
Feldman, D.B., and C.R. Snyder. (2001). "Hope and Meaning in Life: A New Approach to an Old Problem." Unpublished manuscript, Department of Psychology, University of Kansas, Lawrence.
Feldman, D.C., and H.J. Arnold. (1983). *Managing Individual and Group Behavior in Organizations.* New York: McGraw-Hill.
Friedman, R.; M. Kane; and D.B. Cornfield. (1998). "Social Support and Career Optimism: Examining the Effectiveness of Network Groups Among Black Managers." *Human Relations* 51, no. 9: 1155–1177.
Golembiewski, R.T.; R.F. Munzenrider; and J.G. Stevenson. (1986). *Stress in Organizations: Toward a Phase Model of Burnout.* New York: Praeger.
Hewitt, J.P. (1998). *The Myth of Self-esteem: Finding Happiness and Solving Problems in America.* New York: St. Martin's Press.
Jaffe, D.T. (1995). "The Healthy Company: Research Paradigms for Organizational and Personal Health." In *Organizational Risk Factors for Job Stress*, ed. Steven L. Sauter and Lawrence R. Murphy. Washington, DC: American Psychological Association, 13–39.
Karasek, R., and T. Theorell. (1990). *Healthy Work: Stress, Productivity, and the Reconstruction of Working Life.* New York: Basic Books.
Korman, A.K. (1966). "Self-esteem Variable in Vocational Choice." *Journal of Applied Psychology* 50: 479–486.
———. (1967). "Self-esteem As a Moderator of the Relationship Between Self-Perceived Abilities and Vocational Choice." *Journal of Applied Psychology* 51: 65–67.
Kotter, J., and T. Heskett. (1993). *Corporate Culture and Performance.* New York: Free Press.
Landsbergis, P.A.; J. Cahill; and P. Schnall. (1999). "The Impact of Lean Production and Related New Systems of Work Organizations on Worker Health." *Journal of Occupational Health Psychology* 4: 108–130.
Lawler, E.E., III. (1986). *High-Involvement Management.* San Francisco: Jossey-Bass.
Lazarus, R.S. (1999). "Hope: An Emotion and a Vital Coping Resource Against Despair." *Social Research* 66 (2): 665–669.
———. (2000). "Toward Better Research on Stress and Coping." *American Psychologist* 55: 653–678.
Lazarus, R.S.; J. Deese; and S.F. Osler. (1952). "The Effects of Psychological Stress Upon Performance." *Psychological-Bulletin* 49: 293–317.
Lloyd, T. (1990). *The Nice Company.* London: Bloomsbury.
Lovallo, D.P. (1997). "Essays on the Psychology of Competition." *Dissertation Abstracts International: Section A* 58(8–A): 3565.
Maccoby, M. (1988). *Why Work? Leading the New Generation.* New York: Simon and Schuster.
Maslow, A.H. (1965). *Eupsychian Management.* Homewood, IL: Irwin/Dorsey.
McGregor, D. (1960). *The Human Side of Enterprise.* New York: McGraw-Hill.
Munoz-Dunbar, R. (1993). "Hope: A Cross-Cultural Assessment of American College Students." Unpublished master's thesis, Department of Psychology, University of Kansas, Lawrence.
Pylyshyn, Z.W. (1973). "What the Mind's Eye Tells the Mind's Brain: A Critique of Mental Imagery." *Psychological Bulletin* 80: 1–24.
Salzmann, J.C. (1997). "Thriving During Organizational Change: The Role of Metaphors for Change, Op-

timism and Pessimism, and Attributional Style." *Dissertation Abstracts International:* Section B, 58(5–B): 2734.

Schulman, P. (1999). "Applying Learned Optimism to Increase Sales Productivity." *Journal of Personal Selling and Sales Management* 19, no. 1: 31–37.

Sennett, R. (1998). *Corrosion of Character: The Personal Consequences of Work in the New Capitalism.* New York: Norton.

Sigall, H., and R. Gould. (1977). "The Effects of Self-esteem and Evaluator Demandingness on Effort Expenditure." *Journal of Personality and Social Psychology* 35: 12–20.

Simmons, B.L., and D.L. Nelson. (2001). "Eustress at Work: The Relationship Between Hope and Health in Hospital Nurses." *Health Care Management Review* 26, no. 4: 7–18.

Snyder, C.R. (1994). *The Psychology of Hope: You Can Get There from Here.* New York: Free Press.

———. (2000). "Hypothesis: There Is Hope." In *Handbook of Hope: Theory, Research, and Applications,* ed. C.R. Snyder. Orlando, FL: Academic Press, 3–21.

———. (in press). "Hope Theory: Rainbows in the Mind." *Psychological Inquiry.*

Snyder, C.R.; J. Cheavens; and S.T. Michael. (1999). "Hoping." In *Coping: The Psychology of What Works,* ed. C.R. Snyder. New York: Oxford University Press, 205–231.

Snyder, C.R.; C. Harris; J.R. Anderson; S.A. Holleran; L.M. Irving; S.T. Sigmon; L. Yoshinobu; J. Gibb; C. Langelle; and P. Harney. (1991). "The Will and the Ways: Development and Validation of an Individual-Differences Measure of Hope." *Journal of Personality and Social Psychology* 60: 570–585.

Snyder, C.R., Sympson, S. C., Ybasco, F. C., Borders, T. F., Babyak, M. A., & Higgins, R. L. (1996). "Development and Validation of the State Hope Scale." *Journal of Personality and Social Psychology* 70: 321–335.

Snyder, C.R.; T. Tran; L.L. Schroder; K.M. Pulvers; V. Adams, III; and L. Laub. (2000). "Teaching the Hope Recipe: Setting Goals, Finding Pathways to Those Goals, and Getting Motivated." *Reaching Today's Youth* 4, no. 4: 46–50.

Sympson, S. (1993). "Construction and Validation of a State Hope Measure: A Month in the Lives of College Students." Unpublished doctoral dissertation, Department of Psychology, University of Kansas, Lawrence.

Tharenou, P. (1979). "Employee Self-esteem: A Review of the Literature." *Journal of Vocational Behavior* 15: 316–346.

Turner, N.; J. Barling; and J. Zacharatos. (2002). "Working." In *The Handbook of Positive Psychology,* ed. C.R. Snyder and S. Lopez. New York: Oxford University Press, 715–728.

U.S. Bureau of the Census. (2001). "The Employment Situation: August 2001": ftp://146.142.4.23/pub/news.release/empsit.txtl (September 7).

Wagner, P.R. (1996). "Management During Organizational Change: Optimism versus Disillusionment." *Dissertation Abstracts International*: Section A, 56(9–A): 3654.

CHAPTER 25

WHEN THE SPIRIT MOVES YOU

Administration, Law, and Spirituality in the Workplace

TERREL L. RHODES

In recent years there has been an outpouring of books and articles that focus on the need to bring spirituality into the workplace; to acknowledge the role that spirituality plays in people's lives; and to integrate spirituality into the workplace as well as the home (see Greenleaf 1977; Vaill 1989; DePree 1989; Fairholm 1997). The majority of the literature that addresses issues of spirituality and the workplace emanates from the perspective of business management. As with most new management trends, they first appear in the private sector where they are tested and established in the pantheon of business practices before migrating to the public sector. Spirituality and the workplace is no different in this regard than earlier trends such as total quality management, performance budgeting, zero-based budgeting, servant leadership, and so forth.

This chapter will examine some of the recent literature and research focusing on the need for incorporating spirituality into the workplace and the implications for public sector managers. Second, current scientific efforts at identifying the neurophysiological foundations for spirituality will be introduced as a basis for the inability to exclude spirituality from the workplace. Finally, the legal foundations that have begun to emerge regarding spirituality in the workplace will be summarized with regard to public managers.

SPIRITUALITY AND RELIGION

What exactly are we talking about in this debate over spirituality in the workplace? What is all the fuss about? At one level, the entire interest in spirituality in the workplace is a "tempest in a teapot" in that the management principles that have emerged over the past two decades clearly recognize the place of the employee in the workplace as more than just a "cog in the wheel," or a functionary to carry out the dictates of the boss. The worth of the individual in an organization and the recognition that employees have lives that encompass much more than their jobs is already embedded in modern management practices (see, e.g., Lerner and Wanat 1992; Bozeman and Straussman 1984).

One need look no further than the obvious introduction of day care centers, flex time, job-sharing, partner benefits, and family leave to see the recognition of the value and needs of an employee as a part of a family outside and inside the workplace. The provision of time off for employees to vote, to be involved in community service, and to enhance skills through training and development further validate aspects of self-actualization beyond the job. Finally, the incorporation into job descriptions and hiring processes of such characteristics as collaboration, ability to get along with others, respect, responsiveness, commitment, and integrity reflect the need for employing individuals who bring to the workplace values and characteristics related to success-ful organizational outcomes. Regardless of whether these changes in management practices are motivated by increased organizational efficiency or for "higher goals" of employee self-actual-ization, the result is that modern management practice has clearly acknowledged individual needs that extend beyond the workplace skills, abilities, and responsibilities.

On the other hand, the manifestations of valuing the worth of employees as people whose work is only a part of who they are, can be criticized as still failing to encompass the spiritual (White 1994). The advocates for more explicit attention to spirituality in the workplace express their senti-ments in several ways, attempting to define and demonstrate how to include spirituality in the work-place. Some recent examples: Guillory (1997) argues that, "spirituality in the workplace . . . is the integration of holistic principles, practices, and behaviors that encourages the full expression of body, mind, and spirit. These include humanistic and employee-friendly work environments, ser-vice orientation, creativity and innovation, personal and collective transformation, environmental sensitivity, and high performance" (xv). Rabbi Wayne Dosick (2000) places his plea for greater spirituality in the form of a story based on the Ten Commandments of business.

Mitroff and Denton (1999) take the approach of presenting a list of characteristics of spirituality:

- Spirituality is highly individual and intensely personal. You don't have to be religious to be spiritual.
- Spirituality is the basic belief that there is a supreme power, a being, a force, that governs the entire universe. There is a purpose for everything and everyone.
- Everything is interconnected with everything else. Everything affects and is affected by everything else.
- Spirituality is the feeling of this interconnectedness. Spirituality is being in touch with it.
- Spirituality is also the feeling that no matter how bad things get, they will always work out somehow. There is a guiding plan that governs all lives.
- We are put here basically to do good. One must strive to produce products and services that serve all of humankind.
- Spirituality is inextricably connected with caring, hope, kindness, love, and optimism. Spiri-tuality is the basic faith in the existence of those things.

Marcic (1997) places spirituality in the context of the New Management Virtues: trustworthi-ness, unity, respect and dignity, justice, and service and humility. "These management virtues form the philosophical and spiritual foundation for many of the new management concepts" (46–47).

Fairholm, in his 1997 study of nineteen public administrators, argues strongly against current professional management values and practices and for greater spiritualism in the workplace based on Judeo-Christian foundations:

> This inner moral standard comes out of our deepest traditions of right and wrong, out of our sense of spirituality. Spirituality transcends doctrinaire religion. It finds common cause with people of all religious persuasions, and even among those who profess no religion. . . .
> It is everything about me that is nonphysical: my identity, my values, my memories, my sense of humor, and so forth. . . . (6)
>
> The rise of management marks the rise of commitment to a stifling common cause. Uniformity is now the rule. Conformance to a common standard has replaced individuality, individual commitment, and innovation. Conformity, not innovation is the mark of a good employee. (19)

Fairholm then takes a more explicit turn toward linking his critique of modern administration to the need for grounding our thinking about the workplace in Judeo-Christian theology. He argues that American society rests on an implicit, yet pervasive, notion of a social compact between government and the citizens. Although he admits that all criminal, family, business and commercial law, and most legislation have a moral foundation that draws heavily on Judeo-Christian teaching, they are insufficient.

> The Mosaic Law, on the other hand, offers another theory of human relationships. It seeks the basis of it in polity, first in the absolute sovereignty of God, next in the relationship of the individual to God, and then, through God to his countrymen. This theory of human relationship is more germane to spiritual leadership than old and obsolete political theory. . . . While it contradicts none of the common theories, the Mosaic Law lies beneath them all. (1997, 40)

Clearly, there is a range of views on what constitutes spirituality, how to define it, and what the foundational bedrock should be. There are, however, similarities among these authors and among others who argue for the incorporation of spirituality into the workplace. The common factors revolve around a perceived need to acknowledge in a public manner the otherworldly, beyond physical dimensions of humankind. To infuse into the workplace a language of the soul or the spirit that goes far beyond the language of current administrative practice. To hear some of the advocates for spirituality's place in modern administration, for example Fairholm, is to believe that the last twenty years of administrative reform, which, at least in part, responded to calls to recognize the humanness of employees in its many dimensions, never occurred.

Where does this surge of claims for spirituality in the workplace leave us?

BUSINESS AND SPIRITUALITY

In one of the more recent and reasoned presentations of spirituality in the workplace, Mitroff and Denton (1999) create a continuum of business models based on the degree and manner to which they incorporate or foster spirituality into the organizational foundations and operations of business organizations. At the continuum's most pronounced point, Religious-Based Organizations explicitly proclaim God as their foundational chief executive officer and the teachings of the Bible as the guiding principles for conducting business. Moving through the other models—the Evolutionary Organization, the Recovering Organization, and the Socially Responsible Organization—they arrive at the Values-Based Organization.

> Values-Based Organizations are able to separate their guiding beliefs and day-to-day practices from religion and spirituality because they have borrowed the most universal and least controversial of all religious values. (150)
> . . . words having to do with spirituality and soul are off limits for the Values-Based Organization. Although terms such as love, respect, trust, and wisdom are used freely and the concepts they represent are readily accepted, words having any hint of religious or spiritual connotation are rejected outright. . . . This attitude derives from an underlying and strongly held belief that certain words possess the power to do more harm than good . . . religion and spirituality and the words used to express them compete negatively with universal values. (155)

Through their data collection, Mitroff and Denton find some interesting expressions related to spirituality and religion in the workplace. The authors asked their respondents about their positive and negative views of both religion and spirituality: 30 percent of the respondents expressed both positive views of religion and spirituality; a very small percentage (2 percent) had positive views of religion and negative views of spirituality; roughly 60 percent had positive views of spirituality and negative views of religion; and 8 percent had negative views of both religion and spirituality.

The authors conclude their study by creating a Best-Practices model that builds primarily on the Values-Based Organization model as the best foundation for organizations to adopt, but that borrows aspects from each of the other models to make it more explicitly religious and spiritual in its language. Their Best-Practices model appears to recognize the two-thirds of respondents who expressed negative statements about religion, while also providing something for the one-third who reflected the acceptance of religious expressions in the workplace. The clear conclusion from the authors is that modern, successful organizations must include both explicit spiritual and religious language in the organizational mission and operations.

Mitroff and Denton (1999) have attempted to bring the methods of social science research to their discussions to both anchor the argument for managers that spirituality does need to be explicit in the workplace, and to satisfy the standards of evidence required by the academic reviewers of their work for inclusion in the curriculum of colleges and universities. Although their study is one of the most grounded in empirical evidence through a set of surveys and interviews of business executives and human resource directors, the findings are still lacking in generalizability. For example, the survey of human resource directors resulted in an extremely low response rate of 7.5 percent. Their conclusions are supplemented by a series of individual interviews with corporate executives on both coasts of the United States, and although intriguing, drawing any general conclusions from these few interviews and the incredibly low survey response rate, leaves their study very problematic at best (Trevino 2000).

Part of what is revealed is the paucity of empirical evidence related to the role or need for a role for spirituality in the workplace, especially in the public arena. What emerges from the initial attempts to gather empirical evidence is the suggestion that it is appropriate to use spiritual language, but still useful to clearly separate religion and public management, policy making, and service provision.

SPIRITUALITY AND THE PHYSICAL BRAIN

More recently efforts have been made by science to examine the physical basis for spiritual and religious experiences. According to David Wulff, a psychologist at Wheaton College, MA: "Spiritual experiences are so consistent across cultures, across time, and across faiths," which suggests "a common core that is likely a reflection of structures and processes in the human brain" (as quoted in Begley 2001, 53). New imaging capabilities have been developed that allow sophisticated mapping of brain activity. As a result, scientists have begun examining electrical patterns in the brain when patients experience various types of brain activities.

The most recent development has been single photon emission computed tomography (SPECT) imaging of the brain. Images of the brain have been taken immediately after patients have experienced deep spiritual, meditative states.

> As expected, the prefrontal cortex, seat of attention, lit up. . . . But it was a quieting of activity that stood out. A bundle of neurons in the superior parietal lobe, toward the top and back of the brain, had gone dark. This region, nicknamed the "orientation association area," processes information about space and time, and the orientation of the body in space. . . . It

determines where the body ends and the rest of the world begins. . . . Specifically, the left orientation area creates the sensation of a physically delimited body; the right orientation area creates the sense of the physical space in which the body exists.

> With no information from the senses arriving, the left orientation area cannot find any boundary between the self and the world. As a result, the brain seems to have no choice but "to perceive the self as endless and intimately interwoven with everyone and everything," Newberg and d'Aquili write in *Why God Won't Go Away*. The right orientation area, equally bereft of sensory data, defaults to a feeling of infinite space. . . . (Begley 2001, 53)

> Combination of focused attention and heightened emotion superstimulate the brain's arousal system into hyperdrive. One of the brain structures responsible for maintaining equilibrium—the hippocampus—puts on the brakes. It inhibits the flow of signals between neurons. . . . The result is that certain regions of the brain are deprived of neuronal input. One such deprived region seems to be the orientation area, the same spot that goes quiet during meditation and prayer. . . . The result again is "blurring the edges of the brain's sense of self, opening the door to the unitary states that are the primary goal of religious ritual." (Begley 2001, 57)

The advances of science have introduced new dimensions to the discussion of spirituality. The imaging systems provide a foundational physical picture of spirituality. In no way does the research mean that spirituality is simply and only a physically induced state. On the other hand, the research supports the role of the physical brain in creating the sensations and feelings that we associate with spiritual states. (see Woodward 2001) The existence and the inducement of meditative states are typically considered to be beneficial to humans. The argument can be made that no matter where an individual is—at home or at work—that physiological and psychological spiritual events can, and perhaps should, occur. Public managers might, for example, engage in simple actions in the workplace to create quiet space or work environments that would be conducive to meditation or "mental" breaks. The knowledge of physiological functions of the brain might prove useful by providing new ways of structuring conflict situations or stress reduction actions when events or times are particularly challenging.

LEGAL ISSUES

Beyond the moral, ethical, theory, and practice discussions about spirituality and the workplace lies the legal environment that also governs workers, managers, and the work setting. The legal environment has been instrumental in public administration in establishing the rights of those who work in the public arena and the public that receives services and programs through public agencies and individuals.

To date, the bulk of court cases and legal opinions rendered in the general arena of spirituality and religion and the workplace, have revolved around two primary types of cases: (1) cases involving employee benefits, and (2) the role of government in support of free exercise and establishment of religion. Cases directly related to spirituality in the workplace have not yet made their way into the court system as an established legal doctrine. In most instances, the existing court rulings have involved more formal religious beliefs and practices rather than expressions of spirituality itself. Because of the close connection between religion and spirituality as presented by many of the writers on the topic of spirituality who advocate for the explicit incorporation of spirituality into the workplace, the cases revolving around religion and its role in the workplace provide a good starting point for examining the thinking of the courts in this general domain. The cases and the reasoning provided in the opinions also provide a potential preview of the arguments and opinions that could pertain to future cases that would involve spirituality in the workplace.

Several cases that have relevance to our discussion have involved cases of employees being denied benefits because of their beliefs. In the landmark case *Sherbert v. Verner et al., Members of South Carolina Employment Security Commission et al.*, 374 US 398 (1963), an employee was dismissed because she refused to work on Saturday, which was her Sabbath. When she was unable to obtain other employment, she filed for unemployment compensation benefits under the provisions of South Carolina's Unemployment Compensation Act. To be eligible, a claimant must be "able to work and . . . available for work"; and, further, [374 US 398, 401] that a claimant is ineligible for benefits "[i]f . . . he has failed, without good cause . . . to accept available suitable work when offered him by the employment office or the employer. . . ." In an administrative hearing, the Employment Security Commission found that the appellant was restricting her availability for work by refusing to work on Saturdays and therefore disqualified her for benefits because she failed, without good cause, to accept suitable work when offered. On subsequent appeal, the South Carolina Supreme Court upheld the denial of benefits, rejecting the claim that the Free Exercise Clause of the First Amendment protected the employee's right to observe her religious practices. Ultimately, the U.S. Supreme Court overturned the South Carolina Supreme Court and ruled in favor of the claimant's right to exercise her religion and to receive unemployment compensation benefits under the Free Exercise provisions of the First Amendment as applied through the Fourteenth Amendment:

> The door of the Free Exercise Clause stands tightly closed against any governmental regulation of religious beliefs as such, *Cantwell v. Connecticut*, 310 US 296, 303. Government may neither compel affirmation of a repugnant belief, *Torcaso v. Watkins*, 367 US 488; nor penalize or discriminate against individuals or groups because they hold religious views abhorrent to the authorities, *Fowler v. Rhode Island*, 345 US 67; nor employ the taxing power to inhibit the dissemination of particular religious views, *Murdock v. Pennsylvania*, 319 US 105; *Follett v. McCormick*, 321 US 573; see *Grosjean v. American Press Co.*, 297 US 233. On the other hand, [374 US 398, 403] the Court has rejected challenges under the Free Exercise Clause to governmental regulation of certain overt acts prompted by religious beliefs or principles, for "even when the action is in accord with one's religious convictions, [it] is not totally free from legislative restrictions." *Braunfeld v. Brown*, 366 US 599, 603. The conduct or actions so regulated have invariably posed some substantial threat to public safety, peace or order. See, for example, *Reynolds v. United States*, 98 US 145; *Jacobson v. Massachusetts* 197 US 11; *Prince v. Massachusetts*, 321 US 158; *Cleveland v. United States*, 329 US 14.

The U.S. Supreme Court held firmly that individuals do have a right to the free exercise of their religion, even as it relates to the workplace, and to not be discriminated against as a result of that free exercise unless that exercise threatened public safety, peace, or order.

In 1981, the U.S. Supreme Court again ruled on the Free Exercise Clause in a case involving unemployment compensation, this time in Indiana. In the Indiana case, a Mr. Thomas quit his job because of his religious objections to manufacturing arms, although he was willing to accept a position wherein he produced materials that might then be used to create weapons. Having been denied unemployment compensation benefits by the administrative hearing board and subsequent court appeals through the Indiana courts, the U.S. Supreme Court ruled: "Unless we are prepared to overrule *Sherbert, supra,* Thomas cannot be denied the benefits due him on the basis of the findings of the referee, the Review Board, and the Indiana Court of Appeals that he terminated his employment because of his religious convictions" (*Thomas v. Review Board, Indiana Employment Security Division et al.* 450 US 707 [1981]). The lower court findings were reversed and Mr. Thomas received his benefits.

More recently, the U.S. Supreme Court has continued to clarify the Free Exercise provision as it relates to the workplace in *Employment Division, Department of Human Resources of Oregon, et al. v. Smith et al.* 494 US 872 (1990). The case involved an employee who was dismissed from his job for using peyote. The employee claimed that his peyote use was an integral part of his religious practice that was prescribed to facilitate spiritual contact with the other world. The claim rested on the earlier decisions of the Court in *Sherbert v. Verner, supra, Thomas v. Review Board, Indiana Employment Security Div., supra,* and *Hobbie v. Unemployment Appeals Comm'n of Florida,* 480 US 136 (1987), wherein the Court had held that a State could not condition the availability of unemployment insurance on an individual's willingness to forgo conduct required by his religion.

The Court's decisions were typically not simplistic. The Court argued that when they had found the application of a neutral, generally applicable law to religiously motivated action under the First Amendment's Free Exercise Clause to be invalid, the decision had also involved other constitutional provisions such as free speech and freedom of the press. And, that some cases involving compelled expression that had been decided on free speech grounds, also involved freedom of religion (see *Wooley v. Maynard,* 430 US 705 [1977] [invalidating compelled display of a license plate slogan that offended individual religious beliefs]; *West Virginia Bd. of Education v. Barnette,* 319 US 624 [1943] [invalidating compulsory flag salute statute challenged by religious objectors]).

In the 1990 Oregon case the Court was asked to allow an otherwise prohibitive behavior—using a controlled substance (peyote)—because it was accompanied by religious convictions, to be constitutional and free of governmental regulation. The Court firmly refused to do so. The Court further stated:

> Even if we were inclined to breathe into *Sherbert* some life beyond the unemployment compensation field, we would not apply it to require exemption from a generally applicable criminal law. . . . To make an individual's obligation to obey such a law contingent upon the law's coincidence with his religious beliefs, except where the State's interest is "compelling"—permitting him, by virtue of his beliefs, "to become a law unto himself," *Reynolds v. United States,* 98 US, at 167—contradicts both constitutional tradition and common sense.
>
> Values that are protected against government interference through enshrinement in the Bill of Rights are not thereby banished from the political process. . . . Because respondents' ingestion of peyote was prohibited under Oregon law, and because that prohibition is constitutional, Oregon may, consistent with the Free Exercise Clause, deny respondents unemployment compensation when their dismissal results from use of the drug. (*Employment Division, Department of Human Resources of Oregon et al. v. Smith et al.* 494 US 872, 1990)

The Court supported the Free Exercise provisions, but typically in conjunction with other constitutional provisions. When individual free exercise of religion collided with criminal prohibitions, the duty of the State to protect public safety, peace, and order would prevail in most instances.

Beyond employment compensation law, which has been the narrowly constrained arena that most Court workplace rulings related to religious convictions (and spirituality) have been restricted to, the exercise of religion has been the focus of other rulings that have some relevance to public administration. The second major area in which the Court has made a series of rulings related to religious expression is the role of government in endorsing or supporting religious expression.

Another 1963 landmark case addressed this second major legal arena. The public arena in the 1960s was churning with assaults on governmental and societal values, institutions, and practices. Policies that required school prayer and recitation of the Pledge of Allegiance were under attack. In *School District of Abington v. Schempp*, 374 US 203 (1963), and hearkening back to a 1943 Court decision, the Supreme Court addressed mandatory school prayer:

> While the Free Exercise Clause clearly prohibits the use of state action to deny the rights of free exercise to anyone, it has never meant that a majority could use the machinery of the State to practice its beliefs. Such a contention was effectively answered by Mr. Justice Jackson for the Court in *West Virginia Board of Education v. Barnette*, 319 US 624, 638 (1943): "The place of religion in our society is an exalted one, achieved through a long tradition of reliance on the home, the church and the inviolable citadel of the individual heart and mind. We have come to recognize through bitter experience that it is not within the power of government to invade that citadel, whether its purpose or effect be to aid or oppose, to advance or retard. In the relationship between man and religion, the State is firmly committed to a position of neutrality. Though the application of that rule requires interpretation of a delicate sort, the rule itself is clearly and concisely stated in the words of the First Amendment." (*School District of Abington TP., PA v. Schempp*, 374 US 203, 83 S. CT. 1560, 1963)

Again, in *Allegheny County Greater Pittsburgh ACLU*, 492 US 573 (1989), the Supreme Court held that placing a religious display (a creche) in a public building constituted official governmental support of a religion and thus violated the Establishment Clause of the First Amendment and was therefore unconstitutional. However, having religious symbols in a display on public property outside of a governmental building saluting liberty was within the protection of the Constitution by not violating the Establishment Clause.

In a 1994 New York case in which the New York state legislature established a separate school district so that an orthodox Jewish religious sect would not have to send their children to a public school, the Supreme Court declared the legislative action to be unconstitutional. Justice Souter delivered the opinion of the Court:

> because this Act is tantamount to an allocation of political power on a religious criterion and neither presupposes nor requires governmental impartiality toward religion, we hold that it violates the prohibition against establishment. . . . A proper respect for both the Free Exercise and the Establishment Clauses compels the State to pursue a course of "neutrality" toward religion. (*Committee for Public Ed. & Religious Liberty v. Nyquist*, 413 US 756, 792–793, 1973)
>
> . . . We therefore find the legislature's Act to be substantially equivalent to defining a political subdivision and hence the qualification for its franchise by a religious test, resulting in a purposeful and forbidden "fusion of governmental and religious functions." (*Larkin v. Grendel's Den*, 459 US, at 126)

Justice O'Connor concurred, stating that "The Constitution permits '*nondiscriminatory* religious-practice exemption[s],' *Smith*, *supra*, at 890, not sectarian ones" (*Board of Education of Kiryas Joel Village School District v. Grumet*, 512 US 687, 1994).

More recently, in *City of Boerne v. Flores, Archbishop of San Antonio et al.* 521 US 507 (1997), the Court held that zoning laws could apply to religious institutions as to any others even when the laws resulted in a burden on the religious institution if that burden was incidental to the general application of the law. In other words, government neutrality did not mean that *no* burden could be placed on the free exercise of religion.

In an effort to strengthen the free exercise of religion and to restrict the courts' ability to make decisions that limited religious expression, for example, prayers at football games, in classrooms, and so forth, the U.S. Congress passed federal legislation—the Religious Freedom Restoration Act. The Act expanded the conditions for expression of religion and allowed governmental support for and sponsorship of religious conduct and practices. The *Boerne v. Flores* case provided a test for the Restoration Act. The Court found that:

> Broad as the power of Congress is under the Enforcement Clause of the Fourteenth Amendment, Religious Freedom Restoration Act contradicts vital principles necessary to maintain separation of powers and the federal balance. The judgment of the Court of Appeals sustaining the Act's constitutionality is reversed. It is so ordered. (521 US 507, 1997)

The U.S. Supreme Court clearly expressed its determination to continue to prohibit any official governmental support for religion and religious expression while maintaining the government's responsibility to protect individual rights to the free exercise of their religion regardless of what the particular religion was.

All of these cases deal with religion in the workplace or the role of government in the support or endorsement of religions. None of these cases directly relates to issues of spirituality in the workplace. These cases, though, are illustrative for the public administrator in that they reveal central legal tenets that should guide the behavior of public officials and public administrative agencies when considering issues of spirituality in the workplace.

From these cases one can extract two central principles:

1. Individuals cannot be discriminated against because of the exercise of their religious convictions. Religious convictions can be broadly construed to include spiritual convictions (see *Employment Division, Department of Human Resources of Oregon et al. v. Smith et al.,* 494 US 872, 1990). Religious and/or spiritual convictions are not given unlimited freedom, however, especially when they confront criminal laws or general public policies, procedures and laws that affect or burden the exercise of their religious convictions incidentally and in a manner generally applicable to all others; and

2. Governmental agencies and officials cannot engage in behaviors and actions that appear to establish, support, or endorse religious (spiritual) practices, rituals, or symbols. Adopting official or formal policies and procedures that endorse and recognize such practices, rituals, or symbols in the workplace would appear to be suspect from the beginning. The Supreme Court's finding the Religious Freedom Restoration Act to be unconstitutional is a clear example of the continuing legal position on the Establishment Clause.

THE PUBLIC MANAGER

At the risk of being placed in the camp of those opposed to the new insistence on spirituality in the workplace, I would argue that public managers should not be unappreciative of spirits, souls, religious convictions, or appreciation for the virtues and values that make us human. There are, however, widely accepted values that underlie modern public administration and accepted behavior by public managers. These values, or virtues, are most openly and consistently enunciated through formal Codes of Ethics, adopted by organizations representing professional public administrators in this country and around the world.

Religious leaders have frequently been in the forefront of the reform movements that transformed personalized, ward politics into the professional managerial state. It took decades to create a system for providing services to the public that was built on merit, qualifications, fairness, and equity, rather than on personal connections, graft, discrimination, and favoritism. Few in this country would argue for a return to the earlier era of nepotism and corruption. The struggle to encourage professional ethical values and behavior among public managers has been a continuous strand of action and attention over the past century of ongoing administrative growth and reform.

Currently, graduate school curricula embed the teaching of professional and ethical behaviors and values in most public career professional degree programs. The debate over the inclu- sion of spirituality in the curriculum and in the professional roles of public administrators is spreading throughout higher education. The Council of Social Work Education is revising its curriculum policy and accreditation standards for graduate social work degrees and may well include "spiritual development" along with the biological, psychological, social, and cultural factors central to the social worker's philosophy of human behavior (Miller 2001, A-12).

Ethics is founded on moral values. Ethics extols virtuous conduct. Morals and virtues are central to making us human. As Marcic (1997) reports after surveying world religions, "All of the world's religions teach the importance of pure intentions and egoless devotion to virtuous behavior" (111). It would seem that the need to ground managerial principles in religion, re- gardless of the specific religion, is somewhat specious. There appear to be some number of universals, whether they are called principles, values, or virtues that have evolved around the world. Where formal religions have arisen, these same principles and values have become part of the doctrine of the religion or the philosophy.

The literature of public administration is replete with efforts to establish and to name the essential principles and virtues of a good public manager. Stephen K. Bailey (1964) was one of the first to address the challenge for public administrators in a democratic society. Terry Coo- per (1982) reinvigorated the discussion when his *Responsible Administrator* appeared, spawn- ing a continuing search for ethical administrative behavior. John Rohr (1989), Kathryn Denhardt (1991), George H. Frederickson (1997), and others have contributed varied, yet strikingly similar, treatises in the continuing search for core administrative values and principles. Different au- thors approach the search from different perspectives, but all end with a relatively short list of necessary values, principles, or virtues essential for ethical behavior by public administrators.

Kathryn Denhardt (1991) has one of the shorter lists, arguing for the adoption of only three principles and virtues: honor, justice, and benevolence.

> Though virtues do not provide the substantive guidance of moral principle, they are necessary to bring moral principle into practice. . . . In offering a core definition of the meaning and character of a profession, it is valuable to address both the core moral

principles of the profession *and* the qualities of character necessary to interpret those principles and put them into practice, as one is insufficient without the other. (102)

In other words, it is equally important to have core values and to have managers who hold a moral compass shared by the professional community that equips them to act on the core moral principles.

Even Fairholm (1997), in his criticism of current management organizations, finds similar core values "that are important to professionals—integrity/honesty, freedom/independence, fairness/equality/justice" (89). Louis Gawthrop (1998) picks up on the same tension and complementarity that Denhardt argued—the need to integrate political/social/organizational values with virtuous individual administrators who hold personal values. He finds the primary political/organizational values to be justice, equality, freedom, and responsibility. The personal values are prudence, temperance, fortitude, and justice, while the virtues are benevolence, justice, kindness, and unselfishness. The common principle among the three categories is justice, which he argues is not sufficient to hold the three domains together effectively.

The listing and parsing of moral values and virtues can be stretched substantially further by examining other authors' presentations; however, little more is gained. There is already wide agreement among scholars and practitioners about the core moral values in public administration, as well as in managerial good practices. In addition, the qualities or virtues desired in the manager are similarly broadly recognized and shared. "Indeed, James M. Burns (1978) defines transformational leadership as a process in which leaders and followers raise each other to higher levels of morality and motivation" (217). The message of many who argue for more explicit inclusion of spiritual language and behavior (often including religious language) in the public workplace seems not dissimilar to transformational leadership in public administration. It is another way to attempt to restore lost public confidence in the good intentions and purposes of government and public services and officials.

Public administrators, because they are public administrators, must steer clear of couching their transformative efforts in the language of religion. Nor should we as professionals encourage colleagues to attempt to incorporate religious language into the policies, procedures, and actions of the public workplace. Public administration already has a set of core values that encompasses spirituality. None of the values, principles, or virtues requires a discussion of either spiritual or religious dogma or practice. The fact that religion and spirituality share values, principles, and virtues with modern professional management theory is wonderful, but it is neither necessary nor sufficient. The broadly, globally shared principles, values, and virtues exist with religion and in its absence. The challenge for public administrators is not to respond to popular trends, but to establish public policy and actions in conjunction with core values and to hire public employees committed to those core values.

REFERENCES

Bailey, Stephen K. (1964). "Ethics and the Public Service." *Public Administration Review* (spring): 234–243.

Begley, Sharon. (2001). "Religion and the Brain." *Newsweek* (May 7): 50–58.

Bozeman, Barry, and Jeffrey Straussman. (1984). *New Directions in Public Administration.* Monterey, CA: Brooks/Cole.

Burns, James M. (1978). *Leadership.* New York: Harper and Row.

Cooper, Terry. (1982). *The Responsible Administrator.* Port Washington, NY: Kennikat.

Denhardt, Kathryn G. (1991). "Unearthing the Moral Foundations of Public Administration: Honor,

Benevolence, and Justice." In *Ethical Frontiers in Public Management: Seeking New Strategies for Resolving Ethical Dilemmas*, ed. James S. Bowman. San Francisco: Jossey-Bass, 91–113.

DePree, Max. (1989). *Leadership Is an Art*. New York: Doubleday.

Dosick, Wayne D. (2000). *The Business Bible: 10 New Commandments for Bringing Spirituality and Ethical Values into the Workplace*. Woodstock, VT: Jewish Lights.

Fairholm, Gilbert W. (1997). *Capturing the Heart of Leadership: Spirituality and Community in the New American Workplace*. Westport, CT: Praeger.

Frederickson, George H. (1997). *The Spirit of Public Administration*. San Francisco: Jossey-Bass.

Gawthrop, Louis C. (1998). *Public Service and Democracy: Ethical Imperatives for the 21st Century*. New York: Chatham House.

Greenleaf, Robert K. (1977). *Servant Leadership*. New York: Paulist.

Guillory, William A. (1997). *The Living Organization: Spirituality in the Workplace*. Salt Lake City, UT: Innovations International.

Lerner, Allan W., and John Wanat. (1992). *Public Administration: A Realistic Reinterpretation of Contemporary Public Management*. Englewood Cliffs, NJ: Prentice Hall.

Marcic, Dorothy. (1997). *Managing with the Wisdom of Love*. San Francisco: Jossey-Bass.

Miller, D.W. (2001). "Programs in Social Work Embrace the Teaching of Spirituality." *Chronicle of Higher Education* 47 (May 18): A-12.

Mitroff, Ian I., and Elizabeth A. Denton. (1999). *A Spiritual Audit of Corporate America: A Hard Look at Spirituality, Religion, and Values in the Workplace*. San Francisco: Jossey-Bass.

Rohr, John A. (1989). *Ethics for Bureaucracy: An Essay on Law and Values*, 2d ed. New York: Marcel Dekker.

Trevino, Linda Klebe. (2000). "A Spiritual Audit of Corporate America: A Hard Look at Spirituality, Religion, and Values in the Workplace." *Personnel Psychology* 53, no. 3 (autumn): 758–761.

Vaill, Peter. (1989). *Managing as a Performing Art*. San Francisco: Jossey-Bass.

Whyte, David. (1994). *The Heart Aroused: Poetry and the Preservation of the Soul in Corporate America*. New York: Doubleday.

Woodward, Kenneth L. (2001). "Faith Is More Than a Feeling." *Newsweek* (May 7): 58.

COURT CASES

Allegheny County v. Greater Pittsburgh ACLU, 492 US 573 109 S.CT. 3086 (1989).

Board of Education of Kiryas Joel Village School District v. Grumet, 512 US 687 114 S.CT. 2481 (1994).

City of Boerne v. Flores, Archbishop of San Antonio et al. 521 US 507 117 S.CT. 2157 (1997).

Employment Division, Department of Human Resources of Oregon, et al. v. Smith et al. 494 US 872 110 S.CT. 1595 (1990).

Hobbie v. Unemployment Appeals Comm'n of Florida, 480 U.S. 136 (1987).

School District of Abington TP., PA. et al. v. Schempp et al. 374 US 203, 83 S.CT. 1560 (1963).

Sherbert v. Verner et al., Members of the South Carolina Employment Securities Commission et al. 374 US 398, 83 S.CT. 1790 (1963).

Thomas v. Review Board, Indiana Employment Security Division et al. 450 US 707 101 S.CT. 1425 (1981).

West Virginia Bd. of Education v. Barnette, 319 US 624 (1943).

Wooley v. Maynard, 430 U.S. 705 (1977).

CHAPTER 26

SPIRITUALITY AND END-OF-LIFE CARE

JONATHAN P. WEST AND COLLEEN M. WEST

> . . . the secret of the care of the patient is caring for the patient.
> —*Francis Peabody 1927*

INTRODUCTION

The wish to approach death with hope and serenity rather than fear and despair often magnifies spiritual and existential concerns at the end of life. Religion and spirituality can be sources of both emotional support and distress to those with terminal illness that are more likely than nonterminally ill patients and healthy people to acknowledge a spiritual perspective and orientation (Reed 1987). This chapter focuses on spirituality and end-of-life care by providing an overview of the topic, relating it to issues of workplace (hospital, home-care, and hospice settings) spirituality, highlighting some practical uses of this information by health care managers, professional caregivers, patients and their families; and exploring issues of spirituality, death, and multiculturalism.

First, it is necessary to distinguish between religion and spirituality. Daaleman and VandeCreek (2000, 2514–2515) indicate that religion encompasses ". . . the totality of belief systems, an inner piety or disposition, an abstract system of ideas, and ritual practices," while spirituality refers to maintaining a purpose or meaning in life. Spirituality may or may not be linked to religious beliefs, practices, or faith communities. Concepts central to spirituality include: meaningfulness, connectedness, and transcendence. Four definitions of spirituality reflect these concepts: "the way in which people understand their lives in view of their ultimate meaning and value" (Muldoon and King 1995, 336); "a present state of harmony and peace" (Hungelmann et al. 1985, 151); "that which gives meaning to life and draws one to transcendence, to whatever is larger than or goes beyond the limits of the individual human lifetime" (Thomason and Brody 1999, 96); and "a subjective experience that exists both within and outside of traditional religious systems" (Vaughan, Wittine, and Walsh 1998, 497).

Measures of spirituality are complicated to construct. Puchalski (1996) has identified thirty operational measures of spirituality or spiritual well-being (see, e.g., Lynn, Schuster, and Kabcenell 2000). While objective measures are complex and illusive, it is increasingly clear that the goal of achieving a comfortable, appropriate death requires meeting patients' spiritual and religious needs, as well as their physical, social, and psychological needs. Indeed, there is now consensus that assessment, management, and support of spiritual and religious well-being is among the core principles of excellent end-of-life care (Cassel and Foley 1999).

The connection of religion and spirituality with medicine has been the subject of considerable scholarship in recent years. Levin, Larson, and Puchalski (1997) and Waldfogel (1997) briefly reviewed published work on this subject. They cite numerous studies dealing with the "epidemiology of religion" suggesting that religion and spirituality influence health and healing. Specifically, they note research findings that show differences in health status, morbidity, and mortality among religious groups. While acknowledging that spirituality is important in the lives of patients, medical care professionals and educators are less certain about how or whether this should influence their practice or teaching. A small but growing number of medical schools are incorporating religious and spiritual issues into their curriculum. Health care professionals and educators who deal with the terminally ill are likely to be among those most receptive to consideration of religious and spiritual issues.

WORKPLACE SPIRITUALITY

End-of-life care is provided in a variety of settings. Those who are terminally ill may prefer to die at home. Indeed, results of a 1997 U.S. national survey, Spiritual Beliefs and the Dying Process, suggest that this is the preference of 70 percent of adults in a U.S. national survey; however, more recent research by Steinhauser et al. (2000) suggests that this preference to die at home may be overstated. For those who do die at home, the "workplace" of caregivers is the patient's residence. For many, however, the setting for end-of-life care is a hospital, nursing home, hospice, or other institutional environment. Thus, "workplace" in this context varies considerably; however, the importance of spirituality transcends locality of death. We will explore workplace spirituality by focusing on the patient and his/her family as well as various members of the interdisciplinary team providing palliative care.

Spirituality and the Patient

Derrickson (1996) has examined spirituality from a crucial perspective: the spiritual work of the dying. She uses a four-fold framework—remembering, reassessing, reconciliation, and reunion— for conceptualizing the spiritual work in which dying patients are engaged. Spiritual work, in Derrickson's framework, refers to the patient's effort to answer some of the deepest questions of life encompassed by these four recurrent themes. The first theme, remembering, involves life review by a patient that may involve joy, tragedy, or ambivalence; reassessing involves an examination of how a patient has defined himself/herself and how terminal illness affects self-worth; reconciliation includes repairing broken relationships with self, others, organized religion, and God; and reunion encompasses efforts to "disconnect" from this world and "reconnect" with the spiritual world. Derrickson maintains that understanding these themes aids caregivers in helping dying patients by asking existential and spiritual questions with which patients are struggling and by guiding their transitional journey.

The previously mentioned national survey in 1997 by Gallup pollsters sought to determine the nature of care American adults would like to receive near the end of life. A major finding: ". . . the American people want to reclaim and reassert the spiritual dimension in dying." A part of this poll investigated whether and how spiritual beliefs influence the ways people prepare for and cope with death. Most respondents stressed the importance of having someone "present" that could share their fears or concerns as they near death—someone to hold, hug, or touch. Most also identified spiritual comfort as important, including the opportunity to pray alone or with someone, and to have others pray for them. Other forms of desired spiritual support included having someone to help achieve spiritual peace, to read spiritual or inspirational material, and to perform ritual prayers or liturgies. People representing a broad range of spiritual beliefs and from different demographic groups shared this desire for spiritual comfort and attendant support. When asked about the preferred comfort providers, people identified family (81 percent) or close friends (61 percent) much more frequently than doctors (30 percent) or nurses (21 percent).

Other surveys indicate that nearly 80 percent of Americans believe God's power or prayer can favorably alter the course of illness (Wallis 1996); that 70 percent claim religion is central to their lives; that 78 percent feel the need to experience spiritual growth; and that a majority feel that spiritual faith can aid them in recovering from illness (Jones and Gallup 2000). When Steinhauser et al. (2000) asked seriously ill patients, recently bereaved family members, doctors, and other caregivers to rank nine major attributes of end-of-life quality, all groups ranked "coming to peace with God" and "presence of family" second or third in importance following "freedom from pain."

Most Americans would like doctors to address their spiritual concerns, but only a small minority (10 percent) said that their physicians actually did so (Puchalski and Larson 1998). Patient beliefs and expectations can influence their views of physicians. The characteristics people desire in a doctor were explored in the 1997 Gallup survey that asked, "If you were dying, how important would each of these be to you?" The percent saying "very important" was as follows: having a doctor who cares about you (68 percent), having a doctor who knows you well (54 percent), and having a doctor who is spiritually attuned to you (39 percent).

Spirituality and the Affinity Family

Different spiritual concerns are likely to emerge depending on the developmental stage of the dying person. For example, family members of very young children may have difficulty explaining why intrusive treatments or diagnostic procedures are required, why they must be separated from loved ones and treated by strangers, and why they must endure physical pain. Some children may believe their illness is a punishment for wrongdoing. Fosarelli (2001) reports that terminally ill school-aged children are likely to have unanswered questions regarding why they are dying, the unfairness of their condition, and their spiritual/religious concerns (e.g., anger at God, undermining their faith in a loving God). Preteens and early teens, according to Fosarelli, may feel cheated out of opportunities for marriage and parenthood. They are concerned about their appearance and unhappy about disruption of their social network and daily schedule of activities. Older teens are concerned about loss of function (speech, mobility, thought) and may express anger toward God, parents, and/or caregivers. Adult family members and health caregivers are challenged to be honest, sensitive, and understanding in responding to the questions of terminally ill children and adolescents. Field and Cassell (1997) provide helpful suggestions for age-appropriate communication with dying children, including discussion of their spiritual concerns.

For some patients (e.g., AIDS patients) the "affinity family" has replaced the traditional family. Sometimes described as the "caregiving surround," this circle of friends frequently acts collaboratively to create a supportive community of concern around the dying patient (Nuland 1993, 198). The recent PBS television series on dying in America, *On Our Own Terms,* produced by Bill and Judith Moyers, highlighted spiritual issues and ways families, friends, and caregivers can reduce suffering and revive hope among those with life-threatening illness.

In many organizations the "affinity family" may include the community of employees in a particular workplace. Managers of organizations experiencing multiple, simultaneous deaths (e.g., hospitals, police departments, military units) need to consider the spiritual needs of grieving survivors and coworkers. One well-known example of an organization's sensitive, compassionate response to the death of employees is provided by Starbucks Coffee Company. When three of their employees were shot and killed in 1997, Starbucks responded as an "affinity family" for survivors. Among the actions by managers were the following: holding a memorial service celebrating the lives of the deceased, closing all seventy stores in the metropolitan area at 5:00 P.M. that day, attendance at the memorial service by the CEO, reopening the store as a memorial to the slain employees with its net profits devoted to preventing violence and assisting victims of violent crime, and raising reward money for information leading to the arrest and convictions of the perpetrators. This sensitive response to the grief and trauma of employees provided an opportunity for the "affinity family" of the workplace to mourn the loss of their coworkers (Davidson and Doka 1999).

Theorists who have examined dying, mourning, and spirituality identify the various "loss reactions" of those experiencing the death of a loved one. Marrone (1997) classifies these reactions into four phases, one of which he labels psycho-spiritual transformation. This phase involves "a profound, growth-oriented spiritual/existential transformation that fundamentally changes our central assumptions, beliefs, and attitudes about life, death, love, compassion, or God" (Marrone 1999). Patients and those in mourning often seek to rediscover meaning by rekindling belief in traditional religious doctrine, the afterlife, philanthropy, reincarnation, or spiritual renewal; others may experience bitterness and a rejection of previously held religious and spiritual beliefs.

Assessment instruments have been developed for interviews with bereaved family members, asking them how well the patient's emotional and spiritual needs were addressed (see Teno et al. 2000, ch. 9). Both patients and families need emotional and spiritual support in adapting to the deterioration associated with advanced, incurable illness. It is not uncommon for those close to dying patients to experience sadness, frustration, guilt, anger, loneliness, fear, despair, and/or hope. Questions in the assessment instrument include:

> While [PATIENT] was under care of the hospital/hospice/nursing home . . .
> (a) did someone talk with you about your religious or spiritual beliefs? (Probe: If yes, was this done in a sensitive manner? Did you have as much contact of that kind as you wanted?)
> (b) how much support in dealing with your feelings about [PATIENT'S] death did the doctors, nurses, and other professional staff taking care of (him/her) provide *you*— less support than was needed or about the right amount?
> (c) did a doctor, nurse, or other professional staff taking care of [PATIENT] talk about how *you* might feel after the patient's death?
> (d) did a doctor, nurse, or other professional staff taking care of [PATIENT] suggest someone *you* could turn to for help if you were feeling stressed?
> (e) how well did those taking care of [PATIENT] do at *providing emotional support* for you and [PATIENT'S] family and friends. (ch. 9, 1)

Spirituality and Health Care Staff

Physician-patient relationships are extremely important for terminally ill patients. Larson and Tobin (2000) stress the value of "end-of-life conversations" between doctors and dying patients. They indicate that the most productive dialogue is linked to (i) physicians' interpersonal communication skills, (ii) a patient-centered model of care, (iii) a focus on quality of remaining life, and (iv) innovative clinical models for implementing these discussions early in the care process. These authors note the barriers to such communication and the need for teaching communication skills to health care professionals working in end-of-life care. It is important for physicians to understand the meaning of the terminal illness for the patient, including spiritual concerns when voiced.

Findings of the SUPPORT project (1996) indicate that efforts to enhance communication between doctors and patients have not necessarily improved care. The preferences of patients and family are often not effectively communicated to physicians or are poorly understood by them. Specifically, less than half of doctors were aware when their patients preferred not to have CPR, half of do-not-resuscitate orders were written within two days of death, 38 percent of patients who died spent a minimum of ten days in ICU, and patients died with pain (moderate to severe) half of the time. Furthermore, there is some evidence that physicians failed to honor patients' and families' preferences in life-threatening situations: 34 percent continued treatments despite patients' or surrogates' expressed wishes that they be discontinued, 83 percent unilaterally withheld futile treatment, and 82 percent unilaterally withdrew futile treatments (Asch, Hansen-Flaschen, and Lanken 1995). Clearly, further efforts are needed to improve doctor-patient discussions with dying patients, especially when exploring spiritual, existential, and religious issues where physicians differ in their interest, comfort, or skills in discussing such matters.

Some authors suggest that physicians should actively solicit information regarding spiritual concerns. For example, Puchalski (1999) has designed a Spiritual Assessment comprised of four basic questions, summarized by the acronym FICA, stressing Faith, Importance, Community, and Address. The questions include:

> *F:* What is your *faith* or belief? Do you consider yourself spiritual or religious? What things do you believe give meaning to your life?
>
> *I:* Is it *important* in your life? What influence does it have on how you take care of yourself? How have your beliefs influenced your behavior during this illness? What role do your beliefs play in regaining your health?
>
> *C:* Are you part of a spiritual or religious *community*? Is this of support to you and how? Is there a person or group of people you really love or who are really important to you?
>
> *A:* How would you like me, your healthcare provider to *address* these issues in your healthcare? (italics added)

Over sixty medical schools are currently teaching this method and many physicians use it (Lynn, Schuster, and Kabcenell 2000). Puchalski views a "spiritual history" as simply talking with a patient or caregiver about his/her beliefs regarding what is important to him or her (Puchalski and Romer 2000). This can be done as part of the first visit, at the time of physical exams, and at follow-up visits. Puchalski and Romer (2000) identify spiritual questions that often emerge for patients and families facing serious illness: What gives my life meaning? Why is this happening to me? How will I survive this loss? What will happen to me when life ends? While physicians and other caregivers are not expected to have answers to such questions, they can provide support and encouragement to people as they wrestle with these issues, use spiritual beliefs as resources, and refer patients and families to others who might help in their search for answers.

When screening for patients' spiritual concerns, certain questions have been identified (Byock 1997; Lo, Quill, and Tulsky 1999; Quill 2001) that caregivers might find potentially useful:

> Is faith (religion or spirituality) important to you?
> Would you like to explore religious matters with someone?
> What do you still want to accomplish during your life?
> What thoughts have you had about why you got this illness at this time?
> What might be left undone if you were to die today?

What is your understanding of what happens after you die?

Given that your time is limited, what legacy do you want to leave your family?

What do you want your children and grandchildren to remember about you?

Other researchers suggest additional questions for clinicians to use in making a spiritual assessment (see, e.g., Waldfogel 1997, 974).

The growing interest in augmenting medical school curricula in spirituality and medicine is evidenced by nineteen schools having received grant awards supporting such developments (1995–1997), a growing number of applicants for future funding, twenty other medical schools in the United States offering courses on spirituality and medicine, and a total of sixty-one medical schools in the country including these topics in certain classes (Puchalski and Larson 1998; Puchalski and Romer 2000). Also an annual conference cosponsored by the Association of American Medical Colleges (AAMC) and the National Institute for Healthcare Research (NIHR) is held on Spirituality, Culture, and End-of-Life Care.

A self-study program for hospice/palliative care training for physicians was developed by the American Academy of Hospice and Palliative Medicine (AAHPM) in 1997 to meet its goals as well as those of the National Cancer Institute. It contains six learning modules, including one on "alleviating psychological and spiritual pain." Candidates reviewing for AAHPM's written examination can use these self-study modules to prepare. The module on spirituality stresses the importance of physician knowledge, skills, awareness, and presence in providing spiritual care to dying patients. It distinguishes spirituality from religion, discusses assessment of spiritual pain and spiritual healing, and considers the signs and symptoms of spiritual pain and ways to alleviate it. This primer devotes considerable attention to major world religions and their frameworks of meaning for suffering, death, and immortality, as well as nonreligious frameworks of meaning. The module concludes with three clinical situations illustrating the alleviation of spiritual pain. Also, the American Medical Association (1999) has developed and disseminated a program of Education for Physicians on End-of-Life Care (EPEC) that addresses spiritual, cultural, and existential beliefs.

Many health care professionals are hesitant or uncomfortable in addressing religious or spiritual issues with their patients (Schuetz 1995). In part, this may be because physicians or nurses lack either spiritual or educational preparation. Other authors stress the importance of being receptive, respectful, and well informed when caregivers do discuss spiritual or religious issues (Smith 1997). Highfield and Carson (1983) highlight the problem of providing spiritual care to dying patients, finding that nurses' failure to adequately distinguish spiritual from psychological problems led them to pursue inappropriate interventions. There are also questions of who—clergy, nurse, interdisciplinary team—should do the spiritual assessment as well as how and when it should be done, and what is to follow. Various instruments have been developed for use by professional staff (see Millison 1995). Meyers (1989) proposes a SOAP model (S = what the client says, O = what is observed, A = the assessment of need, and P = the plan of action introduced) and suggests that spiritual assessment be conducted during each caregiver-patient encounter. Depending on the spiritual needs identified, the patient might best be served by interventions of nursing, clergy, social work, psychology, or volunteer services.

Research has also supported the idea that not all gravely ill patients wish to discuss spiritual matters with caregivers. Indeed, Steinhauser et al. (2000) did not anticipate their finding that the importance attributed to discussions of the meaning of death was higher for physicians, other care providers, and bereaved family members than for patients.

What caregiver skills are needed to provide effective care in the spiritual process of dying?

Zerwckh (1991) identifies three: listening, diagnosing distress of the human spirit, and affirming the significance of spiritual concerns at the end of life. Other crucial qualities include: realism, hopefulness, truthfulness, conviction or faith, resourcefulness, advocacy, sensitivity, and openness and expectation.

Spirituality and Clergy

The role of clergy in meeting the spiritual needs of dying patients is primarily twofold: being "present" for dying patients to provide spiritual care, and training health care personnel about spiritual issues in death and dying. Clergy can provide comfort to patients by helping them to achieve inner peace and by fostering a trusting and loving relationship with them; they can also comfort survivors by acknowledging their loss, communicating with them about death, and helping them to cope with their grief (Schmidt 2001). They can help health care staff by providing education concerning spiritual issues and belief systems and by offering support in coping with multiple, simultaneous losses attendant to providing end-of-life care. Accredited hospitals respect the patients' right to pastoral counseling by providing a list of available clergy, having a department of clinical pastoral counseling, or employing qualified clinical chaplains (JCAHO 2000a). Data from a U.S. national survey found that more than eight of ten family physicians report referring to clergy and pastoral caregivers in circumstances related to end-of-life care (Daaleman and Frey 1998).

Clergy must be aware, however, that a minority of people identifies the clergy as providers of broad spiritual support at the end of life. Indeed, results of a 1997 Gallup survey indicate that only 36 percent of respondents saw the clergy as providing spiritual comfort at the time of impending death. The division of labor in the last century between medical professionals and the clergy delineated clear boundaries—physicians and nurses provided diagnosis and treatment and the clergy and pastoral caregivers provided comfort to the soul. Today's emphasis on holistic health care emphasizes the team approach to patient care with the clergy as members of the team. However, clergy may often find themselves ill prepared to provide needed support to the acutely or chronically ill and to dying patients and their families (DuBose 2001). This is clearly a subject that needs further study (Field and Cassel 1997).

The Gallup survey suggests that faith communities can play a crucial role in end-of-life care. Such communities can work with patients to address their concerns about the aftermath of death and about issues of guilt, fear, and forgiveness. Clergy and faith communities, with proper training, can provide additional interpersonal contact, discussing concerns of the patient, praying with and for them, and helping them to find spiritual peace. This is especially the case when family or friends are absent. It is not uncommon for culturally sensitive end-of-life caregivers to make provision for religious rituals (e.g., last rites, Islamic rituals, Jewish burial practices).

Ordained clergy as well as lay members can provide pastoral care. A good example of pastoral care as a community endeavor is found in the Care Team concept implemented in Houston, Texas, for people with AIDS. Here Care Teams of a dozen or more members from a congregation receive training to offer care—social, emotional, physical, and spiritual—to terminally ill patients and their families, among others. This team effort involves more than 80 congregations and 1,500 members (Shelp 2001). Patients and their families are provided a "sustaining presence" by compassionate caregivers who focus on the spiritual dimension of their relationship with the families and patients they serve. Similar care teams are working in communities across the country.

Another instructive example is an educational initiative for clergy and laity by the Indianapolis Interfaith Workshop on Care for the Dying. The goal of this initiative is to improve quality of life for seriously ill persons and loved ones throughout the illness and bereavement. Specifically, it seeks to educate clergy on issues related to end-of-life care, to train community volunteers to provide support to patients and families, to explore ways to make rituals surrounding illness, loss. and grief more meaningful, and to create an ongoing community network of caregivers for the seriously ill and those closest to them (Moeller 2001).

Spirituality, Palliative Care, and Hospice

The terms *hospice* and *palliative care* refer to care of the dying patient by "maximizing his or her comfort and dignity through treatment of symptoms as desired by the patient and those closest to him or her" (West and West 1998). Corr and Corr (1992, 434–435) identify four characteristics of hospice care: (i) it is individualized (emphasizing the patient's quality of life); (ii) it is holistic (addressing the whole person); (iii) its services are provided to "patient-and-family units"; and (iv) caregivers comprise a team of "professional skills and human presence." Thus, hospices provide palliative care to terminally ill patients, and palliative care is "the active total care of patients whose disease is unresponsive to curative treatment" (Mackey and Sparling 2000). Mackey and Sparling identify six basic principles of palliative care based on guidelines of the World Health Organization:

1. Affirming life and viewing dying as a natural process;
2. Neither hastening nor postponing death;
3. Providing relief from distressing symptoms and pain;
4. Integrating spiritual and psychological aspects of caregiving;
5. Offering a support structure to assist patients in living as actively as possible until death;
6. Offering a support system that helps families cope during the patient's illness and their bereavement. (460)

Hospice and palliative care is patient centered, attending to the specific needs of each patient and providing "total" pain management, including physical, emotional, psychological, and spiritual pain. The American Geriatrics Society (1995, 57) reinforces this concept: "the care of the dying patient, like all medical care, should be guided by the values and preferences of the individual patient." The Joint Commission on Accreditation of Healthcare Organizations (JCAHO 2000b) Pain Standards (RI1.2) specifies "patient rights are involved in all aspects of their care." It goes on to state, "Patients' psychosocial, spiritual, and cultural values affect how they respond to their care. The hospital allows patients and their families to express their spiritual beliefs and cultural practices, as long as they do not harm others or interfere with treatment." Clearly, respect for patient preferences and rights, including spiritual values, is consistent with quality care.

Hospice is sometimes used as an adjective denoting a philosophy of care for the dying and other times as a noun describing a place or organization. Hospices as organizations are concerned with those near death, their family and friends, and they provide structures and procedures for applying palliative care principles. Health care organizations seeking to improve quality of care often adopt standards to provide benchmarks against which to evaluate performance. Standards are frequently simplistic and can lead to "one-size-fits-all" approaches; however, they can provide a basis for auditing organizational performance. Standardizing the spiritual aspects of palliative care is especially problematic, but there have been attempts to develop valid, reliable, and practical guidelines in this area. One notable example developed by Catterall et al. (1998, 166 as

Table 26.1

Standard of Spiritual Care

Statement
   The spirituality of patients and caregivers is acknowledged by the team, integrated within the care and support provided and resources made available.
Structure
   A spiritual care specialist (usually a chaplain) is readily available to provide and facilitate spiritual care for patients and caregivers.
   The team has systems of communication with persons and bodies connected with different faiths who may be required for spiritual support.
   Individuals have access to privacy and quiet, a room suitable for prayer and reflection and a place for religious observance (usually a chapel).
   There is a suitable place for the patient to be visited after death.
   There is provision within the patient documentation to record spiritual needs.
Process
   Part of the initial multidisciplinary team assessment includes assessment of the spiritual health and care needs of the patient.
   The team incorporates spiritual care into the patient's care plan in accordance with the wishes of the patient, or the patient's advocate.
   There is a multidisciplinary review of the progress of spiritual issues and care needs.
Outcome
   Patients, and their caregivers, state that they are aware of the people and facilities available to them to meet their spiritual care needs.
   The patients and their caregivers indicate that they have been enabled to make progress with their spiritual concerns.

   Source: Catterall et al. 1998, 166; Cobb 2001, 109.

reported by Quill 2001, 109), contains a standard within a fourfold framework including statement, structure, process, and outcome (see Table 26.1). This standard is consistent with the hospice philosophy of integrated, holistic, patient-centered care.

The guiding concept of hospice is "comfort" and the central goal is to help persons to live well until they die or to "maximize the quality of life when the quantity of that life can no longer be increased" (quoted in Magno 1990, 111; Kritz 1995). While palliative care teams and hospices are increasingly common in hospitals, where 85 percent of deaths occur in the United States, they are infrequently found in nursing homes (Rhymes 1990; Vladeck 1995).

Hospice and palliative caregivers address spiritual needs. Abrahm et al. (1996) note that patient psychosocial and spiritual problems typically reflected, among other things, the need for counseling to address anxiety, depression, and/or anger, and the desire for prayer, sacraments, and rituals. Frequently spiritual matters are juxtaposed with issues of death and dying. When the emphasis of treatment regimens shifts from curative to palliative care, patients absorb the realization of impending death and reexamine their lives. As Derrickson (1996) notes, this life-review process may lead patients to broach unresolved problems with family and friends and to confront existential/spiritual questions about the meaning of life and death. Hospice-provided spiritual counselors and caregivers may assist in resolving end-of-life spiritual concerns, or they may refer patients to community- or faith-based groups that are trained to address such concerns (Herbst et al. 1995). Table 26.2 provides a list of Web site addresses of organizations that deal with end-of-life issues.

It is not surprising that hospice philosophy emphasizes spiritual needs because the foundation of the modern hospice movement emerged from a Christian religious tradition. While the term

Table 26.2

Selected Web Sites Related to End-of-Life Care

American Academy of Hospice and Palliative Medicine	www.aahpm.org
American College of Physicians-American Society of Internal Medicine	www.acponline.org
American Geriatric Society	www.americangeriatrics.org
American Hospice Foundation	www.americanhospice.org
American Medical Association	www.ama-assn.org
American Pain Society	www.ampainsoc.org
Americans for Better Care of the Dying	www.abcd-caring.org
Center to Advance Palliative Care	www.capcmssm.org
Community-State Partnerships to Improve End-of-Life Care	www.midbio.org
Hospice Association of America	www.hospice-america.org
Hospice Foundation of America	www.hospicefoundation.org
Hospice and Palliative Nurses Association	www.hpna.org
Last Acts Campaign	www.lastacts.org
National Family Caregivers Association	www.nfcacares.org
National Hospice and Palliative Care Organization	www.nhpco.org
Project on Death in America	www.soros.org/death

hospice was used in the Middle Ages referring to places of rest and refreshment for pilgrims or recovery havens for the poor, the first modern hospice was Saint Christopher's, established in London in 1967 by Dame Cicely Saunders as "a refuge for the dying" (Busby 1993). The mission statement for Saint Christopher's is rooted within this religious tradition. As hospice diffused throughout the world and emerged as a global approach to patient care, its focus shifted from its original religious foundation to a broader, more secular emphasis on relief of suffering. Nonetheless, hospice and palliative care retain an independent concern for the spiritual dimension of care (Daaleman and VandeCreek 2000). This is consistent with the perspective of the World Health Organization (WHO), which defines palliative care as: "The active total care of patients whose disease is not responsive to curative treatment . . . [when] control of pain, of other symptoms, and of psychological, social, and spiritual problems is paramount" (1990, 11).

According to WHO, goals of palliative care include providing the best possible quality of life for the patient *and* family. While spirituality is central to the provision of palliative care, its meaning in the context of hospice has changed. Daaleman and VandeCreek (2000, 2516) note that the original definition of spirituality associated with hospice had a religious emphasis stressing one's "relationship with God or a Divine Other," whereas more recent usages of spirituality refer to "the personal and psychological search for meaning." This uprooting of spirituality from its religious sources has facilitated the acceptance of hospice by those from different cultures and varied faith traditions.

Spirituality and Multiculturalism

Numerous cultural differences in attitudes toward death and dying have been documented (e.g., Ersek et al. 1998; Kagawa-Singer 1998; Koenig and Gates-Williams 1995; Braun, Pietsch, and Blanchette 2000; Irish, Lundquist, and Nelsen 1993). For example, Blackhall and colleagues (1995) find that immigrant families are more likely than others to believe that diagnosis of terminal illness should be withheld from patients and that families are thought to be the appropriate decision-makers in end-of-life care. Parallel themes have been noted among Chinese and Latino cancer patients (Ersek et al. 1998). Regarding removal of life-prolonging interventions, non-Hispanic whites are more likely to forego such extreme measures than either Latinos or African Americans (Caralis et al. 1993; Garrett et al. 1993). Certain cultural subgroups—African-, Chinese-, Filipino-, Iranian-, Korean-, and Mexican-Americans—more frequently agree with commencing/ceasing life-prolonging prescriptions when conditions are hopeless or terminal than European Americans (Klessig 1992). Cultural differences are also evident in spiritual matters related to health. For example, Latinos and African Americans more frequently allude to the role of religion and spirituality in both the physician's ability to cure and the patient's prognosis.

Spiritual factors are clearly prominent for those experiencing terminal illness, the dying process, and death, regardless of cultural background. Laurence O'Connell, chief administrator of the Park Ridge Center in Chicago has described the connection between spirituality and multiculturalism with regard to a Native American ritual. He discusses how ethnic groups turn to their surroundings to explain some of the mysteries of life such as death. Noting the Native American's tie to the land, he recalls an incident when a distraught nun confronted a Native American ritual that puzzled her. An aged Native American woman who was in the nun's care (she was a nurse) was dying. Tribal members were coming to the hospital to remove the dying woman from intensive care to place her in a teepee on the hospital grounds. The nun did not want the patient removed from the hospital, but she was worried and uncertain about how to react. O'Connell explains, "... according to the beliefs of the patient's culture, she [the patient] wouldn't be reunited with the Great Spirit if she didn't die on the soil. When the nun understood that this ritual was an effort to honor the patient's spiritual beliefs, she was enthusiastic about participating in the process," recalls O'Connell (Beckwith 2001).

With regard to the African-American community, researchers have noted the underutilization of palliative care and hospice services. Studies by Crawley et al. (2000) attribute this underutilization to barriers to care including, but not limited to, African Americans' religious and spiritual beliefs. As they note:

> ... rich traditions within the African American community tied to religious and spiritual beliefs and practices reflect a view of death as a "welcome friend," there to assist the decedent in the transition from an earthly existence. This perspective recognizes the inevitability of death that comes at the end of a life marked either by longevity and relatively good health until death or by prolonged suffering in the case of some individuals who are chronically ill. Those who have died may be referred to as having "gone home," a notion that views death as a transition rather than as a final state. (2519)

Puchalski provides the example (cited in Teno et al. 2000) of a Hindu patient who sees elimination of pain and suffering as a major life goal. Believing in reincarnation, he thinks that his spirit will pass on to another life; thus, comfort measures may be emphasized and heroic measures of life support rejected.

Cultural differences can create challenges in health care settings because of different interpretations of illness and treatment, conflicting values related to death and dying, and variations in language use or decision frameworks. In some instances this might lead to the use of interpreters or bilingual "culture brokers" who can clarify values, mediate cultural differences, and encourage truthful communication regarding end-of-life issues. For example, fundamental values held by many Navajos exclude discussion of "bad news," a crucial subject when communicating a terminal prognosis and considering advance-care planning (Carrese and Rhodes 1995; Kaufert and Putsch 1997). Death, dying, and spirituality are sensitive subjects requiring delicate treatment, especially in multicultural environments. DeSpelder (1998) has developed a set of cultural background questions regarding spirituality and death that helps caretakers to understand patients' values and beliefs.

Cultural/spiritual competency should be required as a core dimension of practice for all staff serving the gravely ill. Such competencies require sensitivity to patients' cultural and spiritual orientations and support for the various dimensions of values and beliefs. Caregivers need to be able to assess and explore cultural/spiritual needs and to identify issues that require action. They also need to be prepared to effectively provide both reactive and proactive interventions. Cobb (2001, 113–114) clarifies these two distinctive approaches: Reactive interventions seek to address unanticipated problems, issues, or concerns occurring outside of formal assessments, while proactive interventions are anticipated and grow out of assessments, predictable outcomes linked to current conditions, or new situations with future implications. He cites examples of both reactive interventions (i.e., helping patients interpret "near death" experiences) and proactive interventions (i.e., conflicting beliefs of a dying mother and young daughter regarding life after death requiring interventions by caregivers with competencies in faith development in children and in coping with loss). Participation in training and development programs is crucial when palliative caregivers lack knowledge or skills to address such cultural and spiritual issues. The Last Acts Diversity Committee is developing guidelines, bibliographic references, case studies, and a video to assist in developing cultural competencies for those who care for people at the end of life.

CONCLUSION

Caregivers of terminally ill patients are giving increased attention to the relationship between spirituality and well-being. The "workplace" of such caregivers is determined largely by the physical location of the dying patient, whether in a hospital, nursing home, hospice, or private residence. It is important for caregivers to recognize the spiritual and/or religious values of gravely ill patients and their families, to develop care plans with spiritual needs in mind, and to take into account a patient's particular belief system when administering care. To the extent that caregivers are ill equipped to assess and alleviate spiritual pain, it is important to incorporate into professional training programs not only mastery of technical skills, but also knowledge of spiritual/cultural concerns and interpersonal skills such as active listening, perceptive questioning, and empathetic communication if they are to be effective, compassionate caregivers to seriously ill patients.

Because of the numerous service providers that comprise the interdisciplinary hospice/palliative care team in providing end-of-life care, the "workplace" requires collaborative skills and willingness of caregivers to partner with others to provide integrated, holistic care. Busy physicians, nurses, psychologists, and social workers might be effective in conducting spiritual assessments, while recognizing the need for specialized consultation and referral in efforts to alleviate spiritual pain. Likewise, members of the clergy and faith communities can be valuable allies and collaborators in responding to the spiritual needs of dying patients. Concern about psychospiritual needs should not be limited to the predeath experience of the patient, but also should encompass the bereavement period for surviving family members and close friends of the deceased. No longer can caregivers assume that such concerns are outside their province and irrelevant to their role. The new frontier of medicine and health care must create a "workplace" environment where alleviating suffering is a team effort that addresses the physical *and* spiritual needs of dying patients. This integrative philosophy of comprehensive palliative care is eloquently summarized in ten words from the prayer of Maimonides, a twelfth-century rabbi, physician, and philosopher: ". . . in the sufferer let me see only the human being."

REFERENCES

American Academy of Hospice and Palliative Medicine (AAHPM). (1997). *UNIPAC Two: Alleviating Psychological and Spiritual Pain in the Terminally Ill.* Dubuque, IA: Kendall/Hunt.
Abrahm, J.L.; J. Callahan; K. Rossetti; and L. Pierre. (1996). "The Impact of a Hospice Consultation Team on the Care of Veterans and Advanced Cancer." *Journal of Pain and Symptoms Management* 12, no. 1: 23,31.
American Geriatrics Society. (1995). "The Care of Dying Patients: A Position Statement from the American Geriatrics Society." *Journal of the American Geriatrics Society* 43: 577–578.
American Medical Association (AMA). (1999). *Education for Physicians on End-of-Life Care Project.* Chicago: AMA.
Asch, D.A.; J. Hansen-Flaschen; and P.N. Lanken. (1995). "Decisions to Limit or Continue Life-Sustaining Treatment by Critical Care Physicians in the United States: Conflicts Between Physicians' Practices and Patients' Wishes." *American Journal of Respiratory and Critical Care Medicine* 151, no. 2, Pt. 1: 288–292.
Beckwith, S. (2001). "The Connection Between Spiritual and Cultural Diversity": http://www.lastacts.org/statsite/3540la%5Feln%5Fnewsletter.html (July 6).
Blackhall, L.J.; S.T. Murphy; G. Frank; V. Michel; and S. Azen. (1995). "Ethnicity and Attitudes Toward Patient Autonomy." *Journal of the American Medical Association* 274: 820–825.
Braun, K.L.; J.H. Pietsch; and P.L. Blanchette. (2000). *Cultural Issues in End-of-Life Decision Making.* Thousand Oaks, CA: Sage.
Busby, J. (1993). "Hospice Help for the Dying." *Current Health* 2 (January): 30–31.
Byock, I. (1997). *Dying Well: The Prospect for Growth at the End of Life.* New York: Riverhead Books.
Caralis, P.; B. David; K. Wright; E. Marcial. (1993). "The Influence of Ethnicity and Race Attitudes Toward Advanced Directives, Life-Prolonging Treatments and Euthanasia." *Journal of Clinical Ethics* 4, no. 2: 155–165.
Carrese, J.A., and L.A. Rhodes. (1995). "Western Bioethics on the Navajo Reservation, Benefit or Harm." *Journal of the American Medical Association* 274, no. 10: 826–829.
Cassel, C.K., and K.M. Foley. (1999). *Principles for Care of Patients at the End of Life: An Emerging Consensus Among the Specialties of Medicine.* New York: Milbank Memorial Fund.
Catterall, R.A.; M. Cobb; B. Greet; J. Sankey; and G. Griffiths. (1998). "The Assessment and Audit of Spiritual Care." *International Journal of Palliative Nursing* 4, no. 4: 162–168.
Cobb, M. (2001). *The Dying Soul: Spiritual Care at the End of Life.* Philadelphia: Open University Press.
Corr, C.A., and D.M. Corr. (1992). "Children's Hospice Care." *Death Studies* 16, no. 5: 431–449.
Crawley, L.V.; R. Payne; J. Bolden; T. Payne et al. (2000). "Palliative and End-of-Life Care in the African American Community." *Journal of the American Medical Association* 284, no. 19: 2518–2521.
Daaleman, T.P., and B. Frey. (1998). "Prevalence and Patterns of Physician Referral to Clergy and Pastoral Care Providers." *Arch Family Medicine* 7: 548–553.
Daaleman, T.P., and L. VandeCreek. (2000). "Placing Religion and Spirituality in End-of-Life Care." *Journal of the American Medical Association* 284, no. 19: 2514–2517.
Davidson, J.D., and K.J. Doka. (1999). *Living with Grief.* Washington, DC: Hospice Foundation of America.
Derrickson, B. (1996). "The Spiritual Work of the Dying: A Framework and Case Studies." *Hospice Journal* 11, no. 2: 11–30.
DeSpelder, L. (1998). "Developing Cultural Competency." In *Living with Grief*, ed. K.J. Doka and J.D. Davidson. Washington, DC: Hospice Foundation of America, 100–101.
DuBose, E.R. (2001). "Preparing for Death: Linking Medicine, Spirituality, and End-of-Life Care." *Park Ridge Center Bulletin* (May/June): 3–4.
Ersek, M.; M. Kagawa-Singer; D. Barnes; L. Blackhall; and B. Koenig. (1998). "Multicultural Considerations in the Use of Advance Directives." *Oncology Nursing Forum* 25, no. 10: 1683–1689.
Field, M.J., and C.K. Cassell. (1997). *Approaching Death.* Washington, DC: National Academy Press.

Fosarelli, P. (2001). "And the Children Shall Lead Us: End-of-Life Issues for Children and Adolescents." *Park Ridge Center Bulletin* (May/June): 9–11.

Gallup International Institute. (1997). "Spiritual Beliefs and the Dying Process: A Report on a National Survey." www.ncf.org/reports/program/rpt_fetzer/rpt_fetzer_contents.html (July 6, 2001).

Garrett, J.; R.P. Harris; J.K. Norburn; D.L. Patrick; and M. Danis. (1993). "Life-sustaining Treatments During Terminal Illness: Who Wants What?" *Journal of General Internal Medicine* 8: 361–368.

Herbst, L.H.; J. Lynn; A. Mermann; and J. Rhymes. (1995). "What Do Dying Patients Want and Need?" *Patient Care* (February 28): 27–39.

Highfield, M., and C. Carson. (1983). "Spiritual Needs of Patients: Are They Recognized?" *Cancer Nursing* 6, no. 3: 187–192.

Hungelmann, J.; E. Kenkel-Rossi; L. Klassen; and R.M. Stollenwerk. (1985). "Spiritual Well-being in Older Adults: Harmonious Interconnectedness." *Journal of Religion and Health* 24, no. 2: 147–153.

Irish, D.P.; K.F. Lundquist; and V.J. Nelsen. (1993). *Ethnic Variations in Dying, Death, and Grief.* Levittown, PA: Taylor and Francis.

Joint Commission on Accreditation of Healthcare Organizations (JCAHO). (2000a). *Comprehensive Accreditation Manual for Hospitals: The Official Handbook. Patient Rights and Organizational Ethics Standards* (RI1.3.5). Oakbrook Terrace, IL: JCAHO, RI-16.

———. (2000b). "Pain Standards": http://wwwb.jcaho.org/standard/pm_hap.html (July 6, 2001).

Jones, T., and G. Gallup, Jr. (2000). *The Next American Spirituality: Finding God in the Twenty-First Century.* Colorado Springs, CO: Chariot Victor.

Kagawa-Singer, M. (1998). "The Cultural Context of Death Rituals and Mourning Practices." *Oncology Nursing Forum* 25, no. 10: 1752–1755.

Kaufert, J.M., and R.W. Putsch. (1997). "Communication Through Interpreters in Healthcare: Ethical Dilemmas Arising from Differences in Class, Culture, Language and Power." *Journal of Clinical Ethics* 8, no. 1: 71–87.

Klessig, J. (1992). "The Effects of Values and Culture on Life-support Decisions." *Western Journal of Medicine* 157: 316–322.

Koenig, B., and J. Gates-Williams. (1995). "Understanding Cultural Difference in Caring for Dying Patients." *Western Journal of Medicine* 163: 244–249.

Kritz, F.L. (1995). "A Family Guide to Hospice Care. *Good Housekeeping* 220 (February): 178.

Larson, D.G., and D.R. Tobin. (2000). "End-of-Life Conversations." *Journal of the American Medical Association* 284, no. 12: 1573–1578.

Levin, J.S.; D.B. Larson; and C.M. Puchalski. (1997). "Religion and Spirituality in Medicine: Research and Education." *Journal of the American Medical Association* 278, no. 9: 792–793.

Lo, B.; T. Quill; and J. Tulsky. (1999). "Discussing Palliative Care with Patients." *Annals of Internal Medicine* 130, no. 9: 744–749.

Lynn, J.; J.L. Schuster; and A. Kabcenell. (2000). *Improving Care for the End of Life.* New York: Oxford University Press.

Mackey, K.M., and J.W. Sparling. (2000). "Experiences of Older Women with Cancer Receiving Hospice Care: Significance for Physical Therapy" *Physical Therapy* 80, no. 5: 459–468.

Magno, J.B. (1990). "The Hospice Concept of Care: Facing the 1990s." *Death Studies* 14: 109–114.

Marrone, R. (1997). *Death, Mourning and Caring.* Pacific Grove, CA: Brooks/Cole/Wadsworth.

———. (1999). "Dying, Mourning, and Spirituality: A Psychological Perspective." *Death Studies* 23, no. 6: 495–519.

Meyers, H. (1989). "About Our Children: Spiritual Care in Pediatric Hospitals." *American Hospice Care* 6, no. 3: 12.

Millison, M.B. (1995). "A Review of the Research on Spiritual Care and Hospice." *Hospice Journal* 10, no. 4: 3–18.

Moeller, D.W. (2001). "Caring for the Dying Poor." Unpublished paper presented at the annual meeting of the American Academy of Hospice and Palliative Medicine, June 21–23, Phoenix, AZ.

Muldoon, M., and N. King. (1995). "Spirituality, Healthcare, and Bioethics." *Journal of Religion and Health* 34, no. 4: 329–349.

Nuland, S.B. (1993). *How We Die.* New York: Vintage Books.

Peabody, F.W. (1927). "The Care of the Patient." *New England Journal of Medicine* 88: 877–882.

Puchalski, C.M. (1996). "Spirituality and Transcendence." Paper prepared for conference on measuring care at the end of life, August 27–28.

———. (1999). "A Spiritual History." *Supportive Voice* 5: 12–13.

Puchalski, C.M., and D.B. Larson. (1998). "Developing Curricula in Spirituality and Medicine." *Academic Medicine* 73, no. 9: 970–974.

Puchalski, C.M., and A.L. Romer. (2000). "Taking a Spiritual History Allows Clinicians to Understand Patients More Fully." *Journal of Palliative Medicine* 3, no. 1: 129–137.

Quill, T.E. (2001). *Caring for Patients at the End of Life.* New York: Oxford University Press.

Reed, P. (1987). "Spirituality and Well-being in Terminally Ill Hospitalized Adults." *Research in Nursing and Health* 10, no. 5: 335–344.

Rhymcs, J. (1990). "Hospice Care in America." *Journal of the American Medical Association* 264, no. 3: 369–372.

Schmidt, L.M. (2001). "Searching for Spirituality and Inner Peace: Hundreds Gather at Washington's National Cathedral." *Exchange* 4, no. 3/4: 9–10.

Schuetz, B. (1995). "Spirituality and Palliative Care." *Australian Family Physician* 24, no. 5: 775–777.

Shelp, E.E. (2001). "Pastoral Care as a Community Endeavor: A Sustaining Presence Through Care Team Ministry." *Park Ridge Center Bulletin* (May/June): 7–8.

Smith, D.S. (1997). *Caregiving: Hospice Proven Techniques for Healing Body and Soul.* New York: Macmillan.

Steinhauser, K.E.; N.A. Christakis; E.C. Clipp; M. McNeilly et al. (2000). "Factors Considered Important at the End of Life by Patients, Family, Physicians, and Other Care Providers." *Journal of the American Medical Association* 284, no. 19: 2476–2482.

Support Principal Investigators. (1995). "A Controlled Trial to Improve Care for Seriously Ill Hospitalized Patients: The Study to Understand Prognoses and Preferences for Outcomes and Risks of Treatments (SUPPORT)." *Journal of the American Medical Association* 274, no. 20: 1591–1598.

Teno, J.M.; S.N. Okun; V. Casey; and L.C. Welch. (2000). "Toolkit of Instruments to Measure End of Life Care." *Time:* www.chcr.brown.edu/pcoc/toolkit.htm (July 6).

Thomason, C.L., and H. Brody. (1999). "Inclusive Spirituality." *Journal of Family Practice* 48, no. 2: 96–97.

Vaughan, F.; B. Wittine; and R. Walsh. (1998). "Transpersonal Psychology and the Religious Person." In *Religion and the Clinical Practice of Psychology*, ed. E.P. Shafranske. Washington, DC: American Psychological Association, 483–509.

Vladeck, B.C. (1995). "End-of-Life Care." *Journal of the American Medical Association* 274, no. 6: 449.

Waldfogel, S. (1997). "Spirituality in Medicine." *Primary Care* 24, no. 4: 963–976.

Wallis, C. (1996). "Faith and Healing." *Time* (June 24): 58–63.

West, J.P., and C.M. West. (1998). "Analysis of Comfort Care for the Terminally Ill: The Hospice Approach." *Journal of Health and Human Services Administration* 20, no. 3: 281–299.

World Health Organization (WHO). (1990). "Cancer Pain Relief and Palliative Care" (Technical Report Series 804). Geneva, Switzerland: World Health Organization.

Zerwckh, J. (1991). "Supportive Care of the Dying Patient." In *Cancer Nursing*, ed. S.B. Baird, R. McCorkle, and M. Grant. Philadelphia: W.B. Saunders, 875–884.

CHAPTER 27

FORGIVENESS IN THE WORKPLACE

LAURA YAMHURE THOMPSON AND PATRICIA E. SHAHEN

In this chapter, we examine the role of forgiveness as a response to workplace conflict. We propose that forgiveness is an intrapersonal process that complements and balances the various, interpersonal methods of conflict resolution. Through forgiveness, people reframe transgressions such that their transgression-related thoughts and feelings are transformed from negative to neutral or positive (Yamhure Thompson et al. 2001; Yamhure Thompson and Snyder 2000). This is particularly relevant in the workplace because thinking and feeling more positively creates the opportunity for the forgiving person to productively and effectively engage in their work and workplace relationships. Alternatively, engaging in ongoing anger, vengeance, or avoidance can cause people to remain mired in the conflict and blocked from interacting constructively with their work and coworkers.

Forgiveness is encouraged by major world religions such as Judaism, Christianity, Islam, and Hinduism, and the forgiving nature of religious figures is often salient in religious literature (see Rye et al. 2000). Thus, the concept of forgiveness is closely linked with religiosity for many people. McCullough and Worthington (1999) have described forgiveness as having "dual natures: a common one and a transcendent one" (1141), such that it is both a social-psychological and a spiritual or transcendent phenomenon. In the workplace, a nonreligious approach to forgiveness is essential in order to respect the diversity of employees' beliefs. Therefore, it is advantageous to address forgiveness as a social and psychological process that changes how people view transgressions, and that frees people to feel and be their best in the workplace. Nevertheless, due to the transformational and often profound nature of the forgiveness process, people may choose to relate forgiveness in the workplace to their spiritual or religious beliefs and practices. In fact, research indicates that people frequently use religiously based strategies (e.g., prayer) to help them forgive, even in situations where forgiveness is not presented to them in a spiritual or religious context (Rye 1999).

Forgiveness has been positively linked to spirituality (Emmons 2000; Mahoney and Graci 1999), spiritual wellness (Ingersoll 1996), and religiosity (Enright, Santos, and Al-Mabuk 1989; Webb 1999). Research indicates that the more people consider themselves to be religious or spiritual, the more they value forgiveness and consider themselves to be forgiving (for a review see McCullough and Worthington 1999). However, evidence that religiosity and spirituality are linked to people's actual forgiveness behaviors is mixed (McCullough and Worthington 1999). And other studies have found no correlation between forgiveness and religiosity (Coates 1997). As such, we conceptualize forgiveness as a transformational process that may have religious or spiritual meaning, but that need not be connected with any specific religious or spiritual beliefs or practices.

In this chapter, we will examine the role of forgiveness in the workplace, using a psychosocial conceptualization of forgiveness. We will examine each of the main phases in the journey from transgression to forgiveness. Given that the opportunity and need for forgiveness arise as a result of workplace disagreements, and perceived mistreatments or slights (i.e., transgressions or conflicts), we will first address the processes underlying the perception of transgressions, the ways in which people typically respond to transgressions and conflict, and the effects of conflict in the workplace. Second, we will define and describe the forgiveness process and the benefits of forgiveness. Finally, we will examine forgiveness as a process that complements and balances conflict resolution processes, and we will propose that managers and employees would benefit from training designed to enhance forgiveness skills in the workplace.

TRANSGRESSIONS AND CONFLICTS IN THE WORKPLACE

Expectations and Assumptions About Oneself, Others, and the World
(Figure 27.1, Phase 1)

We will begin by exploring the journey that a person may follow in transforming a transgression into forgiveness. As shown in Figure 27.1, we have divided this journey into five phases. The focus of the first phase is on a person's expectations and assumptions. Many people have examined the ways in which individuals are affected by their beliefs, assumptions, schemas, and expectations about themselves, others, and the world. There are a few positively biased beliefs that most people have (e.g., Beck et al. 1979; Janoff-Bulman 1992; Young and Behary 1998). First, most people expect the world to be meaningful and orderly such that good things happen to good people and vice versa (Janoff-Bulman 1992). They also tend to view themselves as being relatively invulnerable and in control (Janoff-Bulman 1992), and to assume that someone or something is to blame when bad things happen (Miller and Vidmar 1981). People strive to associate themselves with events and outcomes that support their view of themselves, others, and the world, and that they and members of their society value as positive; conversely, people try to avoid being associated with events and outcomes that conflict with their views, and that are perceived as negative (Greenwald 1980).

Despite people's positive expectations and assumptions, workplace conflicts, disagreements, mistreatments, and slights can usher negative events and outcomes into their lives. Such events compel people to wrestle with information that may conflict with, and even shake, their positive expectations and assumptions about themselves, others, and the world in general. We refer to an event as a "transgression" when a person perceives it as conflicting with his or her positive expectations and assumptions. Therefore, by definition, a transgression is strictly a subjective determination depending on one's personal perspective. The source of a transgression can be (a) oneself, (b) another person or group of people, or (c) situations for which no specific people appear to be responsible (e.g., a companywide reorganization) (Yamhure Thompson et al. 2001; Yamhure Thompson and Snyder 2000). Further, people may view a transgression as having multiple sources. For example, employees passed over for a promotion may blame both themselves and their supervisors. Given the brevity of this chapter, we will discuss only transgressions in which another person or group of people is the source of the transgression. However, the principles also can be applied to situations in which the source of the transgression is oneself, or to a situation for which no specific people appear to be responsible.

Throughout this chapter, we will illustrate the five-phase journey from transgression to forgiveness, using an ongoing vignette (which will appear in italics) about an employee named

Figure 27.1 **Summary of the Journey from Transgression to Forgiveness**

1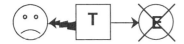

Each person has assumptions and expectations (E) about how he or she, others, and the world "ought" to be.

2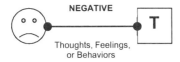

Transgressions (T) violate a person's expectations. The discrepancy between the transgression and the expectations causes dissonance and distress.

3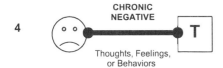

A person develops negative thoughts, feelings, or behaviors about the transgression, transgressor, and related outcomes (T). This constellation of thoughts, feelings or behaviors reflects how the person is relating to the transgression and is therefore called a negative attachment.

4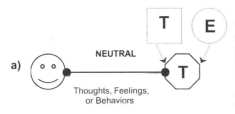

The continuation of transgression-related negative thoughts, feelings, or behaviors (and attempts to cope via negative thoughts, feelings, or behaviors such as angry rumination, retaliation, or avoidance) strengthens the negative attachment between the person and the transgression.

5 **FORGIVENESS:**

a)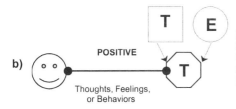

When a person forgives, he or she frames the transgression in a new manner (T in the octagon) and responds to the transgression in ways that do not reinforce transgression-related negative thoughts, feelings, or behaviors. In dialectical terms, the adaptively framed transgression is the synthesis of the transgression and his or her expectations.

b)

Forgiveness may be accomplished by transforming the attachment (i.e., transgression-related thoughts, feelings or behaviors) from negative to neutral (5a) or from negative to positive (5b).

"Bob." As an example of Phase 1, consider the following expectations and assumptions that Bob has about himself and others in the workplace.

Bob is part of a ten-person team working on a group project. Bob sees himself as a competent and productive member of the team. He assumes that his coworkers perceive him in a similar manner, and he expects them to value his contributions and to treat him with respect.

Transgressions Violate Expectations and Create Dissonance and Distress
(Figure 27.1, Phase 2)

In Phase 1 of the journey from transgression to forgiveness, we examined people's expectations and assumptions. In Phase 2, we will focus on how transgressions violate these expectations and create dissonance and distress. When people's expectations about themselves, others, or the world are contradicted, shaken, or even shattered by a transgression, they feel a dissonance between what is and what "ought" to be. Researchers have found that violations of these assumptions and expectations (i.e., transgressions) can cause significant distress and dissonance as people strive to fit the event into their views about themselves, others, and world (see Janoff-Bulman 1992; Janoff-Bulman and Frantz 1997; Janoff-Bulman and Frieze 1983; Janoff-Bulman and Schwartzberg 1991). Because the dissonance caused by transgressions is distressing, people are motivated to resolve the dissonance (Yamhure Thompson et al. 2001; Yamhure Thompson and Snyder 2000). In our vignette, we explore how Bob might perceive an event as violating his expectations and assumptions, and how such an event might create dissonance and distress for him.

One of Bob's team members, Mark, harshly criticizes Bob's contributions during a team meeting. Mark says that Bob's efforts have been harmful, not helpful to the project. Bob is stunned by Mark's criticism because Mark's comments violate Bob's perception of himself as a competent and valued member of the team. Bob's initial response to Mark's comments is to feel defensive and confused. Bob cannot imagine how Mark could think that way about his work. In Bob's opinion, the criticisms Mark raised at the meeting were totally unfounded; and if Mark had a problem with his work, Mark should have spoken directly to him instead of criticizing him unfairly in front of the team.

A Negative Attachment Forms Between the Person and the Transgression
(Figure 27.1, Phase 3)

In Phase 3 of the journey from transgression to forgiveness, the dissonance and distress associated with a transgression typically give rise to transgression-related negative thoughts (e.g., "This has ruined my reputation as a productive team member"), feelings (e.g., anger), or behaviors (e.g., seeking revenge). We use the word *attachment* to refer to the constellation of thoughts, emotions, or behaviors that a person (who is transgressed against) manifests in response to the transgression, transgressor, or the outcomes related to the transgression. Attachment also includes cognitions, affect, or behaviors that arise when one is reminded of the event (Yamhure Thompson et al. 2001; Yamhure Thompson and Snyder 2000).

Bob begins to relate to the transgression and Mark by developing negative thoughts, feelings, and behaviors. For the rest of the day, Bob repeatedly relives the interaction in his mind, and each time, he thinks of things he could have said to defend himself and get even with Mark. Ruminating about the interaction with Mark makes Bob feel increasingly angry and embarrassed. During the following week, Bob gossips to his coworkers about Mark; this makes Bob feel that he is "getting even" with Mark.

Chronic Negative, Thoughts, Feelings, or Behaviors Strengthen the Attachment
(Figure 27.1, Phase 4)

A person may strengthen the negative attachment to the transgression over time by continuing to respond to the transgression in negative ways (Phase 4 of the journey from transgression to forgiveness). The person might experience the transgression-related negative thoughts, feelings, or behaviors as becoming more intense and intrusive, even when the ostensible goal may be to resolve that negative attachment (i.e., to cope with the repercussions of the transgression).

During the following week, Bob strengthens his negative attachment to Mark and the transgression. Bob feels very agitated when he sees Mark enter the room for the next team meeting. Bob feels anger, anxiety, and embarrassment as he remembers Mark's comments from the previous meeting, and Bob's heart beats faster, making him feel more "worked up." Bob finds it difficult to focus on the meeting and participates very little in the group discussions. Over the next week, Bob avoids talking to Mark. In his conversations with other team members, Bob repeatedly criticizes and dismisses Mark's ideas and contributions. Although Bob's behavior makes him feel that he is "getting even" and offers him opportunities to vent his negative emotions, he gets angrier and likes Mark less each time he talks about him. Also, Bob's behavior has numerous potential deleterious effects: it may cause his coworkers to evaluate him negatively (e.g., as petty and bitter), it may make Bob feel even more hostile toward Mark, and it could ultimately elicit retaliation from Mark. Therefore, Bob's angry rumination (i.e., negative thoughts and feelings) and retaliation in the form of gossip (i.e., negative behaviors) perpetuate and strengthen his negative attachment to the original event.

As illustrated by Bob's example, people respond to workplace conflicts in many ways, such as avoidance, sabotage, gossip, overt arguments, and retaliation (e.g., Folger and Baron 1996; Kolb and Putnam 1992). The manner in which people respond is contingent upon their appraisal of (a) their available resources, (b) the event, and (c) the transgressor (Aquino and Bradfield 2000; Aquino, Tripp, and Bies 2001; Bradfield and Aquino 1999). People typically choose to respond in ways that yield some benefits, such as the discharge of negative emotions, decreased contact with the transgressor, or feelings of self-righteousness and empowerment. Although these common responses to workplace conflicts can indeed yield benefits, they may perpetuate or even escalate conflicts.

RELATIONSHIP TRANSGRESSIONS AND WORKPLACE CONFLICTS

We have described Phases 1–4 of the journey from transgression to forgiveness. These four phases concern transgressions. They explain how transgressions violate people's expectations, and how typical responses to transgressions, such as anger, denial, avoidance, hostility, and vengeance, reinforce negative attachments to the transgressions. Next we will explore how transgressions are related to conflicts in the workplace, and their impact on the individual and on the organization.

Conflict is part of the human experience, and workers do not leave their humanness behind when they enter the workplace. Therefore, it follows that conflict is an intrinsic part of people's lives at work (e.g., Kolb and Putnam 1992; Greenhalgh 1999; Wilmot and Hocker 2001). Conflicts in the workplace can be divided into relationship (or affective) conflicts and task-related (or cognitive) conflicts (De and Carsten 1997; Jehn 1995). Relationship conflicts have been defined as "interpersonal incompatibilities among people which typically include tension, animosity, and annoyance" (Jehn 1995, 258), or conflict involving a person's own or group identity, norms, and values (De and Carsten 1997). Task conflicts have been defined as "disagreements among people about the content of the tasks being performed, including differences in viewpoints, ideas and opinions" (Jehn 1995, 258), or conflict involving disputes over scarce resources, procedures, or policies (De and Carsten 1997).

People often experience or commit transgressions when they are involved in relationship conflicts. However, they usually do not experience transgressions when they are involved in task conflicts, unless the task conflicts result in, or stem from, relationship conflicts. Given the overlap between relationship conflicts and transgressions, it is not surprising that relationship conflicts are detrimental to employees and organizations (e.g., Baron 1991; Jehn 1995; Pelled 1995; Roseman, Wiest, and Swartz 1994; Staw, Sanderlands, and Dutton 1981), whereas task-related conflicts typically are not detrimental and frequently enhance productivity (e.g., Baron 1991; De and Carsten 1997; Fiol 1994; Jehn 1995; Putnam 1994; Schwenk and Valacich 1994).

Relationship conflicts are relevant to the area of forgiveness in the workplace because they often stem from or lead to transgressions, and therefore create the need for forgiveness. Task-related conflicts do not create the need for forgiveness. Thus, for the remainder of this chapter, when we refer to workplace conflicts, we mean relationship conflicts, or conflicts that include a relationship component and are not exclusively task-orientated.

Costs of Common Responses to Workplace Conflict

Workplace conflicts are costly to organizations in many ways. First, the negative emotions and thoughts that are hallmarks of these conflicts can adversely affect productivity. For example, anxiety and threat due to workplace conflicts diminish a person's ability to process complex information (Staw, Sanderlands, and Dutton 1981; Roseman, Wiest, and Swartz 1994), and anger and frustration adversely affect group communication and cooperation (Baron 1991). Second, conflict-related behaviors can hamper productivity. People who experience conflicts in a working group tend to (a) withdraw and avoid working with those with whom they experienced conflict (Jehn 1995); (b) reject or fail to assess; new information provided by people with whom they are in conflict; and (c) cause the group to spend time and energy discussing, resolving, or ignoring the conflicts instead of working on the task (Pelled 1995). Third, workplace conflict can lead to lower job satisfaction, lower organizational commitment, and increased intentions to leave the organization (Frone 2000; Hodson 1997). Fourth, when workplace conflicts escalate, they often require third-party interventions, such as mediation, arbitration, or litigation, and such methods of conflict resolution can be expensive to organizations (e.g., Brett, Barsness, and Goldberg 1996). Finally, in addition to taxing the organization's resources directly, conflicts also tax the individual employee's resources; workplace conflict is associated with increased physiological symptoms, depression, and lowered self-esteem (Frone 2000).

In summary, conflict can erode people's ability to (a) do their best work, (b) collaborate effectively with others, and (c) experience satisfaction in their jobs and organizations. Some of the most common responses to conflict tend to perpetuate or escalate the internal and interpersonal conflict experienced by people in the workplace. Therefore, as Martin Luther King, Jr., once stated, "Mankind must evolve for all human conflict a method which rejects revenge, aggression, and retaliation." Forgiveness is one such method for resolving human conflict.

FORGIVENESS

We have explained the first four phases of the journey from transgression to forgiveness. Now, we will consider the fifth and transformational phase of the journey, that of forgiveness itself (Figure

27.1, Phase 5). Forgiveness is an *intra*personal process whereby people reframe the way they think about and relate to a transgression (conflict) such that their attachment to the transgression is transformed from negative to neutral or positive (Yamhure Thompson et al. 2001; Yamhure Thompson and Snyder 2000). Therefore, forgiveness is a process that leads to the resolution of the internal components of conflict and the distress due to a transgression. Because ongoing coping with unresolved conflict requires attention and resources, the resolution of this internal conflict frees a person to expend internal resources in other, potentially more rewarding, arenas such as work and positive relationships. Indeed, empirical evidence indicates that people's level of forgiveness is positively related to their satisfaction with life (Yamhure Thompson et al. 2001).

The essential component of forgiveness is the transformation of the person's transgression-related thoughts, feelings, or behaviors from negative to neutral (Figure 27.1, Phase 5a) or positive (Figure 27.1, Phase 5b). This transformation is accompanied by a reframing of the transgression. Several authors who have studied forgiveness have described this reframing process as the construction of a "new narrative" about the transgression, transgressor, and the forgiver (e.g., Thoresen 2001) whereby "the implications of the original situation are cast in a new light" (Rowe et al. 1989, 242) and "often, the forgiving person is able to see the offender in a more complex way" (Malcolm and Greenberg 2000, 181).

The principles of dialectics can be used to describe how a person reframes a transgression, develops a new narrative, and transforms transgression-related thoughts, feelings, or behaviors. A detailed treatment of dialectics is beyond the scope of this chapter, however we note that dialectical theory has been incorporated into theories regarding the development of thinking in adults (Basseches 1984) and the treatment of a psychological disorder (Linehan 1993).

A main component of dialectical theory is the concept that reality is composed of opposites ("thesis" and "antithesis"), and that these two opposites can be integrated into a new understanding ("synthesis"). Applying this dialectical concept to transgressions and forgiveness, a person's expectations and assumptions could be called the thesis, the transgression the antithesis, and forgiveness the synthesis. That is, when a transgression occurs, a dichotomy is created between that which is (i.e., antithesis/the transgression), and that which the person thinks ought to be (i.e., thesis/expectations and assumptions). The person views the transgression as negative and the expectations as positive. These two apparently dichotomous realities (i.e., the thesis and the antithesis) create tension for the person (i.e., dissonance and distress). The person who forgives is able to resolve that tension by incorporating both the expectations and the transgression into a view of events that contains elements of both (i.e., the synthesis), and which transforms the valence of the person's transgression-related thoughts, feelings, or behaviors from negative to neutral or positive.

Misconceptions About Forgiveness

Definitions of forgiveness vary (e.g., Enright and Coyle 1998; McCullough, Pargament, and Thoresen 2000), and some of the concerns that people have about forgiveness stem from the conflation of forgiveness with other constructs such as forgetting, denial, reconciliation, and pardoning. It is important to distinguish forgiveness from these constructs, in order to establish more clearly what is and is not meant when we refer to the term *forgiveness*.

First, forgiveness is not synonymous with pardoning in that forgiveness does not preclude the option of pursuing justice via appropriate and legally permissible means, provided that the motivation underlying such behavior is not vengeful. Vengeful or otherwise negative thoughts, feelings, or behaviors toward the transgressor reflect a negative attachment that is still active and indicate that forgiveness has not occurred. Therefore, the motivation underlying behaviors toward a transgressor is key in determining whether a behavior is forgiving or not forgiving in nature.

Second, forgiveness does not mean forgetting. The common expression, "forgive and forget" can sometimes lead people to think that they must forget a transgression in order to forgive. However, a person who forgives must acknowledge (at least internally) that a transgression has been committed; and the event certainly is not literally erased from one's mind as a result of forgiving. In addition, at a more subtle level, it is not necessary to behave as if the event never happened or was not a transgression.

Third, forgiveness does not require reconciliation or positive feelings. Reconciliation is not a required part of the forgiveness process. Forgiveness is an *intra*personal process, whereas reconciliation is an *inter*personal process (e.g., Worthington and Drinkard 2000). If those who forgive do develop positive feelings for the persons forgiven, they may choose to pursue reconciliation, but, again, this is not necessary. Similarly, although forgiving may involve the development of positive feelings for the transgressor, our model posits that transformation to a neutral attachment is sufficient for forgiveness (Yamhure Thompson et al. 2001; Yamhure Thompson and Snyder 2000). Some theorists propose that feeling compassion, empathy, and even love for the transgressor is a necessary aspect of forgiveness (Enright et al. 1992; McCullough 2000; Worthington, Sandage, and Berry 2000), but we agree with those who do not view this step as essential (e.g., Tangney et al. 1999).

Fourth, forgiveness is not giving up. Because forgiveness is an internal process, people may not perceive it as an active response. However, research indicates that forgiveness is positively correlated with active coping and negatively correlated with denial and behavioral disengagement (Rasmussen and Lopez 2000). Further, people choose how they respond to conflicts, and forgiveness is one possible choice; it is not the lack of choice or action.

Finally, although forgiveness is positively correlated with acceptance and positive reinterpretation of stressful events (Rasmussen and Lopez 2000), it is not tantamount to condoning. A person who forgives may experience some benefits from the transgression and the attempts to deal with it (e.g., it might have been a good learning experience). However, one does not conclude that the transgression was just, good, or right. People often express the concern that by forgiving they will be letting the transgressor "off the hook." This concern is probably due to the fact that forgiving does preclude reactions such as vengeance, aggression, and retaliation. However, as mentioned earlier, forgiveness does not preclude the pursuit of justice. Further, those who forgive are actually letting themselves "off the hook" by decreasing the negative thoughts, feelings, or behaviors that accompany such unforgiving responses. Refer to Table 27.1 for a summary of the distinctions between forgiveness and other constructs addressed here.

Potential Benefits of Forgiveness

The transgressor is not the primary beneficiary of forgiveness; the forgiver is. However, like ripples in a pond, the positive effects of forgiveness affect those who work with the forgiver, and ultimately benefit the organization. Research indicates that forgiveness is positively related to physiological health, psychological well-being, hope, job satisfaction, and satisfaction with life (e.g., Mauger et al. 1992; Yamhure Thompson et al. 2001; Strasser 1984; Subkoviak et al. 1995; Yamhure Thompson and Snyder 2000; Yamhure Thompson, Snyder, and Hoffman 2001), and that forgiveness is negatively related to hostility, anger, vengeance, physiological symptoms, and rumination or chronic negative thinking about mood and events (Yamhure Thompson et al. 2001; Yamhure Thompson and Snyder 2000).

Table 27.1

Misconceptions About Forgiveness: Forgiveness Distinguished from Other Constructs

Forgiveness versus pardoning
> Forgiving is not synonymous with pardoning. The concept of pardoning has more relevance in the legal arena; it refers to releasing a person from penalties or repercussions of an offense. Forgiving does not preclude pursuing justice, provided that the motivation underlying the pursuit of justice is not vengeful, hostile, retaliatory, or otherwise unforgiving.

Forgiveness versus forgetting, denying, or condoning
> Forgiveness does not mean forgetting or denying a transgression. To forgive, a person must first acknowledge, at least internally, that a transgression occurred. Then a person must reframe the transgression and respond to it in ways that do not reinforce transgression-related negative thoughts, feelings, or behaviors. This reframing is not tantamount to condoning or justifying the transgression.

Forgiveness versus reconciliation
> Forgiveness is an intrapersonal process; the transformation and reframing of a transgression take place within the individual. In contrast, reconciliation is an interpersonal process that takes place between the individual and the transgressor. A person who forgives may choose to pursue reconciliation with the transgressor. However, forgiveness may occur without reconciliation and reconciliation may occur without forgiveness.

Forgiveness versus giving up or being passive
> Forgiveness is sometimes thought to be a passive or choice-less response to a transgression. However, forgiveness requires a person to actively respond to a transgression by reframing it and transforming his or her attachment to it. Giving up implies a lack of choice or action.

Practicing forgiveness also is likely to benefit employees and organizations because the process of forgiveness requires the forgiver to develop and implement skills used in problem solving and conflict resolution. Problem-solving skills are valued in the workplace. In a survey that asked 1,000 executives about the qualities they look for when hiring, problem solving was one of the two most frequently mentioned qualities (Lancaster 1998).

Two of the main problem-solving skills that are used in the process of forgiveness are (a) the ability to generate alternate solutions to problems and (b) the ability to implement those solutions (Jayanthi and Friend 1992). The ability to generate alternate solutions to a problem involves the ability to see things in a variety of ways (i.e., cognitive flexibility). A person who forgives must think flexibly in order to generate a new understanding of the transgression. This new way of framing the transgression is a "solution" to the internal dissonance created by the disparity between the transgression and the person's expectations. Research supports the conclusion that skilled "forgivers" are also skilled in generating alternative solutions to problems. In other words, the higher a person's general tendency to forgive, the greater the person's cognitive flexibility (Yamhure Thompson et al. 2001; Yamhure Thompson and Snyder 2000).

Research also indicates a positive correlation between a person's general tendency to forgive and that person's degree of hope (Yamhure Thompson et al. 2001; Yamhure Thompson and Snyder 2000). Snyder's two-component theory of hope (Snyder et al. 1991) defines hope as the perception of one's own ability to (a) successfully generate alternate pathways to a goal and (b) successfully implement those pathways to the goal. Research on hope indicates that not only do "high-hope" people have a sense of efficacy regarding their ability to generate and implement pathways to their goals, but they also have greater ability to do so than "low-hope" people (Snyder et al. 1991). Therefore, a positive correlation of forgiveness with hope supports the assertion that people skilled in forgiving are also skilled at generating and implementing alternate solutions to problems (when solving the problem is their goal).

Table 27.2

Potential Benefits of Forgiveness

Forgiveness is positively related to:
  Hope
  Satisfaction with life
  Job satisfaction
  Cognitive flexibility (a component of problem solving)
Forgiveness is negatively related to:
  Physiological symptoms
  Anger, Anxiety, Depression
  Vengeance
  Rumination (chronic negative thinking about mood and events)

In summary, people who are more forgiving are less hostile, have better psychological and physiological health, and are more satisfied with their jobs and their lives in general than less forgiving people. Also, people who are forgiving are more adept in two important problem-solving skills (the ability to generate alternate solutions to problems and the ability to implement those solutions). The forgiving person is able to think flexibly in order to gain a new understanding of workplace conflicts, and is able and willing to let go of ineffective, negative thoughts, feelings, or behaviors. Such a person is not only likely to be more productive, but is also more likely to relate to coworkers in a positive and effective manner. Therefore, forgiveness and the skills involved in forgiveness benefit both the individual employee and the organization. Unfortunately, forgiveness is not commonly regarded as a potential response to workplace conflicts. Therefore, people are unlikely to engage in the process of forgiveness early in a conflict. In fact, people may not consider forgiveness until they become aware that their initial responses to the conflict are ineffective or harmful. See Table 27.2 for a summary of the potential benefits of forgiveness.

Bob might begin to consider forgiveness as a response if (a) he realizes that his negative thoughts and feelings about Mark are harming his ability to do his best work and to collaborate effectively with the members of his team; (b) he finds that his coworkers are less sympathetic, or are avoiding or confronting him when he gossips about Mark; (c) his supervisor does not assign him to a new group project because of Bob's lack of participation in group meetings; or (d) the conflict between Bob and Mark escalates and leads to Mark's requesting a third-party conflict resolution process, such as mediation. Once one or several of these events occur, Bob may decide to change how he is responding to Mark, and he may begin the process of forgiveness.

Bob makes conscious efforts to change the way he thinks about Mark and his comments regarding Bob's contributions to the team project. Bob decides to let go of the grudge he has been harboring. He slowly develops a new way of viewing the original event, and his formerly negative thoughts, feelings, or behaviors about Mark become more positive. In contrast to his earlier ways of responding, Bob's more positive responses release him from the distress he has been experiencing each time he is reminded of the conflict with Mark. Bob finds that he is able to interact more productively with Mark, his team members, and his supervisor.

THE ROLE OF FORGIVENESS IN WORKPLACE CONFLICT MANAGEMENT AND RESOLUTION

Problem-Focused Approaches to Conflict

In most organizations, people have access to a variety of processes for resolving their conflicts, including informal problem solving, mediation, arbitration, and litigation. The main objective of these forms of conflict management and resolution is to reach an agreement that solves the problem. They are particularly effective and popular because they keep all parties focused on the problem (or on task-related components of the conflict). However, the relationship components of the conflict are often minimally addressed, if at all, and in many cases they are unresolved by these approaches to conflict. This is particularly true in litigation, an adversarial process that typically results in a "win-lose" solution. While litigation may effectively solve the "problem," it often fails to address, and sometimes amplifies, the relationship or affective conflict. Further, even in methods of alternative dispute resolution that promote "win-win" solutions (e.g., negotiation and mediation), the relationship components of conflict are typically addressed only to the extent that they facilitate the attainment of a mutually agreeable solution to the problem.

Balancing the Problem-Focused Approach with a Person-Focused Approach

The problem-focused methods of conflict management and resolution are well aligned with the purpose of organizations: to get work done. However, even in cases in which win-win solutions are accomplished, if the relationship components of conflict are not resolved, people may experience lingering conflict-related thoughts and feelings, which adversely affect their ability to get their work done. At least one current method of conflict resolution, transformative mediation, is designed to address relationship components of conflict. In contrast to arbitration, litigation, and most mediation processes, transformative mediation is a method of conflict resolution that places a priority on improving the relationship of the disputants as well as on resolving substantive issues (e.g., Bush and Folger 1994). It is a more balanced method of conflict resolution because it addresses both the problem and the interpersonal components of conflict.

Transformative mediation, however, does not directly address the intrapersonal components of conflict. Moreover, it is not accepted or offered in most workplaces because it brings the relationship and emotional conflicts of employees into an official process of conflict resolution, which may not conform with some organizations' approaches to emotions and relationship conflicts in the workplace. Many companies and employees prefer that individuals manage the emotional components of their lives themselves. Therefore, they limit their conflict resolution processes to problem-focused methods and fail to address the relationship or affective components of a conflict.

In contrast to arbitration, litigation, and mediation processes, forgiveness addresses the intrapersonal components of conflicts and can be used to complement the more common, problem-focused methods of conflict resolution. By facilitating the resolution of the intrapersonal aspects of conflict, the process of forgiveness develops and engages the forgiver's problem-solving skills, and perhaps may also open the door to more effective attempts to resolve the interpersonal aspects of conflict. For these reasons, we believe that all employees, including managers and administrators, would benefit from training in forgiveness skills.

Forgiveness Skills Training in the Workplace

Forgiveness skills can be of great assistance to people when they experience transgressions in the workplace. They can be useful at any stage in the conflict resolution process. For example, a person may use forgiveness skills to (a) resolve a transgression internally, which may obviate the need for further conflict resolution; (b) respond effectively to the negative impact of a workplace transgression during an informal or formal conflict-resolution process; or (c) resolve inner feelings of conflict that may linger even after the "problem" has been resolved via a chosen method of conflict resolution.

Sometimes forgiveness occurs without much effort on the part of the forgiver. More often, however, forgiveness requires conscious choice and effort. Whenever forgiveness requires such conscious effort, training regarding the role of forgiveness in the workplace can have various benefits. First, training can increase employees' awareness of forgiveness as a potential response to workplace transgressions. Second, training can make the benefits of forgiveness and the costs of other responses (e.g., avoidance, anger, revenge, and retaliation) more apparent to employees. Third, it can provide employees with the skills to facilitate the process of forgiveness for themselves when they encounter transgressions in the workplace. Fourth, training can develop employees' abilities to problem-solve, to generate alternative solutions, to think flexibly, and to implement solutions. Not only can employees use these skills in the forgiveness process, they can also apply them to their daily tasks in the workplace.

Research regarding the effectiveness of forgiveness interventions with a variety of target groups has demonstrated that it is possible to teach forgiveness skills effectively (Al-Mabuk and Downs 1996; Al-Mabuk, Enright, and Cardis 1995; Coyle and Enright 1997; Freedman and Enright 1996; Hebl and Enright 1993; McCullough and Worthington 1995; McCullough, Worthington, and Rachal 1997; Luskin 1999). However, none of these interventions was designed for use in a workplace setting. There is a need for training programs that can be used to teach forgiveness skills in the workplace. We are currently developing a forgiveness skills workshop and encourage others to do so.

When introducing the topic of forgiveness in the workplace, it is essential to emphasize that forgiveness is not intended to replace formal or informal avenues of conflict resolution; it is a complementary, intrapersonal process. Also, to respect the diversity of employees' religious orientations, a nonreligious approach to forgiveness is important. Forgiveness skills can be taught using a nonreligious conceptual framework that acknowledges the power of forgiveness as a transformational process that results in a new perspective regarding oneself, others, and the world.

CONCLUSION AND FUTURE DIRECTIONS

Conflict is inevitable in the workplace, and research has demonstrated that conflict has numerous deleterious effects on employee productivity, job satisfaction, and well-being. Organizations have recognized this fact and have focused on conflict management and conflict resolution as topics of study and concern (e.g., Cloke and Goldsmith 2000; Greenhalgh 1999; Kolb and Bartunek 1992; Van de Vliert 1998). Although significant advances have been made in the area of conflict resolution, the current methods are primarily problem-focused and frequently fail to resolve the relationship and intrapersonal components of conflicts. Often, although a problem is "solved," employees continue to grapple with lingering negative thoughts, feelings, or behaviors. Thus, the conflict and its detrimental effects frequently continue after substantive issues have been resolved. Therefore, there is a need to provide employees with skills to help them resolve the intrapersonal components of conflicts.

The growing body of research indicates that forgiveness is an effective coping skill that is similar to basic problem-solving skills. Forgiveness enables people to resolve intrapersonal components of conflict by coming to an understanding of the situation that frees them from conflict-related negative thoughts, feelings, or behaviors. This understanding liberates the internal resources that would otherwise be used to cope with those conflicts and allows people to refocus their resources on more productive and satisfying work and relationships.

Thus, forgiveness is a process that can augment the problem-focused methods of conflict resolution most commonly used in the workplace. Further, because research indicates that forgiveness skills can be taught, all employees, including managers and administrators, could benefit from training in forgiveness skills. Although only a few studies have directly examined the role of forgiveness in the workplace (Bradfield and Aquino 1999; Butler 1998), the results of these studies, and of studies regarding the efficacy of forgiveness training, are heartening. The role of forgiveness as a workplace problem-solving and coping skill is a promising area of study that merits further research and application.

REFERENCES

Al-Mabuk, R.H., and W.R. Downs. (1996). "Forgiveness Therapy with Parents of Adolescent Suicide Victims." *Journal of Family Psychotherapy* 7: 21–39.

Al-Mabuk, R.H.; R.D. Enright; and P.A. Cardis. (1995). "Forgiveness Education with Parentally Love-Deprived Late Adolescents." *Journal of Moral Education* 24: 427–444.

Aquino, K., and M. Bradfield. (2000). "Perceived Victimization in the Workplace: The Role of Situational Factors and Victim Characteristics." *Organization Science* 11: 525–537.

Aquino, K.; T.M. Tripp; and R.J. Bies. (2001). "How Employees Respond to Personal Offense: The Effects of Blame Attribution, Victim Status, and Offender Status on Revenge and Reconciliation in the Workplace." *Journal of Applied Psychology* 86: 52–59.

Baron, R.A. (1991). "Positive Effects of Conflict: A Cognitive Perspective." *Employee Responsibilities and Rights Journal* 4: 25–36.

Basseches, M. (1984). *Dialectical Thinking and Adult Development.* Norwood, NJ: Ablex.

Beck, A.T.; A.J. Rush; B.F. Shaw; and G. Emery. (1979). *Cognitive Therapy of Depression.* New York: Guilford.

Bradfield, M., and K. Aquino. (1999). "The Effects of Blame Attributions and Offender Likableness on Forgiveness and Revenge in the Workplace." *Journal of Management* 25: 607–631.

Brett, J.M.; Z.I. Barsness; and S.B. Goldberg. (1996). "The Effectiveness of Mediation: An Independent Analysis of Cases Handled by Four Major Service Providers." *Negotiation Journal* 1, no. 2: 259–269.

Bush, R.A.B., and J.P. Folger. (1994). *The Promise of Mediation: Responding to Conflict Through Empowerment and Recognition.* San Francisco: Jossey-Bass.

Butler, D.S. (1998)."The Effects of Personality and General Health on Choosing Interpersonal Forgiveness in the Workplace." Doctoral dissertation, Georgia State University 1997. *Dissertation Abstracts International* 58: 4498.

Cloke, K., and J. Goldsmith. (2000). "Conflict Resolution That Reaps Great Rewards." *Journal for Quality and Participation* 23: 27–30.

Coates, D. (1997). "The Correlations of Forgiveness of Self, Forgiveness of Others, and Hostility, Depression, Anxiety, Self-Esteem, Life Adaptation, and Religiosity Among Female Victims of Domestic Violence." Doctoral dissertation, California School of Professional Psychology, Fresno. *Dissertation Abstracts International* 58: 2667.

Coyle, C.T., and R.D. Enright. (1997). "Forgiveness Intervention with Post Abortion Men." *Journal of Consulting and Clinical Psychology* 65: 1042–1046.

De, D., and K.W. Carsten. (1997). "Productive Conflict: The Importance of Conflict Management and Conflict Issue." In *Using Conflict in Organizations,* ed. D. De, K.W. Carsten, and E. Van de Vliert. Thousand Oaks, CA: Sage, 9–22.

Emmons, R.A. (2000). "Is Spirituality an Intelligence? Motivation, Cognition, and the Psychology of Ultimate Concern." *International Journal for the Psychology of Religion* 10: 3–26.

Enright, R.D., and C.T. Coyle. (1998). "Researching the Process Model of Forgiveness Within Psychological Interventions." In *Dimensions of Forgiveness: Psychological Research and Theological Perspectives,* ed. E.L. Worthington, Jr. Radnor, PA: Templeton Foundation Press, 139–161.

Enright, R.D.; D.L. Eastin; S. Golden; I. Sarinopoulos; and S. Freeman. (1992). "Interpersonal Forgiveness Within the Helping Professions: An Attempt to Resolve Differences of Opinion." *Counseling and Values* 36: 84–103.

Enright, R.D.; M.J. Santos; and R. Al-Mabuk. (1989). "The Adolescent As Forgiver." *Journal of Adolescence* 1, no. 2: 95–110.

Fiol, C.M. (1994). "Consensus, Diversity, and Learning in Organizations." *Organization Science* 5: 403–420.

Folger, R., and R.A. Baron. (1996). "Violence and Hostility at Work: A Model of Reactions to Perceived Injustice." In *Violence on the Job: Identifying Risks and Developing Solutions,* ed. G.R. VandenBos and E.Q. Bulatao. Washington, DC: American Psychological Association, 51–85.

Freedman, S.R., and R.D. Enright. (1996). "Forgiveness As an Intervention Goal with Incest Survivors." *Journal of Consulting and Clinical Psychology* 64: 983–992.

Frone, M.R. (2000). "Interpersonal Conflict at Work and Psychological Outcomes: Testing a Model Among Young Workers." *Journal of Occupational Health Psychology* 5: 246–255.

Greenhalgh, L. (1999). "Managing Conflict." In *Negotiation: Readings, Exercises, and Cases,* 3d ed., ed. R.J. Lewicki, D.M. Saunders et al. Boston: Irwin/McGraw-Hill, 6–13.

Greenwald, A.G. (1980). "The Totalitarian Ego: Fabrication and Revision of Personal History." *American Psychologist* 35: 603–618.

Hebl, J.H., and R.D. Enright. (1993). "Forgiveness As a Psychotherapeutic Goal with Elderly Females." *Psychotherapy* 30: 658–667.

Hodson, R. (1997). "Group Relations at Work." *Work and Occupations* 24: 426–452.

Ingersoll, R.E. (1996). "Construction and Initial Validation of the Spiritual Wellness Inventory." Doctoral dissertation, Kent State University. *Dissertation Abstracts International* 56: 5827.

Janoff-Bulman, R. (1992). *Shattered Assumptions: Towards a New Psychology of Trauma.* New York: Free Press.

Janoff-Bulman, R., and C.M. Frantz. (1997). "The Impact of Trauma on Meaning: From Meaningless World to Meaningful Life." In *The Transformation of Meaning in Psychological Therapies,* ed. M. Power and C.R. Brewin. New York: Wiley, 91–106.

Janoff-Bulman, R., and I.H. Frieze. (1983). "A Theoretical Perspective for Understanding Reactions to Victimization." *Journal of Social Issues* 39: 1–17.

Janoff-Bulman, R., and S.S. Schwartzberg. (1991). "Toward a General Model of Personal Change." In *Handbook of Social and Clinical Psychology: The Health Perspective,* ed. C.R. Snyder and D.R. Forsyth. Elmsford, NY: Pergamon, 488–508.

Jayanthi, M., and M. Friend. (1992). "Interpersonal Problem Solving: A Selective Literature Review to Guide Practice." *Journal of Educational and Psychological Consultation* 3, no. 1: 39–53.

Jehn, K.A. (1995). "A Multimethod Examination of the Benefits and Detriments of Intragroup Conflict." *Administrative Science Quarterly* 40: 256–282.

Kolb, D.M., and J.M. Bartunek, eds. (1992). *Hidden Conflict in Organizations: Uncovering Behind-the-Scenes Disputes,* vol. 141. Sage focus editions. Thousand Oaks, CA: Sage.

Kolb, D.M., and L.L. Putnam. (1992). "The Multiple Faces of Conflict in Organizations." *Journal of Organizational Behavior* 13: 311–324.

Lancaster, H. (1998). "Managing Your Career: Hiring a Full Staff May Be the Next Fad in Management." *Wall Street Journal* (April 28): B-1.

Linehan, M.M. (1993). *The Cognitive-Behavioral Treatment of Borderline Personality Disorder.* New York: Guilford.

Luskin, F. (1999). "Effects of Forgiveness Training on Psychosocial Factors in College Age Adults." Unpublished doctoral dissertation, Stanford University, Palo Alto, California.

Mahoney, M.J., and G.M. Graci. (1999). "The Meanings and Correlates of Spirituality: Suggestions from an Exploratory Survey of Experts." *Death Studies* 23: 521–528.

Malcolm, W.M., and L.S. Greenberg (2000). "Forgiveness As a Process of Change in Individual Psychotherapy." In *Forgiveness: Theory, Research, and Practice,* ed. M.E. McCullough, K.I. Pargament, and C.E. Thoresen. New York: Guilford, 179–202.

Mauger, P.A.; J.E. Perry; T. Freeman; D.C. Grove; A.G. McBride; and K.E. McKinney. (1992). "The Measurement of Forgiveness: Preliminary Research." *Journal of Psychology and Christianity* 11: 170–180.

McCullough, M.E. (2000). "Forgiveness As Human Strength: Theory, Measurement, and Links to Well-being." *Journal of Social and Clinical Psychology* 19: 43–55.

McCullough, M.E.; K.I. Pargament; and C.E. Thoresen, eds. (2000). "The Psychology of Forgiveness: History, Conceptual Issues, and Overview." In *Forgiveness: Theory, Research, and Practice.* New York: Guilford, 1–14.

McCullough, M.E., and E.L. Worthington, Jr. (1995). "Promoting Forgiveness: A Comparison of Two Brief Psychoeducational Group Interventions with a Waiting-List Control." *Counseling and Values* 40: 55–68.

———. (1999). "Religion and the Forgiving Personality." *Journal of Personality* 67: 1141–1164.

McCullough, M.E.; E.L. Worthington, Jr.; and K.C. Rachal. (1997). "Interpersonal Forgiving in Close Relationships." *Journal of Personality and Social Change* 73: 321–336.

Miller, D., and N. Vidmar. (1981). "The Social Psychology of Punishment Reactions." In *The Justice Motive in Social Behavior,* ed. S. Lerner and M. Lerner. New York: Plenum Press, 145–167.

Pelled, L.H. (1995). "Demographic Diversity, Conflict, and Work Group Outcomes: An Intervening Process Theory." *Organization Science* 7: 615–631.

Putnam, L.L. (1994). "Productive Conflict: Negotiation as Implicit Coordination." *International Journal of Conflict Management* 5: 285–299.

Rasmussen, H.N., and S.J. Lopez. (2000). "Forgiveness and Adaptive Coping." Poster session to be presented at the annual meeting of the American Psychological Association, August, Washington, DC.

Roseman, I.J.; C. Wiest; and T.S. Swartz. (1994). "Phenomenology, Behaviors, and Goals Differentiate Discrete Emotions." *Journal of Personality and Social Psychology* 67: 206–221.

Rowe, J.O.; S. Halling; E. Davies; M. Leifer; D. Powers; and J. van Bronkhorst. (1989). "The Psychology of Forgiving Another: A Dialogal Research Approach." In *Existential-Phenomenological Perspectives in Psychology: Exploring the Breadth of Human Experience,* ed. R.S. Valle and S. Halling. New York: Plenum Press, 233–244.

Rye, M.S. (1999). "Evaluation of a Secular and a Religiously-Integrated Forgiveness Group Therapy Program for College Students Who Have Been Wronged by a Romantic Partner." Doctoral dissertation, Bowling Green State University 1998. *Dissertation Abstracts International* 59: 6495.

Rye, M.S.; K.I. Pargament; M.A. Ali; G.L. Beck; E.N. Dorff; C. Hallisey; V. Narayanan; and J.G. Williams. (2000). "Religious Perspectives on Forgiveness." In *Forgiveness: Theory, Research, and Practice,* ed. M.E. McCullough, K.I. Pargament, and C.E. Thoresen. New York: Guilford, 17–40.

Schwenk, C., and J.S. Valacich. (1994). "Effects of Devil's Advocacy and Dialectical Inquiry on Individuals Versus Groups." *Organizational Behavior and Human Decision Processes* 59: 210–222.

Snyder, C.R.; C. Harris; J. Anderson; S. Holleran; L. Irving; S. Sigmon; L. Yoshinobu; J. Gibb; C. Langelle; and P. Harney. (1991). "The Will and the Ways: Development and Validation of an Individual-Differences Measure of Hope." *Journal of Personality and Social Psychology* 60: 570–585.

Staw, B.M.; L.E. Sanderlands; and J.E. Dutton. (1981). "Threat-Rigidity Effects in Organizational Behavior: A Multilevel Analysis." *Administrative Science Quarterly* 26: 501–524.

Strasser, J.A. (1984). "The Relation of General Forgiveness and Forgiveness Type to Reported Health in the Elderly." Unpublished doctoral dissertation, Catholic University of America, Washington, DC.

Subkoviak, M.J.; R.D. Enright; C.R. Wu; E.A. Gassin; S. Freedman; L.M. Olson; and I. Sarinopoulos. (1995). "Measuring Interpersonal Forgiveness in Late Adolescence and Middle Adulthood." *Journal of Adolescence* 18: 641–655.

Tangney, J.; R. Fee; C. Reinsmith; A.L. Boone; and N. Lee. (1999). "Assessing Individual Differences in the Propensity to Forgive." Paper presented at the annual meeting of the American Psychological Association, Boston, MA, August.

Thoresen, C.E. (2001). "Forgiveness Interventions: What Is Known and What Needs Knowing." In *Forgiveness and Health—The Stanford Forgiveness Project Symposium,* ed. C.E. Thoresen (Chair), Symposium conducted at the annual convention of the American Psychological Association, San Francisco, CA, August.

Van de Vliert, E. (1998). "Conflict and Conflict Management." In *Handbook of Work and Organizational Psychology,* 2d ed., vol. 3, ed. P.J.D. Drenth, H. Thierry et al. *Personnel Psychology.* Hove, England: Psychology Press/Erlbaum (UK) Taylor and Francis.

Webb, J.R. (1999). "Forgiveness and Control: Toward an Understanding of the Dynamics of Forgiveness." Doctoral dissertation, California School of Professional Psychology, Los Angeles. *Dissertation Abstracts International* 60, no. 1: 0379B.

Wilmot, W.W., and J.L. Hocker. (2001). *Interpersonal Conflict,* 6th ed. New York: McGraw-Hill.

Worthington, E.L., Jr., and D.T. Drinkard. (2000). "Promoting Reconciliation Through Psychoeducational and Therapeutic Interventions." *Journal of Marriage and Family Therapy* 26: 93–101.

Worthington, E.L., Jr.; S.J. Sandage; and J.W. Berry. (2000). "Group Interventions to Promote Forgiveness." In *Forgiveness: Theory, Research, and Practice,* ed. M.E. McCullough, K.I. Pargament, and C.E. Thoresen. New York: Guilford, 228–253.

Yamhure Thompson, L., and C.R. Snyder. (2000). *Forgiveness Theory and the Development of the Heartland Forgiveness Scale: Freeing Oneself from the Negative Ties That Bind.* Poster presented at the annual convention of the American Psychological Association, Washington, DC, August.

Yamhure Thompson, L.; C.R. Snyder; and L. Hoffman. (2001). "Forgiveness, Hope, Hostility, Health, and Job Satisfaction in Six Groups of Professionals." Unpublished manuscript, University of Kansas at Lawrence.

Yamhure Thompson, L.; C.R. Snyder; L. Hoffman; S.T. Michael; H.N. Rasmussen; L.S. Billings; L. Heinze; J.E. Neufeld; H.S. Shorey; C.M. Robinson; J.R. Roberts; and D.E. Roberts. (2001). "Development and Validation of a Measure of Dispositional Forgiveness of Self, Others, and Situations: The Snyder Forgiveness Scale (SFS)." Manuscript submitted for publication.

Young, J., and W.T. Behary. (1998). "Schema-Focused Therapy for Personality Disorders." In *Treating Complex Cases: The Cognitive Behavioral Therapy Approach,* ed. N. Tarrier, A. Wells et al. (Wiley Series in Clinical Psychology). Chichester, UK: Wiley, 340–376.

CHAPTER 28

HOW WORKPLACE SPIRITUALITY BECOMES MAINSTREAMED IN A SCHOLARLY ORGANIZATION

JERRY BIBERMAN

This chapter will discuss how workplace spirituality became mainstreamed in two scholarly organizations—the International Academy of Business Disciplines and the Academy of Management. It will discuss how the interest of a few "founding" members interacted synergistically with the interest of a growing number of general members to generate the forming of a track on "Spirituality in Organizations" at the International Academy of Business Disciplines, and, a few years later, a special interest group on "Management, Spirituality and Religion" at the Academy of Management. It will next discuss how the growing member interest in spirituality coincided with a burgeoning appearance of conference presentations and journal publications about spirituality across a variety of business and related disciplines. Finally, it will describe ways in which the experiences and lessons learned in starting the track and interest group can produce information that can be of general use for managers or administrators.

WHY THE INTEREST IN SPIRITUALITY?

There is evidence of a growing interest—in academics and practitioners alike—in spirituality within a work or business setting. This increase in interest prompts the question as to why and how it is occurring. Why the "sudden" interest in writing, research, teaching, and consulting about spirituality in a work setting? Why are conference sessions on spirituality so well attended?

Informal communication with a number of writers and practitioners in the area would suggest that both academics and practitioners who are most involved in this area have become involved because they are feeling "called" or "drawn" to do so. In many cases, the individuals' personal spiritual beliefs, practices, and experiences over the years have led them to combine these experiences and interests with their professional interests and expertise. This was certainly my own personal experience.

In my case, I have been engaging in yoga and meditation practices for over twenty years, and have also been fascinated by Kabala and Jewish and other types of mysticism for over twenty years. While I am Jewish, I teach at a Jesuit school, and have had the opportunity to pray the Spiritual Exercises of Ignatius of Loyola, and have attended a number of religious and nonreligious retreats. I am also fortunate to have been graced with experiencing several transpersonal experiences over the past twenty years. The nature of these intense personal experiences fueled my academic interest in the subject of spirituality, and prompted me to look for connections between this interest in spirituality and my training and expertise in psychology, management, and organizations. So, at least in my case, my desire to make sense of my own personal experiences led to my interest in spirit at work. I initially did not know—nor did I particularly care—that there were a number of other scholars who were simultaneously and independently developing similar interests. I was, of course, happy to learn over time that these other scholars existed, and that they were very willing and eager to collaborate on scholarship and other projects to further spirituality in organizations.

In almost every case, other scholars have told me that their interest in spirituality at work was motivated by their own spiritual practices, beliefs, or experiences. Most also have said that, over time, they have realized how similar the prescriptions for behavior and descriptions of spiritual practices and experiences of the various world religions and other mystical practices are to each other.

In many respects, the personal experiences and growing interest in spirituality among these scholars mirror the growing interest in spirituality in society in general—particularly among the "boomer" generation, which has dabbled in a variety of aspects of spirituality since the 1960s. Some of the interest may be generated from scholars approaching middle to older age and revisiting and questioning their spiritual and religious values and beliefs and how they can use them more congruently in their professional lives.

In any event, the growing scholarly interest in spirituality at work appears to be an excellent example of the principle of "dharma"—where people working and writing in this area are doing so because they feel that doing so is their purpose in life. In other words, they feel that they are being "called" to do so. The interest in spirituality and work of a few "founding" members interacted synergistically with the interest of a growing number of general members to generate the forming of a track on "Spirituality in Organizations" at the International Academy of Business Disciplines, and, a few years later, a special interest group on "Management, Spirituality and Religion" at the Academy of Management.

BIRTH OF A TRACK

The Spirituality in Organizations track of the International Academy of Business Disciplines (IABD) grew out of the personal interests of two of the IABD's active members—Jerry Biberman and Len Tischler. Jerry had been serving as *Proceedings* coeditor and Len Tischler had been serving as the IABD's newsletter editor. Both had had a long previous interest in spirituality, and both had been personally practicing meditation and other spiritual practices for over twenty years. Both had also been personal friends of the IABD's executive director (a devout Muslim), and had good working relations with the association's officers, program directors, and other track chairs.

With the permission of the program chair and the executive director, the track was first included in the IABD's 1997 conference call for papers. That year, four papers and several workshops were presented at the annual conference in Orlando. The papers were also published in the IABD's 1997 Business Research Yearbook (Biberman and Alkhafaji, 1997). The Spirituality in Organizations track has been listed in the call for papers and included in the Business Research Yearbook every year since 1997, and track sessions at each conference have been well attended and received.

IABD presenters began to collaborate in writing and research with other people who had presented at or attended the IABD Spirituality in Organizations track sessions. In addition, they contacted, and began to collaborate with, other researchers whose names were mentioned by people at the track sessions. These collaborations led to journal article submissions and workshop and paper presentations at other conferences—most notably, at the Academy of Management.

SPIRITUALITY AT THE ACADEMY OF MANAGEMENT

The topic of spirituality was first formally addressed at the Academy of Management in a symposium—held in 1997 at the Boston Academy meeting—that had been organized by Lee Robbins. Copresenters with Robbins at the symposium were Judi Neal, Lee Bolman, and David Cooperrider. The symposium was cosponsored by the Organization Development and Change and the Management Education and Development divisions. Robbins remembers the symposium as follows:

> It was scheduled in a small room which would hold about 35 seated and over a hundred people tried to get in with people in the hall outside jockeying for position from which they could hear the session. The session was more participative than normal for the regular program. David talked about the United Religions Initiative; I talked about 12 Step Fellowship spirituality and organizational structure/process; Lee about the impact of his text *Leading with Soul* and Judi about management and spirituality in general. (Lee Robbins, personal communication, July 9, 2001)

A preconference workshop on teaching spirituality was presented at the 1998 academy meeting in San Diego by Judi Neal, Lee Robbins, Jerry Biberman, and Mike Whitty (Neal et al. 1998). That workshop was also cosponsored by the Organization Development and Change and the Management Education and Development divisions and had a large number of attendees. There have been sessions on spirituality at every academy meeting since 1998—each of which has been sponsored or cosponsored by such academy divisions as Organization Development and Change, Management Education and Development, and Social Issues in Management. Each of these divisions had members who were interested in, and supportive of, the topic of spirituality at work. The program chairs of those divisions scheduled preconference workshops and conference symposia and paper sessions related to the topic of spirituality at work. Each succeeding year since 1998 has seen increasing numbers of sessions devoted to spirituality and/or religion, sponsored by one or more existing divisions of the academy, with each session attracting large numbers of attendees.

At the 1999 meeting of the Academy, a petition was circulated among meeting attendees requesting that the Academy Board authorize the formation of a new special interest group on Management and Spirituality. That petition received over two hundred signatures—many of which were obtained from the large audiences that attend the spirituality sessions. In addition to signing the petition, some rather well known and well established academy members, including at least one academy fellow, worked behind the scenes to influence academy members, and particularly the Academy Board, to support the formation of the interest group.

Later that year, the Academy Board approved the formation of the interest group—and the first business meeting of the Management, Spirituality and Religion (MSR) interest group was held at the Toronto Academy meeting in 2000. At that meeting, Jerry Biberman was elected the first chairperson of the interest group. The first full program of the MSR interest group occurred at the 2001 academy meeting in Washington, DC. There were over two hundred academy members registered as members of the interest group in 2001.

The rather rapid formation and approval of the MSR interest group seems to have been fueled by the interest of a large number of academy members—as evidenced by the over two hundred petition signatures and the large number of attendees (typically, over fifty people per session, generally filling each meeting space) at academy sessions on related topics.

RELATIONSHIP TO WORKPLACE SPIRITUALITY

The growing association member interest in spirituality coincided with a burgeoning appearance of conference presentations and journal publications about spirituality across a variety of business and related disciplines. Table 28.1 shows the number of books and refereed journal articles that have appeared on work and spirituality by year, as cited in the Association Spirit at Work (2001a) bibliography. A search of the literature found no academic conference sessions on the topic of spirituality and work prior to 1995, with a proliferation of conference sessions beginning from around 1995 onward.

While the International Academy of Business Disciplines seems to have been the first academic business association to have a track on spirituality in organizations, other business education associations and conferences—including the Eastern Academy of Management, Organization Behavior Teaching Conference, and the Conference of Jesuit Business Educators—began to have sessions on spirituality and related topics beginning around 1996. In the past several years there have even been academic conferences held devoted solely to the topic. In addition, there have been a number of nonacademic business-practitioner-oriented conferences held on related topics. Table 28.2 shows some of the nonacademic conferences and meetings that have been offered just since 2000, as cited in the Association of Spirit at Work's (2001b) Web site.

One of the first academic journals to have published articles specifically on the topic of spirituality and work seems to be the *Journal of Organizational Change Management.* Between 1992 and 1999, that journal published sixty-eight articles that mentioned spirituality, including thirty-six articles with spirituality as their main focus (Boje 2000). In 1999, the *Journal of Organizational Change Management* published two special issues (coedited by Mike Whitty and me [1999a, 1999b]) on spirituality in organizations. Special issues on spirituality and work have also appeared in other journals—including the *Journal of Management Education* and the *Chinmaya Management Review.* In 2000, Jerry Biberman and Mike Whitty edited the first book of readings on the subject (Biberman and Whitty 2000), which has subsequently been adapted for classroom use in several courses teaching spirituality and work that have been developed in business schools throughout the world.

UTILITY OF INFORMATION FOR MANAGERS OR ADMINISTRATORS

Ways in which the experiences and lessons learned in starting the track and interest group may be useful for managers or administrators will now be described. Next, possible challenges that may arise will be suggested.

Lessons learned can be delineated as follows:

- *The importance of having a passion for the subject with which you want to write or work.*
  Individuals' own personal interest in spirituality, own personal experiences with spiritual practices, and the transpersonal experiences they have personally had fuel their interest in learning more about the relationship of spirituality to the workplace. It enables them to stay in dharma. It also enables them to be more aware of other people who share a passion for the subject.
- *The importance of networking with people who share similar interests.*
  Interested scholars have been fortunate to be able to collaborate with scholars from around the world who are also passionate about applying spirituality to work. This collaboration has been facilitated by the ability to send e-mail messages and text files electronically anywhere in the world, making collaboration independent of physical proximity.

Table 28.1

Number of Books and Articles on Work and Spirit Listed by Year

Year	Books	Articles
Pre-1980	24	
1981	4	1
1982	2	
1983		
1984	8	
1985	4	1
1986	5	
1987	8	1
1988	7	3
1989	14	2
1990	20	1
1991	19	11
1992	26	8
1993	32	14
1994	45	19
1995	43	4
1996	40	7
1997	52	17
1998	44	7
1999	25	27
2000	14	3
2001	3	8

- *The importance of timing.*
  As this chapter described, a number of seemingly independent factors interacted in such a way as to facilitate the mainstreaming of spirituality into scholarly organizations and publication outlets. As in the saying "when the student is ready the teacher will appear," it appears as if the field was ready for the topic to appear.

Possible challenges and questions of creating this type of interest group include the following:

- *Understanding of terminology.*
  Spirituality means different things to different people, as does the relationship between spirituality and religion. It is important to understand these differences, and to be able to articulate them. It is also important to understand what other people—especially those who belong to the group—mean by these terms, and to be accepting of the different meanings and interpretations.
- *Avoiding the temptation to proselytize or dictate dogma.*
  While it may be tempting to assume that one's own spiritual path or answers may be the best one, one needs to resist the temptation to act as though he or she has the only correct way or answers. We need to be able to facilitate each person's asking her or his own questions and finding what works best for her or him.
  Occasionally at conference sessions, a session attendee has asserted that her or his religious belief is the only correct one. Group communication and leadership skills were needed to get the session back on track, by honoring that person's beliefs but reshifting the discussion to the topic at hand.

Table 28.2

Nonacademic Conferences on Work and Spirit Held Since 1999

Date of conference	Name of conference	Location of conference
July 22–24, 2002	Living Spirit: A New Dimension in Work and Learning	University of Surrey, Guildford, Surrey, UK
April 21–23, 2002	Spirit and Business Conference	The Sheraton New York Hotel and Towers, New York City
January 18–22, 2002	The 2002 International Conference on Business and Consciousness	Santa Fe, New Mexico, USA
October 19–21, 2001	The Kripalu Consultant Collaborative Fall Meeting	Various locations in New England
July 26–27, 2001	Emerging Ideas in Business Performance: Leadership, Spirituality, and New Economics	Television Centre, London
July 6–8, 2001	Art and Business Management as Art and Science	Castle Borl, Slovenia
July 1–3, 2001	Spirituality in Management	Szeged, Hungary
June 7–9, 2001	The 11th Annual International Conference on Servant Leadership	Sheraton Indianapolis Hotel and Suites in Indianapolis, IN
May 25–26, 2001	The Second International Forum on Management, Ethics, and Spirituality in Montreal	Canada
May 6–12, 2001	Spirituality in the Marketplace	Bon Secours Spiritual Center in Marriotsville, MD
April 27–28, 2001	The Heart of Leadership	Bergamo, in Dayton, OH
March 21–23, 2001	Fourth International Symposium on Spirituality and Business	Babson College, Wellesley, MA
February 7–8, 2001	Team Spirit Annual Conference	Del Mar, CA
February 1–2, 2001	Servant Leadership Retreat	Chapman University, Orange, CA
January 26–28, 2001	Kripalu Consultant Collaborative (KCC) Conferences	Various locations in New England
January 4–5, 2001	Spirituality and Leadership	Center for Creative Leadership in Greensboro, NC
December 2–7, 2000	The 2000 International Conference on Business and Consciousness	Acapulco, Mexico
December 2–4, 2000	The Spirituality, Leadership and Management Network	Ballarat University in Victoria, Australia
August 7–11, 2000	The Institute for Transformative Leadership	
August 5–12, 2000	Learning Disciplines for an Enlightened Society	Shambhala Institute
July 30–August 5, 2000	Millennium Connections: Shaping Profound Societal Change	Denver University
July 28–30, 2000	Conference on Spirituality and Business	Ledgehill, Nova Scotia, Canada
July 12–16, 2000	Art and Business Interdisciplinary Conference	Castle Borl, Slovenia
June 20–23, 2000	The New Soul @ Work Business Conference	Silver Star Mountain Resort, Vernon, British Columbia

June 18–23, 2000	The 46th Annual Creative Problem Solving Institute, CPSI 2000	University of Massachusetts, Amherst, MA
April, June, August, October, and December 2000	Navigating Organizational Change and Transformation in the 21st Century	
June 4–6, 2000	Going Public with Spirituality in Work and Higher Education	
May 3–5, 2000	The Power Paradigm . . . The Emergence of the Corporate Soul	
April 27–30, 2000	Spirituality and Governance: Reuniting the Spirit of America	Washington, DC
April 26–30, 2000	The Art and Mastery of Facilitation: Worlds of Change	Toronto
March 22–24, 2000	Third International Symposium on Spirituality in Business	Babson College
October 14–16, 1999	First Annual Gathering of The International Alliance for Spirit at Work	Rancho Encantado, Santa Fe, NM
September 30–October 3, 1999	Renaissance in the New Millennium	Sunrise Ranch, Loveland, CO
September 22–24, 1999	Heart of Business Conference	Austin, Texas
Fall 1999	International Conference on Spirit at Work	Guatemala

- *Acceptance of diversity.*
  One needs to be accepting of other people's paths or lack of them, without judging the person or the path. Conference sessions have attracted people from a variety of religions and having a variety of spiritual beliefs. It is important for the group to accept the variety of beliefs, and to honor the contributions of each.
- *Avoiding hero worship and self-aggrandizement.*
  One needs to be aware of, and to avoid, the temptation to feel self-important because she or he has found certain answers or had certain experiences—or to think someone else is somehow better for having found certain answers or had certain experiences.

The most important lessons I have learned in exploring the world of spirit at work are as follows:

1. Identify what one is truly called to do (one's dharma) and pursue it with passion.
2. Be respectful of other people and the path they are on.
3. Emotions and intuition are equally as useful and valuable as intellect.
4. The most important principle is to stay in balance.

REFERENCES

Association for Spirit at Work. (2001a). Research bibliography: http://www.spiritatwork.com/research/research.htm#biblio (January 2002).
———. (2001b). Scheduled conferences: http://www.fourgateways.com/newsletr/confer.htm (January 2002).
Biberman, J., and A. Alkhafaji, eds. (1997). "Business Research Yearbook: Global Business Perspectives." *Proceedings of the Ninth Annual International Conference of the International Academy of Business Disciplines*, vol. 44. Orlando, FL; Slippery Rock, PA: International Academy of Business Disciplines, April 10–13, 1997.
Biberman, J., and M. Whitty, guest eds. (1999a). "Spirituality in Organizations," Part I. *Journal of Organizational Change Management* 12, no. 3. West Yorkshire, UK: MCB University Press.
———, guest eds. (1999b). "Spirituality in Organizations," Part II. *Journal of Organizational Change Management* 12, no. 4. West Yorkshire, UK: MCB University Press.
Biberman, J., and M. Whitty, eds. (2000). *Work and Spirit: A Reader of New Spiritual Paradigms for Organizations.* Scranton, PA: University of Scranton Press.
Boje, D. (2000). "Another View: Approaches to the Study of Spiritual Capitalism." In *Work and Spirit: A Reader of New Spiritual Paradigms for Organizations*, ed. J. Biberman and M.D. Whitty. Scranton, PA: University of Scranton Press, xxv–xxxii.
Neal, J.A.; L. Robbins; J. Biberman; and M.D. Whitty. (1998). "The Soul of Great Teaching—Enspiriting Your Career." Preconference development workshop at the Academy of Management 1998 Meeting, San Diego, CA, August 7–12.

CHAPTER 29

OPERATIONAL INTEGRITY

The Gateway to Workplace Harmony and Velocity

KATHLYN T. HENDRICKS AND C. GAY HENDRICKS

The word *integrity* appears in most companies' vision and mission statements. New employees are expected to measure up to the company's integrity standard. Testimonial dinners often extol the recipient's stellar integrity. And when a problem occurs, everybody claims the high moral ground of superior integrity. Yet, no one seems to know how to define or develop integrity.

Our professional and personal passion springs from a lifelong study of the root meaning of integrity, which is wholeness. We have come to understand integrity not as a measure of good-and-bad or right-and-wrong, but an energetic thermostat that gives accurate, current feedback about the organization's creative juice and problem-solving capacity. We have interviewed the top executives of many of the companies who advocate integrity and asked them, "What does integrity mean in the day-to-day life of your organization? How will people know if they are operating in integrity or not? If they are not operating in integrity, what impact does that lapse have on your communication, working alliances, or bottom line?" There appears to be a chasm between the intention and the practice of integrity. For example, the CEO of one of the United States' largest companies couldn't verbalize a working definition of integrity, although the word is a cornerstone of their mission statement. Organizations seem to lack an operational understanding of the integrity skills that give teams, colleagues, and executives the freedom and intellectual momentum to produce breakthrough innovations and resolve the unexpected roadblocks that always arise.

Spirituality flows from the source-spring of integrity and withers without that source. We define spirituality as the quest to find and feel the moving sensations in your body that your mind interprets as connecting you to the cosmos and to other people. So in business, no matter what people are selling to each other, they are also seeking to feel and exchange those sensations. Spirituality cannot flourish in the absence of integrity because the potential spiritual energy of individuals and synergy of groups drains away in power struggles, blame, mistrust, and withholding. In contrast, when organizations stand on a base of integrity, relationships, vision, and creative innovation blossom. Dramas of inclusion and exclusion, replays of old family dramas, and nostalgia about past triumphs and defeats make a poor but common substitute for wholeness and connection. Speculations aside, few practices are actually circulated about how to cultivate the presence of spirit through integrity.

Integrity opens the gate to spirit by acknowledging that we are all connected at a microscopic and macrocosmic level. Yasutani Roshi said that the basic delusion of humanity is to suppose that I am here and you are out there. The fascinating brain research summarized by Drs. Lewis, Amini, and Lannon (2000) confirms humans' lifelong interconnection. "Adults remain social animals: they continue to require a source of stabilization outside themselves. That open-loop design [humans *require* input from others to keep internal systems functioning well] means that in some important ways, people cannot be stable on their own—not should or shouldn't be, but *can't* be" (86). In other words, our very well-being, thinking style, creative output, and harmonious interaction cannot function effectively without nurturing contact with others. Stabilization occurs through what the authors call "limbic resonance." This flow of information between emotional brains actually allows us to share another person's experience and to support each other's well-being through the quality of our exchanges.

We may agree intellectually with the poet Donne's assessment, "No man is an island." However, most people can't truly see or feel their resonance with others because they are seeing through an eons-long mind-body split. People influence each other in thousands of subtle and compounded ways, most of which are so minuscule that only split-frame films can detect them. Emotions, moods, and attitudes are contagious. For example, conversational tones ripple through the organization via the grapevine code that lets everyone know in a matter of minutes the boss's mood or who's about to get fired. Most organizations do not yet realize what Native Americans have held for generations: "There is nowhere in the world to spit."

When we consult for organizations, the first area we examine is their integrity foundation (Hendricks and Ludeman 1996). We have studied whole-body, whole-brain learning for thirty years and have heard thousands of experiences that confirm our theory. When people operate from integrity, personal and professional well-being accelerates tremendously.

The four legs of integrity stand on tangible skills that can be developed with practice: Authentic Speaking and Resonant Listening, Healthy Responsibility, Emotional Literacy, and Impeccable Agreements. We will discuss the problems that arise from lack of skill in each area and the results of reformed wholeness, or integrity.

Organizations perpetuate "The Old Corporate Story" (see Figure 29.1) by skewing the balance of information flow between the cognitive mind and the emotional mind. By favoring the cognitive mind in business, organizations suffer from three types of "thought incoherence" that the physicist David Bohm (1995) has identified:

- Thought denies that it participates in creating thoughts. In other words, thought is the Wizard of Oz saying, "Pay no attention to the man behind the curtain" while making up the illusions that people consider solid and real.
- Thought eventually stops tracking reality and "just goes." For example, getting hold of an assumption about a colleague's motive snowballs into competitive maneuvering that remains under the surface like a burr.
- Thought establishes its own standard of reference for fixing the very problems it contributed to creating. Rather like the Army Corps of Engineers attempting to control the Mississippi River, thought's standards of reality can't control the rich emotional wisdom that weaves through all our decisions.

These systemic thinking errors fuel beliefs that reinforce a sterile view of human potential. For example, a common corporate belief asserts that anyone is interchangeable, especially in the human resources arena. We have heard incredible stories, such as of the man who arrived on Monday morning to find his office locked and his belongings stacked in the hall with his termination notice on top.

More problematic in The Old Corporate Story are the problems that arise by not utilizing each

Figure 29.1 **Example of The Old Corporate Story**

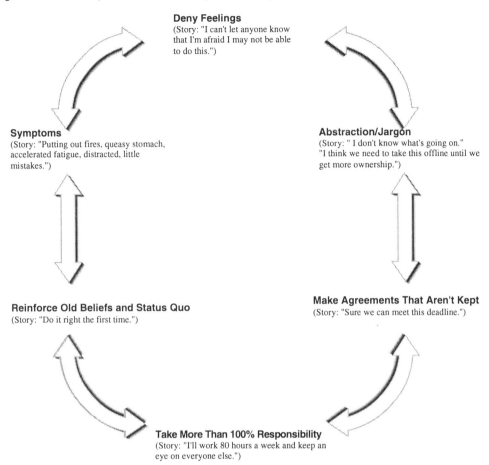

Deny Feelings
(Story: "I can't let anyone know
that I'm afraid I may not be able
to do this.")

Symptoms
(Story: "Putting out fires, queasy stomach,
accelerated fatigue, distracted, little
mistakes.")

Abstraction/Jargon
(Story: " I don't know what's going on."
"I think we need to take this offline until we
get more ownership.")

Reinforce Old Beliefs and Status Quo
(Story: "Do it right the first time.")

Make Agreements That Aren't Kept
(Story: "Sure we can meet this deadline.")

Take More Than 100% Responsibility
(Story: "I'll work 80 hours a week and keep an
eye on everyone else.")

person's full responsibility. In the current model of responsibility, energy is spent in competition rather than cooperation. Colleagues defend territory and dig their heels in rather than negotiate willingly. Coworkers hide possible obstacles and roadblocks to success, such as pertinent information in a strategy meeting. Resources are considered scarce, so managers battle within a limited view of possibility. These operating beliefs lead to turf battles, secrets, gossiping, and symptomatic solutions such as putting out fires.

Operational integrity thrives on change. As organizations reform their wholeness, tangible benefits emerge from the personal to the company level. Personally, staff feels healthy and energetic throughout the day rather than stressed and pressured. Individuals know and utilize a reliable feedback system for assessing their skills. Professionally, people transform their relationship to time, becoming effective, flexible, and adaptable. More interactions involve cooperation rather than stonewalling or defending territory. Collaboration replaces competition, and openness to change invigorates the whole system. Organizationally, each person builds group synergy by contributing unique qualities and skills. The organization designs change rather than chasing it with crisis management. Communication creates synergy rather than power struggle. Higher-quality products and better bottom lines flow from harmony rather than fear.

We have had many executives challenge this model as "pie-in-the-sky," hopelessly idealistic, laughably out of touch with reality. We counter that the old corporate model is not only corrupt, but is bankrupting our health, our families, and our future by ignoring the enormous contribution of the human spirit that speaks through integrity. We have committed to living and teaching in wholeness. We invite you to examine and experiment with these skills (see Table 29.1).

AUTHENTIC SPEAKING AND RESONANT LISTENING—THE MYTHS

One common caveat in business is to hold your cards close to the vest, to never let the "enemy" know what you are really thinking. This strategy is said to preserve a market edge by keeping the competition in the dark. Another commonly held myth is that only fools actually tell the truth to other businesspeople. In a recent seminar, we asked the participants to write their favorite excuses for withholding from others on the flip chart. Here is a partial list:

Reasons for Withholding

1. I don't want to hurt your feelings.
2. This is not important.
3. You won't be able to handle it.
4. This is not the right time.
5. I'll tell you when I figure it out.
6. I feel dumb (foolish) (embarrassed) telling you.
7. I should be able to handle this myself.
8. You must be tired of hearing the same thing.
9. You don't share, so I won't either.
10. This is not worth arguing about.
11. I'll tell you later.
12. If I tell you, it will create a whole new problem.
13. I'm afraid you will get mad (sad) (afraid).
14. Right now you are in a bad mood (tired, etc.).
15. You're in a good mood, and I don't want to bring you down.
16. Now is not a convenient time.
17. I shouldn't dwell on the negative.
18. I'm afraid of what you might say.
19. I don't want to face the truth.
20. I'll tell you when we are alone.
21. I'm figuring out how to word it so I don't push your buttons.
22. You won't like me when you hear it.
23. Nothing can be done about it. It's just the way I am.
24. I'm hoping it will go away by itself.
25. I'll lose something if I tell you.
26. I'm defective; it's just another weird thing about me.
27. I've got too much to do.
28. I missed the right opportunity to tell you.
29. I feel exposed and vulnerable.
30. It has to be perfect!
31. I'll get yelled at.

Table 29.1

Four Pillars of Integrity

1. Emotional literacy
   - To know what you are actually feeling when you feel it
   - To discriminate between different feelings and sensations, for example, between hunger and fear
   - To locate feelings accurately in your body
   - To know the true source of your feelings
   - To be able to talk about feelings congruently in such a way that other people understand
   - To be able to focus attention on feelings until they are no longer an issue
2. Authentic speaking and resonant listening
   - To communicate what is going on in a way that is unarguable
   - To communicate the details of what is going on in any given moment in a way that invites wonder and ... that does not blame anyone
   - To take responsibility for communication until the other person comprehends
   - To be the source and initiator of authenticity in any situation
   - To know the body sensations and experiences associated with authenticity and those associated with withholding
   - To be able to communicate authenticity under duress
   - To listen for accuracy, with empathy, and to promote mutual creativity
3. Impeccable agreements
   - To keep the agreements you make
   - To refrain from making agreements that you do not want to make
   - To select agreements that you do want to make
   - To know how to change agreements if they are not working
   - To come to the realm of making agreements from seeing that keeping agreements increases aliveness rather than seeing that the world is making you do something
4. Healthy responsibility
   - To know how to take 100 percent responsibility/reliably
   - To shift from defensiveness to learning
   - To actively promote and inspire 100 percent responsibility in others
   - To shift readily and easily from blame to wonder

32. If I hold out long enough, it won't matter.
33. I feel guilty about it.
34. Everything will unravel if I tell you about this.
35. I don't have the energy to deal with this.
36. You'll reject me if I tell you.

When people do not know how to speak authentically to each other, words wound. In business settings especially, associates sling words with deadly precision. Here are some examples we have overheard:

- "That is the stupidest idea so far this year!"
- "You always ignore my suggestions."
- "No-brainer—must have been invented for you."
- "Who's responsible for this mess?"
- "You planning on coming in when the rest of us do any time this year?"

Many organizations operate from the perception that if people acknowledge how things actually are, they make it all worse. The ostrich approach governs many businesses and prevents them from navigating change successfully. As Yogi Berra said, "If you don't know where you're going, you will wind up somewhere else."

When people cannot be authentic with each other, they retreat behind masks or roles, which we call personas. Corporate interactions then devolve to popular persona interlocks, such as the Policy Police and the Whiner, or the Supercompetent and the Bumbler. Each company with whom we've consulted has quickly identified their key personas and the predictable, persona-driven bogs they produce.

Spiritually starved businesspeople also downplay the power of listening and relegate it to the dreaded "touchy-feely" garbage heap where many innovations eventually land. In the Vice-Presidents' Institute that Motorola holds for new officers, the most common feedback that colleagues gave to the new Vice Presidents concerned their poor listening skills. New VP's were astounded to hear that others found them obstinate critics, heavy nonverbal signalers (watch checking, sighing, finger drumming), and compulsive interrupters. As another example, two executives in a team building who had worked together for twelve years were unaware that their children played on the same soccer team until they listened to each other describe their issues in balancing home and work life. Colleagues cannot deeply resonate with each other, build on each other's unique contributions, or create synergy to build streamlined innovation from within the myths of inauthenticity.

AUTHENTIC SPEAKING AND RESONANT LISTENING—THE SKILLS

- *To communicate what is going on in a way that is unarguable*
- *To communicate the details of what is going on in any given moment in a way that invites wonder and that does not blame anyone*
- *To listen for accuracy, with empathy, and to promote mutual creativity*
- *To take responsibility for communication until the other person comprehends*
- *To be the source and initiator of authenticity in any situation*
- *To know the body sensations and experience associated with authenticity and those associated with withholding*
- *To be able to communicate authentically under duress*

There is a great deal of research on the health benefits of open communication. The pioneering work of James Pennebaker (1990), among others, has demonstrated a clear connection between authenticity and increased well-being. His research demonstrates that facing, feeling, and expressing "what's so," especially negative feelings, has a tremendous strengthening impact on a person's immune system and overall health. This research contradicts one of the central myths in business: keep your opinions and especially your feelings close to your chest and don't disclose your authentic experience. One of Pennebaker's most intriguing experiments (Spera, Buhrfeind, and Pennebaker 1993) involved a group of long-term, middle-aged businessmen who had lost their jobs due to downsizing. One group of men wrote about their feelings for fifteen minutes on five consecutive days; the control group wrote about trivial items; and a third group engaged in a time-management activity in which they meticulously recorded their job-seeking actions. In a follow-up survey eight months later, the group who had "opened up" about their job loss were more than twice as likely to have found new full-time employment as those in the other two groups. Additionally, these men got their jobs much faster than the other groups.

Most businesspeople confuse authentic speaking with using words as weapons. Or businesspeople confuse clarity with corporate jargon. We can remember how long it took to learn the business jargon that passes for communication in many organizations: "no-brainer," "value-added," "sending the data to the VP of HR," "bottom line," "real time," etc.

In fact, *to communicate what is going on in a way that is unarguable*, which is *to communicate the details of what is going on in any given moment in a way that invites wonder and that does not blame anyone*, promotes connection more quickly than any single communication skill. Authentic speaking brings clarity and economy to conversations, negotiations, and conflict resolution.

So what would this kind of speaking sound like? Here are some examples from our consultations:

Speaking about body sensations:
- "I have butterflies in my stomach."
- "My head feels caught in a vise grip."
- "When you mentioned the report, I held my breath."

Speaking about core feelings:
- "I'm scared . . . sad . . . angry . . . excited."

Speaking about specific thoughts/imaginings/interpretations:
- "I was just imagining you jumping in and taking over."
- "I interpreted your lack of comment as a go-ahead signal."
- "My listening was compromised by the thought, 'You don't like my idea.'"

Speaking about familiar patterns and experiences:
- "When I hurry, I notice I become short with people."
- "Every time the VP of sales comes to our office, my mind goes blank."
- "I realize I have difficulty listening when I feel afraid."

Executives from Bell Labs who learned to communicate unarguably with each other noticed immediately that conversations took less time, produced more specific results, and led to clear agreements that promoted stronger interdepartmental liaisons. Ultimately, they realized that authentic speaking and listening brought new products to market more quickly and directly influenced their bottom line.

To take responsibility for communication until the other person comprehends stands in contrast with the body shop approach that many people take in their communication: "I said it perfectly clearly; you just didn't get it." Or, "what about 'deadline' didn't you understand?" If people learn to look and listen for the impact of their words, they build deep rapport and partnership *while* exchanging the facts and figures to get the job done.

Business partners can best take responsibility for communication by *listening for accuracy, with empathy*, and to promote mutual creativity. Most executives we've worked with think they are good listeners. The feedback from their colleagues and associates suggests otherwise, that most businesspeople are simply waiting for the other person to stop speaking so they can voice an opinion or conclude the item. As one of our friends and consulting colleagues, Ron Bynum, has said, "A conclusion is a place where you got tired of listening and abandoned wonder."

Most people can develop deeper listening skills simply by generating curiosity about what the other person is saying. This skill requires the ability to say, "I don't know," or, "Hmm, I wonder if you have a different perspective that could enrich this discussion." It requires a level of generosity that is squashed by the level of "normal" withholding. Generous listening involves shifting into the other person's world over and over. It acknowledges the need to let go of being right again and again, to know that "we do not see things as they are, we see them as we are. We do not hear things as they are, we hear them as we are" (The Talmud). People can learn to listen, and those who have, say it is the most powerful tool they know.

To be the source and initiator of authenticity in any situation is a senior communication skill that takes practice and commitment to master. Genuine flow and synergy of spirit in business depend on people stepping into authenticity voluntarily and completely. We call this "playing full out," and consider this play the height of cocreativity. The big fun comes from stepping into the unknown armed only with what is real, your experience and your ability to participate in the present interaction. The passivity often rewarded in business was illustrated brilliantly by the recent film *Being John Malkovich*, when the hero steps off the elevator for a job interview on floor 7½. Here everyone stoops, compressing their full height and potential, and distorted postures end in rampant miscommunication.

To know the body sensations and experience associated with authenticity and those associated with withholding locates the speaker accurately. In other words, if you know your own body map of sensations and inner experiences that are associated with withholding, you are much less likely to engage in accusations and power struggles with others in your communications. You are much more likely to say, "Hmm, what am I missing here? What communication am I editing?" For example, working partners often withhold information that they suspect will trouble their colleagues, often using the excuse that they don't want to muddy the waters or create needless upset. The actual reason that truth is withheld is to avoid dealing with the consequences of the disclosure. For example, imagine the initial uproar that might greet:

- "I didn't finish the report and took a shortcut by importing the data that marketing said was nearly foolproof."
- "I didn't agree with your conclusions but waited until after the meeting to gather a group of supporters from the seventeenth floor."
- "I started flirting and dancing quite close with your husband after you left the office party."
- "I made up the statistics."

In contrast, if people can discern when they are withholding and speak something authentic instead, huge icebergs that have been bludgeoning the organization begin to melt, and the flow of interpersonal harmony and creative exchange replace frozen impasses. Communicating an experience that has been held back is often very simple. Listening through the keyhole of someone skilled at communicating withholds might reveal something like this:

- "I drifted off and missed what you just said."
- "I just noticed I was holding my breath. Behind that was a judgment about your proposal. Basically, I disagree with your assumptions and want to find a place where we might meet."
- "I noticed your forehead wrinkling and remembered your critical feedback last quarter. I was shrinking down in my chair hoping you wouldn't notice me."
- "I got confused in the middle of the last paragraph. Could you summarize the point again, please?"
- "Others seem to know what the agreement is, but I lost something from the contract to the discussion. What is our next step?"
- "I've been needing to stretch for a while. I'd like to get up and move around while we continue."

To be able to communicate authentically under duress saves time, energy, and health. This skill evolves from choosing authenticity rather than defensiveness. Even under the gun, the person grounded in integrity will say what is true rather than what is expedient. In our experience, the presence of this skill also reflects a deep, long-term commitment, since duck-and-cover has been rewarded in most organizations.

A person committed to authenticity in speaking and listening is gloriously free. In their presence others feel deeply seen and appreciated. Even if their exchange takes just a few minutes, the resonance level bonds each person more closely. The authentic communicator is not pushed and pulled inside by a multitude of conflicting sensory data. Instead, he or she gives full, undivided attention internally and to the other. They are not doing anything else but what they are doing, and that level of presence inspires and ignites everyone in their paths.

HEALTHY RESPONSIBILITY—THE MYTHS

"Okay, who's responsible for this mess?"

"All right, since I'm responsible for the project, I'll stay tonight and clean up the data."

Sound familiar? Most people confuse responsibility with blame and/or burden. Turf wars over a project are legendary in most companies and foster a sense of responsibility that is linked with alliances, power struggles, and enormous expenditures of energy in blaming and counterblaming. The atmosphere of distrust promoted by these misunderstandings is palpable in many companies. Add the ever-escalating litigation costs promoted by blame- and victim-based structures of responsibility, and you can account for much of the misery and stagnation in organizations.

Here are some symptoms of responsibility imbalances in business that we have observed. See if you recognize any:

Taking less than healthy, 100 percent responsibility:

- Coping quietly, not speaking up when affected.
- Reading mail in meetings you can't stand.
- "Forgetting" deadlines and agreements.
- Blaming others for problems that arise.
- "Nobody told me what to do!"
- "People don't approach me."
- Putting up with ineffective meetings and interactions rather than telling the truth about them and participating in improving them.
- Complaining.

Taking more than healthy, 100 percent responsibility:

- "I'll make you take responsibility for this issue."
- "He was out sick, but I know how to enter the data so I'll just stay late."
- "I'll call everyone on the team to remind them of the deadline."
- Doing others' work for them because you can "do it better."
- Taking over, getting resentful with the workload, giving up.
- Consistently working more hours a week.

Ostrich moves:

- "I was hoping they'd take a piece."
- A manager doesn't take a strong stand when he/she has a strong opinion from the rationale that this stand would cut off others' input.

- "I hold meeting after meeting where I say 'This is open up time' and nobody talks, so I'm not holding any more meetings."
- "Let's have a task force."

Why don't people take 100 percent responsibility? We have noticed that some central issues repeat in most organizations. First, many people create false equations about responsibility. One approach says, if I don't take responsibility but come up with a good excuse, that move equals taking responsibility. Another popular strategy is, "If my strategy isn't working, I'll do what I'm doing more forcefully," equals taking responsibility. In organizations, as in personal relationships, most people prefer to be right and make others wrong rather than to wonder. Most companies promote responsibility problems by not exacting a cost for taking less than 100 percent responsibility. For example, people who consistently come late to meetings (with a good excuse or story, of course) are brought up to date by others. Taking more than 100 percent responsibility is rewarded in many organizations by their compensation plans.

At a deeper level, many people confuse responsibility with "good" and "bad" rather than feedback toward taking healthy, 100 percent responsibility. Bottom line, most people confuse genuine responsibility with blame or burden rather than wonder.

HEALTHY RESPONSIBILITY—THE SKILLS

- *To know how to take 100 percent responsibility/reliably*
- *To shift from defensiveness to openness to learning*
- *To actively promote and inspire 100 percent responsibility in others*
- *To shift readily and easily from blame to wonder*

To know how to take 100 percent responsibility/reliably is the central skill that can shift a business from the bogs to the heights. In order to take 100 percent responsibility, most people need some education about what healthy responsibility looks and feels like. First, responsibility is an action you take, rather than a thing or a point on a graph. Taking responsibility happens over and over during each day as associates face new situations where reliable actions drive the success of the company. Responsibility is a dynamic feedback loop, not a static concept. Taking responsibility involves adjusting actions when you are operating out of more or less than 100 percent responsibility. Just as an airplane gets to where it is going by being off course and adjusting 90 percent of the time, you can take responsibility successfully by noticing the results of your actions and adjusting when you get feedback that your responsibility gyroscope is off kilter.

When you *shift from defensiveness to openness to learning*, you consciously move from blame or burden to ownership. No matter what the situation, you wonder, "What might this have to do with me?" Taking responsibility involves noticing the connections between events. For example, a team member may say during a meeting, "I've noticed that in the last three staff meetings, half the team has been late. I wonder what that is about? I know I've been tempted to continue working on this project deadline rather than come on time." The focus shifts from whose fault to what happened, from finger pointing to what needs to be done.

To shift readily and easily from blame to wonder: This shift has great power. Most people need practice to create wonder rather than blame. If you surf past any current news channel, you'll see a banner saying something like, "Who's to Blame?" We have yet to see a banner that says, "What Needs to Be Done?" Taking responsibility does not mean blaming you or others, which can contribute to stress and defensive maneuvers. If you take responsibility for an old pattern, blaming is an unnecessary addition. You can simply acknowledge what happened, accept the feelings you felt and your interpretations of the event. This acknowledgment frees additional energy to discover what you really want.

For example, a department head at Motorola was embroiled in a turf battle with another department head who just irritated him no matter what he did. In the middle of one of our responsibility activities, he suddenly remembered an incident on the basketball court in college. His coach had been giving him feedback that he had ignored; consequently, he got dropped abruptly from the team. The manager realized that his colleague reminded him of his coach. He had been hearing all his colleague's suggestions through the "coach" filter of failing and being rejected. When he breathed with his feelings about this discovery, he quickly shifted his relationship to his colleague and was able to form an alliance.

Here are some tangible examples of taking healthy responsibility. Imagine the impact on your business if people acted in the following ways:

- Communicating with other colleagues rather than bottling up;
- Sharing discoveries about the connections between actions and results;
- Assuming that everyone can take 100 percent responsibility and allowing them to do so;
- Rewarding keeping of agreements, for example, with appreciation;
- Forming compensation plans where people are rewarded for taking 100 percent responsibility rather than 3000 percent.

Here are some questions that we recommend for developing responsibility skills. They can be used in any situation where people are wondering what 100 percent responsibility might look like.

- What do you notice about your contribution to this situation?
- What might the hidden agenda or payoff be in the way you are participating in this issue?
- What is familiar about my actions, feelings, and responses in this situation?
- How might this dynamic be different if everyone took 100 percent responsibility?
- What can you do differently in this situation to create what you really want?
- How can you look at this situation differently where you participate as the architect or designer?

EMOTIONAL LITERACY—THE MYTHS

How much does it cost to hide your feelings at work? The health costs borne by people's unbalanced lives may be incalculable, but the body of scientific evidence is growing. Oulette, Maddi and Kobasa's research (1984), among others, has firmly established the link between stress and illness. Businesspeople operate under incredible levels of stress and often cannot even take time to deal with the resulting illness. For example, one executive from Motorola had to run his department from his bed for two months when his back went out. The stunted emotional life of millions of businesspeople continues to stymie consultants and support staff who attempt to point out the obvious connection between head and body.

Every second, a massive information exchange is occurring in your body. Imagine each of these messenger systems possessing a specific tone, humming a signature tune, rising and falling, waxing and waning, binding and unbinding, and if we could hear this body music with our ears, then the sum of these sounds would be the music that we call the emotions. . . . We can no longer think of the emotions as having less validity than physical, material substance, but instead must see them as cellular signals that are involved in the process of translating information into physical reality, literally transforming mind into matter. (Pert 1999)

Emotions have been seen as the "soft stuff" for decades, if not generations. In many organizations, showing an emotion is the kiss of death. Why is the official line so anti-feeling? Emotions can't be controlled as easily as graphs and flow charts. The comparatively (to the cognitive mind) messy world of emotions can be frightening if you don't have a map to the territory and a way to navigate all the signals swirling in and around you. In the name of logic and efficiency, terrible wounds are inflicted on business associates daily. Shoes are banged on desks. People get yelled at vigorously enough that spit flies, yet carry on as if everything were normal. The unspoken agreement for most businesses is that feelings get left at the door. They don't belong in the data-driven world of corporations.

The "special feeling" problem also impedes deep connection at work. Most people with whom we have consulted have been mystified and/or terrified by a specific emotion. Anger, sadness, or fear (not to mention the non-PC world of sexual feelings) gets closeted if people haven't learned emotional fluency. For example, in many families only Dad could be openly angry. Children had to go to their rooms until they could behave nicely. This "don't feel" message prevents growing individuals from learning the power of anger to create clear boundaries, to signal social trespasses, or to combat genuine unfairness. Compartmentalization and illiteracy stultifies emotional flow and deep limbic resonance, the true language of the spirit. Without emotional flow at work, people get sick, discouraged, and flat. Most people don't know what they are feeling when they feel an emotion and where those sensations are located in their bodies.

EMOTIONAL LITERACY—THE SKILLS

- *To know what you are actually feeling when you feel it*
- *To discern the difference between feelings and sensations, for example, between hunger and fear*
- *To locate feelings accurately in your body*
- *To know the accurate source of your feelings*
- *To be able to talk about feelings congruently in such a way that other people understand the communication*
- *To be able to focus nonjudgmental attention on feelings until they are no longer an issue*

To know what you are actually feeling when you feel it gives continuity to the dozens of interactions that working people experience every day. We have heard thousands of people describe the confusion caused by ignoring or overriding emotional signals from others and from themselves. When people are present with emotions as they occur, they wield a mighty tool, our inheritance from thousands of generations of savvy ancestors. Those who listen to their emotional voices move more easily into contact and contribution and catch drifts before they form rifts.

Through the research of Gary Schwartz (1990), George Solomon (1985), David McClelland (1985), and others, we learn that ignoring bodily sensations and feelings damages the heart. In contrast, expressing authentic feelings, even so-called "negative" ones, strengthens the immune system. Our whole-body learning approach allows people to build an emotional vocabulary from simple identification and exploration of sensations and other inner experiences.

To discern the difference between feelings and sensations, for example, between hunger and fear creates a freer field of choice. How many meetings have been derailed by the inability to discern between anger and tiredness? How many projects have careened off-track from the confusion between excitement and fear? How much momentum gets lost every week in this confusion? For example, we have personally sat through many off-site meetings where teams literally ate up their creativity.

Cancer research by Lydia Temoshok, a psychologist at UCSF, demonstrated that cancer patients who kept emotions such as anger suppressed (were unaware of their anger) recovered more slowly. She found that the immune systems in those emotionally aware patients were stronger and their tumors smaller (Temoshok and Fox 1984).

To be able to talk about feelings congruently in such a way that other people understand the communication:

> My research has shown me that when emotions are expressed—which is to say that the biochemicals that are the substrate of emotion are flowing freely—all systems are united and made whole. When emotions are repressed, denied, not allowed to be whatever they may be, our network pathways get blocked, stopping the flow of the vital feel-good, unifying chemicals that run both our biology and our behavior. (Pert 1999, 273)

If people know what they are feeling when they are feeling it, they are much better equipped to communicate in a way that promotes emotional resonance and connection. If a person can learn to say, "When you said _____, I felt _____," trust, clarity, and respect result. For example, "When you said the deadline got moved up, I felt scared," will produce a totally different result than stonewalling. Businesses preserve an illusion that people don't know what is going on. In fact, people have to work really hard *not* to know. One of our favorite bumper stickers is, "What are you pretending not to know?"

To be able to focus nonjudgmental attention on feelings until they are no longer an issue: The businesspeople with whom we have worked are very sharp and quick. They grasp concepts fast, even in the emotional realm, then say, "Okay, what do I DO about it?" The paradox of feelings lies in nondoing. Nothing needs to be done with feelings. Feelings are like rivers in the blood that simply need attention, and need simple attention. We teach our students and associates how to give nonjudgmental attention to feelings. They find that feelings flow through, leaving clarity and increased vitality in their wake.

IMPECCABLE AGREEMENTS—THE MYTHS

The most common myth about agreements is that they are actually made and kept. Most people assume that they keep agreements pretty well, except . . . when they are pressed for time, or something important comes up, and so forth. If Woody Allen is truc in saying that being a grownup is just like junior high, only with money, that dynamic shows up most with agreements. How people make and keep agreements will reflect the strength of the other pillars of integrity. *Agreement assessment is the quickest way to diagnose the health of your business.* If people are practicing conscious agreement skills, your business will hum. If not, you can bet that blaming, withholding, lack of listening, and all kinds of miscommunication are also happening on every floor. In our informal surveys, we have determined that a certain percentage of people reliably keep agreements. In other words, they do what they say they are going to do, and they don't do what they say they are not going to do. Guess what this percentage is.*

Why don't people keep their agreements, despite the obvious costs when agreements are broken? In our observation, most people have never gotten over being told what to do and not do with their bodily functions by big authority figures. They tend to confuse business associates with these archaic figures and rebel or give in rather than engaging consciously in making choices. For example, one of our consulting colleagues, Sandra Hill, said that she had never encountered a business team that could make effective decisions as a group, much less develop a reliable protocol for decision-making. Why? Because people get jammed up in power struggles based on their unresolved conflicts with past authority figures.

IMPECCABLE AGREEMENTS—THE SKILLS

- *To keep the agreements you make*
- *To not make agreements that you don't want to make*
- *To know how to change agreements if they are not working*
- *To come to the realm of making agreements with the perspective that keeping agreements increases vitality, rather than viewing the world as making you do something*

To keep the agreements you make sounds simple but is fiendishly difficult for most people to master. *To not make agreements that you don't want to make* counters the "oh sure" problem. "Oh, sure, I can handle that." "Oh, sure, we can fit that into the schedule." "Oh, sure, no problem." When people carefully consider whether they are actually willing to follow up an agreement with action, the entire problem of "buy-in" evaporates. Discussions continue until all parties reach agreement. The time expended on gathering agreement up front looks expensive until you calculate the costs of broken agreements, or even more commonly, fuzzy agreements: missed deadlines, over- or underproduction, departments charging off in totally different directions, and so on.

To know how to change agreements if they are not working: When we bring up this skill in consultations, the usual response is blank faces or the comment, "I thought once I made an agreement I *have* to do what I said." As we all know, drift happens. Any number of unexpected events can alter agreements made in the morning. The ability to change agreements consciously prevents games of chase (e.g., Who was going to do that? Where's the report that was supposed to be on my desk?) and other unconscious methods of changing agreements, such as forgetting, overriding, or ignoring.

The methodology for changing an agreement follows a simple map. Go back through the other pillars of integrity. Open up to any feelings about the current agreement and what you want to change. Tell the truth about your experience. Listen to the other parties' experience and authentic communication. *Then* change the agreement.

To come to the realm of making agreements with the perspective that keeping agreements increases vitality, rather than viewing the world as making you do something: Most people believe that agreements are literally binding. They feel confined and imprisoned by their agreements. The authority confusion mentioned earlier translates into incredibly costly messiness around agreements. If people practiced even a few days of consistently making and keeping conscious

---

*From our surveys, the percentage of people who reliably keep their agreements is 3 percent. Imagine the leap forward in productivity, clarity, and free time that would result from even a slightly higher percentage.

agreements, they would experience enhanced well-being. Feeling more energetic and happier is reinforcing. The practice of conscious agreements leads to knowing your life purpose, taking on meaningful challenges, forming and following a path to what you really want. All these practices increase your vitality and creativity. Suzanne Ouellette's research (Ouellette, Maddi, and Kobasa 1984) underscores a number of physiological and lifestyle markers that are enhanced by being able to make and keep agreements, seek out meaningful challenges, and take healthy responsibility. She calls this combination of traits "hardiness," and finds it composed of: an enhanced sense of healthy responsibility; greeting challenges as an opportunity for growth; and flexibility and adaptability.

The central shift that brings all these skills together is openness to learning. When organizations and their people commit to using each interaction as an opportunity to learn, they can steer toward the organization's goals by choosing openness to learning over and over. The following chart shows you one scale we use to educate clients.

BLAME TO ACCOUNTABILITY SCALE

Accountability is an *action* you take rather than a concept you debate with your colleagues. You consciously move from blame or burden to ownership. Willingness to learn from each moment—as opposed to defending yourself by stonewalling, explaining, justifying, withdrawing, blaming—is the key strategic move that leverages momentum. The great advantage of openness to learning is that you're in charge of it at all times; it's always within your control to shift out of blame into genuine curiosity. This scale was designed to help you make more powerful and rapid shifts into accountability.

High Accountability

+5 Implementing (planning actions, requesting support to follow-up)
e.g., Request feedback about what you could do differently in this situation to create what you really want: "I would really appreciate your direct feedback about ways I can thrive with the changes we're undergoing, especially in . . ."

+4 Taking full responsibility for the issue, the results that were created
e.g., "I see that I've contributed to the confusion about the new configuration in the department by . . ."

+3 Listening generously (able to paraphrase the other person's point of view free of your point of view)
e.g., "I hear you saying that a decision has been made about this issue and that many people have conflicting feelings about it."

+2 Expressing appreciation for the message and the messenger, regardless of delivery
e.g., "Thanks for giving me the heads up on this new timeline so I can start some creative work to meet it."

+1 Genuinely wondering about the issue with an open body posture
e.g., How can I accelerate the velocity in concretely implementing our decisions?

THE KEY TRANSITION MOVE: COMMITTING TO LEARNING:
CHOOSING WONDERING OVER DEFENDING

For example: Could we agree to wonder about this free of our preconceptions? Could we agree to turn this into a learning opportunity rather than fault-finding?

Low Accountability

-1 Showing polite interest outwardly while inwardly clinging to your point of view and/or rehearsing rebuttal
    e.g., mentally planning how to retain all your staff while someone is outlining a cut in personnel
-2 Explaining, interpreting, judging, or going silent
    e.g., withholding the thought, "get to the point already"
    e.g., explaining all the reasons why the new idea couldn't possibly work
-3 Finding fault with the way the message is being delivered
    e.g., "You could have picked a better time, you know."
-4 Blaming someone or something else
    e.g., demanding evidence in a hostile manner
    e.g., "I can't get this goal met because you keep reallocating all my resources."
-5 Creating uproar
    e.g., attacking the messenger, verbally or otherwise
    e.g., enrolling other associates in resisting a change

Research by Schwartz, Jamner and Leigh (1988) supports the vital importance of shifting from defensiveness to openness to learning. Their studies demonstrate the devastating impact of repression on a person's health, in contrast to the significant health boost created by facing and expressing one's experience accurately.

In his groundbreaking work (1990), Peter Senge discusses the devastating effects of defensiveness. Surprisingly, he asserts that defensiveness itself doesn't impede business success. The *concealment* of defensiveness does. For example, disagreeing with a colleague's business proposal is quite common and can be a source of creative innovation. Disguising that disagreement with polite nodding or explanations of the colleague's basic misunderstanding of the business issue sidetrack the company's forward momentum and halt the cocreative synergy of teamwork.

Openness to learning produces vitality in your body/mind, your spirit, and your work. We call that increased vitality ease and flow. What does ease and flow look like, and what does it have to do with bringing spirit to work?

When people practice operational integrity, they raise their thermostat level for experiencing more appreciation, creativity, and collaboration. This expanded state presents a unique problem in human evolution. Human beings are not wired up yet for ease and flow. Survival for millions of years has been based on an ability to suffer, to endure, and to spy the enemy before being spotted. At this point in evolution, humans can choose to actually change their nervous systems to accommodate more joy.

Most people can only sustain a short period of ease and flow before something happens. "Something" in the workplace is often delivered as verbal or nonverbal feedback. For example, you turn in a report that you worked overtime to produce, and your colleague rolls his eyes and sighs. You offer an idea at a meeting; your boss says it's the most ridiculous thing she's ever heard. You're brainstorming with your team and someone across the table leans over to whisper to the person on his left; they both laugh and won't make eye contact with you. Most people have constructed a bunker of maneuvers to defend against these perceived attacks.

In fact, these daily interactions present ongoing opportunities to shift from defensiveness to openness. *The shift is not a one-time event.* We actually call it the shift-and-drift model. We assist clients to see that drifts are a natural part of the business day. Rather than blaming self or others when a drift occurs, we recommend shifting to curiosity and wonder. The shifts described with + numbers on the Blame to Accountability Scale create whole-body, whole-brain states of consciousness. Dan Goleman (1995) made the point that a key health marker is the ability to change states of consciousness by choice. In other words, shifting your perception can shift your whole world.

Here is one example of the impact of openness to learning in the career trajectories of two senior-level executives at Dell Computers. One man was wobbling in the "about to be fired" category. He eagerly embraced the feedback and suggestions he received, brutal as many of them were. He immediately planned and took new actions based on the feedback, and asked for more. In contrast, one of his colleagues, a "golden boy" in one of the European branches, consistently chose to ignore learning opportunities offered by his colleagues and mentors. Within six months, golden boy had lost his job, and the wobbler was heading up a new department.

SUMMARY

People don't need other people; people *require* other people to find their passion and fulfill their purpose. The operational skills of integrity discussed above develop solid and flexible relationships that can propel organizations into this new century. We have never encountered an organizational failure due to lack of technological savvy. We have frequently encountered organizational failure due to lapses of integrity. Integrity can be reformed one skill at a time. Each added skill strengthens the individual and the organization.

Organization and business life can transform dramatically in a short time by building a reliable integrity base. When people operate from authenticity, healthy responsibility, emotional resonance, and reliable agreements, their companies can flourish. Even in the unpredictable fluctuations of local and world events, business can foster wholeness and can return to wholeness when drifts occur. When breakdowns occur, look first to integrity issues. When these are corrected, vision and creativity naturally emerge. When spirit comes to work, work nourishes the spirit.

REFERENCES

Bohm, D. (1995). *The Special Theory of Relativity*. New York: Routledge. Reprint.

Goleman, D. (1995). *Emotional Intelligence*. New York: Bantam.

Hendricks, G., and K. Ludeman. (1996). *The Corporate Mystic*. New York: Bantam.

Jamner, L.; G.E. Schwartz; and H. Leigh. (1988). "The Relationship Between Repressive and Defensive Coping Styles and Monocyte, Eosinophile, and Serum Glucose Levels: Support for the Opioid Peptide Hypothesis of Repression." *Psychosomatic Medicine* 50: 567–575.

Lewis, T.; F. Amini; and R. Lannon. (2000). *A General Theory of Love*. New York: Random House.

McClelland, D.C. (1985). *Human Motivation*. Glenview, IL: Scott Foresman.

Ouellette, S.; S.R. Maddi; and S.C. Kobasa. (1984). *The Hardy Executive: Health Under Stress*. Homewood, IL: Dow Jones-Irwin.

Pennebaker, J.W. (1990). *Opening Up: The Healing Power of Confiding in Others*. New York: William Morrow.

Pert, C. (1999). *Molecules of Emotion: Why You Feel the Way You Feel*. New York: Simon and Schuster.

Schwartz, G.E. (1990). "Psychobiology of Repression and Health: A Systems Approach." In *Repression and*

Dissociation: Implications for Personality Theory, Psychopathology, and Health, ed. J.L. Singer. Chicago: University of Chicago Press.

Senge, P. (1990). *The Fifth Discipline.* New York: Doubleday.

Solomon, G.F. (1985). "The Emerging Field of Psychoneuroimmunology: Hypotheses, Supporting Evidence, and New Directions." *Advances* 2: 6–19.

Spera, S.; E. Buhrfeind; and J.W. Pennebaker. (1993). "Expressive Writing and Coping with Job Loss." Reported in Dreher, H. (1996). *The Immune Power Personality.* New York: Penguin.

Temoshok, L., and B.H. Fox. (1984). "Coping Styles and other Psychosocial Factors Related to Medical Status and to Prognosis in Patients with Cutaneous Malignant Melanoma." In *Impact of Psychoendrocrine Systems in Cancer and Immunity,* ed. G.H. Fox and G.H. Newberry. Toronto: C.J. Hogrefe.

CHAPTER 30

SPIRITUALLY RENEWING OURSELVES AT WORK

Finding Meaning Through Serving

KRISTA KURTH

I don't know what your destiny will be, but one thing I know: the only ones among you who will be really happy are those who have sought and found how to serve.
—*Albert Schweitzer*

Although it may not be apparent how spiritual renewal[1] is relevant to the workplace, there are compelling and objective reasons for exploring such a nontraditional business topic. Even before the new millennium began, increasing numbers of people were sounding a clarion call for spiritual renewal to address the spiritual crisis they believed was taking place in the United States. Evidence suggests that our society has lost its connection with the spiritual foundation necessary to maintain our inherent bond with others and with the divine dimension of life. Given the alienation that tends to accompany such disconnection, and the overemphasis on the material side of life, many people are experiencing a lack of meaning and higher purpose in their lives.

This absence of purpose is especially true in modern organizations that are based on principles of scientific management and the self-interested, materially motivated values of the capitalist economic system. Norman Lear, writing about the state of modern society in "A Call for Spiritual Renewal," asserts that our addiction to the bottom line contributes to our being "estranged from [our] inner life, that invisible wellspring of creativity, morality and faith." He states that, "we need to make room in the culture for a public discussion of our common spiritual life in this desolate modern age. We need to rediscover what is truly sacred" (Lear 1993, CD). Other individuals in the business arena echo Lear's opinion. For instance, both Jack Hawley (1993) and James Autry (1991) advocate making spirituality,[2] love, and service a more serious part of our daily work lives.

The advent of the call for spiritual renewal may be linked, in part, to the baby boomers who, as they reach middle age, are now reassessing their goals and beliefs to discover how they can make their lives more meaningful. It is possible that the large numbers of people in this generation searching for ways to fulfill their potential and contribute something of value to the world have been a factor in the growing interest in this topic. Because most of us spend the majority of our waking hours performing our jobs, it is natural that such self-reflective "coming of age" focuses on finding meaning and fulfillment at work. Some people in particular have discovered that the meaning they are looking for can be found in the process of serving others.

Finding Meaning Through Service

The fact that numerous people find meaning through service is not surprising or new. Most world religions and many well-known philosophers have promoted service to others in alignment with a higher purpose as the means to ultimate fulfillment. Leo Tolstoy wrote that, "The sole meaning of life is to serve humanity." And Chikuro Hiroike (1987), a Japanese scholar who studied the teachings of great sages from various religions, suggested that life's meaning comes from living in accordance with the universal, moral principle of benevolent action; from contributing to the betterment of humankind; and from endeavoring to serve something greater than our own selves in our everyday lives.

Service is a natural expression of spirituality. When we recognize our inherent connection with others, we can be inspired to serve and in the process fulfill a higher purpose and be linked with the deepest part of our selves. This is true whether we are engaged in simple manual labor, like working on an assembly line or waiting tables, or doing something that saves lives, like cancer research. No matter what our job is, if we hold the view of service described below, we can spiritually renew ourselves and find meaning at work.

DEFINING SERVICE

Service is a common term with multiple meanings, ranging from "being in the armed forces" to "rendering homage to God" (Random House 1987). Within businesses and organizations, the term generally refers to customer or volunteer service. The definition of service that forms the foundation of the model presented here is that of *spiritually inspired service.*

While it is similar to customer or volunteer service, in that it involves doing something for others, spiritually inspired service differs significantly in its source of motivation. Whereas businesses often aspire to "better service" as a strategy for getting or retaining customers, or as a means of increasing market share, spiritually inspired service carries no such agenda and is inspired by love and spiritual experience. When we express spiritually inspired service, we feel deeply moved to enhance the long-term welfare of others and, in doing so, we free ourselves from the desire for personal gain. In fact, spiritually inspired service is less about engaging in a particular activity than it is about cultivating a way of being—an intentional presence, grounded in an awareness of Ultimate Reality—that moves us to put our love into action to serve humanity. Spiritually inspired service is *selfless action, inspired and actuated by love and the intent to contribute to the highest good of all, with no immediate concern for personal gain.*

Many major religions and some philosophies have set forth ideas of service, as shown in Table 30.1 on the following page, as a way to achieve deep individual happiness and a means of transforming organizations.

THE ESSENCE OF SPIRITUALLY INSPIRED SERVICE: KEY CHARACTERISTICS

The common attributes in the definitions shown in the table point to the essential nature of spiritually inspired service and distinguish it from secularly motivated service. In its ideal form, spiritually inspired service can be identified by three characteristics.

1. *Spiritually inspired service is inspired by Spirit and actuated by love.* When we are aware of or experience our connection with the Divine (Spirit, Ultimate Reality, God,

Table 30.1

Concept of Service Taught by Major Religions and Some Philosophies

Tradition	Conceptualization of service
Moral philosophy	Altruism—serving others without the expectation of personal gain
Moralogy	Supreme morality—practicing benevolence, having a concern for the development and nourishment of all living beings, renouncing selfish desires, and working for the advancement of morals in organizations and society
Taoism	Wu-wei—learning to be selfless and in tune with the wholeness of the universe
Hinduism/Yoga	Karma yoga—acting, without being attached to particular results, to serve God and enhance the well-being of others
Buddhism	Compassionate action and loving kindness—basing our actions on kindness, compassion, love, and respect for others, while cultivating our speech, thoughts, and deeds to be of positive benefit to others
Confucianism	Jen (human-heartedness or benevolence and love)—having a profound respect for oneself and others, from which flow charity, good faith, and magnanimity
Christianity	Agape and charity and brotherly love—being motivated by love, acting humbly, and surrendering unconditionally to God as in "love your neighbor as yourself"
Islam	Charity and brotherly love—helping to lift the burden of those who are less fortunate, treating others with dignity and courtesy, and appropriately sharing wealth
Judaism	Hesed—being kind to others, showing love for and serving others, even if such actions are inconvenient, inspired by the belief that it is God's will to be of service
Universal model of Ram Dass	Conscious service or compassionate action—working with others in a selfless, loving, and respectful way, and bringing truth and loving kindness into each situation
Siddha yoga	Seva or selfless service—giving one's time and energy without any strings attached and therefore being able to work in total freedom; wholeheartedly acting for God's sake and giving up personal expectations about the results

Allah, Yahweh, Consciousness, or whatever we call it), we naturally feel inspired to serve this same divine essence that exists in all forms of life. The profound sense of love and gratitude that arises when we recognize our basic unity with everything prompts us to want to contribute to the good of all.

2. *Spiritually inspired service involves acting from the part of our being that personifies divine qualities, and focusing on higher intentions and purposes.* In order to put the love that comes from being aware of our connection with the Divine into action, we must draw on the best part of ourselves and cultivate inner qualities that exemplify divine love and compassion. Luckily, these divine virtues exist in all of us and become very accessible when we feel unified with Spirit. When we feel whole and in harmony with ourselves, it is much easier to feel connected with, have compassion for, and serve our families, companies, communities, and the environment. From such a perspective, we are naturally drawn to serve the highest purpose and have the most loving intent in each

situation, such as enhancing the well-being of others, promoting life, and uplifting and transforming society.

3. *Spiritually inspired service combines selfless action and a unique quality of presence.* To serve the highest purpose in any given situation, we set aside our personal agendas and remain detached from the specific outcomes of our deeds while in the midst of performing our work. When we do this it becomes easier to accept what happens in each moment and calmly and spontaneously do what is needed. Essentially, we give ourselves wholeheartedly to what we are doing, and open to the situation as it unfolds (Creel 1970).

We have all touched on this experience in moments when we have been totally absorbed in what we are doing and work flows on its own. In these moments, all of our awareness is focused on what we are doing in the present moment, we "lose ourselves" in what we are doing, and we often experience joy or feel energized. Although for many of us, these moments happen on their own, spiritually inspired service demands that we consciously bring this quality of presence to what we do. Essentially, it is the serene and loving quality of presence that we bring to our actions that is key.

Because the key characteristics of spiritually inspired service are so different from how service and action are typically thought of in the work environment, it requires effort to learn how to express it and continual commitment to its practice. And, because spiritually inspired service relies on our being aware of our spiritual connection, our inner attitudes, and our personal agendas, it requires that we reassess our lives, our actions, and our way of being in the world on a day-to-day basis, including when we are at work.

EXPRESSING SPIRITUALLY INSPIRED SERVICE AT WORK

For those of us choosing to live a spiritually inspired life of service, it is essential that we find ways to perform such service at work since we spend so many hours there and it fills such an important role in our lives. Freud proposed that work is as important to human life as love, giving purpose to our daily lives and allowing us to contribute to the society in which we live. And, while the norms in most of our workplaces may not explicitly support the expression of love and other spiritual values, the workplace is a natural place for us to practice spiritually inspired service. As John Cowan, in *Common Table: Reflections on Community and Spirituality in the Workplace* (1993), says:

> The spirit seeks a workplace. . . . The workplace is the natural home of the spirit. . . . No workplace can be truly alive until we see the divinity within one another, until we experience the breath of life, until we insist that our work will not be the humdrum of a sleeping spirit but a glorious monument to who we really are. (59–61)

Work and spiritual growth go hand in hand. Certainly our work influences our spiritual growth. When we consciously commit to making our work an expression of spiritually inspired service, that work becomes the "grist" for our spiritual "mill." Through the challenges we face in performing spiritually inspired service in the midst of our daily activities, we come face to face with our limitations and our strengths. When we can turn difficult experiences into learning opportunities, we can learn to serve more fully.

Our spiritual growth also influences our work. As we learn to practice spiritually inspired service at work, the work itself takes on a sacred dimension and our daily lives begin to have a spiritual flavor. As the *Bhagavad Gita* suggests, work done in the spirit of selfless, spiritually inspired service becomes worship.

So, how can spiritually inspired service specifically be put into action in the workplace? To begin with, if you are interested in spiritually inspired service, you can learn to express it in any situation or job. The first step is to find a guiding perspective of service that speaks to you, and then begin to experiment with how to integrate that view in your daily life in ways that are appropriate for you and your work situation. For instance, you might choose the principle of "Love your neighbor as yourself" to guide you in your interaction with a difficult coworker. As a result, instead of reacting negatively to the person, you might take the time to understand his or her perspective better, or you might confront him or her in a loving way.

The specific tradition and actions you choose to follow are less important than how you express the spiritual inspiration that underlies your chosen form of service. And, you don't have to think of service at work in "larger than life" terms. You can serve simply by bringing an attitude of love to all of your daily actions. As William Wordsworth describes in his poem entitled "Written in Her Album," "Small service is true service. . . . The daisy, by the shadow that it casts, protects the lingering dewdrop from the sun." Or you might simply follow the advice given in the *Bhagavad Gita:* Don't ask if you like the work or if it is creative or if it always offers something new. Ask if you are a part of work that benefits people. If you are, give it your best. In that spirit, every beneficial job can be a spiritual offering.

A MODEL OF SPIRITUALLY INSPIRED SERVICE AT WORK

As I began my practice of spiritually inspired service, I was curious about how others were expressing similar service at work. So I conducted in-depth conversations with twenty businesspeople actively attempting to express their perspective of spiritually inspired service in their work. Although the specific actions they performed varied, I found enough similarities to develop a four-fold model (See Figure 30.1). [3]

Spiritually inspired service appears in the middle of the diagram, representing the central desire to serve. From this starting point, we can turn our attention to serving the Divine, self, other, and/or community. Each area of focus evokes different intentions that lead to diverse forms of spiritually inspired service at work. Our endeavors take place in one or more of four dimensions: transcendental, personal, relational, and communal.

THE TRANSCENDENTAL DIMENSION

For many of us, choosing to live a spiritual life at work is motivated by a desire to strengthen our connection with the Divine aspect of life, as we define and experience it. This desire naturally leads many of us to cultivate a conscious spiritual awareness and to incorporate spiritual activities into our work lives. If this is true for you, I offer five basic ways for consciously expanding your awareness of the spiritual dimension of life while at work, based on my research and personal experience.

1. *Choose work in accordance with your spiritual values.* Get clear on your purpose in life and your core spiritual values, and then choose a career or job or work environment that offers you opportunities to be spiritually aware during the workday that enables you to serve a higher purpose through your work. Jim,[4] a venture capitalist, says his interest in social investing stemmed

Figure 30.1   **Spiritually Inspired Service at Work: A Four-Fold Model**

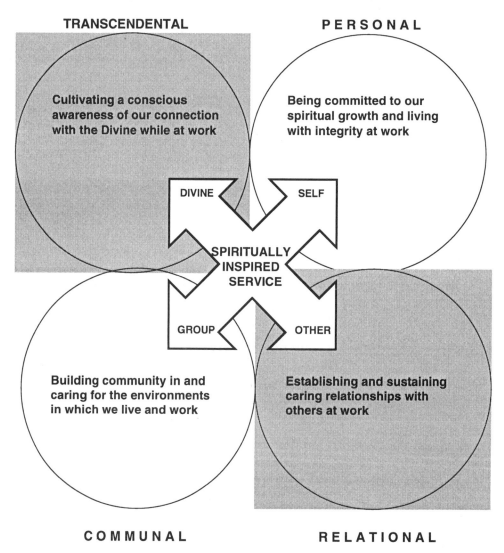

from his spiritual, ethical, and social values. He believes that "everything in everyday life, every-thing you do, should express or be true to your spiritual values." Accordingly, his company invests in areas where they will have a high social impact and make money for investors.

2. *Engage in spiritual practices.* Even if you are aware of work that is in alignment with your spiritual values, you may not have the freedom (inner or outer) or ability to choose the "right" work or working environment. In this case, you can find ways to act in alignment with your spiritual values where you are. You can learn to love what you do by becoming more aware of how you can serve the Divine in your current circumstances. The best way to do this is to engage in spiritual practices that help you expand your awareness of serving the Divine while at work and that help you transcend your personal desires. Various ways to open to a larger perspective are listed below.

- Focus on being fully aware in each moment.
- Invite the Divine presence to inspire you. Doug, the head of a law firm, approaches "most meetings now with the idea that I have to listen more—listen for the voice that is reflecting Thy Will, rather than my will."
- Consciously offer your work to the Divine. Arthur, an entrepreneur retailer, begins his mornings at work by making an "offering [as a] way of remembering . . . why it is that I am working, offering my work to God."[5] Then, throughout the day, he works "to constantly bring my mind back to that place, to that remembrance, to that offering, . . . to that center which is really the same as spiritually inspired service."
- Rely on the Divine for guidance. Keith, a training manager, tries to "honor that voice [the one inside that tells him how to act in accord with his spiritual values], speak the truth, and believe in myself, knowing that as God has called me, I'll be okay."
- Let go mentally and surrender to the Divine. Patrick, the head of an international education firm, opens himself by practicing setting aside his personality during the course of the workday. He is learning to be open and clear enough to become "a channel through which the energy of the universe can flow." Jane, the president of a chemical distribution company, has been focusing on "surrendering to and trusting [the] process [of life by] . . . letting go of the direct result of a given situation, whatever my subjective judgment is on it."
- Engage in prayer and meditation. Will, another venture capitalist, uses meditation to look for the patterns and connections in his work. He explains, "Instead of working hard, this is like standing back and letting the gift appear—what the answer is in terms of relationships, strategies and designs."

3. *Focus on the connectedness of life and seeing the divine in others.* An important method for becoming more aware of the Divine while at work is to look beyond the personal, concrete aspects of life at work. You can do this by intentionally seeing the divine in others with whom you work. Learn to see beyond your colleagues' personalities and pay attention to their essence as human beings, or "That of the Divine in them." Doug, the head of the law firm mentioned earlier, intentionally looks for "the good in people, the God-like quality in people," while Jill, a management consultant, practices noticing the many faces of the Divine—to see that "every person is a different reflection of the divine, [which] shows itself in different ways."

4. *Talk about spiritual issues with others.* You can directly cultivate your awareness of the Divine by talking with others at work about spiritual values, issues, and practices. You might be surprised at the number of people interested in having conversations about spiritual topics. Depending on your working environment, taking this action may require considerable courage. Lee, an organizational consultant, routinely discusses spiritual issues with the members of his organization and incorporates similar dialogues into his work with some clients. He once facilitated a group in which he invited managers and union leaders, who had been at odds for years, to sit in a room and close their eyes together in a moment of silence. Later, they talked about their spiritual lives, which had a positive impact on how they dealt with the organizational issues at hand.

5. *Integrate spiritual practices into organizational activities.* Incorporating spiritual practices into organizational activities is a big step. And, although it is less common and more challenging than individual actions, it appears that more and more organizations are experimenting with including spiritual practices in the way they do things. For instance, you might incorporate spiritual practices into organizational activities in one or more of the following ways:

- Pray, meditate, or have moments of silence together during or before meetings. Management consultant, Jill, meditates with her business partner before meeting with clients. She explains that, "We [take whole breaths] for a couple of minutes and then we are still and can witness what's taking place. . . that's when circulation occurs and that's where life is, where breath is, and love is, and God is." Claire, the president of an international development consulting firm, has someone teach meditation classes during lunch for interested staff members. And Doug, the law firm executive, prays with his staff during meetings. According to Doug, "Every time we get together [for a staff meeting] we have a prayer. And different people offer the prayers. And we have discovered some amazing qualities in individuals. . . . We find that when we turn to that person to ask him or her to pray, that there is a facility there that is very good, that is very strengthening."

- Support dialogue groups, in which employees can talk about spiritual topics. The World Bank and Rodale Press sponsor employee-organized spirit at work groups, while other organizations are using books like *Chicken Soup for the Soul at Work* (Canfield and Rutte 1996) to encourage people to share their personal stories.
- Create a space in the office where people can perform spiritual practices. The EPA has a "quiet" room and Rodale Press has a "kiva" (a Native American sacred space) where employees can go to meditate and reflect. Jane, the chemical distributor, plans to incorporate "meditation, prayer, and intuitive counsel into organizational activities, by creating a room in [her office] or a place where we can have a meditation booth or area."
- Ask for intuitive or spiritual counsel when making decisions. Will and his partners in a venture capital business recognize the "mystical events in life" and occasionally use the Chinese *Book of Changes* (*I Ching*) to gain insight and obtain intuitive information. He and six managers used the book to develop the logo of the company. Jill asserts that her company "uses, as business consultants, people that are intuitive consultants, or psychics. . . . They have been guides to us in terms of ways to think about [our work] experience. One of the critical pieces that came from one of those people was to think of [our business and work] as people coming to a table, where they want to nourish this entity (the business) and also be nourished by it, be supported by it. But, it is that exchange of energy that is going to create an environment that we are going to want to be in."

Obviously, depending on the culture in the organization, it is easier to introduce spiritual practices into some companies than others. Some individuals begin by incorporating spiritual practices into their organizational activities, while others actively seek to structure their organization around shared spiritual values. Tom Chappell, of Tom's of Maine, took a sabbatical to attend Harvard Divinity School, then made major changes in his company based on his religious beliefs and his respect for people and the environment (Chappell 1993). Jane makes a conscious effort to operate her business with integrity and is organizing her company into what she calls a "spiritual hierarchy," one that "operates out of compassion, understanding and commitment and, ultimately, . . . is a gathering of individuals who take turns being leaders," similar to a flock of geese that take turns flying point. Lee, the head of a consulting firm, says his spiritual values and his business "melt together" and that he is trying to live according to his "core values" in all aspects of his work. He is developing a process to use in his work with clients and other organizations that helps others with their "personal mastery" (spiritual development). Will, the venture capitalist mentioned earlier, built his organization around his belief in "right livelihood." He and his partners "brought in some consultants to help build an organization around [spiritual] values and beliefs."

While business owners and organizational leaders have more ability to effect such change, anyone can begin to institute change within their sphere of influence. Other ways in which people are conducting their business activities in accordance with their spiritual values include: (a) hiring people with similar spiritual values; (b) using strategic planning and training classes to help people communicate with each other more genuinely; (c) incorporating an awareness of environmental and social issues into the investment process, hence avoiding companies that pollute and/ or seeking out companies that manufacture beneficial products; (d) encouraging the printing company they use to switch to soy inks, which are better for the environment; (e) holding regular meetings to discuss ways to apply spiritual values in the business on a daily basis; and (f) exploring new ways of thinking about organizations.

As one commercial real estate developer's, Rick's, company grows, he frequently asks himself and others, "How does the emerging organization reflect the will of God?"

THE PERSONAL DIMENSION

Engaging in spiritually inspired service requires that we remain committed to developing ourselves spiritually and that we live with as much integrity and authenticity as possible. Wrestling with the complexities of being *both* human *and* spiritual requires that we participate in ongoing activities and spiritual practices that allow us to grow and expand our expression of selfless service over time. To more fully express spiritually inspired service at work, consider doing the following:

1. *Practice self-reflection and persistent self-inquiry.* Step back from your work, reflect on what you are doing, pay attention to your inner voice, and witness the actions being taken in the organization. As David, a financial consultant, observes, "Inwardly, there has to be some kind of bravery and willingness to deal with the fact [that life and business involve suffering] and to always be willing to drop whatever is going on [externally] and look at what is going on with [in] somebody, . . . with [in] yourself. When you are actually open to what might be happening for somebody else, then you can work with them humanly."

2. *Pay attention to the motivations underlying your actions.* Remaining vigilant of your actions and inner attitudes as you perform your work is the first step in confronting aspects of yourself that get in the way of serving as fully as you would like.

3. *Maintain a positive and accepting attitude toward life.* Walt, a financial director, remarks, "One of the things I have tried to do is not to have any expectations about what [people] ought to be, and in that sense be more willing to accept and try to learn." Instead he said he tries to cultivate a "willingness to accept them as they are and realize God is working in their lives as well as my own." Comparably, Paul, a financial broker, commented that he tries to maintain a peaceful, more detached, approach to his work. He accepts what work comes, "knowing that at some level, everything works out the way it should, even though many times it doesn't appear that way at the time."

4. *Be willing to learn from what life presents you, such as reframing challenging situations into opportunities to learn.* You might ask yourself, as Keith, a technical trainer, does, "What is it that I need to see about this situation? How can I transcend this moment of anger or impatience or intolerance? How can I get reconnected to my deepest Self, to God?"

5. *Keep reminders of the spiritual principles of service on which you choose to base your actions.* Keith also keeps images and quotes at his desk that remind him of his principles, while Jill, a management consultant, uses "whole breathing" as a way of "energizing [her] whole system" and getting in touch with love and God.

Each of these practices and attitudes can help you develop and maintain congruity between your intentions and actions. Like Claire, the CEO of an international development consulting firm, you can ask yourself, "Am I, and are we in the company, doing our best to live up to our commitment of doing no harm in our work?" Or like Jim, a venture capitalist, you can ask yourself and others, "First, are we doing any harm to anybody? Second, is the situation going to further people's fulfillment in the world?"

The Relational Dimension

Because much of our work takes place in the context of relationships and because spiritually inspired service itself is about enhancing the welfare of others, paying attention to the types of relationships we have with people is a key to expressing selfless service at work. When we interact with others out of love, trust, and respect, then we create truly caring relationships. Caring relationships are nonmanipulative. They are rooted in people's genuine interest in getting to know and care for each other because they recognize each person's worth as an individual and a human being. Serving others through caring relationships requires what Erich Fromm (1956) describes as mature love, which entails giving of ourselves, being concerned for others based on our common humanity, accepting responsibility for ourselves and others, willingly responding to the needs of others, and respecting others and seeing them for who they are.

Within the context of organizational life, caring for others can take the forms described by Charles Watson, in *Managing with Integrity* (1991), of leading by serving your followers, treating your coworkers and employees fairly, sharing gains with those with whom you work, supporting others in their work, and having a general concern for others. Such caring can be viewed as putting love into action in the workplace. As James Autry (1991, 13) asserts "good management is largely a matter of love." It involves, says Autry, thinking of others first, going beyond your role to be personal, building relationships with others, being honest, trusting employees, caring about yourself and others, paying attention to people's differences and meeting them where they are, listening to others, opening up and letting go of your management mindset, and recognizing and accepting everyone's humanness.

Practicing spiritually inspired service through caring relationships revolves around treating others with dignity, respect, honesty, trust, and love. It relies on establishing a deep personal connection with those with whom you work. As Walt, a financial director, remarks, "I am simply trying to figure out what it means to love people. And bring some love into the workplace." In addition to treating others with love and respect, caring relationships demand that all parties involved actively support each other's personal and professional growth, respond to each other's needs, trust each other, and communicate openly and honestly with each other.

The Communal Dimension

This dimension of spiritually inspired service centers on building communities and caring for the environments in which we live and work. We can focus our attention on building community in our work team and caring for the environment in our office space or we can focus on our country and the global environment. In either case, community is best described by Scott Peck in *The Different Drum* (1988), as a complex phenomenon requiring an "on-going process of becoming increasingly conscious, living together in freedom and love, and serving together in a way that enables us to use and share our innate talents and gifts" (19–20). Kaz Gozdz, in *Community Building* (1995), describes community similarly and adds that genuine community creates a group of people who are all leaders and who "have the ability to fight gracefully while transcending differences" (58).

Interestingly, if we first focus on spiritually inspired service in the other three dimensions of the model, then the groundwork for building communities in our work environments will already be laid. For, essentially, community involves serving together. When a group has a purpose of service, it sets the foundation on which it can grow, and draws people into something greater than themselves (Peck 1988).

In order to create such a community in your organization, you will need to incorporate spirit, personal authenticity, deep relationships, and honest communication, as well as address any tension related to organizational size and structure, authority, inclusiveness, task definition, rituals, and individuality (Peck 1988). You can also enhance the feeling of community by engaging in organizationally sponsored volunteer activities, building a sense of togetherness through rituals and events, creating an open and trusting atmosphere, allowing for and celebrating diversity, encouraging open communication, working collaboratively with others, and caring for the environment.

APPLICATIONS OF THE FOUR-FOLD MODEL OF SPIRITUALLY INSPIRED SERVICE AT WORK

The Spiritually Inspired Service Model has important implications both for those engaged in research on spirituality in the workplace and for people choosing to renew themselves spiritually and find more meaning in their work. The model itself offers an integrated framework for researching and practicing service, while the four dimensions provide clear alternatives for expressing service. It can serve as a practical guide both for those of you who wish to renew yourselves spiritually in your work and for those of you who wish to research the topic in more depth. For instance, you could research how different practices and actions outlined in the model impact different aspects of work life. Or you could facilitate and study an organizational intervention, where members of the organization agree to apply the model in their company interactions, and see what kinds of challenges they face as well as which actions have the most beneficial impact on the members and the organization as a whole.

Because of the spiritual nature of the topic, one of the best ways to research the efficacy of the model is to experiment with some of the suggested actions to see which ones work best. Whether you are a researcher or an organizational member, consider using the Four-Fold Model to select a dimension in which to focus your attention, and then experiment with different kinds of actions and spiritual practices. You can also use the model to explore those dimensions in which you are already serving and those in which you would like to serve more. For instance, you might ask yourself, "In what way(s) do I currently cultivate an awareness of the divine while I'm at work? How can I connect more fully with the spiritual inspiration in my work? In what ways do I currently cultivate my capacity to serve at work? What can I do to more fully foster my spiritual growth? How can I more fully serve with integrity at work? What new actions can I take to create work relationships that are more caring? In what ways can I build community and care for the environment in which I work?"

The key is to find spiritual practices that work for you and match your values, your individual nature, and where you are in your personal and spiritual development. It is also important to choose actions that replenish you, fit into your workday, and suit you and your organization. For instance, you might choose to quietly bring a spiritual presence to what you do, or actively raise spiritual topics with others, or try to structure your organization around your spiritual values.

If you take a more overt path, be careful to recognize that spiritual ways of being at work are uniquely individual and should not be imposed on others. Because true spiritual expressions are internally inspired by experience and faith, people must choose for themselves whether or not to embrace and express a spiritual way of being at work. This does not diminish your ability to live and work according to your spiritual values or to raise spiritual topics at work. Just be sensitive to and accepting of the differences in values held by other organizational members when you make your spiritual orientation known.

It is particularly important for leaders to be thoughtful about how they communicate with others about spiritual values and practices in the workplace. Because of the amount of authority and influence inherent in leadership positions, organizational members may assume that compliance with the leader's stated outlook is mandatory. Peter Vaill (1990), an organizational consultant who has written about spirituality and leadership, emphasizes the importance of creating a voluntary and safe environment for discussing spiritual issues in the workplace. He proposes that sharing spiritual development with others requires a process of mutual discovery in a nonthreatening environment in which people can experience their spiritual kinship. Only when organizational members can express their beliefs, fears, and desires, can trust be built and true community developed (Peck 1988; Gibb 1978).

One of the most effective ways for leaders to share spiritual values and be responsive to others is by entering into dialogue and "care-full" communication. When you are open, honest, and caring in your interactions with others, and when you genuinely share your personal experiences and struggles, then you create room for others, making it possible for people to learn from each other. Since not much research has been done yet on talking about spiritual values in the workplace, this is an area rich with research opportunities. If you are a researcher, consider investigating the impact on individuals, teams, and organizations of talking about spirituality at work as well as exploring the best ways to discuss spirituality in organizations.

It is particularly important for leaders who choose to incorporate spiritual values into their companies to explore how best to raise the issue. If you are a leader who is introducing spirituality into an established organization, make sure you openly discuss the spiritual values you are considering with other organizational members. Take time to reach agreement on the values you will use to guide the organization and how you will put those values into action. Then communicate the agreed-upon spiritual values to potential employees to facilitate hiring individuals who share similar values.

As you can imagine, or may know from experience, it can be challenging to talk about new ways of being in the workplace. There may be only marginal support in your business or organization for expressing spiritual values or raising spiritual topics. It may require considerable effort and courage on your part to take the risk to share your spiritual values, practices, and experiences. And yet, you will probably find your actions are the catalyst for amazing changes at work that could be researched and/or directly experienced. You might, for example, personally discover more meaning in your daily work life; experience peace and joy in your work; establish deep connections with your colleagues and coworkers; receive support from where you least expect it; enjoy inspiring and contributing to others' personal and spiritual growth; uncover opportunities for changing your organization and the way it works; and spawn increased wisdom, creativity, and productivity.

It would be great if each of us could perform all the actions outlined in this chapter simultaneously and perfectly, and immediately experience each of the benefits above. What is more likely is that we will each build our practice of spiritually inspired service at work one action or attitude at a time, over a long period. Because such service becomes habitual only through continual practice and experimentation, we must be willing to explore each day how to expand our serving at work. In your process of learning to serve, you may want to keep in mind the words of Mother Theresa, "Love has to be put into action and that action is service. Whatever form we are, able or disabled, rich or poor, it is not how much we do, but how much love we put into the doing." If you hold this awareness, then, whether or not you see it happen, your love will shine through in all that you do and make a difference in the world around you.

NOTES

1. Spiritual renewal is defined here as revitalizing ourselves by being aware of and integrating the spiritual dimension into our daily lives. It involves reconnecting with the Divine Essence of life through spiritual practices of some sort; getting in touch with the source of inspiration, inner strength, and wisdom within us; and remembering and acting on what is most important in life.

2. In the context of this chapter, spirituality is differentiated from religion. Certainly people can spiritually renew themselves through participation in a particular religion. However, since spirituality is all encompassing and inherent in all life, individuals do not need to be involved in a traditional religion to spiritually renew themselves. One way of looking at the relationship and difference between spirituality and religion, which Brian Luke Seaward (1997) uses, is to think of spirituality as water, which comes in different forms that are found everywhere, and to think of religions as containers that hold water. Containers that hold water can come in many different shapes and sizes, but water does not need a container to exist.

3. Because the research method I used was qualitative in nature, I want to acknowledge that the model that emerged is not globally applicable. It is most relevant to people who explicitly want to express an idea of spiritually inspired service at work that is like the definition presented in this chapter. And even then, the ideas presented should be individually tested to see how applicable and valid they are for that individual.

4. I use fictitious names throughout the chapter since I do not have permission to use all of my study participant's names. However, the stories are actual examples drawn from my research.

5. Because some people are put off by the use of this word, I wish to explain its use in this chapter. Many of the participants in the study used the word *God* as a way of speaking about the Transcendent Reality because it is a familiar term in our culture. It does not necessarily refer specifically to any one religion's definition. It is used simply as one name for the ineffable transcendent dimension of life.

REFERENCES

Autry, James. (1991). *Love and Profit: The Art of Caring Leadership*. New York: Avon Books.

Canfield, Jack, and Martin Rutte, eds. (1996). *Chicken Soup for the Soul at Work 101: Stories of Courage, Compassion and Creativity in the Workplace*. Deerfield Beach, FL: Health Communications.

Chappell, Tom. (1993). *The Soul of a Business: Managing for Profit and the Common Good*. New York: Bantam Books.

Cowan, John. (1993). *Common Table: Reflections and Meditations on Community and Spirituality in the Workplace*. New York: HarperCollins Business.

Creel, Herrlee G. (1970). *What is Taoism?* Chicago: University of Chicago Press.

Fromm, Erich. (1956). *The Art of Loving*. New York: Harper and Row.

Gibb, Jack. (1978). *Trust: A New View of Personal and Organizational Development*. Cardiff, CA: Omicron Press.

Gozdz, Kazimierz, ed. (1995). *Community Building: Renewing Spirit and Learning in Business*. San Francisco: New Leaders Press, Sterling and Stone.

Hawley, Jack. (1993). *Reawakening the Spirit at Work: The Power of Dharmic Management*. San Francisco: Berrett-Koehler.

Hiroike, Chikuro. (1987). *An Outline of Moralogy: A New Approach to Moral Science*. Chiba-Ken, Japan: Institute of Moralogy.

Lear, Norman. (1993). "A Call for Spiritual Renewal." *Washington Post*, CD (May 30).

Peck, Scott. (1988). *The Different Drum: Community Making and Peace*. New York: Touchstone, Simon and Schuster.

Seaward, Brian Luke. (1997). *Stand Like Mountain Flow Like Water: Reflections on Stress and Human Spirituality*. Deerfield Beach, FL: Health Communications.

Vaill, Peter. (1990). "Executive Development as Spiritual Development." In *Appreciative Management and Leadership: The Power of Positive Thought and Action in Organizations*, ed. Suresh Srivastva et al. San Francisco: Jossey-Bass.

Watson, Charles. (1991). *Managing With Integrity*. New York: Praeger.

CHAPTER 31

ILLUMINATING THE INVISIBLE

IT and Self-Discovery in the Workplace

KIERAN MATHIESON AND CYNTHIA E. MIREE

> The authentic self is the soul made visible.
> —*Sarah Ban Breathnach*

INTRODUCTION

Throughout history, sages have emphasized self-discovery as a vital part of the human experience. Socrates said, "The unexamined life is not worth living." Traditional Buddhist forms suggest that seeing through layers of delusion is central to enlightenment, Jews are asked not to be deluded or seek to delude, and Christians are encouraged to examine their hearts in an effort to understand their motives and behavior.

Many traditions assume the existence of an "authentic self," a set of core beliefs about the self, other people, the universe, and one's role in the world. The authentic self is said to exist even if unacknowledged and unexplored. As a result, with consistent self-analysis, everyone has the potential to manifest this authenticity in all areas of life. Once recognized and articulated, these beliefs offer a sense of meaning. They provide the impetus for consistent action—in other words, action that reflects one's core beliefs—as well as a sense of worth in the "larger scheme of things" (Frankel 1984).

There is a growing interest in the spiritual aspects of work (Gunther 2001). For many in the developed world, the significance of work goes beyond economic utility. Work is part of our identities. It can enhance or impede one's pursuit of authenticity in mind and action. When work and the authentic self are synchronized, work becomes a means of operationalizing our deepest beliefs. When core beliefs and work conflict, however, some people choose to abandon work situations that sap their energy, drain their strength, or violate their basic values. The loss of talent, creativity, and enthusiasm leaves gaps in the workplace that managers must fill.

Many companies are responding to their employees' need for deeper meaning in the workplace by hiring chaplains, supporting prayer groups, or teaching employees about meditation (Conlin 1999; Gunther 2001). When employees integrate their values into day-to-day workplace tasks, both the organization and the workers benefit. Workers approach their jobs with a passion difficult to achieve through external reward systems (Senge 1990). Workplace dissatisfaction and its symptoms, like absenteeism and turnover, fall as employees' attitudes toward work improve.

Supporting this level of individual development within an organization is not easy. Self-discovery is a complex, lifelong process. It draws from concrete experience and philosophical abstraction. It is social, individual, emotional, and intellectual in its makeup. It requires not only perseverance, but also an almost daily commitment to nurturing the pursuit.

Self-aware individuals can live more complete lives. Organizations employing them will benefit from their insights. Workplaces will be more pleasant and creative (Bierema 1996). These positive outcomes prompt the question: What can organizations do to help employees discover their authentic selves?

We think information technology (IT) can help. IT can deepen human experience, as when the bereaved create online memorials, a daughter creates an online gallery of her mother's art, or an extended family shares triumph and tragedy via e-mail and Web sites. Similarly, IT is a tool that can help people with the work of discovering their authentic selves. It doesn't do the work, of course. Rather, just as a poet uses a word processor, seekers can use computers to read others' stories, write their own, explore the thoughts of history's sages, and talk with others about deep questions.

The next section introduces a model of the authentic self at work. We then consider how the authentic self is discovered and developed, with an eye to supporting these processes with IT. Sample IT applications follow.

The Authentic Self in the Workplace

Figure 31.1 captures our view of authenticity in the workplace. The authentic self has three aspects: spiritual, emotional, and cognitive. The first refers to a set of axiomatic principles, or core beliefs. These principles are learned from family and culture, and perhaps reinforced through study of religion and philosophy. We call them "spiritual" because they lie at the core of an individual's self. They are not necessarily associated with religion; atheists have core beliefs. Of course, an individual's behavior is not driven by principles alone, but also by habit, self-interest, and social convention.

The second aspect of this core, emotion, affects thought and behavior. Strong emotion reduces our ability to think analytically, while at the same time pushing us to act (Goleman 1995). Awareness of how emotions affect thought and action can help people overcome emotions' negative effects and enhance their positive ones. Paradoxically, the better one understands how emotions control our thoughts, the less control emotions have.

The cognitive architecture of the human mind limits our ability to use our values. For example, someone might want to judge others on their merits rather than their appearance, but not be able to overcome her stereotyped thinking (Bennett-Goleman 2001). Evolution has molded us to be quick, confident decision-makers, ignoring complexity to make fast fight-or-flight choices (Wright 1994). These innate responses were appropriate for our primitive ancestral environment, but not for modern organizational life, where unconsidered action can have serious consequences (Langer 1989).

Workers in an organization operate in groups. People tend to have relatively dense interactions with workgroup members, thereby influencing each other's spiritual, emotional, and cognitive aspects. Norms are derived from implicit or explicit rules of group behavior. Norms can both help or harm workers and organizations. A norm to "help workers of your own race but not other races" will reduce group performance, while a norm of "no pilfering" can help control costs. All in all, the attributes of individual workers (both functional and dysfunctional) affect the attributes of their groups.

Finally, an employee's workgroup is part of a larger organizational environment. Over time,

Figure 31.1 **Authenticity in the Workplace**

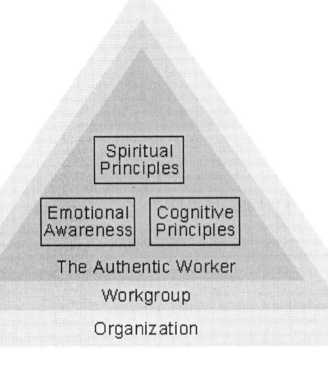

the sum of group behaviors and organizational norms creates a broader climate that can affect both employees and the organization's clients (Schneider, White, and Paul 1998).

DISCOVERING THE AUTHENTIC SELF

The authentic self always exists, even if unacknowledged and incomplete. So self-discovery is, in part, a matter of exposing what is. It's also a matter of development, building a more complete scnse of self through reading, reflection, and social interaction.

Theories of moral development give insight into the process of self-discovery. Unfortunately, the literature is contradictory and incomplete. We won't review it in detail here, but refer the interested reader to Nucci (1987; 1997a) for overviews of moral development theories, Berkowitz (1998) for a unified approach to the definition of a moral person, Huitt (2000) for a description of character education programs, Kohlberg (1976) for a cognitively based theory of moral development, and Nucci (1997b) for a reconciliation of character education and cognitive development approaches.

Notwithstanding the disagreement on moral development, some consistent themes emerge from the literature. These themes, in turn, guided our thinking about how IT can support self-discovery. The first theme is that some people gain a deeper appreciation of moral principles as they mature. Kohlberg (1976) identified three types of moral reasoning: preconventional, conventional, and postconventional. Preconventional reasoning focuses on the outcomes of behavior for the individual: "what's in it for me." Conventional reasoning emphasizes conformity to socially determined rules defining "a good person." In postconventional reasoning, behavior depends on moral principles applied across situations. A postconventional thinker has an emotionally compelling sense of self. It is respect for the self that precludes certain actions and promotes others (Allport 1955). Postconventional reasoning is a sign of moral maturity.

Another theme in the literature is that both feeling (emotion) and thought (cognition) are involved in self-discovery. Strong emotional experiences, such as a brush with death, lead some people to reflect on their deepest beliefs (Brookfield 1998, 295). Empathy, the ability to "step into someone else's shoes" and feel what he or she is feeling, is key to altruism and behavioral change (Goleman 1995). Cognition can help people better manage their emotions, as well as better understand themselves. For instance, some people habitually respond to minor setbacks with feelings of worthlessness. They can learn to challenge this conclusion by asking whether the evidence justifies it (Bennett-Goleman 2001).

The third theme is that self-discovery is both an individual and a social process. People not only learn social mores from those around them, but deepen their understanding of moral principles through discussion. Open dialog is a hallmark of the values clarification movement (e.g., Simon, Howe, and Kirschenbaum 1972).

Finally, there is motivation. Personal emotional experiences, empathy with others' distress, and social influence can encourage people to explore their authentic selves. Respected others—CEOs, sports figures, ministers, coworkers—can prompt someone to think about life's deeper issues, by exhortation, example, or simple conversation. But once the process of self-discovery has begun, what keeps people going? Individual persistence depends in large part on self-efficacy, the belief that success is achievable (Goleman 1995). A second factor is social support. People might either commend or ridicule someone's self-discovery efforts. The more support someone receives, the more motivated he or she will be. Another factor is organizational support. The allocation of resources to spiritual initiatives can legitimize such pursuits in the minds of employees.

WHAT INFORMATION TECHNOLOGY DOES

Now let's turn to IT. What, in general terms, can it do? Once this question is answered, we can suggest how IT can be used for self-discovery.

The first and most familiar IT function is storing and retrieving information, like essays, newspaper articles, and calendars. Information lies on a continuum from structured (with a known format, like a TV listing) to unstructured (with a flexible format, like a poem), and IT can handle both. Multimedia (photographs, video, animation, and sound) adds to information's cognitive and emotional impact. An IT system can search its information base, helping people find what they want.

Additionally, IT is able to structure relatively unstructured information, making it easier to understand and use. Authors structure documents with tables of contents and hyperlinks. Users can add their own information and structure to existing documents. For example, a Web site can let people add their own notes to any page (see Figure 31.2) and collect their scattered notes on a single page. Users can also create new documents. For instance, a user might create an online virtual notebook, adding structure to clarify relationships between thoughts (see Figure 31.3).

Second, IT can also add structure to problem solutions. Checklists and worksheets help ensure that people don't forget important issues. People can store solutions to problems, reusing them as needed. An IT system can present information in different ways. For instance, it can show different

Figure 31.2 **A Page Note**

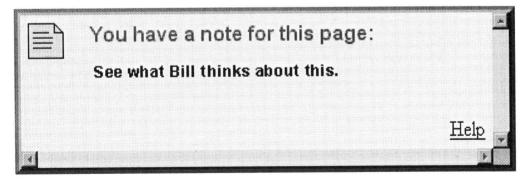

Figure 31.3 **A Virtual Notebook**

graphical charts of the same numerical data. It can also help people learn about a task—why to do it, how to do it, how to evaluate results, how to detect and correct errors, etc. A system can also store the results of an incomplete task so it can be resumed later.

Finally, IT can help people interact with each other. Users can help each other understand information and see how it applies to their own situations. They can evaluate each other's ideas. IT can put physically scattered people in touch. It can do so anonymously, where users do not know each other's real identities.

In sum, IT can (a) store, retrieve, and structure information; (b) add structure to tasks; and (c) help people interact with each other. Certainly there is more IT can do, such as automate processes, but these three are the most relevant to our goals.

SAMPLE APPLICATIONS

We will now identify IT applications that can help people discover their authentic selves. A company could make these applications available over its own intranet, or provide access to them on the Internet. We don't talk about the technology here; our focus is on the more important functional requirements rather than the less important technical details.[1] The discussion is organized around the five elements of the individual authenticity shown in Figure 31.1.

Spiritual Principles

From childhood, people learn spiritual principles from family and culture. They are elaborated through experience, discussion, and contemplation. IT can help someone examine his or her principles and encourage postconventional reasoning (see the section entitled "Discovering the Authentic Self"). First, a system could give people access to others' thoughts on principles, from theological figures like Buddha and Jesus to philosophers like Aristotle, Epicurus, Kant, and Rawls to other system users who choose to share their ideas. The system could also present artistic expressions of spiritual principles, including painting, music, and other nonverbal forms. Page notes (Figure 31.2) and lists of favorite resources would help users organize their thoughts.

Second, the system could show how principles relate to day-to-day workplace life. It can offer scenarios showing how principles lead to greater control over one's life and can be used by the average worker. There could be quotes and personal stories about principle-based living, including stories from business leaders like Edward Simon of Herman Miller who asked, "Why can't we do good works at work?" (Senge 1990, 5). The system could have a "Wisdom Base," where users post spiritual advice they have found valuable.

Third, the system can help people record their principles, using a notebook like that shown in Figure 31.3. Someone might begin with a free-form journal, then summarize ideas in a personal credo. The credo could have hyperlinks back to the journal entries and other documents on which it was based. The notebook could track changes over time for those who want to see how their ideas develop. Tools like spell checking and text search would make the notebook more usable.

Specialized tools can help people structure their thoughts. For instance, LifeStarz (http://www.lifestarz.com) encourages people to think about the dimensions of their life, their values for each dimension, their goals for each value, and the actions they will take to achieve those goals. Users create a series of linked worksheets for each one (see Figures 31.4 and 31.5).

People could contribute their ideas to the system, uploading their own documents to the site's database. Some documents would be restricted to workers in the firm, while others might be available publicly over the Internet. Other users could ask questions of the author, perhaps creating a small discussion forum focused on the author's document. As with discussion forums and chat, users could choose anonymity.

Fourth, the system could help people visualize principles in various ways. Figure 31.6 shows some personal artwork created by LifeStarz. This particular example is designed to be printed, but screen-based animations are also possible. It might be used for discussion, as a memory aid, or simply as decoration.

Fifth, as well as giving users readings on principles, the system could help them induce principles from their preferences. For example, users might describe people they admire. Principles might emerge from these descriptions.

Finally, users could discuss their principles using forums (asynchronous discussion) and chat

Figure 31.4 **Dimensions Worksheet Fragment**

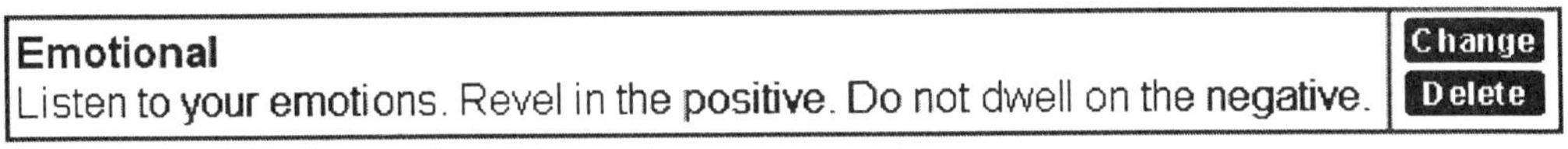

Emotional [Change]
Listen to your emotions. Revel in the positive. Do not dwell on the negative. [Delete]

Figure 31.5 **Editing a Dimension**

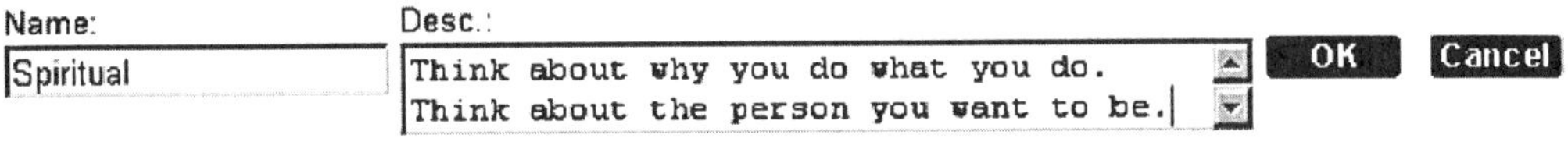

Name: Desc.:

Spiritual Think about why you do what you do. [OK] [Cancel]
Think about the person you want to be.

Figure 31.6 **Personal Artwork**

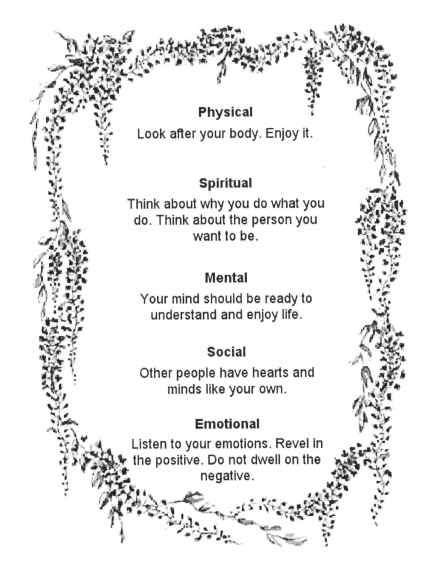

Physical
Look after your body. Enjoy it.

Spiritual
Think about why you do what you
do. Think about the person you
want to be.

Mental
Your mind should be ready to
understand and enjoy life.

Social
Other people have hearts and
minds like your own.

Emotional
Listen to your emotions. Revel in
the positive. Do not dwell on the
negative.

rooms (synchronous discussion). Both support anonymity, making honest communication easier for some. Special guests, such as experts on business ethics, could be invited to participate. The system could store transcripts of the discussions for later reference.

Apart from helping each other discover their principles, discussion helps users from different parts of an organization encourage each other to keep working at it. It can provide support that might not come from a worker's immediate social environment.

Emotional Awareness

Self-discovery includes emotional awareness. IT has a role here as well. If it can't offer primary emotional experiences, IT can help people remember, interpret, and learn from their past experiences.

The system could be designed to help people learn about the emotional structure of the mind and the effect of emotions on thoughts and behavior. It could present instructional material people could annotate (Figure 31.2) and discuss.

Second, users could look back on their lives to gain some insights into their emotional development. Figure 31.7 shows the beginning of a personal timeline, listing significant events in someone's life. Figure 31.8 shows how a system can bring together information about a person who was involved in different events.

The timeline could go into the future, stopping at the person's death. Although thinking about one's mortality can be disturbing, it reinforces the idea that we had better do what we can while we can. The system might ask users to write their own eulogy, imagining what they would like people to say about them when they are dead: Were we kind? wealthy? an achiever? a good spouse? This can help someone decide on the type of person he or she wants to be.

Third, the system could help people develop empathy, the ability to understand others' emotions. It might suggest experiences that could help (e.g., helping an elderly neighbor) and perhaps give contacts for volunteer organizations. It could also tap users' own experiences to build empathy. For instance, they might describe times when coworkers have helped them. They could record how they felt when they received the help, and how they think the other person felt. They could also be asked to remember times when they helped others and recall the emotions involved. Conversely, users could examine the times they have hurt others and been hurt themselves. They could draw their experiences together in a summary document.

Users might also describe their parents, children, spouses, and other important people in their lives. The system might ask, "How do they influence you? How did you influence them? What lessons did you learn? What did you teach? Describe their character. Why do you think they are that way?"

Another way to encourage empathy is to let people read about others' suffering. For example, a gay man might talk about his experience with workplace discrimination. The story would concentrate on the emotions he experienced. It would include video and voice to enhance its impact.

Finally, the system could help people discuss emotional questions with others. Anonymity can be provided here, too. Furthermore, since emotional trauma often requires professional help, the site could describe various forms of psychological counseling and offer contact lists.

Revisiting these emotional experiences can have important organizational implications. Disgruntled workers or those under emotional duress would be able to explore their emotions in a safe context, rather than acting them out with violence or other disruptive actions. By reading documents that users decide to make public, managers could better understand the emotional needs of their employees.

Figure 31.7 **Life Timeline**

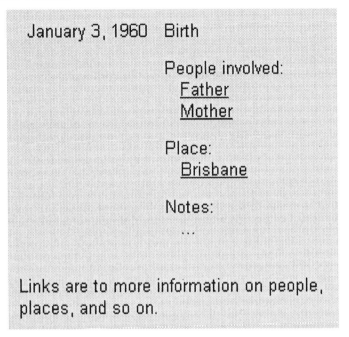

January 3, 1960   Birth

People involved:
Father
Mother

Place:
Brisbane

Notes:
...

Links are to more information on people, places, and so on.

Figure 31.8 **Understanding Another**

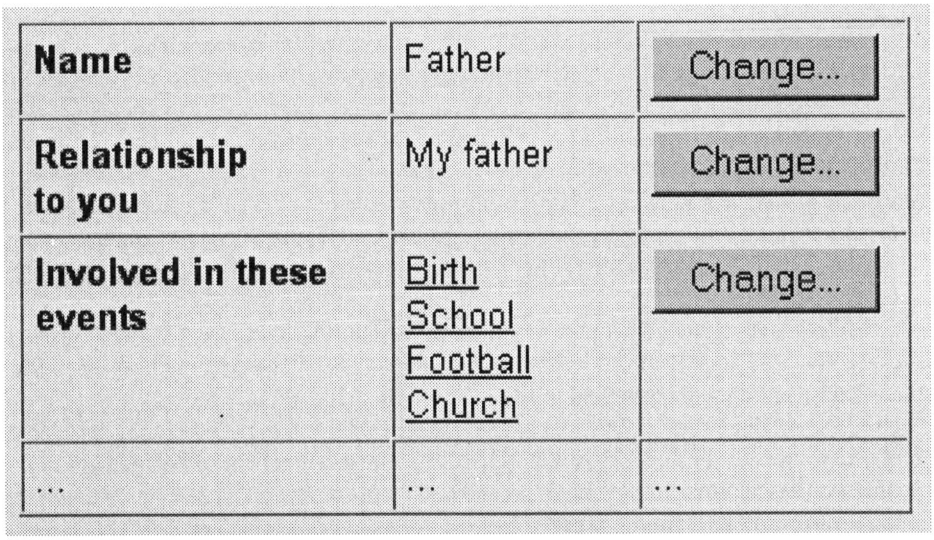

Name	Father	Change...
Relationship to you	My father	Change...
Involved in these events	Birth School Football Church	Change...
...	...	...

Cognitive Awareness

Knowing how to make reasoned choices is an important part of both acting in accordance with one's spiritual principles and making sound business decisions. IT can help. First, people should be aware of the limits of their thinking. People unconsciously frame issues based on their location in the hierarchy, their functional background, or their cultural upbringing (Hodgkinson and Johnson 1994). The system could offer instructional materials on these issues. It could be designed to include exercises demonstrating, for example, how people can be overconfident in interpreting ambiguous workplace situations.

The system could also encourage people to cognitively challenge their own emotional evaluations. For example, users with low self-esteem might list their positive qualities and successes in life and be asked whether their evaluations of themselves are justified.

Third, the system could help people analyze situations and make decisions. For instance, the system could help people use a method for making ethical decisions (see Figure 31.9). The system might also offer material on more general critical thinking skills, including basic numeracy and statistics.

Finally, the system could help people practice using these techniques. For instance, users might review ethical dilemmas and discuss their analyses. If there was agreement on the "best" analysis (although perhaps not on the decision), the system could store it for future users.

Workgroup Interaction

While IT is no substitute for face-to-face conversation, it can help people learn from their interaction with others. For example, the system could be designed to help people understand generic ideas about workgroup interaction, like the value of different skills people bring to workgroups, and how a single individual can dominate a group. The system could offer material on these topics, allowing annotation and discussion.

Second, the system could help people appreciate the specific individuals in the workgroup, their aspirations, core beliefs, skills, and interaction styles. Each individual could post whatever personal information he or she wants to share. Users could keep their own notes on each other, with the system encouraging elaboration of these ideas. For instance, if a user writes that a coworker is distant, the system might ask what evidence warrants this conclusion, why the coworker might be that way, and what the implications are for future interaction. Information confidentiality would be particularly important here.

Third, the system could help people learn how to interact with each other, perhaps supplementing live training. For example, the matter of raising difficult issues in a nonthreatening way could be supported via discussion of this subject with other workers and with (possibly geographically distant) experts.

Fourth, the system could help a group explore its own norms and power structure. Users could discuss positive and negative group norms and decide what to do about them. Anonymity, as a design requirement, would be critical in such a discussion.

Finally, the system could offer tools designed to overcome group interaction problems. For example, a group decision support system (GDSS) [a cluster of networked computers in a meeting room] with anonymous voting could be used to help overcome one individual's dominance of a group (Bostrom, Watson, and Kinney 1992).

Organization Atmosphere

At the organizational level, the system could help people reflect on the relationship between their goals, their workgroup's goals, and those of the firm. It could make organizational goal statements available and clarify each workgroup's contributions to the goals. The system could be

Figure 31.9 **Analyzing Situations**

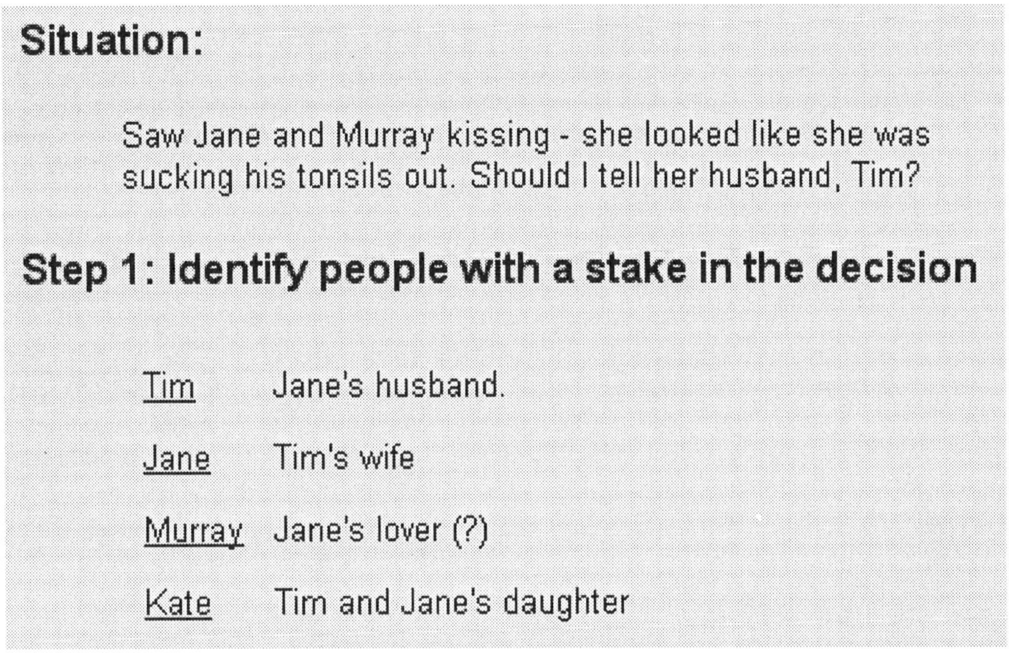

Situation:

Saw Jane and Murray kissing - she looked like she was
sucking his tonsils out. Should I tell her husband, Tim?

Step 1: Identify people with a stake in the decision

<u>Tim</u>   Jane's husband.

<u>Jane</u>   Tim's wife

<u>Murray</u>   Jane's lover (?)

<u>Kate</u>   Tim and Jane's daughter

designed to help people record and organize their thoughts about goal alignment and organization atmosphere. It could facilitate discussion of these issues, again with anonymity.

With the agreement of the participants, the results of these anonymous discussions could be forwarded to management, thereby helping them to better understand how employees view the organization. For instance, workgroup members might feel that the overly competitive atmosphere in their organization neither matches their own behavioral preferences nor facilitates superior firm performance.

CONCLUSION

Computers have reached almost every part of modern society, except for one of life's most important tasks: discovering the self. We feel they have a role here, possibly an important one. An information system won't, or at least should not, tell someone what sort of person he or she ought to be, but it can help someone answer the question for himself or herself.

Our work is in its infancy, and many important issues remain. From a theoretical standpoint, different theories of moral development not only imply different tasks for our systems to support, but are based on different underlying philosophies. For instance, Kohlberg was influenced by Rawls's relatively thinker-independent views of justice. Virtue ethics focuses on developing moral character rather than moral rules. A constructivist view is quite different again, emphasizing the role of individual experience in building personal moral commitments. The tools discussed in the section entitled "Sample Applications" use ideas from all these paradigms. It is unclear which paradigm is "best," or even whether the question is meaningful. Our first prototype self-discovery system, LifeStarz (http://www.lifestarz.com), used a rational Kantian approach. It was useful for some people but confusing and barren for others. We think the best approach at this point is to try various ideas, closely follow users, and see what they prefer and are successful with.

Second, there are issues of measurement. What makes one self-discovery exercise "better" than another? We could argue for some answers. For instance, we think people should know about human emotional architecture. However, relying on outcome assessment alone is difficult since it involves, for example, comparing moralities. We think system assessment will mix measures of outcomes (like knowing some emotion science), process (such as stories written), and attitude (e.g., whether people think the system is useful).

Third, there are many organizational issues associated with self-discovery. Since organizations change as the individuals within them change (Turner 1999), any significant spiritual evolution within the firm necessitates the participation of all (or at least a majority of) employees throughout the firm. Employees who do not participate in self-discovery initiatives may feel pressured to get involved in these programs "for the good of the company." Those who do participate will confront perspectives that conflict with their beliefs or that they find simply offensive. Self-discovery systems could highlight discontentment as people from across the organization come into relatively intimate contact, perhaps for the first time. Conflict between workers and management, and between workers and workers, might increase as they try to reconcile basic differences in outlook. These effects can be reduced by, for example, establishing norms of mutual respect between system users. However, genuine conflict and the challenges associated with managing conflict will still exist.

Is this reason enough for a company to ignore, or even discourage, self-discovery? Not necessarily. Differences in values exist among employees, whether formally acknowledged or not. The problems they create will still occur. Bierema (1996) warns that the short-term savings associated with either ignoring employees' needs for development or treating them with quick fixes are not worth the costs of turnover and lost productivity.

Fourth, what can a firm expect to gain from employee self-discovery? Empirical evidence on the effect of spiritual practices in the workplace is limited at best. The current literature, albeit primarily theoretical, suggests there should be a positive relationship between the use of spiritual practices in the workplace and outcomes like increased productivity, enhanced creativity, a greater sense of individual fulfillment, and higher morale (Turner 1999). Turner (1999) further suggests that these positive outcomes will lead to higher profitability. We would also expect to see less attrition among employees. Gozdz (1995) suggests that the use of self-discovery systems should lead to greater organizational learning, as these communication-intensive, community-building systems may remove barriers to learning. This would be particularly important for firms relying on the creativity of socially connected employees.

Finally, we expect that various types of organizations will use self-discovery systems in different ways. For example, the technology could help nonprofit organizations better define what "success" means. To measure performance, nonprofits typically look at program inputs (e.g., financial contributions) and outputs (e.g., what products and services have been delivered). However, there is growing interest in understanding client outcomes; that is, identifying something that the client is, has, or does in response to the products and service delivered (Plantz, Greenway, and Hendricks 1997). After all, it does not matter how much a nonprofit collects or how many services it delivers if it is not positively changing its clients' lives.

The technology we have described could help a nonprofit's workers and contributors better understand exactly what they are trying to achieve. However, it could be opened to clients as well as employees. This would integrate a key stakeholder into the organizational self-discovery process.

Consider another example where the system could be adapted to an organization. In some industries, there is a significant power imbalance between service providers (e.g., doctors, teachers, clergy, and counselors) and clients. Do these service providers know what clients want from them? Do the clients know what service providers can reasonably offer, and how they can participate more fully in service delivery? The technology we have described could help everyone involved better understand each other.

Are managers ready to take self-discovery seriously? We think most are not. Change on this scale is uncommon in organizations not threatened with extinction. It will take a special type of manager to embrace these changes, one who thinks beyond quarterly returns to life's deepest questions. These people exist in the industrialized world, but we suspect their ranks are thin. In the short term, people will leave the firm, others will transfer within it, goals will be revised, strategies realigned. However, if an organization embraces self-discovery, it could eventually have insightful workers deeply committed to its goals.

NOTE

1. Please contact Kieran Mathieson at the School of Business Administration, Oakland University, Rochester, Michigan, for information about our Web-based prototypes.

REFERENCES

Allport, G. (1955). *Becoming.* New Haven: Yale University Press.

Bennett-Goleman, T. (2001). *Emotional Alchemy: How the Mind Can Heal the Heart.* New York: Harmony Books.

Berkowitz, M. (1998). "The Education of the Complete Moral Person": http://www.uic.edu/~lnucci/MoralEd/aotm/article3.html (June 3, 2001).

Bierema, L. (1996). "Development of the Individual Leads to More Productive Workplaces." *New Directions for Adult and Continuing Education* 72: 21–28.

Bostrom, R.P.; R.T. Watson; and S. Kinney, eds. (1992). *Computer Augmented Teamwork: A Guided Tour.* New York: Van Nostrand Reinhold.

Brookfield, S. (1998). "Understanding and Facilitating Moral Learning in Adults." *Journal of Moral Education* 27: 283–300.

Conlin, M. (1999). "Religion in the Workplace." *Business Week* (November 1): 151–158.

Frankel, V.E. (1984). *Man's Search for Meaning* (rev. ed.). New York: Washington Square Press.

Goleman, D. (1995). *Emotional Intelligence.* New York: Bantam Books.

Gozdz, K. (1995). "Creating Learning Organizations Through Core Competence in Community Building." In *Community Building: Renewing Spirit and Learning in Business*, ed. K. Gozdz. San Francisco: Sterling and Stone, 57–68.

Gunther, M. (2001). "God and Business." *Fortune Magazine* (July 9): 62–74.

Hodgkinson, G., and G. Johnson. (1994). "Exploring the Mental Maps of Competitive Strategists." *Journal of Management Studies* 31: 525–551.

Huitt, W. (2000). "Moral and Character Development": http://chiron.valdosta.edu/whuitt/col/morchr/morchr.html (January 12, 2001).

Kohlberg, L. (1976). "Moral Stages and Moralization: The Cognitive-Developmental Approach." In *Moral Development and Behavior: Theory, Research and Social Issues*, ed. T. Lickona. New York: Holt, Rinehart and Winston, 31–53.

Langer, E. J. (1989). *Mindfulness.* Cambridge: Perseus Books.

Nucci, L. (1987). "Synthesis of Research on Moral Development." *Educational Leadership* 44: 86–92.

———. (1997a). "Moral Development and Moral Education": http://www.uic.edu/~lnucci/MoralEd/overview.html (January 12, 2001).

————. (1997b). "Moral Development and Character Formation." In *Psychology and Educational Practice*, ed. H.J. Walberg and G.D. Haertel. Berkeley: MacCarchan, 127–157.

Plantz, M.C.; M.T. Greenway; and M. Hendricks. (1997). "Outcome Measurement." In *Using Performance Measurement to Improve Public and Nonprofit Performance*, ed. K.E. Newcomer. San Francisco: Jossey-Bass, 13–30.

Schneider, B.; S.S. White; and M.C. Paul. (1998). "Linking Service Climate and Customer Perceptions of Service Quality: Test of a Causal Model." *Journal of Applied Psychology* 83: 150–163.

Senge, P.M. (1990). *The Fifth Discipline.* New York: Currency Doubleday.

Simon, S.; L. Howe; and H. Kirschenbaum. (1972). *Values Clarification.* New York: Hart.

Turner, J. (1999). "Spirituality in the Workplace." *CA Magazine* 132, no. 10: 41–42.

Wright, R. (1994). *The Moral Animal.* New York: Vintage Books.

CHAPTER 32

USING THE EVERYDAY CHALLENGES
OF BUSINESS TO TRANSFORM
INDIVIDUALS AND ORGANIZATIONS

KAZIMIERZ GOZDZ AND ROBERT FRAGER

INTRODUCTION

There is a widely acknowledged need for business organizations to engage in an ongoing process of human resource development. In our consulting capacity, we have developed an approach that uses everyday work practices to enhance both personal and organizational learning and development. This approach keeps the business focused on solving common business problems and prospering in the marketplace, while simultaneously using these real-life business issues as a means of fostering both personal and organizational transformation. Everyday work and developmental growth become seamless, integrated processes, a process we see as synonymous with spiritual growth.

Organizations and individuals grow through thoughtfully developing competencies and systems directly relevant to the real issues facing an organization. In our approach, we facilitate this process by providing a growth-oriented framework for problem solving.

Building on Greenleaf's (1977) work on servant leadership, we assist clients to become more mature and effective leaders, driven by business ideals like service rather than ego gratification. At the same time we help institutions become learning organizations or learning communities, which are capable of responding constructively to the challenges of change. We expand on Senge's (1990, 3) notion that learning organizations "continually expand their capacity to create the results they truly desire."

Transformation in Organizations

Webster's Unabridged Dictionary (1979) defines transformation as: "1. the act or operation of changing the form or external appearance; 2. in biology, change of form in insects, metamorphosis, as from a caterpillar to a butterfly; 3. in alchemy, the change of one metal into another; transmutation of metals [as in the alchemical transformation of lead into gold]." By transformation we mean a major shift in an organization or individual, from one developmental stage to the next. According to developmental theorists, there are clearly measurable, qualitatively different stages of development and maturation, consisting of a series of fundamental transformations from stage to stage.

In the past, psychology has studied the transformation of children into adults but has paid less attention to the transformation of healthy adults into exceptional human beings. Adult transformation instead has been discussed primarily in transpersonal psychology and in the world's great

475

spiritual traditions. Organizational transformation, from average to excellent, has been studied by researchers such as Maslow (1965), Senge (1990), Fisher and Torbert (1995), and Collins (2001).

Our personal and organizational methods of transformation extend the four-quadrant, integral theory of Ken Wilber (Wilber 2000a) and our own four-stage development theory. Our model describes a wide range of individual and organizational functioning, from highly dysfunctional to extraordinary. From our vantage, transformation to higher stages of functioning can be a process that occurs naturally, through ordinary work, in healthy individuals and organizations. There is no duality between the spiritual and daily life; life itself is an integral spiritual process.

CONTENT, PROCESS, AND CONTEXT

In using our approach with businesses, we have found that organizations and individuals can grow through the process of carefully framing complex business issues as vehicles for growth. Central to our approach is the *way* in which we view business challenges.

In a classic discussion of transpersonal therapy, Vaughan (1993) distinguishes the three dimensions of content, process, and context. In working with problems or challenges a business is facing, we have found it helpful to attend to these three dimensions of experience. *Content* refers to the specific issues, tasks, and problems facing an individual or organization. *Process* refers to the ways problems are addressed and solutions sought. *Context,* in our work, concerns the level of development at which individuals and organizations operate. But context also refers to the way in which problems are framed. Ideally, everyday problems are taken as challenges to growth and development. It colors both content and process, and organizes perception and experience.

A good counselor or psychotherapist uses everyday issues and problems to lead a client to greater awareness and deeper insight. We employ the same principles in working with organizations. It is not necessary to teach skills or processes unrelated to the daily tasks of doing business. Our pedagogy uses content-specific business issues as vehicles for psychological and spiritual growth. We avoid special sessions emphasizing human or organizational development alone, because we feel they are artificial and ineffective to the extent they are unrelated to real and pressing business issues.

This approach, which integrates learning disciplines for personal and organizational learning into everyday work, has been applied by the Army in the "After Action Review Process." According to Parry and Darling (2001): "By weaving a disciplined process for learning through experience into the tapestry of ongoing work, an emergent learning practice helps people to use their own experience as a context for generating, refining, and validating knowledge, while enhancing their ability as a unity to 'learn our way through' difficult and complex situations" (1).

We believe that effective solutions to fundamental business problems *require* inner growth and development. When we pay full attention to the content, process, and context of business problems, robust solution of these problems calls forth the need for individuals and institutions to grow to their highest capacity. Conducting business efficiently and effectively is a real challenge, and, when placed in the right context, it can grow people and organizations.

By right context, we mean the understanding that development is possible and healthy, and the realization that some organizational problems can be solved only by individuals who have acquired requisite knowledge and skills and attained a certain level of development. For example, Erik Erikson's (1963, 1964, 1980) developmental theory makes it clear that you cannot expect a fifteen-year-old to be able to handle interpersonal issues involving intimacy. Until an individual has developed a healthy sense of identity and maturity, true intimacy is not yet possible. Working with business in this context can have direct consequences for business performance.

Content

We begin our work with individuals and organizations by looking at the issues and the opportunities our clients perceive in the current moment. We use this content as a springboard for transformation. We have clients changing from an authoritarian management style to a cooperative decision-making management style. The content of our sessions has also included rebuilding work processes and job responsibilities, supporting the upgrade of information technology and accounting software, and educating the workforce to work with a new leadership model. Working with content issues also gives us the opportunity to shape processes and context.

People will rise to the challenge of necessity, especially if they understand that the best way to meet the challenge is to grow and to increase their capabilities. We seek to facilitate this orientation by helping institutions develop a corporate culture that values growth and development, a culture that holds a goal of excellence and not mere survival. Promoting a culture of excellence is an essential step, for in a culture of growth and excellence, the content of the work *is* a spiritual, transformational practice.

Precedents for defining daily life as spiritual practice can be found in the great religious traditions. According to one Taoist master, for example, the ineffable *is* our everyday experience. He defined the Tao as follows: "When you are hungry you eat, when you are thirsty you drink, when you meet a friend you greet him" (Suzuki 1959, 11).

More specifically, by spirituality we mean the daily practice of universal values and ethical principles such as honesty, integrity, and service. These practices lead both individuals and organizations to greater development. Personal religious beliefs are sacred and private and we differentiate them from general spiritual principles. Commitment to high ideals and principles can be discussed in ways consistent with all spiritual traditions.

Process

The term *process* has several meanings. One refers to a particular method of doing something, another refers to moving forward or proceeding toward a particular end. We use both senses of the term. For example, birth is a natural, healthy process that is usually facilitated by midwives or obstetricians, who are also present in case of complications. We act as "midwives" to corporate and individual growth, facilitating the natural processes of transformation and also remaining ready to assist with complications that might abort the growth process.

We help keep organizations *actively* engaged in mature problem-solving processes. Growth results from completing the process of solving complex problems, as participants are called to address the limits of their development as a constraint on their solution options. Another process entails the handling of conflict, in which we promote maturational development of the culture and its people to embrace differences in order to develop a more creative and robust conflict resolution process.

But complex business issues may also require a shift in leadership style. In a large American oil company, the president of a major division was put in charge of a radical reorganization effort (Gozdz 1999). Contrary to his previous approach, he sat down with his staff and let them know that he did not know how to proceed with the project. He admitted he did not know all the variables this project required for success, and asked for all the help and insight they could give him. His staff was amazed, felt much more supportive of their supervisor, and experienced a deep sense of empowerment. At the end of the project, everyone agreed that it would never have succeeded without this more inclusive leadership approach.

This process-oriented approach to organizations is compatible with Cohen and March (1991), who have noted ". . . An organization is a collection of choices looking for problems, issues and feelings looking for decision situations in which they might be aired, solutions looking for issues to which they might be the answer, and decision makers looking for work" (174–175).

Our specific focus on process is via generic processes of problem analysis, hypothesis formulation, and solution implementation. Solving a particular content issue requires identifying ontological (theories of being) and epistemological (theories of knowledge) assumptions. These are translated into a pedagogy (theory of teaching) that supports processes relevant to the client's defined goals.

We establish processes to examine ontological, epistemological, and pedagogical assumptions and, when necessary, to adopt more holistic and sophisticated ones.

Many of the assumptions we offer our clients are shared by the great spiritual traditions. They include the following: (1) All human beings have untapped potential for growth in awareness and capability, (2) each individual is an integral part of the whole of nature, and (3) healthy human beings are called to act in accordance with their higher ideals and values. In turn, we teach that individual transformation and organizational transformation are mutually supportive and that a learning community develops through honest and authentic dialog.

We have found Schein's (1992) emphasis on basic assumptions and Argyris's (1982) theory-in-use methods for building learning organizations useful in developing our own emphasis on linking process awareness to fundamental assumptions. When addressing the content of business issues, we seek to make participants more conscious of the relationship between fundamental assumptions and external actions. By bringing fundamental assumptions into conscious awareness and examining the role they play in decision processes, we facilitate the maturation of these assumptions at individual and institutional levels.

A person or organization's orientation to a particular problem or aspiration is converted by our method from a static stance to a dynamic process. This can be seen as a call for greater growth and development. Much like a five-year-old is developmentally incapable of solving the social problems faced by a teenage sibling, we assume an organization is called to move to a new developmental level in order to handle what is currently a seemingly insoluble problem. We use the process of problem solving as a challenge to grow everyone involved, both individually and organizationally.

We have developed a four-stage model of individual and organizational development to map the process. Our transformational perspective, the movement from one developmental stage to the next, is summarized in Table 32.1. With each stage come greater awareness, greater maturity, and a greater capacity to solve problems and issues. This developmental growth might be called a meta-process underlying content-specific problem-solving processes.

Context

As individuals and institutions shift to higher stages of development, the new stages provide larger and more sophisticated alternatives for problem solving. Developmental shifts also produce greater responsiveness to change, more responsibility concerning matters of social and ecological concern, and added support for the health and growth of a learning community. Perception of content issues and process alternatives is transformed with each developmental revision of our clients' internal and external maps of the world.

Scott Peck clearly describes the way in which the solving of life problems is related to the context of growth and development:

Table 32.1

Basic Elements of the Four Stages

Stage of development	Individual	Institutional
I. Unprincipled	Narcissistic	Self-serving, fear-based management
II. Conventional	Authoritarian	Conservative, obedience-based management
III. Self-Actualizing	Success-oriented	Competitive, team-based management
IV. Integrated	Servant Leader	Cooperative, learning-based management

Problems, depending upon their nature, evoke in us frustration or grief or sadness or lone-liness or guilt or regret or anger or fear or anxiety or anguish or despair. These are uncom-fortable feelings, often very uncomfortable, often as painful as any kind of physical pain, sometimes equaling the very worst kind of physical pain. Indeed, it is *because* of the pain that events or conflicts engender in us that we call them problems. And since life poses an endless series of problems, life is always difficult and is full of pain as well as joy.

Yet it is in this whole process of meeting and solving problems that life has its meaning. Problems are the cutting edge that distinguishes between success and failure. Problems call fourth our courage and our wisdom, indeed, they create our courage and our wisdom. It is only because of problems that we grow mentally and spiritually. When we desire to encour-age the growth of the human spirit, we challenge and encourage the human capacity to solve problems, just as in school we deliberately set problems for our children to solve. It is through the pain of confronting and resolving problems that we learn. (Peck 1978, 16)

The context is our map of the internal and external world, as well as our developmental level. It generates our individual and institutional worldviews and includes the aggregate of all the beliefs, assumptions, and capacities for action that make up this worldview. There are both con-scious and unconscious aspects to context. In his book *Transformative Dimensions of Adult Learn-ing,* Mezirow (1991) addresses both aspects of context with his theory and practice for treating problem solving as a learning process that can lead to perspective transformation. He writes: "Perspective transformation is the process of becoming critically aware of how and why our assumptions have come to constrain the way we perceive, understand, and feel about our world; changing these structures of habitual expectation to make possible a more inclusive, discriminat-ing, and integrative perspective; and, finally, making choices or otherwise acting upon these new understandings" (167). This adult learning is compatible with our meaning of context shift.

Context is a perspective from which we act, and contains current assumptions, future inten-tions, and plans for action. As such, we seek to change contexts by clarifying intentions and promoting greater understanding of the basic assumptions held by individuals and institutions. This growth in awareness leads to developmental growth. We are not concerned with problem solving per se, but with creating the conditions in which the problems are solved by a develop-mental shift. The shift in leadership style mentioned earlier is an excellent example.

Each stage of development provides a new, internal context for action and problem solving as well as new issues to be addressed. Inasmuch as institutional processes reflect internal develop-mental contexts, sophisticated business problems demand developmental growth. It is to this issue that we now turn.

DEVELOPMENTAL THEORY AND LEARNING

Our approach is a developmentally based theoretical method of building learning organizations. Theories of human development describe systematic changes in individuals from conception to death. Chaos and confusion are often part of the change process, but each new stage of development is itself a stable and orderly state.

Two major processes underlie developmental change. One of these processes, *maturation,* refers to biological and psychological development according to a genetic plan. Just as the acorn is preprogrammed to become an oak tree, so, too, is the human embryo preprogrammed to become a mature, healthy adult human being. Developmental psychologists have found that a human maturational blueprint guides all of us through the same developmental changes at similar points in our lives.

A second developmental process is *learning,* which produces relatively permanent changes in our feelings, thoughts, and behaviors. Learning plays a greater role in human behavior and development than in any other species on the planet. In many species, complex behavior patterns have been "hardwired" in their genetic plan. Most human developmental changes stem from *both* maturation and learning. For us, learning is a central human activity, a psycho-spiritual growth process. Improving the quality of learning leads to new stages of maturation and development. In the following section, we will address the issue of learning.

Incremental Versus Stage Learning

Many developmental theorists emphasize the importance of stages in development. Erik Erikson (1963), one of the first developmental psychologists, compares these stages to the stages of embryo development. He calls this an "epigenetic" model, which suggests that each element develops on top of other parts (*epi* means "upon" and *genesis* means "emergence"). Each organ system of the body has its own special time for growth and development that follows a predetermined sequence. Similarly, each stage builds on the development of the previous one. In his developmental model, Wilber (2000a) has stressed the principle that each new stage of development transcends and also includes all those stages that have gone before.

We view learning and maturation as spiritual development processes. Our intelligence and capacity to learn lie at the spiritual core of what it is to be human. When competent people in well-run institutions run up against problems they cannot solve, we treat this as a developmental challenge. We expect them to transcend and include prior competencies within a larger set of options. Essentially, it requires growth. Carl Jung has written that solving significant problems requires us to grow:

> All the greatest and most important problems of life are fundamentally insoluble. . . . They can never be solved, but only outgrown. This "outgrowing" proved on further investigation to require a new level of consciousness. Some higher or wider interest appeared on the patient's horizon. (Jung, cited in Jacoby 1959, 302)

This kind of "solution through growth" is integral to effective business practice.

Single-, Double-, and Triple-Loop Learning

Three types of learning that are linked to maturation must be distinguished. Most problem solving involves *single-loop learning.* The problem is defined and various solutions considered until an effective solution is found. Only immediate solutions of the problem get considered. For example, the thermostat is designed to "solve" changes in temperature by turning on the heat or air conditioning. It completely ignores the causes of those changes, such as a broken window or a fire. In addition, in single-loop learning, no consideration is given to the assumptions underlying the problem.

In *double-loop learning,* possible root causes of the problem are considered. It does not suffice to solve the problem without considering current assumptions; institutional assumptions, system dynamics, and other possible causes of the problem are surfaced in the course of seeking solutions. For example, if a company consistently pays too much for merchandise, a single-loop solution would be to hire a new purchasing agent. A double-loop solution would be to investigate the procedures and assumptions underlying the company's purchasing policies. Double-loop approaches tend to be process-oriented.

A *triple-loop solution* would be to use the problem to investigate not only the immediate issues and the assumptions within the institution, but also to examine deep-seated beliefs or assumptions in the industry or in society bearing on the problem. A triple-loop solution is context-oriented. It expands the developmental level of the situation. The recent work of Fisher, Rooke, and Torbert (2001) has also moved in the direction of triple-loop learning.

An example of triple-loop learning, taken from Gozdz's (1999) research, involves the CEO of a major American oil company, which is transforming into a learning organization. We will refer to him as David Nobel from Grail Oil. During a multiyear transformation process involving about twenty thousand people and at least five operating companies, Nobel made a decision to address diversity and white male privilege. He initiated a companywide diversity-training program and required all senior executives to attend. Then he instructed his senior staff to create and implement diversity-related practices throughout the company.

Nobel's decision to take these actions required him to reflect on his own fundamental assumptions as well as those of his company and of society. This triple-loop learning process exemplifies our approach to transformation because it is directly related to improving business performance while simultaneously fostering developmental growth in the company and its employees.

Triple-loop learning can be a transformational process in which learning allows us to go beyond cultural assumptions and stereotypes and to develop whole new levels of competence and capability. David Nobel fostered triple-loop learning by focusing on his own, his institution's, and society's view of diversity. His specific focus is worth noting:

> There are both personal and business reasons for my emphasis on diversity as part of our transformation effort. All of my growing up experience was conditioned to go against the underlying beliefs upon which diversity initiative was formed. The root of my personal conviction around the diversity issue is shame. I grew up in the "Jim Crow South." It was a time and place in which both race and sex were very clear lines of demarcation and instruments of superiority. That superiority was sanctioned by every institution—the state, church, schools, the family, everything. My ideas and beliefs about women and their "place in society," for example, were formed by the society and times within which I was growing up.
>
> My whole life was conditioned by certain environmental experiences early in life. It was, well, not the way Gloria Steinem would like to see us growing up today. My beliefs about race and gender continued on in my mind and at least in terms of immediate reaction, conditioned my first thoughts. I was a racist, no question. Upon seeing a Black man act in a certain way, I would say "isn't that typical? That's exactly the way 'they are.'" As I started looking at the world around me, I thought about race and gender in our corporation and decided to work on this both personally and in the corporation.
>
> That's why the idea of really examining, not just the surface of things, but looking at a little deeper level produced such a profound personal change in me. It was not until my very

late years, I am sorry to say, that I began to examine and look at things beyond the superficial, beyond the readily apparent. Doing this, I began to reach very, very deep and different conclusions. . . .

On a more intellectual level, I believed there was a very profound case in terms of business to pursue this question of diversity. That's why I put our diversity initiative in place. I did combine business and personal reasons to examine the diversity issue, but my changed thinking and shame were important. I thought, my God, you have lived 50 years with these kinds of wrong and immoral views and acted upon them in many cases. Somehow there is an act of not just good business sense, but of a sense of atonement for wrong personal beliefs involved. (Gozdz 1999, 171)

This example of introspection led to triple-loop learning at Grail Oil as an institution. It produced social learning, institutional learning, and personal learning.

TRANSPERSONAL PSYCHOLOGY

Beyond developmental theory and learning, our approach is firmly rooted in the field of transpersonal psychology and founded on the work of William James, Carl Jung, Carl Rogers, and Abraham Maslow. The best-known transpersonal theorist today is Ken Wilber, whose books are among the most widely read philosophical and psychological works in the world.

Founded in 1969, the field of transpersonal psychology investigates the full range of human experience, from psychotic and neurotic states to states of genius and inspiration. The field focuses on the study of humanity's highest potentials and on the understanding of what Maslow called peak experiences (Maslow 1987). Peak experiences are especially joyous and exciting moments in the lives of every individual and may include mystical and transcendent experiences. Such experiences have been among the most potent influences on human behavior throughout history and have been a major influence on the world's major religions. Transpersonal psychology has been defined as "a healing endeavor that aims at the integration of physical, emotional, mental, and spiritual aspects of well-being" (Vaughan 1993, 160). A major goal is to facilitate the attainment of optimal psychological health, and impulses to adult development and spiritual growth are considered basic in healthy individuals.

Psychology's interest in the transpersonal is recent relative to the actual primary sources from which it has drawn theory and practice. Plato, Buddha, Jesus, Moses, and Muhammad were all transpersonally oriented spiritual teachers and social reformers. Modern transpersonal psychology draws from the wisdom of the world's spiritual traditions and also from over thirty years of research and theory in psychology, particularly in studies of exceptional, high-achieving people. Consistent with a transpersonal approach, human performance research in the business world suggests that high human development is a basic foundation for great business performance (Collins, 2001).

AN INTEGRATED SPIRITUAL TRANSFORMATION APPROACH: THE FOUR-QUADRANT APPROACH TO PERSONAL AND ORGANIZATIONAL GROWTH

A central element in our approach is the four-quadrant model of individual and organizational transformation developed by Ken Wilber. His model (Wilber 1996, 2000a, 2000b) provides a powerful meta-theory encompassing most conceivable approaches to human experience and behavior. This system is particularly valuable in its integration of individual and institutional dynamics.

The development of both individuals and institutions requires what Wilber calls an integral approach to growth. This kind of growth is a four-quadrant process. The variables that generate the four quadrants are individual and collective, and inner and outer, and are shown below.

Individual/Inner: Tacit knowledge, purpose, values, and personal maturity	Individual/Outer: Explicit knowledge, technical skills, and competencies
Collective/Inner: Collective mental models, culture, community	Collective/Outer: Systems, processes, infrastructures

The upper right quadrant refers to the individual viewed objectively and focuses primarily on outer behavior (the traditional domain of academic psychology). The upper left quadrant includes the individual's personal or subjective experiences, including thoughts, feelings, values, and consciousness (major areas of interest for transpersonal psychology). The upper left quadrant includes what Polanyi (1958/1962) called "tacit knowledge." This is that aspect of our knowing that cannot be put fully into words or mental models. As Polanyi suggested, we know more than we can tell. One of the greatest challenges to modern social science is the integration of these two realms, coming to a greater understanding of the interactions of the subjective, inner world and the outer world of action.

The lower left quadrant includes those patterns in consciousness (such as values and beliefs) shared by members of a particular culture or subculture. It includes our institutional or communal mental models and the worldview of an institution or community. The lower right quadrant includes the objective aspects of organizations and societies. Wilber calls these "intersubjective realities" the social system, which includes social institutions, patterns of communication, economic and political structures. We include in this quadrant organizational governance, institutional infrastructure, and processes such as capital spending and budgeting.

These four quadrants interact in any complex behavior and provide a holistic approach to analyzing business situations. In our approach we have often referred to organization and personal transformation. But in Wilber's model, we can see that personal transformation occurs in the upper left and upper right quadrants, and organizational transformation occurs in the lower left and lower right quadrants.

We can relate the upper left quadrant to employees' personal understanding of corporate values and their implications for action. To the extent that an employee consciously grapples with the personal assumptions underlying their decision-making processes, they are reflecting the dynamics of this quadrant.

The upper right quadrant relates to a person's technical business skills and competencies. This might include the ability to generate a capital-spending plan, conduct a variance analysis, or drive a truck. Most training and human resource development lies squarely in this quadrant.

The lower right quadrant includes tangible business structures. These can involve physical plant, drawings, or codified work. Another example is the tangible portion of information systems, such as computer programs, hardware, and tangible aspects of computer networks. It also includes externally codified governance processes such as formal power and authority relationships between a parent company and a subsidiary. We place in this quadrant all tangible infrastructure from company policies, procedures, and systems.

The lower left quadrant is the domain of communal assumptions and mental models. Broadly speaking it is the organization's culture. These components constitute the tacit and explicit collective assumptions from which the organization consciously and unconsciously does business. This quadrant also includes the collective experience of community in a company, an intangible collective reality. We focus on this domain of inner collective reality when we build context at the organizational level. The lower left quadrant includes the tacit learning community within the organization.

Others have been applying Wilber's integral approach to business. Geoffrey Gioja has presented Integral Leadership seminars to many leading companies. Others working with Wilber's ideas include John Forman, Leo Burke, Ian Mitroff, Don Beck, Tony Schwartz, Bill Torbert, and Warren Bennis. Daryl Paulson has shown that there are four major theories of business management, and these are actually the four quadrants—Theory X stresses individual behavior; Theory Y focuses on psychological understanding; cultural management looks at organizational culture; and systems management emphasizes the organization's social systems and its governance.

Nonaka and Takeuchi's (1995) ontology for knowledge creation and Wilber's four-quadrant model suggest that personal and organizational dimensions of knowledge interact at increasing levels of scale on both tacit (internal) and explicit (external) dimensions:

> . . . an organization cannot create knowledge by itself. Tacit knowledge of individuals is the basis of organizational knowledge creation. The organization has to mobilize tacit knowledge created and accumulated at the individual level. The mobilized tacit knowledge is "organizationally" amplified. . . . We call this the "knowledge spiral," in which the interaction between tacit knowledge and explicit knowledge will become larger in scale as it moves up the ontological levels. Thus, organizational knowledge creation is a spiral process, starting at the individual level and moving up through expanding communities of interaction, that crosses sectional, departmental, divisional, and organizational boundaries. (72)

A FOUR-STAGE DEVELOPMENTAL MODEL FOR ORGANIZATIONS AND INDIVIDUALS

Our model was initially inspired by the simplicity and effectiveness of Peck's (1988) four spiritual development stages, distilled from Fowler's (1981) work on stages of faith. We have drawn primarily from two sophisticated spiritual systems—the Zen Ox-Herding pictures and the Sufi stages of the transformation of the self.

The stages of spiritual growth have been graphically represented in Zen Buddhism as the Ox-Herding pictures. The best-known and most respected series is the ten Ox-Herding pictures of Kakuan. This series begins with searching for one's own enlightened nature, Seeking the Ox (one's Buddha Nature), and ends with dedication to service, Entering the City with Bliss-Bestowing Hands.

The seven stages of the transformation of the self in Sufism begins with the egocentric, narcissistic self, the greatest single obstacle to our spiritual development. The final stage is the "pure self," which is completely transparent to the divine.

We have been influenced in developing our four-stage system by Wilber's (1996, 2000a) integration of dozens of psychological and spiritual development systems, and also Graves' theory of cultural developmental stages as developed by Beck and Cowan (1996). Our work has been refined by examining Piaget's (1950) model of cognitive development and Wade's (1996) discussion of developmental psychology from a transpersonal perspective.

We took on the challenge of developing a relatively simple psycho-spiritual model that describes both individual and organizational stages of development for our clients. We wanted a practical tool that is descriptive, easily understood, and immediately useful to businesspeople. It has been used successfully with businesspeople with no prior theoretical knowledge of psychology or developmental theory.

We have used this model in working with organizations. Our clients have found it is a valuable tool that describes their organization and also describes the stages at which their personnel operate. Our model was constructed a priori. It does, however, build on the empirical research of the developmentalists, and it has provided invaluable heuristic insights in our applications in the field. Our model provides a practical map that describes more a set of possibilities than a developmental mandate and is comprised of four stages: Unprincipled, Conventional, Self-Actualizing, and Integral.

STAGE I. UNPRINCIPLED

	Inner	Outer
Individual	Narcissism, unconsciousness	Rule-breaker, obey from fear of punishment
Collective	Short-term profits, *"caveat emptor"*	Arbitrary management, "sweat shops"

Individual

Stage I people tend to be narcissistic and egocentric. Wilber (2000a) has pointed out that Stage I narcissism consists of both the overvaluing of the self and its abilities and also the undervaluing of others and their talents or contributions. Developmental theorists refer to the first stage of development as egocentric, meaning that infants are incapable of taking the role of the other. Wilber (2000a, 17) writes that, "Development, in fact, can be defined as a *successive decrease in egocentrism*" (italics in original).

Narcissists will not forgo their needs for anyone or anything outside themselves and have no regard for any higher authority or principles that might limit their self-seeking motivation. Stage I people insist on having their own way; they seek to control and dominate others in their lives, regardless of the damage this does. In the extreme they are psychopaths, who have no conscience and no sense of compassion.

But Stage I people refuse to admit they have a problem. In some ways, Stage I people have an ego addiction. They become obsessed with protecting their false self-image, their fragile pride, and their narcissistic ego. When threatened, they can easily turn to violence or abuse. Most theories of human nature describe people at the later stages. Theorists rarely discuss this first level of unconscious, self-centered, unprincipled behavior, perhaps assuming that we have all transcended this stage, in spite of the stories of violence, greed, and dishonesty filling our news.

As Peck (1983) has pointed out, Stage I people characteristically exhibit dishonest behavior. Many people still operate, at least part of the time, in this first stage, although most will deny it and try to rationalize their dishonesty. (For example, in a survey of twenty thousand people, over 12 percent admitted they were dishonest and would steal or cheat if given the chance [Case 2000].)

Stage I people only follow the rules (of their company or of society) from fear of punishment. They will break the rules whenever they can get away with it, or they will try and distort the rules and "bend" them in their favor. But one of the hallmarks of Stage I is a lack of consciousness. The Sufis have called this the stage of "waking sleep." Stage I people are heedless of the damage they do and tend to deny or rationalize away their own selfish behavior. They are often quite intelligent and may seem to be effective learners. However, their narcissism distorts their learning. Their learning process is distorted by an ego-centered lens.

Collective

Stage I institutions are dysfunctional for society and for the planet. They follow a philosophy of greed and a sense of being above the law, equating economic power with moral justification for their actions. Their long- and short-term goals are self-serving; Stage I companies despoil and pollute the earth and atmosphere in order to maximize profits. They tend to value short-term profits over long-term gains, and habitually overcharge and underserve their customers. They see the business world as a jungle in which everyone fights for survival and anything goes. Their customer service motto is caveat emptor, "let the buyer beware." They value merciless tactics, like "going for the jugular," as viable, sensible, and even laudable. A common belief is that it is a "dog eat dog" world, and you must cheat others before they cheat you.

Stage I management systems manipulate or withhold information, and support outright lies to customers and also to employees. Their systems are organized to take advantage of both customers and employees as well. Sweat shops around the world that employee disenfranchised adults or use child labor are examples of Stage I businesses.

Stage I institutions are often run by a tyrannical boss, who generally has absolute control over power and economic resources. The person in charge may share power with a few loyal followers. Manipulative, narcissistic leaders govern by developing arbitrary laws to serve their own purposes. Without any possibility of appeal to logical or ethical standards, there is little sense of security or trust among employees and customers alike. Power is exercised absolutely and often crudely or harshly, because there exists no sense of the rule of law or of legitimacy of authority. People are cowed by fear.

STAGE II. CONVENTIONAL

	Inner	Outer
Individual	Attachment to structure	Rule-bound, dogmatic, conformist
Collective	Conservatism	Authoritarian management

Individual

Stage II people are characterized by self-doubt. They seek the comfort of external rules and authoritarian structure because they are afraid to rely on themselves and their own judgment. Relatively healthy Stage II people have more self-confidence. Others cover their self-doubt with a façade of certainty and superiority. The greater the self-doubt, the more Stage II individuals tend to become attached to external rules and rigid conventions.

Research on authoritarianism (Adorno et al. 1950) has found such people tend to be subservient to those above them in the system, and arrogant to those below them. Healthy Stage II individuals temper their authority with a sense of fairness and respect for the rules and values of the system; unhealthy Stage II people can easily become tyrants, even slipping toward Stage I behavior.

Stage II learners tend to be single-loop learners and are uncomfortable with the double-loop process of questioning basic assumptions, because this process threatens their fragile self-concept and rigid belief system. Stage II learners may project a certain attitude of false efficiency, which takes the form of: "Let's just solve this and get on with it!" This means, seek an immediate solution and don't "philosophize" about deeper issues like underlying assumptions.

Stage II business leaders tend to behave like the old generals who insist on refighting the last war, instead of perceiving how current military thinking and technology dictate entirely new strategies. They have certain well-developed skills and knowledge, and they stay unwilling to learn new ways of functioning. In fact, many Stage II people enter the military where they are surrounded by a strong, well-defined, bureaucratic-mechanistic-hierarchical Stage II structure, a structure that provides detailed and specific rules to follow in most aspects of life.

The strict drill sergeant is an excellent illustration of a Stage II leader. The sergeant's tremendous authority over recruits comes from his position as a representative of the system. To question him means to question the system, which is absolutely forbidden.

Collective

The culture of a Stage II institution emphasizes the importance of following the rules. The motto might well be "love it or leave it." The culture demands unconditional acceptance of the system and its rules. Working hard is valued, and obedience is more important than initiative. The atmosphere is often autocratic and patriarchal; family businesses often function as Stage II institutions.

Stage II institutions value rules and regulations. They advocate the old-fashioned management approach of controlling employees' behavior through detailed rules and procedures, and enforcing the rules with threats of punishment. They tend to be conservative and conventional, using the same "time-tested" techniques of manufacturing, marketing, and so forth no matter how economic conditions and customer demands have changed. They value "reliability," which means continuing to do what worked well in the past, no matter what the present requires. Because Stage II institutions tend to remain unresponsive to the need for change, they risk serious danger of failure when markets and competition change.

The structure of the military provides an excellent example of a Stage II institutional structure. There is a clearly defined hierarchy, and the higher up in the hierarchy, the more power one has over those below. Promotion comes from following the rules. Creativity and initiative are rewarded, but only within the limits of the rules. Rank determines the opportunity or tolerance for any creativity.

Stage III. Self-Actualizing

	Inner	Outer
Individual	Commitment to self-development	Rule-maker, hard-working, competitive
Collective	Teamwork, win-lose orientation	Excellence in planning and problem solving

Individual

Stage III people commit to self-development and tend to make growth-oriented choices in their lives. They are present-centered; they experience the world more fully than most people, with concentration and heightened awareness. Maslow (1971) found they have managed to reduce their ego defenses and have become more capable of relating to others and perceiving the world around them with minimal distortion. They develop self-awareness, a clear sense of their own values and tastes, and they act in terms of their inner values. They have also enjoyed "peak experiences," heightened moments in which they felt uplifted and inspired, or in which they functioned at their very best.

Stage III people work hard and often succeed at the goals they set. They tend to be entrepreneurs, and seek to improve both their own skills and capacities and also their organizational system. They are ambitious and want to be recognized and rewarded for their achievements. As a result, working hard and working long hours becomes the norm, often resulting in executive burnout.

Stage III leaders tend to have good judgment and are committed to the values and principles of the organization. They intuitively know which among dozens of problems will become the most important in the long run. Although prone to overwork, they do use their time and energy well.

Stage III learners often employ double-loop learning. They can develop considerable sophistication concerning systems dynamics and the role of institutional assumptions in problem solving. They take as a challenge, not as a threat, the questioning of assumptions underlying organizational processes such as decision-making and implementation. Because they remain ego-oriented, they tend to compete with each other, often at the expense of the larger interests of the organization or at the expense of the relationship between the organization and the social or physical environments.

David Nobel reflects back on the Stage III phase of his career from a Stage IV perspective:

> After about 12 or 13 years of working with Grail in science applications, I began to get into positions of management and business strategy. I approached much of my business work with essentially the same scientific worldview. Instead of doing differential equations, drawing maps of oil finds and so forth, I just worried about columns of numbers that were dollars. My outlook and relationships with other people were still very individualistic. I was not uncaring of other people in the business world, but I was very separated from others. (Gozdz 1999, 162)

Collective

Stage III institutions value growth and innovation. Their motto is "work hard *and* work smart." Competitive Stage III organizations value teamwork, which unconsciously entails a sports-based, "win-lose" attitude. The team orientation stresses cooperation and mutual support among team members, along with the notion that "our team" is out to beat the other teams. Successful competition has great appeal to the ego.

Stage III organizations are skilled at planning and responding to change. Their firms have institutionalized effective structures *and processes* for strategizing, planning, and problem solving. The institution supports and rewards individual effort and success, as well as cooperative teamwork. Initiative gets rewarded with bonuses and promotions. Those who produce the most value for the institution receive promotions the most rapidly. Sometimes, Stage III organizations invest in the personal and interpersonal development of their people in addition to training in required technical skills.

Competition with other institutions is typical, reinforced by the ego orientation of Stage III. Bill Gates certainly illustrates a highly accomplished Stage III entrepreneur, and he built an extremely successful Stage III company, although some might argue that Microsoft's competitiveness became heightened to an extreme, reminiscent of Stage I organizations.

STAGE IV. INTEGRAL

	Inner	Outer
Individual	Commitment to self-transformation, a sense of vocation, connectedness, concern for others	Rule-transcender, servant leadership
Collective	Learning community, embrace change, value customer service	Learning organization

Individual

Stage IV people have begun to drop their ego orientation and have started to operate in a new way. They have generally experienced powerful, transcendent peak experiences of love and connection to the world and to others, and to that which is transcendent (what Maslow called the "Being-values" such as truth, beauty, and honesty). Such experiences tend to increase humility and compassion and decrease self-concern and self-importance. This is real spirituality, which involves moving from ego-based willfulness to a "willingness" to surrender to those forces far greater than self.

This kind of willingness is beautifully described by the great statesman Dag Hammarskjold (1966):

> I don't know Who—or what—put the question. I don't know when it was put. I don't even remember answering. But at some moment I did answer Yes to Someone—or Something— and from that hour I was certain that existence is meaningful and that, therefore, my life, in self-surrender, had a goal. (205)

Underlying all the thoughts and actions of these advanced Stage IV people is a sense of inner and outer unity. They have recognized that, in Zen terms, everything is Buddha; in Sufi terminology, Stage IV people have become "rule-transcendent" because they realize that the best set of rules is only a partial solution, one that does not apply at all times or under all circumstances. They understand through direct experience that the world is not a static, closed system. It is ever-changing, composed of interrelated dynamic processes. Because of this understanding, Stage IV people devote themselves to mastering change, growth, and flexible long-term planning. Stage IV leaders have a clear vision for their company or organization, and they can articulate their vision in clear and inspiring ways.

At Stage IV we find triple-loop learning. Because Stage IV people are aware of the interdependence of all things, they can easily see the importance of questioning social and cultural assumptions as well as their own assumptions and those of their institution. Because of their lack of attachment to ego, this process is never threatening. In fact, Stage IV individuals generally believe it is part of their responsibility as leaders to question deeply these different levels of assumptions.

Stage IV individuals illustrate Robert Greenleaf's concept of servant leadership. As servant leaders, Stage IV people seek to find better ways to serve others' needs—employees and customers alike. They are people-building, not people-using. As we mentioned earlier in our example of triple-loop learning, Stage IV leaders do not only bring out the capacities and gifts of those they work with. They also help others grow to new developmental stages, and in the process to form whole new levels of capacity.

A modern Zen master illustrates the inner state of an advanced Stage IV individual:

When we become truly ourselves, we just become a swinging door, and we are purely independent of, and at the same time, dependent upon everything. Without air, we cannot breathe. Each one of us is in the midst of myriads of worlds. We are in the center of the world always, moment after moment. So we are completely dependent and independent. If you have this kind of experience, this kind of existence, you have absolute independence; you will not be bothered by anything. . . . This kind of activity is the fundamental activity of the universal being. (Suzuki 1970, 31)

Collective

Stage IV institutions enjoy a culture that values flexibility and embraces change and paradox. They have become learning institutions; they understand that the world and the marketplace are constantly changing, and that a healthy institution has to keep learning, growing, and changing in order to keep pace. Stage IV institutions are "world-centric" in their worldview, not bound solely by what is good for the institution. Decisions and strategy relate to the highest values and purpose of the institution within the context of the society and the world at large.

Stage IV organizations do not simply *respond* to change. They plan ahead and organize themselves for the future, actively and creatively meeting future trends. Their planning includes a self-transcendent, good-of-the-whole perspective.

Stage IV organizations function like martial arts masters, always ready to respond instantly and effectively to a threat or an attack from any direction. A master's balanced posture enables freedom of movement in any direction. The master can respond instantly, elegantly, and effectively without having to shift posture in order to act. A martial arts master remains alert and aware, effortlessly taking in all aspects of the environment. As a result, masters are rarely if ever surprised or taken at a disadvantage. Their perceptions are not distorted by expectations or other mental models, so they perceive the world as it is. They remain open for whatever might happen.

Because of their balanced posture, readiness to respond, and sensitive awareness of the environment, Stage IV organizations almost automatically take advantage of change. They seem to be magnets for synchronicities, for favorable "accidents" of fate.

The institutional structure is characterized by functional groups, groups developed to attain specific objectives. A loose hierarchy of authority shifts according to the tasks undertaken. Authority is given according to capacity to handle a given job, not locked into a position on an organizational chart. Stage IV institutions have become flexible, highly functional learning organizations supported by the ideals and values of healthy learning communities. (For us, the term *learning organization* refers to institutional *structure,* or the lower right quadrant in Wilber's model. *Learning community* refers to the lower left communal mental models, assumptions, and culture of an organization. It is a worldview that supports and nurtures the development of all its members.)

Stage IV organizations value service, and they tend to have excellent customer relations. Satisfied customers are one of the great strengths of these institutions. They actively seek feedback from customers and from the marketplace, and they have developed flexible infrastructures responsive to this feedback. Rather than think in terms of competition, Stage IV companies naturally seek cooperative, synergistic, "win-win" solutions.

CONCLUSION

We can summarize some of the major distinctions among the four stages as follows:

Individual Stages

I. Narcissistic	Rule-breaker	Unskilled apprentice (needs constant supervision)
II. Conformist	Rule-bound	Journeyman (needs some supervision)
III. Success-oriented	Rule-maker	Professional (functions independently, creative)
IV. Integrated	Rule-transcender	Master (develops radically new approaches and techniques)

Institutional Stages

I. Self-serving	Arbitrary leadership	Fear-based management
II. Conventional	Authoritarian leadership	Obedience-based management
III. Competitive	Team leadership	Team-based management
IV. Cooperative	Servant leadership	Learning-based management

In this chapter we have outlined a praxis for transforming ordinary business issues into opportunities for personal and organizational transformation, beginning by framing three aspects of our approach: content, process, and context. These are vehicles for development because the specific content of every business issue resides within a particular context.

Our work suggests that spiritual growth is no farther away than our attention to the limits of our current ability. Difficult work challenges are seen as limits of developmental level, which when our clients work through them, produce business results and grow themselves.

But a praxis has to be simple and effective to educate businesspeople quickly and efficiently. Our approach achieves business results and simultaneously promotes awareness of personal and organizational development. As practitioners, we have seen our model achieve this goal for our clients, and we are certain it can serve to link spiritual concerns and business realities for other organizations as well.

REFERENCES

Adorno, T.; E. Frenkel-Brunswick; D. Levinson; and R. Sanford. (1950). *The Authoritarian Personality.* New York: Harper.

Argyris, C. (1982). *Reasoning Learning and Action.* San Francisco: Jossey-Bass.

Beck, D.E., and C.C. Cowan. (1996). *Spiral Dynamics.* Malden, MA: Blackwell.

Case, J. (2000). *Employee Theft: The Profit Killer.* Delmar, CA: Case and Associates.

Cohen, M., and J. March. (1991). "The Process of Change." In *Organization and Governance in Higher Education,* 4th ed. Needham Heights: Ginn Press.

Collins, J. (2001). "Level 5 Leadership: The Triumph of Humility and Fierce Resolve." *Harvard Business Review* (January): 10–17.

Erikson, E. (1963). *Childhood and Society,* 2d ed. New York: Norton.

———. (1964). *Insight and Responsibility.* New York: Norton.

———. (1980). *Identity and the Life Cycle.* New York: Norton.

Fisher D., and W.R. Torbert. (1995). *Personal and Organizational Transformations.* New York: McGraw-Hill.

Fisher, D.; D. Rooke; and W. Torbert. (2001). *Personal and Organizational Transformations: Through Action Inquiry.* Boston: Edge\Work Press.

Fowler, J.W. (1981). *Stages of Faith: The Psychology of Human Development and the Quest for Meaning.* San Francisco: Harper and Row.

Gozdz, K. (1999). "A Transpersonal Heuristic Inquiry Into a Learning Organization Undergoing Transformation." Unpublished doctoral dissertation, Institute of Transpersonal Psychology, Palo Alto, CA.

Greenleaf, R. (1977). *Servant Leadership: A Journey into the Nature of Legitimate Power and Greatness.* New York: Paulist Press.

Hammarskjold, D. (1966). *Markings.* New York: Knopf.

Jacoby, J. (1959). *Complex, Archetype, Symbol in the Psychology of C. G. Jung.* New York: Pantheon Books.

Maslow, A. (1965). *Eupsychian Management: A Journal.* Homewood, IL: Irwin.

———. (1971). *The Farther Reaches of Human Nature.* New York: Viking.

———. (1987). *Motivation and Personality*, 3d ed., rev. R. Frager, J. Fadiman, C. McReynolds, and R. Cox. New York: Harper and Row.

———. (1998). *Maslow on Management.* New York: Wiley.

Mezirow, J. (1991). *Transformative Dimensions of Adult Learning.* San Francisco: Jossey-Bass.

Nonaka, L., and H. Takeuchi. (1995). *The Knowledge-Creating Company.* New York: Oxford University Press.

Parry, C., and M. Darling. (2001). "Emergent Learning in Action: The After Action Review." *Systems Thinker* 12, no. 8: 1–5.

Peck, M.S. (1978). *The Road Less Traveled.* New York: Simon and Schuster.

———. (1983). *People of the Lie.* New York: Simon and Schuster.

———. (1988). *The Different Drum: Community Making and Peace.* New York: Simon and Schuster.

Piaget, J. (1950). *The Psychology of Intelligence.* London: Routledge and Kegan-Paul.

Polanyi, M. (1958/62). *Personal Knowledge.* Chicago: University of Chicago Press.

Schein, E. (1992). *Organizational Culture and Leadership*, 2d ed. San Francisco: Jossey-Bass.

Senge, P. (1990). *The Fifth Discipline.* New York: Doubleday.

Suzuki, D.T. (1959). *Zen and Japanese Culture.* New York: Pantheon.

Suzuki, S. (1970). *Zen Mind, Beginners Mind.* New York: Weatherhill.

Vaughan, F. (1993). "Healing and Wholeness: Transpersonal Psychotherapy." In *Paths Beyond Ego*, ed. R. Walsh and F. Vaughan. Los Angeles: Tarcher.

Wade, J. (1996). *Changes of Mind: A Holonomic Theory of the Evolution of Consciousness.* Albany: State University of New York Press.

Webster's New Twentieth Century Dictionary of the English Language, Unabridged. (1979) New York: Simon and Schuster.

Wilber, K. (1996). *A Brief History of Everything.* Boston: Shambhala.

———. (2000a). *A Theory of Everything.* Boston: Shambhala.

———. (2000b). *Integral Psychology.* Boston: Shambhala.

ABOUT THE EDITORS AND CONTRIBUTORS

Virgil H. Adams III is an assistant professor of psychology and assistant research scientist of gerontology at the University of Kansas. His scholarly interests center around well-being, hope, aging, and minority populations with particular interest in African Americans.

Blake E. Ashforth is the Jerry and Mary Ann Chapman Professor of Business at Arizona State University. He received his Ph.D. from the University of Toronto. His research focuses on identity and identification in organizational settings, socialization and newcomer work adjustment, the dysfunctions of organizational structures and processes, and the links among individual-, group-, and organization-level phenomena. Dr. Ashford recently wrote *Role Transitions in Organizational Life: An Identity-Based Perspective* (2001).

Richard Barrett is an internationally known culture consultant and keynote speaker on values, culture change, and personal transformation. He works with leaders and senior executives in North America, Europe, and Australia to develop values-driven organizational cultures that build human capital, strengthen financial performance, and support sustainable development. Barrett is listed in the *National Register of Who's Who in Executives and Professionals* 2002–2003 edition, is a fellow of the World Business Academy, and is former values coordinator at the World Bank. He is the creator of the "corporate transformation tools" values assessment instruments, and author of the book *A Guide to Liberating Your Soul* and *Liberating the Corporate Soul.*

Jerry Biberman is chair of the management/marketing department and professor of management at the University of Scranton. He writes, teaches, consults, speaks, and conduct workshops in the areas of work and spirituality, workplace diversity, and organization transformation. Biberman is coeditor (with Michael Whitty, professor of management, College of Business, University of Detroit-Mercy) of *Work and Spirit: a Reader of New Spiritual Paradigms for Organizations*, published by the University of Scranton Press. He was a founder and first chair of the Management, Spirituality and Religion interest group of the Academy of Management, and cofounder and track chair of the Spirituality in Organizations track of the International Academy of Business Disciplines.

Michael G. Bowen has taught at the University of Illinois at Urbana-Champaign, the University of Notre Dame, the University of Tampa, and the University of South Florida (USF). He has published scholarly papers and case studies on the "escalation phenomenon," business ethics, leadership, and decision-making. Areas of expertise also include systems thinking and planning, leadership development, community building, managerial decision-making, and group dynamics. Dr. Bowen is currently a visiting professor at the USF, a cofounder of the Leadership House and the Leadership Development Center at USF, and does some management consulting and personal coaching.

Rogene A. Buchholz, Legendre-Soule Professor of Business Ethics, Loyola University New Orleans, has published twelve books and some seventy-five articles in the area of business ethics, social issues in management, and environmental ethics. He has served on several editorial boards and is past chair of the Social Issues in Management division of the Academy of Management.

John B. Cullen is professor of management at Washington State University. He has also served on the faculties of the University of Nebraska, the University of Rhode Island, Waseda and Keio Universities in Japan (as a Fulbright lecturer), and the Catholic University of Lille in France. Prof. Cullen is the author or coauthor of four books and over fifty journal articles. His publications have appeared in journals such as *Administrative Science Quarterly, Academy of Management Journal, Journal of International Business Studies, Journal of Management, Organizational Studies, Management International Review, Journal of Vocational Behavior, American Journal of Sociology, Organizational Dynamics*, and the *Journal of World Business.*

David Efraty earned his Ph.D. from the department of organizational behavior, Weatherhead School of Management, Case Western Reserve University. Currently, he is a professor of management and organizational behavior at the University of Houston Downtown. His research work relates to organizational identification and organizational commitment and their impact on performance and quality of work life.

Gordon E. Dehler received his Ph.D. from the University of Cincinnati and is an associate professor in the organizational sciences program at the George Washington University. His research interests fall under the broad umbrella of organization change, focusing on issues pertaining to the transformation to the "new paradigm," recently incorporating views from critical theory. Specific domains of inquiry address organization architecture, management learning, new product development, constructive deviance, as well as the secular implications of spirituality in work life. His publications have appeared in *Academy of Management Journal, Management Learning, Journal of Management Education, Journal of Managerial Psychology.*

Riane Eisler is a cultural historian and evolutionary theorist and the author of numerous books, including *The Chalice and The Blade, Sacred Pleasure, Tomorrow's Children*, and *The Power of Partnership.* She is president of the Center for Partnership Studies, a founding member of the General Evolution Research Group, a fellow of the World Academy of Art and Science and the World Business Academy, and a member of many editorial boards. Dr. Eisler is the author of over 100 essays and articles for publications ranging from *Futures, Behavioral Science, Holistic Education Review*, and *Political Psychology* to *Brain and Mind, The UNESCO Courier, The International Journal of Women's Studies*, the *Human Rights Quarterly*, and the *World Encyclopedia of Peace.* She has taught at the University of California and Immaculate Heart College in Los Angeles.

Dawn R. Elm is professor of management in the University of St. Thomas College of Business. She has published a variety of articles on ethical decision-making, honesty, and women's issues in journals such as the *Journal of Business Ethics, Human Relations,* and *Business & Society.* Prof. Elm has also contributed to several books on the above subjects published by JAI Press and Oxford University Press. Her research interests include ethical decision-making and spirituality at work. Prof. Elm is a member of the editorial board of the *Journal of Business Ethics* and serves as a reviewer for numerous other journals in the business and society field.

Robert A. Emmons is professor of psychology at the University of California—Davis. His research is at the interface of personality psychology and religion. Emphasis is on the measurement of personal strivings as determinants of subjective quality of life outcomes. Dr. Emmons is a consulting editor for the *Journal of Personality* and *Social Psychology*, a member of the editorial board of the *International Journal of the Psychology of Religion*, and a member of the American Psychological Association, the Society for the Scientific Study of Religion, and the American Academy of Religion. He is the author of *The Psychology of Ultimate Concerns: Motivation and Spirituality in Personality*.

Gerald R. Ferris is the Francis Eppes Professor of Management and professor of psychology at Florida State University. Formerly, he held the Robert M. Hearin Chair of Business Administration and was professor of management and acting associate dean for faculty and research in the School of Business Administration at the University of Mississippi. Dr. Ferris received a Ph.D. in business administration from the University of Illinois at Urbana—Champaign. His research interests are in the areas of social influence processes in human resources systems and the role of reputation in organizations. He is the author of articles published in such journals as the *Journal of Applied Psychology*, *Organizational Behavior and Human Decision Processes*, *Personnel Psychology*, *Academy of Management Journal*, and *Academy of Management Review*. Dr. Ferris serves as editor of the annual series *Research in Personnel and Human Resources Management*.

Robert Frager received his doctorate in social psychology from Harvard University and has taught psychology at Harvard, University of California—Berkeley, and University of California—Santa Cruz. He has led training and consulting programs for businesses for over fifteen years. His research interests include the interaction between social and cultural context and individual behavior and also exceptional human performance. Dr. Frager has been a pioneer in the field of transpersonal psychology, and, in 1975, he founded the Institute of Transpersonal Psychology, an accredited psychology graduate school offering M.A. and Ph.D. degrees. He has coauthored a transpersonally-oriented textbook, *Personality and Personal Growth*, which is now in its fifth edition, and is past president of the Association for Transpersonal Psychology.

Adrian Furnham was educated at the London School of Economics and Oxford and is currently professor of psychology at the University of California—Los Angeles, where he has been for twenty years. He has wide interests in applied psychology and has written thirty-five books and 450 peer-reviewed papers. His first degree was in divinity but he "fell among thieves" and ended up being a psychologist. Dr. Furnham was raised in colonial Africa by parents of British decent and still enjoys travelling. In 2002 he lectured in eighteen countries on all five continents.

Jean-Claude Garcia-Zamor is a professor of public administration at Florida International University. He is also an adjunct professor at Leipzig University in the former East Germany. Dr. Garcia-Zamor is the author of four books and has edited or coedited five others. He also has published extensively in professional journals. He holds a Ph.D. in public administration from New York University.

Robert A. Giacalone is the Surtman Distinguished Professor of Business Ethics in the Department of Management at the Belk College of Business Administration. His areas of research include business ethics, employee sabotage and destructiveness, exit interviewing and surveying, and the impact of employee image management on organizations. He has served as a consultant to numerous organizations and is the author/editor of five books and numerous scholarly articles.

Kazimierz Gozdz is a researcher and organizational consultant specializing in developing learning organizations/communities from a transpersonal perspective. His consulting practice has emphasized corporate transformation and leadership development. He is editor of the anthology, *Community Building: Renewing Spirit and Learning in Business.*

C. Gay Hendricks is Professor Emeritus at the University of Colorado. He is author and coauthor of twenty-four books, including *The Corporate Mystic, Conscious Living,* and *Achieving Vibrance.* Dr. Hendricks is cofounder of The Hendricks Institute, an international learning center that teaches the core skills of conscious living for professionals and organizations. He received his Ph.D. from Stanford University.

Kathlyn T. Hendricks is a member of the Academy of Dance Therapists and has been registered with the American Dance Therapy Association since 1975. She is the coauthor of nine books, including *Conscious Loving, At the Speed of Life,* and *The Conscious Heart.* Dr. Hendricks is also a cofounder of The Hendricks Institute. She received her Ph.D. from the Institute for Transpersonal Psychology.

Peter C. Hill is professor of psychology at the Rosemead School of Psychology in La Mirada, California. Formerly, he was professor of psychology at Grove City College in Grove City, Pennsylvania. He received his Ph.D. in social psychology from the University of Houston. Dr. Hill has written more than forty articles or book chapters and has coedited two books, including *Measures of Religiosity* (1999). He is also the editor of the *Journal of Psychology and Christianity.*

Andrew J. Hoffman is assistant professor of organizational behavior at the Boston University School of Management. He has published more than forty articles and four books, including: *Competitive Environmental Strategy: A Guide to the Changing Landscape* (2000); *From Heresy to Dogma: An Institutional History of Corporate Environmentalism* (2001); *Global Climate Change: A Senior-Level Dialogue* (editor, 1998); and *Organizations, Policy and the Natural Environment* (coeditor, 2002). His research deals with the nature and dynamics of change within institutional and cultural systems. Dr. Hoffman applies that research toward understanding the cultural and managerial implications of environmental protection for industry. He earned a joint Ph.D. in management and civil and environmental engineering from the Massachusetts Institute of Technology.

R. Elliott Ingersoll received his Ph.D. from Kent State University. He is a professional clinical counselor and psychologist in the state of Ohio. He has authored and coauthored several books and papers on topics ranging from spirituality to psychopharmacology. Dr. Ingersoll is currently an associate professor and chairperson of the counseling, administration, supervision and adult learning department at Cleveland State University.

Carole L. Jurkiewicz, Ph.D., is the Milton J. Womack Professor for Developing Scholars at Louisiana State University. Her areas of research interest are leadership and employee performance, ethics, and health care management. She is chairman of the American Society for Public

Administration Section on Ethics and chairs the Research on Gender Committee for the Section on Women in Public Administration. Dr. Jurkiewicz serves on a number of executive boards, and is an organizational consultant for many public, private, and nonprofit organizations. Her work has appeared in numerous scholarly journals, books, and in the popular press.

Susan G. Keortge, Ph.D., is currently an assistant professor of psychology at Westmont College, where she also conducts her professional practice as a licensed clinical psychologist. She earned her doctoral degree in clinical psychology from Washington State University, and completed pre- and postdoctoral fellowships at Harvard Medical School/Massachusetts General Hospital and McLean Hospital. Dr. Keortge practiced at the Beck Institute for Cognitive Therapy and Research in Philadelphia as a senior postdoctoral fellow under the direct supervision of Aaron T. Beck, M.D. She then went on to join a group private practice, also in Philadelphia. She was recently granted the status of founding fellow of the Academy of Cognitive Therapy.

Elisa A. King is a clinical psychology doctoral student at the University of Kansas. Her research interests include the psychology of hope, minority issues, and legal issues.

Robert W. Kolodinsky is assistant professor of management at James Madison University in Harrisonburg, Virginia. He did his doctoral studies in organizational behavior and human resources management at Florida State University. Dr. Kolodinsky has published several journal articles and book chapters, and papers in which he was the primary author have won "best paper" awards at two conferences. He is a three-time small business owner and a small business founder.

Krista Kurth, cofounder and principal of Renewal Resources LLC in Potomac, Maryland, is an executive coach and management consultant who provides services to individuals and organizations around renewal issues. She has been exploring, conducting programs on, and speaking about renewal in the workplace for over a decade. Her own personal experience and her abiding interest in helping people to be more true to themselves at work inspired her original research on spiritual renewal in business. Dr. Kurth delivers presentations on renewal and spirituality in the workplace at local, national, and international events and is coauthor of a book on renewal at work, *Running on Plenty at Work: Renewal Strategies for Individuals*.

Dong-Jin Lee is associate professor of marketing at Yonsei University. His research interest is in the areas of international relationship marketing and quality of life studies. He is currently serving as vice president for publications for the International Society for Quality-of-Life Studies. Prof. Lee gratefully acknowledges support for this study from SUNY-Binghamton. He received his Ph.D. from Virginia Tech.

Richard O. Mason currently teaches in the subject areas of corporate ethics and responsibility, global business environment, and managing emerging technologies. In 2001, he received the LEO (Lyons Electronic Office) Award from the Association of Information Systems for Lifetime Exceptional Achievement in Information Systems. Dr. Mason completed his three-year term on the Graduate Management Admissions Council while researching the areas of business strategy and information systems, social and ethical implications of information systems, and the history of information systems. In 1992, he was elected as a foreign member of the Russian Academy of Natural Sciences in the Information and Cybernetics Sector.

Kieran Mathieson is associate professor of information systems in the School of Business Administration at Oakland University. His research focuses on the use of information technology to help people understand themselves and their values. He has also studied individual technology adoption, how people form beliefs about information systems, and aspects of Web-based information systems.

Daryl McKee is professor of marketing at Louisiana State University, where he teaches in the M.B.A. program. He earned his Ph.D. in marketing from Texas A&M University. Dr. McKee's research interests include marketing strategy, services marketing, marketing ethics, and electronic commerce. The results of his research have been published in the *Journal of Marketing*, the *Journal of the Marketing Research Society*, the *Journal of Personal Selling and Sales Management*, the *Journal of the Academy of Marketing Science*, the *Journal of Macromarketing*, *Journal of Health Care Marketing*, *Economic Development Review*, and other professional and academic journals. Dr. McKee is past president of the Association of Collegiate Marketing Educators (formerly Southwestern Marketing Association) and president-elect of the Technology and Marketing Special Interest Group of the American Marketing Association.

Cynthia E. Miree is an assistant professor of management at Oakland University. Her research focuses on competitive intelligence and specifically explores how the competitive intelligence process can be used by organizations to facilitate the coordination of strategic and tactical intelligence in the sales and marketing functions. In addition, Prof. Miree has an interest in understanding churches and the factors that influence church growth.

Alfonso Montuori is associate professor at California Institute of Integral Studies and a consultant with Lisardco, a leading Bay Area executive development firm. He has also taught at the Saybrook Institute, the College of Notre Dame, and the South-Central University of Technology in Changsha in the People's Republic of China. His research has been in the areas of creativity and innovation, systems and complexity theories, planetary culture, organizational theory, strategy and strategic thinking, and cultural epistemology. His books include *Evolutionary Competence* (1989) *From Power to Partnership* (1993), *Creators on Creating* (coeditor, 1997), and the four-volume series, *Social Creativity* (coeditor, 1999–2000). Prof. Montuori has written articles in publications ranging from the *Academy of Management Review* and the *Journal of Management Education*, and the *Journal of Humanistic Psychology*.

Raymond F. Paloutzian is professor of experimental and social psychology at Westmont College, Santa Barbara, California. He received his Ph.D. in 1972 from Claremont Graduate School, taught psychology of religion at Stanford University, was president of American Psychological Association Division 36 (Psychology of Religion), and was guest professor at Katholieke Universiteit Leuven, Belgium. Dr. Paloutzian wrote *Invitation to the Psychology of Religion* (2d. ed.) and edits *The International Journal for the Psychology of Religion*.

K. Praveen Parboteeah is an assistant professor of management at the University of Wisconsin-Whitewater. He received his Ph.D. in international management from Washington State University. His research interests include the role of social institutions in explaining cross-national differences in organizational behavior outcomes, ethics and ethical climates, innovative teams, and networks.

Pamela L. Perrewé is the Jim Moran Professor of Management and serves as the associate dean for graduate programs in the College of Business at Florida State University. She received her bachelor's degree in psychology from Purdue University and her master's and Ph.D. degrees in management from the University of Nebraska. Dr. Perrewé has focused her research interests in the areas of job stress, organizational politics, and personality. She has published more than sixty book chapters, and journal articles in such journals as *Journal of Applied Psychology, Journal of Management, Journal of Organizational Behavior, Journal of Vocational Behavior, Journal of Occupational Health Psychology, Human Relations,* and *Journal of Applied Social Psychology.* Dr. Perrewé is the co-editor for *Research in Occupational Stress and Well Being* and serves as a member of the editorial review board for *Journal of Occupational Health Psychology, Human Resource Management Review,* and *Journal of Management.*

Jeffrey Pfeffer is the Thomas D. Dee II Professor of Organizational Behavior at the Graduate School of Business, Stanford University, where he has taught since 1979. Pfeffer received his B.S. and M.S. from Carnegie Mellon University and his Ph.D. from Stanford, and has also taught at the University of Illinois and the University of California—Berkeley. He is the author or co-author of ten books including *The Knowing-Doing Gap, The Human Equation,* and *Hidden Value,* as well as more than100 articles and book chapters. He currently serves on the board of directors of five companies, and he has lectured in more than twenty-six countries around the world on the subjects of human resource management, power in organizations, and organizational design.

Barry Posner is dean of the Leavey School of Business and professor of leadership at Santa Clara University. He is co-author of the award-winning and best-selling leadership book, *The Leadership Challenge.* Dr. Posner has also co-authored three other books on leadership—*Credibility: How Leaders Gain and Lose It, Why People Demand It; Encouraging the Heart: A Leaders Guide to Recognizing and Rewarding Others;* and *The Leadership Challenge Planner: An Action Guide to Achieving Your Personal Best.* He is an international renowned scholar who has published more than eighty research and practitioner-oriented articles, in such journals as the *Academy of Mangement Journal, Journal of Applied Psychology,* and *Personnel Psychology.* He has served on the board of directors for several start-up companies and a number of public and community-based organizations. Dr. Posner received his undergraduate degree in political science from University of California—San Diego, his master's degree from the Ohio State University in public administration, and his Ph.D. in organizational behavior and administative theory from the University of Massachussett—Amherst.

Michael G. Pratt is an associate professor at the University of Illinois. His research utilizes theories of identity/identification, symbolism, socialization, and sensemaking in examining the individual-organizational relationship. His current work looks at the blurring of boundaries among work, family, and spiritual life—as well as the role of technology in this blurring. His work has recently appeared in such outlets as the *Administrative Science Quarterly, Academy of Management Journal,* and *Academy of Management Review.* He received his Ph.D. from the University of Michigan.

Kim M. Pulvers is a clinical health psychology doctoral student at the University of Kansas. Her research interests include positive psychology, stress and coping, preventive medicine and public health issues.

Anat Rafaeli is a professor of organizational behavior at the Faculty of Industrial Engineering of the Technion, Israel's Institute of Technology. She received her Ph.D. in industrial and organizational psychology from Ohio State University and has worked at Stanford University, the University of Michigan, INSEAD, and Hebrew University of Jerusalem. Her research examines symbols and emotions in organizations, especially as they relate to service encounters. Dr. Rafaeli has published in journals such as the *Academy of Management Journal* and the *Journal of Applied Psychology,* and she is a member of the editorial board in journals such as the *Academy of Management Review, Organizational Science* and the *Journal of Service Research.*

Kevin L. Rand is a doctoral student in clinical psychology at the University of Kansas. His research interests include positive psychology (e.g., hope) and depression.

Terrel L. Rhodes is vice provost for curriculum and undergraduate studies and professor of public administration. He is the author of three books, including the *Public Managers Casebook.* His teaching and research interests are ethics, policy analysis and program evaluation, and Native American issues.

Sandra B. Rosenthal, Provost Distinguished Professor of Philosophy at Loyola University of New Orleans, has published eleven books and approximately 200 articles on pragmatism and its relation to various issues and movements, and has presented invited formal lectures on pragmatism in China, Poland, and Germany, among other places. She is on the editorial boards of several journals and book series, and has served as president of various professional organizations, including The Charles Peirce Society, The Society for the Advancement of American Philosophy, and the Metaphysical Society of America, and on the executive committee of the American Philosophical Association, Eastern Division. Her more recent books include *Speculative Pragmatism, Charles Peirce's Pragmatism Pluralism, Time, Continuity and Indeterminacy: A Pragmatic Encounter with Contemporary Perspectives*, and *Rethinking Business Ethics: A Pragmatic Perspective*, coauthored with Rogene Buchholz.

Phillip Siegel is on the accounting faculty at Fairleigh Dickinson University. He has previously held positions at University of Houston and San Francisco State University. Siegel is a Certified Public Accountant and has published in *Journal of Accounting, Auditing and Finance; Research in Accounting Regulation; Review Quantitative Finance and Accounting; Journal of the American Taxation Association*, and other peer-reviewed publications.

Patricia E. Shahen has twenty years of mediation and legal experience in employment, personnel, and family matters, and extensive experience leading groups in conflict resolution and team building. During her eight years at the U.S. General Accounting Office, she designed and initiated the Mediation Program, and served as the director, deputy director, and mediation program manager for the Affirmative Action, Civil Rights Office. She also worked as a supervisor, attorney advisor, and trial attorney with the Equal Employment Opportunity Commission; as a partner in a family law practice; and as the managing director of a family mediation practice. Shahen received a B.S. degree from Cornell University and a J.D. degree from the University of Puerto Rico Law School. She is a member of the Virginia State Bar.

David R. Sigmon is a clinical psychology master's student at the University of Kansas. His research interests include positive psychology, offense-taking, and forbearance.

M. Joseph Sirgy is a social/industrial psychologist. He is also a professor of marketing at Virginia Tech and holder of the Virginia Real Estate Research Fellow. Dr. Sirgy has published extensively in quality-of-life research and business ethics. He is currently serving as president of the Academy of Marketing Science and executive director of the International Society for Quality-of-Life Studies. He received his Ph.D. from University of Massachusetts.

Gary S. Smith is professor of history and coordinator of the humanities core at Grove City College. He received an M.Div. from Gordon-Conwell Theological Seminary and a Ph.D. in American History from Johns Hopkins University. He is the editor or author of five books, including *The Search for Social Salvation: Social Christianity and America, 1880–1925* (2000).

C. R. Snyder received his Ph.D. in clinical psychology from Vanderbilt University. He has spent his entire academic career at the University of Kansas, Lawrence, where he has been an assistant professor, an associate professor, a full professor, and in 2001 the Wright Distinguished Professor in Clinical Psychology. A fellow in five divisions of the American Psychological Association (general, teaching, personality and social, clinical, and health), he also is the recipient of numerous teaching awards at his university and nationally, the most recent being the Carnegie Foundation Award for Outstanding Professor in Kansas. He has written five books on hope, and along with his colleague Shane Lopez, has edited the *Handbook of Positive Psychology* (2002).

Bennett J. Tepper is a professor and chair of the department of management at University of North Carolina at Charlotte. He received an M.S. and Ph.D. in organizational psychology from the University of Miami. His research on organizational justice, leadership, and prosocial and antisocial organizational behavior has been published in various outlets including the *Academy of Management Journal, Journal of Applied Psychology,* and *Organizational Behavior and Human Decision Processes.*

Laura Yamhure Thompson is research coordinator of the Heartland Forgiveness Project, a four-year research program funded by the John Templeton Foundation to study dispositional forgiveness. She is a 2001–2002 Ford Foundation Dissertation Fellow and a Ph.D. candidate in the clinical psychology program at the University of Kansas. Thompson received an M.A. in clinical psychology from the University of Kansas and a B.A. in psychology from the University of Virginia.

M. Ann Welsh is an associate professor of management at the University of Cincinnati. Her research interests focus on organizational change with a specific emphasis on the creation of adaptive capacity in individuals and organizations. Current research projects involve managing innovation and new product development; the use of communities of practice in fostering the capacity for change; the role of constructive deviants in promoting change; and a critical examination of management education. Her articles have appeared in *Academy of Management Journal, Academy of Management Review, Administrative Science Quarterly, Management Learning, Journal of Management Education, Journal of Managerial Psychology, Journal of Engineering* and *Technology Management and Research-Technology Management.* Dr. Welsh received her Ph.D. from University of Missouri.

Colleen M. West is a clinical psychologist at the Miami Department of Veterans Affairs Medical Center. She received her Ph.D. from the University of Arizona. Dr. West provides a range of psychological services to medically fragile patients in geriatrics and extended care, including hospice patients. She also educates and trains multidisciplinary health care staff and students in end-of-life issues, and has worked with hospice programs in the United States and Great Britain. Dr. West has co-authored articles in the *Journal of Health and Human Services Administration* and in *Review of Public Personnel Administration.*

Jonathan P. West is professor of political science and director of the graduate program in public administration in the School of Business Administration at the University of Miami. He received his Ph.D. in political science from Northwestern University. Dr. West taught previously at the University of Houston and the University of Arizona. His most recent co-authored books are *Human Resource Management in Public Service* (2001) and *American Politics and the Environment* (2002). He has also published numerous articles and book chapters on public personnel administration, public policy, ethics, and American politics.

Richard D. White, Jr. is the Marjory B. Ourso Excellence in Teaching Professor at Louisiana State University's Public Administration Institute. He has published widely in research areas that include administrative history, public ethics, and moral development. Dr. White received his Ph.D. from Pennsylvania State University.

Iris Vilnai-Yavetz is a Ph.D. candidate at the Faculty of Industrial Engineering and Management of the Technion, Haifa. She received her B.A. in psychology from the Hebrew University of Jerusalem, and her M.B.A. from the School of Business Administration of the Hebrew University of Jerusalem. Vilnai-Yavetz studies the impact of various aspects of the physical environment on the behavior and emotions of customers and service providers. She is especially interested in the influence of the physical environment on the interactions between employees and customers, as part of dynamics of service delivery. Prior to doctoral studies, she held a managerial position in a marketing research and consulting firm in Israel.

Kelly L. Zellars is an assistant professor of management at the University of North Carolina–Charlotte. She received her bachelor's and M.B.A. degrees from the University of Notre Dame, her M.S.T. from the University of Wisconsin–Milwaukee, and her Ph.D. in management from Florida State University. Dr. Zellars has focused her research interests in the areas of job stress and burnout, personality, and perceptions of fairness. She has published in journals such as *Journal of Applied Psychology*, *Journal of Organizational Behavior*, and *Journal of Applied Social Psychology.*

AUTHOR INDEX

SUBJECT INDEX